UNDERSTANDING
INTERCULTURAL COMMUNICATION

UNDERSTANDING INTERCULTURAL COMMUNICATION

SECOND EDITION

Stella Ting-Toomey
CALIFORNIA STATE UNIVERSITY AT FULLERTON

Leeva C. Chung
UNIVERSITY OF SAN DIEGO

NEW YORK   OXFORD
OXFORD UNIVERSITY PRESS

Oxford University Press, Inc., publishes works that further Oxford University's
objective of excellence in research, scholarship, and education.

Oxford New York
Auckland Cape Town Dar es Salaam Hong Kong Karachi
Kuala Lumpur Madrid Melbourne Mexico City Nairobi
New Delhi Shanghai Taipei Toronto

With offices in
Argentina Austria Brazil Chile Czech Republic France Greece
Guatemala Hungary Italy Japan Poland Portugal Singapore
South Korea Switzerland Thailand Turkey Ukraine Vietnam

For titles covered by Section 112 of the US Higher Education Opportunity Act,
please visit www.oup.com/us/he for the latest information about
pricing and alternate formats.

Published by Oxford University Press, Inc.
198 Madison Avenue, New York, New York 10016
http://www.oup.com

Oxford is a registered trademark of Oxford University Press

Library of Congress Cataloging-in-Publication Data
Ting-Toomey, Stella.
  Understanding intercultural communication / Stella Ting-Toomey, Leeva C. Chung. —
2nd ed.
      p. cm.
  Includes bibliographical references and index.
  ISBN 978-0-19-973979-0 (pbk. : alk. paper)
1. Culture shock. 2. Language and culture. 3. Cross-cultural orientation. I. Chung,
Leeva C., 1965- II. Title.
  GN345.6.T57 2011
    303.48′2—dc23   2011021033

9 8 7 6 5 4 3 2 1

Printed in the United States of America
on acid-free paper.

DEDICATION TO OUR BELOVED PARENTS

獻給我最親愛的父母親

To my loving parents: Ting Chun Yen and Wang Shu Chin, this book is dedicated to you. For all your love, sacrifices, resilient spirit, and a lifetime of hard work—I thank you for teaching me caring, considerateness, and adaptability wherever I go. I love you and appreciate your "letting go" of me at a young age and letting me come to America and study. Whatever I've acomplished, I'm an extension of your love and gentle grace.

丁允珠
—Stella Ting-Toomey Wun Chu

To my visionary parents: Chung Dai Tau and Pang Duk Wai, this book is dedicated to you—allowing me the freedom to find my voice, inspiring me through your creative energy, and teaching me to trust intuition and flow, despite life's uncertainties. For all of your love—I thank you both.

程麗華
—Leeva Chung (Ching) Lai Wah

BRIEF CONTENTS

CONTENTS

CHAPTER **3**   **What Are the Essential Cultural Value Patterns?**   *38*

PREFACE

This text, *Understanding Intercultural Communication, Second Edition,* is written for you to increase your appreciation, knowledge, and skills about intercultural communication. With increased globalization and demographic changes in the United States, it is inevitable that you will be communicating with people who are culturally different. Developing constructive, quality intercultural relationships can make life enriching and exciting to ourselves and to people around us.

This book is an introductory text designed for undergraduate students, teachers, and practitioners who are searching for a user-friendly text on the fundamentals of intercultural communication. With the lens of flexible intercultural communication, we thread through an abundance of intercultural material with a very practical theme.

This book emphasizes a strong value-orientation perspective and its effect on intercultural encounters. It also addresses the complex role of cultural–ethnic identity and global–local identity and their relationship to intercultural contacts in our increasingly pluralistic U.S. society.

This text is distinctive because of its well-balanced emphasis on both international intercultural communication issues and U.S. domestic diversity issues. Our pedagogical approach to this book emphasizes a student-empowering philosophy via a tight integration of culture-sensitive knowledge, attitude checkpoints, and pragmatic communication skills necessary to develop intercultural communication flexibility in diverse contexts.

SPECIAL FEATURES

The second edition of *Understanding Intercultural Communication* is a book with many special hooks and original features. For example, it offers first-time students the following:

- A comprehensive *introduction* to all the important concepts of intercultural communication.

- A sound *knowledge base* of contemporary intercultural communication research areas that reflect multiple theoretical viewpoints.
- A *wide-angle lens* to learn about intercultural and interethnic communication concepts drawn from diverse disciplines.
- A *theory-practice emphasis* via the use of timely, real-life news stories and case studies to connect with key concepts in each chapter—starting from Chapter 2 and ending with Chapter 12.
- A text with *accessible language* so that students, teachers, and practitioners of intercultural communication can enjoy reading the book in an interactive manner.
- Simple *tables and figures* to highlight various important intercultural and intergroup communication ideas.
- An intercultural *"do-able" checklist* at the end of each chapter to remind students to practice flexible intercultural communication skills in everyday interactions.

We have also updated many of the favorite features from the first edition and added several new special features in this second edition:

- Beginning with Chapter 2, each chapter opens with *a real-life news event or personal case story* to motivate students to reflect on and explore the connection between the story and chapter concepts.
- *Top Five Jeopardy* boxes throughout the text to increase students' global, pop culture, and domestic diversity literacy.
- *Blog Post* personal narratives, stories, and poems throughout the text to connect abstract intercultural concepts and principles with meaningful understanding.
- *my.blog* enjoyable mini-assessments that promote self-awareness and self-empowerment and also encourage interaction with classmates through deeper dialog.
- *Live-Chat or L-Chat* realistic workplace or interpersonal scenes to illustrate the dynamic, pulsating intercultural message exchange process.
- *Hit-or-Miss* mini-quizzes and mix-and-match questions on current global, international, online, and intercultural issues.
- *Blog Pic* photos to transport students to globally and culturally different communities where they will experience culture shock or cultural ambiguity.
- A well-designed *Instructor's Manual* with many active learning exercises and activities plus instructional tips for managing challenging topics in the intercultural classroom.
- A captivating *Interactive Student Study Guide* that encourages students to read the actual text, reflect on and dialog about the interactive discussion questions, and, on their own, continue their intercultural learning journey by checking out the suggested Web sites, movies, books, and many other global and intercultural resource treasures.

WRITING THIS SECOND EDITION: ASSUMPTIONS AND CHANGES

Five initial assumptions guided the development of the second edition of this text. First, we patiently waited to work on the second edition to harvest the continually maturing insights of the intercultural–interethnic research field and the booming contemporary trends related to intercultural communication. We believe that the time is ripe now (theoretically and practically, for example, updating all Jeopardy Boxes on top five trends in the domestic, intercultural, and international arenas), after a five-year interval, to update this book with fresh research ideas, new perspectives, and the latest global trends and statistics (see, for example, Chapter 11). Second, we wanted students to enjoy learning about the various concepts of intercultural communication. Thus, we have intentionally integrated a carefully chosen set of current, international news cases and real-life personal stories to highlight various intercultural concepts. Third, we wanted to signal to students that there is no one right way to practice competent intercultural communication in the twenty-first century—instead, there are many adventures awaiting them and exciting opportunities to connect with globally and culturally different others. Thus, the recurrent theme in this text is *intercultural communication flexibility*. Fourth, we would like our students to develop a strong global and cultural consciousness via a self-empowered learning process—internalizing the inspiring individual stories and accounts and developing their own personal narratives, explaining them with the aid of the text's concepts. Fifth, we wanted to have fun writing this book together—as a way of celebrating our friendship on a continuous and light-hearted basis. As we approach the ending journey of writing this text, we believe that we have realized our goals with joy and exhilaration!

What are the ***changes or "news"*** in this *Understanding Intercultural Communication, Second Edition*? Based on the thoughtful feedback of students, instructors, reviewers, researchers, and practitioners using this text, and in conjunction with our own teaching and training experiences using this text in the United States, Mexico, Canada, France, Germany, Portugal, Switzerland, South Africa, China, Hong Kong, Japan, and South Korea, we now identify the ***top twenty changes or selected highlights.*** In this innovative second edition, we've:

- Throughout the entire text, called attention to the important role of technology in impacting the intercultural communication message exchange process;
- Updated reasons for studying intercultural communication in Chapter 1;
- Introduced the vital concept of "culture" more quickly by moving its definition from Chapter 2 to Chapter 1;
- Rearranged the "intercultural communication flexibility" theme from Chapter 1 to Chapter 2 and discussed the theme with more depth;
- Included the "motivational" value function in Chapter 3 and updated some of the value dimensions with the GLOBE project research results (see Chapter 3);
- Updated the complex discussion on "multiracial and biracial identity" in Chapter 4;
- Integrated more culture shock stories in Chapter 5 and eliminated some secondary concepts concerning the culture shock "hostility" stage;
- Combined Chapters 6 and 7 into one coherent chapter: Chapter 6 on *What Is the Connection Between Verbal Communication and Culture?*;
- Illustrated the nonverbal chapter (Chapter 7) with many fascinating global nonverbal examples and new facial nonverbal photos;

- Throughout the entire book, updated all photos taken from various countries and reflected individuals from different walks of life, which we now call the *Blog Pic* special feature;
- Updated many of the poignant personal stories and illuminating examples throughout various chapters, which we now label as the *Blog Post* special feature;
- Introduced a popular training model, the Developmental Model of Intercultural Sensitivity (DMIS) in Chapter 8, on the "biases against outgroups" motif and provided a wealth of current news examples on "E.S.P." (ethnocentrism, stereotypes, and prejudice);
- Explained a new intercultural workplace conflict model in Chapter 9 and also emphasized the importance of adaptive code-switching in managing conflict flexibly via lively dialog examples in the *Live-Chat, or L-Chat,* a special boxed feature;
- Inserted sections on online and mobile dating and "relational transgressions and terminations" in Chapter 10 on "intercultural-intimate relationship" challenges and emphasized the bicultural/biracial identity struggles of multiracial kids;
- Updated the entire Chapter 11 on the theme of "global–local dialectical identity" and its impact on intercultural communication and the accompanying communication change patterns in various nations or cultures;
- Revitalized the final chapter, Chapter 12, on the motif of "becoming flexible and ethical intercultural communicators" via the introduction of new concepts, and streamlined a set of ethical guidelines and questions to guide students to formulate their own principled ethical stance;
- Throughout the text, updated the popular *Jeopardy Boxes* (plus also changed from the top ten trends to the top five trends so that students can digest the information more enjoyably) and included intercultural and global statistics up to May 2011;
- Retained the favorite self-assessment *know thyself* feature and renamed it as **my.blog** special feature in this edition;
- Created a new special feature called *Hit-or-Miss* to invite interactive learning through fun global knowledge quizzes and mix-and-match questions; and
- Added more than *250 new references* and deleted some outdated ones.

BOOK DESIGN AND ORGANIZATION

This book is organized in three sections. The first section (Chapters 1–4) lays the foundational framework and concepts of intercultural communication. The reasons for studying intercultural communication and practicing flexible intercultural skills are articulated. Major research areas, such as cultural value patterns (e.g., individualism–collectivism) and cultural–ethnic identity, are explored—especially through the reflections of many cultural voices and personal stories.

The second section (Chapters 5–7) emphasizes the process of crossing cultural boundaries and the dynamic process of intercultural verbal and nonverbal exchange encounters. Topics such as developmental culture shock, language functions, and diverse cultural verbal styles, as well as fun topics such as nonverbal space violations and cross-cultural hand gestures are discussed and accompanied by lively intercultural examples.

The third section (Chapters 8–12) focuses on intercultural–interpersonal relationship development contexts. Important factors such as E.S.P. (i.e., ethnocentrism, stereotypes, and prejudice) are discussed in depth. Practical knowledge and skills to manage intercultural conflict flexibly are proposed. Many animated conflict Live-Chat dialogs and interpersonal examples are used to illustrate the development of intimate intercultural relationships. The contemporary topic of the development of a morphing global–local identity is addressed through a new concept we coined the "e.netizen" individual. We discuss the impact of technology and pop culture and its effect on our shifting value patterns. Finally, a cornerstone theme, becoming an ethical and flexible intercultural communicator, rounds out the book.

Throughout this book, personal stories, poems, news cases, blog pics, fun quizzes, global trend statistics, ethical dilemmas, and practical skill "do-ables" are offered to empower students to engage in active learning and to master the foundational concepts of intercultural communication. At the same time, we strive to give first-time students an accurate and enjoyable basic text to learn about intercultural communication. We want students to come away with a special appreciation for the mindful efforts and the artful skills it takes to communicate across cultures adaptively and flexibly. We want them to also resonate with the identity struggles in various forms as expressed by the diverse voices of multiple individuals in many of the special feature stories.

As we and you begin traversing the landscape of this book, we hope we have succeeded in motivating students and teachers to discover and to explore together: the unfamiliar worlds and some unfamiliar words, the slippery slopes and the diverse terrains, and the vulnerable faces and the amazing voices that struggle to be affirmed and listened to—from within and beyond the classroom instructional setting.

ABOUT THE AUTHORS

Dr. Stella Ting-Toomey is a professor of human communication at California State University at Fullerton (CSUF). She received her Ph.D. at the University of Washington in 1981. She teaches courses in intercultural communication, intercultural conflict theory and practice, and intercultural communication training applications. Stella is the 2008 recipient of the 23-campus wide CSU Wang Family Excellence Award, and the 2007–08 recipient of the CSU-Fullerton Outstanding Professor Award. Stella has published numerous books and over 100 articles/chapters on the topics of intercultural conflict competence and cultural and ethnic identity negotiation process. Her publications have appeared in the *International Journal of Intercultural Relations, Communication Monographs, Human Communication Research, The International Journal of Conflict Management,* and *Communication Research,* among others. Two recent book titles are *The Sage Handbook of Conflict Communication* (with John G. Oetzel) and *Managing Intercultural Conflict Effectively* (Sage; with John G. Oetzel). Stella has held major leadership roles in international communication associations and has served on numerous editorial boards. She has lectured widely throughout the United States, Asia, and Europe on the theme of mindful intercultural communication practice. She has also designed and conducted over 150 intercultural training programs for corporations, universities, and social service organizations. *Understanding Intercultural Communication, Second Edition,* (coauthored with Leeva C. Chung) is her sixteenth book. Stella is an ardent Lakers basketball fan and she plays the piano for fun. She also enjoys walking through the quiet morning campus with her iPod Shuffle blasting beautiful classical music in her ears. Those are her blissful moments.

Dr. Leeva C. Chung is a professor at the University of San Diego (USD). She received her Ph.D. at the University of Oklahoma in 1998. At USD, she teaches in both the Department of Communication Studies and the Department of Ethnic Studies and has won numerous teaching and mentoring awards on campus, most recently the 2011 Davies Award of Teaching Excellence. In addition to teaching abroad, Leeva teaches courses in intercultural communication, ethnic identity, global teams, among others. Her research interests include cultural, ethnic and global identity, aging across cultures, and pop culture. Her recent publications include book chapters in *Cross-Cultural Psychology: A Contemporary Reader* and *Best Practices in Experiential and Service Learning.* Leeva has also published articles in the *Global Media Journal, Journal for Intercultural Communication Research, International Journal of Intercultural Relations, Communication Research Reports,* and *Communication Reports.* In the San Diego community, she serves as a founding member of the San Diego Asian Film Foundation Festival. Leeva is proud to be a native San Franciscan and Giants fan.

ACKNOWLEDGMENTS

If it takes a village to write a book and an entire symphony to make beautiful music, then crafting *Understanding Intercultural Communication, Second Edition*, has been an orchestrated celebration. We are grateful to the many individuals who encouraged and motivated us to bring this work to fruition. First and foremost, we want to thank our many students who have contributed their voices and shared their intercultural experiences with us. Without their unique voices, this book would have been quite abstract. We also want to thank our colleagues and our respective departments at the California State University at Fullerton (CSUF) and the University of San Diego (USD) for providing a supportive environment in which to conduct our writing.

Second, we want to thank John Challice, Vice President and Publisher at Oxford University Press, for his enormous patience and good humor in waiting for the birth of this second edition. Thank you to Mark Haynes, Caitlin Kaufman, Kate McClaskey, Theresa Stockton, and the entire production staff at Oxford for their professional help and their determination to make this book the "shining star" in the intercultural market. We also want to thank our anonymous reviewers for their astute comments and thoughtful suggestions in preparation for the second edition of this text.

We are also indebted to the reviewers who reviewed the previous first edition book: Myrna Cornett-DeVito, Emporia State University; Robbin D. Crabtree, Fairfield University; Fernando Delgado, University of Wisconsin–River Falls; Tina M. Harris, University of Georgia; Armeda C. Reitzel, Humboldt State University; Diana Rios, University of Connecticut; Arvind Singhal, Ohio University; and Candice Thomas-Maddox, Ohio University, Lancaster. We are also thankful for the informal feedback and random conversations from intercultural scholars, instructors, practitioners, and students who contributed many useful insights that guided this revision.

On an individual level, our deepest gratitude and appreciation goes to ALEX FLECKY: your unflappable demeanor when all things go chaotic, your razor-sharp eye in reviewing and proofreading each chapter, and your exceptional organizational skills in keeping track of all the special features in the text are astonishing to behold. We appreciate your poised friendship, sweet kindness, and your grace in moving us forward with faith that we will see the light at the end of the tunnel.

We also extend our special appreciation to Peter Lee, who helped us in preparing the tables and figures in the first edition and additional figures in the second edition. We also thank Ngao for his assistance and feedback with our new figures in this edition. A big thank you to Noorie Baig for all her diligent research assistant help in tasks small and big as we get to the finish line. In addition, we extend our heartfelt thanks to Janet Bennett, the Executive Director of the Intercultural Communication Institute, and all the Portland-Summer Institute of Intercultural Communication Workshop faculty, students, and staff for providing us with a nurturing environment in which to dialog and actively engage ourselves in all things intercultural.

As we wrap up this second edition, foremost in our mind are the late Dr. William (Bill) Gudykunst and the late Dr. Richard (Rich) Wiseman of CSUF—two top-tier intercultural scholars and dedicated teachers with their own distinctive instructional styles in the teaching of intercultural communication effectiveness. We hope to pass on some of their spirit and legacy through the various chapters of this text. We miss them sorely every day as we walk through life without hearing their encouraging words or seeing their familiar, supportive faces.

We would also like to take this opportunity to acknowledge the warm support of many of our splendid students, friends, and families.

FROM STELLA: I extend my special appreciation to many of my undergraduate and graduate students, who let me experiment and test many of the ideas in this book and so embrace "zig-zag learning" as a playful teaching perspective. Your thirst for learning and your hunger for creative teaching tools prompted me to become more risk-taking with each step or dance I performed in the classroom setting. In discovering your passion, commitment, and awakening, I've also uncovered my own joy, passion, and enthrallment for creativity in the intercultural teaching arena. On an everyday basis, your positive energy for learning and your willingness to stretch make me a better teacher every step of the way.

I also want to thank the following individuals for their delightful support and rays of light at different phases of the development of this book: Jennifer Acosta-Licea, Noorie Baig, Andrew Bottom, Annette Bow, Maria Chan-Sew, Jeanine K. Congalton, Tenzin Dorjee, Ge Gao, Jean Hotta, Angela Hoppe-Nagao, Michelle Hu, Atsuko Kurogi, Peter Lee, Shelly Lee, Hiromi Motozuka-Ladino, John Oetzel, HyeKyeung Seung, Miki Yamashita, and Ruifang Zhang. To Annette Bow, your warm and radiant smiles brighten my day every time I step into the main office. To Tenzin Dorjee, I treasure your peaceful friendship and having you as my next-door office neighbor. You've provided me with a serene space to just hang out and sit. To Jean Hotta, our "lonely tree" Monterey conference trip and your always caring friendship mean tons to me. To Peter Lee, I value your long-time friendship, considerate gestures, and steadfast companionship.

I also want to mention the special men in my life: my husband, Charles, and my son, Adrian. To Charles, your kindhearted caring and Irish humor provide me with a safe hammock to take a restful nap. To Adrian, I'm proud that you're making good progress in CSUF graduate school and am enchanted that you continue in my footsteps by majoring in the intercultural communication field. You're my premium joy and bliss in my life. Thank you for being *you*—with lots of hugs and love.

I also want to mention my three special brothers—Tom, Henry, and Victor—to all three of you, I treasure your support in good times and bad. To Big Brother Tom (BBT), thank you for all the coaching advice you've given me to deal with the various life issues these past few years. To Second Brother Henry, I appreciate your fighting spirit and your tenacity to hold on with fortitude. To Youngest Brother Victor, I value your thoughtful attentiveness on many celebratory holidays and birthdays—thank you for remembering all the special occasions and more. Although we are spread out in different corners of the world, you are all constantly in my warm soul and heart.

FROM LEEVA: First and foremost, this book could not have been completed without the thoughtful reflection and feedback from my students, both here and abroad. I extend the biggest shout out and MAHALO—for challenging me, laughing with me, embracing the organized chaos, all of which allowed me to be me. You all have been the x-factor that gives me the passion to teach. (~.~)

I extend the warmest thanks to the following individuals for their unique and exceptional contributions to this book at various developmental and psychological phases: aLx + Min, Alex Bryan, Noorie Baig, Richard Brislin, Joyce Chan, Ling Chen, Adriana Rios-Collins, Chris and Brenna, Kira Espiritu, Eduardo Espinoza, Minh-Ha Hoang, Daniel Jaimes, Leeann Kim, Young Yun Kim, Eveyln Kirkley, Nancy Kuehnel, Gina Lew, Jon Nussbaum, Patricia Plovanich, Mrs. Sutter, Thiagi, Paul Turounet, Joe Whitecotton, and of course, A. Rafik Mohamed. A special thanks to Dean Mary Boyd and the IOG Committee for the time and monetary support that enabled me to find time to finish the book project. To my advocates, Carole and Kristin, thank you for pushing me to fly higher than I thought possible. A special thanks to Catanzaro, for the space and eyes you provided me to get this manuscript done. To MEL, your gifts of Southern etiquette, vicissitude, and real friendship mean the world to me. To O| for your perspective and addicting kpop music—ya!

Grounding me and offering me humor and wit at each turning point of this journey were my friends and ohana, both close and far: <3 to Haeme, Liliana, Toni, Monica, McCroskey, and Lei—you're all a major part of this accomplishment; my pride (Keige, Keean, Justin Garrett, and P); So Jun and May K, resilient women to the end, you both live through me every day; Ngao, for always challenging me to think critically and act responsibly—my love and a special "holla" to you!!; and my incredible "sistas" who empower me at each turn and make me laugh ("ah lai wah fan lai!"): your vigilant protection, no-nonsense attitude, and unconditional love extended to me have given me the strength, confidence, and force to overcome all obstacles and downplay the successes. It is because of both of you that I am and will always be "keeping it real!"

It has been over twenty-two years since I met Stella at SCA (now NCA) and heard her present her top-ranked conference paper. Inspired, I took the unexpected turn into academia and my wish to work with Stella resulted in numerous collaborations together—a path completely unforeseen and still shocking to me. I am most indebted and grateful to Stella—

the yin to my yang or yang to my yin. True to her name, Stella is my North Star, guiding me through difficulty and supporting me in all my (crazy) endeavors. For all the accomplishments I have received, she is a reflection and a large part of each and every one of them. I am truly blessed to have such a *yuan* (or relational karma) connection and an inspiring mentor as a role model and ultimately friend, who embodies the definition of compassion, wisdom, and food partner!

REJOINING VOICES: I would be remiss if I (Stella) did not say anything about my professional relationship with Leeva, and, more important, our friendship. It has been more than twenty years since Leeva was in my interpersonal communication graduate seminar class. We started off in a teacher–student, mentor–mentee relationship. Witnessing Leeva's professional maturation has been one of my life's true blessings. My second blessing was to work on the book twice now with her. Our yin–yang styles complement each other. We laughed together and we sulked together. We might have our disagreements occasionally; however, we are able to uplift each other with a good bowl of Vietnamese *pho* (noodles) and some tasty spring rolls. Leeva—thank you for your light-hearted rhythms when I truly needed those moments to chill and laugh. Thank you also for your unique photographic eye in capturing some of the amazing photos that graced this book. Although the writing of this text has been an exhausting and, simultaneously, a breathtaking journey, the magic of our friendship has outweighed any stress from working on the manuscript.

As partners taking joy in our friendship and energized by our collaboration, we wish you an awe-inspiring journey of intercultural discovery.

FUNDAMENTAL CONCEPTS IN INTERCULTURAL COMMUNICATION

CHAPTER 1

WHY STUDY INTERCULTURAL COMMUNICATION?

CHAPTER OUTLINE

- Practical Reasons to Study Intercultural Communication
  - Adjusting to Global Workplace Heterogeneity
  - Adapting to Domestic Workforce Diversity
  - Engaging in Creative Multicultural Problem Solving
  - Comprehending the Role of Technology in Global Communication
  - Facilitating Better Multicultural Health Care Communication
  - Enhancing Intercultural Relationship Satisfaction
  - Fostering Global and Intrapersonal Peace
  - Deepening Cultural Self-Awareness and Other-Awareness

- Culture: A Learned Meaning System
  - Surface-Level Culture: Popular Culture
  - Intermediate-Level Culture: Symbols, Meanings, and Norms
  - Deep-Level Culture: Traditions, Beliefs, and Values

- Stamping Your Intercultural Passport

As we enter the twenty-first century, direct contact with culturally different people in our neighborhoods, communities, schools, and workplaces is an inescapable part of life. With immigrants and minority group members representing nearly 30 percent of the present workforce in the United States, practicing intercultural communication flexibility is especially critical in today's global world.

Flexible intercultural communication means managing cultural differences adaptively and creatively in a wide variety of situations. The underlying values of a culture (e.g., individual competitiveness versus group harmony) often shape communication expectations and attitudes. How we define a communication problem in a work team and how we approach the communication process itself are also likely to vary across cultures, ethnicities, situations, and individuals. For example, some cultural groups (e.g., German and Swiss work teams) may believe that addressing a workplace problem directly and assertively can be stimulating and spark further new ideas. Other cultural groups (e.g., Chinese and Korean work teams) may believe that approaching a conflict issue indirectly and tactfully can facilitate a more harmonious communication process.

With such layered complexity facing global and domestic diversity issues, we must practice intercultural communication sensitivity when dealing with culturally different others. This chapter examines the reasons why we should understand intercultural communication in diverse contexts. The chapter is developed in three sections. First, we offer several practical reasons why we should pay special attention to the study of intercultural communication. Next, we define the major characteristics of culture. We end by summarizing this first chapter and "stamping" your intercultural passport, continuing you on your intercultural journey.

PRACTICAL REASONS TO STUDY INTERCULTURAL COMMUNICATION

With rapid changes in the global economy, technology, transportation systems, and immigration policies, the world is becoming a small, intersecting community. We find ourselves having increased contact with people who are culturally different. In a global workforce, people bring with them different work habits and cultural practices. For example, cultural strangers may approach problem-solving tasks or nonverbal emotional expression issues differently. They may develop friendships and romantic relationships with different expectations and rhythms. They may also have different communication desires, end goals, and emphases in an intercultural encounter. In this twenty-first century global world, people are constantly moving across borders, into and out of a country. Neighborhoods and communities are changing. In what was once a homogeneous community, we may now find more diversity and cultural values in flux.

The study of intercultural communication is about the study of communication that involves, at least in part, cultural group membership differences. It is about acquiring the necessary knowledge and dynamic skills to manage such differences appropriately and effectively. It is also about developing a creative mindset to see things from different angles without rigid prejudgment. There are indeed many practical reasons for studying intercultural communication. We offer eight reasons here: increased global workplace heterogeneity, increased domestic workforce diversity, engaging in creative problem solving, comprehending the role of technology in global communication, facilitating better multicultural health care communication, enhancing intercultural relationship satisfaction, fostering global and intrapersonal peace, and deepening cultural self-awareness and other-awareness.

Adjusting to Global Workforce Heterogeneity

In this global age, it is inevitable that employees and customers from dissimilar cultures are in constant contact with one another—whether it is through face-to-face, cellular phone, Skype, smart phone, or e-mail

JEOPARDY BOX 1.1   TOP FIVE MOST VALUABLE
GLOBAL BRANDS BY DOLLAR VALUE

Brand name	Industry
1. Coca-Cola	Beverages
2. IBM	Business services
3. Microsoft	Computer software
4. Google	Internet services
5. GE (General Electric)	Diversified

Note: All U.S.-owned.

Source: http://www.interbrand.com/en/knowledge/best-global-brands/best-global-brands-2008/best-global-brands-2010.aspx (retrieved March 20, 2011).

contacts. To begin, do you know which companies have the most valuable global brands? Take a guess and then check out Jeopardy Box 1.1. Workplace heterogeneity on the global level represents both opportunities and challenges to individuals and organizations. Individuals at the forefront of workplace diversity must rise to the challenge of serving as global employees and leaders (Bhawuk & Sakuda, 2009; Moodian, 2010).

Many U.S. Americans are becoming global employees while staying on U.S. soil. An increasing number of computer workers in the United States are freelancing for companies overseas. In just one year, the number of international companies—from the UK, Australia, China, Pakistan, and India—that hired U.S. computer workers to work remotely jumped from 1,429 to 4,285 (Cook, 2010). In addition, hundreds of thousands of U.S. workers are currently working in overseas locations. U.S. corporations spend approximately $25 billion annually on corporate relocation, and they also spend approximately $16 million annually to transfer their employees for overseas assignments (Global Trends Relocation Survey, 2010).

Despite the number of U.S. workers overseas, international relocation researchers estimate that the proportion of U.S. workers who fail in their global assignments (i.e., return prematurely) ranges from approximately 10 percent to 20 percent—with the highest failure rates associated with assignments in developing countries (Global Mobility Effectiveness Survey, 2009). Contrast this with the fact that only

6 percent of assignees from Asia-Pacific–based corporations returned to their home countries before the end date of their international assignments. Although most U.S. international employees are considered technically competent, they may lack effective adaptive intercultural communication skills to interact appropriately and effectively in the new culture (Moran, Youngdahl, & Moran, 2009; Palthe, 2009; Storti, 2009).

Beyond workplace mobility and internationalization, the world's population is aging. Retirement for the 60-and-older ("baby boomer") population has begun, symbolizing a "graying economy" and an expected mass retirement. In the United States alone, the fastest growing part of the workforce will be of retirement age. According to the U.S. Bureau of Labor and Statistics, the percentage of workers over the age of 65 will increase from 15 percent in 2006 to 19.7 percent by 2014 (Kinsman, 2006). Unbelievably, baby boomers, who accounted for 56 percent of full-time workers in 2007, will increase to 65.2 percent by 2014 (U.S. Bureau of Labor Statistics, 2008).

With the upcoming exodus of workers anticipated as a result of retirement, many countries are wondering how to replace the skills and knowledge that will be lost. In Japan, new products and services are being created especially for the retired population, such as health foods, adult education classes, and planned communities (Coleman, 2007). In the United States, many companies are starting mentoring programs to help with older-adult transition issues. The baby boomer is a potential bonanza for innovative global companies planning how to appeal to this aging population that will have money to spend. Equally relevant will be how to retain the important work experience and institutional wisdom that may be lost when this population is no longer working.

Global managers and employees, international human resource groups, global product development teams, multiethnic customer service groups, and international marketing and sales teams can all benefit from mastering intercultural communication competencies (J. Bennet, 2009; Gupta, 2009; Hyatt, Evans, & Haque, 2009). Any groups or individuals that must communicate on a daily basis with culturally diverse coworkers, clients, or customers can reap the rewards of acquiring the awareness, knowledge, and skills of flexible intercultural communication. Intercultural communication knowledge and skills are needed to solve problems, manage conflicts, and forge new visions on both global and domestic levels (Bhawuk, Landis, & Munusamy, 2009; Goleman, Boyatzis, & McKee, 2002).

Adapting to Domestic Workforce Diversity

Even if we do not venture beyond our national borders, cultural diversity becomes a crucial part of our everyday work lives (see Blog Pic 1.1—Workplace diversity). The study of intercultural communication on the U.S. domestic front is especially critical for several reasons. First, according to U.S. Census Bureau, we are now a nation with increased multicultural complexities and nuances—of the nation's approximately 307 million people, 65 percent are whites/non-Hispanics, 16 percent are Latinos/Hispanics, 13 percent are African Americans/blacks, 4.5 percent are Asian Americans, 1 percent reported as American Indians/Alaskan Natives, and 0.2 percent identified themselves as Native Hawaiians and Pacific Islanders. Note that 1.7 percent of the population chose to identify themselves as two or more races.

The most sweeping demographic change in the United States is occurring in the Latino/a population. It is projected that in the year 2050, the Latino/a population in the United States will more than double in size (to approximately 30% of the total U.S. population), followed closely by an increase in the Asian American population (to approximately 9%). The African American population will remain stable (estimated at 15%), whereas the non-Hispanic white population will decline significantly (to approximately 46%) on the national level (Passel & Cohn, 2008). Hawaii, California, and New Mexico are the three most racially diverse states in the United States. Conversely, Maine, Vermont, and West Virginia are listed as the three most homogeneous states, with non-Hispanic whites making up over 93 percent of those states' populations (check out Jeopardy Boxes 1.2 and 1.3). The highest percentage of individuals of mixed-race identifiers were reported to live in Hawaii, Alaska, and California.

Second, we are moving at an accelerated pace with increased foreign-born diversity in the nation. According

Blog Pic 1.1 Workplace diversity has become an inevitable part of our daily life.

JEOPARDY BOX 1.2 TOP FIVE MOST RACIALLY/
ETHNICALLY DIVERSE STATES IN THE UNITED STATES

1. Hawaii	77.3% minority population
2. California	59.9%
3. New Mexico	59.5%
4. Texas	54.7%
5. New York	41.7%

Source: U.S. Census Bureau, http://factfinder.census.gov/servlet/ACSSAFF-People?_submenuId=people_10&_sse=on (retrieved July 17, 2011).

JEOPARDY BOX 1.3 TOP FIVE MOST RACIALLY/
ETHNICALLY HOMOGENEOUS STATES IN THE UNITED
STATES

1. Maine	5.6% minority population
2. Vermont	5.7%
3. West Virginia	6.8%
4. New Hampshire	7.7%
5. North Dakota	11.1%

Source: U.S. Census Bureau, http://factfinder.census.gov/servlet/
ACSSAFFPeople?_submenuId=people_10&_sse=on (retrieved July 17, 2011).

to U.S. Census data for 2010, 36.7 million people representing 12 percent of the total U.S. population are foreign-born nationals. Another 33 million (i.e., 11%) are native born with at least one foreign-born parent, making more than one in five people in the population either first- or second-generation U.S. residents or citizens. Among the foreign born, more than half were born in Latin America, and almost one-third were born in Mexico. Nearly one in three foreign-born individuals entered the country in 2000 or later. Other foreign born were either from Asia or Europe, and the remaining small percentage were born in other regions of the world. Basically, current and future generations in the United States include many individuals whose parents or grandparents were born in a Latin American or Asian region. Thus, the influence of multicultural and diverse customers is expanding in every industry. Auto makers, retailers, banks, and media and entertainment industries must learn to reach out to these multiethnic customers with increased intercultural sensitivity and skills.

Third, skilled and highly educated immigrants (especially in the areas of computer and engineering service industries) play a critical role in U.S. advanced technology industries. The payrolls of leading information technology (IT) companies such as Intel and Microsoft include many highly skilled and foreign-born employees. Many U.S. immigrants have also contributed positively to the social and economic development of the nation. The richness of cultural diversity in U.S. society has led to dramatic breakthroughs in the fields of physics, medicine, science, and technology. Attention to diversity issues bolsters employee morale, creates an inclusive climate in the workplace, and sparks creative innovation (Cortes & Wilkinson, 2009; Rink & Jehn, 2010).

Engaging in Creative Multicultural Problem Solving

Our ability to value different approaches to problem solving and mindfully move away from traditional "either/or" binary thinking can expand diverse options in managing team intercultural problems. According to creativity research (Maddux & Galinsky, 2009; Sternberg, 1999; Tharp & Reiter, 2003; Ting-Toomey, 2010a), we learn more from people who are different from us than from those who are similar to us. At the individual level, creativity involves a process of taking in new ideas and of being thrown into chaos. If the uncertainty or chaos is managed with an open-minded attitude, team members can come up with a synergistic perspective that involves the best of all viewpoints. A synergistic perspective means combining the best of all cultural approaches in solving a workplace problem.

At the small-group level of research, results indicate that the quality of ideas produced in ethnically diverse groups has been rated significantly higher by experts than that in ethnically homogeneous groups (McLeod, Lobel, & Cox, 1996; Oetzel, 2009). Of course, culturally heterogeneous teams also have more conflicts or communication struggles than homogeneous work teams. However, if such conflicts are managed competently and flexibly, the outcome of heterogeneous team negotiations often results in a better-quality product than that produced by a homogeneous team. Many recruiting experts say that they are launching aggressive campaigns to recruit top management candidates who have the leadership experience and the multicultural problem-solving skills in coordinating diverse team issues such as culture, race, gender, sexual orientation, and age. Workplace trend reports indicate that losing an employee can cost a company up to four times an employee's salary. Losing a vital employee with significant ties to a multicultural or diverse community can cost many missed business opportunities and fruitful outcomes.

Culturally and ethnically diverse teams have the potential to solve problems creatively because of several factors. Some of these factors include a greater variety of viewpoints brought to bear on the issue, a higher level of critical analysis of alternatives, and a lower probability of groupthink because of the heterogeneous composition of the group (Oetzel, 2005; Ting-Toomey & Oetzel, 2001).

Comprehending the Role of Technology in Global Communication

As global citizens, we are moving at an incredible rate of speed thanks in large part to the Internet. The Internet is the central hub—the channel that offers us a wide-open space to communicate globally and to connect with individuals from diverse walks of life. More importantly, this hub pulses with a speed and efficiency never seen before. Would you like to connect with your preschool classmate? Within five seconds, you can transport yourself into one of the many social networks and find your long-lost friend. Consider the following startling facts:

1. It took radio more than thirty years to reach 60 million people, fifteen years for television to reach 60 million people, and the Internet three years to reach more than 90 million people;
2. In a one-month period, YouTube.com had 100 million viewers in the United States watching 5.9 billion YouTube videos;
3. Although Google and Yahoo! websites receive approximately 280 million visitors per month, the approximately 116 million Facebook members spend much more time surfing this site (over seven hours per month);
4. Ninety-three percent of U.S. Americans use cell phones or wireless devices; one-third of those are on "smartphones."

Sources: Hof, McWilliams, & Saveri (1998); *"Hulu continues ascent"* (2009).

In this twenty-first century, both individualists and collectivists, regardless of what cultures they are from, are at a crossroads of redefining, exploring, and reinventing their identities (Ting-Toomey, 2010b). On a global scale, new generations of individuals are attempting to create a third identity—a hybrid identity that fuses the global and local cultures together. This global connection is so appealing, and so very persuasive, that it constantly shapes and makes us reexamine who we are or what we want to become. Technology allows us to develop relationships across the barriers of time, space, geography, and cultural–ethnic boundaries. Because 84 percent of U. S. children have home Internet access, spending an average of one and one-half hours per day on the Internet (Rideout, Foehr, & Roberts, 2010), when discussing important issues in intercultural and interracial communication, we can no longer afford to ignore the powerful influence of modern technology (see Blog Pic 1.2).

Technology drives what we listen to, what we download, and what we want to look like. It also forges a sense of global communal belonging when individuals do not relate to their particular cultural or ethnic group membership. While searching for a sense of belonging to a group, individuals end up finding each other in cyberspace. Understanding the impact of technology on every aspect of our lives will allow us to use communication productively—to engage in increased awareness, dialog, and collaboration between the local culture level and the global consumerism level.

By the way, do you know which countries have the highest ratio of Internet users? And which countries have the highest ratio of cellular mobile phone subscribers? Take a guess and check out Jeopardy Boxes 1.4 and 1.5. As we communicate across the globe through various electronic or wireless media, flexible intercultural communication becomes critical in such a global connective environment.

Blog Pic 1.2   We can communicate and connect from anywhere.

JEOPARDY BOX 1.4   TOP FIVE COUNTRIES WITH THE
HIGHEST RATIO OF INTERNET USERS

Country	% of Population Penetration
1. United Kingdom	82
2. (South) Korea	80.9
3. Germany	79.9
4. Japan	78.4
5. United States	78.2

Source: http://www.internetworldstats.com/top20.htm (retrieved March 2011)

Facilitating Better Multicultural Health Care Communication

As borders continue to merge and divide, one area rich in conversation is the state of multicultural health care (Anand & Lahiri, 2009). When Liliana was giving birth to her daughter, the doctor was surprised that her husband, Senel, did not stand by Liliana. He did not coach her along or support her through the various stages of labor. In fact, he was not even in the delivery room to witness the delivery of a beautiful baby girl named Aryana. The doctor was quite perturbed and puzzled. Several months later, during a routine baby check-up, in chatting with Liliana, the doctor finally understood that Senel was not in the delivery room because of his Muslim faith and belief. For Muslims, birth comes through the "house" with a midwife in attendance, a very sacred place, and no man should be inside the room during the baby's delivery. Similarly, Native Indians in Belize and Panama also believe that the father should not be in the delivery room with the mother or the baby or else harm can come to both of them. If you were a trained nurse or health care professional, would you likely be aware of this religious tradition concerning childbirth?

JEOPARDY BOX 1.5 TOP FIVE COUNTRIES WITH THE HIGHEST RATIO OF CELLULAR MOBILE PHONE USERS 2009

Country
1. Montenegro
2. Hong Kong
3. Saudi Arabia
4. Russia
5. Lithuania

Source: http://www.ofta.gov.hk/en/datastat/key_stat.html; http://www.arabianbusiness.com/saudi-arabia-sees-mobile-broadband-users-increase-291245.html; http://www.delfi.lt/news/economy/ITbussines/vel-augo-mobiliojo-rysio-abonentu-skaicius.d?id=29326053; http://www.bit.prime-tass.ru/news/show.asp?id=79606&ct=news; http://www.cgvijesti.net/267703_Na-kraju-2009-vise-od-1-29-miliona-korisnika-mobilne-telefonije.html Retrieved on (retrieved July 17, 2011).

Many immigrants and multicultural citizens have high expectations that health care workers will respect their personal beliefs and health care practices. This is not always the case. For example, Fadiman (1997) documents a case in which a Hmong child became brain-dead after doctors in Merced, California, continuously miscommunicated with the parents. The clash between traditional Hmong beliefs and the role of Western medicine resulted in a tragic incident.

Multicultural health care in this global age is an additional concern because of the aging population. Many must agonize over the rising cost of providing quality care to aging parents and grandparents. They also must struggle with their own cultural and personal values of taking care of their aging parents at home or sending them away to a health care facility.

Additionally, immigrants with limited English skills must often struggle to communicate with the hospital staff, nurses, or doctors to convey a simple message. Many immigrants also use their children as translators—which easily tips the balance between the parental role and the child's role in a status-oriented family system. Worse, even if the child speaks English fluently, she or he may not know how to translate all the medical terms or medication prescriptions for a parent.

In addition, different cultural beliefs and traditions surround the concept of "death." For many U.S. Americans, death is a taboo topic. Euphemisms are often used, such as "He is no longer with us," "She passed away peacefully," "She's in a better place," or "May he rest in peace." There are also a number of different cultural traditions in terms of burial practices. For example, the tradition among Orthodox Jews is to bury the deceased before sundown the next day and to have postdeath rituals that last for several days. When Muslims approach death, they may wish to face Mecca, their holy city in Saudi Arabia, and recite passages from the Qur'an (Purnell & Paulanka, 2008). Some Mexicans hold an elaborate ceremony known as a *velorio*, which may appear like a big party; in fact, they are celebrating the person's life because she or he has actually lived it fully. Likewise, the Irish hold a *wake*, and they eat and drink and celebrate the person's bountiful life. However, if you do not subscribe to any of the foregoing rituals, you would likely find it odd that some of these groups actually laugh and sing and dance during painful periods of grieving.

Concepts such as **ethnocentrism** and **ethnorelativism** and constructive intercultural conflict management skills such as **mindful listening** and **reframing** (as explored in the next few chapters) can serve as foundational building blocks for effective multicultural health care communication. Health care professionals and service providers can all benefit from mastering the knowledge and the skills of adaptive intercultural communication competencies.

Enhancing Intercultural Relationship Satisfaction

A meaningful life often entails deep relationship contacts with our families, close friends, and loved ones. However, with close contact often comes relationship disappointments and expectancy violations. If we already feel inept in handling different types of interpersonal relationships with people from our own cultural groups, imagine the challenges (plus, of course, the rewards) of dealing with additional cultural factors in our intimate relationship development process. Interpersonal friction provides a sound testing ground for the resilience of our intimate relationships.

According to expert researchers in interpersonal conflict (Canary & Lakey, 2006; Cupach, Canary, & Spitzberg, 2010), it is not the *frequency* of conflict that determines whether we have a satisfying or dissatisfying intimate relationship. Rather, it is the *competencies* that we apply in managing our conflicts that will move the intercultural–intimate relationship onto a constructive or destructive path.

Even if we do not venture out of our hometown, the places for people to meet, to socialize, and to date are changing. An interesting phenomenon is online dating, both domestically and globally. In the past, dating was considered a private affair. Now, online dating services, chat rooms, and other social networking services allow people to meet on the basis of criteria they find important. Some people may disclose their ethnicities, and some people may not, in the early stage of courtship and flirting. Brooks (2003) reports that 40 million U.S. individuals date online! With Match.com and other various dating services, the supply is definitely in demand in this "hook-up" age.

With the dramatic rise of intercultural marriages and dating relationships in the United States, intimate relationships are a fertile ground for culture shock and clashes. According to Rosenfeld (2007), more than 7 percent of the nation's 59 million married couples in 2005 were interracial, compared with less than 2 percent in 1970. Alaska is reported as the top-ranked U.S. state with a biracial heritage population, followed by Hawaii and California. The Pew Research Center (*"Almost all Millennials,"* 2010) conducted a study of over two thousand members of the Y (or "Millennial") Generation, those born after 1980. Results indicate that an overwhelming majority, regardless of race, are fine with a family member's marriage to someone of a different racial or ethnic group. When asked about marriage into a group to which they do not belong, nine of ten say they would be fine with a family member's marriage to an African American (88%), a Hispanic American (91%), an Asian American (93%), or a white American (92%). Another finding is that 54 percent have an interracial friend. Teenagers of today are often more receptive to developing close friendships and dating relationships across all racial lines compared with when data tracking began.

On the topic of intercultural family relationship satisfaction, for many U.S. adoptive families, which countries do you think most foreign-born adopted children come from? Take a guess and check out Jeopardy Box 1.6. The U.S. Census Bureau's very first profile of adopted children reveals that 1.6 million adopted kids under age eighteen are now living in U.S. households. Although foreign adoptions are increasing and getting the most headlines, the report shows that 87 percent of adoptees from diverse ethnic–racial backgrounds under eighteen were born in the United States.

As more U.S. families are becoming families of color, the challenge is to grapple with issues of race, ethnicity, and even religion. For example, in a documentary entitled *Off and Running* (http://offandrunningthefilm.com/), Avery Klein-Cloud is your typical sixteen-year-old teenager—who happens to be an African American raised by Jewish adoptive mothers. Avery has two adopted brothers: Samuel, who is biracial (African American and white), and Zay-Zay, who is Korean. Raised with Jewish faith in a lesbian household, Avery goes on a quest to find her birth mother and, as a result, experiences a true identity crisis. At one point, as she struggles with her newfound black identity, she seeks help from a counselor and admits that "I don't know how to be black." Her identity crisis and challenges depict her struggle to find the answer to the question: "Who am I?" Beyond cultural and religious identity questions in many of these multicultural–multiracial family households, other relevant issues include where to live and raise a biracial family, reaching out and making connections with those ethnically similar to the adopted child, and understanding the dilemmas of a child's or an adolescent's multiracial–multiethnic identity development stages.

Understanding the possible internal and external obstacles that affect an intimate intercultural

JEOPARDY BOX 1.6 TOP FIVE COUNTRIES OF BIRTH FOR FOREIGN-BORN ADOPTED CHILDREN UNDER EIGHTEEN IN THE UNITED STATES, 2010

1. China (Mainland)
2. Ethiopia
3. Russia
4. South Korea
5. Ukraine

Source: U.S. Department of State, 2010, http://adoption.state.gov/about_us/statistics.php (retrieved March 25, 2011).

relationship can increase our acceptance of our intimate partners and family members. Intercultural relationship conflict, when managed competently, can bring about positive changes in a relationship. It allows the conflict partners to use the conflict opportunity to reassess the state of the relationship. It opens doors for family members to discuss identity struggles and family dynamic issues. Culture-sensitive, respectful, and empathetic communication can increase relational and family closeness and deepen cultural self-awareness. The power of being understood on an authentic level can greatly enhance relationship quality, satisfaction, and personal insight.

Fostering Global and Intrapersonal Peace

The need for global peace has never been more apparent. A look at the headlines in any international news magazines or newspapers in early 2011 and the headline news spotted: "Tunisia, Algeria, Jordan, Yemen, Egypt, . . . Libya" and the revolutionary protests staged by citizens across the Middle East. The role of technology galvanized the young and the old to come together and demand their citizenship rights, democracy, and freedom. As the famed journalist Fareed Zakaria (2011) notes, "It's too simple to say that what happened in Tunisia and Egypt happened because of Facebook. But technology—satellite television, computers, mobile phones and the Internet—has played a powerful role in informing, educating and connecting people in the region. Such advances empower individuals and disempower the state. . . . Today's technology are all many-to-many, networks in which everyone is connected but no one is in control. That's bad for anyone trying to suppress information" (p. 31).

Not to mention the fact that more than ten years ago, the United States had never experienced terrorism so close at hand as on September 11, 2001, when almost three thousand individuals perished in the attack on the World Trade Center and the Pentagon. The death toll included individuals from many other countries, such as Australia, China, the Dominican Republic, El Salvador, Germany, Ireland, Israel, Japan, and Sweden (http://cnn.com).

In part because of this event, in the past five years interest in pursuing advanced college degrees in Peace

and/or Social Justice Studies has gained tremendous momentum around the world. There are currently over 450 bachelor's, master's, and doctoral programs and concentrations in forty countries and thirty-eight U.S. states to obtain a degree in Peace and Justice (Harris & Shuster, 2007). Programs are varied, such as at Depauw University, where you can major or minor in Conflict Studies, or you can join the Citizen Peacebuilding Program at the University of California, Irvine, or head off to the School of Peace Studies at Kyung Hee University in South Korea, which has been established since 1984.

In addition, other organizations have been dedicated to promoting peace, cultural, and spiritual development, and betterment of humankind. The Kyoto Symposium Organization in California, for example, was founded in 2004 to organize and administer the Kyoto Prize, awarded to individuals who have made "outstanding contributions to the betterment of humanity" (http://www.kyotoprize.org). In 2008, one such recipient was McGill University's Professor Emeritus Charles Taylor. In the Kyoto awards booklet, a beautiful bio and quotation exemplifies why peace and humanitarian tolerance are so relevant in our twenty-first century life: "Dr. Taylor is an outstanding philosopher who advocates communitarianism and multiculturalism from the perspective of holistic individualism. . . . He has constructed and endeavored to put into practice a social philosophy that allows human beings with different historical, traditional, and cultural backgrounds to retain their multiple identities and to live in happiness with each other" (http://www.inamori-f.or.jp/laureates/k24_c_charles/ctn_e.html). This quote summarizes Dr. Taylor's vision, in which he believes that all people, and all groups of people, deserve recognition for their distinctive humanistic qualities despite historical rejections.

To practice global peacemaking, we must hold a firm commitment that considerations of fairness should apply to all identity groups. We must be willing to consider sharing economic and social resources with underprivileged groups to level the fear and resentment factors. We must start practicing win–win collaborative dialogs with individuals or groups we may currently consider our enemies. We must display a mindful listening attitude even if we do not like the individuals or agree with their ideas or viewpoints. In displaying our respect for other nations or groups of individuals, we may open doors for more dialogs and deeper contacts. Human respect is a prerequisite for any type or form of intercultural or interethnic communication.

Global peacebuilding is closely connected to intrapersonal peacebuilding. If we are at peace with ourselves, we will hold more compassion and caring for others around us. If we are constantly angry and fighting against ourselves, we will likely spread our anger and resentment to others. The current spiritual leader of many Buddhists, the Holiness Fourteenth Dalai Lama, made comments on the importance of promoting world peace and thinking of the entire globe as a human family (http://www.dalailama.com/messages/world-peace/a-human-approach-to-peace; see Blog Post 1.1).

Let's also go visit Blog Post 1.2 and read the lyrics by John Lennon. Perhaps by listening to this song, we can engage in some imaginative peacebuilding work in our everyday lives—with our loved ones, families, close friends, classmates, teachers, neighbors, coworkers, and cultural strangers that come our way.

Deepening Self-Awareness and Other-Awareness

The late Tupac Shakur once rapped, *"Words of wisdom, they shine upon the strength of a nation. Conquer the enemy, on with education. Protect thy self, reach with what you wanna do. Know thy self, teach with what we've been through"* (from Shakur's *2Pacolypse Now*, 1991).

As we systematically acquire the building-block concepts and skills to deal with cultural differences, this knowledge base should challenge you to question your own cultural assumptions and primary socialization process. We acquire our cultural beliefs, values, and communication norms often on a very unconscious level. Without a comparative basis, we may never question the way we have been conditioned and socialized in our primary cultural system. Cultural socialization, in one sense, encourages the development of ethnocentrism.

Ethnocentrism means seeing our own culture as the center of the universe and seeing other cultures as insignificant or even inferior (see Chapter 8). As Charon (2004) describes the development of ethnocentrism, "Groups develop differences from one another, so do formal organizations, communities, and societies. *Without interaction with outsiders, differences become difficult to understand and difficult not to judge.* What is real to us becomes comfortable; what is comfortable becomes right. What we do not understand becomes less than right to us" (p. 156).

Without sound comparative cross-cultural knowledge, we may look at the world from only one lens—that is, our own cultural lens. With a solid intercultural knowledge base, we may begin to understand the possible value differences and similarities between our own cultural system and that of another cultural system. We may be able to explain

---

BLOG POST 1.1 "A HUMAN APPROACH TO WORLD PEACE"

Today we are so interdependent, so closely interconnected with each other, that without a sense of universal responsibility, a feeling of universal brotherhood and sisterhood, and an understanding and belief that we really are part of one big human family, we cannot hope to overcome the dangers to our very existence—let alone bring about peace and happiness.

One nation's problems can no longer be satisfactorily solved by itself alone; too much depends on the interest, attitude, and cooperation of other nations. A universal humanitarian approach to world problems seems the only sound basis for world peace. What does this mean? We begin from the recognition mentioned previously that all beings cherish happiness and do not want

suffering. It then becomes both morally wrong and pragmatically unwise to pursue only one's own happiness oblivious to the feelings and aspirations of all others who surround us as members of the same human family . . .

. . . The global population is increasing, and our resources are being rapidly depleted. Look at the trees, for example. No one knows exactly what adverse effects massive deforestation will have on the climate, the soil, and global ecology as a whole. We are facing problems because people are concentrating only on their short-term, selfish interests, not thinking of the entire human family. They are not thinking of the earth and the long-term effects on universal life as a whole. If we of the present generation do not think about these now, future generations may not be able to cope with them.

Source: http://(www.dalailama.com)

why people behave the way they behave from their culture's logic systems or value patterns. Whether you will be utilizing the knowledge and skills right on your own campus, in your classroom setting, in your workplace setting, and/or in your daily interpersonal relationship development contexts, we hope the knowledge building-blocks in this text will improve the quality of your everyday communication lives.

Intercultural knowledge can deepen our awareness of who we are, where we acquired our beliefs and values in the first place, and how we make sense of the world around us. To increase our self-awareness, we must be in tune with our own uncertainties and emotional vulnerabilities. We must understand our own cognitive filters and emotional biases in encountering cultural or ethnic differences. Knowledge brings the power of new insights. New insights, however, can be at times disconcerting and threatening. Confusion is part of the intercultural discovery journey. In this section, we have discussed eight practical reasons for why the study of intercultural communication is such an important topic. We are sure you can add other professional or personal reasons for why you should take a keen interest in this intercultural communication class. With the knowledge and skills gained as an intercultural student, and with imagination and creativity, we hope that you will find yourself applying these intercultural knowledge building blocks and these communication skills in diverse interaction settings. We now

turn to a discussion of the definitional elements of culture.

CULTURE: A LEARNED MEANING SYSTEM

What is culture? This question has fascinated scholars in various academic disciplines for many decades. As long ago as the early 1950s, Kroeber and Kluckhohn (1952) identified more than 160 different definitions of the term **culture**. The study of culture has ranged from the study of its external architecture and landscape to the study of a set of implicit values to which a large group of members in a community subscribe. The term originates from the Latin word *cultura* or *cultus* as in "*agri culture*, the cultivation of the soil.... From its root meaning of an activity, culture became transformed into a condition, a state of being cultivated" (Freilich, 1989, p. 2).

To be a "cultivated" member of a cultural community, the implication is that you understand what it means to be a "desirable and ideal" member of that particular system. It means you have acquired the meanings of "right" and "wrong" actions that produce particular consequences in that cultural environment. It means you have been nurtured by the core values of that cultural community and understand what constitutes "desirable" and "undesirable" behaviors as sanctioned by members of that system.

Culture is basically a learned system of meanings—a value-laden meaning system that helps you to "make sense" of and explain what is going on in your everyday

---

BLOG POST 1.2 IMAGINE

Imagine there's no heaven,
It's easy if you try,
No hell below us,
Above us only sky,
Imagine all the people
Living for today . . .

Imagine there's no countries,
It isn't hard to do,
Nothing to kill or die for,
No religion too,
Imagine all the people
Living life in peace . . .

Imagine no possessions,
I wonder if you can,
No need for greed or hunger,
A brotherhood of man,
Imagine all the people
Sharing all the world . . .

You may say I'm a dreamer,
but I'm not the only one,
I hope some day you'll join us,
And the world will live as one.

intercultural surroundings. It fosters a particular sense of shared identity and solidarity among its group members. It also reinforces the boundary of "we" as an ingroup and the "dissimilar others" as belonging to distant outgroups. *Ingroup identity* basically refers to the emotional attachments and shared fate (i.e., perceived common treatment as a function of category membership) that we attach to our selective cultural, ethnic, or social categories. *Outgroups* are groups from which we remain psychologically or emotionally detached, and we are skeptical about their words or intentions (Dovidio, Hewstone, Glick, & Esses, 2010a, 2010b).

In sum, *culture* is defined in this book as *a learned meaning system that consists of patterns of traditions, beliefs, values, norms, meanings, and symbols that are passed on from one generation to the next and are shared to varying degrees by interacting members of a community.* Members within the same cultural community share a sense of traditions, worldviews, values, rhythms, and patterns of life. We explore some of the key definitional ideas of culture—popular culture, meanings, symbols, norms, values, beliefs, and traditions—in the following subsections.

Culture is like an iceberg: the deeper layers (e.g., traditions, beliefs, and values) are hidden from our view. We tend to see and hear only the uppermost layers of cultural artifacts (e.g., fashion, pop music, and mass-appeal commercial films). We can also witness the exchange of overt verbal and nonverbal symbols (see Figure 1.1). However, to understand a culture—or a person in a cultural community—with any depth, we must match their underlying values coherently with their respective norms, meanings, and symbols.

It is the underlying set of cultural beliefs and values that drives people's thinking, reactions, and behaviors. Furthermore, to understand commonalities between individuals and groups, we must dig deeper into the level of universal human needs. Some universal human needs, for example, can include the needs for security, inclusion, love/connection, respect, control, and creating meaning. Although people in diverse cultures are dissimilar in many ways, they are also alike in many aspects—especially in the deep levels of the needs for human respect, connection, and security. Unfortunately, using the analogy of the iceberg, individuals usually do not take the time or effort to discover the deeper layers of universal human needs and connections.

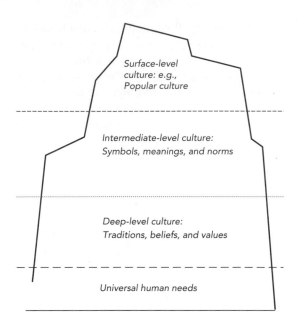

FIGURE 1.1 Culture: An Iceberg Metaphor

Surface-Level Culture: Popular Culture

On the most surface level, we often learn about another culture via the representation of its popular culture (for further examples, see Chapter 11). Popular culture is often referred to as "those cultural artifacts, processes, effects, and meanings that are popular by definition, derivation, or general understanding" (Zelizer, 2001, p. 299). Popular culture covers a wide spectrum of mediums—from pop music to pop gadgets, from pop karaoke to pop icons, and from global TV shows to global hip-hop fashion.

Popular culture (or *pop culture*) basically refers to cultural artifacts or systems that have mass appeal and that infiltrate our daily life. Popular images as portrayed in television, film, advertising, pop music, and even comic strips often reinforce cultural and gender ideologies in a society. The daily bombardment of television is one of our main sources of pop culture. Despite a limited number of women and ethnic minorities on television, for example, the media actually do offer sporadically some strong female gender roles (e.g., *Covert Affairs, Nikita,* and *The Good Wife*) and positive images of ethnic roles (e.g., *Hawaii Five-O, Modern Family,* and *The Game*). It is also important to remember that all popular media are businesses that aim for mass consumption and profit-generating outcomes.

In this context, U.S. popular culture tends to dominate the global market. In 2010, *CSI: Crime Scene Investigation* won the prestigious International Television Audience Award for a Drama TV Series at the Fiftieth Monte Carlo TV Festival. *CSI* has won the award three times in the five-year history of the audience awards and is the highest rated global television show across five continents. The reasons for the global appeal of *CSI* could be because it is a fast-paced suspense drama, featuring attractive-looking actors, and depicting crimes committed and solved smartly within a one-hour span. Furthermore, many U.S. television shows are exported globally, such as *Glee, House, Lost,* and *The Big Bang Theory.* Contemporary television programming of reality shows (e.g., *American Idol, Jersey Shore,* and *Pawn Stars*) appeals widely across multiple national boundaries, especially with global online video streaming.

Furthermore, U.S. popular culture in the category of films also dominates on a worldwide level. Films like *Avatar* and *Inception* reflect the surface layer of U.S. commercial pop culture. Other films, such as *Iron Man, Pirates of the Caribbean,* and *The Bourne Identity,* promote sweeping adventure, romance, open frontiers, and a spirit of exploration—images that reinforce the notion of the United States as a carefree, action-packed, adventure-seeking culture. Although the United States is one of the highest movie-producing countries, do you know what is the top-ranked highest movie-making country? Take a guess and check out Jeopardy Box 1.7, which lists the top five movie-

JEOPARDY BOX 1.7   TOP FIVE MOVIE-PRODUCING COUNTRIES IN 2009

Country	Features Produced
1. India	1,288
2. United States	677
3. China (Mainland)	456
4. Japan	448
5. France	158

Source: http://www.variety.com/article/VR1118012934?refCatId=13&query=france+feature+films+2009+BO (retrieved March 25, 2011).

JEOPARDY BOX 1.8   TOP FIVE MOST POPULAR U.S. NEWSSTAND MAGAZINES

1. Cosmopolitan
2. People
3. Woman's World
4. First
5. US Weekly

Source: Audit Bureau of Circulations, http://www.accessabc.com (retrieved March 25, 2011).

producing countries in 2009. Beyond films, people also receive images of another country via news magazines and television shows. Do you know what are the most popular U.S. newsstand magazines? Take a guess and check out Jeopardy Box 1.8.

Furthermore, icons, such as Disneyland, McDonald's, Coca-Cola, Starbucks, and Nike brand names, in conjunction with pop music, television shows, and films, are some prime examples of global popular culture. Some forms of popular culture have a direct correlation with the culture's underlying values and norms, but other forms of popular culture have been created for sheer entertainment purposes and profit-making objectives. Popular culture is often driven by an economic industry with a money-making target audience in mind. Boosting global appeal is another aspect of popular culture driven by strong economic interests.

As the music industry continues to suffer a severe decline in revenue and rampant piracy issues, music labels are finding alternative ways to evolve and achieve success. Digital downloads are one way. Do you know the top five digital downloads of 2010? Check out Jeopardy Box 1.9. Another alternative is the unique manifestation of hip-hop and rap. Chile's Ana Tijoux was nominated in 2011 for her rap in Spanish in the Grammy category of Best Latin Rock, Alternative, or Urban Album. Korean pop's (K-pop) domination in Asia is slowly infiltrating the United States, with artists like Rain selling out in New York and the Wonder Girls opening up for the Jonas Brothers. Finally, the combinations of ethnic minorities singing hip-hop/rap and social networks (YouTube and Facebook) have appealed to the masses. Take, for example, the group Far East Movement. These Koreatown Los Angeles

JEOPARDY BOX 1.9 TOP FIVE DIGITAL DOWNLOADS FOR 2010

Singer/group	Song	2010 Sales
1. Katy Perry feat. Snoop Dogg	California Gurls	4,398,000
2. Train	Hey, Soul Sister	4.314,000
3. Eminem fat. Rihanna	Love the Way You Lie	4,245,000
4. Taio Cruz	Dynamite	4,083,000
5. B.O.B. feat. Hayley Williams	Airplanes	4,004,000

Source: http://www.billboard.com/charts# (retrieved March 25, 2011).

rappers hit platinum with their song "Like a G6." It was the first time an Asian American group had a No. 1 digital single, eliciting about 10 million views on YouTube.

Some individuals consume a particular form of popular culture (e.g., CNN) as a way to be informed and included in their cultural community. By commenting on the headline news as reported on CNN, for example, individuals have a common symbol to rally around and to trade reactions with one another. Although having some information is better than no information before we visit another culture, all of us must remain vigilant in questioning the sources of where we receive our ideas or images about another culture. For example, the images we have acquired about Colombia, China, Israel, Sweden, and South Africa are often derived from secondhand news media. We should ask ourselves questions such as the following: Who are the decision makers behind the production of these popular images, icons, or sounds? Have we ever had a meaningful conversation with someone directly from that particular culture concerning his or her specific cultural or personal standpoints? Do we actually know enough people from that particular culture who are able to offer us multiple perspectives to understand the diverse reality of that culture? Do we actually have any acquaintances or close friends from that group who could help us to comprehend their culture on both a broad and a deep level?

In other words, we must be more watchful about how we process or form mental images about a large group of people under the broad category of "culture" or "race." Although we can travel in time to many far-flung places through the consumption of various media, we should remain mindful that a culture exists on multiple levels of complexity. Popular culture represents only one surface slice of the embedded richness of a culture. For more popular culture discussions, see Chapter 11.

Intermediate-Level Culture: Symbols, Meanings, and Norms

A **symbol** is a sign, artifact, word(s), gesture, or nonverbal behavior that stands for or reflects something meaningful. We use language as a symbolic system (with words, idioms, and phrases), which contains rich culture-based categories to organize and dissect the fluctuating world around us. Naming particular events (e.g., "formal gathering" versus "hanging out") via distinctive language categories is part of what we do in everyday communication activities. Expressions such as "Where there's a will there's a way" (a U.S. expression) or "The nail that sticks out gets hammered down" (a Japanese expression) reveal something about that culture's attitude toward self-determination or group-value orientation. Intercultural frictions often arise because of the ways we label and attach meanings to the different expressions or behaviors around us.

The **meanings** or interpretations that we attach to a symbol (e.g., a national flag or a nonverbal gesture), for example, can cue both objective and subjective reactions. People globally can recognize a particular country by its national flag because of its design and color. However, people of different cultural or ethnic backgrounds can also hold subjective meanings of what the flag means to them, such as a sense of pride or oppression. Other symbolic meaning examples can include the use of different nonverbal gestures across cultures. An animated "OK" nonverbal gesture sign from the United States, for example, with the thumb and forefinger signaling a circle, can mean money to the Japanese, a sexual insult in Brazil and Greece, a vulgar gesture in Russia, or zero in France.

Cultural norms refer to the collective expectations of what constitutes proper or improper behavior in a given interaction scene. For example, whether we should shake hands or bow to a new Japanese supervisor when being introduced reflects our sense of politeness or respect for the other individual in the scene. However, to enact a proper "getting acquainted" interaction script, we must take the setting, interaction goal, relationship expectation, and cultural competence skills into account.

The **setting** can include the consideration of cultural context (e.g., the interaction scene takes place in Japan or the United States) or physical context (e.g., in an office or a restaurant). The **interaction goal** refers to the objective of the meeting—a job interview meeting is quite different from a chance meeting in a restaurant. A meeting to "show off" that you are an expert about the Japanese culture (therefore, you bow appropriately) is quite different from a chance meeting with a Japanese supervisor in an American restaurant (therefore, maybe a slight head nod will do).

The **relationship expectation** feature refers to how much role formality/informality or task/social tone you want to forge in the interaction. Last, **cultural competence skills** refer to the cultural knowledge you have internalized and the operational skills you are able to apply in the interaction scene. For example, if you do not have a good knowledge of the different degrees of bowing that are needed in approaching a Japanese supervisor, you may make a fool of yourself and cause awkward interaction. You may end up with an improper performance in the "getting-acquainted bowing" scene. By not differentiating the different levels of bowing (e.g., lower bowing for supervisors and shallow bowing for low-ranking staff), you may have committed a cultural bump without conscious realization.

To understand a culture, we must master the operational norms of a culture. However, beyond mastering the prescriptive rules of what we "should" or "should not do" in a culture, we must dig deeper to understand the cultural logics that frame such distinctive behaviors. Although norms can be readily inferred and observed through behaviors, cultural beliefs and values are deep seated and invisible. Cultural traditions, beliefs, and values intersect to influence the development of collective norms in a culture.

Deep-Level Culture: Traditions, Beliefs, and Values

On a communal level, culture refers to a patterned way of living by a group of interacting individuals who share a common set of history, traditions, beliefs, values, and interdependent fate. This is known as the *normative culture* of a group of individuals. On an individual level, members of a culture can attach different degrees of importance to these complex ranges and layers of cultural beliefs and values. This is known as the *subjective culture* of an individual (Triandis, 1972, 1994, 1995). Thus, we can talk about the broad patterns of a culture as a group membership concept. We can also think about the culturally shared beliefs and values as subjectively subscribed to by members of a group, demonstrating varying degrees of endorsement and importance (Ting-Toomey, 2010a, 2010b, 2011).

Culturally shared traditions can include myths, legends, ceremonies, and rituals (e.g., celebrating Hanukkah or Thanksgiving) that are passed on from one generation to the next via an oral or written medium. They serve to reinforce ingroup solidarity, communal memory, cultural stability, and continuity functions. Culturally shared traditions can include, for example, the celebrations of birth, coming-of-age rituals, courtship rituals, wedding ceremonies, and seasonal change celebration rituals. They can also include spiritual traditions, such as in times of sickness, healing, rejuvenation, mourning, and funeral rituals for the dead (M.F. Bennett, 2009).

Culturally shared beliefs refer to a set of fundamental assumptions or worldviews that people hold dearly to their hearts without question. These beliefs can revolve around questions as to the origins of human beings, the concept of time, space, and reality, the existence of a supernatural being, and the meaning of life, death, and the afterlife. Proposed answers to many of these questions can be found in the major religions of the world, such as Christianity, Islam, Hinduism, and Buddhism.

Peering into U.S. culture, do you know what are the top five religions in the United States and which countries have the largest Christian and Jewish populations? Take a guess and check out Jeopardy

JEOPARDY BOX 1.10   TOP FIVE RELIGIONS IN THE UNITED STATES

Religion	%
1. Christianity	78.4
2. Judaism	1.7
3. Buddhism	0.7
4. Islam	0.6
5. Hinduism	0.4

Source: http://religions.pewforum.org/reports (retrieved March 25, 2011).

JEOPARDY BOX 1.11   TOP FIVE COUNTRIES WITH LARGEST CHRISTIAN AND JEWISH POPULATIONS

Top Five Countries with Largest Christian Populations
1. United States
2. Brazil
3. Russia
4. China
5. Mexico
Top Five Countries with Largest Jewish Populations
1. United States
2. Israel
3. France
4. Argentina
5. Canada

Source: Ash (2011, p. 80, 82; based on World Christian Database).

JEOPARDY BOX 1.12   TOP FIVE COUNTRIES WITH LARGEST BUDDHIST, HINDU, AND MUSLIM POPULATIONS

Top Five Countries with Largest Buddhist Populations
1. China
2. Japan
3. Thailand
4. Vietnam
5. Myanmar
Top Five Countries with Largest Hindu Populations
1. India
2. Nepal
3. Bangladesh
4. Indonesia
5. Sri Lanka
Top Five Countries with Largest Muslim Populations
1. Indonesia
2. Pakistan
3. India
4. Bangladesh
5. Iran

Source: Ash (2011, p. 80; based on World Christian Database).

Boxes 1.10 and 1.11. Do you know which are the top five countries with respect to the largest Buddhist, Hindu, and Muslim populations? Take a guess and cross-check your answers with Jeopardy Box 1.12. People who subscribe to any of these religious philosophies tend to hang on to their beliefs on faith, often accepting the fundamental precepts without question. They also tend to draw from their deeply held beliefs to subscribe meanings and explanations for why certain things happen in the cosmic order of life itself.

Beyond fundamental cultural or religious beliefs, people also differ in what they value as important in their cultures. **Cultural values** refer to a set of priorities that guide "good" or "bad" behaviors, "desirable" or "undesirable" practices, and "fair" or "unfair" actions. Cultural values (e.g., individual competitiveness versus group harmony) can serve as the motivational basis for actions (Stringer, 2003). For example, an Israeli psychologist, Shalom Schwartz (1990, 1992; Schwartz & Bardi, 2001), believes that we should understand the underlying motivational values that drive human actions. Those motivational values or basic value needs include the following: satisfying biological needs, social coordination needs, and the survival and welfare needs of the group.

From his various research studies in more than fifty countries, Schwartz has further identified ten value clusters that motivate people to behave the way they do in different cultures. These motivational value clusters or value types include the following: self-direction, stimulation, and hedonism; security, tradition, and conformity; power and benevolence; achievement; and universalism. Although self-direction, stimulation, and hedonism appear to reflect individualistic value tendencies, security, tradition, and conformity appear to reflect group-based, collectivistic value patterns. Power and benevolence seem to reflect whether individuals crave social recognition or deeper meaning in life. Achievement and universalism reflect whether individuals are ambitious and crave material success or whether they are universalistic oriented in wishing for a world at peace and inner harmony. More important, Schwartz's research indicates that a clear structure of values does emerge in reflecting people's underlying needs. The value structure and the relationship between value types appear to be consistent across cultures. However, cultures vary in terms of how strongly or how weakly they endorse a particular cluster of values.

To understand various communication patterns in a culture, we must understand the deep-rooted cultural values that give meanings to such patterns. An in-depth discussion of the contents of cultural values appears in Chapter 3.

STAMPING YOUR INTERCULTURAL PASSPORT

Overall, culture is a complex frame of reference that consists of patterns of traditions, beliefs, values, norms, meanings, and symbols that are shared to varying degrees by interacting members of a community. Oftentimes, our ignorance of a different culture's worldviews or values can produce unintentional clashes between ourselves and people of that culture. We may not even notice that we have violated another culture's norms in a particular communication scene. The result may worsen the intercultural misinterpretation process.

In summary, this chapter discusses several reasons why we should study intercultural communication. In discussing the definition of culture, we explored the three levels of understanding a culture: surface-level, intermediate-level, and deep-level culture. If you have fully understood all the concepts of Chapter 1, you have now earned one stamp on your intercultural passport. You can continue on your journey mindfully—read, observe, notice, experience, and learn. The remaining chapters will address intercultural communication flexibility issues, value dimensions, multilayered identities, verbal and nonverbal communication competence issues, and much more.

CHAPTER 2

WHAT IS INTERCULTURAL COMMUNICATION FLEXIBILITY?

CHAPTER OUTLINE

- Defining Intercultural Communication: A Process Model
  - Intercultural Communication Process: Overall Characteristics
  - Intercultural Communication: Meaning Characteristics

- Practicing Intercultural Communication Flexibility
  - Three Content Components: Knowledge, Attitude, and Skills
  - Three Criteria: Appropriateness, Effectiveness, and Adaptability

- Developing Intercultural Communication Flexibility
  - A Staircase Model
  - An Essential Hook: A Mindful Perspective

- Deepening Intercultural Process Thinking
  - Process Consciousness: Underlying Principles

- Intercultural Reality Check: Do-Ables

I met my wife years ago in San Francisco. It was love at first sight. She was funny, energetic, and incredibly passionate about life. Lili was the last person I thought I would date, much less marry, and part of the reason was our faith. I was born and raised in Turkey and am a Muslim. Lili was a Peruvian native but Jewish. Muslim and Jewish?! Are you kidding me? We worked it out and her parents embraced me as their own child, despite our many differences, as did mine. The true test to our relationship started when we decided to have children. How do we raise our children? After many arguments, discussions, and "if" statements, Lili got pregnant. We had a girl and decided that girls in our family will be raised in the Jewish faith. Should Allah bring me a boy, he would be raised Muslim.

Four girls later, I never regretted that decision. The most amazing moment of my life came when my oldest daughter, Leyla, had her Bat Mitzvah. I went to the temple, wore a *yamaka* (head cap), and became part of the service. Many people who attended could not believe I would do such a thing, but the most important gift I can give my daughter is compassion and love and the realization that religious faith will not divide our family. I was there for the next two Bat Mitzvahs and we have one more to go!

Last year, I took Lili and my family to Turkey. My parents had the opportunity to meet their grandchildren and the very special moment came when as a family we walked together to the Mosque. They were all dressed respectfully in Islamic attire.

—T. Senel, *Father*

To communicate adaptively with culturally different others, we must understand the major characteristics that make up the intercultural communication process. Although both culture and communication reciprocally influence one another, it is essential to distinguish between the characteristics of the two concepts for the purpose of understanding the complex relationship between them. Having already introduced the defining features of culture in Chapter 1, in this chapter we define the term "intercultural communication" for you. Although the idea of "culture" is an elastic concept that takes on multiple shades of meaning, similarly, the concept "communication" is also dynamic and subject to multifaceted interpretations.

In this chapter, we address the following three questions: What is the intercultural communication process? What is intercultural communication flexibility? What are the possible stages in developing intercultural communication flexibility? This chapter is developed in four sections: first, we introduce a culture-based process model to help you understand the "big picture" of the intercultural communication process. Second, we explore with you the concept of intercultural communication flexibility. Third, we introduce a staircase model of developing intercultural communication flexibility. Fourth, we outline general principles to help increase your understanding of the intercultural communication process. We end the chapter with a "Reality Check"—a set of recaps and checkpoints to guide you through your intercultural communication excursions.

DEFINING INTERCULTURAL COMMUNICATION: A PROCESS MODEL

Intercultural communication takes place when cultural group membership factors (e.g., cultural values) affect our communication process. Intercultural communication is often referred to as a symbolic exchange process between persons of different cultures in their attempts to create shared meanings in a given context. In the symbolic exchange process, intentions are inferred and culture-based interpretations are formed.

To increase your alertness to the intercultural communication process, we identify the characteristics of the intercultural communication process in two subsections: the overall characteristics of the process and the specific meaning characteristics of the intercultural exchange process. Figure 2.1 is a graphic model that represents some of the key elements in an intercultural-based process model.

Intercultural Communication Process: Overall Characteristics

Intercultural communication is defined as *the symbolic exchange process whereby individuals from two (or more) different cultural communities attempt to negotiate shared meanings in an interactive situation within an embedded societal system.* The major characteristics of this definition include the following concepts: symbolic exchange, process, different cultural communities, negotiate shared meanings, an interactive situation, and an embedded societal system. Interestingly, the intercultural communication scholar Halualani (2010), in conducting eighty in-depth qualitative interviews, uncovered some interesting distinctions among U.S. students in their conceptualizations of the term "intercultural interaction."

For example, Asian American interviewees focus on the importance of "sameness" (e.g., making them feel equal and comfortable) among diverse individuals and the need to establish "common ground." Latino/a students emphasize the "cultural respect" aspect of intercultural interaction and the importance of recognizing "cultural roots" of the other memberships. African American interviewees focus on intercultural interactions as having "difficult conversations" and recognizing others' stereotypes and prejudices against them. Last, European American students emphasize having intercultural interaction encounters as reflecting their "open-mindedness" and "acceptance of all cultural groups" (Halualani, 2010).

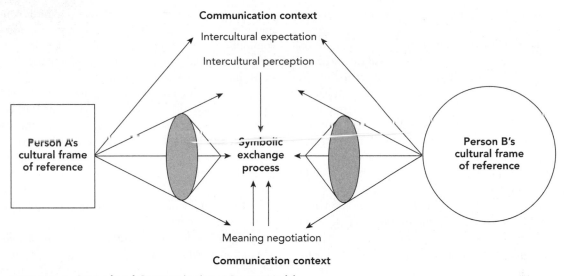

FIGURE 2.1 Intercultural Communication: A Process Model

On a broad-based level, in any intercultural encounter process, individuals use verbal and nonverbal messages to get their ideas across. The first characteristic, **symbolic exchange,** refers to the use of verbal and nonverbal symbols between a minimum of two individuals to accomplish shared meanings. Although verbal symbols represent the digital aspects of our message exchange process, nonverbal symbols or cues (i.e., the smallest identifiable unit of communication), such as smiles, represent the analogical aspects of our message exchange process. Digital aspects of communication refer to the content information that we convey to our listener. The relationship between a digital cue (e.g., the word *angry*) and its interpretation is arbitrary. The word *angry* is a digital symbol that stands for an intense, antagonistic emotional state. The word itself, however, does not carry the feeling: it is people, as symbol users, who infuse the word with intense emotions.

In contrast, analogical aspects of communication refer to the "picturesque" meanings or the affective meanings that we convey through the use of nonverbal cues. Nonverbal cues are analogical because there exists a resemblance relationship between the nonverbal cue (e.g., a frown) and its interpretation (e.g., dislike something). Furthermore, although verbal cues are discrete (i.e., with clear beginning and ending

sounds), nonverbal cues are continuous (i.e., different nonverbal cues flow simultaneously with no clear-cut beginning and ending) throughout the message exchange process. Although verbal messages always include the use of nonverbal cues, such as accents and vocal intonations, we can use nonverbal messages, such as touch, without words. As babies, we acquire or soak up the nonverbal cues from our immediate cultural environment before the actual learning of our native tongue.

The second characteristic, **process,** refers to the interdependent nature of the intercultural encounter. Once two cultural strangers make contact and attempt to communicate, they enter into a mutually interdependent relationship. A Japanese businessperson may be bowing, and an American businessperson may be ready to shake hands. The two may also quickly reverse their nonverbal greeting rituals and adapt to each other's behavior. This quick change of nonverbal postures, however, may cause another awkward moment of confusion. The concept of process refers to two ideas: the transactional nature and the irreversible nature of communication (Watzlawick, Beavin, & Jackson, 1967).

The **transactional** nature of intercultural communication refers to the simultaneous encoding (i.e., the sender choosing the right words or nonverbal gestures to express his or her intentions) and decoding (i.e., the receiver translating the words or nonverbal cues into comprehensible meanings) of the exchanged messages. When the decoding process of the receiver matches the encoding process of the sender, the receiver and sender of the message have accomplished shared content meanings effectively. Unfortunately, more often than not, intercultural encounters are filled with misunderstandings and second guesses because of language problems, communication style differences, and value-orientation differences.

Furthermore, intercultural communication is an *irreversible process* because the decoder may form different impressions even in regard to the same repeated message. Once an encoder has uttered something to a decoder, he or she cannot repeat the same exact message. The encoder's tone of voice, interaction pace, or facial expression will not stay precisely the same. It is also difficult for any encoder to withdraw or cancel a message once the message has been decoded. For example, if a sender utters a remark such as "I have friends who are Japs!" and then quickly attempts to withdraw the message, this attempt cannot succeed because the message has already created a damaging impact on the receiver's decoding field. Thus, the intercultural communication process is irreversible (Barnlund, 1962).

The third characteristic, **different cultural communities**, is defined as a broad concept. A **cultural community** refers to a group of interacting individuals within a bounded unit who uphold a set of shared traditions and way of life (see Blog Pic 2.1).

This unit can refer to a geographic locale with clear-cut boundaries, such as a nation. This unit can also refer to a set of shared beliefs and values that are subscribed to by a group of individuals who perceive themselves as united even if they are dispersed physically. For example, many Jews, who are dispersed throughout the world, tend to perceive themselves as a united cultural community via their shared religious traditions and beliefs.

Broadly interpreted, a cultural community can refer to a national cultural group, an ethnic group, or a gender group. It is, simultaneously, a group-level concept (i.e., a patterned way of living) and an individual's subjective sense of membership or an affiliation with a group. The term *culture* here is used as a frame of reference or knowledge system that is shared by a large group of individuals within a perceived bounded unit. The "objective" boundaries of a culture may or may not coincide with national or political boundaries. The term can also be used on a specific level to refer to a patterned way of living by an ethnocultural group (i.e., an ethnic group within a culture). Beyond the three characteristics of symbolic, process, and cultural communities,

Blog Pic 2.1   Celebrating with traditional dance is an inherent part of cultural communities.

the next section emphasizes the importance of paying close attention to negotiating shared meanings between members of different identity groups.

Intercultural Communication: Meaning Characteristics

The fourth characteristic, **negotiate shared meanings,** refers to the general goal of any intercultural communication encounter. In intercultural business negotiations or intercultural romantic relationships, a first level of concern is that we want our messages to be understood. When the interpretation of the meaning of the message overlaps significantly with the intention of the meaning of the message, we have established a high level of shared meanings in the communication process. The word negotiate indicates the creative give-and-take nature of the fluid process of human communication. For example, if both communicators are using the same language to communicate, they may ask each other to define and clarify any part of the exchanged message that is perceived as being unclear or vague.

Furthermore, every verbal and nonverbal message contains multiple layers of meanings. The three layers of meaning that are critical to our understanding of how people express themselves in a communication process are content meaning, relational meaning, and identity meaning. **Content meaning** refers to the factual (or digital) information that is being conveyed to the receiver through an oral channel or other communication medium. When the intended content meaning of the encoder has been accurately decoded by the receiver, the communicators have established a level of mutually shared content meanings. Content meaning is usually tied to substantive discussion or issues (e.g., business contract details) with verifiable, factual overtones (i.e., "Did you or did you not say that?"). It also involves what is appropriate to say in a particular cultural scene. For example, in many Asian cultures, it is impolite to say "no" directly to a request. Thus, people from traditional Asian backgrounds will tend to use qualifying statements such as "I agree with you in principle; however…" and "Maybe if I finish studying and if you still want to borrow my lecture notes…" to imply a "no" or "maybe"

answer. In most encounters, however, people are more aware of content meaning negotiation than relational or identity meaning negotiation.

Relational meaning offers information concerning the state of the relationship between the two communicators. Relational meaning is inferred via nonverbal intonations, body movements, or gestures that accompany the verbal content level. It conveys both power distance (e.g., equal–unequal) meanings and relational distance (e.g., friendly–unfriendly) meanings. For example, the professor says, "I want to talk to you about your grade in this class," which can be interpreted as either "You're in serious trouble—I can't believe you handed in such a sloppy paper!" or "I'm concerned about your grade in this class—let me know how I can help you." On the relational level, the professor's statement can be decoded as an intimidating–unfriendly request or a caring–friendly statement. The comment can also be decoded with compliance or resistance by the recipient of the message. The relational meaning of the message often implies how the relationship between the communicators should be defined and interpreted. It is closely linked with identity meaning issues.

Identity meaning refers to the following questions: "Who am I and who are you in this interaction episode?" "How do I define myself in this interaction scene?" and "How do I define you in this interaction scene?" (Wilmot & Hocker, 2011). Identity meaning involves issues such as the display of respect or disrespect and identity approval or disapproval. Decoders typically infer identity meanings through the speaker's tone of voice, facial expressions, nonverbal postures, spatial distance, and selective word choices. Nonverbal tones or gestures, however, are highly culture dependent and are oftentimes easily misinterpreted.

For example, the statement: "Maria Montoya? Come over here!" can be rephrased as "Ms. Montoya, when you have a minute, I would really like to talk to you" or "Maria, don't you understand my English? I need to talk to you right now!" or "Dr. Montoya, please, when you have some time, I would really appreciate your advice on this." These different statements indicate different shades of respect accorded to the addressee—depending on the tone of voice and whether the individual is addressed with her title—and also situational and cultural contexts.

The characteristics of content, relational, and identity meaning negotiation constitute the dynamic nature of the intercultural communication process. The process can take place in either a face-to-face or a mediated situation through e-mail, cellular phone, Twitter, blogs, or the teleconferencing context. Thus, the communication situation, the nature of the topical exchange, the relational features, the language use, the technological medium, and the cultural territory in which the exchange took place all have a profound influence on the symbolic exchange process itself.

The fifth characteristic, an **interactive situation,** refers to the idea that every communication episode occurs in a relational context, a psychological context, and a physical context. Throughout this book, we will use **relational context** examples of intercultural acquaintance relationships, friendships, dating relationships, and business relationships to illustrate diverse relationship contexts. A **psychological context,** in turn, refers to our psychological moods (e.g., anxious versus secure), meaning-making interpretations (e.g., perceived meanings of the formal or informal interactive setting), and normative role expectations of a given situation. Last, a **physical context** refers to the immediate physical features (e.g., furniture or seating arrangement in a room, temperature) and layouts surrounding the face-to-face or mediated interaction. We acquire the meanings to these situational features via the primary socialization process of our culture and family system.

The sixth characteristic, **societal embedded system,** refers to the multilayered contexts such as history, politics, economics, social class, formal institutions, and policies, as well as the community or organizational contexts that shape the process and the outcome of the actual intercultural communication encounter (Oetzel, Ting-Toomey, & Rinderle, 2006). Transactional human communication always takes place within an interactive situation and is subjected to the influence of the multilayered factors in the larger societal environment.

We also encourage you to think of additional examples and questions to clarify your own understanding of important concepts that affect the intercultural

communication encounter's conditions, processes, and outcomes. The next section introduces the intercultural communication flexibility perspective.

PRACTICING INTERCULTURAL COMMUNICATION FLEXIBILITY

What is intercultural communication flexibility? How do we know that the individuals in the communication process have communicated inflexibly or flexibly? Intercultural communication flexibility has three content components—knowledge, attitude, and skills. **Flexible intercultural communication** emphasizes the importance of integrating knowledge and an open-minded attitude and putting them into adaptive and creative practice in everyday communication. **Inflexible intercultural communication** stresses the continuation of using our own cultural values, judgments, and routines in communicating with culturally different others.

Whereas inflexible intercultural communication reflects an ethnocentric mindset, flexible intercultural communication reflects an ethnorelative attitude. An **ethnocentric mindset** means staying stuck with our own cultural worldviews and using our own cultural values as the baseline standards to evaluate the other person's cultural behavior. An **ethnorelative mindset**, however, means to understand a communication behavior from the other person's cultural frame of reference (M. Bennett, 1993; J. Bennett & M. Bennett, 2004). In an optimal state of ethnorelativism, a flexible mindset, an alert emotional awareness, and competent interaction behaviors come together and help us to become dynamic, flexible intercultural communicators. In the following sections, we first discuss the three components of flexible intercultural communication. We then discuss the three criteria for evaluating whether the cultural members in the process have behaved flexibly or inflexibly.

Three Content Components: Knowledge, Attitude, and Skills

Knowledge here refers to the systematic, conscious learning of the essential themes and concepts in intercultural communication flexibility. Conscious learning can be developed through formal studying and informal immersion experiences. *Formal studying* can include taking classes in intercultural communication and ethnic-related studies. It includes attending intercultural communication seminars and diversity-related training. It could mean taking a foreign language class or a global history class. *Informal learning* experiences can include international traveling, studying abroad, volunteering for community service, and visiting ethnic neighborhoods, temples, or stores in our own backyard. It includes reading international newspapers and magazines. It could mean putting ourselves in constant contact with culturally different others and learning to be comfortable with the differences.

To digest the knowledge we have learned, we must develop an open mindset and an attentive heart. **Attitude** can include both cognitive and affective layers. The *cognitive* layer refers to the willingness to suspend our ethnocentric judgment and readiness to be open-minded in learning about cross-cultural difference issues. The *affective* layer refers to the emotional commitment to engage in cultural perspective-taking and the cultivation of an empathetic heart in reaching out to culturally diverse groups. It also means we have spent time reflecting on our own identity and emotional vulnerability issues in dealing with the changes within our own affective state. A receptive and responsive attitude serves as the basis to push us forward to communicate adaptively with people from diverse cultural communities.

In developing cognitive and affective openness, we try to intentionally put on a new pair of "glasses" or "lenses" (i.e., the practice of ethnorelative thinking and empathy). A flexible intercultural attitude means engaging in ethnorelative thinking to understand someone else's behavior from her or his cultural point of view. From an ethnorelative lens, we put our ethnocentrism on hold and suspend our hasty cultural judgments.

Skills are our operational abilities to integrate knowledge and a responsive attitude with adaptive intercultural practice. Adaptive communication skills help us to communicate mindfully in an intercultural situation. Many interaction skills are useful in promoting flexible intercultural communication. Some of these, for example, are value clarification skills, mindful tracking skills, attentive listening, verbal code

switching, nonverbal sensitivity skills, and intercultural conflict management tools (see the Intercultural Reality Check section at the end of this and each of the remaining chapters). These skills will be discussed under different topics in later chapters.

Three Criteria: Appropriateness, Effectiveness, and Adaptability

The criteria of communication appropriateness, effectiveness, adaptability, and creativity can serve as evaluative yardsticks of whether an intercultural communicator has been perceived as behaving flexibly or inflexibly (Spitzberg & Cupach, 1984; Ting-Toomey, 1999, 2004, 2010c) in an interaction episode. A dynamic, competent intercultural communicator is one who manages multiple meanings in the communication exchange process—appropriately, effectively, and adaptively. All three criteria can also be applied developmentally to an individual who is attempting to increase her or his mastery of knowledge, an open attitude, and skills in dealing constructively with members of diverse cultures (Csikszentmihalyi, 1996; Wiseman, 2003).

Appropriateness refers to the degree to which the exchanged behaviors are regarded as proper and match the expectations generated by the insiders of the culture. Individuals typically use their own cultural expectations and scripts to approach an intercultural interaction scene. They also formulate their impressions of a competent communicator on the basis of their perceptions of the other's verbal and nonverbal behaviors in the particular interaction setting. The first lesson in communication competence is to "tune in" to our own ethnocentric evaluations concerning "improper" dissimilar behaviors. Our evaluations of "proper" and "improper" behavior stem, in part, from our ingrained cultural socialization experiences. If your friend has never eaten with a knife and fork, this does not mean your friend lacks good manners. Perhaps your friend eats with chopsticks, hands, a spoon, or a combination of these.

To understand whether appropriate communication has been perceived, it is vital to obtain competence evaluations from the standpoint of both communicators and interested observers. It is also critical to obtain both self-perception and other-perception data. We may think that we are acting appropriately, but others may not concur with our self-assessment. Appropriate communication behaviors can be assessed through understanding the underlying values, norms, social roles, expectations, and scripts that govern the interaction episode. When we act appropriately in an interaction scene, our culturally proper behaviors can facilitate communication effectiveness. Instead of saying to your friend, "You're so weird!" you may ask him if he can teach you how to use a pair of chopsticks.

Effectiveness refers to the degree to which communicators achieve mutually shared meaning and integrative goal-related outcomes. Effective encoding and decoding processes lead to mutually shared meanings. Mutually shared meanings lead to perceived intercultural understanding. Interaction effectiveness has been achieved when multiple meanings are attended to with accuracy and when mutually desired interaction goals have been reached. Interaction ineffectiveness occurs when interpersonal goals are mismatched and intercultural noises and clashes jam the communication channels (Gudykunst, 2001, 2005a, 2005b).

Communication effectiveness can improve task productivity. Productivity is closely related to outcome factors, such as the generation of new ideas, new plans, new momentum, and creative directions in resolving the intercultural problem. In an unproductive interaction episode, both sides feel that they have wasted their time and energy in being involved in the interaction in the first place. Both sides feel they have lost sight of their original goals in the stressful interaction episode. In a productive communication exchange, both sides feel that they have mutual influence over the communication process and that they have devoted positive energy in creating the constructive outcome.

Communication adaptability refers to our ability to change our interaction behaviors and goals to meet the specific needs of the situation. It implies behavioral flexibility in dealing with the intercultural miscommunication episode. It signals our mindful awareness of the other person's perspectives, interests, goals, and communication approach, plus our willingness to modify our own behaviors and goals to adapt to the interaction situation. By mindfully tracking what is going on in the intercultural situation, both parties may modify their nonverbal and verbal behavior to achieve a more synchronized communication process. In modifying their behavioral styles, polarized views on the intercultural content problem may also become depolarized or "softened."

Flexible intercultural communication requires us to communicate appropriately and effectively in different intercultural situations, which necessitates creativity, choices, change, and adaptation (Digh, 2008, 2011; Iyengar, 2010; Tharp & Reiter, 2003). By having an open-minded attitude that motivates our behaviors, we generate intercultural interest and curiosity in the intercultural relating process (Gannon & Pillai, 2010; Nwosu, 2009; Van Dyne, Ang, & Koh, 2009).

In sum, to be flexible intercultural communicators, we must be highly imaginative in our assessment of the intercultural contact situation. We also must be behaviorally nimble to decide whether to adapt, to maintain the same posture, or to expect the other person to adapt to our behaviors—depending upon the intentions, process, goals, and people involved in the interactive situation. It takes a flexible mindset to combine the best practices of both cultures to arrive at a creative, synergistic solution (Schaetti, Ramsey, & Watanabe, 2009; Ting-Toomey, 2009). It also takes a well-balanced heart to move beyond the practices of both cultures and utilize a third-culture approach to sensitively bridge the cultural differences. An individual with an open mindset and elastic communication skills is able to flex her or his communication muscles with good timing and can stretch intentionally to interact competently through a diverse range of intercultural terrains.

DEVELOPING INTERCULTURAL COMMUNICATION FLEXIBILITY

To understand intercultural communication flexibility from a long-term developmental viewpoint, we present the staircase model to reinforce your learning and stretch your imagination.

A Staircase Model

Flexible intercultural communication can be conceptualized along the following stages (see Figure 2.2): (1) unconscious incompetence—the blissfully ignorant

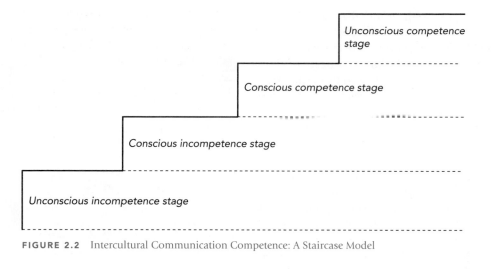

FIGURE 2.2 Intercultural Communication Competence: A Staircase Model

stage in which an individual is unaware of the communication blunders she has committed in interacting with a cultural stranger; (2) conscious incompetence—the semi-awareness stage in which an individual is aware of her incompetence in communicating with members of the new culture but does not do anything (or know how to) to change her behavior adaptively in the new cultural situation; (3) conscious competence—the **"full mindfulness"** stage when an individual is aware of her intercultural communication "nonfluency" and is committed to integrating the new knowledge, attitude, and skills into competent practice; and (4) unconscious competence—the "mindlessly mindful" zen stage when an individual can code switch so spontaneously and effortlessly that the interaction flows smoothly from an "out-of-conscious yet mindful awareness" rhythm (Howell, 1982; Ting-Toomey, 1999).

In the first stage, the **unconscious incompetence stage,** individuals have no culture-sensitive knowledge (nor do they have responsive attitudes or skills) to communicate competently with the host members of the new culture (see Blog Pic 2.1). This is the cultural obliviousness stage or cultural ignorance stage. Cultural members operate from a total ethnocentric worldview. For example, Esteban, who is Cuban American, likes to tell racial jokes about Cubans. Because he is Cuban American, he thinks it is totally acceptable to joke about his own ethnic ingroup. However, some of

his Cuban and non-Cuban friends do not appreciate the jokes at all. They send him nonverbal disapproval signals but he does not get those awkward signals.

In the second stage, the **conscious incompetence stage,** individuals have some notion (i.e., attitudinal openness) that they behave incompetently; however, they lack the knowledge or skills to operate appropriately in the new cultural setting. They do, however, start questioning their own ethnocentric lens and communication habits. For example, Estaban still admits to telling racial jokes out of habit—although he is aware of his terribly offensive behavior.

In the third stage, the **conscious competence stage,** individuals are actively pursuing new intercultural knowledge to improve their communication competencies. Given time and practice, they would probably move from the conscious semicompetence phase to the conscious full-competence phase. In the fully developed conscious competence phase, individuals are able to connect knowledge, a responsive attitude, and skills into competent applications. In the conscious competence stage, individuals try to stay in tune and be fully mindful of the communication process itself and also attend to the outcome goal. They use an ethnorelative lens, rather than an ethnocentric lens, in interpreting what is going on in the intercultural encounter process.

For example, if we decide to spend time in Spain, we must learn new behaviors conscientiously, from *"el punto del sal"* (a Spanish custom that says one should not add salt to a meal until after tasting it, because it shows you doubt the competency of the chef; the food should arrive at the table with the correct amount of salt) to "always wear shoes or slippers inside the house" (bare or stocking feet are unseemly and improper, according to the Spanish culture). Becoming consciously competent can allow you to pick up everyday intercultural meanings and also practice competent intercultural behaviors.

The fourth stage, the **unconscious competence stage**, is the "mindlessly mindful" zen-like stage in which individuals move in and out of spontaneous yet adaptive communication with members of the new culture. They can code switch effortlessly between the two different intercultural communication systems. Their effort appears to be very "seamless"—thus, the notion of "unconscious" competence. For example, once a person becomes conscious of the Spanish custom of always wearing shoes inside a Spanish house, with repeated practice it becomes a spontaneous habit—done without awareness. However, if the same person now travels to Japan, she must learn new rules of behaving (e.g., taking off her shoes before entering a traditional Japanese house and putting on a pair of nice, clean guest slippers). Thus, in any intercultural situation, the most flexible intercultural communicators often rotate between the conscious competence stage and the unconscious competence stage. Through such rotation between stages, the flexible intercultural communicator is constantly updating her knowledge about cultural difference issues and refreshing her attitude in dealing with culturally diverse situations (Gardenswartz & Rowe, 1998, 2009).

If an individual stays in the unconscious competence stage for too long without a humble attitude, cultural arrogance may set in without notice. The individual may easily fall back into the unconscious incompetence stage because of overconfidence or cultural condescension (see Blog Pic 2.2).

An Essential Hook: A Mindful Perspective

Communication flexibility requires us to be sensitive to the differences and similarities between dissimilar cultures. It also demands that we be aware of our own ethnocentric biases when making evaluations

Blog Pic 2.2   Where do you envision yourself on these stairs?

of other people's communication approaches. It also asks us to communicate appropriately, effectively, and adaptively in a culturally respectful manner. A flexible communicator is a well-trained individual with a vast amount of knowledge in the domain of intercultural communication. He is able to make creative connections among cultural values, communication styles, and situational issues.

A flexible communicator is also a mindful cultural scanner (Ting-Toomey 2009, 2010a). To engage in an inward state of mindfulness, an individual must turn inward and look into herself and realize that: (1) her state of identity is closely intertwined with her unconscious cultural conditioning process; (2) her reactive judgments of culturally unfamiliar behaviors are based on her own cultural and personal value priorities; (3) her perceptions and interpretations of culturally "bizarre" behaviors are often based on the insecure feelings of fear and colored by stereotypic images gained from the media; and (4) her lack of knowledge about the unfamiliar others creates further psychological and physical gaps (Ting-Toomey, 2010a).

In addition, to engage in an outward state of mindfulness, a flexible intercultural communicator must learn to: (1) engage in cultural frame switching and see things from the other person's cultural frame of values; (2) connect underlying value patterns with the unfamiliar cultural behaviors and understand the cultural logic of why people behave the way they behave; (3) observe and notice complexity of identity issues and situational issues in any cultural community; and (4) focus on the present moment of the process and listen closely to the repeated words and nonverbal nuances that are being exchanged in the process (Bennett-Goleman, 2001; Canary & Lakey, 2006; Langer, 1989, 1997; Ting Toomey, 2009).

To be flexible intercultural communicators, we must increase the complexity of our intercultural communication knowledge. We must develop a keen sense of alertness on two fronts—one is increasing self-awareness as a cultural and unique being and the other is increasing our awareness of others as complex cultural and unique beings. Furthermore, we must develop a more layered sense of understanding by realizing that many cultural, ethnic, situational, and personal factors shape and, in turn, affect an intercultural miscommunication episode. Being committed to applying divergent and differentiated cultural viewpoints means taking the time and patience to work out the cultural differences constructively. We will lay out some of these ideas in the coming chapters.

DEEPENING INTERCULTURAL PROCESS THINKING

The general goal of intercultural communication is to create shared meanings competently—so that what I intended to say or imply is accurately decoded by the culturally different other and, simultaneously, in a culturally appropriate manner. To communicate effectively and appropriately, a flexible intercultural communicator must develop a keen sense of adaptability and imagination in her or his intercultural connecting process.

Process Consciousness: Underlying Principles

The following guidelines are presented to increase your conceptual understanding of the intercultural communication process. On an everyday intercultural communication level, we must develop an astute sense of mindfulness of the following principles:

PRINCIPLE 1: *Intercultural communication often involves mismatched expectations that stem, in part, from cultural group membership differences.* When we encounter miscommunication in an intercultural interaction process, we experience emotional frustration. Some of the emotional frustration often stems, in part, from cultural differences, mismatched expectations, or ignorance. Intercultural miscommunication takes place when our cultural group membership factors affect, in part, our communication process on either an awareness or an unawareness level.

The cultural membership differences can include deep-level differences, such as cultural worldview differences and value differences. Concurrently, they can also include the mismatch of applying different norms and expectations in a particular communication scene. In practicing mindful intercultural communication, we can develop an understanding of the valuable differences that exist between different cultural groups. At the same time, we also must continuously recognize the commonalities that exist in all humans, across all cultures.

PRINCIPLE 2: *Intercultural communication often involves varying degrees of biased intergroup perceptions.* Biased intergroup perceptions often involve overgeneralizations or stereotypes. The term *intergroup* means viewing the person as a representation of a group membership category and deemphasizing the person's unique attributes. Thus, from an intergroup lens, stereotyping involves an overestimation of the degree of association between stereotypic–psychological traits (e.g., cantankerous, grumpy) and group membership categories (e.g., elderly population). Moreover, stereotyping is also about creating self-fulfilling prophecies. We tend to see behavior that confirms our expectations even when it is absent, and we ignore vital information (e.g., knowledgeable, wise advice) when it is incongruous with our expectations.

When we communicate mindlessly, we do not notice the distinctive qualities of the cultural person with whom we are communicating. Rather, we fall back on our stereotypes to reduce our guesswork and, perhaps, emotional vulnerability level. Although the contents of our stereotypes can be positive or negative, rigidly typecasting selective members of a cultural group into "triangles" and "squares" can perpetuate inaccurate impressions and myths. If we are unwilling to question our rigidly held stereotypes, our intergroup relationships will stay only at a superficial level of contact. Stereotyping, together with an ethnocentric attitude and a prejudiced mindset, can often perpetuate misinterpretation spirals and intergroup conflict cycles.

PRINCIPLE 3: *Intercultural communication involves the simultaneous encoding and decoding of verbal and nonverbal messages in the exchange process.* This is the key assumption to understanding the concept of "process" in intercultural communication. From a transactional model viewpoint, both intercultural communicators in the communication process are viewed as playing the sender and receiver roles. Both are responsible for synchronizing the conversational process and outcome. An effective encoding and decoding process leads to shared meanings. An ineffective encoding and decoding process by one of the two "transceivers" can lead to intercultural misunderstanding.

However, beyond the accurate encoding and decoding of messages on the content level, communicators need to cultivate additional sensitivity along multiple levels (such as relational, identity, and situational meanings) of intercultural understanding. Without a keen sense of cultural decoding competence, we

Blog Pic 2.3 Intercultural incompetence.

are likely to misjudge our intercultural partners' intentions and find ourselves in serious trouble. Without a mindful sense of message encoding, we may say the wrong things in the wrong context and with bad timing. With mindful alertness, we can conscientiously choose words and behaviors that make dissimilar others feel affirmed, included, and listened to.

PRINCIPLE 4: *Intercultural communication involves multiple goals, and the goals people have are largely dependent on how they define the interaction episode.* Echoing the various layers of meaning negotiation, three types of goals are important in an intercultural encounter process: content goals, relational goals, and identity goals. *Content goals* refer to external, substantive issues in the communication process. Some questions we may want to consider are these: What do we want to accomplish in the intercultural negotiation session? What are the content or instrumental interaction goals? What are the potential obstacles and the necessary steps to accomplish our goals effectively? For example, a clear content goal discussion can involve asking a professor to postpone the deadline of a group project or requesting a pay raise from your international boss. We need to think ahead in terms of the cultural or interpersonal obstacles that lie in the path of content goal attainment. We also need to decide whether we should pursue our content goals in an individualistic, assertive manner or in a relational, tactful manner.

Relational goals refer to the socioemotional issues or relational role expectations that are involved in the intercultural negotiation session. We need to examine questions such as the following: What are my role expectations and the other person's role expectations in the intercultural encounter episode? What are the situational conditions that shape the dynamics of the role-encountering process? What are the behavioral requirements, and what is "off limits" in this intercultural interaction scene? A professor from a small power distance value culture (e.g., the United States) may be comfortable with informal discussions with his students in the classroom environment. A professor from a large power distance value culture (e.g., Iran) may expect more formality from students in the classroom setting. However, the same Iranian professor may relax her role expectations at a student-sponsored picnic in the park. To be flexible communicators across cultural lines, we must recognize the interconnected nature of norms, roles, and situations.

Identity goals refer to the projected self-image or self-worth issues in the interaction scene. Identity goals can involve identity respect/disrespect or approval/disapproval postures. It can also be interpreted in connection with our desires to have our cultural, ethnic, gender, disability, professional, and personal images respected in the communication episode. The ability to project a desired self-image or "face" and to have this projected "face" be validated are critical skills in any intercultural negotiation session. *Face* is basically about identity respect issues and other consideration issues within and beyond the intercultural encounter process. In a mindful facework negotiation process, honoring others' face and helping others to save face are ways to manage favorable interactive identities across cultures (see Blog Post 2.1).

PRINCIPLE 5: *Intercultural communication calls for understanding and acceptance of diverse communication approaches and styles.* For example, in an intercultural conflict episode, parties often utilize different communication styles that are consistent with their culture-based values. For some cultures, a conflict with another party should be confronted directly and assertive steps should be taken to resolve the conflict in a clear win–lose direction. In other cultures, a conflict should be avoided at all costs to preserve relational harmony. Mutual face-saving and face-honoring moves may supersede the need to arrive at a clear win–lose

resolution. In fact, conflict negotiators may want to cultivate the image of a win–win conflict process so that both parties can maintain some face, or dignity, before returning to their home cultures.

The cultural preferences for certain communication styles are, of course, mediated by many situational and relationship expectation factors. To embark on an inclusive communication approach, we must learn to be flexible in our verbal and nonverbal styles in dealing with diverse groups. We also must pay close attention to mediating factors—such as situational parameters and interaction goals—in shaping our different communication modes.

PRINCIPLE 6: *Many intercultural encounters involve well-meaning culture bumps or clashes.* Individuals of different cultural communities have learned different interaction forms, for example, eye contact maintenance or avoidance, in everyday conversations. They also tend to use their own cultural scripts to evaluate the competencies of cultural strangers' behaviors. Many intercultural miscommunication episodes start off from culture bumps or clashes. A **culture bump** is defined as a cultural violation on the behavioral level when our meanings do not overlap with one another in viewing the same behavior, which creates communication awkwardness or embarrassment (Archer, 1991). Let us look at Blog Post 2.2.

In this particular story, although David acted in an "unconscious incompetent" manner in the beginning, he caught his own culture bump and moved to the

---

BLOG POST 2.1

As a Mexican American young woman, I've experienced the push and pull of my identity. I feel like half of my life I've been adopting and adapting to the dominant American culture while selectively choosing certain aspects of my Mexican culture to nurture and celebrate.

Growing up, I did not interact much with other Hispanic classmates. In fact, I didn't know how to talk to them. I was constantly surrounded by Caucasians and determined at that time in my young life that this was how everything should be. This was the time that I began to disregard my Hispanic identity. I remember acting aloof when my mother attempted to speak Spanish and I pretended I didn't understand her. Soon thereafter, I remember seeing gardeners (who are stereotypically Mexican

in Southern California) and thinking to myself, I may be Mexican, but I'm not a gardener.

It wasn't until college that I was exposed to the reality of social circumstances, prejudice, stereotypes, and heteronormativity. I realized then how empty my identity had become and how rich it could be with a reacquaintance of my Mexican roots. Yes, I will take up anything and everything that is related to being Hispanic as part of my identity now, it is who I am. To not embrace my Mexican heritage is to not embrace me. I guess that's why I favor diversity in the schools I've attended, and I now have a better perspective on what I want my life to be like as I raise my children up in a world where every ethnicity should be welcomed.

—Jennifer, *college student*

BLOG POST 2.2

In a Poly Sci[ence] class during a group discussion, I was sitting to the right of a man from Saudi Arabia. As I was talking to him, I placed my right ankle on my left knee. I noticed a definite change in his demeanor toward me. After class, I approached him and asked if I had done or said something that offended him. He told me that in the Arab culture, exposing the soles of your shoes while directly speaking to someone is tantamount to giving them "the finger." I apologized for my ignorance; he apologized for his ignorance of my ignorance. We ended up being friendly to one another for the remainder of the semester.

—David, *college student*

"conscious incompetent" stage to inquire about his own communication mistake. A culture bump often ends in more miscommunications and frustration when the two communicators continue to misinterpret each other's behavior as rude or even insulting. A culture bump is about violating another person's cultural norms without malicious intent. More often than not, we commit unintentional culture bumps in a new culture because we have not mastered the norms and the meaning fluency of that new system.

Well-meaning clash basically refers to misunderstanding an encounter in which people are actually behaving in a "socially skilled manner" and with "good intentions" according to the norms in their own culture (Brislin, 1993). Unfortunately, the behaviors that are considered proper or effective in one culture can be considered improper or ineffective in another culture. For example, using direct eye contact is considered a sign of respect in U.S. culture, whereas direct eye contact can signify disrespect in the Thai culture. The term *well-meaning* is used because no one in the intercultural encounter intentionally behaves obnoxiously or unpleasantly. Individuals are trying to be well mannered or pleasant in accordance with the politeness norms of their own culture. Individuals behave ethnocentrically—often without conscious realization of their automatic-pilot verbal or nonverbal routines.

PRINCIPLE 7: *Intercultural communication always takes place in a context.* Intercultural communication does not happen in a vacuum, but is always context bound. Patterns of thinking and behaving are always interpreted within an interactive situation or context. To understand intercultural communication from a contextual viewpoint, we must consider how the physical and psychological settings of the communicators establish the climate or mood of their interaction.

The physical setting can include furniture arrangement, props, color of the room, temperature of the room, and who is in the room. However, and more important, we must understand the psychological or emotional meanings that are attached to the physical setting by the different cultural participants. Additionally, the expected roles of the participants, their relational distance, conversational topics, interaction goals, implicit communication rules, and culture shock factors can all influence the interaction climate. Last, the degree of cultural knowledge, past cultural visiting experience, and competent performance of communication skills form the overall patterns of the communication context.

PRINCIPLE 8: *Intercultural communication always takes place in embedded systems.* A system is an interdependent set of components that constitutes a whole and, simultaneously, influence each other. Our enculturation process (i.e., our primary socialization process at a young age) is influenced by both macro- and microlevel events in our cultural environment. On a macro level, we are programmed or enculturated into our culture via our family and educational systems, religious and political systems, and government and socioeconomic systems, as well as by the paramount influence of media in our everyday life (Oetzel, 2009; Oetzel et al., 2006).

On a microlevel, we are surrounded by people who subscribe to similar worldviews, values, norms, and expectations. We are the recipients and also the preservers of our culture via the daily messages that we trade. However, culture is not a static web. It is a dynamic, evolutionary process. Human beings are also not static individuals—they are changeable. In learning about another culture or dissimilar groups, we can expand our mental landscape and emotional horizon. Through the lens of another culture, we may be able to reinterpret our own identity and culture with fresh visions and insights.

INTERCULTURAL REALITY CHECK: DO-ABLES

In this chapter, we defined intercultural communication and intercultural communication flexibility. In exploring the definition of intercultural communication, we emphasized the importance of using a meaning-centered approach to look at the intercultural communication process. We also covered the components and criteria of intercultural communication flexibility. Finally, the chapter ends with a discussion of a staircase learning model—from unconscious incompetence to unconscious competence—and the role of mindfulness in achieving intercultural communication flexibility.

To be a dynamic, flexible intercultural communicator, you must start practicing some of the ideas you have read in this chapter in your everyday intercultural encounters. Let the learning journey begin. We also urge you to develop a strong "process consciousness" in dealing with cultural strangers. More specifically, we would like you to build on what you've learned so far, keeping the following checkpoints in mind when, in the next chapter, you learn about the value dimensions of a culture:

- A flexible intercultural communicator emphasizes a process-focused approach to intercultural communication.
- A flexible intercultural communicator recognizes the separate, ethnocentric realities that divide individuals and groups.
- A flexible intercultural communicator is willing to suspend evaluative, snap judgments concerning culture-based verbal and nonverbal style differences.
- A flexible intercultural communicator can deal with ambiguities and paradoxes in uncertain intercultural situations.
- A flexible intercultural communicator can communicate appropriately, effectively, adaptively, and creatively through the use of a variety of constructive verbal and nonverbal communication skills.

Intercultural knowledge opens doors to the diverse richness and breadth of the human experience. It reveals to us multiple ways of experiencing, sensing, feeling, and knowing. It helps us to start questioning our own stance regarding issues that we once took for granted. It widens our vision to include an alternative perspective of valuing and relating. By understanding the worldviews and values that influence others' communication approaches, we can understand the logic that motivates and propels their actions or behaviors. The next chapter will discuss some key value patterns around the globe.

CHAPTER 3

WHAT ARE THE ESSENTIAL CULTURAL VALUE PATTERNS?

CHAPTER OUTLINE

- Functions of Cultural Values
  - Analyzing Cultural Values
  - Identity Meaning Function
  - Explanatory Function
  - Motivational Function
  - Ingroup–Outgroup Evaluative Function

- Analyzing Cultural Value Dimensions
  - Discovering Cultural Values
  - Identity: Individualism–Collectivism Value Pattern
  - Power: Small–Large Power Distance Value Pattern
  - Uncertainty: Weak–Strong Uncertainty Avoidance Value Pattern
  - Sex Roles: Feminine–Masculine Value Pattern

- Additional Value Orientation Patterns
  - Value Orientations: Background Information
  - Meaning: Activity Value Orientation
  - Destiny: People–Nature Value Orientation
  - Time: Temporal Value Orientation

- Individual Socialization Development
  - Independent versus Interdependent Self-Construal
  - Horizontal versus Vertical Self-Construal
  - Internal versus External Locus of Control

- Intercultural Reality Check: Do-Ables

Daisy Parales, a local Filipina, was recently promoted to a supervisor for the State of Hawaii. Daisy is now in charge of her former friends, a diverse group of ten clerks in the division. As a caring supervisor, Daisy makes a point to get together with her employees and their families once a month outside of work—usually a fun lunch or picnic at the beach. Her division accepts her more as a family friend than a supervisor.

In the past two months, Daisy has experienced increased frustration and irritation with several of her employees. Whenever Daisy asks them for data analysis or meeting a deadline, they never follow through. They say "yes," but they do not take her requests seriously. Worse, they have even started to talk behind her back or give her an attitude. Daisy has difficulty going to work and feels uncomfortable and very anxious. She thinks, "Where did I go wrong? Was I too friendly? Am I an incompetent supervisor?"

Annual year-end performance reviews are due soon and Daisy does not want to write anything negative, but she will probably have to do so. All these things go against her values and her own caring self-image. What is your interpretation of her plight? What advice can you give Daisy?

Identifying cultural and personal value differences provides us with a map to understand why people behave the way they do in a new cultural setting. It also sheds light on our own behavior and styles of communicating with people from diverse cultural communities. Cultural values form part of the content of our sense of self and answer this question: Who am I in this world? Our sense of self is infused with cultural, ethnic, gender, spiritual, professional, relational, and personal values.

This chapter asks the question: Can we identify some general value patterns of different cultures that will help us to cross cultural boundaries more effectively? The chapter is organized into five sections. We first explore the various functions of cultural value patterns. Second, we discuss the four value dimensions that are critical in influencing people's communication styles. Third, we examine three additional value orientations that affect individuals' cultural boundary-crossing journeys. We then discuss dimensions of personality that may combine with cultural values in shaping people's communication styles. Last, we offer practical checkpoints to remind you to keep these diverse cultural value patterns in mind when crossing cultures.

FUNCTIONS OF CULTURAL VALUES

By peering into the window of another culture, intercultural knowledge can make individuals more reflective of their own ingrained cultural beliefs and values. By understanding where major cultural differences exist, learners can figure creative ways to connect the differences and to find common ground to work with individuals from diverse cultural groups.

Systematic cultural value analysis helps us to grasp the alternative paths that other cultures may prefer in their ways of thinking, valuing, and being. This section defines and explores some of the major functions of cultural value patterns.

Analyzing Cultural Values

Values are shared ideas about what counts as important or unimportant, right or wrong, what is fair or unfair, and what counts as ethical or unethical conduct. Although each of us has developed our unique set of values based on our socialization and life experience, there are also larger values at work on a cultural system level. Cultural values are relatively stable and enduring—values protect a culture in times of crisis and stressful situations (Fiske, 1991; Rokeach, 1972, 1973).

Cultural value patterns form the basic criteria through which we evaluate our own behaviors and the behaviors of others. They cue our expectations of how we should act and how others should act during an interaction. They serve as implicit guidelines for our motivations, expectations, perceptions, and communicative actions. They set the emotional tone for interpreting the behavior of cultural strangers. For example, child labor or animal cruelty is a global topic and what is appropriate in one country may be considered totally inappropriate or unacceptable in another. In Mexico, for instance, school-age child bullfighters receive top billing across the country. These minimatadors are wildly popular across Mexico, and children appearing in many bullrings are not much taller than the bulls they fight (see Blog Pic 3.1). As their appearances have grown more frequent, so too has criticism from those who say they should find a safer extracurricular activity (Lacey, 2008).

Cultural value patterns serve many functions, including the identity meaning function, explanatory function, motivational function, and ingroup–outgroup evaluative function.

Identity Meaning Function

Cultural values provide the frame of reference to answer the most fundamental question of each human being: Who am I? Cultural beliefs and values provide the anchoring points to which we attach meanings and significance to our complex identities. For example, in the larger U.S. middle class, "American" values often emphasize individual initiative and achievement. A person is considered "qualified" or "successful" when he takes the personal initiative to realize and maximize his full potential. The result is recognition and rewards (e.g., a desirable career, six-digit income, coveted car, or dream house) that

Blog Pic 3.1 Minimatadors are popular in Mexico but are controversial elsewhere.

process. The concept of being successful or an "irreplaceable" person, and the meanings attached to such words, stem from the premium values of a cultural community. The identity meanings or significance that we acquire within our cultural community and what we deem as insignificant or inconsequential are constructed and sustained through the everyday communication process.

Explanatory Function

Within our own group, we experience acceptance and approval. We do not have to constantly justify or explain our actions or values. Our commonly shared values are implicitly understood and celebrated via everyday communication rituals. With people of dissimilar groups, however, we must be on the alert and may need to explain or even defend our culture-based behaviors with more effort. For example, in a country that holds Disneyland as a priority, imagine the anger against a new law that allows more stores to open on Sundays. Since 1906, the French have had Sundays off as the day of "rest." Many who oppose the law worry over the loss of this important time set aside for family and Disneyland—an integral part of the French lifestyle (Gauthier-Villars, 2009). Thus, the premium emphasis on personal Disneyland time value serves as the explanatory base for the strong resistance of the French people to open up their stores on Sundays.

When we interact with people from our own cultural group, we can mentally "fill in the blanks" and understand why people behave the way they do. However, when we communicate with people from another cultural group, we need mental energy to try to figure out why they behave the way they behave. We must constantly perform anxiety-laden guessing games to explain away their "bizarre" behavior or attitude. For example, we may be witnessing people using different public displays of affection or saying strange phrases; however, we may remain clueless in terms of why they communicate the way they do. Intercultural misunderstandings may pile up if we do not attach the appropriate cultural values to explain the words and nonverbal gestures that people use in a particular cultural scene (see Blog Post 3.1). What do you think went wrong between Andrew and Paloma? Do you concur with

are tangible and acknowledged by others. A person who can realize his dreams, after overcoming all odds and obstacles, is considered a successful individual in the context of middle-class U.S. culture. Many U.S. celebrities are admired for their "rags-to-riches" stories: Tom Cruise is admired for overcoming dyslexia, hip-hop star Curtis "50 Cent" Jackson overcame being orphaned at age eight, and Sean "Diddy" Combs, born in poverty in Harlem, overcame the murder of his father to become a successful hip-hop artist and music executive.

Valuing individual initiative may stem, in part, from the predominantly Judeo-Christian belief system in the larger U.S. culture. In this belief system, each person is perceived as unique, as having free will, and as responsible for his or her growth and maturation

BLOG POST 3.1   WHY DON'T YOU SAY SWEET THINGS TO ME?
Andrew is an undergraduate student from UCLA studying abroad in Argentina. Andrew's Spanish level and knowledge of the local culture are minimal, but he feels right at home in his new environment. A month into his stay Andrew meets Paloma, a local Argentinean classmate. Although Andrew's Spanish is limited and Paloma cannot speak English, they soon begin dating.

During their first week together all goes well. Andrew takes Paloma out to dinner and they even decide to go to a salsa class. At the beginning of the second week, however, Andrew starts to feel uncomfortable with their relationship. Although he really likes Paloma, she has started to call him pet names. For instance, she will say to Andrew, "mi amor" (my love), "amorcito," (love), "cariño" (darling), and "corazón" (sweetheart). All of these words are terms of endearment for a significant other, which is a positive sign for their relationship.

In Andrew's mind, however, he feels like Paloma is moving too fast. He would never use the English equivalent of "babe" or "honey" until they had been dating for at least a month or two. To make things worse, Paloma becomes upset that Andrew is not returning her terms of endearment. At one point Paloma confronts Andrew and says, "Why don't you say sweet things to me too?" Andrew replies, however, saying, "Although I really like you, I feel like we're moving too fast." This catches Paloma totally off guard and the couple eventually drifts apart.

—*Andrew, college student*

Andrew's relational hesitancy or do you think there is a better explanation for Paloma's use of endearing verbal phrases?

Basically, in an unfamiliar cultural environment, we often have not mastered the deep value-based explanatory system of that culture. We cannot come up with a reasonable guess or interpretative competence as to why people say certain "strange" things and with improper timing in that "strange" cultural context.

Motivational Function

Cultural values also serve as the internal drives for self and others in terms of what rewards are emphasized and what punishments are awaiting you if you violate the basic norms of the cultural community. For example, for cultures that have everyday sayings such as "the person who stands alone excites our imagination," "before cleaning your neighbor's door, you must start cleaning your own door," "the more chefs, the worse the soup," and "where there is a will, there's a way," you will need to motivate and inspire people in that culture with incentive messages that appeal to their personal ambitions, drives, and expectations for individual recognition and approval. In the U.S. culture, for example, when top-ranked professional athletes are paid more than college professors or medical doctors, the value priorities of fierce competition, personal drive, and the importance of winning are in full display and are being rewarded.

Other cultures may have everyday sayings or proverbs such as "it takes a village to raise a child," "one chooses one's friends, but family is from birth," "when spider webs unite, they can tie up a lion," "one finger cannot lift a pebble," and "one arrow can be easily broken, but three arrows—bundled together—cannot be broken lightly." If you understand the primary group-orientation values of such cultures, you may want to connect with people in that cultural community by engaging in more team-based persuasive appeals or emphasize the importance of their family or extended family connection concerns.

Ingroup–Outgroup Evaluative Function

Culture and its accompanying shared values create a comforting buffer zone in which we experience ingroup inclusion and outgroup differences. A shared common fate or a sense of solidarity often exists among members of the same group. For example, within our own cultural group, we speak the same language or dialect, we share similar nonverbal rhythms, and we can decode each other's moods without even speaking. However, with people from a dissimilar membership group, we tend to "stand out," and we experience awkwardness during interaction (Brewer, 1991; Brewer & Miller, 1996)

Boundary arrangements (for example, language differences, national borders, and club memberships) shape our ingroup and outgroup evaluative attitudes when dealing with people who are culturally dissimilar. An *attitude* is a predisposed and learned tendency that influences our thinking pattern. A positive or negative attitude toward other groups is acquired through our cultural socialization, family socialization, and personal life experiences. We begin to think of people who live across the border or who belong to a different language group as those "others," as outsiders. Perceived polarized value patterns strengthen our evaluative attitudes toward ingroup and outgroup interactions. So, if we belong to groups that have positive attitudes toward "getting to the point," we begin to see others outside our groups who speak more indirectly as "less than": they "beat around the bush" and are therefore inferior.

Ingroups are groups with whom we feel emotionally close and with whom we share an interdependent fate, such as family or extended family, our sorority or fraternity, or people from our own cultural or ethnic group. **Outgroups,** on the other hand, are groups with whom we feel no emotional ties, and at times, we may experience great psychological distance from them and even feel competitive against them—they can be our rival fraternity, our wartime enemy, or simply individuals who belong to another cultural identity or ethnic group.

Overall, we tend to hold favorable attitudes toward ingroup interactions because of our perceived shared values and behavioral similarities. Concurrently, we tend to hold unfavorable attitudes toward outgroup interactions because of our ignorance of their cultural values and norms, thus arousing communication fear. Value patterns regulate ingroup consensus and set evaluative standards concerning what is *valued* or *devalued* within a cultural community.

In sum, cultural values serve the identity meaning, explanatory, motivational, and ingroup–outgroup evaluative functions. Communication, in essence, serves as the major hook that links the various channels (e.g., family socialization, educational institution, religious/spiritual institution) of value transmission systems in a coherent manner. Drawing from the various functions of cultural values as discussed above, we can now turn to explore the core value patterns that shape the intercultural communication process.

ANALYZING CULTURAL VALUE DIMENSIONS

Cultural value analysis highlights the potential differences and similarities of value patterns between cultural groups. Despite the difficulties in generalizing about the diverse values in heterogeneous cultures such as India and the United States, it is possible and in fact imperative to engage in such cultural value assessments. Mindful value comparison on a cultural group membership level acts as a critical first step toward better understanding of potential cultural differences and similarities.

This section introduces the cultural value analysis concept and examines four value dimensions: the key value dimension of individualism–collectivism and the other three value dimensions of power distance, uncertainty avoidance, and femininity–masculinity.

Discovering Cultural Values

Based on the comparative studies of a wide range of cultures throughout the world, specific value patterns in different cultures have been uncovered by researchers in the areas of anthropology, cross-cultural psychology, sociology, international management, linguistics, and intercultural communication. Cultural values form the implicit standards by which we judge appropriate and inappropriate behaviors in a communication episode. They are the contents of self that drive our thoughts, emotions, and everyday decision-making processes. They serve to shape the motivation to explain human behavior.

However, cultural value patterns such as individualism and collectivism exist as general value tendencies on a cultural level of analysis. Cultural-level tendencies, however, do not explain the behaviors of all members in a single culture. Family socialization, individual life experience, popular culture, and immigration or intergroup contact experience will all have differential effects on the value formation processes of an individual in a society. If two cultures (e.g., Vietnam and New Zealand) differ on a value dimension (e.g., collectivism), it does not necessarily mean that a particular Vietnamese person is bound to be collectivistic and a particular New Zealander individualistic. It only implies that the average tendencies of the two cultures—on a group membership level—differ in terms of the value characteristics. However, within each culture, wide variations exist on the distinctive culture level and the individual level of analysis. (see, for example, Guo-Ming & Ran, 2009; Manian & Naidu, 2009; Medina-Lopez-Portillo & Sinnigen, 2009; Zaharna, 2009). Although we can say that a majority of individuals in New Zealand subscribe to some form of individualistic values, we should also recognize that some individuals in New Zealand have strong interdependence tendencies. Likewise, although we can say that a majority of individuals in Vietnam subscribe to some form of group-based values, we should also pay close attention to the fact that some individuals in Vietnam have strong "I-identity" attributes. The more pluralistic or "loose" the culture, the more we may find diverse individuals subscribing to diverse norms and belief systems in that culture (McCann, Honeycutt, & Keaton, 2010). Before we discuss the four value dimensions at the cultural level of analysis, let's look at my.blog 3.1. Take a few minutes to complete it before you continue reading.

Identity: Individualism–Collectivism Value Pattern

In reviewing your answer to situation 1 about "solo versus group achievement," if you checked (1a), your value pattern tends toward the "I-identity" end of the spectrum. If you checked (1b), your value pattern tends toward the collectivistic or "we-identity" end of the spectrum. Hofstede (1991, 2001) derived four cultural variability dimensions in his large-scale study of a U.S. multinational business corporation. The corporation has subsidiaries in 50 countries and three regions (the Arabic-speaking countries, East Africa, and West Africa). All together, 116,000 managers and employees in this worldwide corporation were surveyed twice. On the basis of the results, Hofstede (2001) delineated four organizational value patterns across a diverse range of cultures.

Indeed, an international research project, GLOBE ("Global Leadership and Organizational Behavior Effectiveness"), which included two hundred research collaborators in sixty-two nations, has provided additional evidence that the foundational constructs of all four of Hofstede's value patterns, including individualism–collectivism, permeate sixty-two countries. This study's sample size included 17,370 middle managers from three industries—telecommunications, financial services, and food supply—within each nation and at the societal, organizational, and individual levels of analysis (House, Hanges, Javidan, Dorfman, & Gupta, 2004).

Thus, the first and most important dimension that shapes our sense of self is the individualistic–collectivistic value pattern. The other three cultural variability dimensions are power distance, uncertainty avoidance, and femininity–masculinity. We should note that Hofstede's four cultural value dimensions are more related to business or organizational values in different nations. He also argues that ethnic and religious groups, gender, generation, social class, and social structure assert a strong influence on the value patterns within a particular culture. The four value dimensions should be viewed as a first systematic research attempt to compare a wide range of cultures on an aggregate, group level (Hofstede & Hofstede, 2005).

Before you read on, because individualism–collectivism is such an important intercultural value theme, please fill out the brief assessment in my.blog 3.2 and find out your value tendency preference.

Do you subscribe more to individualistic or collectivistic value tendencies? The individualism–collectivism value dimension has received consistent attention from both intercultural researchers and cross-cultural psychologists (Gudykunst & Ting-Toomey, 1988; Ting-Toomey, 2010b; Triandis, 1995). Intercultural scholars have provided evidence that the value patterns of individualism and collectivism are pervasive in a wide range of cultures. Individualism and collectivism can explain some of the basic differences and similarities concerning communication behavior between clusters of cultures.

Basically, **individualism** refers to the broad value tendencies of a culture in emphasizing the importance of individual identity over group identity, individual rights over group rights, and individual needs over group needs. Individualism promotes self-efficiency, individual responsibility, and personal autonomy. In contrast, **collectivism** refers to the broad value tendencies of a culture in emphasizing the importance of the

my.blog 3.1 DISCOVERING PERSONAL VALUE DIMENSIONS

Instructions: The following scenarios reflect four dilemmas. Each situation gives two decision-making alternatives. Use your gut-level reaction and check the answer that you consider best reflects your honest decision under the circumstances.

1. You have two hours to prepare for an examination for one class and an oral report that you and several fellow students will present in another class. The exam score is your own; the oral report earns a group grade. Both are worth 25 percent of your grade in each class. In the two hours, you can only do one well. What should you do?

   a. _____ Study hard for the exam—it reflects your individual achievement.

   b. _____ Prepare for the group report—do not let down your team members.

2. You are deeply in love with a romantic partner from a different cultural background. However, your parents do not approve of him or her because they think it's hard enough to make a relationship work even if the person is from the same culture. What should you do?

   a. _____ Tell your parents to respect your dating choice and decision.

   b. _____ Tell your partner to be patient and try to understand your parents' viewpoint.

3. Your next-door neighbors are partying loudly again and it's already 1:00 a.m. You have an important job interview scheduled for the early morning. You really want to have a good night's sleep so that you can wake up refreshed in the morning. What should you do?

   a. _____ Tell your neighbors to stop partying.

   b. _____ Grin and bear it. You really don't like conflict, and you hope the noise level will die down eventually.

4. Your nephew really enjoys playing with dolls and your niece really enjoys playing with tanks and soldiers. Your sister asks you for advice. Should she be worried about her two kids and their playing habits? What would you say?

   a. _____ Don't worry. There's nothing wrong with boys playing with dolls and girls playing with tanks.

   b. _____ You're right to be concerned. It seems like the kids are confused about their sex-role identity. You should observe them more closely.

Scoring: If you put a check mark on the (a) answers, the answer keys are as follows: *(1a) individualistic, (2a) small power distance, (3a) weak uncertainty avoidance,* and *(4a) "feminine"* patterns.

   If you put a check mark on the following (b) answers, your answers are reflective of the following: *(1b) collectivistic, (2b) large power distance, (3b) strong uncertainty avoidance,* and *(4b) "masculine"* patterns.

   If you have checked some (a) answers and some (b) answers, your values are reflective of a mixed set of value patterns. Review and label your own answers now.

Interpretation: Please continue to read your text under the "Analyzing Cultural Value Dimensions" section for further value interpretations. Your honest answers to the four situations should provide some insight into your personal values. Your responses basically reflect how your individual values shape your interpretations of the four situations. Keep your responses in mind as you read the remainder of this section.

"we" identity over the "I" identity, group rights over individual rights, and ingroup needs over individual wants and desires. Collectivism promotes relational interdependence, ingroup harmony, and ingroup collaborative spirit (see Table 3.1).

Individualistic and collectivistic value tendencies are manifested in *everyday family, school,* and *workplace interaction.* Individualism pertains to societies in which ties between individuals are loosely linked and everyone is expected to look after himself or herself and his or her immediate family. Comparatively, collectivism refers to societies in which ties between individuals in the community are tightly intertwined. Group members view their fate as interdependent with one another. Although they will look after the welfare of ingroup members, they also expect their ingroup

my.blog 3.2 ASSESSING YOUR INDIVIDUALISM AND COLLECTIVISM VALUE TENDENCIES

Instructions: The following items describe how people think about themselves and communicate in various situations. Let your first inclination be your guide and circle the number in the scale that best reflects your overall value. The following scale is used for each item:

$$4 = SA = \textit{Strongly agree}$$
$$3 = MA = \textit{Moderately agree}$$
$$2 = MD = \textit{Moderately disagree}$$
$$1 = SD = \textit{Strongly disagree}$$

		SA	MA	MD	SD
1.	Act assertively to get what you want.	(4)	3	2	1
2.	Be sensitive to the needs of others.	4	(3)	2	1
3.	Be competitive and move ahead.	(4)	3	2	1
4.	Blend in harmoniously with the group.	4	(3)	2	1
5.	Act on independent thoughts.	4	(3)	2	1
6.	Be respectful of group decisions.	(4)	3	2	1
7.	Value self-reliance and personal freedom.	4	(3)	2	1
8.	Consult family and friends before making decisions.	4	3	(2)	1
9.	Voice my personal opinions when everyone else disagrees.	(4)	3	2	1
10.	Be sensitive to the majority views in a group.	(4)	3	2	1

Scoring: Add up the scores on all the odd-numbered items and you will find your individualism score. *Individualism* score: _____. Add up the scores on all the even-numbered items and you will find your collectivism score. *Collectivism* score: _____.

Interpretation: Scores on each value dimension can range from 5 to 20; the higher the score, the more individualistic and/or collectivistic you are. If all the scores are similar on both value dimensions, you are a bicultural value person.

Reflection probes: Take a moment to think of the following questions: Do your values reflect your family of origin's values? How have your values changed over time? What can you do to achieve greater understanding of people from a different value system?

members to look after their interests and concerns throughout their lifetimes.

If you were inclined toward collectivism, what would be your reaction to the popular U.S. television show *Judge Judy*—the judge with an attitude? Her popularity is to the result of her straightforward expressions and impatience with litigants who waste her time. Judge Judy will say, "I'm speaking!," "Liar, liar, pants on fire," "Listen to me: You are an outrageous person," and "Sir, you want to say something to me? Are you sure you want to say something to me?" Will this kind of talk help you to understand a conflict or confuse you somewhat? And if you were individualistic, how would you react to Tiger Mom Amy Chua's (2011) opinion that unlike the Western "lax" parental style, Chinese parents set higher standards, demand more of their children, and believe that their kids can handle more pressure if parents push them to excel on a daily basis?

Hofstede's (2001) research reveals that factors such as national wealth, population growth, and historical roots affect the development of individualistic and collectivistic values. For example, wealthy, urbanized, and industrialized societies are more individualistically oriented, whereas the poorer, rural, and traditional societies are more collectivistically

TABLE 3.1 VALUE CHARACTERISTICS IN INDIVIDUALISTIC AND COLLECTIVISTIC CULTURES

Situations	Individualistic cultures	Collectivistic cultures
General	"I" identity	"We" identity
Family	Nuclear family	Extended family
Relationship	Privacy regulation	Relational harmony
School	Individual competition	Teamwork
Workplace	Personal competence	Ingroup emphasis
Communication	Direct communication patterns	Indirect communication patterns
Personality equivalence	Independent self	Interdependent self

oriented. However, there are some exceptions, especially in East Asia, where Japan, South Korea, Taiwan, Hong Kong, and Singapore appear to retain collectivism despite industrialization.

Individualism is a cultural pattern that is found in most northern and western regions of Europe and in North America. More specifically, high individualism has been found in the United States, Australia, Great Britain, Canada, the Netherlands, New Zealand, Italy, Belgium, Denmark, and Sweden. *Collectivism* is a cultural pattern common in Asia, Africa, the Middle East, Central and South America, and the Pacific Islands. Although less than one-third of the world population resides in cultures with high individualistic value tendencies, a little more than two-thirds of the people live in cultures with high collectivistic value tendencies (Triandis, 1995). High collectivistic value tendencies have been found in Guatemala, Ecuador, Panama, Venezuela, Colombia, Indonesia, Pakistan, Costa Rica, and Peru (Hofstede, 1991). The *top individualist values* emphasized are freedom, honesty, social recognition, comfort, hedonism, and personal equity. The *top collectivist values* are harmony, face-saving, filial piety (respecting parents' wishes), equality in the distribution of rewards among peers (for the sake of group harmony), and fulfillment of others' needs (Triandis, 1995).

Let's check out the following story: Olympic snowboarder Kazuhiro Kokubo caused outrage among the Japanese government officials and patrons at the corner pub during the 2010 Vancouver winter games. When twenty-one-year-old Kazuhiro Kokubo arrived in the Vancouver, B.C., airport, he sported double nose piercings, wearing dark sunglasses indoors, and his team-issued uniform was in disarray, an untucked shirt with his pants hung low below his hips, and a loose tie revealing an unbuttoned shirt. The clincher, which forced the Japan Ski Association to punish him, was when he decided to display his mane of dreadlocks.

Japan's Minister of Education was "not a fan of the hip hop twist to the national uniform" and issued the following statement: "It's extremely regrettable that Mr. Kokubo dressed in a totally unacceptable manner as a representative of Japan's national team. He lacks the awareness that he is participating in the Olympic Games and serves as a representative of our country with everyone's expectations on his shoulders. This should never happen again" (Lah, 2010).

From the Japanese cultural context, the concept of team is compared with an old-fashioned village, where a mayor lords over the other villagers. As a communal-based relationship develops, Mr. Kokubo should have known what to do for the village—he should bring honor and recognition to the village, not shame or failure (Larimer, 2000). This particular example also echoes House et al.'s (2004) two-tiered concept of collectivism: ingroup collectivism and institutional collectivism. **Ingroup collectivism** refers to the sentiment of loyalty and solidarity between the employee and his organization or ingroup community. **Institutional collectivism** refers to the institutional perspective in enforcing ingroup norms, cohesion, and conformity. Obviously, in this case, Mr. Kokuba has violated both the ingroup collectivism spirit and the institutional collectivism expectation.

Overall, researchers have found that different layers of individualism (e.g., emphasizing personal need in the UK or immediate family need in Sweden) and collectivism (e.g., emphasizing work group need in Singapore or caste need in India) exist in different cultures. For each culture, it is important to determine the group with which individuals have the closest identification (e.g., their family, their corporation, their religion) (Brislin & Yoshida, 1994). For example, for the Vietnamese, it is the extended family; for the Japanese, the corporation; for the Irish, the Roman Catholic Church, and so on (see, for example, Oetzel, Arcos, Mabizela, Weinman, & Zhang, 2006).

In addition, *gender differences* exist in adherence to individualistic or relational-based values. U.S. males generally have been found to adhere more to individualistic values than to communal-based values. U.S. females generally have been found to subscribe to communally oriented values (Wood, 2009). However, compared with females in other collectivistic societies, such as Italy and Mexico, U.S. females are still fairly individualistic in their orientation. In their gender identity formation, U.S. males emphasize self-identity separation and competition, whereas U.S. females emphasize other-identity support and relational connection. Gendered groups in many cultures appear to differ in their preferences for individualistic or collectivistic value tendencies.

Our discussion of value patterns appears to be on two opposite poles of a continuum. In reality, many of you probably hold an integrative set of values, such as I-identity *and* we-identity patterns across a diverse range of situations (Ting-Toomey, 2010a). The key is that the more you are attuned to analyzing your own value patterns and those of culturally different others, the more you increase your cultural value awareness quotient. In addition to the individualism–collectivism dimension, another important value dimension is the dimension of power distance.

Power: Small–Large Power Distance Value Pattern

In reviewing your answer from my.blog 3.1 to situation 2 about intercultural dating, if you checked (2a), your value pattern tends toward the small power distance pole. If you checked (2b), your value pattern tends toward the large power distance pole. The power distance value dimension refers to the extent to which individuals subscribe to the ideology of equal power distribution and the extent to which members adhere to unequal power distribution in an interaction episode, within an institution or within a society. Small power distance scores are found, for example, in Austria, Israel, Denmark, New Zealand, Ireland, Sweden,

and Norway. Large power distance scores are found, for example, in Malaysia, Guatemala, Panama, the Philippines, Mexico, Venezuela, and Arab countries (Hofstede, 2001; Hofstede & McCrae, 2004).

People in **small power distance cultures** tend to value equal power distributions, equal rights and relations, and equitable rewards and punishments on the basis of performance. People in **large power distance cultures** tend to accept unequal power distributions, hierarchical rights, asymmetrical role relations, and rewards and punishments based on age, rank, status, title, and seniority. For small power distance cultures, equality of personal rights represents an ideal to strive toward in a system. For large power distance cultures, respect for power hierarchy in any system is a fundamental way of life (see Table 3.2).

In *small power distance family situations*, children may contradict their parents and freely speak their mind. They are expected to show self-initiative and learn verbal articulateness and persuasion. Parents and children work together to achieve a democratic family decision-making process. In *large power distance family situations*, children are expected to obey their parents. Children are punished if they talk back or contradict their parents. The value of respect between unequal status members in the family is taught at a young age. Parents and grandparents assume the authority roles in the family decision-making process.

In *small power distance work situations*, power is evenly distributed. Subordinates expect to be consulted, and the ideal boss is a resourceful democrat. In *large power distance work situations*, the power of an organization is centralized at the upper-management level. Subordinates expect to be told what to do, and the ideal boss plays the benevolent autocratic role. Although the United States scores on the low side of power distance, it is not extremely low. Hofstede (1991) explains that "U.S. leadership theories tend to be based on subordinates with medium-level dependence needs: not too high, not too low" (p. 42). The workplace even has an subtle code of who has power based on where the cubicle, office, or chairs are set up. See if you can guess who has the most seniority in this Hong Kong office (see Blog Pic 3.2).

TABLE 3.2 VALUE CHARACTERISTICS IN SMALL AND LARGE POWER DISTANCE (PD) CULTURES

Situations	Small PD cultures	Large PD cultures
General	Emphasize interpersonal equality	Emphasize status-based difference
Family	Children may contradict parents	Children should obey parents
Relationship	Younger people are smart	Older people are wise
School	Teachers ask for feedback	Teachers lecture
Workplace	Subordinates expect consultation	Subordinates expect guidance
Communication	Informal communication patterns	Formal communication patterns
Personality equivalence	Horizontal self	Vertical self

Small power distance during interaction can easily create misunderstanding and confusion. Negotiating power distance often leads to levels of anxiety and uncertainty. For example, suppose you have an intercultural teacher who wants you to call him "Bill," not "Dr. Gudykunst." Bill is friendly and open to class discussion and enjoys sharing personal stories about his experiences, even those about his life out of the classroom. Perhaps you and the class feel very comfortable with him as an informal, "go to" teacher. But one day, when you receive the result of a group project, you notice your team did not do well at all; Bill made two full pages of evaluative notes commenting on the strengths and weaknesses of the project. You and your team get very upset with Bill.

Your reaction may be caused by the negotiation of different power distance expectations. Believing that Bill is very "friendly" and "easy to talk to," you'll also likely expect that Bill will go "easy" on the grading. These are preconceived stereotypes associated with a small power distance value pattern and correlating that with an informal, easy-going personality style. However, as soon as the teacher plays the large power distance role of an evaluative instructor (and from his perspective he is being a motivating and responsible teacher), it may leave you to think that this "friendly, casual" teacher is actually quite "mean" and "harsh" toward his students.

Blog Pic 3.2 Who has the most seniority?

Uncertainty: Weak–Strong Uncertainty Avoidance Value Pattern

In reviewing your answer from my.blog 3.1 to situation 3 about neighborhood conflict, if you checked (3a), your value pattern tends toward the weak end of the uncertainty avoidance continuum. If you checked (3b), your value pattern tends toward the strong end of the uncertainty avoidance continuum. Uncertainty avoidance refers to the extent to which members of a culture do not mind conflicts or uncertain situations and the extent to which they try to avoid those uncertain situations. **Weak (or low) uncertainty avoidance** cultures encourage risk-taking and conflict-approaching modes. **Strong (or high) uncertainty avoidance** cultures prefer clear procedures and conflict-avoidance behaviors. Weak uncertainty avoidance scores, for example, are found in Singapore, Jamaica, Denmark, Sweden, Hong Kong, Ireland, the UK, and the United States. Strong uncertainty avoidance scores, for example, are found in Greece, Portugal, Guatemala, Uruguay, Belgium, El Salvador, and Japan (see Table 3.3).

Whereas members in weak uncertainty avoidance family situations prefer informal rules to guide their behavior, members in high uncertainty avoidance family situations tend to prefer formal structure and formal rules. Rules and laws are established to counteract uncertainties in social interaction. In *weak uncertainty avoidance family situations*, roles and behavioral expectations are actively negotiated. Children are given more latitude to explore their own values and morals. In *strong uncertainty avoidance family situations*, family roles are clearly established and family rules are expected to be followed closely.

In *weak uncertainty avoidance work situations*, there is a greater tolerance of innovative ideas and behaviors. Conflict is also viewed as a natural part of organizational productivity. In *strong uncertainty avoidance work situations*, there is a greater resistance to deviant and innovative ideas. Career mobility is high in weak uncertainty avoidance cultures, whereas career stability is a desired end goal in strong uncertainty avoidance cultures. If you are a student who enjoys spontaneity and you live life as it comes, would you want to work in Japan? Or if you are a student who enjoys stability and careful planning, would you go on a road trip without maps?

Hofstede (2001) uses the following statements to represent the basic characteristics of *strong uncertainty avoidance organizations:* (1) most organizations would be better off if conflict could be eliminated; (2) it is important for a manager to have at hand precise answers to most of the questions that subordinates may raise about their work; and (3) when the respective roles of the members of a department become complex, specific job descriptions are essential. Members of strong uncertainty avoidance organizations tend to score high on these statements; members of weak uncertainty avoidance organizations tend to score low on them.

During the March 11, 2011, devastating 9.0 earthquake in Japan, residents in Minamisanriku were cut

---

BLOG POST 3.2

My first travel abroad was to Missoula, Montana, USA. I was a visiting Tibetan Buddhist Scholar at a small Tibetan Buddhist Center. During my visit, I had an opportunity to attend a Counseling Psychology Seminar at the University of Montana (UM). I saw a student leaning back in his chair and using another chair to support his stretched legs. He had his feet pointed to his teacher (a professor) and talked while eating his food. All of his behaviors violated my cultural norms regarding teacher–student interaction. Growing up in India, teachers were highly respected and obeyed. When my teachers in high school called my name to ask questions, I would stand up straight like a good soldier and answer their questions respectfully, addressing them as "Sir" or "Ma-

dame." Never could we call them by their first names or even their names without titles such as Sir or Madame. And, we would not dare to eat in class when class was in session. Given this socialization, I was shocked to witness the behavior of this American student in the seminar. I thought he was very disrespectful to his teacher; interestingly, she did not mind it at all. Now I realize students in American schools respect their teachers differently. I was shocked more by pointing feet at the teacher than by his eating in the class. In many cultures feet and shoes are considered dirty and therefore, showing them to a person, especially your teachers, is very disrespectful.

—Tenzin, *college instructor*

TABLE 3.3 VALUE CHARACTERISTICS IN WEAK AND STRONG UNCERTAINTY AVOIDANCE (UA) CULTURES

Situations	Weak UA cultures	Strong UA cultures
General	Uncertainty is valued	Uncertainty is a threat
Family	Dynamic and changing	Reinforce family rules
Relationship	High mobility	Low mobility
School	Challenges are welcome	Routines are welcome
Workplace	Encourage risk-taking	Encourage clear procedure
Communication	Conflict can be positive	Conflict is negative
Personality equivalence	High tolerance for ambiguity	Low tolerance for ambiguity

off completely from the rest of the world after the colossal tsunami swept away bridges, cell phone service, and phone lines. Half of the residents went missing. The survivors banded together for twelve days by assigning jobs according to gender. Women boiled water and prepared food while the men searched for firewood and gasoline. Within days, their community was organized with a clear set of assignments and clear hierarchy. A governing body with clear community rules was set up until help arrived (Fackler, 2011). In this time of crisis, a clear set of survival instructions and directions to avoid further uncertainty, intersecting with large power distance leadership and the spirit of collectivism, contributed to the group's survival for this makeshift community.

Sex Roles: Feminine–Masculine Value Pattern

In reviewing your answer from my.blog 3.1 to situation 4 about toys preference, if you checked (4a), your value pattern tends toward the "feminine" value pole. If you checked (4b), your value pattern tends toward the "masculine" value pole. Distinctive female and male organizational behavior differences are found on the feminine–masculine value dimension.

Femininity pertains to societies in which social gender roles are fluid and can overlap—that is, whatever a woman can do, a man can do; likewise, both women and men are supposed to be modest, observant, and tender, and they are concerned with the ecological quality of their environment. **Masculinity** pertains to societies in which social gender roles are clearly complementary and distinct. Namely, men are supposed to be assertive, masculine, tough, and focused on task-based accomplishment and material success, whereas women are supposed to be more modest, feminine, tender, and concerned with the quality of life (Hofstede, 2001).

"Feminine" cultures emphasize flexible sex role behaviors and "masculine" cultures emphasize complementary sex role domains. Sweden, Norway, the Netherlands, Denmark, Costa Rica, Yugoslavia, and Finland, for example, have high femininity scores. Comparatively, Japan, Austria, Venezuela, Italy, Switzerland, Mexico, and Ireland, for example, have high masculinity scores. The United States ranks fifteenth on the masculine scale (i.e., closer to the masculine value pattern) of the fifty countries and three regions studied (Hofstede, 1998, 2001). Furthermore, House et al.'s (2004) international research project actually subdivided the femininity–masculinity value dimension into two concepts: gender egalitarianism and assertiveness. Whereas gender egalitarianism emphasizes sex role flexibility and fluidity, the concept of high assertiveness stresses the importance of a particular society in encouraging an assertive to aggressive outlook on business task performance and winning (e.g., India and Hong Kong). The counterpart of low assertiveness means a society that promotes modesty, nurturance, and cooperation (e.g., Egypt and Thailand).

Historical roots and family socialization processes concerning gender roles shape the development of the feminine–masculine dimension. In feminine families, both boys and girls learn to be caring and concerned with both facts and feelings. In masculine families, boys learn to be assertive, tough, and ambitious, but girls learn to be nurturing and relational-based. In the Pacific Island nation of Vanuatu, *kastom* refers to the status between males and females. Males have superior status and power, whereas women support their husbands by taking care of the house, caring for the children (UNICEF, 2005).

Feminine families also stress the importance of quality-of-life issues. Masculine families are achievement and success oriented. A feminine workplace merges male and female roles flexibly. A masculine workplace differentiates male and female roles clearly. A feminine organization tends to emphasize quality of work life and family balance issues above and beyond business performance, whereas a masculine organization tends to emphasize the important role of business performance and gross profits (see Table 3.4).

By implication, when one communicates in a feminine organizational culture, one should be sensitive to the flexible sex role norms and roles in that workplace. When one communicates in a masculine organizational culture, one should be mindful of the norms and rules of complementary sex role behaviors in the system. In working for a feminine organization, one should be more mindful of the importance of quality of work/life balance issues. In working for a masculine organization, one should focus more on business achievements and tangible results-based performance.

TABLE 3.4 VALUE CHARACTERISTICS IN "FEMININE" AND "MASCULINE" CULTURES

Situations	"Feminine" cultures	"Masculine" cultures
General	Flexible sex roles	Complementary sex roles
Family	Emphasize nurturance	Emphasize achievement
Relationship	Both take initiative	Males take initiative
School	Social adjustment is critical	Academic performance is critical
Workplace	Work in order to live	Live in order to work
Communication	Fluid gender communication	"Masculine" toughness and "feminine" softness
Personality equivalence	Overlapped gender roles	Clear masculine/ feminine gender roles

Cultural values are deposits of wisdom that are passed from one generation to the next. Simultaneously, they also can serve as cultural blinders to alternative ways of thinking, feeling, motivating, and relating. Although cultural values serve many useful functions, such as those of identity meaning, explanatory, motivational, and evaluative functions, they also reinforce various habitual practices and norms of communicating.

ADDITIONAL VALUE ORIENTATION PATTERNS

Before proceeding to our discussion about the four additional value orientations, take a few moments to answer the questions in my.blog 3.3.

Value Orientations: Background Information

On the basis of their research on Navajo Indians, Latino/as, and European Americans in the Southwest, Kluckhohn and Strodtbeck (1961) proposed a set of universal questions that human beings consciously or unconsciously seek to answer. In addition, the famous cross-cultural anthropologist Edward T. Hall (1966, 1983) also emphasized the study of time and space in conjunction with understanding issues in culture and communication. These intercultural experts observed that human beings in all cultures face this set of common human problems or existential questions. Of the set of proposed questions, the following three questions are the most relevant to our understanding of complementary value patterns: (1) What do people consider meaningful or worthwhile in their everyday activity? (activity value orientation); (2) What is the relationship between people and nature? (people–nature value orientation); and (3) What is the time focus of human life? (temporal value orientation). The value orientations approach assumes that the above questions are universal ones and that all human beings seek answers to these inquiries, whether consciously or unconsciously (Kluckhohn & Strodtbeck, 1961). The answers or solutions to these questions are available in all cultures. However, some cultures have a stronger preference for one particular set of answers than for others. The solutions represent the cumulative wisdom or survival mechanisms of a particular

my.blog 3.3 DISCOVERING PERSONAL VALUE ORIENTATIONS

Instructions: Read each set of statements and check (a), (b), or (c) in each set. The check means the statement sounds very much like your own value preference.

1. _____ a. I feel useless if I am not doing something constructive every day.

   _____ b. I prefer to enjoy life with my full five senses present in each waking moment.

   _____ c. Developing an inner understanding of who I am is more important than any other tangible accomplishment.

2. _____ a. I believe we, as human beings, have a great deal of decision-making power in how we shape and manage our life's destiny.

   _____ b. In my everyday life, I strive to live simply and flow with it, which is closer to the natural world.

   _____ c. I believe that no matter how much we try to plan and control things, a variety of forces operate beyond us and direct our destiny.

3. _____ a. I tend to keep lists of schedules and tasks that I need to accomplish today and tomorrow.

   _____ b. I tend to "go with the flow." Worrying about the past or future is a waste of my time and energy.

   _____ c. I tend to respect older people for their life experience and wisdom.

Scoring: Your answers to the above statements should increase your awareness of your personal value orientation preferences.

Scoring interpretation:

1a = Doing	1b = Being	1c = Being-in-becoming
2a = Controlling	2b = Harmonizing	2c = Yielding
3a = Future	3b = Present	3c = Past

You may want to circle and label all your answers. You will get an initial review of your personal value orientations.

Interpretation: Please continue to read your text under the "Additional Value Orientation Patterns" section for further interpretations.

culture passed from one generation to the next (Bond et al., 2004). The range of potential solutions to these three questions is shown in Figure 3.1.

Meaning: Activity Value Orientation

What do people consider as meaningful—doing or being—in this particular cultural community? The activity orientation further asks the question Is human activity in the culture focused on the doing, being, or being-in-becoming mode? The **"doing" solution** means achievement-oriented activities. The **"being" solution** means living with emotional vitality and being relationally connected with significant others. The **"being-in-becoming" solution** means living with an emphasis on spiritual renewal and regeneration.

Middle-class African Americans, Asian Americans, Latino/a Americans, and European Americans focus on a doing or an achievement-oriented solution, but Native Americans tend to focus on the being-in-becoming mode (Sue & Sue, 1999). However, the doing preference is manifested quite differently among the European American, African American, Chicano/a, Asian American, and Latino/a American groups.

For example, a doing solution among African Americans and Chicano/as means fighting against adversity and combatting racism through social achievements and activism for the good of the community. The doing mode among Asian and Latino/a immigrants in the United States is typically associated

Orientation	Range		
Meaning	Doing (action-oriented)	Being-in-becoming (inner development)	Being (expressive/ emotional)
Destiny	Controlling nature (mastering)	Harmony with nature (flow)	Subjugation to nature (yielding)
Time	Future-oriented (schedule-bound)	Present-oriented (here-and-now)	Past-oriented (tradition-bound)

FIGURE 3.1   Three Value Orientation Patterns. Adapted from Strodbeck (1961) and Kohls (1996).

with working hard and making money to fulfill basic obligations toward family and extended family networks. A doing mode among European Americans is the focus on tangible accomplishments for personal satisfaction.

Furthermore, traditional Africans and African Americans also display a being solution for living. They attach positive meanings to a sense of aliveness, emotional vitality, and openness of feelings. African American culture is infused with "a spirit (a knowledge that there is more to life than sorrow, which will pass) and a renewal in sensuousness, joy, and laughter. This symbol has its roots in African culture and expresses the soul and rhythm of that culture in America" (Hecht, Collier, & Ribeau, 1993, p. 103). Likewise, Latino/a Americans emphasize the being vitality solution. Many traditional Latino/as subscribe to the being mode of activity, which means enjoying the moment to the fullest. Shared celebrations and recreation with close friends and family members often form a sacred part of a Latino/a's lifestyle.

For many traditional Native American groups, the preferred choice is the being-in-becoming mode. Many Native American cultures are oriented toward religious and spiritual preservation. They are concerned with spiritual well-being more than material well-being. Spiritual self-renewal and enrichment are much more important to them than tangible gains and losses. It is also critical to remember that there are 505 federally recognized tribes with 252 different languages. Because each tribe has its own traditions, beliefs, and values, the term "Native American" is broad-based.

Destiny: People–Nature Value Orientation

The destiny value orientation asks this question: Is the relationship between people and the natural (or supernatural) environment one of control, harmony, or subjugation? Many middle-class European Americans tend to believe in mastery and control over the natural environment. For example, right now, Mexico City, the third largest city in the world, is sinking into the earth, as much as eight inches a year. And oddly enough, this problem dates back to the Aztecs, who built Tenochtitlan, the original name of the city, on an island. The increasing population created a need for more drinking water, but the pumping of water from underground aquifers increased the rate of sinking. Crews are working deep underground, digging tunnels in an effort to stave off catastrophe (Hawley, 2010).

By **controlling or mastering their environment**, they can also increase their productivity and efficiency in accumulating material security and comfort. If something goes wrong in a system or organization, they believe they can fix it, change it, or master it. For example, China invested billions of dollars and uprooted 1.25 million people to build a dam across the Earth's third largest river, the Yangtze. Authorities believe the dam will limit the amount of water flowing further downstream and minimize the impact of devastating floods. But environmentalists believe the dam will be an environmental catastrophe (Hvistendahl, 2008). Individuals who endorse a strong "controlling" solution believe that any disaster can be prevented if flaws are detected and fixed accordingly.

Buddhist cultures, such as those of Bhutan, Laos, Thailand, and Tibet, tend to emphasize strongly the harmony-with-nature or **"flowing" value solution**. Their outlook on life tends to emphasize spiritual transformation or enlightenment rather than material gain. Many ethnocultural groups (such as African, Asian, Latino/a, and Native American) in the United States tend to believe in living harmoniously with nature. Many Native American groups, for example, believe that what is human, what is nature, and what is spirit are all extensions of one another. We should learn to live harmoniously with one another because we are all creatures of the same universe. In globally dense cities, how do the people manage to become in harmony with nature? Parks are one example. Check out Blog Pic 3.3, a park located in densely populated Hong Kong, which lies next to a freeway and a congested street.

In contrast, many Polynesian, Middle Eastern, and Indian cultures subscribe to the **subjugation-to-nature** or **"yielding" value solution**. Individuals who subscribe to the yielding solution also tend to be more fatalistic than individuals who subscribe to the controlling nature value solution. Natural disasters in a cultural community such as earthquakes, volcano eruptions, and floods may have contributed to their belief that nature is a powerful force that is beyond the control of individuals (see Blog Pics 3.4.a and 3.4.b).

The best way to deal with nature is to pay respect to it and act humbly in the face of cataclysmic external forces. Individuals who endorse a strong yielding value solution, for example, can be seen in Kalapana, Hawaii. The Goddess of the volcano is known as Pele. In the 1990 lava flow that destroyed the town of Kalapana, several homes were inconceivably spared. The lava "mysteriously circumvented each house sparing it from the destructive fires. After the lava had cooled, offerings to Pele were found on the property that had been saved.... [meanwhile] the town and its infrastructure had been covered in Pele's lava blanket 15 to 25 meters deep" (Iolana, 2006, p. 3). Check out the yielding value solution in Blog Post 3.3 from a 2009 newsletter from a community near Kalapana.

After experiencing centuries of tragedies, wars, and natural disasters, generations of people who have lived in similar disaster-prone cultural communities tend to be more fatalistic in their cultural beliefs. For them, the destiny of life is to "submit" to the supernatural forces that shape their life cycles. These individuals may try their best to meet certain life goals and dreams; however, in the back in their minds, they

Blog Pic 3.3   A park, built with modern design that blends natural landscape within a crowded city.

Blog Pic 3.4.a The aftermath of Katrina. (Photo: Paul Turounet)

Blog Pic 3.4.b The wrath of Hurricane Katrina.

also believe the power of a supernatural force or fate can strike anytime, anywhere. Take another example: East Indian culture, which emphasizes the *law of karma*. **Karma** involves fatalism, which has shaped the Indian philosophical view of life over the centuries. In its simplest form, the law of karma states that happiness or sorrow is the predetermined effect of actions committed by the person either in a present life or in one of his or her numerous past lives. Things do not happen because we make them happen. Things happen because they are *destined* to happen. We can only try so much, and then we should yield to our fate or karma.

BLOG POST 3.3 FROM A HAWAIIAN COMMUNITY NEWSLETTER: *"ASTROLOGICAL PERSPECTIVE ON THEMES OF 2009"*

Several important astrological cycle points give potency to the series of events that will be the key themes of the year. Earthquakes and earth-based or weather events will be part of the things we have to face. These are beyond our control and acts of nature. Hawaii may have more lava output from the volcano. Already the vog [(i.e. like smog, but emanating from volcanic instead of industrial sources] situation is unbearable for some on the Kona coast. Earthquakes could be more of a factor this year."

Source: Ream (2009, p. 4)

Overall, the implication of this value orientation is that although some individuals believe in gaining control over their environment, others believe in the importance of living harmoniously or submissively in relationship to their natural habitat. People who tend to believe in controlling nature would have a stronger sense of the "self-over-nature" approach in dealing with their surroundings. People who tend to subscribe to the "self-with-nature" or "self-under-nature" viewpoint would have a more harmonious or fatalistic approach in dealing with their outer surroundings.

When individuals from different "people–nature" solutions come together, intercultural problems may arise. Individuals from one cultural group are eager to "fix" the environment with huge projects by building dams, levees, and reservoirs, but another cultural group may be deeply offended because the action may provoke the anger of the spirits that inhabit the river being dammed or the terrain being inundated. Flexible adjustment and cultural sensitivity are needed for both cultural parties to reach common ground in their collaborative efforts.

Time: Temporal Value Orientation

The time-sense orientation asks this question: Is the temporal focus in the culture based on the future, present, or past? The **future-oriented time sense** means planning for desirable short- to medium-term developments and setting out clear objectives to realize them. The **present-oriented time sense** means valuing the here and now, especially the interpersonal relationships that are unfolding currently. The **past-oriented time sense** means honoring historic and ancestral ties plus respecting the wisdom of the elders. The House et al. (2004) GLOBE research project also emphasizes the importance of understanding societies that value short-term planning and those valuing long-term planning. An earlier research project, the Chinese Cultural Connection (1987) also emphasized the time dimension in guiding people's actions in different countries. This project identified China, Hong Kong, Taiwan, Japan, and South Korea as long-term planning countries and Sierra Leon, Nigeria, Ghana, the Philippines, and Norway as short-term planning countries.

Those who subscribe to the future value solution (e.g., middle-class European Americans) tend to deemphasize the past, move forward boldly to the immediate future, and strongly emphasize the importance of "futurism" (e.g., the glorification of the youth culture and devaluation of aging). Latino/a Americans tend to have a strong affective response to the present experience—enjoy the face-to-face contact experience while it lasts. Traditional Asian immigrants and Native Americans tend to revere the past—to understand someone or a corporate culture deeply, you must dig down through three generations of history.

Many Africans and African Americans tend to embrace a combination of past–present value solution. As Pennington (1990) observed, "Time is conceived [for Africans] only as it is related to events, and it must be experienced in order to make sense or to become real. The mathematical division of time observed by Westerners has little relevance for Africans" (p. 131). In traditional African societies, people tend to emphasize that something is experienced only at the present moment and that the past and one's ancestors are indispensable in giving meaning to one's present existence. Likewise, the larger French culture has been classified as reflecting the past–present value solutions. For African Americans and the French, the past looms

as a large historical canvas with which to understand the present.

In addition, for many Vietnamese American immigrants, their past profoundly influences their present identities. Many first-generation Vietnamese Americans believe in the Buddhist precepts of karma and rebirth. They believe that an individual's life cycle is predetermined by good and evil deeds from a previous life. Their hope is to achieve eventual spiritual enlightenment. Oftentimes, ancestors are worshiped for four generations after death.

Many Mexican Americans, in contrast, prefer to experience life and people around them fully in the present. Experiencing the rhythms of life in the present and temporarily forgetting about the day's worries is a learned cultural art. Living life fully and relating to family and friends through meaningful connections make intuitive sense to many traditionally oriented Mexicans or Mexican Americans

A potential clash can develop between members of business groups with different time orientations, for example, between members who favor a past–present focus and members who favor a future focus. Business members from the first group want to view everything from the company's history and tradition, but members from the latter group want to bypass the past and plan ahead efficiently for an immediate future. Individuals with a past–present focus have a long-term view of time, whereas individuals with a future focus have a short-term to medium-term view of time.

INDIVIDUAL SOCIALIZATION DEVELOPMENT

Beyond cultural–ethnic group membership values, individuals develop distinctive personal identities because of unique life histories, experiences, and personality traits. We develop our personal identities—our conception as a unique individual or a "unique self"—via our observations of role models around us and our own drives, relational experiences, cultural experiences, and identity construction. To examine individualism–collectivism on an individual level of analysis, Markus and Kitayama (1991) coined the terms *independent construal of self* and *interdependent*

my.blog 3.4 ASSESSING YOUR INDEPENDENT VERSUS INTERDEPENDENT SELF-CONSTRUAL TRAITS

Instructions: Recall how you generally feel and act in various situations. Let your first inclination be your guide and circle the number in the scale that best reflects your overall impression of yourself. The following scale is used for each item:

4 = YES! = *strongly agree—IT'S ME!*

3 = yes = *moderately agree—it's kind of like me*

2 = no   = *moderately disagree—it's kind of not me*

1 = NO! = *strongly disagree—IT'S NOT ME!*

		SA	MA	MD	SD
1.	Feeling emotionally connected with others is an important part of my self-definition.	4	3	2	1
2.	I believe I should be judged on my own accomplishments.	4	3	2	1
3.	My family and close relatives are important to who I am.	4	3	2	1
4.	I value my personal privacy above everyone else's.	4	3	2	1
5.	I often consult my close friends for advice before acting.	4	3	2	1
6.	I prefer to be self-reliant rather than depend on others.	4	3	2	1
7.	My close friendship groups are important to my well-being.	4	3	2	1
8.	I often assume full responsibility for my own actions.	4	3	2	1
9.	I enjoy depending on others for emotional support.	4	3	2	1
10.	My personal identity is very important to me.	4	3	2	1

Scoring: Add up the scores on all the even-numbered items and you will find your independent self-construal score. *Independent self-construal score:* _____. Add up the scores on all the odd-numbered items and you will find your interdependent self- construal score. *Interdependent self-construal score:* _____.

Interpretation: Scores on each personality dimension can range from 5 to 20; the higher the score, the more independent and/or interdependent you are. If the scores are similar on both personality dimensions, you are a biconstrual personality individual.

Reflection probes: Take a moment to think of the following questions: Have your self-construals changed throughout the years? What factors shape your independent or interdependent self-construals? Do you like your own independent and/ or interdependent self-construals? Why or why not?

Source: Scale adapted from Gudykunst et al. (1996)

construal of self. Before you read on, take a few minutes and fill out the brief survey in my.blog 3.4. The survey is designed to find out how you generally think of yourself and your connection with members of groups to which you belong.

Independent versus Interdependent Self-Construal

The terms *independent self-construal* and *interdependent self-construal* (Markus & Kitayama, 1991, 1994) refer to the degree to which people conceive of themselves as separate or connected to others, respectively. **Independent self-construal** involves the view that an individual is a unique entity with an individuated repertoire of feelings, cognitions, and motivations. Individuals with high independent self-construals tend to view themselves as distinct and unique from others and from the context. They use their own abilities and ideas as motivational bases rather than the thoughts and feelings of others. People who have high independent self-construals value personal achievement, self-direction, and competition (Boucher & Maslach, 2009; Harb & Smith, 2009; Santamaria, de la Mata, Hansen, & Ruiz, 2010). When communicating with others, high independents believe in striving for personal goals, being in control of their environment, and expressing their needs assertively. Independent self-construal types tend to predominate in individualistic cultures or ethnic groups (Gudykunst, Matsumoto, Ting-Toomey, Nishida, Kim, & Heyman, 1996; Park & Guan, 2006).

Interdependent self-construal, on the other hand, involves an emphasis on the importance of fitting in with relevant others and ingroup connectedness (Markus & Kitayama, 1991). People who have high interdependent self-construals strive to fit in with others, act in a proper manner, value conformity, and emphasize relational connections. When communicating with others, individuals with interdependent self-construals aim for relational harmony, avoid direct conflicts, and interact in a diplomatic, tactful manner. Interdependent self-construal types tend to predominate in collectivistic cultures or ethnic groups (Park & Guan, 2006).

Independent-self individuals tend to be found in individualistic societies, and interdependent-self individuals tend to be located in collectivistic societies. People of independent self-construal value the ideals, goals, motivations, and identity negotiation process of an "unencumbered self." In comparison, people of interdependent self-construal value the ideals, goals, motivations, and emotions of a "connected self." This connected self binds the person to his or her family, extended family, reference group, neighborhood, village, or caste group. Whereas the independent self emphasizes the basis of the individual as the fundamental unit of interaction, the interdependent self emphasizes relationship or the ingroup as the basic focus of social interaction.

Horizontal versus Vertical Self-Construal

Before you continue reading, fill out the my.blog 3.5 assessment. The survey assesses your horizontal versus vertical personality tendency. Parallel to the above self-construal idea, we can examine power distance from an individual level of analysis. Individuals and their behaviors can be conceptualized as moving toward either the "horizontal self" or the "vertical self" end of the spectrum.

Individuals who endorse **horizontal self-construal** prefer informal–symmetrical interactions (i.e., equal treatment) regardless of people's position, status, rank, or age. They prefer to approach an intercultural problem directly and to use impartial standards to resolve the problem. In contrast, individuals who emphasize **vertical self-construal** prefer formal–asymmetrical interactions (i.e., differential treatment) with due respect to people's position, titles, life experiences, and age. They apply a "case-by-case" standard to assess the right or wrong behaviors in accordance with the roles occupied in the hierarchical network.

The different power distance personality types mean that people will seek different kinds of relationships and, when possible, "convert" a relationship to the kind with which they are most comfortable. Thus, a professor with a horizontal-based self-construal may convert a professor–student relationship to a friend–friend relationship, which may well confuse a student with a vertical-based self-construal who expects a larger power distance in professor–student interaction.

Internal versus External Locus of Control

Let's check out whether you prefer to control your destiny or yield to your fate. Fill out the brief assessment in my.blog 3.6.

Locus of control reflects the destiny value orientation (control vs. yielding) on the cultural level. In terms of the locus of control personality dimension, there are two personality types: internal and external

my.blog 3.5 ASSESSING YOUR HORIZONTAL VERSUS VERTICAL PERSONALITY TRAITS

Instructions: Recall how you generally feel and act in various situations. Let your first inclination be your guide and circle the number in the scale that best reflects your overall impression of yourself. The following scale is used for each item:

4 = YES! = *strongly agree—*IT'S ME!

3 = yes = *moderately agree—*it's kind of like me

2 = no = *moderately disagree—*it's kind of not me

1 = NO! = *strongly disagree—*IT'S NOT ME!

		SA	MA	MD	SD
1.	I generally obey my parents' rules without question.	4	3	2	1
2.	I believe in respecting people's abilities— not their age or rank.	4	3	2	1
3.	I believe teachers should be respected.	4	3	2	1
4.	I respect people who are competent— not their roles or titles.	4	3	2	1
5.	I believe people who are older are usually wiser.	4	3	2	1
6.	I believe all people should have equal opportunities to compete for what they want.	4	3	2	1
7.	I think older siblings should take care of their younger siblings.	4	3	2	1
8.	I believe families should encourage their children to challenge their parents' opinions.	4	3	2	1
9.	I value the advice of my parents or older relatives.	4	3	2	1
10.	I respect parents who encourage their children to speak up.	4	3	2	1

Scoring: Add up the scores on all the even-numbered items and you will find your horizontal self score. *Horizontal self* score: _____. Add up the scores on all the odd numbered items and you will find your vertical self score. *Vertical self* score: _____.

Interpretation: Scores on each personality dimension can range from 5 to 20; the higher the score, the more horizontal and/or vertical you are. If the scores are similar on both personality dimensions, you have both personality traits.

Reflection probes: Think of your own family system some more. Do your parents encourage you to speak up and express your emotions? Do they enforce family rules flexibly or strictly? Do you like all the family rules? Or do you rebel against them? Discuss your family socialization experience and family rules with a classmate.

(Rotter, 1966). Internal locus of control individuals have a strong mastery-over-nature tendency, and external locus of control individuals have a strong yielding-fatalistic tendency.

Individuals with **internal locus of control** tend to emphasize free will, individual motivation, personal effort, and personal responsibility over the success or failure of an assignment. In comparison, individuals with **external locus of control** emphasize external determinism, karma, fate, and external forces shaping a person's life happenings and events. Internal locus of control is parallel to the notion of mastery over nature (i.e., controlling value), and external locus of control is parallel to the notion of subordination to nature (i.e., yielding value). Internal-locus individuals believe in the importance of free will and internal control of

Instructions: Recall how you generally feel and act in various situations. Let your first inclination be your guide and circle the number in the scale that best reflects your overall impression of yourself. The following scale is used for each item:

4 = YES! = *strongly agree*—IT'S ME!
3 = yes = *moderately agree*—it's kind of like me
2 = no = *moderately disagree*—it's kind of not me
1 = NO! = *strongly disagree*—IT'S NOT ME!

		SA	MA	MD	SD
1.	I believe I'm the master of my own destiny.	4	3	2	1
2.	I generally yield to my luck or fate in doing things.	4	3	2	1
3.	I am driven by my own motivation and effort.	4	3	2	1
4.	"Mother Nature" is usually in charge and wins.	4	3	2	1
5.	I am in charge of my own future and planning.	4	3	2	1
6.	I believe it is difficult to transcend fate.	4	3	2	1
7.	I believe personal willpower can conquer everything.	4	3	2	1
8.	I do my best and then let fate take over.	4	3	2	1
9.	I believe I have complete control of what will happen tomorrow.	4	3	2	1
10.	Life is unpredictable—the best we can do is to flow with our fate.	4	3	2	1

Scoring: Add up the scores on all the odd-numbered items and you will find your internal locus of control score. *Internal locus of control* score: _____. Add up the scores on all the even-numbered items and you will find your external locus of control score. *External locus of control* score: _____.

Interpretation: Scores on each locus of control can range from 5 to 20; the higher the score, the more internal and/or external you are. If the scores are similar on both personality dimensions, you subscribe to both personality traits.

Reflection probes: Think of the major decisions in your life (e.g., where to go to college, where to live, buying a car, or whom to date), and reflect on the following questions: Where did you learn your self-determination attitude? Or where did you learn your yielding attitude? How do you think your locus of control attitude influences your everyday decision making? What do you think are some of the strengths and limitations of being a high internal locus of control person or a high external locus of control person?

one's fate. External-locus individuals believe in trying their best and then letting fate take over.

Some individuals plan their actions in terms of the internal locus of control tendency, and others contemplate their life events along the external locus of control tendency. Perceived control of one's destiny exists in varying degrees in an individual, across situations, and across cultures (Leung & Bond, 2004; Rotter, 1966). In terms of gender socialization differences,

for example, males tend to endorse internal locus of control, and females tend to endorse external locus of control in a wide variety of cultures (Smith, Bond, & Kagitcibasi, 2006; Smith, Dugan, & Trompenaars, 1996). The translation is that males in many cultures are more motivated by internal drives and a doing/fixing approach, and females tend to be more contextual and being-oriented in their attempt to flow with their external environment.

To engage in competent identity-support work, we must increase our awareness and accuracy levels in assessing others' group membership and personal identity issues. There are many more identities (e.g., social class, sexual orientation, age, disability) that people bring into an interaction. However, for the purposes of this interculturally focused book, we shall emphasize cultural and ethnic identity issues and their relationship to communication.

INTERCULTURAL REALITY CHECK: DO-ABLES

This chapter has reviewed seven value patterns that we believe can explain some major differences and similarities that exist between clusters of cultures on a global level. The four value dimension patterns are individualism–collectivism, power distance, uncertainty avoidance, and feminine–masculine. The additional three value orientations are meaning, destiny, and time value patterns.

We have also identified distinctive personality types that carry their own unique stamps in their communication styles. We will be using these seven cultural value patterns and some of the unique personality styles to discuss and explain a variety of intercultural communication behaviors and relationships in the next few chapters.

To start off, to be a flexible intercultural communicator at the values clarification level, here are some recommended guidelines and skills:

- When entering a new culture, learn to practice the mindful O-D-I-S method. The mindful O-D-I-S method refers to mindful observation, description, interpretations, and suspending ethnocentric evaluations.
- Rather than engaging in hasty, negative evaluations, O-D-I-S analysis is a slowing-down process that involves learning to *observe* attentively—the verbal *and* nonverbal signals that are being exchanged in the communication process. Skipping the mindful observation process when confronted with different patterns of

behavior often leads to unconscious incompetent behavior.

- After mindful observation, we should then try to *describe* mentally and in behaviorally specific terms what is going on in the intercultural interaction (e.g., "He is not making direct eye contact with me" or "She is standing about six feet away from me while we're chatting"). Description is a clear report of what we have observed, including a minimum of distortion. It also means refraining from adding any evaluative meaning to the observed behavior.
- Next, we should generate *multiple interpretations* to make sense of the behavior we are observing and describing. Interpretation is what we think about what we see and hear (e.g., "Maybe from his cultural value framework, avoiding eye contact is a respectful behavior; from my cultural perspective, this is considered rude."). The important thing to keep in mind is that there can be multiple interpretations for any description of an observed behavior (e.g., "She is shy," "She is just doing her cultural thing," or "She just got Lasik eye surgery.").
- We may decide to respect the differences and *suspend* our ethnocentric evaluation. We may also decide to engage in open-ended evaluation by acknowledging our discomfort with unfamiliar behaviors (e.g., "I understand that eye contact avoidance may be a cultural habit, but it makes me feel uncomfortable."). Evaluations are positive or negative judgments concerning the interpretation(s) we attribute to the behavior (e.g., "I like the fact that she is keeping part of her cultural norms" or "I don't like it because I've been raised in a culture that values the use of direct eye contact.").
- Additionally, learn to observe a wide range of people in a wide range of situations in the new cultural setting before making any premature generalizations about the people's behavior in that culture. For example, we may want to observe a wide variety of people (and in a wide range of contexts)

from this cultural group to determine whether eye contact avoidance is a cultural custom or an individual trait.

Cultural and ethnic values shape the content of our identity on a group membership level. The more we are willing to dig deeper into our own value lens and understand our own socialization process, the more we can understand why we form quick, evaluative judgments concerning other people's "bizarre" way of thinking and behaving. Taken together, we believe that the four essential value dimensions (i.e., identity, power, uncertainty, and sex role) and the three value orientation patterns (i.e., meaning, destiny, and time) all shape our outlook on the intercultural communication meaning construction process and its expected outcome in a particular cultural community.

CHAPTER 4

WHAT ARE THE KEYS TO UNDERSTANDING CULTURAL AND ETHNIC IDENTITIES?

CHAPTER OUTLINE

- Family and Gender Socialization
  - Families Come in Different Shapes
  - Gender Socialization and Interaction Patterns

- Group Membership: Intercultural Boundary Crossing
  - The Process of Acculturation and Enculturation
  - Systems-Level Factors
  - Individual-Level Factors
  - Interpersonal Face-to-Face and Network-Level Factors
  - Mass Media–Level Factors

- Group Affiliation and Identity Formation
  - Cultural Identity Conceptualization
  - Ethnic Identity Conceptualization

- Ethnic–Racial Identity Change Process
  - Cultural–Ethnic Identity Typological Model
  - Racial–Ethnic Identity Development Model
  - Multiracial and Biracial Identity

- Intercultural Reality Check: Do-Ables

Growing up as a former Jehovah's Witness, color or ethnicity was not something that really was part of my focus in life. Although being biracial (half Croatian and half Jamaican) was part of my heritage, it did not have an impact on my life. Religion was my core identity and belief system. It wasn't until my freshman year in high school during a math class that I really understood that there was a bigger world of distinction. A fellow student turned to me during class and blurted out, "Oh my god, Alex—You are black!" At that moment, I realized that I did not really know what that meant. Growing up in a predominantly white neighborhood and constantly being surrounded by my mother's Eastern European friends and other Jehovah's Witnesses, I had limited experience and a lack of emotional connection to my black side. Although kids in school would call me Carlton (from the *Fresh Prince of Bel Air* TV show), I didn't see any similarity between myself and him. As a result, throughout my life, I have become used to people trying to fit me into a category or a box I don't fit in. I see myself as a collage of collided identities but, one whole: Me!

—aLx, Part 1, *Web Designer*

Individuals acquire and develop their identities through interaction with others in their cultural group. On a daily basis, we acquire the meanings, values, norms, and styles of communicating. We struggle with and against these identities, whether imposed or acquired. The above two scenarios highlight two very common questions we ask ourselves: Who am I? Who are you? Grappling with these identity issues is profoundly influenced by our cultural socialization, family socialization, and acculturation and identity change processes. For many, the result is a struggle between an individual's perceptions of being "different" coupled with the inability to blend in with both the mainstream culture and the ethnic heritage. More important, our identities are multifaceted, complex, and intersected. Although culture plays the larger role in shaping our view of ourselves, it is through multiple channels that we acquire and develop our own set of ethics, values, norms, and ways of behaving in our everyday lives. For example, through the direct channel of family, values and norms are transmitted and passed on from one generation to the next. Parents teach their children about right and wrong and teach acceptable or unacceptable ways of behaving through the words they use and through their role-modeling actions.

This chapter is organized into five main sections. We first explore the theme of family and gender socialization. We then discuss the factors that shape the ups and downs of intercultural boundary crossing. Third, we explore issues concerning cultural identity and ethnic identity conceptualization. Fourth, we explain two ethnic identity development models. We also discuss the experiences of being a multiracial or biracial individual. Finally, we offer do-ables for increasing your cultural identity self-awareness skills and also cultural identity other-validation skills.

FAMILY AND GENDER SOCIALIZATION

Early on, children internalize what to value and devalue, what to appreciate and reject, and what goals are important in their culture through the influence of their family system. Additionally, teenagers and young adults may be influenced, to a certain extent, by the pervasive messages from pop culture and the social media. It is through pervasive cultural value patterns—as filtered through family and media systems—that persons define meaning and values of identities, such as ethnicity, gender, and identity types (Lucey, 2010).

The term **identity** is used in this chapter as the reflective self-conception or self-image that we each derive from family, gender, cultural, ethnic, and individual socialization processes (Ting-Toomey, 2005a). It is acquired via our interaction with others in particular cultural scenes. Identity refers to our reflective views of ourselves and of other perceptions of our self-images—at both the social identity and the personal identity levels (Crisp, 2010a; Jackson, 1999, 2002; Wetherell & Mohanty, 2010). Before you continue

reading, fill out the my.blog 4.1 survey. The survey assesses how much your social and personal identities influence your everyday communication.

Social identities include cultural or ethnic membership, gender, sexual orientation, social class, religious affiliation, age, disability, or professional identity. **Personal identities** include any unique attributes that we associate with our individuated self in comparison with those of others (Reicher, Spears, & Haslam, 2010). Seeing yourself as independent, smart, loyal, or funny are examples of personal identities. Regardless of whether we are conscious of these identities, they influence our everyday behaviors in a generalized and particularized manner.

In this section, we explore some important ideas about family and gender socialization processes. In the following main section, we will discuss immigrants' intercultural boundary-crossing factors.

Families Come in Different Shapes

In all cultures, family is the central communication hub. Although all cultures and societies have webs

my.blog 4.1 ASSESSING THE IMPORTANCE OF YOUR SOCIAL AND PERSONAL IDENTITIES

Instructions: The following items describe how people think about themselves and communicate in various situations. Let your first inclination be your guide and circle the number in the scale that best reflects your overall value. The following scale is used for each item:

$$4 = SA = \textit{Strongly Agree}$$
$$3 = MA = \textit{Moderately Agree}$$
$$2 = MD = \textit{Moderately Disagree}$$
$$1 = SD = \textit{Strongly Disagree}$$

		SA	MA	MD	SD
1.	My group memberships (e.g., ethnic or gender) are important when I communicate with others.	4	3	2	1
2.	My personality usually comes across loud and clear when I communicate.	4	3	2	1
3.	I am aware of my own ethnic background or social roles when I communicate.	4	3	2	1
4.	My personality has a stronger influence on my everyday interaction than any social roles.	4	3	2	1
5.	I am aware of ethnic or gender role differences when I communicate.	4	3	2	1
6.	I tend to focus on the unique characteristics of the individual when I communicate.	4	3	2	1
7.	Some aspects of my ethnic or social roles always shape my communication.	4	3	2	1
8.	I believe my personal identity is much more important than any of my social membership categories.	4	3	2	1
9.	If people want to know me, they should pay more attention to my professional or student role identity.	4	3	2	1
10.	My unique self is more important to me than my ethnic or cultural role self.	4	3	2	1

Scoring: Add up the scores on all the odd-numbered items and you will find your social identity score. *Social identity* score: _____. Add up the scores on all the even-numbered items and you will find your personal identity score. *Personal identity* score: _____.

Interpretation: Scores on each identity dimension can range from 5 to 20; the higher the score, the more social and/or personal you are. If all the scores are similar on both identity dimensions, you emphasize the importance of both social and personal identities in your everyday communication process.

Reflection probes: In the first encounter with a stranger, do you usually try to understand the social role identity or personal identity of the stranger? Why? Do you primarily share your social role identity or personal role identity information with a stranger? What factors (e.g., work situations, classroom situations, or attraction) usually prompt you to exchange either more social role data or more personal identity data in your communication process?

of family relationships, the structure changes across time and cultures (Lucey, 2010). First and foremost, we acquire some of the beliefs and values of our culture via our primary family system. The rules that we acquire in relating to our parents, grandparents, siblings, and extended families contribute to the initial blueprint of our formation of role, gender, and relational identities. Through communication within the family, we learn to deal with boundary issues, such as space and time and power dynamics (e.g., which parent or siblings hold the power status).

Families can be defined in many ways. The **traditional family** consists of a husband–wife, father–mother pair with a child or children, a father working outside the home, and a homemaker-mother. In the United States, the traditional family is the exception, never the rule, limited to upper- and middle-class heterosexuals. Historically, most U.S. families have had at least two wage earners. The **extended family** consists of extended kinship groups, such as grandparents, aunt and uncles, cousins, and nieces and nephews. For example, Native Americans, Hawaiians, and Filipino families often include extended family networks that contain several households. These integrative households include parents, children, aunts, uncles, cousins, and grandparents. The **blended family** refers to the merging of different family systems from previous marriages. The **single-parent family** refers to a household headed by a single parent. In many U.S. households, parents are single, and men and women can be single parents to their children.

We can also think of two possible family types in the family decision-making process: the personal family system and the positional family system. Some of the major characteristics of the **personal family system** include the emphasis on personal, individualized meanings, negotiable roles between parents and child(ren), and the emphasis on interactive discussions within the family (Bernstein, 1971; Haslett, 1989). Democratic families try to emphasize different family members as unique individuals. Democratic parents are consultative in their decision-making process. They hold family meetings to solicit input in major family decision issues. They are explicit in their communication styles, and they encourage experimentation and individual initiative

in their children. They try to foster individualistic and small power distance value patterns in the family system. They act more like friends to their children than authority figures (Guerrero, Andersen, & Afifi, 2010).

Comparatively, the **positional family system** emphasizes communal meanings, ascribed roles and statuses between parents and child, and family rule conformity. Positional families emphasize the importance of holding the hierarchical power structure in the family exchange process. Individuals have different status-based authority and responsibilities in a positional family system. Authoritarian parents, from a positional family framework, are demanding and directive. They expect their children to obey family rules without question. They do not believe in having to explain the reasons behind their disciplinary actions to their children (Guerrero et al., 2010). Many positional family systems exist in collectivistic, large power distance cultural regions (see Table 4.1).

In the United States, a growing number of families are formed by differences, whether visible or invisible. Families in this century will reflect more diversity of self conceptions, live within four or five generations of relational connections, and refigure themselves across the lifespan (Galvin, 2006). As a result of our interaction with our family and peers, we directly and indirectly acquire the various value patterns in our culture. Although no single family can transmit all the value patterns in a culture, families who share similar cultural and ethnic ties do have some family value patterns in common. Family serves as the primary value socialization channel that creates a lasting imprint on our communicative behavior. It also cues our perceptions and

TABLE 4.1 CHARACTERISTICS OF PERSONAL VERSUS POSITIONAL FAMILY SYSTEMS

Personal family system	Positional family system
Individual meanings	Communal meanings
Democratic decision making	Authoritarian decision making
Negotiable roles	Conventional roles
Children can question	Children should obey
Small power distance	Large power distance

interpretations concerning appropriate gendered-based interpersonal behaviors. Recall Chapter 1, where we discussed the increase of adoption of children from overseas. As more families are formed by differences, this visible difference clearly changes the dynamics of family and social interaction. Check out the story of Gina and her process of adoption (see Blog Post 4.1).

Gender Socialization and Interaction Patterns

The gender identities we learned as children affect our communication with others. They affect how we define ourselves, how we encode and decode gendered messages, how we develop intimate relationships, and how we relate to one another. Gender identity, in short, refers to the meanings and interpretations we hold concerning our self-images and expected other-images of femaleness and maleness.

For example, females in many cultures are expected to act in a nurturing manner, to be more affective, and to play the primary caregiver role. Males in many cultures are expected to act in a competitive manner, to be more emotionally reserved, and to play the breadwinner role. The orientations toward femaleness and maleness are grounded and learned via our own cultural and ethnic practices. Children learn appropriate gender roles through rewards and punishments they receive from their parents in performing the "proper" or "improper" gender-related behaviors. In the United States, feminine-based tendencies, such as interdependence, cooperation, and verbal relatedness, are often rewarded in girls, whereas masculine-based tendencies, such as independence, competition, and verbal assertiveness, are often promoted in boys.

Gender researchers observe that young girls and boys learn their gender-related behaviors in the home

---

BLOG POST 4.1

Adopting a child takes faith and fate. If you're Chinese it simply takes luck. I'm Chinese. My parents are immigrants from southern China. I was raised on believing in good luck and bad luck. We were raised to remember our ancestors. If we did, good luck would shine on us. If not, bad luck would be unleashed on us. Even today, occurrences around me are evaluated by whether good or bad luck was involved. So for me adopting a child was all about luck.

My husband and I chose to adopt. He was adopted. As potential adoptive parents, my husband and I had to really "think" about what type of baby we were willing to make part of our family. Besides considering what kind of baby are you willing to accept, you invariably ask, does race matter? My husband is white. I am Chinese. Did we want a white baby? How about a Latino or Chinese baby? How about a mixed race baby? For us, we ultimately decided race did not matter.

Our search gave us the options of looking here in the United States or overseas. Ultimately we decided to concentrate on China. There was a need in China to find families for abandoned female babies. Growing up in a traditional Chinese family, I understood how girls were regarded . . . frankly, not so great. I also knew how young female infants were being discarded in favor of the prospect of conceiving a baby boy. For us, China was the place to go to find a healthy baby.

We journeyed to China with a group of twenty sets of prospective American parents. We were required to be in the country for two weeks. We were exposed to Chinese culture, we saw historic Chinese landmarks, and we were encouraged to buy an abundance of trinkets and goods with our American dollars. Yes, even as adopting babies, we were exposed to capitalism, Chinese style!

Before we left China as a group, the Chinese officials gave all of the American parents—and their brand new Chinese babies or toddlers—a gift. It was a red cloth filled with dirt from China. The Chinese officials said they wanted the babies to literally "own" a piece of China. They wanted the new Americans to always know "where" they had come from. They wanted the children to know that China had not abandoned them.

During my husband's and my adoption tour in China, we were told about a Cantonese saying. "These Chinese babies given up for adoption did not find the right stomach to grow in, but they found the right door." And that door is opened all the time. My Jewish husband and I have had the opportunity to open that door of "good luck" more than once. We adopted two precious daughters from China. For us, our two beautiful and strong daughters from China are symbols of good luck. Others might say our daughters are the lucky ones. However, I would submit the "good luck" is my husband's and mine. Our promise to Chinese officials was to raise them well. With some good luck we are doing that.

—Gina, *adoptive mother*

and school and in childhood games. For example, in the United States, girls' games (e.g., playing house, jump rope) tend to involve either pairs or small groups. The girls' games often involve fluid discussion about who is going to play what roles in the "playing house" game, for example, and usually promote relational collaboration. Boys' games (e.g., baseball, basketball), on the other hand, involve fairly large groups and have clear objectives, distinct roles and rules, and clear win–lose outcomes. The *process* of playing, rather than the win–lose outcome, is predominant in girls' games in the larger U.S. culture (Maltz & Borker, 1982; Tannen, 1994). One researcher (Wood, 2009) concludes that girls' games enable U.S. females to form the expectations that communication is used to create and maintain relationships and respond to others' feelings empathetically rather than for individual competitiveness. In contrast, boys' games prompt U.S. males to form the expectations that communication is used to achieve some clear outcomes, attract and maintain an audience, and compete with others for the "talk stage."

Moving beyond the U.S. cultural context to illustrate, in traditional Mexican culture, child-rearing practices also differ significantly in socializing girls and boys. At the onset of adolescence, the difference between girls and boys becomes even more markedly apparent. The female is likely to remain much closer to home and to be "protected and guarded in her contact with others beyond the family.... The adolescent male, following the model of his father, is given much more freedom to come and go as he chooses and is encouraged to gain much worldly knowledge and experience outside the home" (Locke, 1992, p. 137). Gender identity and cultural–ethnic identity intersect and form part of an individual's composite self-conception.

However, Lorber (1994) and Kimmel (1992) argue that the whole point of the gender system today is to maintain structured gender inequality—to produce a subordinate class (women) that can be exploited as workers, sexual partners, childbearers, and emotional nurturers. Thus, gender is a socially constructed status created in a particular societal system (Tagg, 2008). Our gender identities are created, in part, via our communication with others. They are also supported and reinforced by existing cultural structures and practices.

GROUP MEMBERSHIP: INTERCULTURAL BOUNDARY CROSSING

The journey for immigrants, from identity security to insecurity and from familiarity to unfamiliarity, can be a turbulent or exhilarating process. The path itself has many ups and downs, twists and turns. In such a long, demanding passage, an incremental process of identity change is inevitable. This section explains immigrants' acculturation experiences and explores some of the key factors that shape immigrants' outlooks concerning their adopted homeland.

The Process of Acculturation and Enculturation

The intercultural **acculturation** process is defined as the degree of identity change that occurs when an individual moves from a familiar environment to an unfamiliar one. Intercultural acculturation, however, does not happen overnight. It is a gradual, incremental lifetime identity transformation process. The larger the gap between the two cultures, the higher the degree of identity vulnerability that immigrants will experience in the new culture (Berry, 2008; W. Chen, 2010; Halualani, 2008). Which are the top five countries with the highest percentage of immigrants? And which are the top five countries of origins for U.S. immigrants who arrived in the year 2010? Take a guess, and check out Jeopardy Boxes 4.1 and 4.2.

The immigrant group comprises those who generally have voluntarily moved across cultural boundaries, but those in the refugee group often have involuntarily done so for reasons of political, religious, or economic oppression. Unlike tourists and sojourners, immigrants and refugees usually aim for a permanent stay in their adopted country (hereafter, the term *immigrants* will also include refugees). Although there are some similar adaptation patterns (e.g., initial stress and culture shock) in these diverse groups, the means, goals, and motivation to adapt vary.

The term acculturation refers to the incremental identity-related change process of immigrants and refugees in a new environment from a long-term per-

JEOPARDY BOX 4.1 TOP FIVE COUNTRIES WITH THE HIGHEST ESTIMATED NET NUMBER OF IMMIGRANTS PER 1,000 POPULATION

Country	Estimated net number of immigrants as a percentage of national population
1. Andorra	77.25
2. Qatar	75.9
3. United Arab Emirates	71.4
4. Monaco	70.11
5. Kuwait	62.11

Source: U.N. Population Policies 2005, http://books.google.com/books?hl=en &id=YgSsp6S1qnkC&printsec=frontcover&source=web&ots=kXSuhAamCt&s ig=nf3BbgP2FUT4tFxHgFC1ZrZO_8A&sa=X&oi=book_result&resnum=7&ct= result#v=onepage&q&f=false (retrieved July 17, 2011); United Nations Publications (2006); World Population Policies 2005 (Population Studies Series).

JEOPARDY BOX 4.2 TOP FIVE COUNTRIES OF ORIGIN FOR U.S. IMMIGRANTS

Country
1. Mexico
2. The Philippines
3. India
4. China
5. Vietnam

Source: U.S. Census Bureau, Foreign-Born Population by Citizenship Status and Place of Birth, http://www.census.gov/compendia/statab/cats/population/native_and_foreign-born_populations.html (retrieved July 17, 2011).

spective (Redfield, Linton, & Herskovits, 1936). The change process of immigrants often involves subtle change to overt, more extensive change. Acculturation involves the long-term conditioning process of newcomers in integrating the new values, norms, and symbols of their new culture and developing new roles and skills to meet its demands. Let's take a look at Blog Post 4.2.

Enculturation, on the other hand, often refers to the sustained, primary socialization process of strangers in their original home (or natal) culture wherein they have internalized their primary cultural values. For example, a U.S. immigrant born in Egypt would be *enculturated* into an Egyptian identity, but slowly *acculturated* into U.S. culture (in some amount) once he or she immigrates. The same immigrant can be a *bicultural* individual if he or she relates strongly to both cultures (see the section on "Ethnic–Cultural Identity Change Process"; see also, Tadmor, Hong, Chiu, & No, 2010; Ward, 2008; Waters, 1990). Let's take a look at a follow-up story by Laleh in Blog Post 4.3, which is about her own ethnic identity struggles.

What is your reaction to Laleh's story? Have you ever thought about physical appearance and ethnic identity belongingness and exclusion issues? Have you ever felt excluded because you do not look mainstream enough? Beyond physical markers, of course, many factors influence the immigrants' acculturation experience—from self-identification factors, to systems-level factors (e.g., receptivity of the host culture), to individual-level factors (e.g., individual expectations) and also interpersonal-level factors (e.g., formation of social networks).

Systems-Level Factors

Systems-level factors are those elements in the host environment that influence newcomers' adaptation to the new culture (Y. Y. Kim, 2005). In this section, we shall emphasize the need and responsibility of both the host society and the immigrants to learn from each other—to create an inclusive, pluralistic cultural community.

Three observations can be made with regard to adaptation. First, the host culture's *socioeconomic conditions* influence the climate of adaptation (Puentha, Giles, & Young, 1987). When the host culture is economically strong, people appear to be more tolerant and hospitable toward newcomers. When economic conditions are harsh, natives have a more difficult time keeping jobs, and often immigrants become the scapegoats for local economic problems. For example, immigrants are often perceived as competing for scarce resources, such as new jobs and promotion opportunities, and taking away the job opportunities of cultural insiders. Anti-immigration policies make it difficult to adjust easily because natives are motivated with a "fear of being swamped by people of a different culture" (Thatcher, 1978).

Second, a host culture's *attitudinal stance* on "cultural assimilation" or "cultural pluralism" produces a spillover effect on institutional policies (as well as on

BLOG POST 4.2

I was thinking about those factors we discussed in class about what makes an immigrant's stay successful. Being raised in a family [whose members] are all immigrants from Iran, I feel somewhat closely related to what other immigrants have to experience. My grandparents had to learn to adapt to living in a completely different world from [the place] they still call home. I am not so sure that either set of my grandparents was too successful. They came to America in their early seventies, so they were retired. But my grandparents on my mom's side had to leave a lot of their material belongings behind, because there was a revolution in Iran and they had little time to leave the country. So not only did they have to adjust to living in a new culture, but they [also] had to adjust to losing most of their material possessions. I think that resilience and flexibility are two huge factors that my maternal grandmother [is] still working on to this day.

Growing up, I never really saw her try to learn about American culture. She felt more comfortable speaking with Persian friends, finding Persian stores, watching or listening to her Persian programs on television and radio. I am not saying that my grandmother has been wrong for doing these things, but I am noticing that she does not really have much interest in making her permanent stay here "successful."

My maternal grandfather, on the other hand, took ESL classes at night at the local high school and learned to make his way around a grocery store, speaking with the cashiers and knowing the exact change to give them. He was definitely more motivated to adjust to this huge change. Support networks have been really crucial to my grandmother's life. My father helped her apply for a green card. Family friends who also came from Iran years earlier gave her a sense of security and comfort. There is an Iranian television station in Los Angeles where she can find out all about the news of America as well as Iran. She watches it all day long. I can hear the TV on sometimes at 3:00 a.m. And she gets so excited telling me the latest news she has heard.

This is a part of my life that really separated me from the rest of my classmates from elementary school until now . . . the feeling of being different and not quite fitting in with the rest of the kids. The question: What does it mean to live a successful immigrant experience in this country? It can mean so many different things to so many different people. The answer also depends on so many factors. I can see that in their unique yet separate ways, my grandparents [are] quite successful in adapting to this new culture. They use different strategies to deal with the changes surrounding them.

—Zahra, *college student*

BLOG POST 4.3

I have always been reminded of how different I am. . . . This is how minorities are visible. It is interesting how the definition of an "American" can be so clear-cut to some and totally unclear to others. Anyway, in this American culture, it seems so easy for people to determine who is NOT an American or at least not American enough.

To tell you a story, . . . some time ago I had planned to get a nose job. I knew exactly why I wanted to change my nose: it was a typical Persian big nose. I used to be so self-conscious about my nose that I would walk behind everyone so that they could not see my profile if I were standing side by side with them.

Both my parents are in support of me getting a nose job, but I have always been so hesitant to actually go through with the procedure. I realized if I do so, I would be erasing an ethnic identity that should be kept as a part of me.

—Laleh, *college student*

attitudes of the citizenry) toward newcomers' adaptation processes (Kraus, 1991). The main effect of the "cultural assimilation" stance demands that strangers conform to the host environment. In contrast, the "cultural pluralist" stance encourages a diversity of values (e.g., as supported by Canadian "multicultural" policies), providing strangers with wider latitude of norms from which to choose in their newfound homeland. European countries are facing serious criticism for their "anti" immigration sentiment. In the Netherlands, potential Dutch citizens must take a compulsory thirty-minute computerized examination and watch a video to test their readiness to be a citizen. The film features gay kissing and topless women emerging from a crowded beach, both which would make Muslim immigrants uncomfortable (Mutsvairo, 2006). Other European Union (EU) countries have stricter measures. In Italy a law now requires Italian proficiency for permanent residency permits—after five years of legal residence. Immigrants from outside the EU must prove they can speak basic German in Austria five years after receiving their residency permit—or they may be fined or be in jeopardy. In Britain, the government has enforced a stricter requirement for English language competency and immigrants must prove their command of "Britishness"

HIT-OR-MISS 4.1 SAMPLE QUESTIONS FROM THE "TEST OF BRITISHNESS"

See if you "Hit" or "Miss" as you answer these questions from the "Test of Britishness":

1. Where is Cockney spoken?
   a) Liverpool
   b) London
   c) Glasgow

2. What are MPs?
3. Who is head of the Church of England: The Queen or Archbishop of Canterbury?
4. In addition to Great Britain, the Queen is monarch over which countries?
   a) The Bahamas
   b) Canada
   c) Jamaica
   d) New Zealand

5. Which two telephone numbers can be used to dial for emergency services?
   112, 123, 555, 911, 999

Answers:

1. *b) London*
2. *Members of Parliament.*
3. *The head, called the "Supreme Governor" of the Church of England, is the ruling monarch—currently Queen Elizabeth.*
4. *All of the above, and also Antigua, Australia, Barbados, Barbuda, Belize, Grenada, the Grenadines, Nevis, Northern Ireland, Papua New Guinea, Saint Kitts, Saint Vincent, the Solomon Islands, Saint Lucia, and Tuvalu.*
5. *112 and 999. 112 was adopted in 1991 as a universal SOS for all emergency services throughout Europe.*

Adapted from S. Freeman, S, *Times Online*, October 31, 2005. Would you pass the Britishness test? Retrieved March 28, 2011, from http://www.timesonline.co.uk/tol/news/uk/article584918.ece?token=null&offset=0&page=1

---

with multiple choice questions (D'Emilio, 2011; see Hit-or-Miss 4.1).

In France, French Muslim women were officially banned from wearing their face veils in public beginning April 11, 2011. President Nicolas Sarkozy claimed that the "niqab" veils (with just a slit for the eyes) "imprison women and contradict the secular nation's values of dignity and equality" (Rustici, 2011, p. 1). The French law will fine any women who wear the niqab 150 Euros (equivalent to US $215) or they must attend special citizenship classes. Public opinion in the streets of Paris appears to be mixed. Measures like these do keep immigrant groups feeling like "guests" or even "unwelcome suspects" in their adopted countries they now call home. Whether members of the host culture perceive strangers as nonpersons, intruders, aliens, visitors, or guests will influence their attitudes and behaviors toward the strangers.

Third, *local institutions* (e.g., schools, places of work, social services, and mass media) serve as firsthand contact agencies that facilitate or impede the adaptation process of sojourners and immigrants. Following the prevailing national policies, local institutions can either greatly facilitate strangers' adaptation process (e.g., via language help programs or job training programs) or produce roadblocks to the newcomers' adaptive experience. At public schools, varying degrees of receptivity and helpfulness of teachers toward immigrant children can either help the children to feel "at home" or leave them to "sink or swim." Whether the attitudes of local children in the classrooms are favorable or unfavorable can also produce a pleasant or hostile climate for these immigrant children during their vulnerable adaptive stages. Getting used to a strange language, unfamiliar signs, and different expectations and norms of a new classroom can be overwhelming for recent immigrant children.

Whereas some cultures make greater distinctions between insiders and outsiders, some groups have built-in mechanisms to facilitate the socialization of newcomers. Immigrants are marginalists to a new culture. They often need help and coaching to learn the inner workings of a culture. To the extent that insiders of a new culture treat the newcomers with dignity, inclusion, and respect, they experience identity confirmation and connection. To the extent that newcomers or minority members (including second- or third-generation families) are long treated as borderline persons (e.g., by asking third-generation Russians where they came from and when will they return "home"—when their home culture is right here in the United States), they experience identity frustration and dislocation.

The combined systems-level factors can create either a favorable or an unfavorable climate for the newly arrived strangers. Obviously, the more favorable and receptive the cultural climate toward the arrival of strangers, the easier it is for the strangers to adapt to the new culture (Y. Y. Kim, 2001, 2003, 2004). The more help the newcomers receive during the initial cultural adaptation stages, the more positive are their perceptions of their new environment.

Individual-Level Factors

Having status as a permanent resident evokes a mixture of emotional and work-related stress. Immigrants often have more family worries and acculturation issues than do short-term sojourners. The sense of "no return" (i.e., for immigrants) versus "transitory stay" (i.e., for sojourners) produces different motivational drives for newcomers to acquire the new core rituals, symbols, and scripts suited to their new home.

Many immigrants uprooted themselves because of a mixture of "push" *motivational factors* (e.g., political, religious, and/or economic conditions) and "pull" *motivational factors*. The new culture's attractions (pull factors) may include better chances for personal advancement and better job opportunities, greater educational opportunities for the children, an improved quality of life for the family, a better standard of living, and democratic cultural values (Ward, Bochner, & Furnham, 2001). For example, in Ireland,

tens of thousands are joining in a new wave of emigration, leaving for the UK, newer European Union countries (e.g., Poland, Czech Republic), France, and Germany because of Ireland's economic malaise. The severe financial crisis in Ireland is spurring a wave of emigration that threatens to decimate the country's population (Chazan & Thomson, 2011). Greece has offered both push and pull motivations over the years. It is the first point of entry for immigrants to the EU from countries such as Turkey and the Middle East, so many immigrants were pulled to stay in this EU county to take advantages of its benefits and opportunities. Now, with Greece in severe financial crisis, it is creating a push motivation for these same immigrants to return to their home countries (Kakissis, 2011). In sum, the motivational orientation of people leaving their homelands can greatly affect their expectations and behaviors in the new culture.

Cultural knowledge and interaction-based knowledge about the host culture serve as critical factors in the process of adaptation. Cultural knowledge can include information about the following: cultural and ethnic history, geography, political and economic systems, religious and spiritual beliefs, multiple value systems, and situational norms. Interaction-based knowledge can include language, verbal and nonverbal styles, diversity-related communication issues (e.g., regional, ethnic, and gender differences within a culture), and various problem-solving styles.

Fluency in the host culture's language, for example, has been found to have a direct positive impact on sociocultural adaptation, such as developing relationships with members of the host culture (Ward & Kennedy, 1993) and ability to access health care (Fassaert, Hesselink, & Verhoeff, 2009). In contrast, language incompetence has been associated with increased psychological and psychosomatic symptoms (e.g., sleeplessness, severe headaches) in immigrants to the United States from India (Krishnan & Berry, 1992). For elderly Chinese and Korean immigrants to the United States, language incompetence is associated with social isolation, feelings of insecurity, and difficulty in making friends (Mui, Kang, Kang, & Domanski, 2007). Beyond language fluency, interaction-based pragmatic competence (such as knowing when to say what appropriately, under what situations) is critical in adapting to a new environment.

Additionally, *demographic variables*, such as age and educational level, have also been found to affect the success of adaptational effectiveness. Younger children have an easier time adapting to the new culture than adults, and individuals with higher educational levels tend to adapt more effectively than do individuals with lower educational levels (Ward, 1996, 2004; Ward et al., 2001). We should note here that most of the cited studies are based on sojourners' and immigrants' experiences in the settings of Australia, Canada, the United States, the Netherlands, and more recently Germany. Thus, the research conclusions summarized in this chapter are reflective of acculturation norms in individualistic cultures more than in collectivistic cultures.

Finally, on the individual level analysis, contributing to the success of adapting is the personality resilience of the boundary-crossing immigrant or refugee. This x-factor, *resilience or personal strength*, can make or break the process of long-term acculturation. Sensitivity to rejection or fear of interaction may cause individuals to stay within their ethnic community and never venture out, but others who have more resilience enjoy the challenge of communicating with those who are unfamiliar.

Interpersonal Face-to-Face and Network-Level Factors

Face-to-face (F2F) and network-level factors can include face-to-face networks (e.g., social networks), mediated contact factors (e.g., mass media), and interpersonal skills factors (Y. Y. Kim, 2005). First, let's check out Blog Post 4.4.

Blog Post 4.4 illustrates how London is grappling with individuals from all points across the globe, living together in communities across the city. This vibrancy only adds to the complexity of communication between majority–minority members and across intergenerational lines.

Ethnic communities and enclaves form as immigrants move from their homeland to communities in their new adopted land. These communities provide critical support during the initial stages of immigrants'

BLOG POST 4.4

London in 2005 is uncharted territory. Never have so many different kinds of people tried living together in the same place before. What some people see as the great experiment of multiculturalism will triumph or fail here . . . 30% of London residents had been born outside England—that's 2.2 million people, to which we can add the unknown tens of thousands who didn't complete a census form. And even this total takes no account of the contribution of the city's second- and third-generation immigrants, many of whom have inherited the traditions of their parents and grandparents. Altogether, more than 300 languages are spoken by the people of London, and the city has at least 50 non-indigenous communities with populations of 10,000 or more. Virtually every race, nation, culture and religion in the world can claim at least a handful of Londoners.

—L. Benedictus, *UK Guardian*, 2005

adaptation process. This observation is based on the idea that if ethnic clusters or niches in the ethnic community are strong and available as a supportive network, then immigrants may find supportive role models and mentors to assist with the transition and with culture shock. Locals can engage in appropriate and effective identity-validation messages (e.g., "I was lonely and confused when I first got here") that instill hope and confidence among those in transition.

A supportive social network serves as a buffer zone between a newcomer's threatened identity, on the one hand, and the unfamiliar environment on the other. Overall, studies of immigrants' network patterns have yielded some interesting findings. Research indicates that the more a newcomer participates in the dominant group's activities, the more favorable his or her attitudes toward the native culture (Y. Y. Kim, 2005). These contact networks are often viewed as the "healing webs" that nurture the adaptive growth and inquiry process of newcomers. Both close ties (e.g., relatives, close friends) and weak ties (e.g., acquaintanceships with neighbors, schoolteachers, grocers) provide important identity and informational support functions. In fact, it has been speculated that oftentimes the latter, weaker connections may help newcomers to locate their first job or solve their everyday problems (Adelman, 1988; Granovetter, 1973).

With cell phones, Skype, and apps, many immigrants can use technology to assist with language as well. Social media serves to aid and assist immigrants to stay in contact with friends and relatives living in their home towns. The Internet also helps with adaptation to the new culture; one study suggests that as immigrants stay in their new country, over time they become less likely to surf websites that originate in their home country and more likely to communicate with local individuals through the Internet (G. M. Chen, 2010).

Mass Media–Level Factors

Mass media play a critical role in the initial stages of adaptation. Because of language barriers, immigrants tend to reach out to ethnic newspapers, magazines, radio, and TV programs when such media resources are available in the local community (Y.Y. Kim, 2005). Ethnic media tend to ease the loneliness and adaptive stress of the new arrivals. The familiar language and images are identity affirming and offer newcomers a sense of comfort and identity connection in the unfamiliar environment. For example, in a 2010 Nielsen report (http://www.np.nielsen.com) on Hispanic media use, Spanish-speaking households mainly watch Spanish-language television. In addition, 72 percent of Hispanics have computers—89 percent with Internet access. Forty-seven percent of households with Internet access will watch Spanish-related Internet: movies, videos, or listening to music. One-third of Spanish-speaking households listen to Spanish radio for at least thirty minutes and over 50 percent will read a Spanish paper for thirty minutes a day. How popular is Spanish-language television? Univision is currently ranked as the fourth most watched broadcast network among all adults aged eighteen to forty-nine, surpassing NBC and CBS (Radio and Television Business Report, 2011). Popular shows like *Eva Luna* and *Theresa* propelled the network to the top spot on Friday, April 1, 2011.

Mass media may influence and guide the adaptation process—but this is a broad-based influence. Establishing personal relationship networks is deeper. Through the mass media (especially television), immigrants receive a smorgasbord of information concerning a broad range of host national topics, but without much informational depth. In contrast, through personal network contacts, newcomers learn about the host culture from a smaller sample of individuals, revolving around a narrower range of topics, but with more depth and specific personal perspectives.

In any successful intercultural learning process, members of the host culture must act as the gracious hosts, and newcomers must act as the willing-to-learn guests. Without collaborative efforts, the hosts and the new arrivals may end up with great frustrations, miscommunications, and identity misalignments.

We discussed how as individuals and families adapt and acculturate into the mainstream culture, the structural features of the social environment, perceptions, and motivations at the individual level may be powerful tools of connection or discord. The struggle to balance ethnic group affiliation with connecting to mainstream assimilation is a second main intersection of identity development among immigrants, ethnic children, and bi-/multiracial children. We now address the framework of identity development and grapple with the intersection and complexity of how individuals at different change points negotiate and define who they are (see also, Gonzalez, Houston, & Chen, 2011).

GROUP AFFILIATION AND IDENTITY FORMATION

Our *social identities* consist of cultural or ethnic membership identity, gender identity, sexual orientation identity, social class identity, age identity, disability identity, or professional identity. With regard to ethnic identity, social identity consists of two important elements. The first is knowledge of social group membership. Our self-concept comes, in part, from the knowledge we have of our sociocultural group membership (Tajfel, 1979). The second element is emotional significance. If we place high value on the emotional significance of group membership, the result is positive group membership esteem. As a result, the more strongly one identifies with the group, the more bias one shows in favor of his or her group against salient outgroups (Brewer, 1997, 2010; Brewer & Pierce, 2005; Crisp, 2010a, 2010b).

Analyzing the link between social identity and group membership is revealing. Among European Americans, ethnicity is symbolic. A *symbolic identity* "fulfills the need to be from somewhere. An ethnic identity is something that makes you both special and simultaneously part of a community. It can come to you involuntarily through heredity, and at the same time, it is a personal choice" (Waters, 1990, p. 150). European Americans can choose to be individuals apart from their ethnic heritage group or they can choose to claim an ethnicity, such as "Irish American," "Swedish American," or "French/German American." Celebrating an ethnic holiday as a symbolic gesture or being a "representative" for the group is an example of symbolic identity. But rites of passage among Mexicans, such as a quincenera or a bar/bat mitzvah among Jewish groups, are not simply symbolic.

For some ethnic groups in the United States, such as African Americans, personal choice or having a symbolic identity is not a choice. Ethnic individuals can be "marked" or "assigned" to categories ascribed by other groups on the basis of physical characteristics or skin color. Ethnicity is generally not a voluntary choice for all groups because it can be imposed. Orbe (1998), for example, has developed a theory called the **co-culture theory**. He claims that African Americans, because of their position in the larger U.S. society, develop a complex ethnic–cultural standpoint. He contends that in each society, "a hierarchy exists that privileges certain groups of individuals: In the United States these groups include men, European Americans, heterosexuals, the able-bodied, and [the] middle and upper class" (Orbe, 1998, p. 11).

Ethnic differences shape who we befriend and even marry, yet they weaken down the generational line. As each generation is removed from the original immigrant generation, the erosion of ethnic linkage naturally results. According to Alba (1990), individuals having weak identities with the historical ethnic group have a greater tendency to marry out of their ethnic group than individuals with strong ethnic identities. The main reason is that individuals with weaker ethnic identities are perceived as less ethnic and as sharing more things in common with the dominant group than individuals who strongly identify with their ethnic group.

Social identity explains the behavior of an ethnic individual with regard to group membership—how different groups perceive their own and others' group membership identity issues. It is also about marking ingroup–outgroup boundaries as well as majority–minority group relations issues. In being aware of our multifaceted self-conception, we can also develop a deeper awareness of the complex, multifaceted identities of culturally different others. We begin our discussion with cultural identity.

Cultural Identity Conceptualization

All individuals are socialized within a larger cultural membership group. For example, everyone born and/ or raised in the United States has a sense of what it means to be "American" (in this book, to avoid ambiguity, we shall use the term "U.S. American"). However, minority group members or biracial members are asked "Where are you from?" more often than mainstream white U.S. Americans. Let's look at Gitanjali's (1994) musing in Blog Post 4.5.

Alternatively, if you are very comfortable with your own cultural identity, and more important, if you look like everyone else in the mainstream culture, you may not even notice the importance of your cultural membership badge until someone asks you "Where are you from?" in your overseas travels. Before you continue, fill out the brief assessment in my.blog 4.2. This brief survey explores your sense of identification with the larger U.S. culture.

We gain access to cultural group memberships during our formative years. Our cultural identities

---

BLOG POST 4.5 INTERVIEW EXCERPTS

What is your nationality?

I don't know.

I wish I had a dollar for every time someone asked that question.

What is your nationality?

Maybe it's just an obsession.

Yeah, maybe it's you!

What is your nationality?

My mother's a Zebra and my father's a Martian.

So, what's your nationality? Is it a secret?

--Gitanjali (1994, p. 133)

my.blog 4.2 ASSESSING THE DEGREE OF IMPORTANCE OF YOUR CULTURAL IDENTITY AND MARGINAL IDENTITY

Instructions: Recall how you generally feel and act in various situations. Let your first inclination be your guide and circle the number in the scale that best reflects your overall impression of yourself. The following scale is used for each item:

4 = YES! = *strongly agree—IT'S ME!*
3 = yes = *moderately agree—it's kind of like me*
2 = no   = *moderately disagree—it's kind of not me*
1 = NO! = *strongly disagree—IT'S NOT ME!*

		SA	MA	MD	SD
1.	It is important for me to identify closely with the larger U.S. culture.	4	3	2	1
2.	I do not feel a sense of belonging at all to the larger U.S. culture.	4	3	2	1
3.	I usually go by the values of the overall U.S. culture.	4	3	2	1
4.	I feel very confused about my membership in the larger U.S. society.	4	3	2	1
5.	I feel very comfortable identifying with the larger U.S. society.	4	3	2	1
6.	I often feel lost concerning my cultural membership.	4	3	2	1
7.	The overall U.S. culture is an important reflection of who I am.	4	3	2	1
8.	I feel anxious thinking about cultural membership issues.	4	3	2	1
9.	I am an "American," period.	4	3	2	1
10.	I feel like I live on the borderline of the larger U.S. society.	4	3	2	1

Scoring: Add up the scores on all the odd-numbered items and you will find your U.S. cultural identity score. *U.S. cultural identity* score: _____. Add up the scores on all the even-numbered items and you will find your marginal cultural identity score. *Marginal cultural identity* score: _____.

Interpretation: Scores on each identity dimension can range from 5 to 20; the higher the score, the more cultural and/or marginal you are. If the scores are similar on both identity dimensions, you have a mixed identity pattern: that means sometimes you feel very "American" and sometimes you feel confused about your cultural identity membership.

Reflection probes: Take a moment to think of the following questions: What does it mean to be an "American"? Do you think your answers would be very similar or very different from your family members? How so? For the most part, how would you label your cultural or ethnic self? Do you have a strong sense of pride or confusion about your cultural identity? Why? Compare your answers with those of a classmate.

Source: Scale adapted from Ting-Toomey, et al. (2000).

influence whom we befriend, what holidays to celebrate, what language or dialect we are comfortable with, and with what nonverbal gestures we are at ease in expressing ourselves. Furthermore, physical appearance, biological/racial traits, skin color, language usage, self-appraisal, and other-perception factors all enter into the cultural identity construction equation. The meaning and interpretation that we hold for our culture-based identity groups are learned via direct or mediated contacts (e.g., mass media images) with others. **Cultural identity** is defined as the emotional significance that we attach to our sense of belonging or affiliation with the larger culture. To illustrate, we can talk about the larger Danish cultural identity or the larger Australian cultural identity. To understand cultural identity more specifically, we must discuss cultural identity salience.

Cultural identity salience refers to the strength of affiliation we have with our larger culture. Strong associations of membership affiliation reflect high cultural identity salience. Weak associations of membership affiliation reflect low cultural identity salience. The more strongly our self-image is influenced by our larger cultural value patterns, the more we are likely to practice the norms and communication scripts of the dominant, mainstream culture. Salience of cultural identity can operate on a conscious or an unconscious level. We should also clarify here that the concept of "national identity" refers to one's legal status in relation to a nation, but the concept of "cultural identity" refers to the sentiments of belonging or connection to one's larger culture. To illustrate, as an immigrant-based society, residents in the United States may mix some of the larger cultural values with those of their ethnic-oriented values and practices. To negotiate cultural and ethnic identities mindfully with diverse cultural–ethnic groups, we must understand in depth the content and salience of cultural *and* ethnic identity issues.

Ethnic Identity Conceptualization

Before you continue reading, complete the brief scale in my.blog 4.3. By checking out your scores, you should have a better understanding of your identification with your ethnic heritage group.

Ethnic identity is "inherently a matter of ancestry, of beliefs about the origins of one's forebears" (Alba, 1990, p. 37). Ethnicity can be based on national origin, race, religion, or language. For many people in the United States, ethnicity is based on the countries from which their ancestors came (e.g., those who can trace their ethnic heritage to an Asian or a Latin American country). Most Native Americans—descendants of people who settled in the Western Hemisphere long before Columbus, sometime between twenty-five thousand and forty thousand years ago—can trace their ethnic heritage based on distinctive linguistic or religious practices.

Although new forensic technologies (DNA typing) open up opportunities for ethnic ancestry research (e.g., Zuni ancestors came from Japan), many African Americans still may not be able to trace their precise ethnic origins, or traditional ways of living, because of pernicious slavery codes (e.g., a slave could not marry or meet with an ex-slave; it was forbidden for anyone, including whites, to teach slaves to read or write) and the uprootedness forced on them by slaveholders beginning in the 1600s (Schaefer, 2009). Last, many European Americans may not be able to trace their ethnic origins precisely because of their mixed ancestral heritage. This phenomenon stems from generations of intergroup marriages (say, Irish American and German American marriages or mixed Irish/German American and Polish American marriages and the like), starting with their grandparents or great-grandparents.

Ethnicity, of course, is based on more than one's country of origin. It involves a subjective sense of belonging to or identification with an ethnic group across time. To understand the significance of someone's ethnicity, we also need to understand the ethnic value content and the ethnic identity salience of that person's ethnic identity in particular. For example, with knowledge of the individualism–collectivism value tendencies of the originating countries, we can infer the *ethnic value content* of specific ethnic groups. Most hyphenated Americans (e.g., Asian Americans) who identify strongly with their traditional ethnic values tend to be collectivistic. European Americans who identify strongly with European values and norms

my.blog 4.3 ASSESSING THE DEGREE OF IMPORTANCE OF YOUR ETHNIC IDENTITY AND BICULTURAL IDENTITY

Instructions: Recall how you generally feel and act in various situations. Let your first inclination be your guide and circle the number in the scale that best reflects your impression of yourself. The following scale is used for each item:

4 = YES! = *strongly agree*—IT'S ME!

3 = yes = *moderately agree*—it's kind of like me

2 = no = *moderately disagree*—it's kind of not me

1 = NO! = *strongly disagree*—IT'S NOT ME!

		SA	MA	MD	SD
1.	I have spent time to find out more about my ethnic roots and history.	4	3	2	1
2.	I subscribe to both sets of values: my ethnic values and the larger U.S. cultural values.	4	3	2	1
3.	My family really emphasizes where our ancestors came from.	4	3	2	1
4.	I have close friends from both my ethnic group and the larger U.S. culture.	4	3	2	1
5.	My family practices distinctive ethnic traditions and customs.	4	3	2	1
6.	The values of my own ethnic group are very compatible with the larger U.S. cultural values.	4	3	2	1
7.	I feel a sense of loyalty and pride about my own ethnic group.	4	3	2	1
8.	It is important for me to be accepted by both my ethnic group and the overall U.S. culture.	4	3	2	1
9.	The ethnic group I belong to is an important reflection of who I am.	4	3	2	1
10.	I feel comfortable identifying with both my ethnic heritage and the overall U.S. culture.	4	3	2	1

Scoring: Add up the scores on all the odd-numbered items and you will find your ethnic identity score. *Ethnic identity* score: _____. Add up the scores on all the even-numbered items and you will find your bicultural identity score. *Bicultural identity* score: _____.

Interpretation: Scores on each identity dimension can range from 5 to 20; the higher the score, the more ethnic and/ or bicultural you are. If all the scores are similar on both identity dimensions, you have a mixed ethnic/bicultural identity pattern: that means at the same time you identify closely with your ethnic heritage, you also identify closely with the larger U.S. culture.

Reflection probes: Take a moment to think of the following questions: Are the values of your ethnic group compatible or incompatible with the larger U.S. cultural values? How do you reconcile the differences? Do most of your friends see you as an American or see you as a member of a particular ethnic group? Which way do you like to be perceived? Why? Compare your answers with those of a classmate.

Source: Scale adapted from Ting-Toomey, et al. (2000).

(albeit on an unconscious level) tend to be oriented toward individualism. African Americans might well subscribe to both collectivistic and individualistic values—in blending both ethnic African values and assimilated U.S. values—for the purposes of survival and adaptation.

Beyond ethnic value content, we should address the issue of ethnic identity salience. The role of *ethnic identity salience* is linked closely with the intergroup boundary maintenance issue across generations (e.g., third-generation Cuban Americans in the United States). Ethnic identity salience is defined as the subjective allegiance and loyalty to a group—large or small, socially dominant or subordinate—with which one has ancestral links (Edwards, 1994). Ethnic identity can be sustained by shared objective characteristics, such as shared language or religion. It is also a subjective sense of "ingroupness" whereby individuals perceive themselves and each other as belonging to the same ingroup by shared historical and emotional ties. However, for many ethnic minority group members living in the larger U.S. society, a constant struggle exists between the perception of their own ethnic identity issue and the perception of others' questioning of their ethnic heritage or role. Oftentimes, this results in a sense of both ethnic and cultural rootlessness. Let's take a look at Elaine Kim's story (1996, p. 357) in Blog Post 4.6.

Thus, ethnic identity has both objective and subjective layers. Ethnicity is, overall, more a subjective reality than an objective classification. Although political boundaries (e.g., delimiting Chechnya—formerly the Chechno-Ingush Autonomous Soviet Socialist Republic—from Russia) may change over generations, the continuation of ethnic boundaries is an enduring, long-standing phenomenon that lasts in the hearts and minds of its members. Ethnicity is basically a biological inheritance wherein members perceive each other as emotionally bounded by a common set of traditions, worldviews, history, heritage, and descent on a psychological and historical level.

The process of identity formation is concerned with how individuals understand the implications of their ethnic identity or other social identities. We communicate who we are on a daily basis. Our identities have a profound influence on when we

BLOG POST 4.6

Because I spent my early years living as something of a freak within mainstream American society, I decreed that there was no way to be "Asian" and "American" at the same time. I often longed to be held securely within the folds of a community of "my people." Like many other Asians born in the United States, I was changed forever when I visited Korea at the age of twenty—when I saw my relatives for the first time.

Finding myself among so many people similar to me in shape and color made me feel as though I came from somewhere and that I was connected in a normal way to other people instead of being taken as an aberration, a sidekick, or a mascot, whose presence was tolerated [only] when everyone was in a good mood.

But like other U.S.-born Asians, I came to understand that there is no ready-made community, no unquestioned belonging, even in Korea. For as soon as they heard me speak or saw me grin like a fool for no reason, as soon as they saw me launch down the street swinging my arms, as soon as they saw me looking brazenly into people's eyes when they talked, they let me know that I could not possibly be "Korean."

—Elaine Kim, 1996

feel secure, when we are at our most vulnerable, and when we feel obligated to mask our authentic selves. We struggle with and against our identity. But how can we connect identity with a cross-cultural frame? Making a distinction between cultural variability and ethnic identity salience is clear. The sociocultural construction of the self may be one of the key factors in understanding the context of cultural differences. Using the identity pulls of security–vulnerability and inclusion–differentiation, we can understand that it is not easy to place ourselves or place others in clearly marked "identity" categories (Ting-Toomey, 2005a).

Moving beyond general cultural and ethnic identity issues, many majority–minority group identity models have been developed to account for the identity change process of immigrants and minority group members. Let us now explain two identity models concerning ethnic–cultural identity development processes.

ETHNIC–RACIAL IDENTITY CHANGE PROCESS

Immigrants and ethnic minority group members, in the context of intergroup relations, tend to be keenly sensitive to the intersecting issues of ethnicity and culture. For ethnic minority members, the perceived imbalanced power dimension within a society often leads them to draw clear boundaries between the dominant "power holder" group and the nondominant "fringe" group (Collier, 2001, 2005; Orbe, 1998; Orbe & Spellars, 2005). The one model that seems to capture the essence of immigrants' adaptation process is that of Berry and associates' fourfold identity typological model (Berry, Kim, & Boski, 1987).

Cultural–Ethnic Identity Typological Model

To understand how ethnic individuals see themselves in relation to both their ethnic group and the society at large, ethnic and cultural identity salience can be viewed as a fourfold model that emphasizes an individual's adaptation options toward ethnic identity *and* larger cultural identity maintenance issues (see Figure 4.1).

According to Berry (1994, 2004), immigrants who identify strongly with ethnic traditions and values and weakly with the values of the dominant culture subscribe to the traditionally based or *ethnic-oriented identity* option. These individuals emphasize the value of retaining their ethnic culture and avoid interacting with the dominant group. As a result, there is an implication of a higher degree of stress that occurs through contact with the dominant group and also a higher degree of separation from the dominant group. Individuals who identify weakly with their ethnic traditions and values while identifying

strongly with the values and norms of the larger culture tend to practice the *assimilated identity* option. They tend to see themselves or want to see themselves as "American," period.

Other individuals who identify strongly with ethnic tradition maintenance, and at the same time incorporate values and practices of the larger society, develop the *bicultural identity* or integrative option. An integrated individual feels comfortable being a member of both cultural groups. Nguyen and Benet-Martinez (2010) studied the issue of bicultural or integrated identity and concluded that individuals with high bicultural integrated identity tend to see themselves as part of a hyphenated culture (e.g., Korean culture + American culture) and find the two cultures largely compatible, whereas individuals with low bicultural integrated identity tend to see themselves as living "in between cultures" and see the two cultures as conflicting or disparate.

Finally, individuals who identify weakly with their ethnic traditions and also weakly with the larger cultural worldviews are in the *marginal identity* state. They basically have disconnected ties with both their ethnic group and the larger society and often experience feelings of ambiguity, invisibility, and alienation.

To illustrate this model, a second-generation Asian American or Latino/a American can commit to one of the following four ethnic–cultural identity salience categories: Asian or Latino/a primarily, American primarily, both, or neither (Chung & Ting-Toomey, 1999; Espiritu, 1992). Systems-level, individual, and interpersonal factors, added together, have a net influence on immigrants' adaptive experience, their identity change process, and the subsequent intergenerational adaptation and communication issues.

In terms of explaining ethnic identity patterns among ethnic individuals in their everyday lives, Berry's model may not totally fit the actual reality. For example, the four choices do not explain why some groups who chose to assimilate did not necessarily "blend in" with the majority culture. Assimilation may be slower or simply may not take place. Hurh and Kim (1984) argue that Korean Americans adopt an "adhesive adjustment" in the United States, which means although they may adopt the ways of the dominant

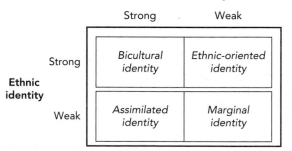

FIGURE 4.1   Cultural-Ethnic Identity Typological Model. *Source*: Data from Berry et al. (1987).

culture, especially on the behavioral dimension, there remains a strong and persistent sense of affective attachment to the Korean culture. Thus, we may want to analyze immigrants' acculturation process from multiple levels: cognitive, affective, and behavioral, plus self-identification and other-identification perspectives in diverse macro- and microsituational settings (Y.Y. Kim, 2009).

Racial–Ethnic Identity Development Model

Alternatively, from the racial–ethnic identity development framework, various models have been proposed to account for the racial or ethnic identity formation of African Americans (e.g., Cross, 1978, 1995), Asian Americans (e.g., Sue & Sue, 1999), Latino/a Americans (e.g., Ruiz, 1990), and European Americans (e.g., Rowe, Bennett, & Atkinson, 1994). Racial–ethnic identity development models tend to emphasize the oppressive–adaptive nature of intergroup relations in a pluralistic society.

From this framework, racial–ethnic identity salience concerns the development of racial or ethnic consciousness along a linear, progressive pathway of identity change. For example, Cross (1971, 1991) has developed a five-stage model of African American racial identity development that includes pre-encounter (stage 1), encounter (stage 2), immersion–emersion (stage 3), internalization (stage 4), and internalization–commitment (stage 5). Helms and associates (e.g., Helms, 1993; Parham & Helms, 1985) have amended and refined Cross' five-stage model (i.e., integrating the concept of *worldview* in each stage) into four stages: pre-encounter, encounter, immersion–emersion, and internalization-commitment (see Figure 4.2).

The *pre-encounter* stage is the high cultural identity salience phase wherein ethnic minority group members' self-concepts are influenced by the values and norms of the larger culture. In this stage, individuals are naive, unaware of being ethnic group members. They may define themselves as Canadian, American, or Australian. The *encounter stage* is the marginal identity phase, in which a new racial–ethnic realization is awakened in the individuals because of a "racially shattering" event (e.g., encountering racism) and minority group members realize that they cannot be fully accepted as part of the "white world." The *immersion–emersion stage* is the strong racial–ethnic identity salience phase, in which individuals withdraw to the safe confines of their own racial–ethnic groups and become ethnically conscious. Last, the *internalization–commitment stage* is the phase in which individuals develop a secure racial–ethnic identity that is internally defined and at the same time are able to establish genuine interpersonal contacts with members of the dominant group and other multiracial groups. One example we use to highlight the stages is a true story that happened to one of us (see Blog Post 4.7).

With the increase in minority groups living in the United States, the question of identification with group membership is an important concern. The range of issues, as we have shared with you, is enormous. One of the common threads is trying to figure out who we are in the context of a culturally pluralistic nation. How can we all learn to get along? How can we reconcile our own identity struggle and

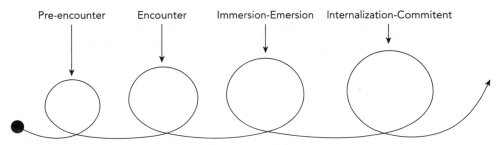

FIGURE 4.2   Racial-Ethnic Identity Development Model

BLOG POST 4.7

Although my high school consisted of primarily black and Asian students, I felt more comfortable hanging around with white kids, who made up 7 percent of the school. I am Chinese American, but at the time, I thought I was white. I befriended a girl named Susan. She was from the South and we became fast friends. In our senior year, Susan and I had to debate each other in our civics class about controversial topics. By the end of the debate, unknown to me, Susan was very angry at my "controversial stance" comments.

I remember sitting down after the last of the three topics. I heard her say, "Well, if you don't like it here and you have a problem with the rules of our country, you need to go back to where you came from!" I looked across at her and started to laugh at our mutual friend named Dana. Dana was black. I said, "Ha ha, Dana, she is talking about you!" She said, "Oh, no way, girl! She ain't talking about me, she's talking about you!" I turned to Susan and asked her if she was talking to me. She said yes, that if I did not like it here I should just pack my suitcase and go back to where I belong.

I was stunned into complete silence. I was born in America. I considered myself to be American. My friends were mostly white. What more did I have to do? But at that particular moment, I realized that I was the "other," foreign and an outsider to this country. I could dye my hair, wear the trendy clothes, speak the language, but I would NEVER be accepted as fully American. I never spoke to Susan again. When I graduated, I went to college and minored in ethnic studies. I took classes that helped me reconcile my conflict and the internal battle of who I am…, and what is the history of Chinese and Asian Americans in the United States. I learned Mandarin. I took a semester off and went to China, traveled around to "find myself." I came back and even worked in a Chinese restaurant for two years.

What I learned from all of my experiences is that although I will never be perceived as fully Chinese or American, I am normal. I accept this as my reality. I work on my identity every day, challenging myself to represent and express both voices.

—Leeva, *college instructor*

---

search processes? How do all these identity struggles manifest themselves in our everyday stereotyping process and ethnocentric views? How can we utilize the dynamic tensions and the best of different worldviews from diverse cultural groups to construct a meaningful "U.S. American" culture? These are important issues that await us in our development to be ethical intercultural communicators in the twenty-first century.

With the increase in minority groups transcending boundaries and borders, the question of identity development is important because individuals born into a particular ethnic group are usually lumped into one single category by the larger society. The processes involved in identity construction and identity perception are complex, but one of the common threads is the fact that this ethnic group is too often seen as one homogeneous, stereotypical group. Thus, questions of group homogeneity and intergroup distance are being addressed among social identity theorists. Understanding the complexity of the interrelationship between cultural identity and ethnic identity and how that affects the use of diverse communication strategies poses a major challenge for future intercultural communication researchers

Multiracial and Biracial Identity

Figures from the 2010 U.S. Census report an increase in the mixed-race population—small in number, but growing fast. In 2000, only 2.4 percent of the U.S. population identified themselves with more than one race. Census officials calculate that over ten years, there has been almost a 50 percent growth rate in this group's numbers. The multiracial population is overwhelmingly young, and American Indians and Native Hawaiians and Pacific Islanders are the most likely to report being of more than one race. African American and Euro-American are the least likely (Saulny, 2011b).

Most intriguing are individuals who are identifying themselves as multiracial, instead of choosing one ethnicity. In some states, such as Nevada, Pennsylvania, North Carolina, Mississippi, Kentucky, and Tennessee, the number of individuals identifying themselves as "multiracial" in the 2010 Census increased more than 50 percent from the 2000 Census figures. In Georgia, the increase was over 80 percent (Saulny, 2011a). As a result, there are more biracial couples with biracial children. In addition, recall from Chapter 1 the increase of domestic and international adoption that has resulted in multiracial families. As complex as ethnic identity is, the additional layer of multiracial and hybrid conceptualizations appears to be an urgent intercultural area of scholarly focus.

Brewer's (2010) social identity complexity theory discusses how complex social identity formation can be understood from four patterns (intersection, dominance, compartmentalization, and merger); this theory holds great promise for understanding this fascinating and complex topic. *Intersection* refers to a compound identity in which two (or more) social membership categories (e.g., female Latina lawyer) can be crossed to form a singular, unique social identity. Individuals with this compound, singular identity also feel more connected with others who share these compound yet singular identity experiences. *Dominance* means the individual adopts one major social identity (e.g., lawyer) and other social membership categories (e.g., being female and being Latina) are subordinated or embedded underneath the dominant professional role identity category of being a "lawyer."

Compartmentalization refers to how one social identity category serves as the primary basis of identification in a particular setting (e.g., the importance of the lawyer category in the law firm) and a gear shift occurs to another primary identity persona in a different context (e.g., being a good Latina mom at home). Finally, *merger* means the awareness of crosscutting social identity memberships in selves and recognizing multiple groups as significant others who share some aspects of this complex, social identity self. According to Brewer (2010), the intersection pattern is low in identity complexity and low in multiple group inclusion, whereas the merger pattern is high in identity complexity and high in multiple group inclusivity.

In sum, multiracial individuals are increasing in number and proportion, and they live on the margins or the borderland between two or more cultural groups. What triggers the strength of a chosen identity? This depends on with whom they are interacting through time and space, their code-switching ability, and the diverse situations in which they find themselves (Shih, Sanchez, & Ho, 2010; van Meijl, 2010). Shih, Sanchez, and Ho (2010) emphasize the importance of an individual's appraisal process in assessing the rewards and costs of identity switching in biracial individuals.

Identity switching is different from frame switching in that frame switching emphasizes cultural and cognitive identity awareness issues, whereas identity switching involves the switching of deeper affective identity belonging and identity distancing issues. Some of the rewards of identity switching include self-presentation in the most advantageous group membership light, increased social membership self-esteem, and defused negative identity stereotypes and threats. Some of the costs include fragmentation of self-identity, unstable self-concept leading to poor mental health, and overly malleable racial identity also spilling over to poor psychological health (Shih et al., 2010). Finally, let's check out our last story in Blog Post 4.8 and reflect on their picture together in Blog Pic 4.1. The story is a continuation of the first story told in this chapter.

Let's go back and review both stories of aLx and Min, which reflect intersecting multilayered identity issues on top of ethnic identity conceptualizations. An individual who is associated with a particular ethnic group may not actually behave or subscribe strongly to her or his ethnic values, norms, or behaviors, such as aLx or Min. In other words, skin color does not automatically guarantee consistent ethnic ingroup membership and affiliation (e.g., in the case of Min, he looks Korean but was adopted by a white couple when he was only six months old). Even more confusing is the intersection of the many complex identities that come into play: religious, biracial, and sexual orientation. aLx tried hard to understand the complexity of his biracial ethnic identity (Croatian and Jamaican mixed), religious identity (Jehovah's Witness), gender identity, and sexual orientation identity. It becomes very clear that many individuals want to find attachment and a sense of secure belonging via a particular group membership. However, in the end, they may find such sense of security and understanding only with individuals who have gone through similar identity struggles and collision forces.

What is your reaction to aLx and Min's story? How important do you think it is to "fit in" if you don't feel like you have a particular or singular ethnic or social membership group to identify with? Unfortunately, many ethnic minority Americans strive hard to be "Americans," but are constantly

BLOG POST 4.8

At sixteen, on a Tuesday afternoon, I had a defining moment. I realized I was gay. I knew my faith would not allow such a contradiction. I was put in a predicament because I knew that I could not tell my mother or I would be disfellowshipped (i.e., shunned by all family and church members). However, I knew that it was something about myself that I could not change. I decided to slowly stop going to church until I was no longer going. While this upset my mother tremendously she still holds out hope that I will return to the church one day.

After college I met Min—who shared complex layers of identity like myself. Min is a Korean American who was adopted at six months by a white couple from Minnesota. When we met, Min was a "queer" identified woman and is now a transgendered male. Like me, he grew up in communities that were predominantly straight, white, and religiously conservative. We shared common childhood and adult experiences of being marginalized and lumped into boxes we didn't fit into.

Min loves to say we have collided identities—that the parts of ourselves that have been socially constructed by others as "right" or "wrong," or that whether it is our racial identities or whom we love—are constantly colliding or crashing with our own authentic selves and also creating an empowered whole. While we know that we will be constantly labeled, mislabeled, and marginalized, we have supported one another in asserting who we are and how we truly view ourselves. Because our friendship is rooted in unconditional acceptance and understanding, our bond is strengthened by each other's courage, growth, and self-discovery—our intertwined lives spark us moving forward to discover and to behold.

—aLx, Part 2, *Web designer*

Blog Pic 4.1   aLx + Min, friends who share multilayered identities.

reminded by the media or in actual interactions that they are not part of the fabric of the larger U.S. society. Ethnic individuals have consistently embraced, adopted, and formed ethnic identities and alliances with others despite assimilation pressures within the society. aLx and Min both represent a kind of Venn diagram—individuals sharing space as intersections of these identities come together, finding commonality and a sense of belonging. Just as individuals like aLx and Min struggle with religion, ethnicity, and sexual orientation, choosing one identity does not negate the others. It just means the other identities are patiently waiting for their exploration and discovery.

INTERCULTURAL REALITY CHECK: DO-ABLES

The intersection of culture, communication, and identity holds hope for improving and fine tuning our understanding of crossing boundaries. An intercultural lifestyle demands both negotiation and flexibility to navigate through life's daily mine fields. The process of self-discovery is never easy; it may be filled with trials and tribulations, clashes and bumps. However, with the understanding of how we can support, embrace, and understand those who are different from us, their layered and complex identities can open our minds and eyes to the diverse richness of the human spirit.

To understand the person with whom you are communicating, you must understand the identity that s/he deems important. For example, if the person strongly values his or her cultural identity, you must find ways to validate and be responsive to the cultural identity; or if the person strongly values his or her sexual orientation identity above and beyond his or her other layers of membership, you must uncover ways to affirm the positively desired sexual orientation. We can discover identity issues that are desirable to the individuals in our everyday intercultural encounters through practicing the following communication skills:

- *Mindful listening:* Mindful listening demands that we pay thoughtful attention to both the verbal and the nonverbal messages of the speaker before responding. Listen attentively with your senses and check responsively for the accuracy of the meaning decoding process on multiple levels. Learn to listen responsively, or ting (this Chinese word for listening means "attending mindfully with our ears, eyes, and a focused heart"), to the sounds, tones, gestures, movements, nonverbal nuances, pauses, silence, and identity meanings in a given intercultural situation. Mindful listening essentially involves a consciously competent shift of perspective, taking into account not only how things look from your identity perspective but also how they look and feel from the other's identity perspective.
- *Identity validation skills:* When a person perceives authentic and positive identity validation, he or she will tend to view self-images positively. When a person perceives identity rejection, he or she will tend to view self-images negatively. Positive identity validation can be expressed through verbal and nonverbal confirming messages, such as recognizing group-based and person-based identities, responding sensitively to their moods and emotional states of mind, and validating other people's experiences as real.

Of all the operational skills, identity validation is a major skill to master in flexible consciously competent practice. By paying attention to the cultural stranger and mindfully listening to what he or she has to say, we signal our intention of wanting to understand the multilayered identity of the stranger. By conveying our respect and acceptance of group-based and person-based differences, we encourage intercultural trust, inclusion, and connection. Through active verbal and nonverbal confirmation skills, we reaffirm the intrinsic worthiness of the dissimilar other. In learning from people who are culturally different, both hosts and new arrivals can stretch their identity boundaries to integrate new ideas, expand affective horizons, and respect diverse lifestyles and practices.

CROSSING CULTURAL AND COMMUNICATION BOUNDARIES ADAPTIVELY

CHAPTER 5

WHAT IS CULTURE SHOCK?

CHAPTER OUTLINE

When I found out I got accepted into the JET program in Japan to teach, I was super excited. Even though I spoke no Japanese, I was motivated to learn as much as I could—I craved any kind of adventure. But I never realized how "western" I was until I sat down with three Japanese teachers and tried to plan my first lesson. My mind was functioning in a linear pattern of "first, next, last," while the Japanese teachers were discussing, thinking in silence, examining every single detail, and consensus building. Just as I was contemplating shoving a sharp pencil into my skull, a consensus was reached and the lesson plan was finished—three hours later!

After the lesson (first time EVER conducting a class!), I asked one of my Japanese colleagues for some constructive criticism regarding a specific activity. Was it good? Should I do it again? Should I make some changes? "Maybe."

"Maybe" was the extent of the feedback I received. And then it dawned on me: I had been living in Japan for almost two months now and I was yet to hear the Japanese word "iie" (no). For two solid months, absolutely no one has said "no" to me directly. What an adventure!

—K. Abbott, *Graduate Student*

Millions of global citizens cross cultural boundaries every year to work, to study, to engage in government service, and to volunteer their time in global humanitarian work. Likewise, millions of international students, cultural exchange teachers, artists, scientists, and business people come to the United States to learn, to teach, to perform, to experiment, and to conduct business. When individuals move from their home cultures to a new culture, they take with them their cultural habits, familiar scripts, and interaction routines. For the most part, these old cultural habits may produce unintended clashes in the new culture.

Culture shock is about the stress and the feeling of disorientation you experience in a new culture. If you are temporarily visiting (sojourning to) a new culture for the first time, it is likely that you will experience some degree of cultural shock. Even if you do not plan to go overseas to work in the next few years, international classmates and coworkers may be sitting right next to you—working side by side with you. By learning more in depth about their culture shock experiences, you may develop new knowledge, display more respectful attitudes, and learn to apply more flexible intercultural skills in communicating with your international coworkers or classmates. This chapter asks three questions: What is culture shock? Can we track meaningful patterns of the intercultural adjustment process? What are some creative strategies we can use when we are crossing cultural boundaries and encountering culture shock problems?

This chapter is divided into four sections. We first address the role and definition of culture shock. We then explain two intercultural adjustment models that many sojourners or international students find useful. Third, we explore the concept of reentry culture shock. Finally, we present a set of do-able checkpoints to guide you through your international discovery journey.

UNPACKING CULTURE SHOCK

Culture shock is an inevitably stressful and disorienting experience. Let's check out the story in Blog Post 5.1.

People encounter culture shock whenever they uproot themselves from a familiar setting and move to an unfamiliar one (e.g., relocating from Lima, Peru, to Gatlinburg, Tennessee, or making the transition as a high school senior to a college freshman). Because culture shock is unavoidable, just how we manage culture shock will determine the adaptive process and outcome.

Culture shock is, first and foremost, an emotional experience. Intense emotions are involved in combination with behavioral confusion and inability to think clearly. Both short-term sojourners and long-term immigrants can experience culture shock at different stages of their adaptation. Sojourners, such as cultural exchange students, businesspersons, diplomats, journalists, military personnel, and Peace Corps volunteers, often play temporary resident roles with a short to medium span of stay. This section covers the definitional characteristics

of culture shock, discusses the pros and cons, describes factors that affect the culture shock experience, and provides some initial helpful tips to manage the culture shock experience.

Characteristics of Culture Shock

Before you read this section, work through my.blog 5.1 and check out your culture shock index when you encounter an unfamiliar environment.

Culture shock basically refers to a stressful transitional period when individuals move from a familiar environment into an unfamiliar one. In this unfamiliar environment, the individual's identity appears to be stripped of all protection. Previously familiar cues and scripts are suddenly inoperable in the new cultural setting. Let's check out a brief story in Blog Post 5.2.

For many international students or sojourners, the previously familiar cultural safety net has suddenly vanished. Communication scripts have changed. From how to say a proper "hello" to how to say a proper "goodbye" in the new culture, every interaction moment could create unintentional awkwardness or

---

BLOG POST 5.1

Three American universities accepted my undergraduate applications—one in Hawaii, one in Ohio, and one in Iowa. Because I had no clue as to how one university differed from another, I wrote down the names of the universities on three pieces of paper and asked my then nine-year-old brother, Victor, to pick one with his eyes closed. He picked Iowa. I decided fate had called me to the University of Iowa. Iowa City, in those days, was an all-white campus town. The university campus was huge—spread out and cut off by a river running through it. I was one of the first group of international students being admitted to the university from Asia.

Life was composed of a series of culture shock waves in my first few months there. From overdressing (I quickly changed my daily skirts to jeans to avoid the question: "Are you going to a wedding today?") to hyperapprehension (e.g., the constant fear of being called upon to answer questions in the "small power distance" classroom atmosphere). I experienced intense loneliness and homesickness at times. The months flew by quickly, however.

—Stella, *college instructor*

---

stress. Unfamiliarity creates perceived threat, and perceived threat triggers fear and emotional vulnerability.

An anthropologist named Oberg (1960) coined the term *culture shock* over five decades ago. He believed that culture shock produces an identity disorientation state, which can bring about tremendous stress and pressure on the well-being of an individual. Culture shock involves (1) a sense of identity loss and identity deprivation with regard to values, status, profession, friends, and possessions; (2) identity strain as a result of the effort required to make necessary psychological adaptation; (3) identity rejection by members of the new culture; (4) identity confusion, especially regarding role ambiguity and unpredictability; and (5) identity powerlessness as a result of not being able to cope with the new environment (Furnham, 1988). An identity disorientation state is part of the culture shock experience.

my.blog 5.1

Recall the last time you traveled to an entirely new place or an unfamiliar environment. Think of that initial experience and put a check mark by the words that best capture your feelings:

Awkward	_____	Bizarre	_____
Disoriented	_____	Energized	_____
Excited	_____	Exhausted	_____
Embarrassed	_____	Surprised	_____
Alive	_____	Anxious	_____
Insecure	_____	Intense	_____
Challenged	_____	Rewarded	_____

In fact, Ward et al. (2001) discuss the *ABC's of culture shock* in terms of the affective, behavioral, and cognitive disorientation dimensions. *Affectively*, sojourners in the initial culture shock stage often expe-

---

BLOG POST 5.2 CULTURE SHOCK: AN INTERVIEW FOR A CUP OF TEA

My first visit abroad was to Missoula, Montana, USA. I was a visiting Tibetan Buddhist Scholar at a small Tibetan Buddhist Center. One day Carleen, my friend, took me to Starbucks in the downtown. I had to go through an interview to get a cup of tea! I stood in the line to order a cup of tea and the girl at the counter asked me, "What kind of tea?" She listed a couple of teas, including herb tea that I had no clue about. She had no Lipton Tea which I wanted so I settled with English Breakfast Tea. I assumed she would provide milk in my tea but she did not. So I asked for milk to which she said, "Do you want half and half, whole milk, or 2 percent?" I had never heard these choices in my life so I asked for regular milk. She looked baffled and waited for my answer. I looked at Carleen who said half and half would be fine. I like sweet tea so I asked if I can get some sugar and she asked me, "Would you like sweetener or this or that?" I had no idea of these choices so I said, "Sugar, please." Finally, I sat at a table with Carleen who had gotten her coffee. When Carleen finished her coffee, the girl refilled her cup but she did not ask me if I wanted more tea. I said, "Could you give me some more tea?" She said, "You need to pay first." I was a bit shocked and frustrated. I told Carleen that I would rather buy tea materials and make good tea for myself than go through this "tea interview and discrimination experience." We both had a good laugh. She took me to Safeway to buy tea materials and I could enjoy my tea in peace. (In India, "tea" is understood as sweet tea with milk. I did not know all the American choices for tea, milk, etc.).

—Tenzin, *college instructor*

rience anxiety, bewilderment, confusion, disorientation, and perplexity as well as an intense desire to be elsewhere. *Behaviorally*, they are at the confusion stage in terms of the norms and rules that guide communication appropriateness and effectiveness. They are often at a loss in terms of how to initiate and maintain smooth conversations with their hosts and how to uphold themselves in a proper manner with the proper nonverbal cadences. *Cognitively*, they lack cultural interpretive competence to explain many of the "bizarre" behaviors that are occurring in their unfamiliar cultural settings.

Culture shock is sparked by the anxiety that results from "losing all our familiar signs and symbols of social discourse. These signs or cues include a thousand and one ways in which we orient ourselves to the situations of daily life: when to shake hands and what to say when we meet people, when and how to give tips" (Bochner, 1986, p. 48). Despite having repeated practice in these interactions in our own culture, we are not aware of its taken-for-granted significance until we are away from our culture. When we start feeling very inept in the new cultural environment and when our peace of mind is jolted suddenly, we start realizing the importance of intercultural learning and intercultural competence skills (Berg & Paige, 2009).

Pros and Cons of Culture Shock

Culture shock can have both positive and negative implications. Negative implications include three major issues: (1) psychosomatic problems (e.g., headaches, stomachaches) caused by prolonged stress; (2) affective upheavals consisting of feelings of loneliness, isolation, depression, drastic mood swings, and interaction awkwardness caused by the inability to perform optimally in the new language; and (3) cognitive exhaustion caused by difficulty in making accurate attributions.

On the other hand, culture shock, if managed effectively, can have the following positive effects on the newcomer: a sense of well-being and heightened positive self-esteem, emotional richness and enhanced tolerance for ambiguity, behavioral competence in social interaction, cognitive openness and flexibility, and an enhanced optimism about self, others, and the everyday surroundings. Culture shock creates an environment and an opportunity for individuals to experiment with new ideas and coping behaviors. It forces individuals to stretch beyond the usual boundaries of thinking and experiencing.

Approaching Culture Shock: Underlying Factors

The following factors have been found to influence why people manage their culture shock experience differently: motivational orientations, personal expectations, cultural distance, psychological adjustment, sociocultural adjustment, communication competence, and personality attributes.

Sojourners' **motivational orientation** to leave their home countries and enter a new culture has a profound influence on their culture shock attitudes. Individuals with voluntary motivations (e.g., Peace Corps volunteers) to leave a familiar culture and enter a new cultural experience tend to manage their culture shock experience more effectively than do individuals with involuntary motivations (e.g., refugees). Furthermore, sojourners (e.g., international students, tourists) encounter less conformity pressure than do immigrants because of their temporary visiting role. Host cultures often extend a more friendly welcome to sojourners than to immigrants or refugees. Thus, sojourners tend to perceive their overall international stay as more pleasant and the local hosts as more friendly than do immigrants or refugees.

Personal expectations have long been viewed as a crucial factor in the culture shock management process. Expectations refer to the anticipatory process and predictive outcome of the upcoming situation. Two observations have often been associated with such expectations: The first is that realistic expectations facilitate intercultural adaptation, and the second is that accuracy-based positive expectations ease adaptation stress (Pitts, 2009; Ward, 1996). Individuals with realistic expectations are psychologically prepared to deal with actual adaptation problems more than are individuals with unrealistic expectations. Furthermore, individuals with positive expectations tend to create positive self-fulfilling prophecies in their successful adaptation (e.g., believing relocation is a great move and your positive thinking affects your actions); negative expectations tend to produce the opposite effect.

Most international students tend to carry positive expectation images concerning their anticipated sojourn in the new culture (Sias, Drzewiecka, Meares, Bent, Ortega, & White, 2008; Ward et al., 2001). Overall, realistic and positively oriented expectancy images of the new culture can help to facilitate intercultural adaptation for both business and student sojourners. Expectations influence newcomers' mindsets, sentiments, and behaviors. A positively resilient mindset helps to balance the negative stressors a newcomer may encounter in his or her adaptive efforts.

Overall, sojourners tend to encounter more severe culture shock when the cultural distance between their home cultures and the host society is high. **Cultural distance** factors can include differences in cultural values, language, verbal styles, nonverbal gestures, learning styles, decision-making styles, and conflict negotiation styles, as well as in religious, sociopolitical, and economic systems. Interestingly, however, when sojourners expect low cultural distance, they may actually encounter more intercultural frustration. These individuals become less culturally astute in dealing with the hosts from a perceived similar language/cultural background (e.g., British dealing with Aussies in Australia; Columbians from Columbia dealing with Mexicans in Mexico). Because of this "assumed similarity" factor, cultural differences may be glossed over; guests may overlook the vast differences in political or business practices or they may start using disparaging remarks in attacking the personality traits of their new cultural hosts. Both hosts and guests may encounter more frustrations without realizing that they are caught up in an understated culture clash spiral.

Psychological adjustment refers to feelings of well-being and satisfaction during cross-cultural transitions (Ward et al., 2001). Chronic strain, low self-esteem, and low mastery have a direct effect on adjustment depression. As cultural distance widens and stress level increases, newcomers must use different strategies to deal with such differences.

To counteract psychological stress, researchers recommend the use of positive self-talk strategies and positive situational appraisal strategies (Chang, Chua, & Toh, 1997; Cross, 1995). Positive self-talk strategies (e.g., giving yourself a pat on the back for being so adaptive in the new culture, rewarding yourself with a nice treat for mastering all the intricacies of saying "no" in this new culture without actually saying "no!") can create a more resilient mindset. A resilient mindset can deal with the bombarded stimuli more effectively (Ting-Toomey, 2005).

Positive situational appraisal strategies involve changing perceptions and interpretations of the stressful events or situations. For example, you start to talk yourself into taking more Italian-speaking classes from the "mean" teacher and reframe the situation: the "mean and demanding" teacher is actually helping you to master your Italian faster than the "nice" teachers. Research indicates that the use of cognitive coping strategies (i.e., positive self-talk and situational reinterpretation) is associated with lower levels of perceived stress and fewer symptoms of depression in East Asian students in Singapore (Ward, 2004). Thus, cognitive reframing appears to soften the psychological stress level for East Asian students who are attempting to adapt to a collectivistic cultural environment. The nature of the stressful event and the degree of control and success that the students can assert on the distressing situation may explain this finding.

Sociocultural adjustment refers to the ability to fit in and execute appropriate and effective interactions in a new cultural environment (Ward et al., 2001; see Table 5.1). It can include factors such as the quality or quantity of relations with host nationals and the length of residence in the host country (Gareis, 2000; Kudo & Simkin, 2003; Mortensen, Burleson, Feng,

TABLE 5.1 CHARACTERISTICS OF PSYCHOLOGICAL ADJUSTMENT VERSUS SOCIOCULTURAL ADJUSTMENT

Psychological adjustment	Sociocultural adjustment
Stress management	Relationship management
Psychological-related	Network-related
Perceptual interpretation	Relationship quality
Intrapersonal control	Host culture receptivity
Digging in	Reaching out
Cognitive reframing	Sociocultural climate

& Liu, 2009). International students, for example, report greater satisfaction with their host culture when host nationals take the initiative to befriend them. It has also been revealed that international students' friendship networks typically consist of the following patterns: (1) a primary, monocultural friendship network that consists of close friendships with other compatriots from similar cultural backgrounds (e.g., Nigerian international students developing friendship ties with other African students) (Brown, 2009; Matusitz, 2005); (2) a bicultural network that consists of social bonds between sojourners and host nationals, whereby professional aspirations and goals are pursued (Holmes, 2005; Lee, 2006); and (3) a multicultural network that consists of acquaintances from diverse cultural groups for recreational activities (Furnham & Bochner, 1982). Research further indicates that greater sociocultural adjustment and social support in the new cultural environment are associated with lower levels of

depression and hopelessness in international students (Lee, 2006, 2008; Lin, 2006; Paige & Goode, 2009; see my.blog 5.2).

Overall, culture-specific knowledge, language fluency, more extensive contact with host nationals, and a longer period of residence in the host culture are associated with lower levels of sociocultural difficulty in the new culture (Kohls, 1996; Ward, 1996). In addition, the host culture's receptivity to new arrivals, the degree of cultural conformity expected, and the current political climate of open-door versus closed-door attitudes toward international students and visitors can also either facilitate or create roadblocks to sojourners' sociocultural adjustment process.

In the intercultural **communication competence** field, researchers have identified the following components as critical to sojourners' adjustment process (Deardorff, 2009; Spitzberg & Changnon, 2009): culture-sensitive knowledge, motivation to adapt, the

---

my.blog 5.2 ASSESSING YOUR SOCIAL SUPPORT CIRCLE

Think of a stressful situation in which you have made a major transition (e.g., from high school to college; from an old job to a new job; from home to living on your own), read each item, and circle **T = True** or **F = False**. In this new environment, you actually have friends or acquaintances:

1.	To listen to you and talk with you whenever you feel lonely or depressed.	T or F
2.	To reassure you that you are supported and cared for.	T or F
3.	To explain things and to make your situation clearer and easier to understand.	T or F
4.	To spend some quiet time with you whenever you do not feel like going out.	T or F
5.	To explain and help you understand the local culture and communication issues.	T or F
6.	To provide necessary information to help orient you to your new surroundings.	T or F
7.	To help you interpret things that you don't really understand.	T or F
8.	To tell you about available choices and options.	T or F
9.	To show you how to do something that you didn't know how to do.	T or F

Scoring: Add up all your answers on TRUE.

Decoding: 1–3 = low social support; 4–6 = moderate social support; 7–9 = high social support.

Interpreting: The higher your score, the greater your social support circle. The greater the social support circle, the easier it is for you to adjust to your transitional phase in a new environment.

Source: Adapted from Ong (2000). "The Construction and Validation of a Social Support Scale for Sojourners: The Index of Sojourner Social Support." Unpublished master's thesis, National University of Singapore, as cited in Ward et al. (2001), p. 89.

activation of appropriate and effective communication skills, the mastery of culture-based contextual rules, and the achievement of conjoint outcomes between the intercultural communicators. On the behavioral tendency skills level, intercultural competence scholars also emphasize the following mindset tendencies and skillset (Gudykunst, 2005a, 2005b; Pusch, 2009): mindfulness, cognitive flexibility, tolerance for ambiguity, behavioral flexibility, and cross-cultural empathy.

According to Pusch (2009), *behavioral flexibility* refers to "the ability to adapt and accommodate one's own behavior to people from other groups," and *cross-cultural empathy* means "being able to participate in another person's experience in your imagination; thinking it intellectually and feeling it emotionally. The ability to connect emotionally with people and showing compassion for others, and being able to listen actively and mindfully" (p. 70). Whereas intercultural scholars emphasize the importance of communication competence skills and then sociocultural and psychological adjustment factors, cross-cultural psychologists tend to emphasize the importance of psychological adjustment and then sociocultural adjustment and communication competence skills (Gudykunst, 2005b, 2005c; Matsumoto, Yoo, & LeRoux, 2010).

In regard to **personality attributes**, such personality traits as high tolerance for ambiguity (i.e., high acceptance of ambiguous situations), internal locus of control (i.e., inner-directed drives and motivations), personal flexibility, and mastery can contribute to generally good adjustment and positive psychological well-being. Interestingly, Ward (2004) also suggests a "cultural fit" proposition, which emphasizes the importance of a good match between personality types (e.g., extraversion and introversion) of the sojourners and the host cultural norms. For example, we can speculate that independent-self sojourners may be more compatible with individualistic cultural norms, whereas interdependent-self sojourners may be more compatible with collectivistic cultural norms. The synchronized match between a particular personality type and the larger cultural norms produces a "goodness of fit" and possibly cultivates a positive adaptive experience for the visiting residents.

Initial Tips to Manage Culture Shock

The fundamental need for newcomers in an unfamiliar culture is addressing the sense of emotional insecurity and vulnerability. The more competent newcomers are at managing their identity threat level, the more they are able to induce effective adaptation outcomes (Matsumoto, Yoo, & LeRoux, 2010).

New arrivals can defuse their perceived threat and, hence, anxiety level by (1) increasing their motivations to learn about the new culture; (2) keeping their expectations realistic and increasing their familiarity concerning the diverse facets of the new culture (e.g., conducting culture-specific research through readings and diverse accurate sources, including talking with people who have spent some time in that culture); (3) increasing their linguistic fluency and learning why, how, and under what situations certain phrases or gestures are appropriate, plus understanding the core cultural values linked to specific behaviors; (4) working on their tolerance for ambiguity and other flexible personal attributes; (5) developing strong ties (close friends) and weak ties (acquaintanceships) to manage identity stress and loneliness; and (6) being mindful of their interpersonal behaviors and suspending ethnocentric evaluations of the host culture.

INTERCULTURAL ADJUSTMENT: DEVELOPMENTAL PATTERNS

The term **intercultural adjustment** has been used to refer to the short-term and medium-term adaptive process of sojourners in their overseas assignments. Tourists are different from sojourners in that tourists are visitors whose length of stay exceeds twenty-four hours in a location away from home and who have traveled for voluntary, recreational holiday-enjoyment purposes. Sojourners, on the other hand, are temporary residents who voluntarily go abroad for a set period of time that is usually related to task-based or instrumental purposes. Both tourists and sojourners can, of course, experience culture shock—especially when the country they visit is very different from their own (see Blog Pic 5.1). In fact, do you know where the top five worldwide tourist destinations are? Take a guess and then check out Jeopardy Box 5.1. Where do you think

Blog Pic 5.1 Does this bowl of "goodness" look appetizing?

JEOPARDY BOX 5.1 TOP FIVE WORLDWIDE TOURIST DESTINATIONS, 2010

Country
1. France
2. United States
3. Spain
4. China
5. Italy

Source: World Tourism Organization (August, 2010), http://www.unwto.org/facts/eng/pdf/highlights/UNWTO_Highlights10_en_HR.pdf (retrieved April 23, 2011).

JEOPARDY BOX 5.2 TOP FIVE COUNTRIES OF ORIGIN OF VISITORS TO THE UNITED STATES, 2010

Country
1. Canada
2. Mexico
3. United Kingdom
4. Japan
5. Germany

Source: U.S. Department of Commerce, Office of Travel and Tourism Industries (March, 2010), http://www.tinet.ita.doc.gov/outreachpages/download_data_table/Fast_Facts_2010.pdf (retrieved April 23, 2011).

JEOPARDY BOX 5.3 TOP FIVE TOURISM CITIES IN THE UNITED STATES, 2008–2009

City	State
1. New York	New York
2. Miami	Florida
3. Los Angeles	California
4. Orlando	Florida
5. San Francisco	California

Source: U.S. Department of Commerce, Office of Travel and Tourism Industries (2009), http://www.tinet.ita.doc.gov/outreachpages/download_data_table/2009_States_and_Cities.pdf (retrieved April 23, 2011).

most tourists to the United States come from (i.e., their countries of origin)? What do you think are the top five tourism cities in the United States? Take a quick guess and check out Jeopardy Boxes 5.2 and 5.3. A tourist, while visiting another country, can be a welcome guest, a nuisance, or a downright intruder in a sacred land. Tourists, their hosts, and businesses/service providers all weave together interdependently to form impressions, to trade, and to share some memorable moments through brief encounters and amusing contacts.

Sojourners, however, are typically individuals who commit to a temporary residential stay in a new culture as they strive to achieve both their instrumental and their socioemotional goals. *Instrumental goals* refer to task-based or business or academic goals that sojourners would like to accomplish during their stay in a foreign country. *Socioemotional goals* refer to relational, recreational, and personal development goals during their sojourning experience. Thus, a Peace Corps volunteer might take an overseas assignment for a year or two for both task and personal enrichment purposes. A business person might accept an international posting for between three and five years. A missionary might go for a longer period, and military personnel are often posted overseas for shorter "tours of duty." Each year, for example, over 1.3 million students worldwide choose to study outside their countries. Right now, there are approximately 690,000 international students studying in different U.S. colleges with the explicit aim of getting their college degrees here. They also bring $20 billion into the U.S. economy via out-of-state tuition and living expenses. In fact, do you know where most of the international students come from? Take a guess and check out Jeopardy Box 5.4. Do you know what are the top pick countries for U.S.

JEOPARDY BOX 5.4 TOP FIVE COUNTRIES OF ORIGIN OF INTERNATIONAL STUDENTS TO THE UNITED STATES, 2009–2010

Country
1. China
2. India
3. South Korea
4. Canada
5. Taiwan

Source: Institute of International Education. (2010). *Top 25 Places of Origin of International Students, 2008/09–2009/10: Open Doors Report on International Educational Exchange.* http://www.iie.org/en/Research-and-Publications/Open-Doors/Data/International-Students/Leading-Places-of-Origin/2008-10 (retrieved April 23, 2011).

JEOPARDY BOX 5.5 TOP FIVE STUDY ABROAD LEADING DESTINATIONS FOR U.S. COLLEGE STUDENTS, 2008–2009

Country
1. United Kingdom
2. Italy
3. Spain
4. France
5. China

Source: Institute of International Education. (2010). *Top 25 Destinations of U.S. Study Abroad Students, 2007/08–2008/09. Open Doors Report on International Educational Exchange.* http://www.iie.org/en/Research-and-Publications/Open-Doors/Data/US-Study-Abroad/Leading-Destinations/2007-09 (retrieved April 23, 2011).

student-abroad programs? Take a guess and check out Jeopardy Box 5.5.

Indeed, most of the international students come from communal-oriented cultures, such as China, India, South Korea, Canada, and Taiwan, and they study in California, New York, and Texas (Institute for International Education [IIE], 2011). There are also approximately 260,330 U.S. students nationwide who embark on one-year study-abroad programs. The favorite study-abroad destinations of U.S. college students are the UK, Italy, Spain, France, and China (IEE, 2011). However, the number of U.S. students studying in Chile, South Korea, and Peru increased by more than 25 percent, whereas the top four destinations dropped in popularity. Students surveyed cited personal growth, new perspectives on world affairs, and career enhancement as some of the reasons for why they opt to go abroad to study. Beyond instrumental goals, international exchange sojourners also pursue socioemotional goals or fun activities, such as developing new friendships with the local students and hosts, visiting local marketplaces and museums, and learning about local histories, sports, and folk crafts (check out Hits-or-Misses 5.1, 5.2, 5.3).

In the remainder of this section, we explore the developmental models of the short- to medium-term adjustment process of sojourners. By understanding the developmental phases of intercultural adjustment, we can increase our competencies in dealing with our own and others' change process.

HIT-OR-MISS 5.1 TOP FIVE U.S. UNIVERSITIES ENROLLING INTERNATIONAL STUDENTS

See if you "Hit" or "Miss" as you name the top five U.S. universities that enroll the highest numbers of international students:

1. _____ (California)
2. _____ (Illinois)
3. _____ (New York)
4. _____ (Indiana)
5. _____ (New York)

Answers: 1: USC (University of Southern California); 2: University of Illinois–Urbana-Champaign; 3: NYU (New York University); 4: Purdue University; 5: Columbia University.

Source: International Institute of Education. Retrieved March 25, 2011, from http://www.iie.org

The U-Curve Adjustment Model

A number of researchers have conceptualized the sojourner adjustment process from various developmental perspectives. An interesting consequence of these stage-oriented descriptive models centers on whether sojourners' adaptation is a U-curve or a W-curve process. In interviewing over two hundred Norwegian Fulbright grantees in the United States, Lysgaard (1955) developed a three-phase intercultural adjustment model that includes (1) initial adjustment, (2) crisis, and (3) regained adjustment:

(1) is the optimistic or elation phase of the sojourn-ers' adjustment process, (2) is the stressful phase, when reality sets in and sojourners are overwhelmed by their own incompetence, and (3) is the settling-in phase, when sojourners learn to cope effectively with the new environment.

Drawing from the above ideas, Lysgaard (1955; see also Nash, 1991) proposed the U-curve model of the sojourner adjustment process, suggesting that sojourners pass through an initial honeymoon phase, then experience a "slump" or stressful phase, and finally pull themselves back up to an effective phase in managing their assignments abroad. In extending the U-curve model, Gullahorn and Gul-lahorn (1963) proposed a six-stage W-shape model, with successive honeymoon, hostility, humorous, at-home, reentry culture shock, and resocialization stages. Expanding the ideas of Gullahorn and Gul-lahorn, we have developed the following seven-stage revised W-shape adjustment model to explain sojourners' short-term to medium-term adjustment process (see Figure 5.1).

The Revised W-Shape Adjustment Model

The revised W-shape adjustment model consists of seven stages: the honeymoon, hostility, humorous, in-sync, ambivalence, reentry culture shock, and reso-cialization stages. The model applies especially to international students' experience abroad. Take a look first at Blog Post 5.3 and check out the experience abroad of one college student, Laleh.

In the **honeymoon stage**, individuals are excited about their new cultural environment. This is the ini-tial landing phase in which everything appears fresh and exhilarating. Sojourners perceive people and events through pleasantly tinted (or rose-colored) glasses. Nonetheless, they do experience mild bewil-derment and perplexity about the new culture; they also experience bursts of loneliness and homesickness. However, overall, they are cognitively curious about the new culture and emotionally charged up at meet-

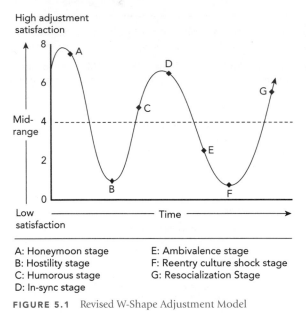

High adjustment satisfaction

A: Honeymoon stage
B: Hostility stage
C: Humorous stage
D: In-sync stage

E: Ambivalence stage
F: Reentry culture shock stage
G: Resocialization Stage

FIGURE 5.1 Revised W-Shape Adjustment Model

ing new people. They may not completely understand the verbal and nonverbal behaviors that surround them, but they are enjoying their initial "friendly" contacts with the locals.

Check out the story in Blog Post 5.4.

In the **hostility stage**, sojourners experience major emotional upheavals. This is the serious culture shock stage in which nothing works out smoothly. This stage can occur rapidly, right after the glow of the honeymoon phase is over and reality sets in sooner than expected. At this stage, sojourners experience a major loss of self-esteem and self-confidence. They feel consciously incompetent and emotionally drained in many aspects of their life. Many of these sojourners

can either become very aggressive/hostile or totally withdrawn. Anderson (1994), for example, identifies three types of "culture shockers" as follows: (1) the early returnees—those who tend to use aggressive or passive aggressive strategies to deal with the "hostile" environment and exit prematurely back to their home cultures; (2) the time servers—those who are doing a minimally passable job with minimal host contact and who are emotionally and cognitively "serving their time," but eagerly looking forward to returning home; and (3) the participators—those who are committed to adjust in an optimal manner and participate fully in their new culture and who take advantage of both instrumental and socioemotional learning in the new environment.

The "early returnees" tend to use *pounce* strategies or passive aggressive strategies and blame all the problems on the new culture. They constantly use their ethnocentric standards to compare and evaluate the local practices and customs. They exit their overseas assignments prematurely because of their interpretations of a stressful "hostile" environment and the "uncivilized" people they have to deal with on a daily basis (Brown, 2009). Yiping, a young woman from China who had been studying in the United States for seven months, complained to her friends and Chinese international classmates: "This semester, you must *talk* to earn your participation points in the classroom. We have three parts of the grade in this class. One third is discussion participation, the other two-thirds is writing articles. So if you don't talk, you lose one third of your points. So you have to talk. Talking is so exhausting! And it's not just talk, you know, from the material. You need to say what you *think* about it. But in China, you just

---

BLOG POST 5.3 INTERCULTURAL ADJUSTMENT—HONEYMOON STAGE

W-Shape Model Narrative . . .

I feel like I went through several of the stages of culture shock while I was doing a Junior [Year] Abroad study program in Spain. The honeymoon stage was great. This was right when I got there. I thought that everything was wonderful. I didn't really miss being at home because I was doing so many new and exciting things.

I was traveling through the south of Spain, who would ever think that there was something better than that? I was having such a good time and didn't really seem to even notice that I was so far away. I thought that Spain was a great place. I wasn't able to see any of the downfalls. I would practice my Spanish with as many people as I could find. It was a very exciting time. I would say that this period lasted for about two weeks, while I was traveling through Spain.

—Laleh, *college student*

BLOG POST 5.4 INTERCULTURAL ADJUSTMENT— HOSTILITY STAGE

Then the *hostility stage* hit. I think that the turning point was the first night when I was at my señora house. This experience was a huge shock to me. The apartment that I was living in was about a sixth of the size of my house. I was sharing a room that was the size of a shoebox. Needless to say I was really unhappy, at first. The minute that I got there it really hit me that I was living in another country for a long time without my family. To make things even worse, the room had no windows. All I wanted to do was go home. I didn't want to be in this little apartment with some woman that I didn't know, who didn't speak a word of English. I immediately called my dad crying. I told him that I wanted to come home and that I wasn't going to stay in Spain for a whole semester. After about a half an hour of listening to me whine and cry, my dad told me that I had to stay because he knew that that was what I really wanted and that this was just a bump in the road. He told me that I would get used to things and that everything would be all right. I thought that he had gone crazy.

The following few weeks were full of ups and downs. I was in an environment [in which] I didn't know what to do. I didn't even know where to buy the basic things that I needed. I felt like I was in a whole other world that didn't exist to me before. I had to learn how to take public transportation, which is something that I had never done before. After countless times of getting on the wrong bus, I finally figured it out. I would get frustrated because I wasn't able to express what was going on, because I was able to put together only the most basic of sentences.

—Laleh, *college student*

remember the expert answer.... We have one, and only one correct answer. That's my educational experience in China. But here it's like, okay, no right answers. Everyone is good. Every answer is correct. You just need to give your own perspective loudly and with back-up evidence. I'm so worn-out from talking and stressed all the time. I'm here to learn from the expert professors, why do they care about my opinions? I'm so ready to go home to China now!"

The "time servers" tend to use *avoidance* strategies. They use either physical avoidance or psychological withdrawal strategies to avoid interacting with host members. They do their job or fulfill their role in moving ahead in attaining their instrumental goals. However, they are fairly dissatisfied in the socioemotional connection area and feel quite isolated. They also tend to engage in wishful-thinking strategies and counting the days until they can go home. In an interview, Mariko, who had been studying in the United States for seventeen months, described her problem with her roommate and how she handled it: "Sometimes when I'm tired or not feeling very well, it appears on my face. And my American roommates started to tell me how small my eyes are. 'You are Japanese, and your eyes are usually small, but it's getting smaller, and smaller, and I couldn't see them.' I took it as a joke at first. But she kept telling me this stuff. I kind of get used to that, because she usually does that. But the problem is, she couldn't stop. Even though I tried to show that I was becoming annoyed, like, "Please stop it. I'm too tired right now." ... I don't know but she always says those kinds of things without being afraid of being misunderstood.... Whenever I tried to tell her about my problems, she started telling me it's my cultural background, or tried to talk about her own problems instead.... But she was never really respectful or caring of me. I now tried to avoid my roommate and stayed in the library more. I'm secretly trying to look for a new place to stay and looking for a new roommate to room with. I'm now counting down my months when I can go home and sleep on my own cozy futon bed."

The "participators," on the other hand, use active commitment strategies to realign their identities with the new culture. They try to engage in positive self-talk and positive situational appraisal strategies. They also intentionally develop new communication competence practices to connect with their new culture. They are committed to using an ethnorelative lens to view things from the other culture's frame of reference (Iyer, 1989). With the help of supportive networks, incremental task goal progression, and their personal emotional resilience, many sojourners can pull themselves out from the hostility stage and arrive at the recovery curve. Natalia, a Columbian student who has been in the United States for eighteen months, talked about how her attitude changed to become more of a participant in U. S. culture: "I think it changed when I started applying (for the master's program). Because I see that I will stay here for two years or more. So that's a lot of

---

BLOG POST 5.5   INTERCULTURAL ADJUSTMENT—
HUMOROUS STAGE AND IN-SYNC STAGE

The *humorous stage* was a little bit more enjoyable. I did have many times when I found myself doing something wrong and was able to laugh at myself. Once I was able to laugh about it and not worry so much about what I was doing, I felt a lot better. However, I still haven't gotten the hang of the whole kissing on both cheeks when you meet. I will still offer them my hand and they will be leaning in to kiss me. It is like an awkward first date goodbye. I do not think that I fully experienced that in-sync stage. I feel like I became more accustomed to what was

going on, but I was never completely comfortable with many of the "strange" cultural situations. The longer I stayed there the more I got used to things. However, I was still wishing that things could have been more like home. I never understood why you couldn't just go in somewhere and order a nice turkey sandwich. There were little things that would get on my nerves on a daily basis, but I was able to work through them. I guess I became more in sync with what was going on around me. I knew what I needed to do to get what I wanted, which was a big accomplishment.

—Laleh, *college student*

---

time. Then in this process, I have to start to make new American friends, and not to talk too much with the same friends in Colombia.... I make a decision to participate more in the American culture—watch more American news, talk more to American students in class, and learn to visit Professors in their office which I'm not used to back home. I want to really know how the American mind ticks, why they all seem so confident and carefree!"

Now let's check out Blog Post 5.5, the humorous stage description.

At the **humorous stage**, sojourners learn to laugh at their cultural *faux pas* and start to realize that there are pros and cons in each culture—just as there are both good and evil people in every society. They experience a mixture of stress–adaptation–growth emotions (Y. Y. Kim, 1988, 2005), such as small frustrations and small triumphs. They are able to compare both their home and their host cultures in realistic terms, and they no longer take things as seriously as in the hostility stage. They can now take a step backward and look at their own behavior and reactions objectively. Taskwise, they are making progress in attaining their instrumental goals (e.g., achieving their MBA degree or acquiring new business skills). They are beginning to form new friendships and social networks. These sojourners eventually arrive at the next stage.

At the **in-sync adjustment stage**, sojourners feel "at home" and experience identity security and inclusion. The boundaries between outsiders and insiders become fuzzier, and sojourners experience social acceptance and support. They are now easily able to interpret "bizarre" local customs and behaviors. They

may be savvy enough to speak the local language with flair, even catching some verbal jokes and puns and perhaps responding with a one-up joke. They may now even act as role models or mentors to incoming sojourners from their home cultures. During the in-sync adjustment stage, sojourners develop a sense of trust and empathy and a wide spectrum of other positive emotions. They become much more creative and adaptive in the new environment. They are capable of making appropriate choices in connection with any new situations that may arise, just as they arrive at a "comfort level" of their sojourn. However, they must get ready to pack their bags and go home.

Let's check out Laleh's ambivalent feelings in Blog Post 5.6.

In the **ambivalence stage**, sojourners experience grief, nostalgia, and pride, with a mixed sense of relief and sorrow that they are going home. They recall their early awkward days when they first arrived and they count all the new friends they have made since then. They also look forward eagerly to sharing all their intercultural stories with their family members and old friends back home. They finally say goodbye to their newfound friends and their temporarily adopted culture.

At the **reentry culture shock stage**, sojourners face an unexpected jolt (see the "Reentry Culture Shock" section that follows). Because of the unanticipated nature of reentry shock, its impact is usually much more severe, and returnees usually feel more depressed and stressed than they did with entry culture shock. There is a sharp letdown (e.g., their friends or family members have no interest in hearing all their

BLOG POST 5.6 INTERCULTURAL ADJUSTMENT—
AMBIVALENCE STAGE

I had two different experiences with the ambivalence stage. When I was leaving to come home for Christmas, I had a feeling like I hadn't accomplished everything that I wanted to, which was why I decided to stay for another semester. There were so many things that I still wanted to do, and I felt that if I didn't stay for another semester that I would be cheating myself out of more wonderful cultural experiences. The second experience that I had with the ambivalence stage was quite different. When it was getting to the end of the second semester, I was totally ready to go home. I was ready to get out of there three weeks before school was over. I was tired of not being able to communicate like I wanted to. I had all my bags packed and [was] ready to take off and share all my wonderful stories with my family and friends.

—Laleh, *college student*

wonderful intercultural stories) and identity chaos: the greater the distance (i.e., on the cultural values and communication dimensions) between the two cultures, the more intense the reentry shock. Additionally, the more integrated into and time spent in the abroad country, the more difficult this stage becomes. By now, however, most sojourners have become resourceful and resilient individuals. They can recycle some of the commitment strategies they used abroad to pull themselves through to the next stage.

In the **resocialization stage**, some individuals (i.e., the resocializers) may quietly assimilate themselves back to their old roles and behaviors without making much of a "wave" or appearing different from the rest of their peers or colleagues. They bury their newly acquired ideas and skills together with the pictures on their Facebook page and try not to look at them again. Looking at these pictures can only cause identity dissonance and disequilibrium. Other individuals (i.e., the alienators) can never "fit back" into their home cultures again. They are always the first to accept an overseas assignment. They feel more alive abroad than at home. For example, Jenny, a college junior, has been to Spain, Italy, Mexico, and Hong Kong on study-abroad programs. She confessed feeling unease and restlessness at her own university and will spend the next semester in Argentina. Jenny, an alienator, may eventually become a global nomad who claims the global world as her home base rather than any single place as her national cultural affiliation.

Finally, yet other individuals (i.e., the "transformers") are the ones who act as agents of change in their home organizations or cultures. They mindfully integrate their new learning experience abroad with what is positive in their own culture (Brown & Brown, 2009; Brown & Holloway, 2008). They apply multidimensional thinking, enriched emotional intelligence, and diverse angles to solve problems or to instigate change for a truly inclusive learning organization. Geeta, from India, studied in the United States for two and one-half years and reflects on the experience as she returns to her home culture: "The U.S. has helped me become more assertive in a respectful way, not aggressive though. The ways of the U.S., this whole concept about space, about individualism versus collectivism, that certainly has merits. Although it has its demerits, it has some merits, too. And I think I'm inculcating those, because I think that makes me a stronger person. Saying 'no' cordially and not feeling guilty about it, that is something I've learned after coming here. And placing my own needs as important as the needs of others, and considering my own wants and needs as a priority is an eye-opening experience for me."

Transformers are the change agents who bring home with them a wealth of personal and cultural treasures to share, actively and responsibly, with colleagues, friends, and families. They do so with interpersonally sensitive skills—something hey've learned in the foreign environment. They have no fears of acting or being perceived as "different" or being situated in the "outgroup" category; they now have a "taste" of what it means to be different (however, this taste of difference is qualitatively different from the "difference" that many minority members experience in their everyday lives). They are comfortable in experiencing the cultural frame-shifting process, for example, being individualist and becoming collectivist, interacting in low context style with one set of individuals and switching to a high-context approach with another set of folks (Nguyen & Benet-Martinez,

2010). They practice a "third culture" approach in integrating and activating the best practices of both cultures and creatively fuse them into a third culture perspective outlook in decision making and problem solving. They are more compassionate and committed than before about social injustice issues and human rights issues on a global scale. Transformers are the individuals who have acquired (and are always in the process of acquiring) mindfulness, compassion, and wisdom.

Culture Shock: Peaks and Valleys

In sum, the revised W-shape adjustment model basically emphasizes the following characteristics, which can influence the progress of the sojourners' identity change process: (1) They must understand the peaks and valleys, and positive and negative shifts, that constitute identity change in an unfamiliar environment, realizing that the frustration-and-triumph roller coaster ride is part of the change-and-growth process. (2) They must be aware and keep track of their instrumental, relational, and identity goals in the new culture; success in one set of goals (e.g., making new friends) can affect triumph in another set of goals (e.g., newfound friends can help to solve a school-related problem). (3) They must give themselves some time and space to adjust; they should keep a journal or blog to express their daily feelings and random thoughts, and they should also keep in touch with people in their home culture via Facebook, letters, e-mails, and Skype. (4) They must develop both strong ties (meaningful friendships) and weak ties (functional social connections, e.g., with supportive teachers, caring counselors, or friendly grocers) to cushion themselves and seek help in times of crisis. (5) They must reach out to participate in the host culture's major cultural events—art and music festivals, parades, local museums, or national sports—and immerse themselves in this once-in-a-lifetime experience and learn to enjoy the local culture as much as possible.

The patterns of the revised W-shape adjustment model consist of back-and-forth looping movements within and between stages. Length of sojourn, alone or with family, degree of adaptation commitment, degrees and types of communication competence (e.g., linguistic competence), first-time visit versus repeated visit, and realistic versus unrealistic goals are some other factors that will propel either progressive or regressive loops along the W-shape model. Remember the story from the opening chapter? Let's explore more of Ms. Abbott's experiences in Blog Post 5.7 to understand the flow of choppy waters of the model.

Church (1982) and Ward (2004), in reviewing the literature on these developmental models, comment that both the U-curve and the W-shape models appear to be too general and do not capture the dynamic interplay between sojourners' and host nationals' factors in the adjustment process. In addition, sojourners adapt and learn at different rates. The support for both models is based on one-time cross-sectional data (i.e., one-time surveys of sojourners) rather than longitudinal data (i.e., collection of surveys at different points during sojourners' two-year adjustment). More controversial is the debate as to the initial phase (i.e., the *honeymoon stage*) of adjustment. Research (Adler, 1997; McLachlan & Justice, 2009; Osland, 1995; Rohrlich & Martin, 1991) indicates that international students and managers both tend to experience severe identity shock (i.e., the *hostility stage* comes very early, side by side with the fleeting *honeymoon stage*) in the early phase of their sojourn abroad. However, the overseas stressors also motivate them to become more resourceful and resilient in their search for new knowledge and skills in managing the alien environment.

Despite some of the limitations of the developmental models, their positive implications are that they offer us a developmental portrait of the culture shock experience, illustrate that the culture shock process is filled with peaks and valleys, and contribute to a holistic understanding of the psychological, affective, and identity changes in the new arrivals. Additionally, in the W-shape model, we are made aware of the importance of understanding the role of *reentry culture shock*.

REENTRY CULTURE SHOCK

The phenomenon of reentry culture shock has received increased attention from intercultural researchers (Martin & Harrell, 1996, 2004; Sussman, 1986). Reentry shock involves the realignment of one's new identity with a once-familiar home environment. After

BLOG POST 5.7 BACK AND FORTH ALONG THE W-SHAPE ADJUSTMENT MODEL

After graduating from the university, I moved to Japan to teach English in Japanese public school as a member of the JET Program. Upon my arrival to Japan, I spoke no Japanese, knew nothing about Japanese culture, and had no formal experience teaching children. My true purpose in coming to Japan was to escape the reality of getting a 9–5 job in America and to continue on my adventurous quest to see as much of the world as I possibly could.

I graduated with a degree in Political Science with a minor in Communication, got high marks, and considered myself a fairly intelligent person. But moving to the Japanese countryside rendered me an illiterate mute, unable to read even the simplest signs or communicate with the second graders I taught. It was an incredibly humbling experience to walk into a grocery store and not be able to read a single label, or have your third grade students check the penmanship of your hiragana characters.

What proved to be the real challenge in my daily life in Japan was communicating across cultures with the teachers I work with. Although the language barrier is an obvious hurdle, the many layers of Japanese culture and the context in which they conduct business was the most fascinating aspect of my experience. I found myself surrounded by a tangled web of unspoken rules, titles, hierarchy, formality, and cultural idiosyncrasies. Every day was a puzzle that I could not solve, but appeared easy and natural through the eyes of my coworkers. It was the process of solving this puzzle that left me either laughing hysterically or crying alone in a rice patty at the end of each day (mood depending).

I taught a class of fifth graders one day that were particularly unruly, difficult to control, and boisterous. The homeroom teacher willingly helped me gain control of the classroom, calmed the children down, and we finished up the lesson. She thanked me profusely for the lesson and I carried on my day, assuming it was a success. It wasn't until a few days later that my supervisor told me that the fifth grade teacher was displeased with the class activity and wanted me to make several changes to my lesson plan before the next session. I felt bad about the lesson, but I was confused as to why the teacher didn't just tell me herself, or why my supervisor waited three whole days to discuss this and what I perceive as now ancient history with me. And I realized the lessons I learned.

I always considered myself a highly logical person, working and thinking in a linear pattern, moving quickly from A to B and on to C; I assumed that this was the only logical way to do things. But the Japanese way of thinking moves in circles, darting from one end to the other, forming a web that is impossible to follow, moving forward and back, up and down, with seemingly no end in sight. It is a different type of logic and thinking all together, but it works if one is willing to observe closely, and with patience.

The reason that I haven't heard anyone say "no," or the reason that the supervisory teacher did not approach me with her concern up front, is because being frank and direct is a Western communication value—something so rude that a Japanese person would never consider doing. I realized that the teacher was afraid to offend me by telling me I was wrong. I now finally understand the difference between the direct, low-context and the subtle, high-context communication style by this cultural immersion process.

—K. Abbott

living abroad for an extensive period of time, reentry culture shock is inevitable.

Let's check out Kari's reentry feelings in Blog Post 5.8.

This identity realignment process can sometimes be more stressful and jolting than entry culture shock because of the unanticipated nature of one's own identity change and the accompanying change of one's friends and family.

Reentry Culture Shock: Surprising Elements

According to research (e.g., Chang, 2009; Osland, 1995), the often unanticipated, surprising elements that affect reentry culture shock include the following:

1. Sojourners' identity change—the newly acquired values, emotions, cognitions, role statuses, managerial methods, and behaviors are, surprisingly, not a "good fit" with the once-familiar home culture;

2. Sojourners' nostalgic and idealized images of their home culture—sojourners tend to remember the positive aspects of their culture and forget its negative aspects during their experience abroad, and thus, the reentry reality often produces a strong jolt;

3. Sojourners' difficulty in reintegrating themselves into their old career pathway or career roles because of their new cultural lenses;

4. Sojourners' letdown in their expectations as to close ties with family members and friends who

BLOG POST 5.8   REENTRY CULTURE SHOCK

I had problems readapting after spending a year in Italy. I have been feeling stuck in this reentry period for a little longer than normal. I feel like there is no one else who feels like I do; everyone else seems to transition effortlessly. But in a way, I feel bad for those people. I think that the reason that I feel the way I do is because I absorbed so much when I was there. I completely opened myself up to whatever new culture I came across, and this had a direct impact on how I look at things. . . . Though I seem to be temporarily stuck in the depression phase of it all, I would rather feel like this than to have let the experience pass me by with no impact at all.

—Kari, *college student*

have become more distant because of the long separation;

5. Family and friends' lack of interest in listening to the sojourning stories of the returnee and their growing impatience with her or him;

6. The home culture's demand for conformity and expectations for old role performance;

7. The absence of change in the home culture (e.g., the old system or workplace looks stale and boring in comparison with the overseas adventure) or too much change (e.g., political or corporate upheavals), which can also create immense identity disjunction for the recent returnees.

Thus, reentry culture shock can be understood from three domains: the returnees' readiness to resocialize themselves in the home environment, the degree of change in the returnees' friendship and family networks, and the home receptivity conditions. Sussman (1986) recommends that on the individual level, awareness of change should be a major component of reentry training as individuals face a wide range of psychological and environmental challenges. Pusch and Loewenthall (1988) further recommend that preparation for a successful return should include (1) the recognition of what sojourners are leaving behind and what they have gained in their assignments abroad; (2) the emotional costs of transition; (3) the value of worrying (i.e., anticipating and preparing for difficulties that may occur); (4) the need for support systems and ways to develop them; and (5) the necessity of developing one's own strategies for going home.

Resocialization: Different Returnees' Profiles

Adler (1997) identifies three profiles of returnee managers in relationship to the specific transition strategies they employ: resocialized returnees, alienated returnees, and proactive returnees. *Resocialized returnees* are the ones who do not recognize having learned new skills in the new culture. They are also psychologically distant from their international experience. They try to use the fit-back-in strategy and resocialize themselves quietly into the domestic corporate structure. They typically rate their reentry experience as quite satisfactory.

The *alienated returnees*, on the other hand, are aware of their new skills and ideas in their experience abroad. However, they have difficulty in applying their new knowledge in the home organizations. Rather, they try to use the "distance-rejective" strategy of being onlookers in their home culture. Of all the three types, they are the most dissatisfied group.

The *proactive returnees* are highly aware of changes in themselves and the new values and skills they have learned overseas. They try to integrate the new values and practices learned from the sojourning culture into the home culture and develop an integrated outlook in their reentry phase. While abroad, the proactive managers tend to use proactive communication to maintain close ties with the home organization via formal and informal means. They also have a home-based mentor to look after their interests and pass on important corporate information. Their mentor keeps the home-based headquarters informed of the sojourner's achievements while abroad.

Proactive managers might report the acquisition of the following skills in their assignments abroad: alternative managerial skills, tolerance of ambiguity, multiple reasoning perspectives, and ability to work with and manage others. They further report that the new skills improve their self-image and self-confidence. Not surprisingly, returnees who receive validation (e.g., promotions) from their bosses and recognition from their colleagues report higher reentry satisfaction than do returnees who receive no such validation or recognition (Adler, 1997).

INTERCULTURAL REALITY CHECK: DO-ABLES

In this chapter, we explored culture shock as we crossed cultural boundaries. We explained the pros and cons and looked at some of the factors of why people manage culture shock differently.

We also talked about the developmental ups and downs of culture shock and suggested tips to manage culture shock adaptively. Last, we emphasized the importance of paying attention to reentry culture shock issues.

Overall, here are some practical tools for managing sojourners' culture shock effectively:

- Newcomers should realize that culture shock is inevitable. It is an unavoidable experience that most people encounter when relocating from a familiar environment to an unfamiliar one.
- New arrivals should understand that culture shock arises because of the unfamiliar environment, when one is bombarded and saturated with unfamiliar cues. Developing a realistically positive outlook in viewing their one-time experience as a precious adventure and doing some positive reframing of surprising events may help to lower their stress level

- Making an effort to establish broad-based contacts with members of the host culture and learning to communicate with them can increase local knowledge and reduce such feelings of vulnerability. Cultivating a deeper, supportive friendship network and easing themselves into the new setting can also help to restore the identity equilibrium state.
- Likewise, the more members of the host culture extend a helping hand and the more they attempt to increase their familiarity with the new arrivals, the more they can increase the n*ewcomers' sense of security and inclusion.
- Culture shock is induced partly by an intense feeling of incompetence. By seeking out positive role models or mentors, newcomers may be able to find reliable and competent cultural bridge persons in easing the stress level of their initial culture shock experience.
- Newcomers should realize that culture shock is a transitional affective phase of stress that ebbs and flows from high to low intensity. New arrivals must hang on to a resilient sense of humor and emphasize the positive aspects of the environment rather than engaging in prolonged concentration on its negative aspects, realizing that these "growing pains" may lead to long-term personal and professional growth and development.

CHAPTER 6

WHAT IS THE CONNECTION BETWEEN VERBAL COMMUNICATION AND CULTURE?

CHAPTER OUTLINE

- Human Language: Distinctive Features and Rule Patterns
  - Distinctive Language Features
  - Multiple Rule Patterns

- Appreciating Diverse Language Functions
  - The Cultural Worldview Function
  - The Everyday Social Reality Function
  - The Cognitive Shaping Function
  - The Group Membership Identity Function
  - The Social Change Function

- Verbal Communication Styles: A General Framework
  - Defining Low-Context and High-Context Interaction Patterns
  - Direct and Indirect Verbal Styles
  - Self-Enhancement and Self-Humbling Verbal Styles
  - Beliefs Expressed in Talk and Silence

- Intercultural Reality Check: Do-Ables

Around the world, languages are disappearing. In the past five hundred years, an estimated half of the world's languages, from Etruscan to Tasmanian, from Alaska to Australia, hundreds of languages around the world are teetering on the brink of extinction—some being spoken by a single person. More than half of the world's seven thousand languages are expected to die out by the end of the century, often taking with them irreplaceable knowledge about the natural world. There are five hotspots where languages are vanishing most rapidly: eastern Siberia, northern Australia, central South America, Oklahoma, and the U.S. Pacific Northwest. To identify the five hotspots, three main criteria are used:

1. The diversity of languages spoken,
2. The level of endangerment to the tongue,
3. The scientific documentation of a language.

Languages die a slow death because people simply abandon their native tongues when they become surrounded by people speaking a more common language.

—Stefan Lovgren, *National Geographic News,* 2007

Indigenous people refer to groups who are rooted to a particular place by history, traditions, legends, rituals, and language. According to expert linguists, an indigenous language dies every two weeks. For example, you will never again hear anyone speaking Laghu of the Solomon Islands or signing in Old Kentish Sign Language used by the Kamilaroi tribe of New South Wales (Tobin, 2011). With the death of a language comes the death of a people's way of thinking, living, and relating, their traditions, folklore, legacies, and centuries of irreplaceable knowledge and wisdom.

We use language to communicate, to agree and disagree with people, to make and decline requests, or to enforce politeness and defuse tension. Language frames our perceptions and interpretations of everyday events that are happening in our cultural community. It is a taken-for-granted aspect of our cultural lives. Without language, we cannot make sense of the cultural world around us. We cannot pass on the wisdom of our culture from one generation to the next.

We acquire meanings for words (e.g., "winning," "relational karma") or phrases (e.g., "that's what I think I deserve") from the value systems of our culture. Although language can easily create misunderstandings, it can also clarify misunderstandings and reduce tension. The "linguistic categories" we use every day serve as a kaleidoscope that captures our multiple realities.

In this chapter we explore the relationships among language, verbal communication, and culture. This chapter is organized into four main sections: the first section explores the basic features and rule patterns of human language; the second section examines the different functions of languages across cultures; the third section identifies low-context and high-context communication characteristics; and the last section offers checkpoints and do-ables of how to deal with language and verbal communication difficulties when crossing cultural boundaries.

HUMAN LANGUAGE: DISTINCTIVE FEATURES AND RULE PATTERNS

Language is an arbitrary, symbolic system that labels and categorizes objects, events, groups, people, ideas, feelings, experiences, and many other phenomena. Language is also governed by the *multilayered rules* developed by members of a particular sociocultural community. Although broad similarities exist among languages, variations remain in the sounds, written symbols, grammar, and nuances of meaning of an estimated 6,700 language varieties across worldwide cultures. This section examines the four distinctive features of language: arbitrariness, abstractness, meaning-centeredness, and creativity. It also examines the multilayered rules of language usage in relationship to culture.

To do a quick check, do you know what are the top five countries that have the most native English and Spanish speakers, respectively? Take a quick guess, and check out the answers in Jeopardy Boxes 6.1 and 6.2.

JEOPARDY BOX 6.1   TOP FIVE COUNTRIES WITH THE MOST ENGLISH-LANGUAGE SPEAKERS

Country	Approximate number of speakers*
1. United States	215,423,557
2. United Kingdom	58,100,000
3. Canada	17,694,830
4. Australia	15,581,329
5. Ireland	4,122,100

*People for whom English is their native tongue.

Source: Adapted from Ash (2011, p.104; based on Ethnologue Database).

Distinctive Language Features

Arbitrariness

Human language is arbitrary in phonemic (i.e., sound unit) and graphic representation (i.e., alphabet or characters). Language is viewed as an arbitrary symbolic system because the words that are strung together have

Country	Approximate number of speakers*
1. Mexico	106,770,268
2. USA	50,000,000
3. Spain	46,184,857
4. Colombia	44,937,600
5. Argentina	40,275,837

*People for whom Spanish is their mother tongue.

Source: Adapted from Ash (2011, p.104; based on Ethnologue Database)

no innate meaning. It is people in a speech community who attach shared sounds and common meanings to words that they use in their everyday lives. For example, the word "player" has no real meaning in its sounds and letters, yet in English we interpret these sounds and letters as having a particular intimate meaning. Even sign language, as "spoken" by deaf people, is arbitrary in nature in terms of the use of different nonverbal gestures. There are many different culture-specific sign language varieties (e.g., American, British, and Chinese).

By three months, infants have acquired the ability to imitate some aspects of vowel sounds that they hear (Kuhl & Meltzoff, 1996). Through continuous reinforcement, children learn to retain sounds that are most familiar to their ears and tongues and drop off other nonessential sounds. Universally, children first acquire speaking and comprehending skills, then reading and writing skills. Whereas all children have the capacity to utter all the sounds in all languages, this linguistic competence tapers off as they reach puberty.

Abstractness

Language, however, also allows humans to engage in abstract thoughts or hypothetical thinking. Because of this unique feature, we can plan for our intercultural journey, daydream, and fantasize about the infinite possibilities of our potential experience abroad. Our ability to use different linguistic categories to imagine ourselves in different locations, in different time zones, and in different social interaction scenes is truly a unique human language feature.

The more we move away from concrete, external phenomena, the more we engage in the process of language abstraction. In many instances, language creates intercultural friction because it is such an abstract, imprecise instrument. We can use language to provoke tension, create conflict, reduce stress, flirt with others, and also uplift the spirit of others (Farb, 1973; Ting-Toomey & Chung, 2005).

When we perceive that the use of our language causes anxiety and uncertainty in our intercultural interaction, we may want to force ourselves to go "down the ladder" of symbolic abstraction—to use more concrete wordings or alternative verbal approaches to discuss the problematic interaction. Likewise, we should also develop a sense of cultural sensitivity when we communicate with individuals from a linguistic system that values tactful, "abstract" verbal styles.

Meaning-Centeredness

To understand a cultural stranger's language usage, we must acquire both the dictionary meaning of a word and the subjective meaning of a word or phrase. In any language, two levels of meaning exist: denotative meaning and connotative meaning. The **denotative meaning** of a word emphasizes its objective, dictionary definition shared and recognized by the majority members of a linguistic community. The **connotative meaning**, on the other hand, stresses the subjective, interpretive meanings of a word constructed by individual members based on their cultural and personalized language experience.

For example, the word *hook up* can have the objective, denotative meaning of "an arrangement of mechanical parts" or "an alliance or cooperation." However, from the connotative meaning construction level of informal U.S. English usage, cultural members may interpret the meaning of *hook up* as a casual sexual encounter or dealing drugs.

In addition, translation problems and jokes that involve different meaning misunderstandings abound at the global level: "Things come alive with Pepsi" has been translated into German as "Pepsi can pull you back from your grave!" Mazda's car "Laputa" has been translated into Spanish as *la puta*, which means "the prostitute." The American Dairy Association's "Got milk?" campaign in Spanish was changed after it was realized that "¿Tienes leche?" translates as "Are you lactating?" In 2009, the debut of the "Audi RS6 White Power" automobile from Germany was renamed "Audi RS6 Avant" after complaints, accusations, and negative publicity flooded car blogs, news sites, and forums across the Internet. Take a look at Blog Pics 6.1.a and 6.1.b.

These translation problems or jokes often occur because of the crossover confusion between literal or denotative translation emphasis and cultural connotative inaccuracy. Even if the literal or denotative translation were accurate, the "objective" meaning often creates a very strange or even hilarious effect. The challenge for translators is to understand the specific intention and meaning of the original phrase and then to adjust appropriately the meaning of the phrase with regard to the cultural context and the situational appropriateness of the other language application (see also, Kwon, Barnett, & Chen, 2009).

Creativity

There are three distinctive elements in the linguistic creativity feature: productivity, displacement, and the meta-communicative feature (Crystal, 2010). The productivity element refers to the immense creative capacity children and adults have—to say things never spoken before once they have mastered the basic "recipe" of a language. By the time children with normal language development patterns reach their fourth birthday, they have already internalized the exceedingly complex structure of their native tongue. Add a couple more years and children will possess the entire linguistic system, allowing them the ability to utter and understand sentences they have never heard before. Parents do not have to teach their children every sentence in their language system. Once they have mastered the common vocabulary and grammatical structure of their native tongues, children can creatively spit out coherent sentences from their mouths via a creative reconfiguration of words.

Furthermore, individuals in all linguistic communities also have the capacity to talk about things far away in time and space (i.e., the displacement element) and to use language (e.g., via oral history, poetry, parables, stories, or songs) to pass on their heritage, lessons learned, memories, and wisdom from one generation to the next. It also means that individuals can garner their creative potential to use language mindfully (i.e., meta-communication) for mutual collaboration and understanding. Alternatively, language can be used to disseminate hate-filled propaganda, bully others, express prejudice, wage war, and engender destruction. Let's check out Blog Post 6.1—an original poem, "Words," by Win Garcia.

Can you relate to this poem? Can you visualize his experience? Can you picture the hurting image of the word *wetback* versus the healing image of the word *love*? Language can be a healing and a hacking instrument. It can be used mindfully to uplift and support others' desired identities; it can also be used to "cut

Blog Pic 6.1.a Sometimes the meaning gets lost in translation.

Blog Pic 6.1.b Brand name confusion?

BLOG POST 6.1 WORDS

All their words were weapons
and they were aimed at me
"Wetback" was the chosen word
that others shot at me

I can feel the humiliation
I do remember the pain
how could an entire nation, I thought,
call me by an evil name?

Now the tide has shifted
for many of us "meek,"
we seem to be uplifted
by our refusal to be weak

I see their offspring walk about
attempting to hold on,
to their ideal of "sameness"
that is forever gone

Though I sometimes reminisce
about those painful years,
the words for me are different now
they range from "sir" to "dear"

I know that words are weapons
for many I have heard,
there are no needs for weapons here
only needs for loving words

Source: From Win Garcia, "Words" (an original poem).
Copyright © 2004 by Win Garcia. Reprinted by permission.

JEOPARDY BOX 6.3 TOP FIVE MOST WIDELY SPOKEN LANGUAGES WORLDWIDE

Country (language)	Approximate number of speakers
1. Chinese (Mandarin)	845,000,000
2. Spanish	329,000,000
3. English	328,000,000
4. Hindustani*	242,000,000
5. Arabic#	221,000,000

*Hindi and Urdu are essentially the same language: Hindustani. As the official language of Pakistan, it is written in modified Arabic script and called Urdu. As the official language of India, it is written in the Devanagari script and called Hindi.

#Includes sixteen variants of the Arabic language.

Source: Adapted from http://www.ethnologue.com/ethno_docs/distribution. asp?by =size#2 (retrieved March 28, 2011).

down" or degrade others' primary identities. The bottom line is that language is the key to the heart of a culture.

Multiple Rule Patterns

What are the top five languages spoken by most inhabitants of the world? Take a guess and check out Jeopardy Box 6.3. All languages are constructed with words or symbols that are arranged in patterned ways, that is, they are rule governed. Most native speakers have difficulty clearly articulating the rules of their own language. Native speakers often operate on the unconscious competence stage of language usage because they can converse fluently within their own linguistic community without needing to overworry about the rule patterns of their everyday language usage (see, for example, Bolden, 2008). We introduce the following rule patterns of language here: phonology, morphology, syntactics, semantics, and pragmatics.

Phonological Rules

The **phonological rules** (or **phonology**) of a language refer to the different accepted procedures for combining phonemes. **Phonemes** are the smallest sound units of a word. For example, some of the phonemes in English are [k], [sh], [t], and [b]. Native speakers of English, for example, may possess an intuitive sense of how to utter these sounds, such as *kick, shame, tree,* and *butter;* however, they may not be able to articulate the how and why of the phonetic rules for producing these sounds. Although the English language has forty-five phonemes, other languages have a range of phonemes spanning anywhere between fifteen and eighty-five.

Linguistically speaking, everyone who communicates speaks with an accent because **accent** means the inflection or tone of voice that is taken to be characteristic of an individual. Our inflection and tone of voice are unique. Members of subcultures who are native speakers of the same language can also be identified as having accents. In such cases, the distinctive accent is attributed to shared group membership interacting within a common space (Wyatt, 1995). Many Bostonians, for example, claim that they can differentiate the Italian, Irish, and Jewish groups in their city by the way they articulate their /o(r)/ vowel sound (e.g., in words like "start" and "park").

The issue of accents becomes apparent because technology has been in the forefront of speech and speech-to-text recording. Cell phones have the "voiceprint" app, which allows you to record your own unique voice saying the names in your address book and instead of dialing, you just say, "Call Catanzaro." In our modern times, speech-to-text technology is becoming rampant, where a person can speak into a device that then produces written text of what was said, thus justifying the use of "accent-free" language. In 2011, Sprint was the first U.S. cell phone carrier to integrate Google Voice across its entire handset lineup, which allows a Google search by speaking the search term into the phone.

Morphological Rules

The term **morphological rules** (or **morphology**) refers to how combinations of different sounds make up a meaningful word or part of a word (e.g., "lead" and "er-ship" form "lead-er-ship"; or words such as "caff-eine" and "flow-er"). In English and many other European languages, morphemes that are required by grammar are often put at the end of words as suffixes (i.e., "is going" and "is sleeping" contain the morpheme "ing," which indicates that an activity is currently in progress; or in adverb form as in "worth-less" and "mind-less").

Languages develop different rules on the basis of cultural conventions that are passed down from one generation to the next. Once we have internalized the language sound habits of our culture, it is much more difficult to learn another set of linguistic conventions. In Swahili, the grammatical information indicating verb tense appears at the beginning as a prefix (*law* = "to go," and *nalaw* = "is going"; or *sun* = "to sleep," and *nasun* = "is sleeping"). Thus, in the Swahili morphological system, individuals are in a state of preparation before actually doing something. Interestingly, well-trained Russians who speak fluent English will still give themselves away when they pronounce the letter "t" in the English sentence such as "Tomorrow is a town hall meeting." The Russian "t" is pronounced by contact between the tip of the tongue and the upper teeth, unlike English, which pronounces "t"

by making contact between the tongue, just back of its tip, and the upper gum ridge.

When we hear nonnative speakers chatting, we often view the morphological sounds of their foreign language as undetermined patter and may even get annoyed when their intonations sound unfamiliar and out of the range of our language tones. Again, we should practice linguistic empathy in many intercultural occasions because we should remember that once a child reaches four years old, she may have internalized the sound habits of her native-tongue language. Instead of evaluating harshly the "off-kilter" sound system of a foreign speaker, we should extend respect for any individual who tries to master and practice a second or third language in her later years.

Syntactic Rules

The **syntactic rules** (or **syntactics**) of a language refer to how words are sequenced together in accordance with the grammatical practices of the linguistic community. The order of the words helps to establish the meaning of an utterance. It is also reflective of the cultural notions of causality and order.

In English grammar, for example, explicit subject pronouns are used to distinguish self from other (e.g., "I cannot give you the report because Manuela is still working on the conclusion section."). In Chinese grammar, explicit pronouns, such as "I" and "you," are deemphasized. Instead, conjunctive words, such as "because" (*yinwei*), "so" (*suoyi*), and "then" (*juo*), appear early in the sentence to pave the way for the rest of the story. For example, the following statement illustrates this point: "*Because* of so many snow storms, *so* the report has then not been handled properly, *then* we're now one week behind the deadline."

Chinese syntax establishes a context and contingent conditions and then introduces the main point, but English syntax establishes the key point and then lays out the reason (Young, 1994). Likewise, in Spanish, there are two different verb forms to address the past tense, depending on how the action occurred in the past, whereas English is a "matter-of-fact" language with fewer ways to address the past tense. The syntactic rules of a language—in interaction with the cultural value system—assert tremendous power on people's thinking and reasoning patterns within a culture.

Semantic Rules

The **semantic rules** (or **semantics**) of a language concern the features of meaning we attach to words. Words themselves do not have self-evident meanings. It is people within a cultural language community who consensually establish shared meanings for specific words and phrases.

The concept of "meaning" is tied closely to how we interpret the incoming verbal message in a culturally relevant and situationally relevant manner. To truly understand what someone is saying from another linguistic community, we must understand three affective (or connotative) features of meaning: the evaluative feature (i.e., good–bad), the potency feature (i.e., strong–weak), and the activity feature (i.e., fast–slow) (Osgood, Suci, & Tanenbaum, 1957).

For example, your cultural classmate says, "I am totally committed to this project" with the affective connotations of "good, strong, *and fast.*" This particular cultural member thinks that the project will be completed before spring break. The other cultural member echoes the same phrase, but with the affective connotations of "good, strong, *but slow*" (i.e., I will mull over our project, meet a couple more times, and we'll do it after break). Although both teammates have similar meaning reactions concerning the "good and strong" portions of the concept concerning "commitment," they differ significantly on the activity feature of "fast versus slow."

Further culture-based meaning misunderstandings could take place, for example, if both U.S. and Russian conflict negotiators cannot agree on the semantic meaning of words such as "compromise" or "collaboration." U.S. American negotiators generally regard compromise as inevitable and desirable. Russian diplomats, on the other hand, consider compromise a sign of weakness, a retreat from a correct and morally justified position. Russian conflict negotiators, therefore, are prepared to "wait out their opposite numbers in the expectation that time and Russian patience will produce more concessions....Chess is a Russian national pastime, and Russians negotiate in the same way they play chess, planning several moves ahead" (Richmond, 1996, pp. 150–151).

Pragmatic Rules

The **pragmatic rules** (or **pragmatics**) of a language refer to the contextual rules that govern language usage in a particular culture. Pragmatics concerns the rules of "how to say what to whom and under what situational conditions" in a speech community (Hymes, 1972). A **speech community** is defined as a group of individuals who share a common set of normative expectations and communication rules regarding appropriate or inappropriate interaction practices in a community (Byram, 2009; Carbaugh, 1996; Lee & Park, 2011; Philipsen, 1997, 2010).

Let's check out the following critical incident in Blog Post 6.2.

BLOG POST 6.2

Amaya works in the English Tutorial Lab on campus at Seoul University and spends a lot of time discussing the subtleties and intricacies of English with Korean students. She loves her job and finds each day she learns something new from the students who stop by for some advice. For the last year, Amaya had worked closely with Seung-Ho on improving his writing skills in his English technical papers. She felt at ease with Seung-Ho and felt she could tell jokes and make observations about Korean life in general and Seung-Ho would respond back with a hearty laugh.

One day in the cafeteria, Amaya saw Seung-Ho and his guy friends eating lunch. She stopped by to say hello and see how he was doing. Seung-Ho introduced his friends to Amaya and said, "Amaya, my girlfriend is coming here soon and I want you to meet her. She will be writing her first English analytical paper and I encouraged her to talk with you. Will you be at work later?"

Amaya smiled and replied, "Of course, Seung-Ho, no problem. If I can change the way you use the word from 'totally' to 'completely' in your research papers then I can work with any hot mess! Come by before five." Seung-Ho was visibly upset by this comment. He excused himself with as much politeness as possible and left the table with a sullen face. Amaya left the cafeteria in complete confusion.

If Amaya asked for your help to understand this communication episode, how would you analyze the intercultural interaction? Your analysis could include any of the following possible explanations: (1) Seung-Ho was testing Amaya to see if she was interested in him—Amaya's enthusiasm to meet his girlfriend irritated him and caught him off guard; (2) In South Korea the politeness norm is to pay attention to the gender hierarchy—Amaya did not show enough cultural sensitivity to Seung-Ho and his guy friends; (3) Seung-Ho interpreted Amaya's remarks as offensive and insulting.

What would be your analysis of this communication incident? You can answer number (1), (2), or (3). However, if you choose (3), congratulations! Amaya's remark (i.e., "I can work with any hot mess!") was negatively interpreted by Seung-Ho. The term "hot mess" can have at least two meanings. "Hot" has a feature of temperature and "mess" has a feature of organization. When we combine "hot + mess," the concept takes on a whole new meaning. Amaya used the idiomatic term "hot mess," as in the context of having thoughts being in disarray but maintaining some beauty in a very informal, American English way. However, "hot mess" also describes a situation, behavior, or someone's appearance that is disastrously distasteful. Seung-Ho must have thought that this was the meaning Amaya had in mind. He probably felt that the remark sounded patronizing and also caused him to lose face in front of his Korean guy friends.

Amaya and Seung-Ho actually have two language problems here: the semantic problem and the pragmatic problem. The semantic problem is caused by the different meaning interpretations of the term "hot mess." The pragmatic problem is that Seung-Ho perceived Amaya's remark about his use of "totally" and "hot mess" as out of context and insulting, especially in front of his friends.

What can Amaya do now? After hearing your language analysis, Amaya may want to use a perception check with Seung-Ho. She may want to approach Seung-Ho and apologize for her unintended unconsciously incompetent behavior. Amaya may ask probing questions about Seung-Ho's sudden exit and sullen expression. Seung-Ho may also take the initiative to reflect on his own confusion concerning Amaya's rude comment. Seung-Ho may raise his own awareness and realize perhaps he misinterpreted the term "hot mess." Seung-Ho may tell Amaya that he doesn't mind that she jokes with him in English on a one-to-one basis in the English Tutorial Lab setting; however, in the public cafeteria setting, he doesn't want his friends or professors to witness their casual bantering style.

Someone learning a new language will have difficulty understanding something so subtle as what happened between Amaya and Seung-Ho—unless a culturally sensitive language tutor can explain the semantic meaning and the pragmatic rule of the phrase. Furthermore, Amaya may really need to polish her understanding of the pragmatic rule of whether to use informal English in front of ingroup or outgroup members when interacting with Seung-Ho. The truth is that most people learning or even teaching the language do not have this kind of opportunity to reflect so carefully on these rules.

Paying close attention to the multilayered rules of everyday language usage in a new culture may be a good start to move you from conversing at the unconscious incompetence stage to the conscious incompetence stage and, hopefully, lead to the conscious competence staircase level. Linguistic rules give rise to the diverse functions of languages across cultures and answer the question of why language plays such a critical role within each culture (Dougherty, Mobley, & Smith, 2010; Park & Guan, 2007, 2009). Language is an integral part of both a sense of identity and the mindset that goes with it.

APPRECIATING DIVERSE LANGUAGE FUNCTIONS

Cultural value orientations drive language usage in everyday lives. If a culture has a high individualism value index (e.g., Canada and Ireland), words and phrases such as "I," "me," "my goal," "my opinion," "self-help," and "self-service" tend to appear as part of everyday parlance. If a culture has a high collectivism value index (e.g., Costa Rica and Nigeria), phrases such as "our work team," "our goal," "our future together," and "we as a group" are part of the everyday lexicon.

In this section, we identify the diverse functions of languages across cultures as the cultural worldview function, the social reality function, the cognitive shaping function, the group identity function, and the social change function.

The Cultural Worldview Function

To really connect with a culture, we must understand the language of a cultural group. To understand language in context, we must understand the fundamental worldview that drives particular language reasoning processes in particular situations. **Worldview** refers to our larger philosophical outlook or ways of perceiving the world and how this outlook, in turn, affects our thinking and reasoning patterns. Intercultural experts have proposed two worldviews that divide Western and non-Western cultures: the linear worldview and the relational worldview (Stewart & Bennett, 2005).

A *linear worldview* emphasizes rational or analytical thinking that is based on an objective reality. A *relational worldview* emphasizes holistic or connected thinking that is based on a contextual reality. The language systems of the linear worldview tend to emphasize beginning with either facts and figures or models and theories and uses two reasoning patterns: inductive and deductive reasoning (see Table 6.1).

Inductive reasoning refers to the importance of facts and evidence to make a claim. Facts are important because they are objective. A claim is not valid until proven with concrete facts and tangible figures. The U.S. American reasoning process has been identified as following an inductive reasoning pattern or a linear inductive persuasion style. For example, any case that goes to trial in a U.S. court follows such a persuasion style in court. **Deductive reasoning**, on the other hand, refers to the primacy of conceptual models or big principles to start and then moves on to specific analytical points of inferences and factual conclusions. The European (e.g., France) to East European styles (e.g., Russia) of reasoning have been identified as reflective of a broadly deductive reasoning pattern (Stewart & Bennett, 2005). For example, the Russians will start with an agreement in principle (i.e., the big picture) and then fill in the details step

by step based on linear deductive reasoning process (Glenn, 1981).

Alternatively, the language systems of the *relational worldview* emphasize the importance of concerns about relational loyalty and trust, extended family connections, and ingroup membership dignity and honor. Thus, individuals operating from the relational worldview language system avoid the use of extreme polarized and direct wordings in their everyday interactions. For example, the Chinese language and worldview pattern avoids using the polarized ends (e.g., love–hate, good–evil, rich–poor) to comprehend the nature of the universe. Instead, the Chinese language pays close attention to the quality of the spectrum of emotional expressions (e.g., "not that bad," "I like," "I very like," "I not too like"), which in English are polarized (e.g., *like* and *dislike*).

The relational worldview language patterns also reinforce the notion of different forms of spiral reasoning styles—from the dramatic to the subtle. Members in many Arab cultures, for example, tend to use the **dramatic spiral reasoning** style such as effusive metaphors, stories, parables, and a wide range of flowery adjectives to reinforce a point. Thus, the dramatic conversation styles of many of the Arabic cultures often tend to emphasize image over digital content and form over function. Members of Italian, Slavic, Jewish, and many African cultures, for example, also have a tendency to use demonstrative speeches, vivacious similes, and spirited narratives to dramatize the emotional impact of their message. Many Asian and Native American cultures, however, may resort to using the **understated spiral reasoning** style, including subtle messages, implied hints, reserved talks, relational reasons, and tactful nonverbal gestures to convey an intended meaning and context. Blog Post 6.3 is a Zen story (Pearmain, 1998, p. 119) that illustrates an understated mode of storytelling.

The Everyday Social Reality Function

Everyday language serves as a prism or mirror through which individuals emphasize "important" versus "unimportant" events out there or "interesting" versus "uninteresting" value priorities in a cultural speech community. For example, in Mexico, Spanish words such as *machismo* (i.e., masculinity, physical

TABLE 6.1 LINEAR WORLDVIEW AND RELATIONAL WORLDVIEW: A COMPARISON

Linear worldview	Relational worldview
Rational thinking	Connected thinking
Objective reasoning	Context-based reasoning
Facts and evidence	Context and relationship
Polarized interpretation	Continuum interpretation
Analytical dissecting mode	Holistic big-picture mode
Tangible outcome	Long-term relational outcome

BLOG POST 6.3   A ZEN STORY

Once upon a time, two Buddhist monks were on a journey to a distant monastery when they came to a river. There on the bank sat a young woman. "I beg you," she asked, "could you carry me across? The current is strong today and I'm afraid I might be swept away."

The first monk remembered his vows never to look at or touch a woman, and so, without so much as a nod, he crossed through the heavily flowing currents and soon reached the other side. The other monk showed compassion and bent down so that the woman could climb upon his back to cross the river. Although she was slight, the current was strong and the rocky bottom made it difficult crossing. Reaching the other side, he let the woman down and went on his way.

After some hours journeying down the dusty road in silence, the first monk could no longer contain his anger at the second for breaking their vows. "How could you look at that woman?" he blurted out. "How could you touch her, let alone carry her across the river? You've put our reputation at stake."

The first monk looked at his companion and smiled. "I put that woman down way back there at the river bank, but I see that you're still carrying her."

What do you think of the above story? Can you rewrite the story to reflect a more linear mode of storytelling? Which persuasive mode do you prefer, the linear mode or the spiral mode? Why? In addition to the linear versus the spiral mode of persuasion, we can also consider the implications of the self-credentialing and self-humbling modes of persuasion.

strength, sexual attraction), *marianismo* (i.e., a woman's submissiveness, dependence, gentleness, and remaining a virgin until marriage), *respeto* (i.e., showing proper respect for authority, such as parents and elders), and *familismo* (i.e., the importance of family and the extended family network) infiltrate individuals' everyday social experiences, and they are used as yardsticks to measure self and others' appropriate role performance.

Our everyday language has repeated categories that capture our social experience and ultimately shape our cultural and gendered expectations (Brabant, Watson, & Gallois, 2010; Lee & Park, 2011). For example, the usage of everyday English idioms in the U.S. corporate world or in conflict context such as "That was a slam dunk," "This will be a game changer," and "Wow you hit that out of the park," reflect a strong doing and gaming metaphor in corporate U.S. culture.

Moreover, on the personal level, English speakers tend to use explicit pronouns of "I," you," and "my" to express an opinion or solicit an idea such as "I totally disagree with you," 'What do you think?" "I'm doing a fact check," or "My bad!" Furthermore, the term "self" is common in daily English, for example, self-service, self-help, self-made, self-regard, self-importance, self-interest, etc. which reflects the individualistic value motif. In contrast, Korean speakers use more implicit and ambiguous words. Instead of appearing to be assertive, they use more qualifiers such as "maybe," "perhaps," "probably," "excuse me," or "sorry" at the beginning of a sentence in substitution for the explicit use of the "I" pronoun in an up-front manner.

The Cognitive Shaping Function

Language also serves as a strong filter between what we think and how our thinking pattern is shaped by the grammatical structure of our language system. Benjamin Whorf (1952, 1956), drawing from the work of his mentor, Edward Sapir (1921), tested the "language is a shaper of ideas" hypothesis. By comparing the Hopi Indian language with European languages, Whorf (1952) found that language is not only a vehicle for voicing ideas but also "the shaper of ideas." He further emphasized that the grammatical structure of a language shapes and constitutes one's thought process. This grammatical structure is entirely culture based and, as such, language, thinking, and culture are integral parts of a mindset system.

Whorf cited several examples from the Hopi language: (1) The Hopi language does not possess a discrete past–present–future grammatical system as in most European languages; instead, it has a wide range of present tenses based on the observations of the speaker, such as "I know that she is sleeping at this very moment" or "I am told that she is sleeping." (2) The Hopi language does not use a cyclic noun, such as "days" or "years," in the same manner as countable quantities, such as eight women or eight men; instead, it emphasizes the concept of "duration" when conceiving time. Thus, the Hopi equivalent for the English statement "They stayed eight days" is "I know that they stay until the seventh day." (3) English speakers tend to use spatial metaphors in their sentences (e.g., "time is up," "I'm on top of it," or "I'm running low"), but the Hopi language tends to emphasize events that are happening in the here and now.

By linking cultural worldview and thought pattern together, one achieves the Sapir–Whorf hypothesis, also known as the *linguistic relativity hypothesis*. The grammars of different languages constitute separate conceptual realities for members of different cultures. We experience different thoughts and sensations via our linguistic systems. For example, the structure of the future tense in Spanish tells us a great deal about the notion of the future in Spain. In Spanish, statements made about the future signal probability rather than certainty. A Spanish speaker will prefer the statement closer to the English "I may go to the market" (*"Puedo ir al mercado"*) instead of "I will go to the market" to indicate the probability of an action in the future rather than the certainty of that action. The future, for many Spanish-speaking people, represents an unknown in time and space: many things can happen later this afternoon or tomorrow—they are beyond the control of individuals.

After reviewing extensive studies on the Sapir–Whorf hypothesis, Steinfatt (1989) concluded that although the *weak* form (i.e., language helps to shape our thinking patterns) of the linguistic relativity hypothesis received some support, no conclusive evidence can be drawn to support the *strong* form (i.e., language completely determines our thinking patterns). Sapir and Whorf were trailblazing pioneers in linking language with culture and, as such, they left a major contribution to the study of intercultural communication.

The Group Membership Identity Function

Language represents a rallying point for evoking group sentiment and shared identity. Language serves the larger cultural–ethnic identity function because it is an emblem of group solidarity. In speaking a common

tongue, members signal ingroup ties and outgroup separation. The core symbols and linguistic categories of a group often express ethnic and nationalistic sentiment. By virtue of its powerful and visible symbolism, language maintenance issues are worth fighting and dying for—from many ethnic groups' perspectives. For example, the disputes between Anglophones and Francophones over the use of English or French in Canada's Quebec province and the heated debates over whether Pidgin and Ebonics (i.e., Hawaiian English and Black English) are languages or dialects in the United States reflect the significant role of the group membership function of language. The debate over Ebonics recently reignited in 2010 when the U. S. Drug Enforcement Administration announced it was hiring nine Ebonics translators to assist them with their drug enforcement efforts in the southeastern United States. "Unfortunately, the use of the term 'Ebonics' in the public sphere raises a red flag," said Walt Wolfram, linguistics professor at North Carolina State University. "(T)he term has been politicized and racialized" (McDonald, 2010).

Some cultural members develop enormous membership loyalty to and pride in speaking their native tongue, but other members derive tremendous flexibility in their ability to code-switch. Code-switching means switching to another language or dialect to increase or decrease intergroup distance. For example, many African Americans have developed different verbal strategies to deal with the stigma attached to Black English (or Ebonics—*ebony* and *phonics*) by the dominant group. Black English is a distinctive rule-governed language (Hecht, Collier, & Ribeau, 1993; Hecht & Ribeau, 1984) that gained public attention in 1996 as a result of a proposal by the Oakland California School Board to use African American English in teaching Standard English in the Oakland School District (Applebome, 1996). Many African Americans are able to code-switch using mainstream American English in formal or work-related settings and then switch to Black English with familiar others in casual settings for the purpose of forging group identity and connection (Helms, 1993; Parham & Helms, 1985).

On purely linguistic grounds, all languages are created equal. However, in all linguistic struggles, a fierce competition exists: "Not between languages themselves but, rather, between language communities or linguistic interest groups" (Edwards, 1994, p. 205). Matters of group membership, power, and status interlock with societal perceptions to form attitudes toward different language varieties in the larger cultural context.

The Social Change Function

Twenty years ago, we did not have words like *texting, ipad,* and *refudiate* or use *Facebook* or *Google* as verbs. They are now part of our everyday vocabulary. As innovative social beings, we are the creators of the social tool of human language. We are also at times trapped by the habits of our own linguistic system.

Let's do the my.blog 6.1 poll here before you read on.

Although some people may assume that women are included in such male generic terms as *mankind,* research has demonstrated conclusively that "masculine generics are perceived as referring predominantly or exclusively to men. When people hear them, they think of men, not women" (Wood, 2004, p. 152). For example, the use of male generic language in English—words such as *businessman* or *fireman* used in Western society or the use of "man" in the Bible that refers to gender inclusivity—tends to elevate men's experience as more valid and make women's experience less prominent. To the extent that the language of a culture makes men appear more visible and concurrently makes women seem invisible, the perceptions generated from such biased language usage create biased thinking. By flexibly changing some of our linguistic habits (e.g., changing *fireman* to *firefighter, mankind* to *humankind*), we can start transforming our thinking patterns through the use of gender-equitable terms.

Beyond language habit change, two interesting trends are taking place. The first interesting trend is the language change in the U.S. sports and global social scenes. For example, in the United States, it is common for a sports fan to hear one minute left to go as "a buck" and seconds as "change." With 1:12 left in a game, you can say "there is a buck and change left in the game." On the international language change scene is the issue of language borrowing. For example, in Malyasia, "gwai-lo size" refers to a very large "Western size" portion of food. In the indigenous communities around the town of Juchitán, Mexico, local Zapotec people have made room for a third category of sexual orientation, which they call "muxes" (pronounced MOO-shays). Muxes, derived from the Spanish "mujer," or woman are men who consider themselves women and live in a socially sanctioned netherworld between the two genders (Lacey, 2008). Or if one is on the Internet, Germans will say "im Internet surfen" (*"Pukka German,"* 2011). Global language borrowing can indicate an ingroup connection and solidarity function, an added status, or a necessary convenience.

The second interesting trend under the social change heading is integrating brand names into everyday language and, as a result, you cannot tell the product from the brand. In the South (Texas, Oklahoma), ordering a Coke refers to any soft drink. In Latin America, when people want a pack of razors, they ask for "Gillettes;" if they want a whirlpool bath, they ask for a "Jacuzzi" (Bianchi & Sama, 2003). Domestically, with an increase in the popularity of rap music, English is now up for grabs. Called a new "bilingual" English, this is a way for street kids, or the music industry, to promote the inclusion of the slang and jargon of rap music into everyday vocabulary.

To close this section, let's check out how much social change has occurred in your Internet linguistic literacy. Do you know what the following abbreviations ALAP, 420, FTW, and NSFW stand for in cyberspace? Check out the answers in Hit-or-Miss 6.1.

---

my.blog 6.1

Using your gut-level response, whom do you picture when you read the following words? Circle your answer quickly.

Businessman?	Man	Woman
Nurse?	Man	Woman
Technician?	Man	Woman
Cook?	Man	Woman
Mailman?	Man	Woman
Librarian?	Man	Woman
Fireman?	Man	Woman
Stewardess?	Man	Woman
Freshman?	Man	Woman
Mankind?	Man	Woman

VERBAL COMMUNICATION STYLES: A GENERAL FRAMEWORK

Before you continue reading, let's do my.blog 6.2 to check out your verbal style preference.

Why did you find some of the behaviors irritating? Where did you acquire your own verbal habits or rituals? What cultural or personal values influence your verbal styles? Do you notice any style differences between females and males in your culture? How so? Do you communicate very similarly in different situations? Or do you switch your verbal styles to adapt to different interaction situations?

Defining Low-Context and High-Context Interaction Patterns

Hall (1976) claimed that human interaction, on a broad level, can be divided into low-context and high-context communication systems. In **low-context communication**, the emphasis is on how intention or meaning is expressed through explicit verbal messages. In **high-context communication**, the emphasis is on how intention or meaning can best be conveyed through the embedded contexts (e.g., social roles or positions, relationship types, intergroup history) and the nonverbal channels (e.g., pauses, silence, tone of voice) of the verbal message (see Table 6.2).

In general, low-context communication (LCC) refers to communication patterns of direct, matter-of-fact tone, transparency, assertiveness, and sender-oriented values (i.e., the sender assumes the responsibility to communicate clearly). In the LCC system, the speaker is expected to be responsible for constructing a clear, persuasive message that the listener can decode easily. The value priority in the LCC style is "say what you mean, mean what you say" as a mode of respect for verbal honesty and personal accountability. In comparison, high-context communication (HCC) refers to communication patterns of indirect, tactful nonverbal tone, diplomatic talk, self-humbling speech, and receiver-sensitive values (i.e., the interpreter of the message assumes the responsibility to infer the hidden or contextual meanings of the message [Ting-Toomey, 1985]). In the HCC system, the listener or interpreter of the message is expected to "read between the lines" and infer the nonverbal subtleties that accompany the verbal message. The value priority in the HCC style is "don't say anything that will hurt the other's feelings" as a mode of interpersonal sensitivity for other-centric consideration (see country examples of LCC and HCC in Table 6.3). Of course, the broad-based LCC and HCC communication style

TABLE 6.2 LOW-CONTEXT COMMUNICATION (LCC) AND HIGH-CONTEXT COMMUNICATION (HCC): VERBAL PATTERNS

LCC patterns	HCC patterns
Individualistic values	Collectivistic values
Linear logic	Spiral logic
Direct verbal style	Indirect verbal style
Matter-of-fact tone	Understated or animated tone
Informal verbal style	Formal verbal style
Verbal assertiveness or talkativeness	Verbal reticence or silence

TABLE 6.3 COUNTRY EXAMPLES OF LOW-CONTEXT AND HIGH-CONTEXT COMMUNICATION

LCC examples	←———————→		HCC examples
Germany	USA	Saudi Arabia	Japan
Switzerland	Canada	Kuwait	China
Denmark	Australia	Mexico	South Korea
Sweden	UK	Nigeria	Vietnam

L-CHAT 6.1

KALENE (knocks on her neighbor's screen door): Excuse me, it's past 11 o'clock already, and your loud music and dancing around are really disturbing my sleep. Please stop your jumping and banging around right away! I have an important job interview tomorrow morning, and I want to get a good night's sleep. Some of us *do* need to pay rent!

KAINOA (resentfully): Well, this is the only time I can rehearse! I have an important audition coming up tomorrow. You're not the only one that's starving, you know. I also need to pay my rent. Stop being so petty!

KALENE (frustrated): I really think YOU'RE being VERY ANNOYING and INTRUSIVE! There is an apartment noise ordinance, you know. And if you don't stop banging around immediately, I'm going to file a complaint with the apartment manager and he could evict you . . .

KAINOA (sarcastically and turning up the music louder): Whatever! Do what you want. I'm going to practice as loud as I want. Don't bother to ask for my autograph when I become a Hollywood star!

L-CHAT 6.2

MRS. TRAN: Hello, Mrs. Nguyen. . . . Your son Minh-Ha is entering his high school karaoke contest, isn't he? I envy you, because you must be so proud of his talent. You must be looking forward to his future as a pop singer. . . . I'm really impressed by his enthusiasm—every day, he practices so hard, for hours and hours, until late at night . . .

MRS. NGUYEN: Oh, I'm so sorry . . . Minh-Ha is just a beginner in karaoke singing. We don't know his future yet. . . . He is such a silly boy singing so late. We didn't realize you can hear all the noise next door. I'll tell him to stop right away. I'm so sorry about all your trouble, it won't happen again.

---

usage also varies—dependent strongly also on generational ethnic identity issues, individual-level personality traits, relationship types, interaction goals, and situational contexts.

LCC is illustrated by the following dispute between two European American neighbors in L-Chat 6.1.

In contrast, the following interaction in L-Chat 6.2 involving two Japanese housewives illustrates their use of *HCC*.

In L-Chat 6.1, Kalene and Kainoa spell out everything that is on their minds with no restraints. Their interaction exchange is direct, to the point, bluntly contentious, and full of face-threat verbal messages. L-Chat 6.1 represents one possible low-context way of approaching a disagreement. Although the first example represents an unproductive scenario, Kalene and Kainoa might actually turn their dialog around and obtain a more productive outcome by identifying their common interests (e.g., urgency of the job search or rent payment due) and exploring other constructive options (e.g., closing the windows or practicing in another room). They can use the strengths of low-context, "explicit talk" in dealing with the disagreement openly and nonevaluatively.

In L-Chat 6.2, Mrs. Tran has not directly expressed her concern over Minh-Ha's singing with Mrs. Nguyen because she wants to preserve her face and friendship. Mrs. Nguyen correctly "catches the drift" and apologizes appropriately and effectively before any real conflict with Mrs. Tran escalates. L-Chat 6.2 represents one possible high-context way of approaching a disagreement because even a minor disagreement is perceived as a major face-threat situation. If Mrs. Tran were the neighbor of Kainoa in L-Chat 6.1, Kainoa might not be able to read between the lines of Mrs. Tran's verbal and, more important, nonverbal message. Kainoa might be clueless that a disagreement was simmering between them and might actually take Mrs. Tran's verbal message literally as a compliment—and continue late-night practices!

Overall, LCC patterns emphasize direct talk, self-enhancement, informal interaction, and the value of talkativeness. In comparison, HCC patterns stress indirect verbal style, verbal self-humbling pattern, status-sensitive formal interaction, and the importance of silence (see, for example, Park & Guan, 2006, 2009; Park, Lee, & Song, 2005). The following sections discuss in detail some of these low-context and high-context verbal habits in different cultures

Direct and Indirect Verbal Styles

Mannerism of speaking frames *how* a message should be interpreted or understood on a continuum. Individuals in all cultures use all of these verbal styles to a certain degree, depending on assumed identities, intentions, interaction goals, relationship types, and the situation. However, in individualistic cultures, people tend to encounter more situations that emphasize direct talk. In contrast, in collectivistic cultures, people tend to encounter more situations that emphasize the use of indirect talk.

The direct and indirect styles differ in how they reveal the speaker's intentions through tone of voice and the straightforwardness of the content in the message. In the **direct style**, statements tend to reveal the speaker's intentions with clarity and are enunciated with a forthright tone of voice. In the **indirect style**, statements tend to camouflage the speaker's actual intentions and are carried out with a softer tone. For example, the overall U.S. American style often calls for clear and direct communication. Phrases such as "give me the bottom line," "call it like you see it," and "what's your point?" are some examples. In contrast, in a request situation, U.S. Americans tend to use a straightforward form of request, but Koreans tend to ask for a favor in a more roundabout and implicit way to sound not so imposing or demanding. The Koreans are not the only indirect group. Let's demonstrate a pair of contrastive "airport ride request" scenes in L-Chats 6.3 and 6.4 between two Irish Americans and two Latinas:

In the Latina conversation, requests for help are likely to be implied rather than stated explicitly and directly. Indirect requests can help both parties to save face and uphold smooth harmonious interaction. When Daniela detects a request during a conversation with Essie, she can choose to offer help, pretend she does not understand the request, or apologize that she cannot take Essie to the airport with a good reason. An implicit understanding generally exists between

---

L-CHAT 6.3

ALAINE: We're going to the Orange Bowl in Miami this weekend.

PATRICK: What fun! I wish I were going to the game with you. How long are you going to be there? [*If she wants a ride, she will ask.*]

ALAINE: Three days. By the way, we may need a ride to the airport. Do you think you can take us?

PATRICK: Sure. What time?

ALAINE: 10:30 p.m. this coming Saturday.

PATRICK: All right. No problem.

L-CHAT 6.4

ESSIE: We're going to the Orange Bowl in Miami this weekend.

DANIELA: What fun! I wish I were going to the game with you. How long are you going to be there?

ESSIE: Three days. [*I hope she'll offer me a ride to the airport.*]

DANIELA: [*She may want me to give her a ride.*] Do you need a ride to the airport? I'll take you.

ESSIE: Are you sure it's not too much trouble?

DANIELA: It's no trouble at all.

two high-context communicators. They do not need to overtly state their request or use an overt "no" to state their opinion overtly, thus hurting the feelings of the other high-context collectivist.

Intercultural misunderstanding, however, becomes highly probable when Essie communicates with Patrick. They each rely on their own cultural scripts to inform them of what to expect in the interaction. Let's look at L-Chat 6.5 of the "airport ride request" dialog, this time between Essie and Patrick (adapted from Gao & Ting-Toomey, 1998, p. 77).

It should be obvious that Essie emphasizes the indirect verbal style and Patrick emphasizes direct verbal style. Because neither has knowledge of high-context and low-context differences, a misunderstanding is inevitable. In high-context conversations, negative responses, such as "No," or "I disagree with you," or "I cannot do it" are not stated overtly. Instead, apologetic expressions with qualifying reasons, delayed decisions, or indirect expressions are used.

If the conversational patterns of people from different cultural or ethnic groups at some point annoy you, think about the stylistic level of conversation. For example, although the British are indirect in comparison with U.S. Americans, the Japanese would not find them to be in the least bit indirect. Becoming flexible intercultural communicators means fluid code-switching between the low-context and high-context message system on both the verbal and the nonverbal

levels and in accordance with the situational norms and rules of the cultural context.

Self-Enhancement and Self-Humbling Verbal Styles

Another verbal pattern is the spectrum between self-enhancement and self-humbling verbal style. The **self-enhancement style** emphasizes the importance of drawing attention to or exaggerating one's credentials, outstanding accomplishments, and special abilities. The **self-humbling style**, on the other hand, emphasizes the importance of downplaying oneself via modest talk, restraint, hesitation, and the use of self-deprecation message concerning one's performance or effort. For example, let's check out L-Chat 6.6, a conversation between Bernardo Lara, who is from Puerto Rico, and Pierre LaFont, who is from Switzerland.

Verbal self-humbling or self-effacement is a necessary part of Puerto Rican American politeness rituals. In Swiss or U.S. culture, we encourage individuals to "sell themselves and boast about their achievements." Otherwise, in a performance review or job interview session, who would notice the accomplishments from a self-effacing individual? However, the notion of merchandising oneself does not sit well with many Latin American, Asian, and Native American groups. "After 25 years working for California Transportation," says Dai, a retired worker, "I thought I would be given a window when we moved offices. I never got one. I assumed my supervisors would see that I deserved it. I never asked." Dai believed that if his performance is exceptional, his supervisors will notice his stellar performance and take appropriate, appreciative action. However, from the Western cultural standpoint, an exceptional performance must be documented with concrete evidence and in an explicit manner to catch the attention of busy supervisors. This difference is probably caused by the observational-centric value of the collectivistic HCC pattern, as opposed to the sender-centric value of the Western LCC pattern.

All cultural characterizations and comparisons are in the eye of the beholder more than with the behavior of the beheld—these are relative differences

---

L-CHAT 6.5

ESSIE: We're going to the Orange Bowl in Miami this weekend.

PATRICK: What fun! I wish we were going to the game with you. How long are you going to be there?

ESSIE: Three days. [*I hope he'll offer me a ride to the airport.*]

PATRICK: [*If she wants a ride, she'll ask me.*] Well, have a great time.

ESSIE: [If he had wanted to give me a ride, he would have offered it. I'd better ask somebody else.] Thanks. I'll see you when I get back.

L-CHAT 6.6

BERNARDO LARA: Thanks for making the time to see me, Mr. LaFont.

PIERRE LaFONT: What's on your mind?

BERNARDO: Well, I heard from Haeme, the production assistant, that there will be open auditions for the new play But Can He Dance?

PIERRE: Yes, this is true.

BERNARDO: Well, I think this is good. It's an excellent play.

PIERRE: Yes?

BERNARDO: Well, I've been working on designing sets for the past four years, and all have been well received. My work in this theater has never faltered, and I never missed work. [pause] See, I was hoping to get a chance to audition. And since this play is so close to my experience . . .

PIERRE: Oh! You want to audition. I understand. Why do you want this part?

BERNARDO: Well, as I said, I enjoyed the play. And I always wanted to get my foot into the acting business . . .

PIERRE: But you're an amazing set designer. Why are you qualified for this role?

BERNARDO: Actually, the role would give me more money. I have my sister's children who will come to live with me. They need to attend a better high school and college. With more money, I can at least afford to have them both stay in my house.

PIERRE: Bernardo, are you serious? You want this role because you have kids coming to live with you? There are many people who have qualifications in acting, such as degrees and training. So this doesn't make any sense to me at all!

BERNARDO: But Mr. LaFont, I've worked overtime, triple time, covered people who were sick, and never shrugged off any of my duties. I just wanted a chance to audition for this role.

PIERRE: Bernardo, who will design the set?!

Beliefs Expressed in Talk and Silence

Words like violence
Break the silence
Come crashing in
Into my little world
Painful to me
Pierce right through me
Can't you understand . . .

Depeche Mode, "Enjoy the Silence," 1991

This British single of 1991 captures the momentary need for peace and quiet that will be ruined with words. Silence can oftentimes say as much, if not more, than words. Although silence occurs in interaction contexts in cultures around the world, how silence is interpreted and evaluated differs across cultures and between persons. Hall (1983) claims that silence, or *ma*, serves as a critical communication device in many Native American and Asian communication patterns. *Ma* is much more than pausing between words; rather, it is like a semicolon that reflects the inner pausing of the speaker's thoughts. Through *ma*, interpersonal understanding is made possible in many high-context cultures. Although silence may hold strong contextual meanings in high-context cultures, prolonged silence is often viewed as "empty pauses" or "ignorant lapses" in the Western rhetorical model.

From the high-context perspective, silence can be the essence of the language of superiority and inferiority, affecting such relationships as teacher–student, male–female, and supervisor–employee. The process of refraining from speaking can have both positive and negative effects. In some situations, such as members in the Apache, Navajo, and Papago Indian tribes, silence is appropriate in contexts where social relations between individuals are unpredictable, role expectations are unclear, and relations involve high levels of ambiguity (Basso, 1970; Covarrubias, 2007).

Do you use talk to "break the ice" and reserve silence for your most intimate relationships? If so, this is typical of European American styles. In France people tend to engage in animated conversations to affirm the nature of their established relationships; in the absence of any such relationship, silence serves

between cultural and ethnic groups, not absolute differences. By understanding such nuanced and layered differences, we can learn to accept or even to adapt to some of these culture-based verbal style differences.

the French as a neutral communication process. This is why in the elevator, in the street, or on the bus, people don't talk to each other readily in France. This is a seemingly inexhaustible source of misunderstanding between the French and U.S. Americans, especially because "these rules are suspended under exceptional circumstances and on vacation (and therefore on the train, on the plane)....U.S. Americans often feel rejected, disapproved of, criticized, or scorned without understanding the reason for this hostility" (Carroll, 1987, p. 30).

The mode of speaking, in short, reflects the overall values and norms of a culture. The cultural modes of speaking in many speech communities reflect the hierarchical social order, family socialization, asymmetrical role positions, and power distance values of the different cultures. Intercultural miscommunication can thus often occur because of the different priorities placed on talk and silence by different groups. Silence can serve various functions, depending on the type of relationship, the interactive situation, and the particular cultural beliefs held. Silence can also serve as a powerful means of sharing or persuasion.

INTERCULTURAL REALITY CHECK: DO-ABLES

In this chapter, we've explored the diverse features, rules, and functions of language across cultures. We have identified four distinctive language features (arbitrariness, abstractness, meaning-centeredness, and creativity), discussed the five functions of the relationship between language and culture (cultural worldview, social reality, cognitive shaping, group membership identity, and social change functions), and explained the particular characteristics of low- versus high-context verbal communication patterns. Listed here are some checkpoints for you to communicate flexibly when you are using your native language (e.g., English) when communicating with a nonnative English-speaking audience or individuals with a different communication style. To be flexible verbal communicators, try to practice the following guidelines:

- *Understand languaculture.* Have a basic grasp of the features of the languaculture that you will be encountering. *Languaculture* emphasizes the necessary interdependent tie between language and culture (Agar, 1994). The rule patterns of a particular language, from syntactic rules to semantic rules, reflect a speaker's worldviews, values, and premises.
- *Practice verbal tracking.* Pay close attention to the content meaning of the message. Remember that everyone speaks with an accent. Move beyond the accent and track the intended content meaning of the speaker.
- *Practice verbal patience.* Use verbal empathy and patience for nonnative speakers from a different culture. We can try to slow our pace, choose less complex words, consciously pause, and try to rephrase restatements to convey the same intended content meanings.
- *Pay attention to nonverbal tone of voice.* You can be saying the same words; however, your tone of voice can convey your intercultural patience or impatience, receptivity or skepticism. The tone of voice often expresses relational and identity meaning of your verbal content message.
- *Use multiple modes of presentation.* Use visual restatements, such as pictures, graphs, gestures, or written summaries, to reinforce your points. Likewise, if you sojourn to another country, use similar strategies to cross-check for understanding of the meaning of the message from your target audience.
- *Master the cultural pragmatic rules.* Understand the importance of pragmatic rules—you can be linguistically fluent in another culture but still act unconsciously incompetent!
- *Understand the basic differences of low-context and high-context communication patterns.* Be aware of your own ethnocentric tendency to negatively evaluate the opposing high-context and low-context interaction characteristics.
- *Practice verbal code-switching mindfully.* Both low-context and high-context communicators need to practice the figure-eight dance of switching fluently between low-context style and high-context style

in accordance with situational norms, individual relationship distance, communication intention, and desired outcome.

Intercultural miscommunications often occur because individuals use cultural-laden linguistic habits to communicate and interpret each other's verbal messages. Fortunately, by staying flexible in our intercultural verbal encoding and decoding process, we may be able to catch our own verbal mistakes or miscomprehensions. To be flexible intercultural communicators, we must understand the combined package of *both* verbal and non-verbal communication styles to promote better intercultural understanding

CHAPTER 7

WHAT ARE THE DIFFERENT WAYS TO COMMUNICATE NONVERBALLY ACROSS CULTURES?

CHAPTER OUTLINE

- The Impact of Nonverbal Communication
  - Making Sense of Nonverbal Communication
  - One Code, Countless Interpretations
  - Verbal and Nonverbal Comparisons

- Forms of Nonverbal Communication
  - Physical Appearance
  - Paralanguage
  - Facial Expressions
  - Gestures
  - Haptics

- Boundary Regulations
  - Regulating Interpersonal Boundaries
  - Environmental Boundaries
  - Psychological Boundaries
  - Regulating Time

- Intercultural Reality Check: Do-Ables

All of us, a thousand times a day, read faces. When someone says "I love you," we look into that person's eyes to judge his or her sincerity. When we meet someone new, we often pick up on subtle signals, so that even though he or she may have talked in a normal and friendly manner, afterward we say, "I don't think he liked me," or "I don't think she's very happy." We easily parse complex distinctions in facial expression. If you saw me grinning, for example, with my eyes twinkling, you'd say I was amused. But that's not the only way we interpret a smile. If you saw me nod and smile exaggeratedly, with the corners of my lips tightened, you would take it that I had been teased and was responding sarcastically. If I made eye contact with someone, gave a small smile and then looked down and averted my gaze, you would think I was flirting. . . . The face is such an extraordinarily efficient instrument of communication that there must be rules that govern the way we interpret facial expressions. But what are those rules? And are they the same for everyone?

—Malcolm Gladwell, 2002

As you can see in the example above, nonverbal communication is both a conscious and an unconscious aspect of our everyday life. We can communicate with people in total silence but still convey many complex emotions. We take for granted the importance of our facial expressions, not realizing the impact a smile can make during an introduction, a sales pitch, or an argument.

Nonverbal messages serve many functions in intercultural situations. If our verbal messages convey the literal and content meanings of words, then nonverbal messages carry the undercurrent of strong identity and relational meaning. For example, nonverbal communication has been called a "relationship code" because nonverbal cues are often the primary means of signaling a relationship with others. We use nonverbal cues to relate messages that may be too embarrassing or direct to disclose out loud. The use of verbal messages involves human intention, but nonverbal messages can be intentional or unintentional. For example, a popular pair of blue jeans on the market today is a brand called Mavi. Mavi, which means blue in Turkish, is a blue jean company based in Turkey. If you wear these jeans in places where people speak Swahili (Tanzania and Kenya), many people may look at you in horror or laugh out loud. The name of your jeans in Swahili means "cow dung!"

Nonverbal communication occurs with or without verbal messages. Nonverbal messages provide the context for how the accompanying verbal message should be interpreted and understood. They can either create confusion or clarify communication. But more often than not, nonverbal messages can create intercultural friction and miscommunication because (1) the same nonverbal signal can mean different things to different people in different cultures, (2) multiple nonverbal cues are sent, and (3) there are many display rule variations to consider, such as personality, gender, relational distance, socioeconomic status, and situation.

This chapter is organized in four sections. We first discuss the nature of nonverbal communication. We then address different forms of nonverbal communication with many lively intercultural examples. Third, we discuss an important area of nonverbal communication: boundary regulation of space and time. We conclude with a set of do-ables, reality checkpoints to facilitate better understanding of nonverbal intercultural communication.

THE IMPACT OF NONVERBAL COMMUNICATION

Nonverbal communication is a powerful form of human expression. It is everywhere, omnipresent, affecting aspects of our lives. Nonverbal messages are often the primary means of signaling our emotions, our attitudes, and the nature of our relationships with others. These messages can be intentional or intentional, quick to read, or oblivious in meaning. Suppose Miki spots Abdul in a café surrounded by his books and iPad, talking on his cell, and sitting with a friend. As she prepares to walk away, Abdul glances up and nods at Miki. "Oh, I really wanted to come over and say hi, but you look really busy!" Did Abdul send an unintentional nonverbal message? Sometimes we signal messages that were not intended, like "do not disturb me." On the other hand, if Miki approached Abdul's table and as soon as she made eye contact Abdul quickly looked away, is this message intentional? Miki may interpret this as an "I'm too busy" or "I'm not interested right now" message. Within two seconds, nonverbal messages can oftentimes express what verbal messages cannot express—and they are assumed to be more truthful than verbal messages. Many nonverbal experts estimate that in every encounter, about 65 percent of the meaning of a message is inferred through nonverbal channels (Burgoon, Guerrero, & Floyd, 2010). Nonverbal messages signify who we are, based on what we wear, how we speak, and how we present ourselves.

Just how important is nonverbal communication? Think about our sensitivity to air travel and terrorism attacks in our airports. Around the world, countries are investing in various measures to ensure the safety of their citizens. The failed 2010 Christmas Day attack on a U.S. airliner triggered a new wave of scrutiny of the U.S. government's approach to aviation security. Airport screeners are now trained by the Federal Bureau of Investigation (FBI) to look for deception clues during routine questioning. In Canada and the United States, undercover agents are being trained to recognize any suspicious behavior. Vancouver has specially trained airport screeners walking around the airport looking out for suspicious nonverbal behavior (Burritt, 2011). In the United States, thousands of undercover air marshals are trained to spot behavioral signs of stress, fear, and deception (*Profile: Training of Air Marshals*, 2010).

Making Sense of Nonverbal Communication

Nonverbal communication is defined as the message exchange process involving the use of nonlinguistic and paralinguistic cues that are expressed through multiple communication channels in a particular sociocultural setting. *Nonlinguistic cues* can include nonverbal eye contact, smiles, touch, hand gestures, or even silence. *Paralinguistic cues* refer to the tone of voice, pitch, or volume of the sounds that accompany a verbal message. *Multiple channels* refer to how the meaning of nonverbal messages can be simultaneously signaled and interpreted through various outlets such as facial expressions, body movements, voice characteristics, hand gestures, spatial relationships, and the temporal and physical environment in which people are communicating. *Sociocultural setting* emphasizes the importance of how cultural norms and expectations shape the standards by which we evaluate nonverbal appropriateness or inappropriateness in a particular cultural situation (Santilli & Miller, 2011).

In essence, nonverbal communication transcends spoken or written words (Hickson, Stacks, & Moore, 2004). Our culture shapes the display rules of when, with whom, what, where, and how different emotions should be expressed or suppressed. Nonverbal display rules are learned within a culture. Cultural value tendencies, in conjunction with many relational and situational factors, influence cross-cultural nonverbal behaviors. A recently graduated Mexican student, Lalo, recalls, "When I was younger and with my sister, we used to turn off the sound of the telenovela [limited-run televised dramas popular in Latin America] and make up our own dialogue. We always based it on the body language and the facial expressions; it was so funny!"

Nonverbal cues are the markers of our identities. The way we dress, the way we talk, our nonverbal gestures—these tell something about who we are and how we want to be viewed. We rely on nonverbal cues as "name badges" to identify what groups we belong to and what groups we are *not* a part of. All of these cues are interpreted through the mediation of stereotypes. Our accent, posture, and hand gestures further give our group membership away. For example, many Latinos who were born in the United States are used to people assuming that they do not speak English fluently. Eduardo, who worked at a steak restaurant, remembers a customer who refused to order from him because "he would not understand what I wanted." Eduardo had many experiences dealing with prejudiced attitudes and presumptions, but is also quick to point out that "this does not happen all the time. When it happens I try not to let it piss me off."

It takes astute observation and deep understanding of a culture to decode nonverbal cues or messages accurately. Just imagine the difficulty interpreting a five-minute conversation between an Italian friend and a Nigerian friend, with variations in their body and hand movements, facial expressions, eye contact, tones of voice, and even the amount of space between the two. Many misunderstandings occur when trying to infer meanings behind nonverbal codes, especially if it is someone who comes from a different cultural background than your own. Nonverbal communication is a powerful communication system. It is, in a nutshell, the heartbeat of a culture. Language may be the key to the heart of a culture, but it is nonverbal communication that embodies the rich and nuanced meanings of a culture.

Nonverbal communication is fascinating: we become curious about how some cultures think about and interpret their world through their nonverbal ways of being. Nonverbal communication includes very subtle microcues to even concrete features such as winking, eyebrow raising, body postures, fashions, accessories, and object displays on a desk that communicate a message during an interaction. Most important, nonverbal communication always has some form of social meaning, although no words may be spoken.

Nonverbal messages can be used without words, can provide the backdrop to interpret the verbal message, and can create miscommunication. Although nonverbal gestures can sometimes clarify a verbal message, most of the time, nonverbal messages also can create tremendous intercultural confusion. There are no set nonverbal "dictionary rules" to follow in sending and interpreting nonverbal cues or messages. Instead, nonverbal communication is oftentimes ambiguous, but at the same time more believable or convincing than words.

For example, many global cities offer dance festivals, featuring modern and traditional dances from across the world. You can watch Balinese *legong*, Latin *rhumba*, and Filipino *tinikling*, to name a few. Each dance type offers us a unique way of expression, with intricate and complicated movements. Each dance has hand gestures that represent or complement the verbal message. Gestures for love and various types of water and fish are all accompanied by particular nonverbal codes. However, some of these codes are communicated without the use of words. If you are not familiar with the local cultural code, interpreting the meanings of the gestures will be almost impossible and will allow plenty of room for inaccurate judgments.

One Code, Countless Interpretations

People send a variety of nonverbal cues during each interaction. This creates an interpretive ambiguity. The same nonverbal cue can mean different things to different people in different cultures. One example of a situation in which this may happen is giving the thumbs up sign (i.e., thumb up and fingers in a fist), which means "all right" or "OK" in the United States and Britain but can signal a condemnation meaning in Thailand and a downright insulting meaning in Afghanistan, Iran, Nigeria, and parts of Italy and Greece. Misunderstandings occur because of the mismatched bumps between the original cultural gesture's intention and a variety of cultural decoding possibilities (See Blog Pic 7.1).

Many nonverbal communication situations carry a variety of messages and meanings. If a friend gives you

Blog Pic 7.1   What are these teens communicating?

a "high five" after you make a basket (as in basketball) in the United States, your friend is congratulating you on your shot. This nonverbal code is purposeful, and the meaning is intended to congratulate you. During an intercultural encounter, conflict and confusion may occur for two simple reasons. First, the same nonverbal signal can mean different things to different people in different cultures. For example, the "OK" sign in the United States can mean the number *zero* in France, can mean "$" in Japan, and can be interpreted as an obscene gesture in Spain. Second, a variety of hand signals can also carry the same meaning. For example, the beckoning or "come here" gesture is done in the United States by curling one's index finger and waving it toward oneself. However, in Italy, Japan, the Philippines, and South Korea, the "come here" hand gesture sign is conveyed via placing the palm downward and making a cupping or sweeping motion with the fingers.

Verbal and Nonverbal Comparisons

Although the use of a verbal message is an intentional communicative act from the sender, nonverbal messages are constantly being interpreted by eyewitness others—even if the gesture has no particular intentional meaning from the sender. Whereas verbal messages emphasize content meanings, nonverbal messages stress analogical or relational meanings via the tone of voice or other body expressive cues. Whereas the use of a verbal message can be very strategic, the use of nonverbal behaviors can be both intentional (e.g., by the clothes that we wear and how we want to present ourselves) and unintentional, as interpreted by the perceiver.

Nonverbal cues can also be used independently or together with a verbal message. When used with verbal messages, they relate to verbal messages in five different ways. Nonverbal cues can repeat, contradict, substitute, complement, and accent verbal messages (Knapp & Hall, 2009). We will briefly use some examples to illustrate these concepts.

Nonverbal communication can simply *repeat* the verbal message. If you are going to get your hair cut, oftentimes the barber or stylist will ask you how much hair you want cut. You will most likely tell him or her the number of inches followed by a confirmation with your fingers. In this example, a nonverbal gesture repeats the verbal message. Another common example you can try is to ask a friend what a "goatee" or "soul patch" is. They will likely tell you that it is hair on a person's face—while stroking their face at the same time.

Nonverbal communication can *contradict* the verbal message. You can contradict a message, or you can enhance it. When Nevaeh plays poker, if she thinks she has a winning hand, she complains out loud that she has a poor hand, but she always fiddles with her hair and avoids eye contact. Unfortunately, her friends are able to see through her bluff immediately. Contradicting a verbal message is a form of leakage, showing our true feelings when we try to hide them. Adults rely more heavily on nonverbal cues for indications of feelings and verbal cues for information about other people's beliefs or intentions.

Nonverbal communication can *substitute* for the verbal message. If you are driving through any border patrol area at an international border crossing, officers will use specific hand gestures to tell you if you need to stop or continue driving. Using a horizontal hand gesture across your neck signals that you want to someone to stop what they are doing. Water skiers usually use a set of hand gestures to indicate whether they want the boat driver to speed up, slow down, or cut the motor off completely. The nonverbal message is clear, and no verbal message is needed to clarify the meaning.

Nonverbal communication can *complement* the verbal message. Patting a teammate on the back and saying "Epic! What an awesome job!" complements the words that are spoken. The nonverbal look in your teachers' eyes or downward facial expressions that accompany their verbal reprimands can clearly illustrate the verbal messages and signal their disappointment. These nonverbal messages function to support the meaning of the verbal messages.

Nonverbal communication may also *accent*, or emphasize, parts of a verbal message. If you like to **bold** some words on a paper or use *italics*, these are accents. Slamming your hand down on the table during a meeting and saying "Focus!" will accent the importance of paying attention.

We learn how to use nonverbal communication very early on. Although some similarities in nonverbal messages and meanings cut across different groups, flexible intercultural communicators can learn that different nonverbal cues are sometimes appropriate and sometimes inappropriate in different cultural settings and with different identity groups (Andersen, Hecht, Hobbler, & Smallwood, 2003).

FORMS OF NONVERBAL COMMUNICATION

To fully understand the significance of nonverbal communication for our communication behavior, we must examine the variety of nonverbal behaviors used by people in our daily life across cultures. There are seven different forms of nonverbal communication: physical appearance, paralanguage (vocal cues), facial expressions, kinesics (body movements), haptics (touch), oculesics (eye contact), and proxemics (space). In this and the next main sections, we will now illustrate each and note their diverse nonverbal functions.

Physical Appearance

Our physical appearance affects our daily interactions with others. Physical appearance includes body type, height, weight, hair, and skin color. Along with our appearance, we wear clothing, and we also generally display artifacts. **Artifacts** are ornaments or adornments we use to communicate just by wearing the actual item. Both artifacts and clothing serve as markers of our unique or subcultural identity. Jewelry, shoes, glasses, gloves, nail polish, tattoos, tongue, facial, and body piercings, and face painting communicate our age, group membership, socieconomic status and class, personality, and gender. We rely on nonverbal cues as a form of comparing ourselves with other groups (Burgoon, Buller, & Woodall, 1996). They can reflect both cultural trends and unique personalities. Famous singers, such as Usher, Pink, Fergie from the Black Eyed Peas, and Eminem sport multiple piercings.

Nonverbal cues can provide clues for us to determine the specific time in history. You may remember that leg warmers or jheri curls were trends in the 1980s and baggy jeans were very fashionable in the 1990s, as were emo hairstyles in the 2000s. Tattoos and body piercings (e.g., eyebrows, lip, and navel) have been used at various times in history. Traditional Polynesian cultures (e.g., Samoa, Tonga, Maori of New Zealand) have used tattoos and piercings as indicators of class, status, and roles. Trendy now, these traditional tattoos and piercings are common and adopted to express individual difference.

These cues serve as identity markers of the individual and also the practices of the larger culture. For example, rap singer Lil Wayne takes pride in his Louisiana roots, so much so that he has a map of the state on his back and the number 17, from the 17th ward in New Orleans. Sporting more than one hundred tattoos, each significant symbol represents his life history for others to view. At the same time, traditional tattoos (e.g., in Hawaii) have been used to signal pride in the rich history that "represents" past ancestors. We (the authors) polled our students informally in two classes (approximately 140 students) and found that the female students had more tattoos than the male students. Interestingly, tattoo artist Kahiki reports that once a person gets a tattoo, they are more likely to get another. Indeed, tattoos reinforce identity belonging among members of tight-knit groups, such as gangs, fraternities, and sororities.

Artifacts can also place a person in a particular status or class. Visit any hospital and you can tell a doctor from a nurse. The doctor typically wears a white coat; nurses wear scrubs. Uniforms in Japan are worn to differentiate among entertainers, students, workers, and supervisors. A funny thing about artifacts: we make so many judgments about what a person decides to wear. Chee Ling, for example, a former international student in Oklahoma, was shocked when she went back home to work in Malaysia. She noticed the pressure for more women to keep up with the latest designer trends. Although she lives paycheck to paycheck, she is a consumer of designer labels—Louboutin heels, Tiffany jewelry, and a Chanel bag—to keep up with fashion trends. The status issue surrounding nonverbal display accessories is common throughout big cities in Asia.

Adornment features, such as clothing, jewelry, cosmetics, and accessories, in different cultures also reflect complex cultural and personal identities. Based on our stereotypic knowledge of a particular group, we look for validation of our expectations via nonverbal cues and surface adornment features. We also engage in stereotypic attitude and even in using direct discriminatory gesture such as the Ashish's *tikka* story in Blog Post 7.1.

Traditional face painting techniques are surface adornment features that are thought to be the foundation of modern cosmetics. In our world today, the cosmetics industry makes a large amount of money marketing traditional styles worn in specific cultures. For example, Indian women traditionally henna their hands on special occasions, such as marriage, birth, and death. But pop stars, such as Madonna and Prince, use henna as an enhancement to their looks.

One last aspect of artifacts and clothing is impression management. As we become an international community, the need to look global (or, actually, Hollywood *Western*) has some interesting implications. As the winds of globalization sweep through, beauty is not only a trend in the United States. For example, we can find aspects of selling and marketing plastic surgery around the world. According to the Biennial Global Survey (2009), Japanese and Korean women have increasingly used plastic surgery to widen their eyes in a relentless drive to attain the Western image of beauty. In South Korea, calf slimming is quite popular. But the most controversial procedure is leg lengthening. Young

BLOG POST 7.1

We moved to California in the early 1990s when I was ten years old. It was a tough transition and my parents really missed India. I liked it here, but the school system was very different. I will never forget about the day I was sent home early from school.

It was *Raksha Bandan*, an Indian festival that celebrates the bond between sisters and brothers. My sister tied a colorful *raakhi* (a sacred thread) that symbolized her love for me. My sister also put a *tikka* (red mark on forehead) as she prayed for me.

When I got to school, my classmates started making fun of my formal clothes and of the *tikka* on my forehead. Unlike the other kids, I used to wear shirts and slacks to school, because I was used to wearing a uniform to school. One boy told me, "You look weird with your third eye." The taunting did not stop and I was getting really frustrated. The same boy tried to wipe off my *tikka* and break off the *raakhi* my sister gave me. I punched and hit him in retaliation. My teacher caught me hitting

my classmate, but she did not wait to hear my side of the story. She sent me to the school counsellor who talked to me then took me home.

My parents were angry that I had misbehaved and beat up another kid. I tried explaining to them that I was made fun of for my clothes and *tikka*. Then the counsellor then suggested to my parents that they should "dress me in more Western clothes, so that I don't stand out." She also suggested that I try to fit in more and not display the 'red dot' in school, so that my adjustment can go easier. Within a year, we moved back to India. My parents found it too hard to adjust and did not want us to forget our cultural traditions. Thirteen years later my sister and I migrated back to California . . . She continues to tie me a *raakhi* every year, but she makes sure that it does not have fancy decorations and it is less colorful. And I continue to wash off my *tikka* before I go to work.

—Ashish, *college student*

Korean, Russian, Chinese, and Iraqi women desire leg lengthening surgery to grow taller in hopes that they can compete globally and stand as tall as their Western counterparts.

According to a 2006 documentary, "Nose, Iranian style" filmmaker Mehrdad Oskouei considers contemporary Iran in the midst of an epidemic of nose jobs. In fact, Iran is called "the nose job capital of the world" (Oskouei, 2006). This may seem shocking in a place where women are required to cover their hair and conceal the shape of their bodies with a hijab. Unfortunately, with the Western (or U.S.-centric) facial beauty standard in mind, some beautiful Iranian women are still not content with their noses. Body alterations definitely serve the nonverbal function of intentional identity management.

If used successfully, artifacts and body alterations can enhance an individual's self-esteem and appearance. However, if used haphazardly or if the operation fails, they can also strip away an individual's remaining self-confidence or distinctive personality. One would do well to proceed with caution when thinking of body alteration techniques or operations to enhance one's face or body image. At the same time, if a safe operation can raise someone's self-image, others may need to learn to accept that person's choice or decision and give any needed support.

Paralanguage

Beyond artifacts, another form of nonverbal communication that gives away our cultural, ethnic, and gender identity is paralanguage. **Paralanguage** is the sounds and tones we use in conversation and the speech behavior that accompanies the message. Simply put, it is *how* something is said, not *what* is said. The nonword sounds and characteristics of speech are called **paralinguistic features**. Aspects of paralinguistic features include a variety of voice qualities, such as the following:

- *Accent:* how your words are pronounced together;
- *Pitch range:* your range of tone from high to low;
- *Pitch intensity:* how high or low your voice carries;
- *Volume:* how loudly or softly you speak;
- *Articulation:* if your mouth, tongue, and teeth coordinate to speak precisely or to slur your words;
- *Rate:* the speed of sound or how quickly or slowly you speak.

Each of these characteristics may be represented on a continuum. For example, U.S. Americans often interpret and mimic the sounds of Cantonese speakers, a dialect of Chinese, as "whiny" and "loud and screaming," typically associating their sounds with old kung fu movies. In contrast, Arabs oftentimes evaluate the speaking style in the United States as unexpressive, cold, distant, and harsh. Whatever the perspective, members of different cultures use their own cultural nonverbal standards as guidelines for proper or improper ways of speaking and for evaluating others.

Through the use of paralanguage, we encode a sense of self via different nonverbal features and behaviors. People tend to use their own standards to judge others through nonverbal markers. Some of these markers can be intentionally sent, but others can be unintentional. If you raise your voice during a conversation, the interpretation is that you must be irritated or angry. However, ethnic or cultural groups raise their voices because it indicates sincerity or authenticity. For example, some African Americans tend to have emotionally expressive voices and are passionate about their conversation points (Orbe & Harris, 2008). This is commonly mistaken for anger. This is also true in other cultural groups. Fatima, a college sophomore from Iran (or Persia, as some Iranian Americans prefer to call their country), recalls that the norm in her culture is to speak in a loud voice, repeat points, and pound on the table for emphasis. In her house, both the men and the women speak in an emotionally expressive, loud voice that might be misinterpreted as a display of anger. If someone who does not understand Farsi observes a conversation between two Persians, he might think that the two people talking sincerely about something are actually mad at each other. Fatima says, "My stepfather is constantly thinking that my mother and grandmother are arguing about something, but they are actually carrying on a normal conversation."

Paralanguage can change the meaning of a sentence simply by accenting different words, depending on the way you say them:

What's up with *that*?
What's up *with* that?
What's *up* with that?
What's up with that?

Or, try the statement "Are you serious?!" by varying the sounds with a classmate. In hearing or conversing in a foreign language, we often cannot pick up subtle vocal changes that may help us understand that either playfulness or sarcasm is intended by the speaker. If you don't pick up the nuances of playfulness or humor in the voice, for example, misunderstandings will affect your relationship with the speaker. You can unintentionally offend, frustrate, or hurt someone without realizing how powerful your voice sounds. Additionally, your vocal message may be misunderstood and inappropriately judged.

Facial Expressions

We sense the feelings and attitudes of strangers from the nonverbal messages we receive during an interaction. One important form of nonverbal communication that conveys feelings and attitudes is kinesics. Kinesics comes from the Greek word *kinesis*, meaning "movement." **Kinesics** is the study of posture, body movement, gestures, and facial expressions. The face is capable of producing about 250,000 different expressions. Nonverbal researchers generally agree that there is relative universality in the decoding of basic facial expressions (Matsumoto, Olide, Schug, Willingham, & Callan, 2009).

It appears that there is consistency across cultures in our ability to recognize at least seven emotions in an individual's facial expressions. We can refer to these recognizable facial emotions by the acronym **SADFISH: S**adness, **A**nger, **D**isgust, **F**ear, **I**nterest, **S**urprise, and **H**appiness (Richmond & McCroskey, 2000). People are able to recognize not only the emotion but also the intensity of emotion and often the secondary emotion being experienced. Take a look at the following photos in Blog Pic 7.2.

On a general level, different cultural groups have interpreted these various facial expressions with a high degree of accuracy. However, the ability to recognize specific emotions on the SADFISH list may vary from one specific culture to the next. For example, studies indicate that students in the United States are better at identifying anger, disgust, fear, and sadness than are Japanese students (Matsumoto & Juang, 2003; Safdar et al., 2009). The reason is that Japanese students learn at a very young age to suppress their facial emotions because this display can be threatening to others and also create disharmony in their everyday relationships. In another study, East Asian participants inadequately distinguished the universal facial expressions of fear and disgust (Jack, Blais, Scheepers, Schyns, & Caldara, 2009). Rather than distribute their observations evenly

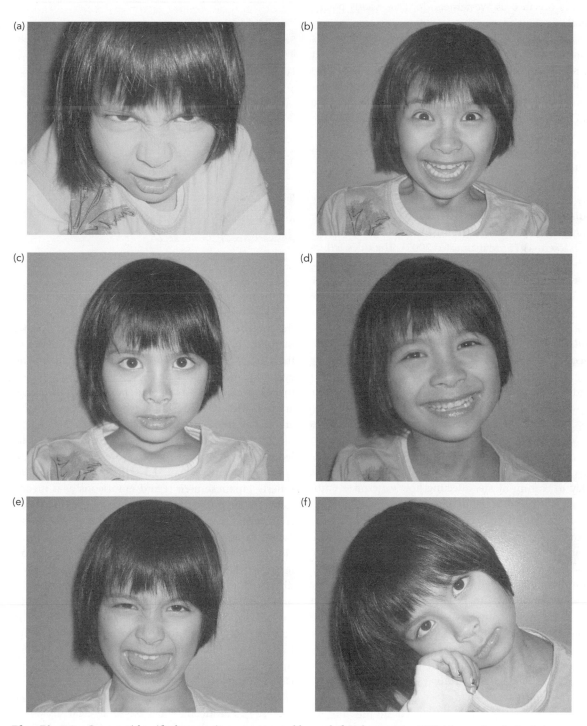

Blog Pic 7.2 Can you identify the emotions represented by each facial expression? Which one is missing? *Answers: (a) anger; (b) surprise; (c) fear; (d) happiness; (e) disgust; (f) sadness. Missing: interest.*

across the face as Westerners do, East Asians persistently fix their gaze in the eye region.

As you can see, identifying facial expressions through a photograph is actually quite difficult. What is more interesting is that children, when asked, have trouble displaying these emotions on their faces when prompted. The special difficulty in interpreting the two facial emotions of disgust and anger only fuels the problem of having the "correct" answer of what the expression looks like. Part of this problem has to do with cultural display rules.

There are cultural differences in the display rules we use for expressing emotions. **Cultural display rules** are the procedures we learn for managing the way we express our emotions (Andersen, 2007; Ekman & Friesen, 1975; Matsumoto, 2009). The rules tell us when it is or is not acceptable to express our emotions. For example, in individualistic cultures, it is acceptable to express anger or disgust alone or in the presence of others. In collectivistic cultures, anger and disgust are not expressed in public, especially in front of individuals with higher status. For example, in Indonesia, people will be quiet and hide their feelings if they are angry with their boss, but those in Australia (an individualistic culture) will openly express their anger toward their boss.

Cultural display rules have changed with advances in technology and the Internet. As we progress with our advanced technology, sending messages via Twitter, text, and Facebook has resulted in a more efficient way to communicate, affecting how we express emotions. The use of icons in text messages became popular because of the great need to replace long sentences, words, and expressions of our feelings with quick keyboard symbols. Universal icon expressions have become a significant way to converse without face-to-face interaction. These give senders everywhere the ability to talk with others without having to explain in detail the weight of their feelings. Can you guess what some of these symbols or sounds represent? Chrchrchr or xa-xa-xa? These express laughter. Expressing laughter online (e.g., LOL) has a variety of differences. How laughter is expressed in writing varies by the sound and interpretation of the laugh. (See Hit-or-Miss 7.1).

How about cultural differences in the use of emoticons? South Koreans and Japanese tend to use

---

HIT-OR-MISS 7.1   LOL QUIZ

See if you "Hit" or "Miss" as you try matching these "laughing" examples to their country/countries:

Letter:

1.	_____ jajaja	(a) South Korea
2.	_____ chrchrchr	(b) Mexico
3.	_____ ㅋㅋ or ㅎㅎ	(c) Russia and Bulgaria
4.	_____ 呵呵	(d) Turkey, Brazil, Sweden, and Hungary
5.	_____ õà-õà-õà	(e) China
6.	_____ hihihi	(f) Germany

Answers: 1b; 2f; 3a; 4e; 5c; 6d

---

emoticons with expressive eyes and a neutral mouth (^_^), whereas U.S. Americans vary the direction of the mouth, :) and :(for example. One study (Yuki, Maddux, & Masuda, 2007) showed that students in the United States are not as sensitive to cues in the eyes and mouth because they badly misinterpreted the meaning assigned to popular emoticons from Japanese culture. Do you know what the most popular emoticons are in Japan? (See Hit-or-Miss 7.2.)

Research regarding the use of emoticons is varied. Asians also tend to use more emoticons than U.S. Americans (Kayan, Fussell, & Setlock, 2006). Elderly Japanese men regard emoticons as a means to overcome the restrictions that computer-mediated communication places on interpersonal communication (Kanayama, 2003), and Indian Web forums also use more emoticons than their German counterparts (Pflug, 2011). Remember in Chapter 6 we discussed the differences between LCC and HCC patterns. Both Korean and Indian cultures are considered HCC cultures, whereas the U.S. culture is considered a LCC culture. It seems logical to infer that high-context folks have a stronger urge to fill in the nonverbal contextual gaps than their Western U.S. counterparts.

Despite the popularity, frequency, and success of the use of emoticons, there are some clear disadvantages to text messaging and icons in general. First,

---

HIT-OR-MISS 7.2 POPULAR JAPANESE EMOTICONS

See if you "Hit" or "Miss" as you match these popular Japanese emoticons with their emotion:

Letter:

1. _____ (^_^)		a. joyful
2. _____ (>_<)>		b. mellow
3. _____ (ToT)		c. grinning
4. _____ (ˉ — ˉ)		d. apologizing
5. _____ (≧∇≦)		e. shocked
6. _____ (ˉ □ ˉ ;)		f. surprised
7. _____ (˚ Ä ˚)		g. crying
8. _____ (——;)		h. worried
9. _____ (´ — `)		i. troubled
10. _____ m(_ _)m		j. laughing

Answers: 1j; 2i; 3g; 4c; 5a; 6f; 7e; 8h; 9b; 10d

Source: http://whatjapanthinks.com/2006/08/14/
japans-top-thirty-emoticons/

---

many people who use icons and text messages on a daily basis can talk about an exact time and place in which they were misunderstood or their words were taken the wrong way after sending out a message. Reading emoticons in a message does not replace the depth of feelings a person has tried hard to convey. Second, joking around and sarcasm are difficult to interpret. Many people complain that they spend much time putting out the flame of a potential conflict because a sentence was misrepresented. For example, by writing WTF or wtf without contextual cues, or a smile to infer a joke, as a result, your friend may "dislike" you on Facebook. The crossover effect between reading an emoticon versus decoding a real-life facial expression can cause further intercultural confusion. This discussion also takes us back to the importance of understanding paralanguage and how misunderstandings can take place because of sarcasm or joking as inferred through the tone of voice more so than facial expressions.

Gestures

Gestures are culturally specific and significant forms of nonverbal communication. In fact, they are much more elaborate and more frequently used in Italian culture than in U.S. culture. The four basic categories of hand gestures and body movements (Ekman & Friesen, 1975) have been categorized as *emblems, illustrators, regulators,* and *adaptors.*

Emblems are gestures that substitute for words and phrases. The nonverbal gesture replaces the need to speak. For example, when you shrug your shoulders to say "I don't know," this is an emblem. An emblem for Filipinos is using the lips to point to an object, a direction, or a person. Emblems are usually gestures or movements that are displayed with clear intent and are recognized by members of your ingroup. Greeting rituals, gestures to call someone over, peace or insult gestures, and head bobs indicating "yes" or "no" are emblems. Every culture has a large variety of emblems with specific meanings and rules of their displays (see Blog Pic 7.3). However, emblems can contribute to intercultural misunderstandings or conflicts. For example, emblems may hold contradictory meanings in different cultures. A "fist" among African Americans signified "Black Power" in the 1970s. But a fist can also trigger a fighting stance. Putting your thumb and index finger together and making a circle with your other three fingers straight can mean "OK." In Japan, this means money, in France it means "zero" or "worthless," and in Venezuela and Turkey, gesturing to someone in this way implies that they are a homosexual.

Joe Whitecotten, an anthropologist, tells a colorful nonverbal story that highlights potential misunderstandings. Check out Blog Post 7.2. This fun story is an example of emblems that are culture specific and the basis for potential misunderstanding (see also Blog Pic 7.4).

Illustrators are nonverbal hand gestures that we use along with the spoken message—they literally illustrate the verbal message. When you are describing a shape, such as a heart, you are likely to make round angles with your thumbs and touch your fingers together. If you "talk with your hands" and use mostly hand gestures, then you are a person who enjoys

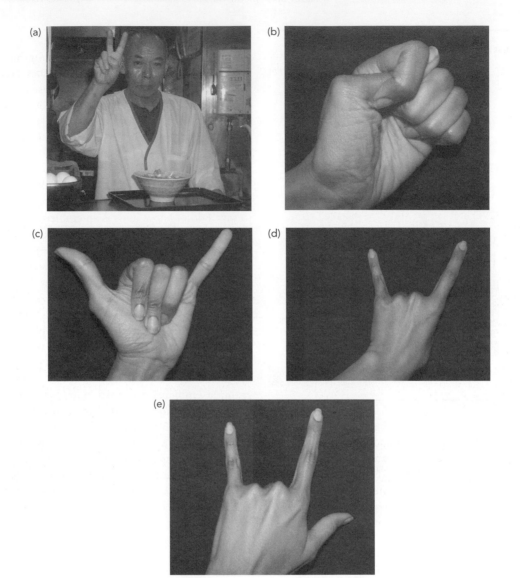

Blog Pic 7.3 How many intercultural hand gestures can you decode? *Answers: (a) U.S. peace; (b) Asian swear; (c) Hawaiian hang loose; (d) Texan hook 'em horns; (e) American Sign Language love.*

expressive illustrators. Egyptians and Italians generally use broad, full arm gestures to illustrate points when they are speaking, more so than the reserved British and Asian groups.

We are so used to making these spontaneous non-verbal movements that it is very difficult to reverse them or make inappropriate gestures. Many people wonder why Asian groups don't use more illustra-tors. The answer is that Asians prefer to focus more on the interaction process and consider the use of too many hand gestures distracting, rude, and even undisciplined.

Regulators are nonverbal behaviors we use in con-versation to control, maintain, or "regulate" the pace

BLOG POST 7.2

I spent a lot of time in Italy. As a huge football fan, I can only imagine the confusion that would happen if the Italians were watching U.S. college football between the University of Oklahoma (OU) and University of Texas at Austin.

The OU fans always hold up their index finger (which means "We are Number 1!"), and the Texas fans respond with a sign holding up the index finger and the little finger simultaneously (which means "Hook 'em, Horns," referring to their mascot, the Longhorn).

To the Italian, these gestures would have very different meanings. The index finger means "Up yours," like the middle finger in American culture, and the simultaneous index finger and little finger signifies "You are a cuckold." This is one of the worst insults you can give to an Italian male, because it means that his wife (or girlfriend) has cheated on him because he is sexually inadequate.

—Joe, *college instructor*

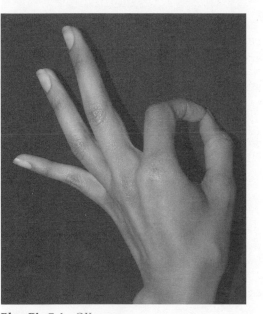

Blog Pic 7.4   OK gesture.

Blog Pic 7.5   Thumbs up.

and flow of the conversation. When we are listening to someone, we acknowledge the speaker by nodding our head and adjusting or maintaining eye contact, and we make paralinguistic sounds (e.g., "mm-hmm," "really," "no kidding!"). Next to emblems, regulators are considered culturally specific nonverbal behaviors. These are also the most rule-governed kinesic behaviors. Regulators act as the nonverbal traffic signal to control the dynamics of a conversation. For example, in the United States, when we interrupt a speaker with "Really?" we are in agreement, we are assisting them with their story, or we are showing them that we are paying attention to their story. If we are in China,

saying "Really?" while a person is talking is considered rude and inappropriate.

We learn regulators at a very young age. We use them at lower levels of consciousness. Depending on what region you are visiting, vocal segregates, such as "Sure, you're right" in the U.S. South and *"Neh neh"* among Korean elders can be classified as nonverbal regulators. These agreement words mean "I am hearing you," but the literal translation in English of the latter is "yes" to those who do not speak Korean.

Adaptors are habits or gestures that fulfill some kind of psychological or physical need. Some adaptors are learned within a culture (e.g., covering the mouth when we sneeze or covering the mouth when we laugh aloud). Others are more automatic (e.g., scratching an itch on your head, picking your nose). Most adaptors are not intended to communicate a message. However, some of these habits can be considered rude in the context of another culture. For example, in a meeting, when you are listening with your arms folded across your chest, some people may assume that you do not want to talk with others, but you may actually feel cold. In the library, you may notice that while studying, some people consistently play with a pen or pencil with their fingers. You may think they are nervous, but they are merely concentrating. In today's iPhone world, some individuals can be texting and Googling and at the same time conversing with their friends. Some of their friends may accept their behavior and even respond in kind; others may be irritated and frustrated at such rude nonverbal inattentive behavior.

Haptics

The nonverbal function of **haptics** examines the perceptions and meanings of touch behavior. Different cultures encode and construe touch behavior to be either appropriate or inappropriate. Past research indicates that touch behavior is used to fulfill five communicative functions: as a greeting ritual, to express affection, to be playful, to have controlling behavior, and to have task-related functions (Andersen, 2007).

Different cultures have different rules about touch. For example, same-sex touch and handholding in Malaysia, China, Sudan, Japan, Nepal, and Saudi Arabia are considered acceptable and part of daily life because contact among the opposite sex is inappropriate. This is better known as "PDA," or the public display of affection. In the United States, same-sex handholding pertains to the gay/lesbian/bisexual community. However, opposite-sex handholding is an appropriate PDA in the United States. Latino/as from Latin American cultural regions tend to engage in more frequent touch behaviors than do U.S. Americans and Canadians. But it is important to remember that the touch behaviors in both the Arab and the Latin American cultures are usually confined to same-sex touching, not opposite-sex touch (see Blog Pic 7.6).

Blog Pic 7.6　President Bush holding hands with Saudi Arabian royalty.

Blog Pic 7.7　President Obama bowing to Japanese Emperor Akihito.

There are also differences among high-, moderate-, and low-contact cultures (Ting-Toomey, 1999). French, Russians, Latin Americans, and Italians are members of high-contact cultures. **High-contact cultures** often look each other in the eye directly, face each other, touch and/or kiss each other, and speak in rather loud voices. East Asians and Asian Americans, such as Chinese, Japanese, and Indians, are members of low-contact cultures. **Low-contact cultures** often engage in little if any touching, preferring indirect eye gazes and speaking in a lower tone. The United States, Canada, and Australia are **moderate-contact cultures**, which is a blend of both. Research (Remland, 2003; Remland, Jones, & Brinkman, 1995) also reveals that southern Europeans touch more than northern Europeans. After observing one thousand couples at many train stations in different countries, nonverbal researchers found that the highest frequency of touching—from the most frequent to the least frequent touch cultures—occurs in descending order as follows: Greece, Spain, Italy, Hungary, Germany, Belgium, England, Austria, and the Netherlands. The researchers also pointed out that much of the intercultural haptics or touch research depends heavily on gender, age, context, duration of the relationship, and personality factors.

In addition, individuals from high-contact cultures can also bother those from a low-contact culture to a great extent. Let's check out Melissa's story and her semester abroad in Blog Post 7.3.

Let's also briefly examine nonverbal situational appropriateness. The "buttock pat" is an excellent example of a situational touch cue. This is used in many professional male sports teams across the globe. The pat is a sign of encouragement, team bonding, and congratulations for a job well done, and it has spread to European sports. Outside the sports context, the fear of touch among U.S. males is high. Therefore, knowing the appropriate context, individual likes and dislikes, and appropriate relationship is vital in intercultural nonverbal communication.

BOUNDARY REGULATIONS

How do you deal with space? For example, when you enter a classroom for the very first time, do you "claim" your area? Do you park yourself on the seat, put your bag down, and own it from this moment on? When the class meets again, do you sit in the identical seat? How do you feel if someone else is sitting in your seat?

Space and time are boundary regulation issues. As human beings, we are territorial animals (see Blog Pic 7.8).

We claim and mark our territory. When someone or something invades our territory, we become much more sensitive to the invasion. It is a feeling of vulnerability and a threatening experience. Marking our territory has more to do with psychological ownership than physical ownership. This is the feeling we have of owning a particular spot. If our territory becomes a precious commodity, we react without taking a moment to think about our behavior and our actions, because we

---

BLOG POST 7.3

I have always been very close with all of my aunts, cousins, grandmas, parents, and siblings. We have always shared our great affection for one another with plenty of kisses and hugs. But with my parents, I am definitely more intimate with my mother. I have noticed that in a lot of Mexican families, the father is the guardian, the role model, and the authority figure. [The parents] usually keep a little distance between themselves and their children (daughters in particular). My dad is a lot less affectionate than my mom. But my mother and my two sisters and I are very affectionate with one another—we touch, hug, and kiss all the time.

—Melissa, *college student*

Blog Pic 7.8 Doorways, windows, or gates regulate inner and outer space.

feel violated. Friends and colleagues in San Francisco will complain when someone "parks in their spot." Although parking is free, finding a space is sometimes impossible, so the violation feels even stronger if one's psychologically owned spot is invaded.

In the next section, we discuss four broad themes of boundary regulation issues: interpersonal boundaries, environmental boundaries, psychological boundaries, and temporal regulation.

Regulating Interpersonal Boundaries

Before you begin this section, take a my.blog 7.1 poll to determine your interpersonal space orientation.

Edward T. Hall was one of the first anthropologists to write extensively about how we "mark" and define our territory. This is the study of proxemics. **Proxemics** is the study of space between persons, physical contact, and the inner anxiety we have when people violate our space. In the United States, according to Hall, we have four spatial zones: intimate, personal, social, and public (Hall, 1959, 1966). The *intimate* zone is zero to eighteen inches. This space is reserved for those who are closest to us, such as family, an emotional situation, and our close friends. The *personal* zone is from eighteen to forty-eight inches, reserved for closer friends, some acquaintances, and colleagues. *Social* zones occur in a larger event, such as a party, at forty-eight inches to twelve feet. Finally, the *public* zone is any distance that is twelve feet or more. Any violation of these zones can result in feelings of anxiety or discomfort.

What constitutes appropriate personal distance for one cultural group can be perceived as crowding by another group. The average conversational distance of personal space for European Americans is approximately twenty inches. The average personal space of many Latin American and Caribbean cultures is fourteen to fifteen inches. In Saudi Arabia, the ideal conversational distance is only nine to ten inches. Personal space serves as a hidden dimension of intercultural misunderstanding and discomfort.

Personal space is our unconscious protective territory that we carry around with us and deem sacred, nonviolable, and nonnegotiable. Although members of all cultures engage in the claiming of space for themselves, the experience of space and space violation varies across cultures and gender groups. Many of our U.S. students agree: in a movie theater with plenty of open seats, most male friends will leave an empty seat between them. But females will watch the movie together, sitting right next to each other. Let's check out a fun, nonverbal space story in Blog Post 7.4.

Environmental Boundaries

In addition to our interpersonal space, we also have boundaries related to our environment. **Environmental boundaries** are defined as the claimed sense of space and emotional attachment we share with others in our community. Concepts of territory and identity are interconnected because we usually invest time, effort, emotion, and self-worth in places that we claim as our primary territories. Our home territory or immediate environment asserts a strong influence on our everyday lives.

---

my.blog 7.1

On the following continuums, place a check mark where you would place yourself spatially when communicating with

	0″	12″	24″	36″	48″
Strangers:					
Acquaintances:					
Teachers:					
Classmates:					
Parents:					
Siblings:					
Same-sex friends:					
Opposite-sex friends:					
Romantic partners:					

BLOG POST 7.4

When I was in the airport in Tel Aviv, Israel, there was no such thing as an orderly line or an open space in the shuttles. People were practically enmeshed in one another, [and] you would be staring at the back of someone's head or armpit. This was actually quite humorous for me. As soon as I learned how people squeezed themselves in front of a counter, I did the same.

It was interesting for me to watch my stepfather's transformation. In the beginning of our trip, he was incredibly disturbed by the lack of space between strangers. But by the end of our trip, he was the one rushing up to the counters, and he would not even flinch when an Israeli man would practically have his nose inside my stepfather's back (he is very tall). If my stepfather had kept to Hall's regulations for space depending on the relationship, he would not have lasted as long as he did in a country that redefines those regulations.

—Nadia, *college student*

Lewin (1936) addressed the significance of how the environment influences our behavior with the following formula: $B = f(P, E)$ in which B = *behavior*, P = *person*, and E = *environment*. This means that our *behavior* is defined by the *persons* interacting as well as the *environment* in which the communication takes place. For example, middle-class neighborhoods in Canada and the United States are very different from the middle-class neighborhoods in many Latin American, Middle Eastern, and Asian cultures, and these environments influence how people in those cultures behave.

In the United States, a home in a typical middle-class neighborhood is physically separated from the community by a fence, a gate, a yard, a lawn, or some combination of these. Homes often symbolize an individual identity related closely with the owner. Environmental boundaries within the home are exercised through the use of separate bedrooms, private bathrooms, and many locks. In contrast, the middle-class neighborhood in Mexico is designed so that houses are integrated with a central plaza, possibly containing a community center and a church. Homes do not have many locks inside the house and many family members share bedrooms and bathrooms. U.S. middle-class homes appear to reflect individualistic qualities, and Mexican middle-class homes appear to promote collectivism and group-based interaction.

Cultural groups have different expectations concerning the specific functions of different rooms in the house. For example, in cultures such as China, Korea, and Japan, the proper way to entertain guests is in a formal restaurant, because the home is "not worthy" of entertaining guests. In contrast, many Arabs, like U.S. Americans and Canadians, do not mind entertaining guests in their homes. Many Arab homes reserve a specific formal room to entertain guests, and the guests may not see any other part of the house until trust is established in the relationship. Many U.S. American hosts showcase the house with a grand tour. This informal tour happens within the first minutes of arrival, before settling in. In many Arab homes, separate quarters are also reserved for male and female activities. This is also true in many traditional Korean homes.

In other related room functions, traditional Japanese and Korean homes do not make clear distinctions among the living room, dining room, and bedroom. Thus, when close friends are invited over, it is critical for them to remove their shoes before entering the multipurpose space, the floor of which is covered with straw mats used for sitting and sleeping. This practice is also common among homes in Hawaii. Removing your shoes and slippers before entering an apartment, condo, or home is a norm. Countries such as Japan and Indonesia have clear distinctions between the bathroom and the toilet. The bathroom is used strictly for bathing. From this cultural perspective, to mix up bathing (a cleaning function) and toileting (a dirtying function) is against their code of civility and personal hygiene.

Many individualistic cultures encourage a home environment that is unique to the owner, but many collectivistic cultures encourage communal-type home settings. These cultural norms have been gained from early childhood, where individuals learn via observation, how to manage space and boundary issues through social roles, furniture setting, and proper interaction rules to be performed in each room. We turn now to psychological space and privacy regulation issues.

Psychological Boundaries

How do you feel when someone breaks an unspoken rule about nonverbal space invasion—stands close to you in an empty elevator? Sits in front of you in an empty theatre? These small examples can be defined as psychological space. If you have ever lived or visited densely populated cities such as Hong Kong and Mumbai and Bangkok, you have probably dealt with psychological space crowding issues. Crowded conditions make it almost impossible for people in many major Asian or Latin or Middle East cities (e.g., Shanghai, Seoul, Sao Paulo, Buenos Aires, Cairo, Istanbul, etc.) to experience privacy as it is known in the United States (i.e., being alone in a room). *Intrapersonal space* refers to the need for information privacy or psychological silence between the self and others. Let's do a quick my.blog 7.2 poll and explore your need for privacy.

Although privacy regulation is a major concern in many Western social environments, the issue may not be perceived as critical in collectivistic-oriented cultures. In fact, even the concept of privacy is construed as offensive in many collectivistic cultures (see Blog Pic 7.9). For example, the Chinese words that closely correspond to the concept of privacy are those for *secretive* and *selfishness.* These words imply that many Chinese feel that relational interdependence comes before the need for personal privacy in everyday interactions.

Another aspect of psychological space is creating the mood or atmosphere of a room. Many people will invest money on the practice and art of feng shui. **Feng shui** literally means "air" and "water" in Chinese. Used for thousands of years, feng shui is the philosophy of combining elements to attain good energy within a room, a building, or an area. For example, many feng shui experts believe that if your bed directly faces a door, all of your good energy and luck will flow out of the room. This basic example is one of many used to design harmony within a house or room. Currently, there are feng shui designers, architects, and counselors in the United States and worldwide. Some may spend a few years in Hong Kong to take feng shui lessons to best serve clients who believe in this art of geomancy (which means the art of making predictions based on patterns of spatial locations and directions). Feng shui lessons include the serious study of the chi, or the flow of energy as perceived in Taoism, to build suburban houses. Creating this form of psychological space promotes a more harmonious living condition. There are even feng shui magazines online, for example, http://www.fengshuiprophet.com.

The magazine offers categories of religion, classical versus traditional feng shui, and articles such as "Why feng shui can't be considered a science."

If cultural groups do not emphasize categories for "privacy" and "solitude" to guide everyday interactions, then such categories may not be a critical part of their everyday social reality. Language, in conjunction with multiple nonverbal cues, directs our perceptions and attitudes toward the functions of space and time. Psychological and physical boundaries protect our levels of comfort and safety. Space is a powerful way to mark and define our ingroup and outgroup boundaries in this regard.

---

my.blog 7.2

Use your gut-level reaction and circle "yes" or "no" to the following privacy violation scenes. Do you usually get irritated or stressed out when someone . . .

Enters your room without knocking:	YES	NO
Parks in your favorite spot:	YES	NO
Stands close to you in an elevator:	YES	NO
Sits too close to you in a movie:	YES	NO
Sits in your favorite spot in the classroom:	YES	NO
Walks on your lawn:	YES	NO
Peeps at your e-mails:	YES	NO
Interrupts you:	YES	NO
Stands too close to you:	YES	NO
Touches your arm in conversations:	YES	NO

Regulating Time

Let's do the my.blog 7.3 survey on time orientation. Are you a monochronic-time person, a polychronic-time person, or a bichronemic-time individual? Please read on.

Temporal regulation is defined as the attitudes we have about time. The study of time is known as the study of chronemics. **Chronemics** concerns how people in different cultures structure, interpret, and understand the time dimension.

We are in a constant struggle with time. The faster we go, the faster we want to go. The faster we go, the more impatient we become. Modern computer gadgets take advantage of our need for time by producing faster results. Do you have no time to make dinner? Mod-

Blog Pic 7.9 An Asian office building.

ern appliances can chill a can of soda in one minute, a bottle of wine in ten, or cook a whole roasted chicken in four minutes. E-mails and texts are faster than sending hand-written letters. The efficiency of receiving e-mails results in an urgency to reply. Our life stages (birth, development, aging, sickness. death) are closely tied in with the sense of time. Our religious or spiritual beliefs, in terms of where the universe begins and ends and where life begins and ends, are two time-related worldview considerations. Cultural patterns of time designate when and how we should start the day; when we should eat, take a break, work, play, sleep, and die; and whether and how we will reincarnate.

We are all affected by the norms and values of time from our own culture. More often than not, we don't realize this until a norm or value has been violated in some way. For example, if you are doing business in Madrid and you are not familiar with the working hours there, you will be completely thrown off by the pattern of the day. Spaniards often start work at 10:00 a.m., have lunch at 3:00 p.m., get back to work at 5:00 p.m., work until 8:00 p.m, and have a light dinner at 10:00 pm.

In 2009, French workers averaged fewer hours per week than workers in most developed nations, which is thirty-five (Fleck, 2009). Many workers in France complain that the country's thirty-five-hour workweek, adopted in January 2000, makes it too hard to work. What other countries do you think work the shortest hours per week and the longest hours per week? Take a guess and check out Jeopardy Box 7.1.

As you can see, workers in South Korea average around a forty-seven-hour workweek (while Turkey topped the chart at a forty-nine hour workweek) despite legislation in 2004 imposing a forty-hour, five-day work week. This includes employees of government corporations, banks, and all large corporations. The pressure to work lengthy hours with short vacations is part of the South Korean hard work Confucius ethics' practice (Olson, 2008).

Hall (1983) distinguished between two patterns of time that govern different cultures: the *monochronic-time schedule* (*MT*) and the *polychronic-time schedule* (*PT*; see Table 7.1).

According to Hall and Hall (1987), MT and PT are polar opposites. People in **monochronic-time** (MT) cultures pay close attention to clock time and do one thing at a time. In MT cultures, people use time in a linear way, employing segments to break up time into

my.blog 7.3 ASSESSING THE IMPORTANCE OF YOUR SOCIAL AND PERSONAL IDENTITIES

Instructions: Recall how you generally feel and act in various situations. Let your first inclination be your guide and circle the number in the scale that best reflects your overall impression of yourself. The following scale is used for each item:

4 = YES! = *strongly agree*—IT'S ME!

3 = yes = *moderately agree*—it's kind of like me

2 = no = *moderately disagree*—it's kind of not me

1 = NO! = *strongly disagree*—IT'S NOT ME!

		SA	MA	MD	SD
1.	Time is not necessarily under our control.	4	3	2	1
2.	It's very important for me to stick to a schedule.	4	3	2	1
3.	I'm very relaxed about time.	4	3	2	1
4.	Meeting deadlines is very important to me.	4	3	2	1
5.	Unexpected things happen all the time—just flow with it.	4	3	2	1
6.	I get irritated when people are not on time.	4	3	2	1
7.	It's OK to be late when you're having a wonderful conversation with someone.	4	3	2	1
8.	I like to be very punctual for all my appointments.	4	3	2	1
9.	I'm more concerned with the relationship in front of me than clock time.	4	3	2	1
10.	I keep an appointment book with me all the time.	4	3	2	1

Scoring: Add up the scores on all the even-numbered items and you will find your monochronic-time preference score. *Monochronic-time preference* score: _____. Add up the scores on all the odd-numbered items and you will find your polychronic-time preference score. *Polychronic-time preference* score: _____.

Interpretation: Scores on each time dimension can range from 5 to 20; the higher the score, the more monochronic and/or polychronic time tendencies you have. If the scores are similar on both time dimensions, you are a bichronemic-time communicator.

Reflection probes: Take a moment to think of the following questions: Do you like your monochronic and/or polychronic time tendencies? Why or why not? Where do you learn your sense of time or clock rhythms? How do you think you can deal effectively with people who have a very different time preference from you?

scheduled and divided allotments so a person can concentrate on one thing at a time. The schedule is given top priority. The United States, Germany, and Switzerland are classic examples of MT-time cultures. Students attending college or a university belong to an MT culture as well. For example, a college student, Kris, has a thoughtful view of time: "I think that my generation in particular has an interesting view of time. I think that we idealize the past, seeing it as being far much more fun and happy than it probably was. We tend to de-value the present, making it seem worse than it is…because when you're in it, it is harder to see the bigger picture. We also tend to view the future as being scarier than it will be. Like: *What will we do after graduation? What's next?* seems to be the current theme of our lives. My mom commented on it once, telling me that I do not know how to just do nothing. I constantly have to be doing something. In fact,

JEOPARDY BOX 7.1 LONGEST AND SHORTEST WORK HOURS, 2009*

Longest work hours

Country	Average work hours per week
1. Turkey	49.4
2. South Korea	46.6
3. Greece	42.5
4. Czech Republic	41.4
5. Chile	41.1

Shortest work hours

Country	Average work hours per week
1. The Netherlands	30.6
2. Norway	33.9
3. Denmark	33.7
4. Switzerland	35.1
5. Germany	35.7

*Note: From a select cohort of thirty-five countries.

Organisation for Economic Co-Operation and Development. http://stats.oecd.org/Index.aspx?DataSetCode=ANHRS (retrieved April 23, 2011).

TABLE 7.1 CHARACTERISTICS OF MONOCHRONIC AND POLYCHRONIC TIME

Monochronic time	Polychronic time
Clock time	Situational time
Appointment time	Flextime
Segmented activities	Simultaneous activities
Task-oriented	Relationship-oriented
Future-focused	Past/present-focused
Tangible outcome perspective	Historical perspective

this weekend, I could not fully enjoy hanging out with friends because I was thinking about all of the homework I'm going to be doing all day on Sunday."

People in **polychronic-time** (PT) cultures pay attention to relational time (involvement with people) and place more emphasis on completing human transactions than on holding to schedules. For example, two polychronic Spaniards conversing on a

BLOG POST 7.5

We've lived in Morocco for three years now, and each time we change the clocks (ahead in Spring and back in Summer), we are always asked the same questions during the week of the change. Our conversations go something like this:

> James: Said, do you want to get together for coffee on Sunday afternoon around 4 p.m.?
> Said: Yes, that would be great!
> James: Okay, see you at 4 then.
> Said: Is that the old 4 or the new 4?

Some change right away, but other people will continue to operate on the old time for a couple of weeks and so we will have this sort of conversation regularly. It is interesting to see how another culture views time. Although the clocks will have changed, in the mind of many Moroccans it is not necessarily a fixed thing. Could you imagine explaining to your boss on Monday morning if you show up an hour late, "Oh, I am still operating on the old time?" This is just another reminder that in Morocco, we are living in a very relationally based culture and not a time-oriented one.

—James, a U.S. American living in Marrakesh

street corner would likely opt to be late for their next appointment rather than abruptly end the conversation before it came to a natural conclusion. For Hall and Hall (1987), Arab, African, Latin American, Asian, and Mediterranean cultures are representative of PT patterns (see Blog Post 7.5). One example of a place with PT cultural patterns is countries in Africa. For many Africans, time creates group harmony and participation among the members (Pennington, 1990). Group connectedness can be seen in the dances and drumming. Time for traditional Africans is viewed as organic rather than mechanical.

When PT and MT people hang out together, disagreements and misunderstandings often occur, for example, in planning a road trip. An MT traveling companion will feel comfortable if the car has GPS installed, if hotel or hostel rooms are confirmed, if a daily schedule is planned, and so on. The PT person will respond by waiting to do these things just prior to departure. As Joyce from Singapore says, "This drives me crazy. I hate waiting until the last minute to do things, and he hates to do too many things in advance. We plan trips around our e-fares to save money so that means sometimes we don't even know where we are going until a few days before we leave."

To be flexible, we must work toward living with both types of time orientations. This adds a lot of spontaneity to life. To quote from Ralph Waldo Emerson, "Finish each day and be done with it. You have done what you could. Some blunders and absurdities no doubt crept in; forget them as soon as you can. Tomorrow is a new day; begin it well and serenely and with too high a spirit to be encumbered with your old nonsense."

Studies indicate that members of individualistic cultures tend to follow the MT pattern, whereas members of collectivistic cultures tend to follow the PT pattern (Hall, 1983). Members of individualistic cultures tend to view time as something that can be controlled and arranged. Members of collectivistic cultures tend to view time as experientially based (i.e., living and experiencing time fully rather than mechanically monitoring clock time).

Now let's do a quick my.blog 7.4.

Hall (1959) made distinctions for arriving late in the United States in accordance with chunks of time within five minutes. Therefore, in the above question, if you are five to ten minutes late, you are in the "mumble something" time, and you offer a small statement. "Slight apology" time is ten to fifteen minutes late, and therefore you are required to apologize. "Mildly insulting or serious apology" time is fifteen to thirty minutes late, so you are expected to offer a persuasive reason for your tardiness. The last two, "rude" time (thirty to forty-five minutes) and "downright insulting" time (forty-five to sixty minutes), are both unacceptable. Time is omnipresent. Chronemic cues allow us to manage our intercultural interactions and facilitate clearer understandings regarding this form of nonverbal communication. Studying chronemics gives us a better understanding of the rhythmic dance of time.

In sum, it is so easy to draw conclusions about people without understanding their culture. When someone from a different culture does not look you in the eye, it is easy to jump to the conclusion that he or she disrespects you, is shy, or is not interested. However, some cultural groups believe that looking someone in the eye is disrespectful. Before drawing any conclusions from watching people's actions, engage in a conversation and find meaning behind the

---

my.blog 7.4

Your MT friend is waiting for you at a restaurant. What will you say if you are

5–10 minutes late? _____
10–15 minutes late? _____
15–30 minutes late? _____
30–45 minutes late? _____
45–60 minutes late? _____

---

gestures. Nonverbal cues communicate status, power, ingroup and outgroup differences, and unique identities. In attempting to understand within-culture and across-culture nonverbal variations, look to interpersonal sensitivity, respect, and open-minded attitudes as good first steps in gaining nonverbal entrance to a culture.

INTERCULTURAL REALITY CHECK: DO-ABLES

In this chapter, we have discussed the importance of nonverbal communication across cultures. More specifically, we have explored artifacts and clothing, paralanguage, facial expressions, various nonverbal hand gestures, haptics or touch, and cross-cultural regulation of space and time (see the answers to Blog Pics 7.2 and 7.3). Each form of nonverbal communication reflects our larger cultural values and also expresses our unique personalities and identities. More important, the situation in which the nonverbal behavior takes place is quite critical in adding meaning to our accurate interpretation.

To be a flexible nonverbal communicator across cultures, be mindful of your own nonverbal behaviors and signals that you send, intentionally or not. Be cautious when you interpret unfamiliar gestures and nonverbal behaviors in a new culture. We present you with a set of nonverbal points to consider in communicating across cultures:

- Be flexible when you observe and identify nonverbal display rules. Your observation and initial reaction may not match the rules across cultural groups. Flexibility allows you to be patient when you observe and match identities, status, distance, expectations, and appropriate nonverbal behaviors in various situations.

- Go deeper: different meanings and expectations of nonverbal norms and rules are more than what one sees; there is typically a deeper-than-surface explanation. This may help you move toward an alternative explanation and a clearer picture.
- Remember that **what** someone says is not as important as **how** it is said. It is important to be aware of one's actions when expressing feelings in words. Sometimes a person can portray a more serious and unfavorable tonal presence than the intended meaning.
- As a flexible nonverbal communicator, express emotions and attitudes that correspond to your comfort level but, at the same time, be adaptive and sensitive to the appropriate nonverbal display rules in a particular situation and within a particular cultural community.
- Because nonverbal behavior is oftentimes so ambiguous and situation dependent, learn to be less judgmental and more tentative in interpreting others' unfamiliar nonverbal signals.

We form impressions of others oftentimes based on superficial nonverbal cues and stereotypes that we derived from our media images. The next chapter will move us to a discussion on the ethnocentric viewpoints that we form and the stereotypic images we bring to bear when we encounter culturally unfamiliar others.

MANAGING CHALLENGES IN INTERCULTURAL RELATIONSHIPS FLEXIBLY

CHAPTER 8

WHAT CAUSES US TO HOLD BIASES AGAINST OUTGROUPS?

CHAPTER OUTLINE

I was having lunch at the university restaurant with my work colleagues when I glanced over at the other table. The table was beautifully decorated with rose petals and fancy packages. The women that were going to be seated were immaculately dressed. I could see the Couture, Chanel, and Gucci. I was curious and walked over to their table. "Excuse me, your table is so beautiful. I was wondering what the special occasion was?" One woman smiled and replied, "We are celebrating friendship day. We do this every year. By the way, may I have a glass of ice tea, no cubes please?" I was totally stunned. "I am so sorry, I did not introduce myself. I am an Assistant Dean in the College of Arts and Sciences." The white woman apologized and ended with, "I thought you were the Maître D—I mean, the Head Maître D."

As an African American woman who has worked on this campus for over a decade, I am still disappointed and somewhat dismayed that, after all of these years, color matters. It is a daily reminder that I am different. For those who are ignorant (and/or racist), this is a teaching moment, and for me, these moments keep me grounded and motivated me to keep being a change agent—with my students and others who I may encounter daily.

—Pauline, *Assistant Dean*

This real-life experience is just a speck of the millions more around us. Ask anyone: "Have you ever been mistreated or stereotyped by others?" and the answer would be "Yes!" However, if we ask the same person whether they are prejudiced or carry prejudicial feelings, we may get a resounding "No!" These examples illustrate two very important points about interactions with people from cultural groups other than our own. First, we usually experience interaction anxiety because we do not have enough information about unfamiliar others—or the stereotypic information we have about others needs to be updated. This lack of knowledge can lead to misunderstanding, or incompetent communication, or both. If we don't have enough information about cultural strangers, this may trigger cultural or ethnic–racial identity separation or distinctiveness.

Second, if we have only partial norms and rules to direct us through the communication interaction, we may fall back into using stereotypes. Although some stereotypes may have an aspect of truth, many group-based stereotypes are inaccurate. The scenario above is the classic recipe for intergroup misunderstandings and prejudice. Communicating with strangers from other cultural groups involves the interplay between ingroup and outgroup membership boundaries.

This chapter is organized into five sections. First, three key principles of human perception will be discussed. Second, biased intergroup filters such as ethnocentrism and stereotypes will be explored. Third, we will examine the effects of interactions with those who are different from ourselves and how we engage in intergroup attribution biases. Fourth, we will examine the shattered lens of prejudice, discrimination, and racism. Concrete suggestions are given to filter out stereotypes, minimize prejudice, and find a sense of peace in our chaotic world. Last, we recommend do-able checkpoints to deal with ethnocentrism and prejudice issues.

HUMAN PERCEPTION TENDENCIES: SOME GENERAL PRINCIPLES

As a reminder, culture shapes the way we see our world. Our vision of the world and information we absorb occurs through a complex filtering process. Both cognitive (mental) and affective (emotions) filters serve as a set of invisible glasses we wear to interpret and evaluate behaviors of intercultural strangers. These glasses allow us to see the world around us, make sense of the world, and interpret behaviors around us. But glasses can limit and distort our vision, making it difficult to accurately see what is directly in front of us.

Human **perception** is the process of selecting cues quickly from the environment, organizing them into a coherent pattern and labeling such a pattern, and interpreting that pattern in accordance to our expectation. Perception is typically a quick three-step process of *selective attention, selective organization,* and *selective interpretation.* Each of these steps is heavily affected by our cultural conditioning process.

Selective Attention

In the **selective attention process**, we pick out cues quickly from our cultural landscape. In an unfamiliar environment, we tend to pay closer attention to the cues that match our own salient identities (e.g., same age group), cues that are distinctive from the group (e.g., different skin color), and cues that serve our interaction expectations or goals (e.g., shaking hands greeting ritual). Because it is impossible to pick up every detail or stimulus that we receive in an overloaded environment, we thus selectively choose from the incoming data. The selective attention principle can explain part of the opening story: the white woman was quickly drawn to the distinctive feature (i.e., skin color) of Assistant Dean Pauline. Her selective attention to skin color also paired quickly with the expected identity role of Assistant Dean Pauline in that university restaurant setting. In other words, the white female diner quickly formed a stereotypic, cognitive map concerning an African American female's role in the restaurant setting.

Beyond skin color, another distinctive feature can be someone's accent. For example, if someone's accent does not match their "looks," we will tend to concentrate more on the sound of the distinctive voice, pitch, or tone. You may be asking yourself, "Where is this accent from?" rather than listening to what the person is saying. Another characteristic of the quick-step selection process is observing any change in the environment, including changes in people's behavior. Have you ever walked into a very noisy class when everyone suddenly gets quiet? You may start checking out the way you dress and wonder whether the students are staring at you—only to find out they are actually looking at the teacher walking quietly behind you.

Culture, family, media, interaction goal, and context all play a big part in what we selectively choose to pay attention to in our everyday environment.

Selective Organization and Labeling

The second step in the perception process is the **selective organization and labeling process**. Our culture and the language we speak guide us to aspects of our environment that we consider relevant. We have learned from our cultural/ethnic socialization to organize our perceptions by grouping similar objects, people, or things together and labeling them with a symbol or name. Concurrently, we also organize objects, people, or things into the "other" category with a label.

Thus, returning to the opening story, the white woman who incorrectly classified Assistant Dean Pauline as the Maître D or Head Maître D was probably using a two-category language system in her mindset: "dinner guests" and "servers." As she organized her thoughts in her mind, she also put Assistant Dean Pauline as a prototype of "black female restaurant waitress." Despite her apology, the apology actually further reflected her unconscious perceptual bias in action.

How you choose to organize your perception and "name" your perception depends on your identities, values, attitudes, language labels, and the context. For example, people commonly use simple names and only a few categories to catalog colors, such as purple, orange, blue, and so forth. Clothing buyers from H&M assign these broad-based colors to their clothes.

However, if you are a fabric buyer specialist (i.e., your professional role identity) for Banana Republic, you probably use more distinctive labels to identify the different shades of blue (e.g., *periwinkle*, *baby*, *sky*, *royal*, and *navy blue*) and you may even assign gender to them. For instance, you might assign *military blue* for men but *regatta bay* for women. Meanwhile, those outside the fashion industry might not even perceive such nuanced color distinctions in their everyday life. Although language labels can help to impose some order and predictability to our chaotic environment, they can also delimit our thinking and create serious misunderstandings. Once we create the labels, our interaction script tends to follow the labels that we have created inside our heads.

We also tend to fill in missing information to round off our perception into a more comprehensive whole or a complete picture. Suppose you are at the airport and you see a man pushing a child in a baby stroller. You will "fill in" your inference that the man is the father and the child is his. This "filling-in-the-blank" tendency is derived from the meanings that we form in our everyday living. Because of cultural and personal experience differences, every individual has his or her own unique perceptual processes and filling-in-the blank moments. If we're doing this in our own cultural community, many of our guesses could be accurate or not too far off. However, if we're doing the guessing in a new cultural community, we may be totally off base in our filling-in the blank moments.

Selective Interpretation

The last step in human perception is **selective interpretation**. Interpretation allows us to attach meaning to the data we receive, and this includes our expectations. Expectations involve what we anticipate and predict about how others will communicate with us during an interaction.

Expectations are the filters of our perceptions of others. We have an image of how we expect people to behave in a given situation in accordance to our own identity role and our perceived identity role of others. If a person violates our expectations, we will become surprised and emotionally aroused and pay more attention to this person's strange behavior (Burgoon & Burgoon, 2001).

Thus, in the opening story, both the white female diner and Assistant Dean Pauline were caught off guard. The white female diner perceived herself as a restaurant guest who was being approached by an African American waitress. Meanwhile, Assistant Dean Pauline perceived herself in the professional dean's role and was trying to be friendly and gracious in inquiring about the get-together of the well-coiffed female diners around the beautifully decorated table. Both were caught by surprise when the intergroup–interpersonal interaction script did not go as intended.

These three perceptual filters (selective attention, selective organization, and selective interpretation) act as major barriers to effective intercultural communication. Ineffective communication between cultural groups often occurs because we assume that we perceive and interpret other people's behavior in an objective, unbiased manner. The reality, however, is that our perceptions of others are highly subjective, selective, and biased. However, by being more mindful of the biased mindset we carry inside our mental map, perhaps we can "catch ourselves" more often and counter our preconceived expectations with flexible adjustments (Brewer, 2010). In practicing flexible communication, we are ready to try on different styles and shades of eyeglasses—to learn to see things from different lenses. We turn now to a discussion of two major intergroup filters that affect communication with unfamiliar others.

BIASED INTERGROUP FILTERS: ETHNOCENTRISM AND STEREOTYPES

Ethnocentrism and Communication

In the United States, three particular sports were invented and developed within: U.S. football, basketball, and baseball. Over the years, all three sports developed a national championship competition. The winner of the U.S. football competition is named the Superbowl "World" Champion; in baseball, the "World" Series is played for the U.S. championship; and until 1986, the National Basketball Association's top team was the NBA "World" Champion. This illustrates the ethnocentric tendency of U.S. sports: these championships are not played

globally, internationally, or across borders, yet the winners are declared champions of the "world!" This despite the fact that the single most popular sport in the world, by far, is soccer (called "football" in many nations). The Federation Internationale de Football Association (FIFA) World Cup is truly a world competition.

Before continuing your reading, fill out the brief my.blog 8.1 survey. The assessment is designed to help you determine the degree of your ethnocentrism tendencies (See also Blog Pic 8.1).

Ethnocentrism comes from two Greek words and can be broken down into its components. *Ethno* refers to "one's own ethnic or cultural group," and *centrism* means that "one's own group should be looked upon as the center of the world." **Ethnocentrism** means that we consider the views and standards of our own ingroup as more important than those of any outgroup. Outgroups are at a disadvantage because we constantly make judgments based on our own group's standards and values. Examples of standards include beliefs that one's own group practices the correct religion, knows how to treat people with respect, employs the best ways of educating their children, and votes for the most qualified political candidates (Brislin, 2003; Verkuyten, 2010). If depicted visually, ethnocentrism would be the core (i.e., our valued ingroup is in the center), and all outgroups are placed at the periphery, the outside (see Blog Post 8.1).

Ethnocentrism has a way of allowing us to focus specifically on events that matter more on our soil

Blog Pic 8.1   Boundary regulation among birds.

my.blog 8.1 PROBING YOUR ETHNOCENTRISM TENDENCIES

Instructions: The following items describe how people generally think about themselves and their cultural groups. Let your first inclination be your guide and circle the number in the scale that best reflects your overall agreement with the statement. The following scale is used for each item:

4 = YES! = *strongly agree*—IT'S ME!
3 = yes = *moderately agree*—it's kind of like me
2 = no = *moderately disagree*—it's kind of not me
1 = NO! = *strongly disagree*—IT'S NOT ME!

Generally speaking . . .	SA	MA	MD	SD
1. I believe my culture offers the best lifestyles compared with other cultures.	4	3	2	1
2. I like routines and a stable environment.	4	3	2	1
3. My culture is very advanced in comparison with other cultures.	4	3	2	1
4. I don't like ambiguous or uncertain situations.	4	3	2	1
5. My culture provides the best opportunity for its members to achieve their goals.	4	3	2	1
6. I get very stressed in unfamiliar settings.	4	3	2	1
7. My cultural group has the most expressive language and vocabulary.	4	3	2	1
8. I don't like to approach strangers for anything.	4	3	2	1
9. My culture has a very rich history and traditions.	4	3	2	1
10. I get quite intimidated thinking of living in another country for more than a year.	4	3	2	1

Scoring: Add up the scores on all the odd-numbered items and you will find your ethnocentrism score. *Ethnocentrism* score: _____. Add up the scores on all the even-numbered items and you will find your tolerance of ambiguity score. *Tolerance of ambiguity* score: _____.

Interpretation: Scores on each attitude dimension can range from 5 to 20; the higher the score, the more ethnocentric and/or intolerant of ambiguity you are. If the scores are similar on both attitude dimensions, you are high on cultural ethnocentrism and high on your fear of ambiguous situations.

Reflection probes: Take a moment to compare your scores with a classmate's. Think of the following questions: Where did you learn your attitudes about your own culture and its value compared with other cultures? What fears do you have in approaching new or unfamiliar situations? Why? How do you think you can prepare yourself more effectively in dealing with new cultural situations and cultural strangers?

---

than ten thousand miles away. This relates back to our discussion of proxemics: whatever is closer to us has a little more value. There are many examples of ethnocentric tendencies. The previous example with sports events assumes that U.S. teams are the best, although they are playing teams only within U.S. borders. The two Chinese characters for *China* translate as the "Middle/Central Kingdom." The characters or pictographs for *China*, first written more than four thousand years ago during the Hsia dynasty, are translated as "the center of the universe." Take a look at a nation's world atlas; it is not surprising that every nation depicts its own country in a central position on the map, with neighboring states shown as peripheral.

BLOG POST 8.1

My husband, Don, was at a self-serve gas station a few years ago and, while in line, a white middle-aged customer became angry when the Korean American cashiers communicated to each other in Korean. He yelled, "Speak English. This is America!" Then he turned to my (also white and middle-aged) husband and angrily stated that those foreigners ought to go back to where they came from. My husband realized that the angry man just assumed he'd agree with the comments because they looked alike, and my husband wanted to let everyone within earshot know that he completely disagreed with the angry man. So, he responded by loudly saying, "Oh, no. I don't agree. I like them. I want more of them to come to our country." This silenced the impatient man, and my husband hoped it indicated, to everyone else who heard, that not all white middle-aged men were the same.

—Alex, *college instructor*

Blog Pic 8.2 Is this really a better bakery?

Ethnocentrism is a defense mechanism used to view our culture as superior to other cultures and thus we perceive our way of life as the most reasonable and proper. As a result, we expect that all other groups should follow our way of living and behaving (Said, 1978). Where does ethnocentrism come from? Like our perceptions, ethnocentrism is reinforced and learned through a cultural socialization process. We favor ingroup standards and communication practices because we are familiar and feel secure with those standards and norms. Ethnocentrism can also consist of both implicit and explicit attitudes toward outgroup members' customs or behaviors (Leyens & Demoulin, 2010; Stephan & Stephan, 2001; Tausch & Hewstone, 2010).

As human beings, we display ethnocentric tendencies for three reasons: (1) we tend to define what goes on in our own culture as *natural* and *correct* and what goes on in other cultures as *unnatural* and *incorrect*; (2) we tend to perceive ingroup values, customs, norms, and roles as universally applicable; and (3) we tend to experience distance from the outgroup, especially when our group identity is threatened or under attack (Triandis, 1990). As we interact with outgroup members, our ethnocentric tendencies may be blurred by our perception of privilege. Privilege is an "invisible package of unearned assets" (McIntosh, 2002, p. 424) that one is oblivious to, but we can count

on this backpack we carry around with us each day. This privilege can be based on color, ethnicity, gender, social status, geographical location, etc. By assuming even on an unconscious level that we "deserve" certain rights over others, this attitude represents one aspect of ethnocentric thinking. Let's take a look at the following infamous example.

In April 2011, Marilyn Davenport, an official with the Orange County (California) Republican Central Committee, forwarded a photo she had received in her e-mail box to several other committee members. It depicted a chimpanzee "family" with President Barack Obama's face overlaid onto the young chimp's. After her actions became public, Davenport defended herself in a press conference by saying, "I think it is only racist when the intent in my heart is racist, and that was not my intent" (Wisckol, 2011).

Ms. Davenport provides a sad but rich example of how we communicate ethnocentrism and racism. In fact, ethnocentrism comes in different gradations. Lukens (1978) used the communicative distances of indifference, avoidance, and disparagement to discuss the *communication degrees* of ethnocentrism. The **distance of indifference** (i.e., low ethnocentrism) reflects the lack of sensitivity in our verbal and nonverbal interactions in dealing with dissimilar others. From the use of insensitive questioning approaches to the use of "foreigner talk" (i.e., exaggeratedly slow speech or a dramatically loud tone of voice, as if all foreigners were deaf and mentally challenged), the speech pattern serves as a reminder that these strangers are different.

The **distance of avoidance** (i.e., moderate ethnocentrism) reflects attempted linguistic or dialect switching in the presence of outgroup members, as well as displayed nonverbal inattention (e.g., members of the dominant group maintain eye contact only with members of their group) to accentuate ingroup connection and avoidance of outgroup members.

Finally, the **distance of disparagement** (i.e., high ethnocentrism) refers to the use of racist jokes or hate-filled speech used to downgrade outgroup members. For example, if you ask about the photo that Ms. Davenport forwarded, most people living in the United States and the world would interpret the photo as racist. Even the Orange County Republican Party Chairman, Scott Baugh, understood this, saying, "The e-mail is racist whether she intended it or not" and calling for Davenport's resignation.

To counteract rigid ethnocentric attitudes, J. Bennett and M. Bennett (2004) developed the Developmental Model of Intercultural Sensitivity (DMIS) to capture how individuals *experience* cultural difference via various change zones. The core assumption behind the DMIS is that as an individual experiences cultural difference in a more complex and nuanced manner, her competence in dealing with cultural differences increases. The DMIS identifies three "states" of ethnocentrism and three "states" of ethnorelativism. Each

state reflects a particular cognitive worldview expressed in certain kinds of attitudes and behaviors related to cultural difference.

The three states of ethnocentrism include denial of cultural difference, defense against cultural difference, and minimization of cultural difference. *Denial of cultural difference* is the state in which one's own cultural difference is experienced as the only real one. Other cultures are avoided by maintaining psychological or physical isolation. If "dissimilar others" impinge on our ingroup existence, we may act aggressively to eliminate the difference. *Defense against cultural difference* is the state in which one's own culture (or adopted culture) is experienced as the only good one. The world is organized as "we" versus "them"—we are the "superior" group, and they are the "inferior" one. Individuals in this state are highly threatened by outgroup members and they tend to be hypercritical of outgroups. Alternatively, individuals can also experience a "reverse defense" state in which their "adopted culture" is viewed as far superior to their homeland culture. *Minimization of cultural difference* is the state in which elements (e.g., nonverbal eye contact system or value dimensions) of one's own culture are viewed as "universals." Individuals under this state tend to proclaim that beyond superficial food customs or holiday celebration differences, at the core, we are all the same, the same like my preferred behavior or values in my own cultural group (Bennett, 1993; Bennett & Bennett, 2004; see Figure 8.1).

The next set of three states reflects the development of ethnorelativism. The three ethnorelative states include acceptance of cultural difference, adaptation to cultural difference, and integration of cultural difference. *Acceptance of cultural difference* is the state in which one's own culture is experienced as one of many possible diverse and complex cultural experiences. Individuals at this state are curious and respectful of cultural differences on the cognitive level. *Adaptation of cultural difference* is that state in which the experience of another culture yields perceptual shifting—seeing things from the other cultural angle—and also behavioral adaptation appropriate to that cultural frame of reference (e.g., viewing "lateness" differently and following nonverbal "polychronic" behaviors, based on new culture's norms and practices).

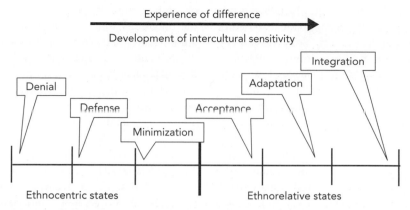

FIGURE 8.1 A Developmental Model of Intercultural Sensitivity (DMIS). *Source*: Adapted from J. Bennett and M. Bennett (2004).

Integration of cultural difference is the state in which the individual intentionally (on cognitive, behavioral, and affective levels) incorporates diverse cultural worldviews into one's identity and is able to transform polarized value sets into complementary value sets. She can also communicate fluidly as a cultural bridge person or a cultural mediator in a culturally effective and also globally humanistic leadership direction (Bennett, 2009; Pusch, 2009).

Stereotypes and Communication

Stereotypes are exaggerated pictures we create about a group of people on the basis of our inflexible beliefs and expectations about the characteristics or behaviors of the group (Lippman, 1936; Stephan & Stephan, 1992, 1996). Before we discuss the concept of stereotypes further, let's check out the following story in Blog Post 8.2.

Group membership (e.g., Hawaiians, Texans, Tea Party, engineers, dancers, and stylists) conjures certain stereotypic images in our mental map. A *stereotype* is an overgeneralization toward a group of people without any attempt to perceive individual variations. Stereotypes contain the content of our social categories. A stereotype can refer to a subconsciously held belief about a membership group. The content of stereotypes can convey both positive and negative information (e.g., "Asians are good in math" or "French people are arrogant"). Thus, we use preconceived images in stereotyping a large group of individuals without

BLOG POST 8.2

I remember one incident, in particular, in which my graduate advisor's support was critical in encouraging me to move on. The incident was a conversation between myself and a professor when he explained why I did not receive a full-year teaching assistantship like the rest of the TA's. The exchange went something like this: "Stella, it's not that you're not good. It's just that life is like a horse race. Some horses get the first prize, and others are runners-up. . . . With your accent, it's just very difficult for you to make it to first place. . . . What I'm trying to say is . . ."

My heart sank upon hearing those words. At that moment, I genuinely had serious doubts about whether I belonged to this very Americanized "speech" communication discipline. It was my advisor's (Dr. Mae Bell) comforting words and academic faith in me that held me together in those days. It was also what my husband (Charles) said to me that echoes still: "Stella, you should go back and tell your professor, what happens in a real horse race is that most people bet on the wrong horse—they have chosen poorly."

—Stella, *college instructor*

tending to individual variations (Fiske, Cuddy, Glick, & Xu, 2002; Fiske & Russell, 2010). When we stereotype French people as rude or believe that Asians can do math, we may be basing our stereotypes on past observations, media images, or what we have heard from others. The stereotype may stem from two to three communication incidents with just a handful of French people. Nevertheless, we devise categories that frame the expectations and meanings we attach to people's behaviors or actions in general.

According to the Stereotype Content Model (SCM), we form stereotypes of individuals based on their national or group identity along two dimensions: low–high warmth dimension and low–high competence dimension (Cuddy, Fiske, & Glick, 2008). The *perception of warmth* dimension is guided by whether our nation (or our group) is in competition or cooperation with another nation. So, for instance, low-warmth countries (or groups) would be those with which we believe there is competition between our country (or group) and the other country. This perception may help to create U.S. individuals' stereotype of, for instance, Germans or rich people as lacking warmth. The *perception of competence* dimension is guided by whether we perceive the particular nation (or group) has low status or high status (Cuddy et al., 2009). This perception may help to create U.S. individuals' stereotype of, for instance, Haitians or the elderly as lacking in competence. In a study testing intergroup stereotypes from their own and other EU countries, individuals were found to stereotype nations as low

on both warmth and competence features (e.g., hostile outgroups), high on both warmth and competence features (e.g., own ingroups and allies), low on warmth and high on competence (e.g., Germany and the UK), and high on warmth and low on perceived competence (e.g., Portugal, Spain, and Italy; Smith, Bond, & Kagitcibasi, 2006, p. 226; see Figure 8.2).

Let's check out another example. One midsummer day in 2009, a police officer in Cambridge, Massachusetts, got a call about a residential burglary in progress. The suspect was trying to enter the home through a window. Arriving at the scene, the officer encountered an African American male who claimed he was the homeowner and had trouble unlocking his door after it became jammed. After his arrest based on "disorderly conduct," the reality was that this gentleman was a famous Harvard professor, Professor Henry Louis "Skip" Gates Jr., and he was also the homeowner. This racial profiling of "burglar" and "black man" made news around the world because of the question: would the same thing happen if the entering male

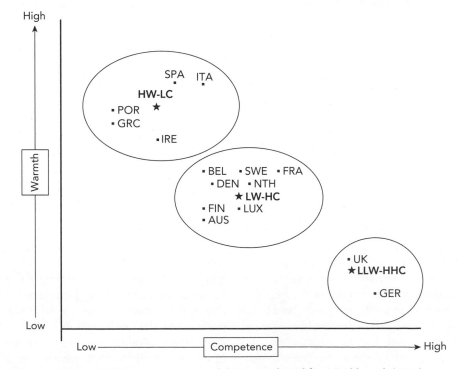

FIGURE 8.2 A Two-Dimensional Stereotype Content Model. *Source*: Adapted from Cuddy et al. (2009). Note: HW-LC = high warmth–low competence; LW-HC = low warmth–high competence; LLW-HHC = lowest warmth–highest competence.

were white? President Obama invited both individuals to the White House for a "beer summit" to discuss the incident. Although the controversy has died down, there is no doubt that stereotypes played a part in this unfortunate incident (see also, for example, Ben-Porath & Shaker, 2010).

There are also times that we may have absolutely no information about a new category and we may need to create new assumptions or guesses to ground this unique grouping (Brabant, Watson, & Gallois, 2010). For example, if we learn that someone is *transgendered*, we tend to be instantaneously guided by the language category of transgendered—if we have one at all. With limited explanation of describing such a person, you may start with "a person who wants to be another gender." This is only partially true: A transgendered male or female is not only unhappy as a member of that particular sex (or gender) assigned, he or she feels psychologically detached by the anatomical structure of the body, particularly the genitals. Min, who has undergone sexual reassignment from female to male, says he was physically a normal female but believed he *belonged* to the other sex and wanted to *function* as a male. We may be so captivated by the distinctive features of a label or naming process that oftentimes we may forget to pay close attention to his or her other rich, social membership qualities or complex, unique traits.

Many factors shape our mindscape. One reason people stereotype is because of language usage. Paired words in the English language, for example, often encourage polarized thinking: straight or gay, us and them, females and males, blacks and whites, to name a few. Although polarized language usage allows us to manage our social environment more efficiently, polarized perceptions often lead us to interpret the social world as either good *or* evil, fair *or* unfair, and right *or* wrong. Beyond language and selective personal experience, the contemporary media play a critical role in shaping our stereotypes about our own group and those of others.

Stereotypes: We Are What We Watch

Media images shape the way we view dissimilar others from different cultural–ethnic groups. As a result, we associate different stereotypes as "character types" or as specific ethnic groups who represent the associated images (Mastro, Behm-Morawitz, & Kopacz, 2008). For example, film directors Chris O'Brien and Jason Witmer (2003) produced a documentary about how Hollywood stereotypes the Native American. This confirms Bird's (1999) research, who observed that American Indian males are often cast as "doomed warriors" who are strong and attractive but are also often cast as either sidekicks or loved by strong, independent-spirited white women (e.g., *The Last of the Mohicans*). Or there is the wise Indian elder, who has abundant knowledge and is the source of ancient wisdom. African Americans and Latino/as do not have it any easier. According to Orbe and Harris (2008), African American males are typically relegated to comedic roles and belong to certain stereotypes, such as Sambo (lazy and content), Uncle Tom (quiet and respectful), and Buck (athletic and sexually powerful). African American women, however, are depicted as either sexually enticing or asexual and nurturing mammies. Latina/os have been relegated to roles identified as sensual and "firey" (Cortes, 2000, 2002) criminals or bandits, and buffoons (Pieraccini & Alligood, 2005).

But there is hope for us who care about what we watch. In 2000, Dora the Explorer served as the first original children's television programming to increase viewers' appreciation and awareness of Latino culture, introduce the Spanish language, and enhance preschoolers' appreciation for the value of communicating in another language. So popular was this series, a spinoff, "Go, Diego, Go!," was created and another, "Ni hao Kai-lan," features young Kai-lan Chow who speaks both English and Mandarin Chinese (http://www.nickjr.com). These programs are very popular, teaching U.S. children that their peers come in many ethnicities and may speak different languages.

It is inevitable that all individuals stereotype. The key to dealing with the issue effectively is to learn to distinguish between inflexible stereotyping and flexible stereotyping. *Inflexible stereotyping (or mindless stereotyping)* holds on to preconceived and negative stereotypes by operating on automatic pilot. We use rigid language labels to typecast a wide range of individuals that fit the label. We dismiss information and evidence that is more favorable to the outgroup, and we presume one member's behavior represents all members' behaviors and norms. We are also rigid in our preconceived attitude and are unwilling to change our early-formed impressions or evaluations (see Table 8.1).

In comparison with inflexible stereotypes, we must address the characteristics of *flexible stereotyping (or mindful stereotyping)*. Essentially, to be more flexible in our preconceived notion of unfamiliar others, we need to be "mindfully minding our mind" as we form our stereotypes of outgroup members. We must recognize that we often form stereotypes of others based on the three reactive processes of human perception (selective attention, organization/labeling, and interpretation) as mentioned earlier in the chapter. However, as we engage in flexible or mindful stereotyping, we should treat our language labels or interpretations as the "first best guesses." We should engage in open-ended interpretive process versus premature closure process. Refraining from typecasting an entire group on the basis of slim evidence, or no evidence, is also a good first step. Using loose, descriptive categories rather than polarized, evaluative categories is another way to mindfully *flex* our stereotypic picture of an identity group. Using a qualifying statement (e.g., "sometimes," "a few people from that group," etc.) or a contextual statement (e.g., "when in this situation") to frame our interpretations allows an outgroup member to be an individual with multifaceted traits and *not* just a representative of an entire group. This is a critical de-stereotyping step. Finally, being open

to new information and evidence gives us an opportunity to get to know, in-depth, the most important membership and personal identities of the individuals within the group (Brewer, 2010; Schmidt & Hewstone, 2010).

Flexible stereotyping allows us to be more open-minded, and inflexible stereotyping makes us short-sighted. Flexible stereotyping reflects a willingness on our part to change our loosely held images based on diversified, direct face-to-face encounters. Interacting with individuals who are different from us can be uncomfortable at times. We may even feel nervous or anxious because of their strange behaviors or unfamiliar accents. By being aware of our own zone of discomfort and admitting that we are anxious or confused in terms of how to approach the cultural stranger, we may be taking a solid step forward, moving from inflexible stereotyping to flexible relating and connecting. *Perceptions, ethnocentrism,* and *stereotypes* provide the contents of our filtering process. We now move on to the outcome, our response to intercultural outgroup members.

MARKING INGROUP–OUTGROUP MEMBERSHIP BOUNDARIES

Us versus Them

As a brief reminder, social identity theory is the study of ingroup and outgroup membership, specifically how your emotional attachment to a social group plays a key role in the formation of your social and personal identity. Ingroup members are people with whom you feel connected, such as family members and close friends, whereas outgroup members are those from whom you feel emotionally and psychologically detached, such as strangers or an opposing religious group (Pettigrew, 1978; Pettigrew & Tropp, 2008; Phoenix, 2010). Hanging out with your ingroup gives you a sense of security and belonging, and being around the outgroup gives you a foundation for comparison—especially in stacking up all the pros about your wonderful ingroup and all the negatives about the outgroup values, norms, and behaviors (Brewer & Miller, 1996).

In this frame, an ingroup is perceived to have positive value for the self because of perceived similarity.

TABLE 8.1 INFLEXIBLE/MINDLESS VERSUS FLEXIBLE/MINDFUL STEREOTYPING

Inflexible stereotyping	Flexible stereotyping
Automatic-pilot reaction	Mindful of categorization
Rigid categories	Open-ended categories
Premature closure	First best-guesses
Polarized evaluations	Loose interpretations
Information distortion	Information openness
Unwilling to change categories	Willingness to change categories

The more I praise my ingroup, the more I'm complimenting myself based on shared similar traits. The comparison is even more polarized if the comparison is with another group that competes for the same reward resources (e.g., a rival high school). Social groups in the United States pledge their loyalty in many ways: wearing fraternity and sorority shirts and emblems, getting tattoos associated with gang membership, buying team jerseys, and putting one's "game face" on during sporting events. This ethnocentric loyalty to and preference for our own group increases both our self-esteem and our esteem of our group, resulting in even stronger ingroup ties. For example, Wisconsin's Green Bay Packers football fans are known as "cheeseheads." Cheeseheads wear crazy cheese-shape hats and feel great camaraderie with other cheeseheads, although outgroup members think this is very weird.

When in- and outgroups communicate with each other, intergroup communication occurs. **Intergroup communication** happens whenever individuals belonging to one group interact, collectively or individually, with another group or its members in terms of their ingroup identification (Sherif, 1966). The **ingroup favoritism principle** states that there is positive attachment to and predisposition for norms that are related to one's ingroup. Ingroup favoritism highlights our desired ingroup and personal identities by also rejecting the outgroup identity. Countless research studies across cultures and racial groups (see Devine, Hamilton, & Ostrom, 1994; Leyens, Yzerbyt, & Schadron, 1994). indicate that people in all cultures and ethnic–racial groups tend to behave with strong ingroup favoritism and outgroup biases and prejudice.

Group Membership Struggles

Membership in an ingroup is a matter of degree and variation. If norms, values, and social relationships within an ingroup influence the communication patterns of group members, the influence of the group on one particular individual should depend on the extent to which one shares the norms (Kim, 1988, 2000). Admission to the ingroup and acceptance by the ingroup, on the basis of shared norms and values, are interrelated: the more an individual associates with the ingroup, the greater the conformity that is expected

and reinforced. At the same time, if the ingroup does not approve of an individual's behavior, it can reject the ingroup member. Because of this variation in conformity among ingroup members, the boundary lines of ingroup and outgroup are sometimes blurred.

Although our ingroups offer us a sense of belonging and security, they also have the power to reject us. Chung (1998) interviewed Korean Americans and Vietnamese Americans in Oklahoma to understand why and when individuals felt like outgroup members within their own group. She found two explanations. First, despite the fact that some perceived themselves to be part of their ethnic group with strong ties, during ingroup interactions ingroup members treated them like outgroup members—because they appeared to be more "American." Those interviewed shared statements such as, "I think I am very Vietnamese and American at the same time, but each of the two groups perceives me as not totally one or the other"; "Koreans think I am too American, but at the same time I am really a true Korean." In one sense, both groups believed this person was not a clear "fit" in accordance with their stereotypic group images. This implies a sense of marginality because to associate with the two groups, an individual tries to claim ties with both cultures. Most groups or cultures have difficulty accepting difference and so rejection or marginalization can occur.

The second explanation has to do with the context and status of the individual with whom one interacts. For example, a twenty-nine-year-old graduate student of Vietnamese ethnic descent who was born in the United States said, "The elders are very traditional and conservative. If everything is not done in a traditional manner...they think I am too 'American.' People do not see you for who you are, they only see that you are different, therefore you must be bad" (Chung, 1998, p. 62).

The context can embody a strong set of ethnic traditions and values that are associated with status, age, and deference. Traditional Asian values emphasize the importance of reserve and formality in interpersonal relations, for example, and these values reflect the biggest communication problems among different generations of Korean Americans and Vietnamese Americans. The struggle often implies reconciling the conflict between the need to retain ethnic values and the need to pursue the prevalent American cultural values—individualism and equality of respect.

You may also have experienced some of this ingroup–outgroup boundary tension. If you ever felt like an outsider in your own ingroup, then several important questions arise: how do you negotiate your loyalty and attachment when interacting with your ingroup? Must you conform in all ways? What behavioral cues among your ingroup members are considered "different" enough to distance you from your ingroup? If you spend time interacting outside the boundary of your ingroup, does this strengthen your connection with the outgroup(s)? There indeed is a tension between meeting our need for security and inclusion through strong loyalty to our ingroup, but at the same time retaining our own individual unique identity and also not engaging in prejudice and discrimination toward outgroups.

Intergroup Attribution Biases

One of the outcomes of interacting with outgroup members is intergroup attributions. The intergroup attribution process helps us to make sense of our encounters by allowing us to interpret and evaluate outgroup members' behavior (Dovidio, Hewstone, Glick, & Esses, 2010a, 2010b). Every day, we try to figure out why people behave the way they do. If *expectations* refer to our anticipations of what will happen in a given interaction, **attributions** are the explanation—the meaning of why people behave as they do. We use assumptions and built-in social categories to explain behaviors or events occurring around us (see Figure 8.3).

There are three biases that typically occur during intergroup encounters. The first is known as the **fundamental attribution error**. A Chicano student, Fernando, gives an example:

> If a competitor or someone I dislike goes on a job interview and doesn't get it, I'd say something like, "It's because he's lazy and stupid, that's why he didn't get the job." Now if *I* went to a job interview and didn't get it, I would say something like, "It's because of the economic meltdown, budget cuts, or foreigners coming in to grab my job."

In Fernando's example, with competitors or strangers, we tend to engage in negative attributions by *overestimating negative personality factors* in explaining a stranger's negative event and *underestimating situational factors*. However, if we personally encounter a negative event, we want to protect our self-image by using situational factors to explain away the negative episode. In Fernando's example, he would not attribute his own failure to being "lazy" or "stupid"; his failure must be the result of factors outside his control.

The second attribution bias is called the **principle of negativity**. We typically place more emphasis on negative information concerning our competitors or outgroup members. That is, bad news catches our eye more than good news, and we often fall back on negative stereotypes when interacting with outgroup members. For example, if Rafik holds a negative bias against Talia, an outgroup member, when his coworkers ask him what he thinks of her, Rafik will pick out the one or two negative incidents he has observed and ignore all of her positive qualities.

The third attribution, **favorable self-bias and other-derogation principle**, arises from positive events concerning our own behavior versus a stranger's behavior (Dovidio, Hewstone, Glick, & Esses, 2009). For example, if you were pulled over for speeding and got cited with a warning (a positive event), you will be likely to attribute this to your safe driving record (positive dispositional attribution). However, if a cultural stranger gets only a warning, you may attribute this to luck or a negative, or derogatory, factor (e.g., knew the cop, manipulated or bribed the cop). This tendency to favor ourselves and our ingroup in explaining our success and to create derogatory explanations for others' or outgroup successes is all too common.

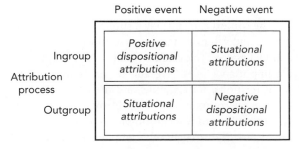

	Positive event	Negative event
Ingroup	Positive dispositional attributions	Situational attributions
Outgroup	Situational attributions	Negative dispositional attributions

Attribution process

FIGURE 8.3 Ingroup and Outgroup Attribution Differences

There are many comparisons between individualistic and collectivistic cultures in how we view situational versus personality traits. For example, one study compared how U.S. and Japanese students attribute success, or failure, in a particular memory task. U.S. students tended to remember a greater number of successful incidents and they explained their success in terms of their positive personal qualities and abilities. Japanese students, in contrast, remembered a greater number of failed incidents and tended to attribute their failures to lack of ability, which reflects what some term the *self-effacement bias* in those from collectivistic cultures (Kashima & Triandis, 1986; Smith & Bond, 1998; Smith et al., 2006).

SHATTERED LENS: PREJUDICE, DISCRIMINATION, AND RACISM

Before we discuss issues of prejudice, let's check out the poem in Blog Post 8.3: "looking at the world from my key hole," by Feven Afewerki.

Prejudice: Multiple Explanations and Functions

A young child picks up behavioral cues from family members, the educational system, peer groups, mass media, and the general socialization process. These cues signal who belongs to the ingroup and who belongs to the outgroup. The term **prejudice** generally describes an individual's feelings and predispositions

---

BLOG POST 8.3 LOOKING AT THE WORLD FROM MY KEY HOLE

i am racist and prejudice
looking at the world from my key hole
i am afraid to use my key
to open the door
and meet the morning sun of openness
the wind of change
the storm of the unexpected
when will i face the sun, the wind, and the storm
looking at the world from my key hole

Copyright © Feven Afewerki. (Born in Eritrea (Northeast Africa). Graduate Student at California State University, Long Beach.) Used by permission of the author.

---

toward outgroup members in a pejorative or negative direction. However, prejudice can actually refer to either negative or positive predispositions and feelings about outgroup members—you can be indiscriminately for or against members of a particular group.

In the intercultural context, prejudice is a sense of antagonistic hostility toward a group as a whole or toward an individual because she is a member of that group. Such feelings are based on a "faulty and inflexible generalization. It may be felt or expressed" (Allport, 1954, p. 7). This hostility toward outgroup members stems from biased judgments made with little evidence to support the overgeneralization. Most people who hold prejudices do not interact with members of other groups because they believe it is a waste of their time.

How does prejudice happen? To understand how the development of prejudice occurs, Schaefer (2009) outlined four explanations on the societal reaction level:

1. **Exploitation theory** views power as a scarce resource: To maintain higher status and power, one restrains those of lower status to improve one's own group position and security. Many people believe that the "glass ceiling"—meaning no minority has an equal opportunity at high-ranking positions—is an example of exploitation theory.

2. **Scapegoating theory** suggests prejudiced individuals believe that they are the victims of society. If something is not going well in their life, they will blame a minority group instead of accepting the basic responsibility for some other type of failure (e.g., bad economy, lack of skills).

3. An **authoritarian personality approach** emphasizes personality features of the individual, including a rigid observance of (or adherence to) conventional norms, complete acceptance of authority, and a high concern for those in power.

4. A **structural approach** to prejudice stresses the climate in one's society whereby institutions

promote a "pecking order" among group members. For example, under Japanese law, anyone who was born abroad or whose parents or grandparents were born abroad is considered a foreigner, and foreigners have no voting rights.

Schaefer's set of explanations allows us to understand the development of prejudice by connecting concepts such as power, class, and position. These concepts serve as deep-seated barriers that are usually unpredictable and difficult to overcome.

Prejudice also serves multiple communication functions on an everyday justification level. First, a prejudiced mindset acts as an *ego-defense mechanism*, acting as a shield to protect our fragile egos. For example, individuals can blame outgroup members for a failed event and, thus, protect their long-held values, beliefs, and standard ways of operation. Second, in our chaotic world, we have a need for *regularity*. To maintain this regularity, individuals view their own cultural values, norms, and practices as the proper and civilized ways of thinking and behaving. For example, some people may be disgusted by the idea that Latina/os actually eat *menudo* (tripe soup). A comment such as "Why can't they eat normal soup like us?" reflects this function of prejudice.

Another reason why people engage in prejudiced remarks is that they *lack accurate cultural knowledge*. Knowledge takes time and energy to acquire. It is faster to defend the areas of knowledge we have already and to ignore the unfamiliar. For example, if our ingroup is proficient in computer programming, we may see outgroup members who have not learned to master computer programming as incompetent and backward. Finally, individuals engage in prejudiced communication to collect ingroup *rewards* and *approval*. Individuals can collect intangible rewards (e.g., approval, laughs) from their ingroup by acting out consensual beliefs.

The examples of these functions of prejudice allow us to understand the nature of the hostile and biased attitudes toward outgroup members. Some persons hold more prejudice than others, and prejudice also operates in conjunction with the context. We typically swing back and forth when dealing with our feelings of prejudice. Some individuals may display favorable attitudes toward one minority group but demonstrate strong racist attitudes against another. Some individuals may harbor no deep resentments against outgroups until their identity status is seriously threatened or challenged by the arrival of other groups. Check out Blog Pics 8.3 and 8.4.

Prejudiced Remarks or Innocent Jokes?

Prejudiced behaviors take many forms. One aspect includes "innocent" remarks or biased jokes. Let's think about this question for a moment: Do innocent remarks or biased jokes directed at an individual or ethnic group make them tolerable or acceptable? Christian Lander was an ordinary Internet copywriter in 2008 when he had an idea to poke fun of himself and other Euro-Americans. Thus, *stuffwhitepeoplelike. com* was born. In the first week, the site received two hundred hits daily, jumping to six hundred, and by the end of the month, 3 million hits had been received (Rodriguez, 2008). Some of the things white people like—multilingual children, shorts, coffee, and organic food—were written with humor and sarcasm and sparked diverse observations. His satire has inspired a number of spinoffs, such as Stuff Brown People Like, Stuff Educated Black People Like, and Stuff Gay Parents Like.

Blog Pic 8.3 Salt and pepper shakers sold in a European store. Would you buy them?

The question then remains: Where do we draw the line? When is an ethnic joke just a joke, a form of prejudice, or a racist remark (see Blog Pic 8.3)? Is it "OK" to see it as a joke if the humor comes directly from your ingroup? Reflect on some of the recent jokes you have received online or via friends. How many are based on intergroup stereotypes or some forms of prejudice?

So, where do we draw the line? This question is difficult to answer. The main problem has a lot to do with our boundaries and the intention of the person who made the comment. We can argue that this form of ignorance has no malice or intent to offend. We can understand that in the unconscious incompetence stage (recall Chapter 2), individuals do not realize that they are making comments that are hurtful, offensive, and intolerant.

But with the Internet, offensive comments may be broadcast to the world, offending many. Recall the incident when in 2011, UCLA student Alexandra Wallace posted her "rant" online, disparaging Asian students for using cell phones in the library, who say things like "ching chong, ling long, ting tong" ("Racial rant," 2011). Alexandra issued an apology and many would argue that we should move on and forget about her video; she meant no harm. However, communication is not only about intent; it is also about consequence or impact. When in doubt, we must be mindful of our words and deeds—many times, words can actually inflict more emotional scars and pain than any physical damage.

Making comments with or without the intent to offend, hurt, and directly attack is still a mindless act. Making a video that cannot be erased completely invites and incites groups to make ethnic or racist jokes against each other. Pitting one group against another is a hurtful, pernicious act and generates more polarized reactions on a downward spiral. On the upside, "the tools that can be deployed by the so-called cyberbullies are also freely available to those they harass" (Pell, 2011). For example, Jimmy Wong responded to Wallace's comments by writing an original song and posting it on YouTube, with lyrics such as "I pick up my phone and sing…Ching Chong, it means I love you; Ling Long, I really want you; Ting Tong, I don't actually know what that means." Wong believes that his sharp wit in response to the rant can "destroy the power of racism and turn it into something positive" ("Racial rant," 2011).

Beyond mocking someone's accent, individuals can also hold prejudice against people on the basis of skin color, cultural or religious practices, or sexual orientation. The very first South Korean star to come out was Hong Seok Cheon. Mr. Hong concealed his homosexuality for years but when he decided to come out in 2003, he was fired from his variety show and "fellow actors shunned him, teenage boys hurled abuse at him in the street, his parents suggested that the [entire] family should commit suicide for the shameful disclosure, and the job offers vanished, leaving Hong to ponder the wreckage of a once successful life" (Chu, 2003, p. A3). In a country that values traditional Confucian principles, rigid norms about sex role differentiation make it virtually impossible to be "accepted" if one behaves in a different way. The following year, *Time Magazine* honored Mr. Hong as the first Korean celebrity to come out of the closet, and he was selected as the 2004 Asian Hero. Despite his lone fight against prejudice in South Korea and scarce roles for him, Mr. Hong has found success as a restaurateur and an internationally recognized activist.

Four Discriminatory Practices

A prejudiced attitude, in any form, is difficult to censure and avoid. Prejudice is a biased mindset. Discrimination, however, refers to the verbal and nonverbal

Blog Pic 8.4   Darky Gifts. Would you shop here?

actions that carry out prejudiced attitudes. According to Feagin and Feagin (2011), four basic types of discriminatory practices exist in a society: (1) isolate discrimination; (2) small-group discrimination; (3) direct institutional discrimination; and (4) indirect institutional discrimination.

When an ingroup member engages in **isolate discrimination**, harmful verbal and nonverbal action is intentionally targeted toward an outgroup member. This discriminatory behavior occurs on an individual basis. It ranges from the use of racist slurs to violent physical action. Read the story about Lee Ann Kim, telling about her first job in Missouri (see Blog Post 8.4). What would you have done in her shoes?

When a band of individuals from an ingroup engages in hostile and abusive actions against outgroup members, this is known as **small-group discrimination**. These actions do not have explicit support of the larger organizational or community network. Controversy regarding scarves is a perfect example. In 2009, the Equal Employment Opportunity Commission reported that over eight hundred Muslim women filed workplace discrimination complaints in the United States, up 20 percent from the previous year (http://www.eeoc.gov). College sophomore Hani Khan was fired from her job as a stockroom clerk at Hollister Company when she refused to remove her head scarf because it violated the company's "look policy" (Bello, 2010). And Southwest

---

BLOG POST 8.4 A TRUE STORY—LEE ANN KIM, ANCHOR, CHANNEL 10 NEWS, SAN DIEGO

In 1995, I got a job offer as the weekend anchor from the NBC station in Springfield, Missouri. At the time, I was working as the main news anchor in Tuscaloosa, Alabama, which was a very small news market located an hour outside of Birmingham. While most Asian Americans cringe at the thought of living in the South, frankly, my experience in Alabama was a positive one. There were no burning crosses or men in white sheets. The region had already gone through so many lessons of the Civil Rights Era, and since there were many African Americans who lived in the South, people of color weren't as big of a deal.

Little did I know that my employment there would make broadcast history. I was described in Springfield's local newspaper as "the first person of color to ever anchor the news in Springfield." Located an hour north of the Arkansas border, Springfield—or the Ozarks, as it is commonly referred to—[is] nearly 99 percent white, and anyone who was an ethnic minority seemed to be [among] the few immigrant Chinese who ran the drive-through Chinese restaurants.

Race was never made an issue with my coworkers, who welcomed me with open arms. However, out in the community, I was constantly reminded of how I was different. Almost daily, people would ask me, "How did you learn how to speak English so well?" Or "Where do you come from?" "How come your eyebrows are so high above your eyes?" Although these questions may seem ignorant and sometimes offensive, they were asked with genuine curiosity. Simply, this community was not familiar with diversity.

On the second weekend on the job, I was driving into work when I noticed our station's huge, white satellite dishes [had been] vandalized. Overnight, someone had spray painted them with

swastikas and the words "F*** you N*****" and "N***** go home." "That's funny," I thought, "there aren't any African Americans around here." As I entered our newsroom, I was surprised to see my news director and general manager there since it was a Saturday. They were huddled with other coworkers, and the way they looked at me made it instantly clear that the racist graffiti outside had something to do with me. "Are you okay?" they asked me. "Yeah, I'm fine," I answered. There was a pause. Then the epiphany came.

"Wait. That graffiti outside, that's about me, isn't it?" I exclaimed. My bosses and coworkers stood there, uncomfortably silent, then nodded their heads. It was later explained to me that our proximity to Arkansas and lack of diversity in Springfield made it an active region for the KKK, who considered anyone that was not white and Protestant as the "N" word. Frankly, I wasn't the least bit threatened by the whole incident. "At least we know they're watching," I said to everyone jovially, which managed to break the tension. My colleagues seemed much more offended by the vandalism than I was.

The way I see it, people respond to change in different ways. In this case, someone wanted to scare me because of their own insecurities and ignorance. Instead of scaring me, it gave me motivation to be the best journalist I could be, proving to that community that someone who looks like me can speak perfect English and cover the news as well as any white journalist. And hey, maybe people will eventually see beyond my eyes and think of me as an American. I stayed in Springfield for exactly a year before taking my current job in San Diego. But during that year, I became the unofficial corporate hog farm reporter. It was an experience I will always embrace.

—Lee Ann Kim, *first-person story and real name used with permission*

Airlines made a public apology after Irum Abassi, a graduate student and mother of three, was thrown off a flight because the crew thought her behavior was "suspicious." As the flight was getting ready to take off, an airline attendant heard Ms. Abassi say "It's a go" on her cell. She had actually said "I have to go." This "us versus them" mentality is one of the pernicious outcomes of small-group discrimination.

If there is a community-prescribed endorsement of discrimination, we can call this **direct institutional discrimination**. Such practices are not isolated incidents but are carried out routinely by a large number of individuals protected by the laws of a large-scale community. For example, blatant institutional discriminatory practices against Japanese Americans were carried out in World War II. Over 110,000 Japanese Americans were forced to leave their homes and taken to live in shabby internment camps in California and Oregon.

Historically, the Chinese were the only group to be "banned" from entering the United States. On May 6, 1882, Congress passed a bill prohibiting Chinese laborers from entering the United States. In 1902, the Chinese Exclusion Act was made permanent. To this day, no other immigrant group has ever been banned from entering. When the act was lifted in 1943, older and younger Chinese women were finally able to join their families after years of separation. The exclusion act hits close to home with me (Chung). If this act had not been lifted, my grandmother would never have seen her husband and her son again. The seventeen years my grandmother waited to reunite with her husband and son were extremely long, heartbreaking, and painful.

Indirect institutional discrimination is a broad practice that indirectly affects group members without intending to. For example, the Standard Aptitude Test (SAT) serves as an indirect discriminatory tool. The test uses a "homogenized" standard—a strong white, middle-class orientation that assesses the mathematical and verbal fluency level of *all* high school seniors—and is, thus, an example of indirect institutional discrimination. Along with high school grades, the SAT is supposed to predict academic performance of first-year college students. Critics have long attacked the SAT as unfair because it tends to favor students who have wealthier families,

attend better schools, or have access to test-preparation courses and tutors. From personal experience, we agree.

In my inner-city public school (Chung), we did not have the tools and equipment to prepare seniors to take the test. There was no budget, preparatory class, or strong honors program. The majority of (single) parents were not middle or upper class and did not have the means to pay for test preparation. The unfair advantage and use of such "standardized" instruments in diverse populations in the United States have led to an exclusion of group members seeking better educational and, hence, brighter economic opportunities for their future. Without intending to, an institution has discriminated against these group members on an unequal playing field.

Different Types of Racism

The direct effect of discrimination and its very practice is racism. Racism can be summarized by the three following principles:

- Feelings of superiority based on biological or racial differences, or both,
- Strong ingroup preferences and solidarity; rejection of any outgroup that diverges from the customs and beliefs of the ingroup, and
- A doctrine that conveys a special advantage to those in power (Jones, 1997, p. 373).

People have racist attitudes and engage in racist practices because of many factors. One such factor is internal fear. Fear gives rise to our emotional fragility and vulnerability. When individuals worry that their cultural or social habits are being threatened, they may want either to pounce or flee. Racism includes not only verbal insults but also what is *unspoken*. There are three basic examples of racism we will discuss: racial profiling, perpetuating stereotypes, and hate crimes (Dovidio, Gaertner, & Kawakami, 2009).

Racial Profiling

Ever since 9/11, complaints about **racial profiling** have escalated across the globe and in the United States, from New York to Texas. The New York Police Department's (NYPD) policy called "Stop and Frisk" resulted in over 600,000 stops by police in 2010 (Wharton, 2011). The

Center for Constitutional Rights found that over 87 percent of those stopped were Latinos and Blacks and only 8–10 percent were whites. What supports these statistics as clear evidence of racial profiling that was being enforced by the NYPD is the fact that whites comprise 44 percent of the population. In Lubbock, Texas, a report was published showing that whites had lower rates of arrests and searches during traffic stops than black and Hispanic drivers (Pyle, 2011).

Perpetuating Stereotypic Images

Racism is displayed as a "top-down phenomenon" (Jones, 1997). This occurs when members of the majority group present their group in a positive light and the minority in a negative light. The whole process is couched in terms of "protecting the majority group's image of fairness and objectivity, while making disparaging or condescending remarks about those other groups" (Jones, 1997, p. 385). For decades, minority groups in the United States have seen stereotypic depictions of themselves in popular films. Even today, scholars (Glenn & Cunningham, 2009) have indentified long-running black stereotypes such as "mammy" and "Uncle Tom" in such recent films as the *Matrix* series, *Bringing Down the House*, *The Green Mile*, *Nurse Betty*, and *Bruce Almighty*. All of these films depict blacks in a "helping" role, which may seem positive at first glance, yet when looked into more deeply, this help "primarily exists in spiritual and/or folk knowledge as opposed to intellectual cognition, which suggests that Blacks have yet to receive full acceptance in the minds of Whites" (p. 149). Carefully view films and other forms of media you consume; stereotypes may be playing out before your eyes.

Hate Crimes

A **hate crime** is typically motivated by hostility to the victim as a member of a group (e.g., on the basis of ethnicity/race, disability, age, religion, gender, or sexual orientation). These crimes may include such acts as physical assault, assault with a weapon, harassment, vandalism, robbery, rape, verbal harassment, an attack on people's homes or places of worship, and even murder. They can occur anywhere: in schools, in the workplace, on the Internet, in public places, and in the home. Unfortunately, proving a hate crime can be difficult because the authorities must show that a victim was purposely selected for the hateful behavior because she or he is a member of a group. In San Francisco, two separate incidents—an assault of several Mexican men while the suspects yelled "white power" and the knifing of a black man who was homeless—have given prosecutors increasing concern about these crimes (Burack, 2011). In Texas, Harry Glaspell, a European American, pleaded guilty to setting fire to playground equipment at an Arlington mosque. Previously, he had yelled ethnic and religious slurs at attendees of the mosque (U.S. Department of Justice, 2011).

In addition to racially and religiously motivated hate crimes, one's sexuality and sex role identity can lead to hate crimes and even death. The National Center for Transgender Equality and the National Gay and Lesbian Task Force 2011 report found that 35 percent of the transgendered population had been physically or sexually assaulted at one time or another. The most famous historical transgendered hate crime is the case of Brandon Teena. In 1993, two men attacked Brandon after finding out that Brandon was anatomically female. Despite threats of retaliation, Brandon reported the attack to police, identifying the attackers. The city police and county sheriff departments did nothing. Three days later, the same young men killed Brandon; this tragedy became memorialized in the 1999 film *Boys Don't Cry*. The struggle still continues. Hate crimes range from small incidents to racially motivated incidents to violent death.

Bullying, including cyberbullying, can be associated with hate crimes. Cyberbullying has become so prevalent that several states are considering laws addressing its perpetrators and the U.S. government created a Web site dedicated to this trend (Pell, 2011). The connection between bully and target is so seamless that hate speech can often spread more rapidly than its originator ever intended. Data from both the National Youth Violence Prevention Resource Center (http://www.safeyouth.gov) and the Health Resources and Service Administration (http://www.hrsa.gov) indicate one in three students is involved in bullying; bullying behavior has increased by 5 percent; and kids who are obese, gay, or have disabilities are 64 percent more likely to be bullied.

The tragedy of Tyler Clemente is an illustration of the devastating impact of bullying. The eighteen-year-old student committed suicide after finding out that his roommate had secretly videotaped his sexual encounter with another male and posted the video online (http://www.abcnews.com). His roommate may not have meant to act so maliciously, but as a result of his actions, one person, and an entire family, lost a precious and treasured life. Emotional insecurity or fear in the psyche of the perpetrator is one of the major causes of hate crimes. When individuals fear losing power or control, they may lash out aggressively. They may also fear outgroup members, who may bring alternative values, lifestyles, and norms that challenge the comfort zone of the ingroup (Richeson & Shelton, 2010; Schmidt & Hewstone, 2010).

This primal fear triggers a host of other powerful emotions such as confusion, frustration, hostility, anger, anxiety, and hate. Although some of these feelings may be legitimate and need mindful redirection, others have absolutely no merit.

Reducing Prejudice and Discrimination

Reducing our own prejudice and discriminatory practices does not have to be difficult. Just by gaining accurate knowledge and being open-minded, we have started walking along a mindful path. Changing the way we feel or confronting our own vulnerable spots has a lot to do with the intentional reframing of how we view ourselves and others. Here are four practical guidelines to observe:

1. Start by being honest with yourself. Question everything you have learned and gained from your socialization process. Do retain the learning experiences from your cultural or family socialization process but also confront unchecked biases and ethnocentric attitudes. Ask yourself, "What is causing me to react this way?" "Where or from whom did I learn this?" "Am I basing my reactive judgment on accurate facts, or is my reaction based on a subjective interpretation about an outgroup member's behavior?"

2. Check yourself before you evaluate the behavior of an outgroup member. Ask yourself, "Am I overgeneralizing? Am I using a well-balanced attribution process?" A bias will be created by judging someone too quickly so that the interaction goes in a predictable manner. To engage in effective intercultural communication, taking the time to really know someone—without relying on preconceived stereotypes—can save long-term heartaches and headaches.

3. Remember that negative images concerning outgroup members will distort your perceptions. If you harbor any form of prejudice against outgroup members, you have just bought into the principle of ingroup favoritism and outgroup negativism.

4. Communicate your feelings by addressing them in the most comfortable forum. If you observe, read, or hear something that is remotely unfair, then raise your voice assertively (see Blog Post 8.5).

In essence, we must continue to dialog about these culturally sensitive issues. Many times, such discussions can be painful or even hurtful. But the fact that we are willing and able to express indignation at the pain, humiliation, anguish, frustration, and despair shows that we care. We can be change agents. In our partnership dialogs, we must be sensitive to those who suffer but not be overwhelmed by our emotions to the point of paralysis or inaction. *There is no right way to do the wrong thing.* Listening with an open mind, an open heart, and emotional alertness may help both ingroups and outgroups to connect on a deeper level.

BLOG POST 8.5

In February 2011, two hosts of the BBC's television show *Top Gear* made an attempt at a humorous analysis of a Mexican sports car by saying Mexican cars are going to be "lazy, feckless, flatulent, overweight, leaning against a fence asleep looking at a cactus with a blanket with a hole in the middle on as a coat" (http://www.topgear.com). This and other comments sparked angry e-mails from Mexicans, a boycott of the BBC by Mexican radio, a public lawsuit, Internet complaints, and angry letters to the British newspapers. The ambassador of Mexico in England also demanded a public apology. As a result of many individuals raising their voices and objecting to the racist statements, the BBC issued a long apology for the rude and mischievous comments.

INTERCULTURAL REALITY CHECK: DO-ABLES

To become more *flexible communicators* during intergroup encounters, we must understand the basic concepts that form mindset filters, such as ethnocentrism, stereotypes, and prejudice. In this chapter, we talked about key factors that cause us to hold biases against outgroups. These key factors are selective perception, ethnocentrism, and inflexible stereotypes. In addition, we also discussed intergroup attribution biases with many vivid, yet painful, examples. We also explained the underlying reasons why people engage in prejudiced thinking and discriminatory acts. To round off our discussion, we pose the question for you: what will you do to become a change agent? How can you make a difference?

- *Start with a clean slate.* Be flexible with your first best guesses. Look below the surface of the iceberg and remember that appearances or looks often do not represent an individual's multifaceted self. The more you remind yourself with a "clean slate" mentality, the less clutter in terms of flexible communication with dissimilar others.
- *Use your most precious gift: your brain.* You have the ability to think carefully about how you are thinking and how others are thinking and behaving. By being open to multiple perspectives, you can conclude, "I don't behave that way. But I will suspend my judgment or final decision until I understand how this behavior meets or does not meet the expectations of the other person's culture."
- *Continue learning, reading, and gaining knowledge about those who are around you.* We all come from different paths. Let your teacher and other classmates help you—stay humble in your learning, but do form your own flexible judgments as you cumulate your learning in this class. Be active and take part of the change you want to see happening in your community, your university, your world.
- *Remember, all of us are works in progress.* Analyzing your ethnocentric tendencies in an honest manner forces you to consider your deep-rooted beliefs, values, and habitual ways of thinking. This type of self-exploration brings to the forefront all of the issues you did not think existed with "you." "Do I have prejudices? Make judgments about others? Speak and behave insensitively? Never!" That is what you used to say. Be committed to becoming mindful and astute in reading your own ethnocentric biases.
- *Monitor inflexible stereotyping of outgroup members.* Know that you cannot *not* stereotype in social interaction. Because stereotyping is an inevitable process, you must monitor your typecasting process of outgroup members and your ingroups. Thus, you have to engage in flexibly "minding" your own social categorization process.

CHAPTER 9

HOW CAN WE MANAGE
INTERCULTURAL CONFLICT FLEXIBLY?

CHAPTER OUTLINE

- Intercultural Conflict: Cultural Background Factors
  - Culture-Based Conflict Lenses
  - Intercultural Workplace Conflict Grid
  - Intercultural Conflict Perceptions
  - Intercultural Conflict Goal Issues
  - Perceived Scarce Resources

- Intercultural Conflict Process Factors
  - Defining Conflict Styles
  - Cross-Cultural Conflict Styles
  - Cross-Ethnic Conflict Styles and Facework

- Flexible Intercultural Conflict Skills
  - Facework Management
  - Mindful Listening
  - Cultural Empathy
  - Mindful Reframing
  - Adaptive Code-Switching

- Intercultural Reality Check: Do-Ables

In a tiny Chicago suburb, Ms. Safoorah Khan was hired as a new teacher to teach math in a middle school. She worked there for only nine months when she made an unusual request. Ms. Khan wanted to perform the Hajj, the pilgrimage to Mecca in Saudi Arabia, which every adult Muslim is supposed to make at least once in a lifetime—if they are physically and financially able to. Ms. Khan wanted three weeks off. Millions of devout Muslims from different countries travel to Mecca each year. The Chicago school district, faced with losing its only math lab instructor during the end-of-semester marking period, said no. Ms. Khan, a devout Muslim, resigned and made the trip anyway. U.S. Justice Department lawyers examined the same set of facts and reached a different conclusion—that the school district's decision concerning Ms. Khan's request to visit Mecca amounted to outright discrimination against her. They filed an unusual lawsuit, accusing the district of violating her civil rights by forcing her to choose between her job and her faith. The case is still pending.

J. Markon, *Washington Post*, 2011

Although this case is still pending, questions remain: Whose perspective should we accommodate? Was Ms. Khan forced to choose between her job and her religious freedom? Did the school board of Berkeley-Illinois have grounds to deny Ms. Khan's unpaid leave request? Regardless of the outcome, cases like Ms. Khan offer businesses and organizations an opportunity to practice conscious communication competence in dealing with employees of diverse group membership identity backgrounds. Although each workplace conflict situation may be unique, by asking the right questions and generating multiple win–win alternatives, we can begin to prepare ourselves for an increasingly diverse workforce.

With this in mind, we begin Chapter 9 with unpacking how individuals coming from two different cultural communities bring with them different filtered lenses with which to look at their intercultural conflict encounters.

Intercultural conflict often starts with different expectations concerning appropriate or inappropriate conflict behavior in an interaction scene. Different cultural members often have contrasting images of how conflict should be properly handled. In this chapter, we first explore some cultural background factors that influence the escalation of an intercultural conflict episode. Next, we take a close look at important conflict process factors, such as cross-cultural conflict styles and facework behaviors. Third, we introduce some steps and skills in managing intercultural conflict flexibly. Finally, we identify specific do-able checkpoints to help you in managing different intercultural conflicts mindfully.

Conflict occurs whenever we are fighting over some incompatible goals or unmet emotional needs. We define **intercultural conflict** as the implicit or explicit emotional struggle or frustration between persons of different cultures over perceived incompatible values, norms, face orientations, goals, scarce resources, processes, and/or outcomes in a communication situation (Ting-Toomey, 2005b, 2009; Ting-Toomey & Oetzel, 2001). Intercultural conflict in and of itself is not necessarily bad. Instead, it is how we approach the conflict and how we manage the conflict that often shapes the process and determines the outcome. If the different cultural members continue to engage in rigid or ineffective conflict styles, the miscommunication can easily spiral into a polarized conflict situation.

INTERCULTURAL CONFLICT: CULTURAL BACKGROUND FACTORS

Let us look at the following communication episode between Gabi (a Latina American student) and Roy (a Filipino American student). Gabi and Roy are in the library discussing their team project due the next day (see L-Chat 9.1).

In the L-Chat 9.1 dialog example, Gabi and Roy tend to make different attributions concerning what's going on with their classmates and also engage in different conflict styles. An intercultural conflict episode often involves complex, multilayered factors. These factors include different cultural conflict lenses, different conflict perceptions, different conflict goals, and different viewpoints on scarce resources. Let's examine two different conflict lenses that result from individualistic and collectivistic cultural patterns.

Culture-Based Conflict Lenses

In Chapter 3, we looked at the value patterns of individualism and collectivism. Cultural value patterns such as individualism and collectivism often color our conflict attitudes, expectations, and behaviors when we are involved in emotionally frustrating episodes (Cohen, 1987, 1991). Different cultural lenses and assumptions serve as the first set of factors that contributes to initial intercultural irritations.

Before you continue your reading, fill out the my.blog 9.1 conflict lens assessment and get a sense of what your conflict lens, or worldview, looks like.

L-CHAT 9.1

GABI (irritated): Where's the rest of our group? What's up with that?! You know, we've already been waiting fifteen minutes. Text them again.

ROY (trying to appease Gabi): I did already. They know we're supposed to meet at the library. They're probably looking for parking. Toyea and Cruz both have to take the freeway, and it's rush hour.

GABI (still irritated): Whatever the case may be, we've got a deadline to meet. You know Toyea and Cruz better . . . you've had two classes with them, right? Are they always like this? I did all my work already and my time is limited today.

ROY (in a soothing tone): Chill. Toyea and Cruz are cool. They're really creative and pull their own weight. If we want an "A," we definitely need the research data that they have for the pitch to be awesome . . . it'll be fine!

GABI (impatient): K. Wait a sec. I'm just gonna play Angry Birds.

(ten minutes later)

GABI (really agitated now): No flippin way! They're not here yet? Did they text?

ROY (in an apologetic tone): Nope . . . but I think they're on their way. They won't flake on us!

GABI (really fed up now): This is so crazy and disrespectful of my time! I have way too many things going on to keep waiting for them to show up. Considering that I did all my work already. . . . It's so irritating! It's this kind of thing that ABSOLUTELY DRIVES ME NUTS working with groups!

ROY (in a conciliatory tone): Look. Why don't you just give me your write-up? I can incorporate your ideas with Toyea and Cruz. I'm sure they'll show up soon. I don't mind waiting for another fifteen minutes. We'll just meet before class tomorrow.

Let's start with the value patterns of individualism and collectivism. For example, for individualists or independent-self personality types, intercultural conflict resolution often follows an outcome-oriented model. Using an **independent-self conflict lens**, a person often views conflict from (1) a content conflict goal lens, which emphasizes tangible conflict issues above and beyond relationship issues; (2) a clear win–lose conflict approach, in which one person comes out as a winner and the other person comes out as a loser; (3) a "doing" angle, in which something tangible in the conflict is broken and needs fixing; and (4) an outcome-driven mode, in which a clear action plan or resolution is needed. Have you ever noticed that during team presentations in class, a team member may say, "For my part of the project, I did . . . ." This person makes every effort to bring attention to his or her individual accomplishments. From this individualistic conflict lens, the person wants to stand out and be noticed for all of his or her task accomplishments.

Comparatively, for collectivists or interdependent-self personality types, intercultural conflict management often follows a "process-oriented" model. Using an **interdependent-self conflict lens**, a person often views conflict from (1) a relational process lens, which emphasizes relationship and feeling issues; (2) a win–win relational approach, in which feelings and "faces" can both be saved; (3) a "being" angle, in which relational trust must be repaired and loyalty must be amended to preserve relational harmony; and (4) a long-term compromising negotiation mode that has no clear winner or loser in the ongoing conflict. For example, team projects are often difficult for collectivists because they are always the ones who will stay up all night working on the last-minute presentation details—especially when one or two members have failed to carry the workload that was distributed. In their team presentations, collectivists will also often use phrases such as "as a team, we . . . " and "we worked hard" to save the team face and put the best group face forward.

Overall, independent-self types are concerned with conflict outcome closure, whereas interdependent-self types are concerned with interpersonal and ingroup face-saving and face-honoring process issues. These implicit conflict lenses or assumptions taint many intercultural perceptions and orientations concerning antagonistic conflict episodes (see Table 9.1).

Intercultural Workplace Conflict Grid

The second set of background factors takes into consideration the global workplace situation, especially in incorporating the value dimension of small–large

my.blog 9.1 ASSESSING YOUR INDIVIDUALISTIC AND COLLECTIVISTIC CONFLICT LENSES

Instructions: The following items describe how people think about themselves and communicate in various conflict situations. Let your first inclination be your guide and circle the number in the scale that best reflects your overall value. The following scale is used for each item:

> 4 = YES! = *strongly agree*—IT'S ME!
> 3 = yes = *moderately agree*—it's kind of like me
> 2 = no = *moderately disagree*—it's kind of not me
> 1 = NO! = *strongly disagree*—IT'S NOT ME!

In most conflict situations, I try to . . .	SA	MA	MD	SD
1. Consider the interests and needs of the other person.	4	3	2	1
2. Win and feel good about myself.	4	3	2	1
3. Focus on the conflict process.	4	3	2	1
4. Focus on the concrete conflict outcome.	4	3	2	1
5. Listen carefully to what the other person is telling me.	4	3	2	1
6. Be assertive to get my viewpoint across.	4	3	2	1
7. Work toward some compromise.	4	3	2	1
8. Be decisive in terms of how the conflict should work out.	4	3	2	1
9. Be sensitive to mutual face-saving issues.	4	3	2	1
10. Be certain to protect my own self-image.	4	3	2	1

Scoring: Add up the scores on all the even-numbered items and you will find your individualistic conflict lens score. *Individualistic conflict* lens score: _____. Add up the scores on all the odd-numbered items and you will find your collectivistic conflict lens score. *Collectivistic conflict lens* score: _____.

Interpretation: Scores on each conflict lens dimension can range from 5 to 20; the higher the score, the more individualistic and/or collectivistic you are. If all the scores are similar on both conflict lens dimensions, you are a bifocal conflict lens person.

Reflection probes: Compare your scores with a classmate's. Take a moment to think of the following questions: What factors shape your conflict lens? Do you come from a conflict-approach or a conflict-avoidance family? Do you know that individualists tend to approach conflict and collectivists tend to avoid conflict? What do you think are the pros and cons of either approaching a conflict directly or dealing with a conflict indirectly? How can you deal with conflicts constructively when you and your conflict partner have very different conflict lenses?

power distance on top of the value dimension of individualism–collectivism. In combining both individualism–collectivism and small–large power distance value patterns, we can discuss four predominant corporate value conflict approaches that result from forming a grid based on the individualism–collectivism continuum and small–large power distance continuum: impartial, status-achievement, benevolent, and communal (Ting-Toomey, 2009, 2010c). The *impartial approach* reflects a combination of an individualistic and small power distance value orientation; the *status-achievement approach* consists of a combination of an individualistic and large power distance value orientation; the *benevolent approach* reflects a combination of a collectivistic and large power distance value orientation; and the *communal approach* consists of a

TABLE 9.1 INDIVIDUALISTIC AND COLLECTIVISTIC CONFLICT LENSES

Individualistic conflict lens	Collectivistic conflict lens
Outcome-focused	Process-focused
Content goal-oriented	Relational goal-oriented
Doing-centered	Being-centered
Use personal equity norms	Use communal norms
Self-face concern	Other-face concern
Low-context conflict styles	High-context conflict styles
Competitive/dominating behaviors	Avoiding/obliging behaviors
Conflict effectiveness	Conflict appropriateness

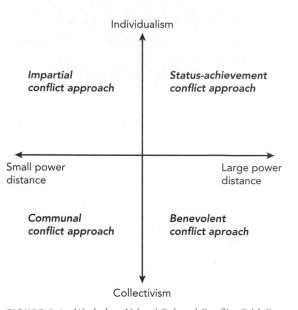

FIGURE 9.1 Workplace Values' Cultural Conflict Grid: Four Conflict Approaches

combination of collectivistic and small power distance value orientation (see Figure 9.1).

Before we continue, let us look at the background information that paves the way for the U.S./Japan Conflict Case Example, below. The background context is as follows (adapted from Clarke & Lipp, 1998, pp. 232–233): A Japanese multimedia subsidiary in the United States had just completed a very successful year. All of the company goals were met or surpassed. As a result, the annual sales conference was held at the Disneyland Resort Hotel in California. Many of the salespeople brought their spouses to the conference, to celebrate and enjoy a well-earned vacation. The audience at the corporate dinner celebration consisted of mostly American salespeople and their spouses and some Japanese technical support personnel. The Japanese president gave a brief welcome speech in halting English, but the audience appreciated his remarks. Given this background, the following event sequences take place:

A U.S./Japan Conflict Case Example

Next, the American director of sales, William Bates, got up and introduced the Japanese vice president, Satoshi Ota-san. They had planned ahead of time to give two short motivational speeches to kick off the conference. Ota-san was about fifty years old, and he had used the previous two weeks to memorize his carefully prepared speech in English. When Ota-san

stood up, his posture was rigid, his face was serious, and his tone sounded harsh. Here is what he said:

> Thank you for your hard work this fiscal year. We have broken many records, *but* … we need to be careful and not to settle down so easily. We need to keep up our fighting spirit! Our competition is working to defeat us at this very minute while we are celebrating. You have done a good job … but you must do more and aim higher. There is no time for frivolous activities. You must prepare yourselves to work twice as hard this coming year. The company has invested a lot of money in new manufacturing facilities. These facilities are producing our new product lines. It is your duty and loyalty to this company to sell these products as efficiently as possible. You must not fail! You must not let your guard down! You must not be content! I hope you will do a better job in the new fiscal year. Thank you.

The American audience sat in stunned silence during most of Satoshi Ota-san's speech. The American director of sales, William Bates, stood up quickly, physically backed away from the Japanese vice president of sales, and with an awkward smile said:

> Disregard everything he just said. We are here to celebrate your fantastic achievements this year!

We have outperformed all our competitors this past year and your success is far beyond expectations. So give yourselves a big round of applause, and let the festivities begin!

The audience applauded. Bates gave the signal to the hotel staff to serve the dinner. For the rest of the conference, the tension between Satoshi Ota-san and William Bates was palpable, and most of the other Americans were irritable.

What went wrong here? Why did Mr. Bates physically back away from Mr. Ota? What did you, the reader, think of Mr. Ota's reaction to Mr. Bates' (i.e., "Disregard everything he just said.") comment? Can you identify all the culture-based collision bumps in the above critical incident? Can the conflict clashes between the two key characters be reconciled? What corporate conflict approach did Mr. Ota practice? What conflict reactions did Mr. Bates exhibit?

Before we reveal the answers, let us explore more in depth the conceptual frames of the four corporate conflict approaches. Overall, managers and employees around the world have different expectations of how a workplace conflict episode should be interpreted and resolved—depending on whether the workplace culture emphasizes impartial, status-achievement, benevolent, or communal conflict interaction rituals. More specifically, for example, in the *impartial approach* (a combination of individualism and small power distance) to workplace conflict, the predominant values of this approach are personal freedom and equal treatment (Smith, Dugan, Peterson, & Leung, 1998). From the impartial conflict approach lens, if an interpersonal conflict arises between a manager and an employee, the manager has the responsibility to deal with the conflict in an objective, upfront, and decisive manner. The employee is sometimes invited to provide feedback and reactions to the fact-finding process. He or she can also ask for clear justifications and evidence from the manager. In an equal-rank employee–employee conflict, the manager would generally play the "impartial" third-party role and would encourage the two employees to talk things over and find their own workable solution. Managers in large corporations in Denmark, the Netherlands, Sweden, and Norway appear to practice the impartial conflict communication approach (Hofstede, 2001, 2009).

Alternatively, from a *status-achievement approach* (a combination of individualism and large power distance) to conflict, the predominant values of this approach are personal freedom and earned inequality. For example, in France, employees often feel that they have the freedom to voice directly their complaints about their managers in the workplace (Storti, 2001). At the same time, they do not expect their managers to change much because they are their bosses and thus, by virtue of their titles, hold certain rights and power resources. The managers, meanwhile, also expect conflict accommodations from their subordinates; subordinates may be free to complain, but the manager is the authority and makes the final decisions. When the conflict involves two same-rank coworkers, the use of upfront conflict tactics to aggressive tactics is a hallmark of the status-achievement approach. Ting-Toomey and Oetzel (2001) also observed that U.S. management style often follows a combined impartial approach and status-achievement approach: the larger U.S. culture emphasizes that with individual hard work, personal ambition, and fierce competitiveness, status and rank can be earned and status cues can be displayed with pride and credibility.

Based on the empirical work of the GLOBE project (Carl, Gupta, & Javidan, 2004), many managers in other parts of the globe tend to see themselves as interdependent and at a different status level than others. That is, these managers think of themselves as individuals with interlocking connections with others and as members of a hierarchical network. They practice the *benevolent approach* (a combination of collectivism and large power distance value patterns) in approaching a conflict problem. The term "benevolent" implies that many managers play the authoritative parental role in approaching or motivating their employees. Two values that pervade this approach are obligation to others and asymmetrical interaction treatment. Countries and large corporate cultures that predominantly reflect the benevolent approach include most Latin and South American nations (e.g., Mexico, Venezuela, Brazil, and Chile), most Asian nations (e.g., India, Japan, China, and South Korea), most Arab nations (e.g., Egypt, Saudi Arabia, and Jordan) and most African nations (e.g., Nigeria and Uganda; Hofstede, 2001).

For many large East Asian corporations, for example, Confucian-driven hierarchical principles promote a type of parent–child relationship between the manager and the subordinate. Under the benevolent conflict approach, although a manager can confront her or his employees to motivate them to work harder, it is very rare that subordinates will directly challenge the manager's authority during a conflict interaction. However, subordinates might opt for using passive-aggressive or sabotage conflict strategies to deal with workplace tensions or frustrations. In dealing with low-importance conflicts, managers would consider using the "smooth over" relational tactics or subtle pressure tactics to gain employees' compliance. However, in dealing with high-importance conflicts, benevolent managers could act in a very directive or autocratic and controlling manner. They might also practice preferential treatment by treating senior employees more favorably than junior employees or family network friends more generously than peripheral workplace members.

Last, the *communal approach* (a combination of both collectivism and small power distance value orientation) is the least common of the four conflict workplace approaches. The values that encompass this approach are authentic interdependent connection to others and genuine equality via respectful communication exchanges at all levels. Research to date has shown that Costa Rica is the only country found to fit this approach (Hofstede, 2001). Nonprofit mediation centers or successful start-up small businesses also appear to practice some of the communal decision-making behaviors and participatory democracy so that everyone has a say, and they also often take turns to rotate democratic leadership. In the communal approach, the importance of mindful listening skill, interpersonal validation skill, and collaborative dialog skill are emphasized (Barge, 2006; Domenici & Littlejohn, 2006).

After reading the explanation of the four corporate conflict approaches, we hope you have increased your knowledge on these complex values issues. If you answered earlier that in the critical incident Mr. Ota used a benevolent approach to motivate his audience, your answer is correct. Mr. Ota's approach included high authority and also treating the employees as a parent might try to motivate children. In addition, if you answered that Mr. Bates' conflict reactions reflected both impartial (e.g., based on objective facts: the American sales force had a banner year) and status-achievement (e.g., they all worked ambitiously to attain this well-deserved event recognition) conflict approaches, you also earn an "A" grade. Clearly in this conflict case example, the Americans and the Japanese carried different cultural assumptions about the meaning of a sales conference celebration event and the meaning of a motivational speech.

From the "status-achievement" corporate worldview, for example, Mr. Bates and the American audience were expecting an "individual status-recognition celebration" event. Many of them brought their spouses to mark the festivity and to enjoy a fun-filled vacation. They expected complimentary accolades and positive motivational messages. Instead, all they heard were what seems to them direct criticism and insults. From the benevolent corporate worldview, Mr. Ota (and perhaps some of the Japanese technical staff) viewed this context as another occasion to "motivate" the sales workforce to work harder and to plan productive sales strategies collectively. Also, Mr. Ota had tried so hard for the prior two weeks to memorize his motivational speech in English, and he thought for sure that the celebration occasion in Disneyland itself sent a strong positive signal to the employees that the company already valued their hard work and dedicated effort. However, Mr. Ota was also looking forward to the special occasion to further motivate his sales employees to reach their highest professional potential and personal best. Mr. Bates' awkward smile and his cavalier phrase "Disregard everything he just said" created enormous face loss for Mr. Ota and also for the corporation's Japanese president who was in attendance.

A knowledgeable, third-party intercultural consultant—or an intercultural consulting team—who understands the deep cultures and the corporate cultures of both Japanese and the U.S. societies can help bridge the widening chasm between these two cultural conflict parties. Understanding the underlying, unspoken value clashes and the misconstrued assumptions between the American and Japanese attendees would serve as a good first step to reconcile the cultural and corporate expectancy differences.

Intercultural Conflict Perceptions

The third set of background factors involves conflict perceptions and orientation. Conflict involves both perception and interaction. **Conflict** is an aggravating disagreement process between two interdependent parties over incompatible goals and the interference each perceives from the other in her or his effort to achieve those goals (Wilmot & Hocker, 2011).

The primary perception features of intercultural conflict are the following: (1) conflict involves intercultural perceptions—perceptions are filtered through our lenses of ethnocentrism and stereotypes; (2) ethnocentric perceptions add biases and prejudice to our conflict attribution process; and (3) our attribution process is further complicated by dealing with different culture-based verbal and nonverbal conflict styles. Recall that ethnocentrism is defined as the tendency to view our cultural practices as the *right* way and to rate all other cultural practices with reference to our standards. Similarly, when members of a culture believe that their own approach is the only *correct* or *natural* way to handle conflict, they tend to see the conflict behaviors of other cultures as *deviant* from that standard. A rigidly held ethnocentric attitude promotes a climate of distrust in any intercultural conflict. In real-life conflict scenarios, individuals often practice ethnocentric behaviors and polarized attributions without a high degree of awareness.

For example, Ben-Porath and Shaker (2010) asked black and white research participants to read the same news story about Hurricane Katrina that hit the New Orleans region (the deadliest Atlantic storm arrived on August 29, 2005, resulting in the deaths of 1,836 individuals and the evacuation of 300,000 residents) and the aftermath humanitarian disaster. Overall, blacks hold the government much more responsible for the human tragedy that followed Hurricane Katrina than whites. The expert researchers conclude that "blacks overwhelmingly believed that the consequences of Katrina were a product of government incompetence or indifference in the face of suffering of an overwhelmingly black population. That the inclusion of images [a black image or a white image of an individual holding a large bag as he walks on a New Orleans highway, and also photos of a survivor joined by a small group of same-race victims on the

highway] did not lessen blacks' perception of government responsibility speaks to the durability of these attitudes" (Ben-Porath & Shaker, 2010, pp. 462–463). In comparison, white readers who saw the images of survivors of the storm held the federal government less accountable than black readers who viewed those same images or no images at all.

Moving beyond the attribution biases in the aftermath of the catastrophic Hurricane Katrina disaster, let's check out another example. Read the following conversation in L-Chat 9.2 between Ms. Rebecca Levine (a Jewish American supervisor) and Mr. Manuel Morena (a recent South American immigrant) in a U.S.–South American joint venture firm, which illustrates the different conflict styles and attribution processes.

In L.Chat 9.2, Ms. Levine uses an assertive, emotionally expressive verbal style in dealing with the conflict. Mr. Morena, on the other hand, uses a hesitant, indirect verbal style in answering her questions. Ms. Levine uses a *straight talk* low-context approach in dealing with the work problem, whereas Mr. Morena uses a *face talk* high-context approach in dealing with the issue. If both had a chance to understand concepts such as LCC and HCC styles, they might arrive at a better understanding of each other's behavior.

Ms. Levine is using her low-context style to evaluate Mr. Morena's behavior (e.g., "Manuel Morena is trying to one-up me") and Mr. Morena is using his high-context script as a baseline to evaluate Ms. Levine's "rude and overbearing" behavior. Better outcomes could result if both were consciously competent: Ms. Levine might engage in a private conversation with Mr. Morena rather than engage in such direct face-threat behavior in public. Mr. Morena, on the other hand, might learn to be more direct and forthcoming in answering Ms. Levine's questions and use fewer pauses and hedges in his conflict interaction style.

Intercultural Conflict Goal Issues

The fourth set of cultural background factors involves conflict goal issues. The perceived or actual differences in an intercultural conflict often rotate around the following three goal issues: content, relational, and identity (Wilmot & Hocker, 2011; Ting-Toomey, 2010c).

L-CHAT 9.2

MS. LEVINE (in the main office): Manuel, where's your project report? You said you'd get it done soon. I need your part of the report so that I can finish my final report by the end of this week. When do you think you can get it done? [Attribution: *Manuel Morena is such a slacker. I should never have trusted him with this time-sensitive document. I thought I was giving him a break by putting him in charge of this report.*]

MR. MORENA (hesitantly): Well . . . Ms. Levine . . . I didn't realize the deadline was so soon . . . I'll try my best to get it done as soon as possible. It's just that there are lots of details I need to cross-check and sources I need to verify, and I'm waiting for Mr. Nam to get back with me . . . [Attribution: *Ms. Levine is sure a tough lady. Anyway, she is the supervisor. Why didn't she tell me the exact deadline early on? Just last week, she told me to take my time on the report. She knows that verifying sources takes a lot of time! I'm really confused. In Venezuela, the supervisor always tells the workers what to do.*]

MS. LEVINE (frustrated): Manuel, how soon is soon? I really need to hear about your plan of action. You can't be so vague in answering my questions all the time. I believe I've given you plenty of time to work on this report already. [Attribution: *Manuel Morena is trying to be sneaky. He doesn't answer my questions directly at all. I wonder if all Venezuelans are that sneaky? Or maybe he isn't comfortable working for a Jewish American? Or a female? Anyway, I have to press him to be more efficient and responsible. He's in America. He has to learn the American way.*]

MR. MORENA (after a long pause): Well . . . I'm really not sure, Ms. Levine. I really don't want to do a bad job on the report or disappoint you. I'll try my best to finish it as soon as possible. Maybe I can finish the report next week. [Attribution: *Ms. Levine is a real pushy boss. She doesn't seem to like me and she's causing me to lose face in front of all my peers. Her voice sounds so harsh and loud. I've heard that American people are hard to work with, and she is really something —rude and overbearing. I'd better start looking for a new job tomorrow.*]

By **content goals**, we mean the practical issues that are external to the individuals involved. For example, an interfaith couple might argue about whether they should raise their children to be Muslim or Mormon, or an intercultural couple might disagree about whether they should raise their children as bilinguals or monolinguals. Intercultural business partners might argue about whether they should hold their business meetings in Montreal, Hamburg, or Atlanta. Content conflict goals also affect the perceptions of relational and identity goals.

The phrase **relational conflict goals** refers to how individuals define the particular relationship (e.g., intimate vs. nonintimate, informal vs. formal, cooperative vs. competitive) or would like to define it in the interactive situation. Relational conflict goals also involve mismatched relationship expectation issues. For example, individualists generally crave more privacy and collectivists generally desire more connectedness in an intimate relationship. The struggle to define *independence* and *interdependence* can cause chronic relationship problems in many intercultural couples.

In a business setting, if one business partner (from Sydney) opts to scribble a note and fax it to another international partner (from Jakarta), the latter might view this gesture as a signal of disrespect for proper professional distance. The Jakartan partner perceives the informal gesture of a scribbled note as a violation of formal business exchange. However, the Sydney business partner may not realize that he or she has committed a *faux pas* by sending this casual message; the informal note was actually intended to indicate "pleasant friendliness" and "closer distance" for the sake of establishing a relaxed working atmosphere.

Research shows that across many cultures, females tend to be more comfortable addressing relational conflict goal issues than males (Ting-Toomey, 1991; Wood, 1997). Males, in comparison, tend to prefer addressing content conflict goal issues and with more ease than pursuing relational conflict topics. In addition, from the collectivistic cultural standpoint, relational conflict goals usually take precedence over content goals. The rationale from the collectivistic point of view is that if the relationship is in jeopardy, it is useless to spend time talking about practical or content issues. Identity goals, however, are paramount to both individualists and collectivists, as well as to males and females, across a wide range of conflict situations.

The phrase **identity-based goals** means face-saving and face-honoring issues in a conflict episode.

They are basically about self-respect (face-saving) and other-consideration (face-honoring) issues in a conflict situation (Ting-Toomey & Cole, 1990). Recall from Chapter 4 that identity-based goals can involve respectful or disrespectful attitudes concerning three identity issues in conflict: cultural, social, and personal. For example, although an interfaith couple is arguing about which religious faith they should instill in their children (cultural or social identity), they are also asserting the *worthiness* of their own particular religious beliefs (personal identity). To the extent that the couple can engage in a constructive dialog about this important issue, the conflict can act as a catalyst for their relationship growth. However, many intercultural or interfaith couples may not possess the necessary conflict skills to deal with important identity issues constructively (Karis, 2009; Kennedy & Sakaguchi, 2009; Rustogi, 2009; Ting-Toomey, 2009; Toyosaki, 2011).

At a minimum, in any conflict scene, conflict parties should realize that they are interdependent in the relationship or within the workplace system. If they were not interdependent, they could just walk away from the conflict scene without the necessity of fighting over incompatible goals. For example, in L-Chat 9.2, Ms. Levine is dependent on Mr. Morena to finish his report before she can put her final report together. Ms. Levine's final report to senior management can mean a promotion or more name recognition for her in the firm. However, Mr. Morena is dependent on Ms. Levine to give him a good performance review for his potential year-end bonus. Thus, both have personal and mutual interests in resolving the conflict. Unfortunately, oftentimes culture-based conflict styles and behaviors lead to intercultural collisions in the negotiation process. With their views of the situation distorted by ethnocentric lenses and mindless stereotypes, both parties in the conflict may be stuck in their polarized positions and perceptual views. They must learn new conflict management skills to disengage from their set behaviors and to free themselves from their negative conflict loops.

Perceived Scarce Resources

The fifth set of background factors is perceived scarce resources. *Conflict resources* are tangible or intangible

rewards that people want in a dispute. The rewards or commodities may be scarce or perceived as scarce by individuals in the conflict. Perceived scarce resources may spark the initial flame behind the conflict.

Tangible resources include how much money to spend on a smart phone, an iPad, or choice of prime location for a vacation. Some tangible commodities are indeed scarce or limited (e.g., only one promotion available for three workers). Other tangible resources are only *perceived* to be scarce (e.g., not enough parking spaces for everyone—when abundant spaces are reserved for administration) rather than actual scarcity. **Intangible resources**, however, may include deeply felt desires or emotional needs, such as emotional security, inclusion, connection, respect, control, and meaning issues. Recurring conflict between two or more individuals often involves unmet (or frustrated) intangible needs rather than conflicting tangible wants. Scarce intangible resources can be real or perceived as real (e.g., two men fighting for the perceived lack of attention from their boss) by individuals in the conflict episode. Both tangible and intangible resources can be managed constructively or destructively, depending on whether the disputants are willing to spend the time and energy in probing the underlying concerns and needs of the other conflict party.

Rothman (1997), and intercultural conflict expert, recommended the following three techniques in negotiating scarce resources in a conflict situation: differentiation, expansion, and compensation. **Differentiation** means taking an active stance to acknowledge the different cultural perspectives and lenses in a conflict situation. At the same time, the conflict parties display good faith in addressing the conflict by dividing up the large puzzle into different pieces or slices. They also strive to maintain constructive momentum to keep on moving forward to reach a shared goal or vision. For example, twin sisters are fighting over a CD. One actually wants the disc, and the other actually wants the cover. By articulating their basic needs in a collaborative dialog format, the sisters can share the CD productively without the need to compromise or make unnecessary concessions.

Expansion means an active search for alternative paths or creative solutions to enlarge the amount, type, or use of available resources (e.g., using existing resources in imaginative ways or cultivating new resources) for mutual gains. For example, the twins may want to make their own music and draw their own CD cover. They can also learn to work together to mix resources (e.g., artwork and music) for mutual gains. When both parties are guided by shared goals or dreams as they search for creative alternatives, they can reduce rigid stereotypes and see each other's humanity more clearly.

Last, **compensation** means conflict parties can offer exchanges or concessions for conflict issues they value differently. For example, one twin sister desperately wants the disc to play at her sorority party that night, but the other twin had planned to take it with her on an overnight driving trip. One twin can offer money to the other (e.g., monetary compensation that is worth more than the price of the original CD) to compensate for the time and effort it takes to go and buy another CD—thus reflecting the compensation technique via seeking out other pragmatic alternatives. As Rothman (1997) notes, "pieces of peace, that one side may offer the other in exchange for something else, can be powerful in fostering confidence and advancing the constructive cycle of cooperation" (p. 64). Culture-sensitive collaborative dialog helps the disputants come to recognize their positive interdependence in a mindful manner.

Through flexible conflict communication skills, the conflict parties may invent creative alternatives or paths to generate additional resources for mutual gain. In this section, we have discussed four cultural background factors—culture-based conflict lenses, intercultural conflict perceptions, conflict goals, and perceived scarce resources—that influence an actual intercultural conflict negotiation process. We now turn to a discussion of important conflict process factors.

INTERCULTURAL CONFLICT PROCESS FACTORS

The following section draws from the conceptual explanations of Ting-Toomey's (1988, 2007a, 2007b) face-negotiation theory and presents some interesting research findings concerning conflict styles and facework behaviors in diverse cultural and ethnic groups. **Face** is really about socially approved self-image and other-image consideration issues. **Facework** is about the verbal and nonverbal strategies that we use to maintain, defend, or upgrade our own social self-image and attack or defend (or "save") the social images of others. For example, when others confront us with face-threatening conflict messages, we are likely either to engage in defensive facework strategies or to flee the scene altogether to recoup our face loss. The following section discusses three approaches to the study of conflict style and defines each conflict style. It then describes some cross-cultural and cross-ethnic conflict styles and facework behaviors.

Defining Conflict Styles

Check out my.blog 9.2, which contains a short questionnaire designed to assess broad conflict styles. Take a couple of minutes to complete it now. The higher the score in the left-hand column, the more direct or low context you are in your conflict style. The higher the score in the right-hand column, the more indirect or high context you are in your conflict style. Overall, **conflict communication style** refers to patterned verbal and nonverbal responses to conflict in a variety of frustrating conflict situations (Ting-Toomey & Oetzel, 2001). There are three approaches to studying conflict styles: the dispositional approach, the situational approach, and the systems approach.

A **dispositional approach** emphasizes that individuals do have predominant conflict style tendencies in handling a wide variety of conflict situations in different cultures. Conflict style is learned within the primary socialization process of one's cultural or ethnic group. It also depends highly on one's dispositional or personality traits. For example, an extrovert will tend to use a more dominating or expressive style, but an introvert will tend to use a more avoiding or obliging style. By extension, a cultural trait approach means particular cultures (e.g., collectivistic cultures) on a systems-based level would also exhibit certain predominant conflict style tendencies (e.g., using more obliging or avoidance conflict patterns). A **situational approach**, on the other hand, stresses the importance of the conflict topic and the conflict situation in shaping what conflict styles will be used in what types of relationships and in what contexts, or both of these. Situational factors such as the conflict topic, situation, relationship type, time pressure, and conflict goals can have a strong influence on whether we will engage in the conflict or avoid the conflict altogether. A **systems approach** integrates both dispositional and situational approaches. It recognizes that most individuals have predominant conflict style profiles because of strong cultural and family socialization conflict scripts. However, individuals also modify their styles on the basis of the particular conflict situation and on their partners' responses and reactions to their conflict behaviors. Among other factors that influence conflict style are intergroup conflict histories, ethnocentric filters, prejudiced mindsets, mood, and conflict competence skills (Hammer, 2009; LeBaron, 2003). We take a systems approach in understanding most cross-cultural conflict style issues in this chapter.

---

my.blog 9.2 GENERAL CONFLICT STYLE ASSESSMENT

Instructions: Consider several conflict situations in which you find your goals or wishes differing from those of another person. How do you usually respond to those conflict situations?

Following are some pairs of statements describing possible behavioral responses. For each pair, circle the "A" or "B" statement that is **most characteristic of your own conflict behavior in most conflict situations.**

1.　　A. I attempt to stand firm in my conflict requests.

　　　　B. I do my best to soothe the other person's feelings and tend to the relationship.

2.　　A. I tend to take time to understand the background context of the conflict story.

　　　　B. I tend to separate conflict task issues from conflict relationship issues.

3.　　A. I try to verbally defend my position to the best of my ability.

　　　　B. There are often times that I shy away from facing the conflict person or problem.

4.　　A. I try to downplay the importance of the conflict disagreement.

　　　　B. I tend to be direct in expressing my conflict feelings.

5.　　A. I try to show him or her the logic and reasons of my position.

　　　　B. I emphasize that our relationship is much more important to me than the conflict itself.

6.　　A. I'm usually firm in pursuing my conflict goals.

　　　　B. I'm usually sensitive to the fact that other people might hear our conflict arguments in public.

7.　　A. I can usually figure out whether the other person is angry by tuning in to her or his feelings.

　　　　B. I like to get potential conflicts out on the table as soon as I am aware of the problem.

8.　　A. I usually try to persuade the other person that my way is the best way.

　　　　B. I try not to discuss the problem in front of others.

9.　　A. I usually apologize just to soothe feelings and soften the conflict situation.

　　　　B. I believe in dealing with conflict in an up-front, honest manner.

10.　　A. I usually articulate and assert my conflict goals clearly.

　　　　B. If it makes the other person happy, I sometimes flow along with his or her wishes.

11.　　A. I try to do what is necessary to avoid useless tensions.

　　　　B. I am usually firm in pursuing my conflict intentions.

12.　　A. I try to postpone facing the issue until I have had time to think it over.

　　　　B. In most conflict situations, I press to get my conflict points made.

Continued

my.blog 9.2 CONTINUED

Scoring: Circle the letters below that you previously circled on each previous item of the questionnaire.

Scoring interpretation:

1.	A	B
2.	B	A
3.	A	B
4.	B	A
5.	A	B
6.	A	B
7.	B	A
8.	A	B
9.	B	A
10.	A	B
11.	B	A
12.	B	A

Total number of items circled in each column:

Left column: _____   **Right column:** _____

[LCC]   **[HCC]**

Scoring: Add up the circled items on the left-hand column and you will find your low-context conflict style score. *Low-context conflict style* score:_____. Add up the circled items on the right-hand column and you will find your high-context conflict style score. *High-context conflict style* score:_____.

Interpretation: Scores on each general conflict communication dimension can range from 0 to 12; the higher the score, the more low context and/or high context you are in your general conflict behaviors. If the scores on both columns are similar, you tend to use both direct/low-context, and indirect/high-context conflict approaches.

Reflection probes: Take a moment to think of the following questions: Is your family a "low-context" conflict engagement family or a "high-context" conflict avoidance family? Do you have a consistent approach in dealing with conflicts or do you switch conflict styles often? Are you happy with your own conflict approach? Do your cultural or ethnic groups value a low-context or a high-context approach in dealing with various conflict situations? Why? Share some of your conflict perspectives and stories with a classmate.

Without realizing it, over the years you probably have developed some patterned conflict styles to deal with various conflict issues. You may be the individual who exits from any conflict scene or gives in easily to keep the peace. Or you may be the diametrically opposite type—the one who gets stimulated by a conflict-challenging environment. Many researchers conceptualize conflict styles along two dimensions. For example, Rahim (1992) based his classification of conflict styles on the two conceptual dimensions of concern for self and concern for others.

The first dimension illustrates the degree (high or low) to which a person seeks to satisfy her or his own conflict interest or face need. The second dimension represents the degree (high or low) to which a person desires to incorporate the other's conflict interest. The two dimensions are combined, resulting in five styles of handling interpersonal conflict: dominating, avoiding, obliging, compromising, and integrating.

Before you continue reading, take the fun test in my.blog 9.3 and obtain your specific conflict style scores.

The five-style conflict model represents one way of conceptualizing these different conflict style tendencies (see Figure 9.2).

The **dominating** (or **competitive/controlling**) **style** emphasizes conflict tactics that push for one's own position above and beyond the other person's interest. The dominating style includes aggressive, defensive, controlling, and intimidating tactics. The **avoiding style** involves dodging the topic, the other party, or the situation altogether. This style includes behavior ranging from glossing over the

my.blog 9.3 ASSESSING YOUR SPECIFIC FIVE CONFLICT STYLES

Instructions: Recall how you generally communicate in various conflict situations with acquaintances. Let your first inclination be your guide and circle the number in the scale that best reflects your conflict style tendency. The following scale is used for each item:

4 = YES! = *strongly agree—IT'S ME!*
3 = yes = *moderately agree—it's kind of like me*
2 = no = *moderately disagree—it's kind of not me*
1 = NO! = *strongly disagree—IT'S NOT ME!*

		SA	MA	MD	SD
1.	I often "grin and bear it" when the other person does something I don't like.	4	3	2	1
2.	I "give and take" so that a compromise can be reached.	4	3	2	1
3.	I use my influence to get my ideas accepted in resolving the problem.	4	3	2	1
4.	I am open to the other person's suggestions in resolving the problem.	4	3	2	1
5.	I generally give in to the wishes of the other person in a conflict.	4	3	2	1
6.	I usually avoid open discussion of the conflict with the person.	4	3	2	1
7.	I try to find a middle course to break an impasse.	4	3	2	1
8.	I argue the case with the other person to show the merits of my position.	4	3	2	1
9.	I integrate my viewpoints with the other person to achieve a joint resolution.	4	3	2	1
10.	I generally try to satisfy the expectations of the other person.	4	3	2	1
11.	I try not to bump up against the other person whenever possible.	4	3	2	1
12.	I try to play down our differences to reach a compromise.	4	3	2	1
13.	I'm generally firm in pursuing my side of the issue.	4	3	2	1
14.	I encourage the other person to try to see things from a creative angle.	4	3	2	1
15.	I often go along with the suggestions of the other person.	4	3	2	1
16.	I usually bear my resentment in silence.	4	3	2	1
17.	I usually propose a middle ground for breaking deadlocks.	4	3	2	1

Continued

my.blog 9.3 CONTINUED

18. I am emotionally expressive in the conflict situation.   4   3   2   1

19. I dialog with the other person with close attention to her or his needs.   4   3   2   1

20. I do my best to accommodate the wishes of the other person in a conflict.   4   3   2   1

Scoring: Add up the scores on items 1, 6, 11, and 16 and you will find your avoidance conflict style score. *Avoidance style* score: _____. Add up the scores on items 2, 7, 12, and 17 and you will find your compromising conflict style score. *Compromising style* score: _____. Add up the scores on items 3, 8, 13, and 18 and you will find your dominating/competing conflict style score. *Dominating style* score: _____. Add up the scores on items 4, 9, 14, and 19 and you will find your integrating/collaborating conflict style score. *Integrating style* score: _____. Add up the scores on items 5, 10, 15, and 20 and you will find your obliging conflict style score. *Obliging style* score: _____.

Interpretation: Scores on each conflict style dimension can range from 4 to 16; the higher the score, the more you engage in that particular conflict style. If some of the scores are similar on some of the conflict style dimensions, you tend to use a mixed pattern of different conflict styles.

Reflection probes: Compare your conflict style scores with a classmate's. Take a moment to think of the following questions: Where did you learn your conflict style tendencies? What do you think are the pros and cons of each specific conflict style? When you are having a conflict with someone from a different culture, how would you address the different conflict style issues? What skills do you need to practice more to be a culturally sensitive conflict negotiator?

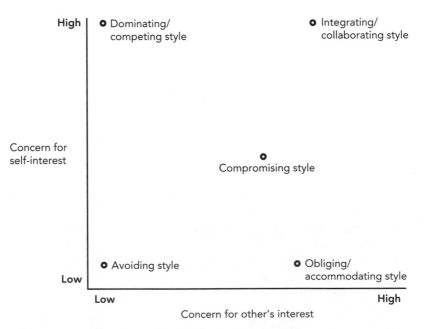

FIGURE 9.2   A Five-Style Conflict Model: A Western Approach

topic and denying that conflict exists to leaving the conflict scene. The **obliging** (or **accommodating**) **style** is characterized by a high concern for the other person's conflict interest above and beyond one's own conflict position. Individuals tend to use the obliging style when they value their relationship more than their personal conflict goal. They tend to either smooth over the conflict or give in to the wishes of their conflict partners. The **compromising style**, however, involves a give-and-take concession approach to reach a mid-point agreement concerning the conflict issue. In using the compromising style, individuals tend to use fairness appeals, trade-off suggestions, or other quick, short-term solutions. It is an intermediate style resulting in some gains and some losses for each party. Finally, the **integrating** (or **collaborative**) **style** reflects a commitment to find a mutual-interest solution and involves a high concern for self-interest and also a high concern for the other person's interest in the conflict situation. In using an integrative style, individuals tend to use nonevaluative descriptive messages, qualifying statements, and mutual-interest clarifying questions to seek common-ground solutions. This is the most time-consuming style of the five conflict styles. Johnson (1986) equated the five different styles to the following animals: shark = *dominating style*, turtle = *avoiding*, teddy bear = *obliging*, fox = *compromising*, and owl = *integrating*.

It should be noted here that in the U.S. conflict research literature, obliging and avoiding conflict styles are often described as being negatively disengaged (i.e., *indifferent* or *fleeing* from the conflict scene). However, collectivists do not necessarily perceive obliging and avoiding conflict styles as negative. For example, collectivists often use these two conflict styles to maintain mutual-face interests and ingroup harmony (Ting-Toomey, 1988). From the collectivistic cultural lens, obliging and avoiding styles can be viewed as two very constructive, face-sensitive conflict styles.

Cross-Cultural Conflict Styles

Face-negotiation theory helps to explain how individualism–collectivism value patterns influence the use of diverse conflict styles in different cultural situations (Ting-Toomey & Kurogi, 1998; Ting-Toomey & Takai, 2006). The premise of the theory is that members who subscribe to individualistic values tend to be more self-face-oriented and members who subscribe to group-oriented values tend to be more other- or mutual-face-oriented in conflict negotiation. The face orientation, shaped by the various cultural, personality, and situational factors, frames our different motivations to use different conflict styles. Individuals who are more self-face-oriented tend to use a direct, low-context conflict style to assert their rights in a conflict situation. Individuals who are more other-face- or mutual-face-oriented tend to use an indirect, high-context conflict style to maintain other or mutual face and to preserve relational harmony (Oetzel, Garcia, & Ting-Toomey, 2008). The more independent or individualistic you are, the more likely you are to use a linear logic, low-context approach in managing your conflict. The more interdependent or collectivistic you are, the more likely you are to use a spiral logic, high-context approach in dealing with your conflict (Okabe, 1983).

Research (e.g., in China, Hong Kong, Japan, South Korea, Taiwan, Mexico, and the United States) clearly indicates that individualists tend to use more self-defensive, dominating, and competitive conflict styles in managing disputes than do collectivists. In comparison, collectivists tend to use more integrative and compromising styles in dealing with conflict than do individualists. It is important to point out that in the research literature focusing on individualists, the compromising style often connotes task-based compromises—you have to give something tangible to get something back and reach a midpoint compromising solution. However, for collectivists, the term "compromise" often means relational give-and-take concessions from a long-term reciprocity perspective. In other words, by "giving in" during a particular conflict episode, both have the mutual understanding that each individual has taken turns giving in. Finally, research also indicates that collectivists tend to use more obliging and avoiding conflict styles in a wider variety of conflict situations than do individualists (Cai & Fink, 2002; Oetzel, Garcia, & Ting-Toomey, 2008; Oetzel et al., 2001; Ting-Toomey et al., 1991; Ting-Toomey, Yee-Jung, Shapiro, Garcia, Wright, & Oetzel, 2000).

It is interesting to note that whether the conflict is with a member of the ingroup or a member of an outgroup also clearly affects how collectivists manage conflict. Chinese, for example, are more likely to pursue a conflict with an outgroup member and less likely to pursue a conflict with an ingroup member than U.S. Americans (Leung, 1988). Likewise, Japanese tend to use a competitive/dominating conflict style with outgroup members and an obliging style with ingroup members more than do U.S. Americans. For U.S. Americans, whether they are having a conflict with an outgroup member or an ingroup member does not seem to influence their predominant conflict styles (Ting-Toomey & Oetzel, 2001; Ting-Toomey & Takai, 2006).

On the personal attributes level, independent-self individuals tend to use more competitive/dominating conflict styles than do interdependent-self individuals, and interdependent-self individuals tend to use more avoiding, obliging, integrating, and compromising styles than do independent-self individuals (Oetzel, 1998, 1999). Thus, to gain an in-depth understanding of an individual's conflict styles, we must understand his or her cultural conditioning process, personality attributes, and ingroup–outgroup conflict situations (Oetzel, Arcos, Mabizela, Weinman, & Zhang, 2006; Oetzel & Ting-Toomey, 2003; Ting-Toomey, 2007a, 2007b; Ting-Toomey & Oetzel, 2001).

Cross-Ethnic Conflict Styles and Facework

In terms of different ethnic conflict styles and facework behaviors, most conflict research has focused on European American conflict styles in both interpersonal and organizational conflict domains. Overall, European Americans tend to prefer solution-based conflict strategies and tend to compartmentalize socioemotional conflict issues separately from task-based conflict issues more than do African Americans (Ting-Toomey, 1985, 1986). European Americans also tend to use more dominating/controlling conflict strategies in dealing with romantic relationships than do Asian Americans (Kim, Lim, Dindia, & Burrell, 2010).

Distinctive conflict styles and facework strategies exist within different ethnic groups in the United States (Orbe & Everett, 2006). The following section first addresses African American conflict styles and then Asian American, Latino/a American, and Native American conflict style orientations.

African American Conflict Styles

African American conflict styles are influenced simultaneously by both individualistic and collectivistic values. At the same time that traditional African values are collectivistic (e.g., community, interdependence, being at one with nature, and church/religious participation) and large power distance-based (e.g., respecting grandparents and pastors), they are also in constant struggle against the power dominance of whites in white-privileged U.S. society (Asante & Asante, 1990).

The white-privileged social position refers to a primarily favored state of whites holding power over other minority groups in all key decision-making avenues (McIntosh, 1995). There is also a tendency for European Americans or whites to view racism episodes as individual acts rather than as part of a problematic, power-imbalance institutional package. Thus, assertive conflict styles and emotionally expressive facework behaviors may be one method by which African Americans uphold self- and ingroup-membership dignity.

Research also reveals that African Americans tend to be more emotionally engaged in their conflict approach, whereas European Americans tend to be more emotionally restrained in their conflict discussions (Ting-Toomey, 1986). The *black mode* of conflict is high-keyed (e.g., energetic, nonverbally animated, and emotionally expressive), whereas the *white mode* of conflict is relatively low-keyed (e.g., dispassionate, nonverbally disciplined, and emotionally restrained; Collier, 1991, 2001; Kochman, 1981, 1990). Let's check out L-Chat 9.3. Zoe, a European American, is the movie director, and Blake, an African American, is the screenwriter. Melody, a European American, is the producer.

Overall, in a conflict situation, African Americans tend to prefer an emotionally engaged, assertive mode of conflict discussion, but some European Americans tend to prefer an analytical, neutral-tone mode in controlling their conflict emotions. It is also interesting that, according to cross-ethnic conflict research (Ting-Toomey et al., 2000), African Americans who identify

L-CHAT 9.3

ZOE: So, Blake, what's your opinion about our film? What's the best action plan?

BLAKE (enthusiastically): I think we need to go back and reshoot the conclusion. The ending is useless and we've had more complaints, and we need closure.

ZOE: (analytically): Melody, what do you think?

MELODY (analytically): Zoe, I think the ending is doable. It just needs to be tweaked with a better soundtrack.

BLAKE (with an animated voice): ARE YOU KIDDING ME?? We did this last time and the movie bombed! Using music to cover up the flaws doesn't support this movie and just DOESN'T WORK!!

ZOE (takes a deep breath): Are you finished, Blake? Good—then here's the plan. Given the time constraint, think about tweaking the ending with music. Melody, contact Kristi in the production department and see how much it'll cost to bring in some hard rock music. Also, set up a prescreening test for . . .

BLAKE (interrupts Zoe): Zoe, it's NOT GONNA WORK! Remember last time . . .

ZOE (losing her cool): OK, BLAKE! I heard you the first time already. Now . . .

BLAKE (raising his voice and trying hard to be heard): I'm serious, Zoe. We're gonna end up losing money . . .

Zoe (in a take-charge voice): ALL RIGHT, enough is enough, BLAKE! I don't know what YOU think I can do. You seem to ALWAYS be challenging my decisions . . .

strongly with the larger U.S. culture tend to use a more give-and-take compromising style in conflict than African Americans who identify weakly with the larger U.S. culture. As a complex and diverse group, many African Americans have an integrative system of individualistic and collectivistic values. Their affectively laden conflict pattern is strongly influenced by ethnic/cultural values, social class, and reactions to racial oppression factors (Cross, 1991; Cross, Smith, & Payne, 2002).

Asian American Conflict Styles

In terms of Asian American conflict orientation, research shows that the philosophy of Confucianism strongly influences proper facework and conflict enactment. Confucius was a Chinese philosopher of practical ethics who lived from 551 to 479 B.C.E. His practical code of conduct emphasizes hierarchical societal structure and appropriate family role performance. Confucianism remains the fundamental philosophy that underlies many Asian cultures (e.g., China, Taiwan, Singapore, South Korea, and Japan). Some core Confucian values are dynamic long-term orientation, perseverance, ordering relationships by status, having a sense of shame, and emphasizing collective face saving (Chen, 2001; Chen, 1997; Gao & Ting-Toomey, 1998). A collective or interdependent sense of shame includes the constant awareness of other people's expectations of one's own performance and the concern for face-losing behaviors.

Asian Americans who adhere to traditional Asian values tend to use avoiding or obliging conflict styles to deal with a conflict at hand. They sometimes also use "silence" as a powerful, high-context conflict style. Moreover, they may resort to third-party help—especially from trusted family members or networks—to mediate the conflict situation. Asian Americans who identify strongly with the larger U.S. culture tend to use an integrative conflict style to find content solutions to the conflict more than do Asian Americans who tend to identify weakly with the larger U.S. culture (Ting-Toomey et al., 2000).

Given the diversity of the Asian American population, we should also pay close attention to the country of origin, immigration experiences, acculturation, generation, language, family socialization, and levels of ethnic and cultural identity importance that create tremendous distinctions among and within these multiple groups.

Latino/a American Conflict Styles

In the context of traditional Latino/a Americans' conflict practices, *tactfulness* and *consideration of others' feelings* are considered important facework norms. Tactfulness is conveyed through the use of other-oriented facework rituals, such as the use of accommodation (i.e., "smoothing over") and avoidance conflict behaviors (Garcia, 1996; Hecht, Ribeau, & Sedano, 1990).

For example, in Mexican American culture, the word *respeto* connotes the honor, respect, and *face* that we accord to listeners in accordance with their roles and hierarchical statuses. In Mexican American culture, facework is closely related to family loyalty, honor, name, respect, and extended family approval. Thus, well-mannered and diplomatic facework behaviors are preferred in managing conflicts in the Mexican American ethnic community. Avoidance conflict style is sometime preferred over a head-on confrontative style in dealing with minor or midrange conflict issues. Collectivism and large power distance values are the underlying value patterns that frame the Latino/a American conflict expectations and attitudes. In dealing with annoying conflict situations, however, it has also been found that Latino/a Americans who identify strongly with their traditional ethnic values tend to use more emotionally expressive conflict styles than Latino/a Americans who do not strongly identify with their traditional ethnic values (Ting-Toomey et al., 2000).

With the tremendous diversity that exists under the "Latino/a American" label, we would do well to increase the complexity of our understanding of the values and distinctive conflict patterns of each group (e.g., Puerto Rican group, Cuban group, or Mexican group).

Native American Conflict Styles

In comparison, Native Americans prefer the use of verbal restraint and self-discipline in emotional expressions during conflict. Some of the value patterns of Native Americans that have been identified by researchers are the following: (1) sharing—honor and respect are gained by sharing and giving; (2) cooperation—the family and tribe take precedence over the individual; (3) noninterference—one is taught to observe and not to react impulsively, especially in meddling in other people's affairs; (4) time orientation—Native Americans tend to be more present-oriented than future-oriented and believe that life is to be lived fully in the present; (5) extended family orientations—there is a strong respect for elders and their wisdom and generational knowledge; and (6) harmony with nature—the tendency is to flow with nature and not want to control or master one's outer environment (Sue & Sue, 1999).

Given these value patterns, we can infer that in terms of emotional expression, Native Americans

tend to be more other- and mutual-face-sensitive in dealing with disputes in their everyday lives. Out of consideration for the other person's face, they use more emotionally understated expressions in trying to resolve their conflict peacefully. They are also likely to go to a third-party elder to solicit wisdom in resolving the conflict issue and, thus, help each other to maintain face. They also tend to use more deliberate silence in conveying their displeasure. Communal and large power distance values frame many Native Americans' nuanced emotional expression styles.

However, given the fact that there are over five hundred Native American tribes, any generalizations should serve only as preliminary cultural knowledge (rather than rigid stereotyping) that helps us to be more consciously competent in generating alternative viewpoints in interpreting an entangled conflict situation. We should realize that, for example, Native Americans who live on or near reservations are more likely to subscribe to traditional values, whereas other Native Americans may adhere to predominant, mainstream values or a set of bicultural values (Ting-Toomey & Oetzel, 2001).

FLEXIBLE INTERCULTURAL CONFLICT SKILLS

Flexible intercultural conflict management depends on many factors. One key factor is the ability to apply adaptive conflict communication skills. This section identifies five skills that are critical to flexible intercultural conflict management: facework management, mindful listening, cultural empathy, mindful reframing, and adaptive code-switching (see Blog Pic 9.1).

Facework Management

Facework skills address the core issues of protecting our own communication identity during a conflict episode and, at the same time, allowing us to deal with the communication identity of the other conflict party. All human beings value the feeling of *being respected and being accepted*—especially during vulnerable conflict interactions. How individuals protect and maintain self-face needs and, at the same time, how they learn to honor the face needs of the other conflict

Blog Pic 9.1   Conflict among coworkers may result in frustration.

party very likely differs from one culture to the next and from one particular conflict scene to the next.

On a general level, both individualists and collectivists must learn to *save face* strategically and *give face* appropriately to each other during a conflict episode. **Self-oriented face-saving behaviors** are attempts to regain or defend one's image after threats to face or face loss. **Other-oriented face-giving behaviors** are attempts to support others' face claims and work with them to prevent further face loss or help them to restore face constructively. *Giving face* means not humiliating others, especially one's conflict opponents, in public.

For *individualists having conflicts with collectivists, giving face* means acknowledging collectivists' ingroup conflict concerns and obligations. Further, it means learning to mindfully listen and hold a mutual-orientation perspective in the conflict process, learning to apologize when you are part of the conflict problem, and giving credit to the teamwork or family members that frame the collectivists' action or accomplishment. For *collectivists having conflicts with individualists, giving face* means honoring others by expressing your ideas (or opinions) actively with other conflict parties in a

candid manner, engaging in explicit verbal acknowledgment and feedback during a conflict negotiation process, recognizing the person's abilities and complimenting his or her unique contributions, and understanding the differences between acting assertively, passively, passive aggressively, and aggressively (see Blog Pics 9.1 and 9.2).

Mindful Listening

Mindful listening is a face-validation and power-sharing skill. In a conflict episode, the disputants must try hard to listen with focused attentiveness to the cultural and personal assumptions that are being expressed in the conflict interaction (see Table 9.2). They must learn to listen responsively or *ting* (the Chinese word for listening means "attending mindfully with our ears, eyes, and a focused heart") to the sounds, tone, gestures, movements, nonverbal nuances, pauses, and silence in a given conflict situation. In mindful listening, facework negotiators tend to practice dialogic listening, one-pointed attentiveness, mindful silence, and responsive words and posture.

By listening mindfully, conflict disputants can learn to create new categories in interpreting the

Blog Pic 9.2   Business negotiations conducted in a social setting.

TABLE 9.2 MINDLESS VERSUS MINDFUL LISTENING CHARACTERISTICS

Mindless listening	Mindful listening
Ethnocentric lens	Ethnorelative lens
Reactive approach	Proactive/choice approach
Selective hearing	Attentive listening
Defensive posture	Supportive posture
"Struggle against"	"Struggle with"
Judgmental attitude	Mindful reframing
Emotional outbursts	Vulnerability shared
Coercive power	Shared power
Positional differences	Common interests
Fixed objectives	Creative options
Win–lose/lose–lose outcome	Win–win synergy

unfolding conflict sequences. *Creating new categories* means learning to apply culture-sensitive concepts to make sense of conflict variation behaviors. We can also practice mindful listening by engaging in paraphrasing and perception-checking skills. **Paraphrasing skills** involve two characteristics: (1) summarizing the content meaning of the other's message in your own words and (2) nonverbally echoing your interpretation of the emotional meaning of the other's message. The summary, or restatement, should reflect your tentative understanding of the conflict party's content meaning, such as "It sounds to me that…" and "In other words, you're saying that…." You can also try to paraphrase the emotional meaning of the disputant's message by echoing your understanding of the emotional tone that underlies her or his message. In dealing with high-context members, your paraphrasing statements should consist of deferential, qualifying phrases, such as "I may be wrong, but what I'm hearing is that..." or "Please correct me if I misinterpret what you've said. It sounded to me that...." In interacting with low-context members, your paraphrasing statements can be more direct and to the point than with high-context members.

Moving beyond paraphrasing, **perception-checking** (see Chapter 8 on intergroup bias) is designed to help ensure that we are interpreting the speaker's nonverbal and verbal behaviors accurately during an escalating conflict episode. Culturally sensitive perception-checking statements involve both direct and indirect perceptual observation statements and perceptual verification questions. They usually end with questions. For example, a perceptual statement can be "You look really confused. I mentioned the deadline to check out was noon. It is now 2 p.m. Did you understand the time? Or is there something else that may not be clear? [pause]." Perception checking is part of mindful observation and mindful listening skills, to be used cautiously in accordance with the particular topic, relationship, timing, and situational context.

Mindful listening involves a fundamental shift of our conflict perspective. It means taking into account not only how things look from your own conflict perspective but also how they look and feel from the other conflict partner's perspective. Over time, mindful listening can lead to the development of cultural empathy.

Cultural Empathy

Cultural empathy has two layers: cultural empathetic understanding and cultural empathetic responsiveness (Ridley & Udipi, 2002; Broome & Jakobsson Hatay. 2006). **Cultural empathy** is the learned ability of the participants to understand accurately the self-experiences of others from diverse cultures and, concurrently, the ability to convey their understanding responsively and effectively to reach the "cultural ears" of the culturally different others in the conflict situation.

Some suggested cultural empathy techniques (Pedersen, Crethar, & Carlson, 2008; Ridley & Udipi, 2002; Ting-Toomey, 1999, 2010c) include the following: (1) check yourself for possible cultural biases and

hidden prejudices in the conflict episode, (2) suspend your rigidly held intergroup stereotypes, (3) do not pretend to understand—ask for clarification, (4) use reflective time and appropriate silence to gauge your own understanding of the other's conflict perspective, and (5) capture the core conflict emotion, metaphor, meaning, and facework theme of the other conflict party and echo the theme back to the conflict party in your own words—with carefully phrased responsive words and gestures.

Mindful Reframing

Mindful reframing is a highly creative, mutual-face-honoring skill. It means creating alternative contexts to frame your understanding of the conflict behavior. Just as in changing a frame to appreciate an old painting, creating a new context to understand the conflict behavior may redefine your interpretation of the behavior or conflict event. **Reframing** is the mindful process of using language to change the way each person defines or thinks about experiences and views the conflict situation (Keaten & Soukup, 2009).

This skill uses language strategically for the purpose of changing the emotional setting of the conflict from a defensive climate to a collaborative one. Through the use of neutrally toned (to positively-toned) language, reframing can help to soften defensiveness, reduce tension, and increase understanding. The following are some specific suggestions for mindful reframing: (1) restate conflict positions into common-interest terms, (2) change complaint statements into requests, (3) move from blaming statements to mutual-focused, problem-solving statements, (4) help those in conflict recognize the benefits of a win–win synergistic approach, and (5) help conflict parties understand the "big picture."

Reframing is a critical conflict management skill because how you *frame* the conflict event may change how you respond to it (Putnam, 2010). In sum, competent intercultural conflict management requires us to communicate flexibly in different intercultural situations, which necessitates adaptation. Constructive conflict management requires us to be knowledgeable and respectful of different worldviews and multiple approaches to dealing with a conflict situation (Canary & Lakey, 2006; Cupach, Canary, & Spitzberg, 2010). It requires us to be sensitive to the differences and similarities between individualistic and collectivistic cultures. It also demands that we be aware of our own ethnocentric biases and culture-based attributions when making quick or hasty evaluations of other people's conflict management approaches (Coleman & Raider, 2006).

Adaptive Code-Switching

Intercultural code-switching is conceptualized as "the act of purposefully modifying one's behavior in an interaction in a foreign setting in order to accommodate different cultural norms for appropriate behavior" (Molinksy, 2007, p. 624). To qualify as an intercultural code-switching situation, a situation must have norms that are either unfamiliar to the switcher or in conflict with values central to the switcher's identity. Central to Molinksy's (2007) conceptualization are two psychological challenges that must be met: code-switchers must execute the new behavior in such a manner that insiders of the culture judge the task performance and behavioral performance dimensions as appropriate to the context, and second, the code-switchers are eventually able to form a coherent sense of "identity dimension" via seeing the meaningful relevance of the behavior in context.

In sum, intercultural code-switching refers to intentionally learning and moving between culturally ingrained systems of behavior relevant to the situation at hand. Thus, individuals who have mastered the deep value structures of a culture (such as individualism and collectivism and other core culture-specific values) and the situational norms of an intercultural conflict episode can code-switch adaptively via an astute culture-sensitive situational analysis.

To extend this line of thinking, there are two possible modes of code-switching. *Behavioral or functional code-switching* refers to surface-level verbal and/ or nonverbal code-switching, especially for multicultural workplace survival and adaption. In contrast, *dynamic or integrative code-switching* is an internal and external synchronized dance of fluid figure-eight movements in which the dialectical tensions of individualism–collectivism (or any other seemingly contrastive value dimensions) within oneself are resolved or harmonized. Externally, the communication styles of this hybrid individual are also assessed as adaptive, appropriate, and effective. Lengthy foreign living experiences, bicultural and multicultural individuals growing up in a diverse household, third culture children's adaptation experiences, and a willingness to encounter differences have been found to enhance creative tendencies within individuals (Leung, Maddux, Galinsky, & Chiu, 2008; Maddux & Galinsky, 2009).

INTERCULTURAL REALITY CHECK: DO-ABLES

To summarize, there are many complex factors that shape an intercultural conflict episode. In addition to the different culture-based conflict lenses, individuals use very different conflict styles and facework behaviors to approach a conflict situation. The latest research on cross-national and cross-ethnic conflict styles illustrated the struggles in an intercultural conflict negotiation process. Five specific communication skills—*facework management, mindful listening, cultural empathy, mindful reframing*, and *adaptive code-switching*—were recommended as starters to practice competent intercultural conflict management.

Some specific recommendations can also be made based on differences in individualistic and collectivistic styles of conflict management. These suggestions, however, are not listed in any order of importance. To deal with conflict constructively in a collectivistic culture, *individualists must do the following:*

- Be mindful of the mutual face-saving premises in a collectivistic culture, especially the use of specific facework skills in managing the delicate balance of humiliation and pride, respect and disrespect, and shame and honor issues.
- Practice patience and mindful observation: Take five seconds before verbally articulating your feelings. Be mindful of past events that bear relevance to the present conflict situation and also limit the number of verbal *why* questions—because collectivists typically focus on the nonverbal *how* process.

- Practice mindful listening skills: Attend to the sound, movement, and emotional experience of the other person. This indicates that one person is attending to the other person's identity and relational expectation issues; remember that the word *listen* can become *silent* by rearranging the letters.

Some specific recommendations also can be made for collectivists in handling conflict with individualists. When encountering a conflict situation in an individualistic culture, *collectivists must do the following:*

- Engage in an assertive style of conflict behavior that emphasizes the right of both parties to speak up in the conflict situation and respects the right to defend one's position; learn to open a conflict dialog with a clear thesis statement and then systematically develop key points.
- Assume individual accountability for the conflict decision-making process: use "I" statements when expressing opinions, sharing feelings, and voicing thought processes; assume a sender-responsible approach to constructively manage the conflict;

learn to ask more *why* questions and probe for clear explanations and details.

- Engage in active listening skills: engage in active verbal paraphrasing and perception-checking skills to ensure that the other person thoroughly understands each point; learn to occasionally disclose emotions, attitudes, and experiences within the conflict process itself; do not rely solely on nonverbal signals or count on other people to gauge personal reactions.

To manage intercultural conflict flexibly we must be prepared to take alternative cultural perspectives into consideration. If another party is an interdependent-self collectivist, we may want to pay attention to his or her "process-oriented" assumptions during our conflict negotiation. If others are independent-self individualists, we may want to be sensitive to their "outcome-oriented" assumptions during the conflict negotiation. Flexible intercultural conflict management means using culture-sensitive communication skills to manage the process and outcome of conflict adaptively and productively.

CHAPTER 10

WHAT ARE THE CHALLENGES IN DEVELOPING AN INTERCULTURAL-INTIMATE RELATIONSHIP?

CHAPTER OUTLINE

- Developing Intercultural-Intimate Relationships: Invisible Challenges
  - Cultural–Ethnic Membership Values
  - Love Expectations and Expressions
  - Autonomy–Connection Issues
  - Communication Decoding Issues

- Intercultural-Intimate Relationship Attraction: Facilitating Factors
  - Perceived Physical Attractiveness
  - Perceived Similarity
  - Cross-Cultural Self-Disclosure Comparisons
  - Online Disclosure of Affection
  - Third-Party Matchmakers: Online and Mobile Dating
  - Intercultural–Interracial Romantic Relationship Development

- Intercultural-Intimate Conflict: Obstacles and Stumbling Blocks
  - The Encounter: Prejudice and Racism
  - Countering Racism and Prejudice: Coping Strategies
  - Relational Transgressions and Terminations

- Raising Secure Bicultural Children
  - Bicultural Identity Struggles
  - Cultivating a Secure, Multifaceted Identity

- Intercultural Reality Check: Do-Ables

At twenty-two, I was a fiercely independent, nontraditional Jain Indian woman who lived in the United States with my parents. For a number of reasons, I decided to pursue an arranged marriage, shocking the closest of my friends. When I came back from India with my husband, my parents were the envy of all their friends. Not only was I the oldest daughter, but I acquiesced and chose a traditional arranged marriage. After one month together, imagine the realization that he was the biggest mistake of my life! My husband was not the man he claimed to be. But my parents were adamantly against the "D" word. "Grin and bear it," they advised me. They refused to become the outcast of the entire community, shamed and embarrassed. So I ignored it and put on a happy face.

After two long years of misery, depression, and suffering, I filed for a divorce. But what a cost . . . my parents no longer speak to me. It was and still is a devastating experience to me. I am now branded as a tainted woman. I recently moved out of the state and am slowly reclaiming my life back again.

Mona

To many East Asian Indians who have decided to pursue arranged marriages or are pressured to follow the traditional path, Mona's relational situation is not an exception to the rule. However, from the lens of our own cultural view, we may read the situation with shock and awe. Why would any independent woman choose to go to India and marry an individual whom she has never dated or barely even knows? What part did *love* play in this arranged marriage? What is the role of *passion* in this relationship pairing? Why should Mona "grin and bear" a miserable marriage? Didn't her parents care enough about her to support her "D"-word decision?

If we probe deeper into how different cultures handle intimate relationship issues, we may learn more about the challenges, decisions, and creative solutions that occur as they deal with different relationship problems. Their decisions may open our eyes to diverse ways of communicating in an intimate relationship. According to Guerrero et al. (2011), *intimacy* is "related to the degree to which people communicate affection, inclusion, trust, depth and involvement conveyed in a variety of ways" (p. 18). Intimate relationships can include deep friendships, romantic relationships, and close family relationships.

This chapter examines the challenges individuals face in forming voluntary intercultural-intimate relationships. The discussion first addresses the relationship challenges that individuals face when they come from diverse cultural value systems. Next, it identifies the facilitating factors that prompt relational partners to be attracted to each other. Third, the chapter addresses particular obstacles that some couples face when they desire to move the relationship to marital bonding stages. Fourth, it explores issues of raising secure, bicultural children. Finally, there are do-able guidelines for developing a healthy intercultural-intimate relationship. Understanding the challenges, facilitating factors, obstacles, and rewards of an intercultural-intimate relationship can help us to be more mindful and patient in dealing with our own diverse intimate relationships.

DEVELOPING INTERCULTURAL-INTIMATE RELATIONSHIPS: INVISIBLE CHALLENGES

Before we discuss why individuals are attracted to one another across cultural or ethnic lines, we need to look deeper into the cultural "iceberg" (remember Chapter 3) and explore the semihidden values that come into play in any relationship. Let's first revisit some familiar terms, such as individualism and collectivism, and draw out their implications for culture-based relationship expectations. Then everyone can investigate some communication decoding issues that may cause relationship misunderstandings.

Cultural–Ethnic Membership Values

Our cultural values (*individualism* and *collectivism*) influence our behaviors and our needs when we are in a close relationship, such as the need for *autonomy* and *connection*. Recall the core building block of individualism–collectivism lies in its relative emphasis on the importance of the "I" identity and the "we" identity (see Chapter 3). "I" identity members (e.g., Australians and Norwegians) tend to emphasize personal and relationship privacy issues. In contrast, "we" identity cultural members (e.g., Guatemalans and Costa Ricans) tend to emphasize family and ingroup network connection issues (see Table 10.1). From the collectivistic frame, relationship development is closely intertwined with the fate of others within the ingroup (Ting-Toomey & Takai, 2006; Wang & Chen, 2010; Wang & Lui, 2010). For example, Mona opted for the traditional path of an arranged marriage early on. She wanted the approval and acceptance of her family and extended family network in the very beginning. Although she suffered in her miserable arranged marriage right after the first month, she did not want to cause her family or extended family network to *lose face* or to be embarrassed on her behalf within the Indian ingroup community. This explains why her first choice was to "grin and bear it."

TABLE 10.1 INDIVIDUALISTIC AND COLLECTIVISTIC RELATIONSHIP ORIENTATIONS

Individualistic orientation	Collectivistic orientation
I-identity relationship expectations	Ingroup relationship pressures
Couple's privacy and autonomy needs	Ingroup's connection and concerns
Voluntary personal commitment	Family and social reactions
Low-context emotional expressions	High-context emotional expressions
Unique relational culture	Conventional relational culture

Despite some individualistic and collectivistic cultural differences, it is also important to know that in nearly all of thirty-seven cultural samples studied (Buss et al., 1990), both females and males endorsed *mutual attraction-love, dependability, emotional stability, kindness-understanding,* and *intelligence* as top-ranked mate-selection criteria. Overall, the greatest cultural variation is found in the attitude toward *premarital chastity.* Respondents in China, India, Nigeria, Iran, and Zambia (i.e., reflective of collectivistic values) differ from those of the continental United States and Western Europe (i.e., reflective of individualistic values) in placing a premium value on premarital chastity.

Love Expectations and Expressions

How do we define love? The word *love* can have many different connotations and at times can be very confusing. The term love can be used seriously or casually—depending on what culture you're from. Researchers simply cannot offer a clear definition of love. However, perspectives on love have been developed to distinguish love from liking, for example, comparing different types of love and liking as a triangle (Sternberg, 1988) or researching the different ideologies of love such as diverse love styles (J. A. Lee, 1977; Levine, Aune, & Park, 2006). In fact, individuals in the United States have different beliefs about romantic relationships and these different ideas suggest how different stages of relational initiation, maintenance, and termination play a critical role in intimate-interpersonal relationships based on love styles.

Just as people vary on how they conceptualize love, expectations concerning love across cultures vary as well. Although passionate love (affection, sexual desire, and attraction) is valued where family ties are weak (e.g., as in the larger U.S. culture), passionate love is diluted where family ties are strong (e.g., in South Korea and Pakistan). Romantic passionate love has been found to be a critical component in the "falling in love" stage of many individualists (Gao, 1991), thus the emphasis in individualistic cultures is on this kind of love regardless of the partners' cultural backgrounds or social standing (Kline, Horton, & Zhang, 2008). This is one of the reasons why individualists believe that getting married without love appears to be a disastrous decision. For example, our interviewee, Cailee (a college student), comments:

> In my opinion you cannot have love without attraction. That is my bottom line. Both terms can have very diverse meanings but with the same root. They connote a behavior and a feeling that motivate and drive people to connect with one another. They can be used for or against you and you need to understand why you're attracted to another person and fall head-over-heels in love with no regrets.

Cailee's view really represents the ideal in individualistic cultures, which is that romantic love is the central part of many love relationships, and that attraction chemistry is common during the initial stages of any romantic love relationship. In individualistic cultures, people typically want to "fall in love" (which sometimes involves intense dating procedures) and then either get married or move on to another dating partner. Romantic love, however, often poses major relational paradoxes. Although intimate partners desire to "lose" themselves in a romantic love-fused relationship, many of them also struggle with their desires for independence and personal freedom. Intercultural love experts Karen and Kenneth Dion (1996) concluded that the high divorce rate that characterizes "U.S. society is due in good part to the culture's exaggerated sense of individualism" (p. 286). They observe that in the United States, subscribers to "expressive individualism" face the following dilemmas in romantic relationships:

> First, one can "lose" one's self and the feeling of personal autonomy in a love relationship, feeling used

and exploited as a result. Second, satisfying the autonomous needs of two "separate" individuals in a love relationship obviously becomes a difficult balancing act. Third, the spirit of American individualism makes it difficult for either partner in a relationship to justify sacrificing or giving to the other more than one is receiving. Finally, and inevitably, Americans confront a fundamental conflict trying to reconcile personal freedom and individuality, on the one hand, with obligations and role requirements of marital partner and parent, on the other. (p. 286)

However, research indicates that many collectivists value companionate love (strong friendship and commitment) more than passionate love in romantic relationships (Gao, 1991). For example, some traditional collectivists (e.g., India, Iran, South Korea, and northern Nigeria, in which arranged marriages are still the norm) prefer to get married and then take their time to fall in love. Essentially, love is more pragmatic. In collectivistic cultures, ingroup harmony and cohesiveness are emphasized over individual needs and desires. From this particular value framework, the value of love as caregiving, doing things for one another, carrying out your relational obligations and role responsibilities, and tending to the relationship from a long-term perspective takes precedence over romantic ideals (Kline, Horton, & Zhang, 2008; Rosenblatt, 2009). Thus, for some collectivists, the meaning of being *in love* takes long-term commitment, reciprocal loyalty, and time to cultivate. They can also continue to learn to fall in love after their marriages. Alternatively, as they learn to grin and bear it, they may also have a change of heart and learn to accept the flaws and virtues of their lifetime partners (see Jeopardy Box 10.1).

Expert researchers on love, Kline, Horton, and Zhang (2008), also examined cultural differences in communicating love by comparing young adults from the United States and East Asian countries of China, Japan, and South Korea. The U.S. American and East Asian international students answered questions about their attitudes, beliefs, and behaviors related to love and friendship and also expectations concerning marriage. The results showed that East Asian respondents were more likely to believe that marriage is about *trust*, *caring*, and *respect* and that it takes *hard work*; U.S.

JEOPARDY BOX 10.1 TOP FIVE WEDDING SONGS IN THE UNITED STATES, 2009

Song	Artist
1. "From This Moment On"	Shania Twain/Bryan White
2. "At Last"	Etta James
3. "Power of Love"	Celine Dion
4. "I Cross My Heart"	George Strait
5. "Unchained Melody"	Righteous Brothers

Source: http://www.weddingzone.net/p-top50t.htm (retrieved April 22, 2011).

American respondents were more likely to believe that love in marriage is *essential* and *unconditional*.

East Asian students also tended to express love and affection in close friendships predominantly through "talking" activities such as having dinner together and drinking together, whereas U.S. American students tended to express love and affection in close friendships during activities (e.g., sports and exercise, going to movies or concerts, and shopping) along with having dinner and drinking together. In expressing love and affection in marriage, both groups had the same notions about important vehicles for expressing love: talking, having dinner together, doing things together, and physical intimacy. Both groups also subscribed to the importance of having similar beliefs, faithfulness, and commitment in marital relationships, more so than in close friendship relationships (Kline et al., 2008).

Autonomy–Connection Issues

In developing a relationship between individuals from two contrastive cultures, friends or romantic partners often face the choice of how to handle autonomy and connection issues without going crazy (see Blog Pics 10.1.a and 10.1.b). *Autonomy* is the need for personal privacy and regulated space in a relationship. *Connection* is the need for the merging of personal and psychological space. Independent-minded partners often view autonomy–connection struggles as a delicate high-wire act, constantly balancing the "me–we" dialectical forces (Baxter & Montgomery, 1996). In contrast, interdependent-minded partners often see autonomy and connection as a quadrangular juggling act, a "me–we–they–they" dance performance in the

(a)

(b)

Blog Pic 10.1 (a) Looking for love. (b) Intercultural-intimate relationship takes hard work.

intimate relationship and among their respective family/friendship connective networks. As a result, the intimate partners believe the romantic relationship will never be truly free from the grip of their family obligations, duties, and extended family reactions.

Further, in terms of relational commitment issues, individualists would tend to expect voluntary personal commitment from their partners in approaching their intimate relationships. However, for collectivists, structural commitment in an intimate relationship may be more important than (or at least on an equal footing with) personal commitment in a long-term romantic relationship. Here **personal commitment**

means an individual's desire or intent to continue the relationship based on his or her subjective emotional feelings and experiences; **structural commitment**, on the other hand, means the individual takes into consideration various external social and family reactions in deciding to either continue or terminate a relationship (M. Johnson, 1991). As in the opening scenario, Mona has opted for the importance of structural commitment over personal feelings, and, therefore, stays in her miserable arranged marriage for another two long years before seeking the "D" word.

As a result of the struggle with the autonomy and connection pulls, one other outcome among the individualistic cultural mindset is the phenomenon known as the "hook up" culture. Hooking up carries a wide range of meanings, but is linked to consensual sexual activities with no pretense of starting a committed relationship between young, mostly college-age students (Bogle, 2008). Bogle (2008) interviewed seventy-six U.S. college students over a span of five years and offered us some insights into how contemporary young men and women are grappling with the sexual realities in U.S. culture. Check out the following hook-up interview dialog (Bogle, 2008, p. 177) in which one female interviewee was complaining about her "hook up partner" to KB:

> Shana: He's not ready to commit. He wants to keep playing and I just can't sit around here anymore because it hurts too much.
> KB: Other girls?
> Shana: Yeah.
> KB: So he wants to be involved with you, but wants it to be a nonexclusive thing?
> Shana: [Right so]...then it comes to the point where he says: "We have to talk." And I'm like: "Oh great [sarcastic tone] Here we go again"...We are famous for having talks.
> [He says] "I want to make sure we are on the same page, that you realize that I am still not ready to commit to you. I see us in the future together but not right now."

Although many U.S. college students recognize hooking up as the pathway to a potential romantic relationship, a hook-up encounter does not guarantee any deep commitment beyond the in-the-moment interpersonal encounter. An intimate relationship is already a complicated affair between two attracted partners within the same cultural community; imagine the complexity of intercultural romantic attraction, especially in conjunction with communication decoding issues (Imahori & Cupach, 2005).

Communication Decoding Issues

Many interesting things can happen in an intercultural relationship development journey. For example, let us consider the following incident in Blog Post 10.1. Olivia and Jose are classmates in the basic intercultural communication class at the University of Hawaii. Olivia is an ethnic mix of Hawaiian and African American, and Jose is from Brazil .

To minimize initial interaction anxiety, two cultural strangers must be at least proficient in a shared language and the use of the everyday slang and idioms of a culture (Gudykunst, 2003, 2004). Moreover, it is critical for the native language speaker to develop cultural sensitivity for a relational partner who is not a native language speaker. That is, even if Jose had understood the idiomatic phrase "chill" (or the word *date*, as in "dating" and not a fruit on the tree), Olivia's dating request might still have hit a brick wall because of the masculine gender role expectations in Brazil. Thus, beyond a shared language and an open-minded attitude, in-depth knowledge of the other's cultural values, expectations, idioms, nonverbal moves, and dating rituals would have greatly helped Olivia to accomplish her "chill" goal.

Although individualists often use a low-context, direct verbal approach in initiating, maintaining, and ending a close relationship, collectivists often use a high-context, indirect approach in dealing with relationship formation and development issues. Take, for example, the South Korean blockbuster hit movie, *My Sassy Girl*. The main character, Kyeon-Woo, has deep emotional feelings for the Girl, a young woman he met accidently on a train and feels responsible for. Kyeon-Woo is never explicit about his deep emotional feelings for the Girl he continues to love for years—even after two separations. When they are finally reunited at the end, his emotional exchange with his relational partner is very subtle and nuanced. There is no public display of affection. There is only mutual silence and holding hands under the table, with warm tenderness. In the United States, we often scoff at such emotional understatement as shyness. In an individualistic culture, it is instead expected that relational partners would engage in active verbal self-disclosure with phrases such as "I love you" and "I miss you." *My Sassy Girl* was remade in the United States with a similar story line. In this version, the main character, Charlie, serves as the narrator to explain his entire background and situation. Charlie has no problem revealing his feelings to the girl, Jordan, and displaying affection for her. With a beautiful, passionate kiss at the end, Jordan reveals her true passion for him in an overt self-disclosure mode.

The contrasting elements are very reflective of the differences between the two cultures. The Korean

---

BLOG POST 10.1

After three weeks of small talk and group work, Olivia was thinking of asking José out. After the intercultural class, Olivia got up the courage to talk with José. She stopped him and said, "José, what are your plans this weekend? Do you wanna chill?" José was dazed and confused.

As a newly arrived Brazilian international student on campus, José had pretty decent English proficiency. But he did not understand the word *chill* as meaning either "to relax and get together informally" or "to relax at a place to watch futbol." He was quite confused by the meaning of the word chill in this context. Had he even understood it, this request—from José's collectivistic,

masculine viewpoint—might well have come too early in their initial acquaintance.

José was a bit embarrassed and hesitated to answer. Meanwhile, Olivia felt like a fool and made an excuse to leave. Both José and Olivia experienced emotional embarrassment in this interaction episode. José, looking at the expression of Olivia, realized that he somehow had offended or insulted her. Olivia, on the other hand, did not realize that Jose was having verbal decoding problems with the word chill. Nor did she realize the different gender role expectations concerning initiating a dating request from the Brazilian viewpoint. She just felt awkward and embarrassed. Both parties experienced emotional anxiety and information uncertainty.

version speaks more for itself rather than through the characters' dialog. The audience generally must reach conclusions about the actors' emotions on their own based on the actors' reactions, responses, and the nuanced chemistry between Kyeon-Woo and the Girl. In the U.S. version, the growing chemistry between Charlie and Jordan was obvious and clear. From the collectivistic cultural lens, if you love someone, you reveal it through your attentiveness and sincere caring actions. For collectivists, love is in the details of paying attention to the other person's needs, desires, and wishes and the fact that you are also ready to sacrifice yourself on your relational partner's behalf. If both individuals are from the HCC zone, they will be able to understand each other's implicit caring gestures. However, in relationships where relational partners come from different communication styles, they may carry diametrically opposed expectations and experience major communication decoding problems.

To address such problems, relational partners must make a strong commitment to communicate in a culture-sensitive manner and to decode both the content and the relational meanings of the communication exchange process. This means learning to truly understand her or his relational partner's beliefs, values, needs, and interaction styles, as well as how she or he interprets core identity and relationship issues.

INTERCULTURAL-INTIMATE RELATIONSHIP ATTRACTION: FACILITATING FACTORS

Attraction is an unspoken energy that drives people together. The force of attraction can be sudden or developed slowly across time. There are clear cultural-based influences that affect the initial attraction between two individuals: perceived physical attractiveness, perceived similarity, self-disclosure, and intercultural–interracial intimate relationship development. Along with several other items, each of these will be discussed in this section.

Perceived Physical Attractiveness

Physical attraction happens when one is attracted to a person's appearance, such as the body, eyes, hair, or clothes. Ryan (2004) found the force of attraction in Western cultures has to do with our facial features:

men should have prominent cheek bones, a big smile, and strong jaw line; women need a small nose and chin, with high eyebrows and narrow cheeks. In addition, usually the extroverts, from the Western cultural perspective, are more likely to be perceived as attractive and are more likely to develop multiple romantic relationships.

Recent research evidence indicates that physical attractiveness is critical to initial attraction, but so are cultural differences regarding what is attractive behavior or what are attractive character traits. For example, attractive persons are perceived to be high in potency in the United States (i.e., high energy and enthusiasm); however, Koreans perceive attractive persons to be high in integrity and concern for others (Wheeler & Kim, 1997). In the initial stage of relationship development, individuals are often concerned with creating a favorable impression in the presence of others so that others can either be attracted to them or at least find them likable. Thus, an individual may interact in a way that seems to exude attractive qualities (from his or her own perspective) to create a favorable impression; unfortunately, this person may still not be perceived as very attractive to an individual from another culture.

Impression formation and *interpersonal attraction* are two intertwined concepts. Physical attraction is closely associated with overall perceived attractiveness. Overall perceived attractiveness, in turn, is related to desirable personality attributes, such as appearing sensitive, kind, sociable, pleasant, likable, and interesting. Attractive people are also evaluated as more competent and intelligent (Ross & Ferris, 1981).

In comparing U.S. and Japanese perceptions of facial attractiveness, U.S. college students have consistently rated smiling faces (both American and Japanese faces) as more attractive, intelligent, and sociable than neutral faces. The Japanese students, on the other hand, have rated smiling faces as more sociable but not necessarily more attractive or intelligent. They actually perceive neutral faces as more intelligent than smiling faces. They also do not perceive smiling faces as more attractive than the neutral faces (Matsumoto & Kudoh, 1993).

In terms of perceived credibility, facial composure and body posture appear to influence our judgments of whether individuals appear to be credible (i.e., high social influence power) or not credible (i.e., low social influence power). In some Asian cultures (e.g., South Korea and Japan), for example, influential people tend to use restrained facial expressions and to practice postural rigidity. In U.S. culture, however, animated facial expressions and postural relaxation are associated with credibility and positive impression formation (Burgoon et al., 2010). Overall, it can be concluded that perceived attractiveness or credibility is in the eye of the beholder. The meaning of such concepts reflects social agreements that are created and sustained through cultural nonverbal practices (check out the bridegroom and the bride in Blog Pic 10.2).

Perceived Similarity

Perceived similarity refers to how much people think others are similar or dissimilar to themselves. It implies the perception of shared views in beliefs, values, attitudes, communication, interests, and/or hobbies. For example, Morry (2005) found that same-sex

Blog Pic 10.2 Celebrating a nontraditional wedding on the beach.

friends perceived themselves to be happier individuals the more they reported being similar to their friends. The similarity–attraction perspective (Byrne, 1971) has received intense attention in intergroup–interpersonal attraction research for the past three decades. The argument behind this perspective (with a distinct individualistic-based focus) claims that individuals are motivated to maintain or increase their positive self-evaluation by choosing to associate with others who reinforce dimensions relevant to the self (i.e., birds of a feather flock together).

The similarity–attraction hypothesis supports this assumption: a positive relationship exists between perceived similarity and interpersonal attraction (Berscheid & Reis, 1998). There are three possible explanations to account for this hypothesis: (1) we experience cognitive consistency if we hold the same attitude and outlook in our relationship; (2) cognitive consistency reinforces our ego and provides identity rewards and affirmation; and (3) with similar others, we tend to invest less time and energy in managing relational vulnerable feelings, which gives a boost to interpersonal attraction.

In the context of intergroup–interpersonal attraction, perceived similarity takes on a variety of aspects, such as perceived cultural–racial similarity. For low-prejudiced individuals, race is a nonissue, but perceived physical attractiveness is the decisive factor in intergroup attraction (Byrne, 1971). In contrast, for high-prejudiced individuals, racial dissimilarity is viewed as creating insurmountable barriers to intergroup attraction. Additionally, research studies indicated that the more the relational partners in initial interethnic encounters hold similar viewpoints concerning communication orientations (e.g., ways to support each other's self-concepts, ways to comfort each other), the more they are attracted to each other (Gudykunst, 2004; Lee & Gudykunst, 2001).

In addition, people may be attracted to dissimilar strangers if they have repeated chances to interact with them under favorable contact conditions and with a positive mindset. Proximity, together with perceived similarity, definitely influences initial intercultural attraction. Rachel, a college senior says, "During the first year of college, Jamal lived one floor down and I never met him. I never went to his co-ed floor. I only hung out with those around me. By chance, I met him in the library last semester and realized he lived one floor right below me! We became fast friends and I regret I never met him until close to graduation." We can communicate only with people we meet via face-to-face situations or in cyberspace. Proxemic nearness to others creates more interaction opportunities. With repeated interaction opportunities, individuals may uncover important attitudinal and communication similarities (e.g., relationship philosophy, family outlook, similar communication styles, and common interests) and thus increase their confidence in relating to each other (see also, Shackelford, Schmidt, & Buss, 2005).

Cross-Cultural Self-Disclosure Comparisons

Self-disclosure involves the intentional process of revealing exclusive information about ourselves to others that the other individuals do not know. The study of self-disclosure is related to social penetration theory (Altman & Taylor, 1973; Chen & Nakazawa, 2010). Generally, social penetration theory says that interpersonal information progresses from superficial, nonintimate self-disclosure to more deep-layered, intimate self-disclosure. This developmental process also involves the **breadth** (i.e., number of topics we are comfortable and willing to disclose to reveal our dynamic self) and **depth** (i.e., intimate layers that reveal our emotionally vulnerable self) of self-disclosure. Deep-layered self-disclosure, as the pinnacle of intimacy, is defined as an individual's willingness to reveal exclusive private information and especially vulnerable identity information to a significant other.

In any relationship, verbal revelation and concealment act as critical gatekeepers in moving a relationship to greater or lesser intimacy. Both the willingness to reveal something about yourself and the willingness to pay attention to the other person's feedback about you are necessary to build a trusting intercultural friendship or romantic relationship (Gibbs, Ellison, & Lai, 2011; Jiang, Bazarova, & Hancock, 2011; Joseph & Afifi, 2010). Verbal self-disclosure often follows a *trust-risk dilemma*. To trust someone, you must be willing to take some risks to share some unique information about yourself. Through taking the risk, you may also

have established an initial trusting cycle in the interpersonal relationship. However, you may also have to worry about your friend betraying the exclusive information you have just shared. Before continuing with this section, fill out the my.blog 10.1 self-disclosure survey. The survey is designed to help you understand your degree of readiness for self-disclosure to strangers versus best friends.

The term **public self** refers to those facets of the person that are readily available and are easily shared with others; the term **private self**, on the other hand, refers to those facets of the person that are potentially communicable but are not usually shared with generalized others (Barnlund, 1975). We can disclose information concerning the different parts of the public self (e.g., tastes and interests, work and studies, attitudes and opinions, money) and the private self (e.g., family secret issues, personality traits, body image or self-image issues). Barnlund (1989) found that the Japanese tend to have a relatively small layer of public self and a relatively large layer of private self. In contrast, his research revealed that U.S. Americans have a larger layer of public self and a smaller layer of private self. Sharing information concerning either the public or the private self is conducted through relational openness. The Japanese have been found to be more guarded with regard to disclosing their inner attitudes and private feelings in initial relationship development stages and they self-disclose with a slower, polychronic time rhythm. In comparison, U.S. Americans are more responsive in disclosing and reciprocating information of a personal, private nature and tend to move faster from the acquaintance relationship to the intimate friendship level, with monochronic time rhythms.

In examining the self-disclosure patterns of East Asian international students from four different countries (China, Japan, South Korea, and Taiwan), Y. W. Chen (2006) found that East Asian students self-disclosed slightly more in intracultural friendships than intercultural friendships. In addition, they perceived the disclosure of attitudes and opinions, tastes and interests, studies or work, and personality as "superficial topics," whereas they considered the sharing of information on money and financial matters and body and appearance "intimate topics." However, there was

my.blog 10.1 ASSESSING YOUR READINESS TO SELF-DISCLOSE TO STRANGERS VERSUS BEST FRIENDS

Instructions: Recall how you generally feel and communicate in various situations. Let your first inclination be your guide and circle the number in the scale that best reflects your overall impression of yourself. The following scale is used for each item:

4 = SA! = Strongly agree!
3 = MA = Moderately agree
2 = MD = Moderately disagree
1 = SD! = Strongly disagree!

Generally speaking, I readily disclose to *strangers* about the following topics:	SA	MA	MD	SD
1. My interests and hobbies.	4	3	2	1
2. My goals and dreams.	4	3	2	1
3. My work or study situations.	4	3	2	1
4. How much money I make.	4	3	2	1
5. My political opinions.	4	3	2	1
6. My racial beliefs and viewpoints.	4	3	2	1
7. My dream dates.	4	3	2	1
8. Conflicts with family members.	4	3	2	1
9. My feelings about my face.	4	3	2	1
10. My feelings about my body.	4	3	2	1
11. My positive qualities that I really like.	4	3	2	1
12. My own negative personality traits.	4	3	2	1

Generally speaking, I readily disclose to *my best friends* about the following topics:	SA	MA	MD	SD
1. My interests and hobbies.	4	3	2	1
2. My goals and dreams.	4	3	2	1
3. My work or study situations.	4	3	2	1
4. How much money I make.	4	3	2	1
5. My political opinions.	4	3	2	1
6. My racial beliefs and viewpoints.	4	3	2	1
7. My dream dates.	4	3	2	1
8. Conflicts with family member.	4	3	2	1
9. My feelings about my face.	4	3	2	1
10. My feelings about my body.	4	3	2	1
11. My positive qualities that I really like.	4	3	2	1
12. My own negative personality traits.	4	3	2	1

Continued

my.blog 10.1 CONTINUED

Scoring: Add up the scores on all the "strangers" disclosure items and you will find your strangers disclosure score. Strangers disclosure score: _____. Add up the scores on all the "best friends" items and you will find your best friends disclosure score. Best friends disclosure score: _____.

Interpretation: Scores on each self-disclosure dimension can range from 12 to 48; the higher the score, the more you are ready to self-disclose to strangers and/or best friends on a variety of topics. If the scores are similar on both item sets, you are equivalent in your readiness to self-disclose to both strangers and best friends.

Reflection probes: Check out your two scores with a classmate. Interview each other and ask each other the following questions: Where did you learn your self-disclosure habits? Do you come from a low self-disclosive family or a high self-disclosive family? How do you feel about people who self-disclose too much? How do you feel about people who self-disclose too little?

Source: Scale adapted from Barnlund (1989).

---

no clear distinction concerning the amount of self-disclosure and the revealing of positive–negative content of self-disclosure in those two friendship types: they generally self-disclosed the same type and amount of information to acquaintances as to intimate friends.

In a follow-up study, Chen and Nakazawa (2010) investigated the self-disclosure patterns of U.S. American students in intercultural and interracial friendship types. In the study, students reported on either their intercultural friendships (between a U.S. citizen and a non-U.S. citizen) or their interracial friendships. The research findings indicate that the level of relational intimacy plays a strong role in self-disclosure patterns: as relational intimacy level increases, friends have greater intent to disclose, they disclose in greater amount and depth, and they also engage in more honest/accurate self-disclosure. These findings were the same for both intercultural and interracial friendship situations; respondents report equivalent levels of reciprocal self-disclosure.

Furthermore, in comparing self-disclosure patterns in Japanese and U.S. American students, Kito (2005) discovered that both groups were drawn to their newfound friends because of perceived similarity. Japanese respondents cite togetherness, trust, and warmth as their top friendship priorities, whereas the U.S. Americans cite understanding, respect, and sincerity as top friendship indicators. It seems that whereas Asian collectivists emphasize an interpersonal "relationship atmosphere" of harmony and warmth, American

individualists emphasize the intrinsic friendship qualities of "being oneself" and "self-transparency" or honesty.

Overall, individualists have been found to engage in more active self-disclosure than collectivists across topics and different "targets," or receivers (e.g., parents vs. friends). When comparing Japanese and U.S. groups, both agreed on their disclosure *target* preferences in the following order: same-sex friend, opposite-sex friend, mother, father, stranger, and distrusted acquaintance (Barnlund, 1989). U.S. college students consistently score themselves higher in their overall amount of self-disclosure than Japanese and Chinese college students. Female college students also report a significantly higher amount of self-disclosure than male college students, regardless of culture (Ting-Toomey, 1991).

Thus, self-disclosure is one of the key factors in developing a personal relationship in any culture or ethnic group. One other way to understand self-disclosure in more depth is to check out the Johari Window. The label "Johari" takes its name from Joseph Luft and Harry Ingham—the first names of the window's creators. The window can be conceived as having four panels: *open, hidden, blind,* and *unknown* (see Figure 10.1).

On a broad level, the *open panel* is defined as information known to self and also information known to generalized others or a specific person. The *hidden panel* is defined as information known to self but unknown to others. The *blind panel* is defined as information not known to self but known to others. Last,

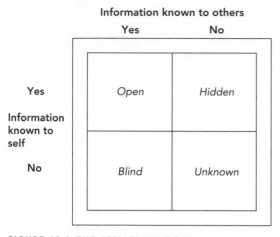

Information known to others

	Yes	No
Yes **Information known to self** **No**	Open	Hidden
	Blind	Unknown

FIGURE 10.1 THE JOHARI WINDOW

the *unknown panel* is defined as information not known to self or to others. One example of this is based on a true story. Two interethnic college friends shared a close friendship, including much sharing about their dating experiences. After graduation, they took a vacation together. While having dinner on the second day of their vacation, the conversation turned deep. One friend, processing all the information and the conversation, came out (admitted she was gay) to the other friend. This surprised them both. The gay friend had no idea until then that she was, in fact, gay. Because of the deep self-disclosure conversation and perceived acceptance, the one friend actually helped the other friend to sort out some of her core identity issues in a very spontaneous yet authentic manner.

Individuals who have big open panels and small hidden panels are more willing to disclose and share information about themselves compared with individuals with small open panels and big hidden panels. The blind panel can shrink in size by paying attention to feedback and comments from others. The blind area means we are unaware (or in denial) that such attitudes (e.g., sexist, racist, and homophobic attitudes) or behaviors (e.g., gay bashing) exist in us, but our friends actually observe those attitudes or behaviors. Through obtaining feedback from others, information that we are previously unaware of becomes known to us. The mysterious panel, the unknown area, at first glance seems strange. However, we can deduce that the unknown panel exists in all of us because there is always something surprising

or new to discover about ourselves and others—through new learning, traveling, life experiences, or meditations about the unconscious self.

Self-disclosure and intimacy are interdependent: appropriate self-disclosure can increase intimacy, and increased intimacy prompts more self-disclosure. Self-disclosure develops interpersonal trust, emotional support, and mutual identity validation. However, self-disclosure can also open up the vulnerable self to hurt, disappointment, and information betrayal.

Online Disclosure of Affection

Although verbal and nonverbal self-disclosure during face-to-face communication has been discussed, social network sites are providing an alternative way to disclose feelings or attraction to another. The most popular social networking site is Facebook, with 500 million active users worldwide. According to Facebook (2011), 50 percent of active users log on in any given day and spend over 700 billion minutes per month logged on. A typical "Facebooker" has 130 friends. With so much time spent on Facebook, how people develop and maintain friendships and how they communicate together change the typical rules of interpersonal relationship engagement. According to Choi, Kim, Sung, and Song (2011), whereas U.S. college students held larger but looser online social networks, Korean college students maintained denser but smaller online social networks. Whereas U.S. students tend to emphasize "bridging" interaction strategies to accumulate large and more extended social networks, Korean students tend to stress "bonding" interaction strategies to solidify deeper social connections on Facebook. By the way, what do you think are the top five ways that U.S. college students express affection via Facebook? Take a guess and jot down your hit-or-miss answers in Hit-or-Miss 10.1.

Third-Party Matchmakers: Online and Mobile Dating

Online dating and matchmaking has evolved, transformed into a multibillion dollar concept and practice. Once marked with negative connotations, online dating services provide the easiest way to meet others without forming the need to move toward forming serious ties or commitment (Romm-Livermore, Somers,

How do you express affection for your close friends on Facebook? Write down the first five things that come to mind and then see how closely your expressions of affection match respondents' in a recent study.

To express affection for my close friends through Face-book, I . . .

1. _____

2. _____

3. _____

4. _____

5. _____

Answers: 1. Send them a wink ;). 2. Post pictures with one another. 3. Add love comment on their wall. 4. Comment on their wall. 5. Comment on their pictures.

Source: Mansson and Myers (2011, p. 162).

JEOPARDY BOX 10.2 TOP FIVE INTERNET DATING SITES

Site	Number of subscribers
1. Match.com	29 million
2. Chemistry.com	14 million
3. Perfectmatch.com	11 million
4. Eharmony.com	9 million
5. Spark.com	1 million

Source: http://www.consumer-rankings.com/dating/ retrieved July 17, 2011

Setzekorn, & King, 2009). James John, a graduate student, recently joined and reflected, "A year ago, as a college senior, I would have laughed at the mere idea of it. I joined Match.com just to see what it was about and I was blown away. It's like a secret society. I ran across so many people I know that would never have told me they were on it, let alone I would have never guessed. There are all kinds of people and very attractive (which I never expected!). I'm only five days in. I told my buddies about it and they all laughed. They were blown away. I jumped in, now everyone seems to be jumping in. A week later I got text messages from two buddies who have also signed up!"

Online dating has become a widespread, explosive global phenomenon. Mobile dating or "mobile romance" appears to be equally popular. Using the same online dating services, subscribers can register, text their location, and find profiles of people in the same zip code range. Technology aids in the heavy reliance on cell phone/text culture, which appeals mainly to younger users (Coleman & Bahnan, 2009). More than half a billion users around the world subscribe to online services (Kale & Spence, 2009). Do you know the top five online dating sites for 2011? Check out Jeopardy Box. 10.2.

Aside from the traditional dating sites, there are also specialized dating and social sites among like-minded people in terms of religion (Christian and Jewish), vegans, "Goths," and spiritual seekers.

The curiosity of online versus offline courtship development is intriguing for some researchers. How does online dating work? According to Whitty (2009), there are five phases of courtship. In phase one, the *attention phase*, an individual selects an attractive photograph to post, chooses a screen name to represent himself or herself, and crafts a skillful profile. If these three methods connect with another individual and attract attention, phase two occurs. In this second phase, the *recognition phase*, virtual flirting occurs, which is sending a wink, a kiss, or some icon to represent an interest to the other party. Phase three is the *interaction phase*, the shortest phase, which may take place via e-mail, instant messaging, or texting. With the absence of traditional cues of flirting, many emoticons are used (see Chapter 7) to express interest. These first three phases reflect the strategic self-presentation used by individuals to communicate who they are in cyberspace. In the virtual world, individuals can be ambiguous and creative and can play without the fear of face-to-face outright rejection. It is interesting to note that with the global reach and the safety of the Internet, online dating has moved to countries with historic patterns of arranged dating. The fourth phase, the *face-to-face meeting phase*, refers to the "screening out process" in which partners check each other out for physical chemistry or sexual arousal attraction. They are also checking to see whether the actual person matches the online profile. The meeting is usually scheduled in a safe public space and with a limited time restriction. Last, the fifth phase, the *resolution phase*, refers to the decision-making phase to decide whether to see each other offline again and/or to also continue using the online dating site to check out other potential dating partners. Conflict arises when one partner takes herself off the site and the other partner is discovered still using the dating site actively.

Take for example Ignighter.com, a U.S. dating Web site created by three founders in their mid-twenties. The site focuses on group dates in which "one member, serving as a point person, could arrange a date—a movie, say, or a picnic in Central Park—with a group of other people and thereby take the awkward edge off typical dates" (Seligson, 2011, p. BU1). Although the dating site was not very successful in the United States, it attracted hundreds of users per day in India—making it India's fastest growing dating Web site. The average age of users is 23.5, and the service connects individuals into groups who chat through messaging; the service also arranges group dates—to movie viewings, restaurant meals, and going to clubs together (Seligson, 2011). This lucrative business of searching for love online is booming in China as well. In a country with relationship worries and the pressure to be married by the age of thirty, millions of Chinese are using online dating services as the answer. C. C. Jiang (2011) reports that online dating sites in China attracted approximately 3 million subscribers in 2010 and is predicted to increase even more in the upcoming five years for busy Chinese professionals (Seth & Patnayakuni, 2009).

Intercultural–Interracial Romantic Relationship Development

Research on intercultural romantic relationships examines both its challenges and its benefits (Leeds-Hurwitz, 2009). In discussing interracial intimate relationship development, Foeman and Nance (1999) concluded that interracial couples move through the following stages of "racial" awareness and awakening in their intimate relationship process: racial awareness, coping, identity emergence, and relationship maintenance. The first stage, *racial awareness*, refers to the gradual awakening stage when the partners in the

interracial relationship become conscious of each other's views and societal views on intimate racial relationship matters. The second stage, *coping*, refers to the struggles the couple must face in gaining approval from their families and friends and the strategies they come up with in dealing with such external pressures. In the third stage, *identity emergence*, both partners gain a new sense of security and bravely announce their intimate relationship to their families and ingroups. The fourth stage, *relationship maintenance*, refers to the continuous hard work the couple must face in dealing with new challenges such as having children, moving to new neighborhoods, and meeting new social circles.

Despite the many pressure points in an intercultural–interracial relationship, many intimate couples often mention the following relationship rewards in their intercultural/interracial relationships (Karis & Killian, 2009; Romano, 2003; Rutsogi, 2009; Ting-Toomey, 2009; Visson, 2009): (a) experiencing personal enrichment and growth resulting from the day-to-day opportunity to continuously clarify their own beliefs, values, and prejudices; (b) developing multiple cultural frames of reference resulting from the opportunity of integrating multiple value systems such as "doing" *and* "being," "controlling" *and* "yielding"; (c) experiencing greater diversity and emotional vitality in their lifestyles because of participating in different customs, ceremonies, languages, celebrations, foods, and cultural network circles; (d) developing a stronger and deeper relationship with their partner because they have weathered intercultural prejudice and racist opposition and arrived at a forgiving, healing place; and (e) raising open-minded, resourceful children who see the world from a multicultural lens and have the ability to be "at home" wherever they find themselves.

These stages of challenge and benefit provide an overall picture of intercultural romantic relationships. With the increase in cultural and ethnic diversification in the United States, the likelihood of being attracted to members of other cultures and races will also increase (Karis, 2009; Llerena-Quinn & Bacigalupe, 2009; Ting-Toomey, 2009). Age, generation, ethnic identity, and racial–intergroup attitude appear to be four important predictors of interethnic dating and marriage. For example, Firmin and Firebaugh (2008) uncovered that one's age and generation appear to be two key predictors for intimate relationship formation: younger people and succeeding generations are more open to interracial dating than older and preceding ones. The later the generation in the United States, the more likely the individuals in that generation tend to date outgroup members. Additionally, the less prejudice they perceive in intergroup relations, the more likely they are to be open to date members from that group. For example, third-generation Asian Americans are five times more likely to marry outside their ethnic group than first-generation Asian Americans (Kitano, Fujino, & Sato, 1998).

Chung and Ting-Toomey (1999), in examining interethnic dating attraction in Asian Americans, found that the strength of individuals' ethnic identities was related to intergroup attraction and dating. Individuals with assimilated, bicultural, or marginal identities have a greater tendency to date outside of their own groups than those who view their ethnic identities and traditions as very important aspects of their self-concept. There were also times during which individuals were attracted to culturally dissimilar others because they perceived their partners as typical, or atypical, of their own culture. This means that people do activate their stereotyping process in initial intercultural attraction stages—be they positive or negative stereotypes. In addition, there may also be a **"Romeo and Juliet" effect** at work in an intercultural-intimate relationship: the more the respective families are against this intimate relationship, the more the couple wants to rebel against their parents and "do their own thing" and, therefore, they find each other even more attractive (Ting-Toomey & Chung, 2005).

Martin, Bradford, Drzewiecka, and Chitgopekar (2003) surveyed European American young adults regarding their openness to and experience with interracial dating. The results indicate that respondents who were raised in more diverse neighborhoods and who had diverse acquaintances were significantly more likely to date outside their race. Reasons given for encouraging interracial dating included compatibility, physical and sexual attraction, and curiosity. Reasons offered for discouraging interracial dating included lack of desire, lack of proximity, and personal, familial, or societal pressure. Levin, Taylor, and Caudle (2007),

in a longitudinal study examining interracial dating patterns from over two thousand college students (from diverse racial–ethnic backgrounds), uncovered that students who exhibited lower levels of ingroup favoritism bias, intergroup anxiety, and ingroup identification were more likely to date members of other racial and ethnic groups during college. In addition, students who dated outside their group more during college showed less ingroup favoritism bias and intergroup anxiety at the end of their college experience (see also, Shelton, Richeson, & Bergsiekar, 2009).

In contrast to this general finding, Asian American students who dated outside their group more during college also felt more pressure *not* to socialize with or date members of other groups at the end of their college experience. Latinos/as whose families had been in the United States for more generations were also more likely to date intercultural–interracial partners. Latinos/as also reported experiencing less bias directed against them as intergroup dating partners than other minority groups because of both historical factors and physical characteristics. Interestingly, intergroup dating in college was less prevalent among those who had a greater proportion of precollege ingroup friendships. The influence of such close friendships and particular ingroup attitudes (e.g., intergroup anxiety and prejudice) may outweigh opportunities to branch outward and seek interracial–intergroup dating opportunities.

In June 2010, the Pew Institute reported a study on interracial marriages in the United States. Among their findings for 2008 are the following:

- 14.6 percent (one in seven) of new marriages in the United States were between spouses of different ethnicities.
- 22 percent of marriages in the West were interracial or interethnic, compared with 13 percent in both the South and the Northeast and 11 percent in the Midwest.
- 22 percent of all black male newlyweds married outside their race, compared with just 9 percent of black female newlyweds.
- 40 percent of Asian female newlyweds married outside, compared with 20 percent of Asian males.
- Intermarriage rates doubled between 1980 (6.7%) and 2008 (14.6%).

- More than one-third of adults (35%) say they have a family member who is married to someone of a different race.

For the most recent percentage breakdown of interracial and interethnic marriages in the United States, see Table 10.2. The label "whites" in Table 10.2 refers to the dominant white group in comparison to members of co-culture or minority group status (Pew Research Center, April 2011).

INTERCULTURAL-INTIMATE CONFLICT: OBSTACLES AND STUMBLING BLOCKS

Intercultural and interracial dating or marriage is fertile ground for culture clash and obstacles (Note: *intercultural* will be used in conjunction with *interracial* for

TABLE 10.2 RACIAL AND ETHNIC INTERMARRIAGE IN THE UNITED STATES

Group	Total Number	Bride	Groom
Whites Marrying Hispanics	118,000	White 53%	White 47%
Whites Marrying Asians	43,100	White 21%	White 74%
Whites Marrying Blacks	32,300	White 75%	White 25%
Whites Marrying Native Americans	14,600	White 48%	White 52%
Hispanics Marrying Blacks	12,600	Hispanic 73%	Hispanic 27%
Hispanics Marrying Asians	6,700	Hispanic 42%	Hispanic 58%
Blacks Marrying Asians	3,700	Black 20%	Black 80%

Source: Pew Research Center (cited in *National Geographic*, April 2011, p. 20). Population: *Marrying Out* (April 2011). *National Geographic*, p. 20.

ease). There are many sources of intercultural-intimate conflict. **Intercultural-intimate conflict** is defined as any antagonistic friction or disagreement between two romantic partners caused, in part, by cultural or ethnic group membership differences. Some of the prominent conflict sources are cultural–ethnic value clashes (see the first section), prejudice and racism issues, and raising bicultural and biracial children (Karis & Killian, 2009; Visson, 2009). This section examines prejudice and racism reactions in the everyday environment of the romantic couple. It also explores the different coping strategies that couples use to counter racist attitudes and includes a discussion of identity issues in raising a bicultural child.

The Encounter: Prejudice and Racism

When it comes to encountering prejudice and racism, the experiences of interracial or intercultural couples may be different. Some of these couples may appear to outsiders to be an ingroup or intracultural relationship because of their physical similarities (e.g., a couple made up of a Mexican American and a Guatemalan may have similar skin color and other physical features, yet they derive from different cultures). These couples can choose to reveal their differences to outsiders. But, for interracial and some other intercultural couples, the visible differences are inescapable to all (e.g., an Asian American married to an African American or a European American dating a Latina). These couples must find different ways to cope with various family and social group reactions as well as with each other's reactions toward the role their ethnic group plays in their relationship.

Although the emotional reactions from outgroup members range from complete acceptance to utter ostracism, the couple's reactions in considering ethnicity as a factor in their relationship can also range from deep understanding to total dismissal.Conflict often arises when intercultural couples have to deal with the dilemma of whether to talk about matters of race or racism in their surrounding environment and within their own relationship context.

Prejudice is about biased, inflexible prejudgments and antagonistic feelings about outgroup members. However, racism is about a personal/institutional belief in the cultural superiority of one race and the perceived inferiority of other races (Jones, 1997).

Racism also refers to the practice of power dominance of a "superior" racial group over other "inferior" races. Couples often encounter initial conflict when marriage plans are discussed with their respective parents. Reactions can range from responses of support, acceptance, rejection, or fear to outright hostility. For example, let's look at Gina's family's response from the following interview excerpt (Gina is a European American woman planning to marry an African American man):

> Well, when I told my parents, they both looked kind of shocked, and then my father sort of blew up. He was yelling and screaming and told me that I had just thrown my life away and was I happy about that. But the whole time, I didn't hear my mother say anything against us. Later, after my father went to bed, she came up to me and told me that while she couldn't go against my father's wishes, she just wanted to make sure that I was happy. (McNamara, Tempenis, & Walton, 1999, p. 76)

Or consider the family response to James (an African American), when he announced his plans to marry a Euro-American woman:

> My father was absolutely against my marrying a white woman. He said I was a traitor to my race and that I was not giving black women a chance at a wonderful life. He would not talk to Donna, would not see her under any circumstances, and we did not talk to each other for over five years. (McNamara et al., 1999, p. 84)

For many ethnically homogeneous families, fear is the basic reason for opposition to an intercultural marriage. Their reasons can include societal or community disapproval, fear for the general physical and emotional well-being of the couple, fear of ostracism, and self-esteem issues concerning their biracial grandchildren (Frankenberg, 1993). As one European American woman commented,

> I am sitting in a small restaurant with my daughter, my husband, my grandson, and my son-in-law. I look at my two-year-old grandson. I have a warm feeling and think to myself, "This is my first grandchild." Then my pleasure dissolves into anxiety as I realize that everyone in the restaurant is looking at us. My grandson is brown. My son-in-law is black. And my daughter is no longer mine. (Crohn, 1995, p. 90)

In terms of societal reactions, one of the most common problems experienced by intercultural couples is the blatant, open stares from strangers. In addition to the stares, prejudicial treatment by some restaurant servers and real estate agents and racism within their own workplace may deeply disturb the couple's relationship. For example, read Russell's (an African American husband) comments:

> We go into a restaurant, together, with our children. We will order the meal and when we are done, the waitress hands us separate checks. Like she is saying "There is no way you two could be together." And here we are sitting with our children, who are obviously fair-skinned: whom does she think they belong to? (McNamara et al., 1999, p. 96)

Finally, simply because the partners are in an intimate relationship, there is no guarantee that they are free of racism or matters of race in their own evolving relationship. In times of anger and conflict, couples may have expressed racial epithets or racial attitudes to vent their frustrated feelings, and these expressions can seriously hurt each other. Although some of the words may have been exchanged in a joking/teasing or sarcastic way during an intimate conflict, those words or phrases can be taken as hurtful, racist comments.

Sometimes a nonminority partner's indifference to or ignorance of a racial issue may actually perpetuate a racist worldview. Gloria (an African American woman married to a European American man) said in an interview,

> I told him someone yelled, "nigger." I was on the corner down there; I was with the baby, just driving by. And his first reaction is, "Well, what did you do to provoke that?"...And I thought, "That's the difference between being black and white. Why would I have to do anything to provoke it?" (Rosenblatt, Karis, & Powell, 1995, p. 240)

This nonminority partner's insulated stance toward racism issues reflects his lifelong privilege of being a white male in a predominantly white society (see McIntosh, 1995). The concept of white privilege refers to the invisible entitlement that confers dominance or power resources for whites. Thus, white males can walk down the street at night without the need for awareness of potential racist remarks directed at them without cause or drive their cars routinely without the need to be particularly concerned with racial profiling issues by the police on the highways.

Fortunately, not all European Americans have such a chilling, indifferent reaction to racism issues faced by their intimate partners. As Adam (a European American male married to an African American female) commented,

> It takes being open to your own racism. It's all well and good to be sensitive to others in how they react to you, but you ought to be a little bit sensitive when you can and recognize your own mistakes, try to learn why what you've just said or done offended your partner…for example, there's an experience where Wanda would say, "Yeah, I understand that," and I say, "I don't understand it. What was happening? Help me out here." (Rosenblatt et al., 1995, p. 243)

When two intimate partners bring to their relationship strong identities as members of two different minority groups, they may be hypersensitive to identity conflict issues. The following heated debate between Alan (with a strong sense of African American identity) and Sara (with a strong sense of Jewish identity) illustrates this point:

ALAN: How can you know what it means to be discriminated against? You grew up in a comfortable, safe neighborhood. You got to choose whether or not you revealed to others that you were Jewish. My ancestors were brought here as slaves.

SARA: I can't believe you're saying this stuff. You know that I lost great-aunts and great-uncles in the Holocaust. You don't have any monopoly on suffering. What right does the past give you to say how we lead our lives? (Crohn, 1995, p. 171)

Alan and Sara's identity conflict issues—cultural, racial, and religious identities—obviously tapped into very intense, core emotions in their own identity construction. They will need time to really get to know the identity of each other and to find meaningful ways to connect to each other's cultures as well as their own.

Countering Racism and Prejudice: Coping Strategies

In dealing with prejudice and racism outside their relationship, some couples may talk about racism issues

as a lifetime project, whereas others dismiss them as inconsequential. Some reinforce the idea that to deal with prejudice issues, they must learn to be honest about prejudices that they carry within themselves. Other couples try to keep matters of race a small part of their relationship and focus their attention more on love, grocery shopping, raising children, doing the laundry, washing the dishes, planning vacations, and handling all the details of a shared life (Rosenblatt et al., 1995). In addition to race issues, emotional issues (e.g., work stress, money, sex, housework, and a new baby) are the most common topics of marital squabbles (Gottman & Silver, 1999). These are the frequent "emotional tasks" that couples have to deal with in their everyday lives and that often reveal their very different cultural and personal perspectives on how to approach such issues.

Most interracial couples, however, have developed specific coping strategies to deal with recurring prejudice and race situations. These coping strategies include *ignoring/dismissing* (especially for minor offenses, such as staring or nasty comments), *normalizing* (thinking of themselves and appealing to others to treat them as "normal" couples with marital ups and downs), and *withdrawing* (avoiding places and groups of people who are hostile to interracial couples). In addition, they use *educating* (outreach efforts to help others to accept interracial couples), *confrontation* (addressing directly the people who insult or embarrass them), *prayer* (relying on faith to solve problems), and *humor* (adding levity in distressing situations) to ease or ward off the pains of racism (McNamara et al., 1999). Partners usually use ignoring/dismissal coping strategies to deal with minor threats but use more direct strategies—such as educating and confronting—when countering major racist comments or slurs.

Because the discussion of any racial or religious identity issue is so complex and emotionally charged, most couples actually avoid the topic altogether in their own relating process. However, refraining from dealing with identity issues (especially from the beholder's viewpoint) is like "buying peace for your relationship on a credit card. You may enjoy the temporary freedom from anxiety you 'purchased' by avoiding the difficult topics, but when the bill finally comes due, the 'interest' that's accumulated in the form of resentment and regret may be devastating" (Crohn, 1995, pp. 183–184). Partners in an intercultural-intimate relationship often wonder whether their conflicts are a result of genuine differences of opinion, personality clashes, cultural value differences, or the prejudiced attitude of one of the partners. To achieve a genuine understanding of these intertwined issues, couples must learn to listen, to probe for accuracy, and to listen some more. As a final example, let's listen to the following comments by an African American male who is married to a white female:

> If I had to pick the perfect wife that I could have, she is very close to it.... She knows me better than anyone else... [and] she helps me a lot too. I like to talk to her and trust her and the fact that we both trust each other was there from the start. I know that she is really sensitive to issues of race and that is because we have experienced so much together. But I also know how difficult that has been for her. So I always try to keep her feelings in the front of my mind. I can't do anything about my race, but I can do something about how it affects her, at least sometimes I can. She does the same for me, which means that we are always thinking of each other. That's one of the reasons why I think we have lasted for so long—we are a lot stronger because we are really sensitive to the problem. (McNamara et al., 1999, p. 150)

A fundamental acceptance of the cultural–racial and religious aspects of a partner's identity and a mutual willingness to explore cultural codes, as well as a mutual openness in discussing racism issues, can facilitate greater relational satisfaction. Whether we are in an intimate intracultural or an intercultural relationship, we will do well to regard each interpersonal relationship as if it is an intercultural one.

Relational Transgressions and Terminations

Individuals involved in intimate romantic relationships of any kind may experience unfortunate relational transgressions (e.g., affairs, flirting with others). Zhang, Ting-Toomey, Dorjee, and Lee (2012) explored how U.S. American college students and Chinese college students might differ when they respond to their dating partners'

Internet relational transgressions. Overall, they found that U.S. respondents tend to prefer leaving the relationship ("exit" response) and/or to communicate anger ("anger voice response") more so than Chinese respondents in reacting to an episode of online emotional infidelity. Comparatively, Chinese respondents tend to prefer loyalty, passive neglect, and third-party help responses. It seems that for the Chinese respondents, loyalty is a passive-active strategy: a patient, self-disciplined reaction helps to tone down upfront confrontation and it would not aggravate the conflict situation further. Furthermore, whereas seeking help from family and close friends might seem to be passive in the U.S. American mindset, it is actually an active strategy for Chinese participants because it shows that the individual is caring and committed to the intimate relationship and that he/she is actually doing something to salvage the relationship by seeking third-party advice. Both culture groups, however, also preferred the use of a high degree of integrative, "win–win" problem-solving as a response to their partner's online infidelity.

Furthermore, the researchers (Zhang et al., 2012) also uncovered that participants with different levels of self-construal differed when they responded to their dating partners' relational transgressions. High independent self-construal participants tend to prefer exit and anger voice responses, whereas high interdependent self-construal participants prefer the use of integrative voice and third-party help-seeking responses. Ting-Toomey, Oetzel, and Yee-Jung (2001) also found that biconstrual individuals (those who are high on both independent and interdependent traits) tend to have the most diverse conflict repertoires to deal with a conflict situation in comparison to independent, interdependent, and ambivalent (low on both independent and interdependent traits) personality types. However, the degree of intimacy between the conflict partners, the nature of the conflict, and the conflict context greatly influence individuals' expectancies concerning appropriate and effective conflict behaviors and outcomes in different intercultural/interracial conflict situations.

Moving beyond interracial/interethnic communication styles and response to transgressions, Bratter and

King (2008) used data from the 2002 National Survey of Family Growth to examine divorce rates for interracial couples in comparison to same-racial couples. The study revealed that overall, interracial couples have higher rates of divorce, particularly for those marrying during the late 1980s. Compared with same-race white/white couples, they found that black male/white female marriages and Asian male/white female marriages were more prone to divorce. Interestingly, those involving white male/non-white female marriages and Hispanic/non-Hispanic marriages tended toward lower risks of divorce.

Researchers continue to focus on understanding these more fragile interracial marriages. Although they cannot conclude that race is the cause per se of divorce, it does seem to be associated with higher risk of divorce or separation (Zhang & Van Hook, 2009). One notable finding is that there is a consistent elevated divorce rate for white females in interracial marriages. This distinctive couple type may experience added stress caused by negative reactions from strangers and diminished support from family and friends. In addition, it may be that white mothers may be perceived as "unqualified to raise and nurture non-white offspring because of their lack of experience in navigating American culture as a minority" (Bratter & King, 2008, p. 170). Yancey (2007) notes that white females reported encountering more racial incidents with their black husbands (e.g., inferior restaurant service, racial profiling, and racism against their children) and more hostilities from families and friends compared with other interracial pairings. Such unwelcoming reactions and the distancing environment from both racial ingroups may add additional strain and social isolation to this type of interracial marriage.

Finally, not all is perfect in the online community. Eighty-one percent of the top divorce U.S. attorneys say that during the past five years they have seen an increase in the number of U.S. divorce cases using Facebook evidence (American Academy of Matrimonial Lawyers, 2010). Facebook is now viewed as the unrivaled leader for online divorce evidence with 66 percent of attorneys surveyed citing it as the primary source.

RAISING SECURE BICULTURAL CHILDREN

The common refrain from many intercultural marital couples is, "We were doing fine until the kids came along." Most intercultural parents easily slip back into their own childhood memories and use their own family models to discipline, to guide, and to raise their children. In the context of bicultural family socialization, some of these parents may hold conflicting values and attitudes in teaching their children "good" from "bad" behaviors or "proper" from "improper" ways of communicating with their grandparents, parents, siblings, or extended family members. There are two themes in this section: raising bicultural–biracial children and helping children to develop a secure identity.

Bicultural Identity Struggles

In any intimate relationship, the topic of raising children is a major stress point. But add intercultural factors to this mix and both parents and children have multiple options to choose from and to follow. Do you remember our story from Chapter 2, when the Muslim father and the Jewish mother struggled with interfaith issues in raising their bicultural children? His story, along with other interfaith and intercultural couples' stories, can be expressed through the following reflective questions: Does one parent have a greater intensity when identifying with her or his cultural or ethnic group (or religious faith) than the other? What degree of involvement do members of the immediate and extended families play in the child's life? What is the cultural and religious composition of the environment, neighborhoods, and schools? Do parents reach a mutually satisfactory outcome regarding an identity path for the family and in raising the child? Take a minute and read the poem "What Is the Color of Love?" in Blog Post 10.2. Discuss your reactions and feelings with your classmates.

Bicultural children and transadopted children often face more identity issues and complexity during various stages of their life cycle development. Decisions about which group to identify with, which label they prefer, and the context that triggers an identity are part of the bicultural identity struggles among children and adolescents. In addition, there are four identity forms many bicultural children claim for themselves: (1) **majority-group identifiers**—these children identify with the parent from the dominant culture or religion, and they may or may not publicly

BLOG POST 10.2 WHAT IS THE COLOR OF LOVE?

he came to me
he saw through me
and he gave me his heart
we found harmony
so much in common
though we were from worlds apart
when I saw him
I loved him and he loved me
what could be simpler to see
but clouds of fear hovering near
coloring the truth
afraid to let it be . . . let it be
we had a son
and being half black
he asked some hard questions
at six, while building sand
castles at the beach
he said, "mommy I wonder
what people think
seeing a Black kid with a
Japanese lady?"
at seven, he watched a white

neighbor scream at me
"you should be ashamed for
having a Black child!"
and my son said
"mommy is there something
wrong with that lady?"
at eight years old he came home
from school one day and said
"why do some people hate
Black folks so much?"
I didn't know how to answer
But I hope he never runs out of questions
love so strong
like a simple song
it made two worlds into one
but I'm still left with a child's question
what is the color of love?
what is the color of love?

Source: Miyamoto, N. "What Is the Color of Love?" In A. Ling (Ed.), *Yellow Light: The Flowering of Asian American Arts* (pp. 330–331).

acknowledge the identity of their other parent (in this case, from a minority-group background); (2) **minority-group identifiers**—these children identify with the parent who is a minority, and they may either acknowledge that their other parent is from a different background or deny (or minimize) their dual heritage background; (3) **synthesizers**—children who acknowledge the influence of both aspects of their parents' cultural backgrounds and synchronize and synthesize the diverse aspects of their parents' values into a coherent identity; and (4) **disaffiliates** (i.e., "none of the above" identifiers)—children who distance themselves or claim not to be influenced by their parents' cultural backgrounds, and they often create their own identity labels and rebel against any existing label that is imposed on them as part of a particular racial or cultural group (Crohn, 1995).

Children or teenagers at different developmental stages may experience the emotional highs and lows related to their sense of self. They may opt for different identity forms—depending on their peer group's attitudes, their parents' socialization efforts, their own self-identity explorations, and the larger society's support or rejection of such an identity search process (see Blog Post 10.3).

Cultivating a Secure, Multifaceted Identity

Developing a secure identity is a lifelong commitment that requires resilience and skill development. In essence, it means maintaining flexibility. This is not an easy task. To achieve bicultural competence with living in two or more cultures, LaFromboise, Coleman, and Gerton (1993) outline dimensions we believe may help bicultural individuals:

- Have knowledge of the cultural values and beliefs of each group;
- Have a positive attitude toward both minority and majority groups;
- Have the confidence that one can live effectively within the bicultural groups without compromising one's individual identity; and
- Be grounded.

To facilitate a stronger dialog between parents and children regarding cultural and religious identity

BLOG POST 10.3 *"I WANT TO BE PINK!"*

When I was three years old, I wondered why my skin color was so different from my newborn baby sister. My mother tells me that I asked, "Why am I blue? Why can't I be pink like my sister?" as I pointed to the brown skin on my arm. I must have been concerned that I was irregular or odd because I didn't have the same skin tone as my sister. I never met my biological father, who did have a dark complexion, so I unknowingly used my mother and baby sister as the models for what I should have looked like. For me, as a child, I think I was mostly concerned with looking like my sister because I wanted to be reassured that I was part of the family. I thought to myself, "Wait, why do I look different? I want to be part of this family very much, so I should change my skin tone!" Given my experience, I think to myself how troubling (mental strain, anxious, confusion) it can be for some children who grow up not knowing or having a blueprint to compare themselves to.

I didn't know any better as a child; my identity was shaped by my surroundings and of course by those closest to me. I was very young, but I made an age-old observation that as human beings, we want to find similarities between others and ourselves. As an adult, I look back at my childhood inquiry as a reminder to embrace diversity, because in the end, we all want to belong.

—J. Acosta-Licea, *college student*

issues, here are some practical guidelines. First, take time and make a commitment to work out a family identity process as early in your relationship as possible; understand the important aspects of your own and your partner's cultural–ethnic and religious identity. Second, make time to listen to your children's identity stories and experiences; their ambivalence is oftentimes part of a normal, developmental process. Learn not to judge or be hurt by their truthful revelations. Third, try to provide your children with plenty of cultural enrichment opportunities that celebrate the diversity of both of your cultures; offer them positive experiences to appreciate and synthesize the differences (Crohn, 1995; Ting-Toomey, 2009).

Fourth, be truthful in dealing with prejudice and racism issues; nurture a secure sense of personal self-esteem and self-worth in your children regardless of how they wish to identify themselves. Parents should model constructive, assertive behaviors in confronting prejudice and racism issues. Finally, recognize that your children will grow up and choose their own path; keep the dialog open and let your young children or teenagers know that you will always be there for them. A secure home environment, listening to their stories with patience and interest, giving them room or space to grow, and finding meaningful ways to relate to who they are and are becoming are some very basic means that parents can use to signal their heartfelt caring and mindful presence in their children's lives.

To conclude this chapter, we should recognize that in any intercultural-intimate conflict, it is difficult to pursue all "my needs" or all "your needs" and come up with a neat conflict resolution package. In most intimate conflicts, couples who engage in constructive conflict tend to cultivate multiple paths in arriving at a mutually satisfying destination (see Blog Post 10.4).

These couples learn to listen to their partners' viewpoint with patience, and they are open to reconsidering their own position. They are committed to understanding their partners' cultural beliefs, values, intimacy lenses, and relational expectations. They are also willing to actively share and self-disclose their vulnerabilities, dreams, and hopes. Finally, they are able to inject humor and to laugh with each other in times of stress. They are also able to be mindfully there for their small children and adolescents—in their quest for cultural and personal identity meanings.

INTERCULTURAL REALITY CHECK: DO-ABLES

This chapter focused on the challenges in developing intercultural-intimate relationships. We explored different culture-based relationship expectations concerning love, autonomy and connection, and communication issues. We discussed the facilitating factors—perceived physical attractiveness, perceived similarity, self-disclosure, offline and online dating, and some intercultural–interracial romantic relationship research findings—that shape the ebbs and flows of an intercultural-intimate relationship. The pressures that an intercultural couple face in dealing with various racism issues and also the increasingly important topic of raising bicultural–biracial

---

BLOG POST 10.4 AN INTERFAITH MARRIAGE: DEVELOPING A THIRD CULTURE OUTLOOK

I was with my boyfriend for three and a half years before he proposed to me. Our religious differences were known, but overlooked by us . . . until we got engaged and had to plan our wedding. Both of us were born and raised in India and had moved to USA for further education. My father is a Muslim by birth, my mother a staunch Protestant Christian. My fiancé and his parents are Hindu. I grew up Christian. Both my fiancé and I are not extremely religious, or at least consider ourselves not to be.

How do you put these contrasting religions together? How should we plan our interfaith wedding? There were four ways to resolve this issue: we could choose to display one identity and ignore the other; display no identity at all and have a legal ceremony that forgoes all ritual elements; figure out a way to combine both religious and cultural traditions into a single ceremony; or display different identities in separate events.

After countless hours of discussion with my fiancé and parents, we agreed that each of our religious rituals was important to each of our identities, and it was also important for us to consider our parents' desires. But there was no way we could fit it all into one ceremony. The thought of trying to combine the bridal attire would be a recipe for disaster—Hindus wear white to a funeral, and red for their wedding; imagine me wearing a white bridal gown on my wedding day?

The last option is what seems to be working for us—separate the two. The result is planning for a four-day wedding, one for each side of the family, four different wedding ensembles, and plan for multiple, yet distinct ceremonies. However, even this is easier said than done. It took us several months to help each other understand the different rituals in each faith; it also took time to convince each of our parents to understand the other side. I could not understand why the Hindu wedding had to take place on an auspicious day at a particular time that was decided by a priest and he could not understand why I wanted to get married in the church I was raised in.

My identity was questioned, and I could not understand or explain why I am at a "culture-pluralistic" stage, where I assume that as an interfaith couple we have a "tapestry marriage;" we will have to constantly work on our differently colored threads, to combine a complex fabric for the future.

—Noorie, *college student*

---

children were presented. These and other obstacles are best handled by culture-sensitive dialog, genuine relational commitment, and extra attention to cultural, ethnic, and relational identity development issues.

The following do-able guidelines are drawn from the preceding discussion of various challenges and stumbling blocks that face an intercultural-intimate couple. They may help you in managing diverse intimate relationship issues:

- Pay close attention to culture-based challenges in developing an intercultural-intimate relationship.
- Be mindful that individualists and collectivists hold different expectations concerning communication issues, such as dating requests or self-disclosure.
- Be sensitive to your relational partner's family reaction issues. Learn to deal with the individualistic and collectivistic value gaps adaptively.
- Be committed to developing a deep friendship with your intimate partner as a cushion to deal with both internal and external stressors down the road.

- Be unconditionally accepting of your partner's core personality. You must make your partner feel that you try hard to understand the cultural and religious (or nonreligious) contexts that she or he is coming from.
- Be flexible in learning the communication styles of your intimate partner and learn to code-switch from direct to indirect styles or from verbal to nonverbal attending behaviors.
- Be responsive to the "emotional tasks" awaiting you in your intimate relationship and learn to share them responsibly and with enjoyment.
- Be diligent in depositing emotionally supportive messages into your relationship. Research (Gottman & Silver, 1999) confirms the validity of the "5-to-1 ratio"—you must deposit five positive messages in your intimate relationship to counteract one negative message.
- Be positive in your relationship memories. Research indicates that the more you engage in positive relationship memory reflections, the more you will think positively about the current state of your intimate relationship.

CHAPTER 11

WHAT ARE THE COMMUNICATION ISSUES FACING A GLOBAL IDENTITY?

CHAPTER OUTLINE

My friend and I went to go see a documentary, Isaiah's Children, about the exodus of Sudanese refugees and their journey to Israel at the Black Film Festival. The story was moving, humbling, and inspiring. One scene showed a handful of Sudanese refugees gathered together singing their outcries and as they repeated the verse, my friend leaned over and asked, "Is that guy wearing a *50 cent* shirt?" I looked, and sure enough, he was! We looked at each other in disbelief.

I thought about a recent interview with rapper Jay-Z. Jay who told Oprah, "I have a very interesting take on the cultural impact of hip hop and it's a strong one...I think that hip hop has done more for racial relations than most cultural icons....This music didn't only influence kids from urban areas; it influenced people all around the world. People listen to this music all around the world."

—Adriana Rios-Collins

The Royal Wedding of William and Kate, even more dramatic breaking international news of the past few months, was a three-front war for screen time with viewers via TV, computer, and mobile devices, such as iPhone and iPad apps. With the blossoming of the Web and social media platforms, every news organization has to have its own dedicated Twitter feed and Facebook page for the event, along with fashion programming and news coverage that work across platforms.

—S. Thielman and L. Barraclough, *Daily Variety*, April 2011

In this global reality of endless on and off buttons, highly techno-savvy netizens (Internet citizens) have emerged from their "intersected" cities from across the ocean and are changing our outlook and the composition of our social and personal identities. We have learned to multitask what we watch and how we watch news and entertainment. The reality is that there is little room for tradition as we make room for the next best thing. The power of the Internet has transformed how we gather information and who we compare ourselves with, changing as the wind blowing or the latest trend. One day it's in and the next, well, it's out! And boy, how this has affected our global vision indeed. Role models, brands, and music are not limited to the confines of the United States. Our music trendsetters, Bruno Mars, Lady Gaga, and Ke$ha, for example, are just as popular overseas as they are here. But now we have crossover global music makers, such as the Wonder Girls (South Korea) and Adele (the UK). With no promotion or fanfare outside his country, Korean pop singer Taeyang, a member of the boy band Big Bang, released his solo album and the record immediately hit No. 1 on iTunes in Canada and No. 2 in the United States. We must take a moment to sit down and reflect on how modern technology has influenced the development of our changing identity and communication styles.

The concern of this chapter is twofold: first, how does technology and pop culture shape contemporary identities on a global level? Second, what is the impact of this global self on intercultural communication? Let's begin with a definition of the background of a contemporary identity through a new concept we, the authors, have coined, the e.netizen identity. Next, we explore some of the important issues that individuals face as active technology users and communicators at the global level. Third, the effect of popular culture on the development of a contemporary identity is explained. Finally, the chapter concludes with some checkpoints for daily intercultural practice.

A s we enter the decade of the 21st century, the Internet is no longer an optional resource. It is a fundamental tool encountered in every aspect of our lives. We rely on it for business, information, education, communication, and personal expression. We use it at our offices, in our homes, on desktops, laptops, and even on our phones.... the Internet might be the most powerful economic tool since the invention of the printing press.

—Anna Ashoo, *SF Chronicle*, February 6, 2011

WIRED AND ON: THE ROAR OF THE INTERNET

Marching toward the persistent beat, we simply cannot resist the tempting rhythm of the Internet. The migration toward cyberspace is a way of life, an unchartered territory of time and space. We are now netizens, citizens of the Internet, contributing to the Internet's use, growth, and great possibilities for cultural and social change. How powerful is the Internet? In the United States alone, for the past five years, "Americans have doubled the hours they spend online, exceeding their television time and more than tripling the time they spend reading newspapers or magazines. Most now play video or computer games regularly, about 13 hours a week on average. By age 21 the average young American has spent at least three times as many hours [playing video or computer games than] reading" (Saletan, 2011, p. 7). Clearly, we are all influenced and shaped by the time we spend sitting in front of a screen.

The Internet as Our Central Station

For better or worse, the Internet is our central station, the hub that offers us a wide-open space to communicate globally and to connect with individuals from diverse walks of life. More important, this hub pulses with speed and efficiency. The Internet gives us a common language—English—with which to communicate and bond with fellow global citizens—over 536 million to be exact (Internet World Stats, 2011). The English language, in operation with virtual reality, hooks people together on an instantaneous global level (Norris, 2009). This global connection is so appealing, so "hip," and so very persuasive that it constantly shapes and reshapes our sense of composite self. Let's take a Hit-or-Miss 11.1 break. (Can you guess what are the top five Internet languages used on the Web?)

How was your answer? The Internet allows users to develop relationships across the barriers of time, space, geography, and cultural–ethnic boundaries. Of course, we realize that this global space is also a very privileged space—accessible only to members and cultural groups who have the access and means to afford such technological resources and updates. It also privileges individuals who can use English comfortably as a medium of Internet communication. It has been estimated that approximately 605 million people use the Internet on a daily basis, and they e-mail each other across diverse age groups and diverse cultural boundaries—from Mongolia to Argentina and from Iceland to New Zealand (http://www.nua.ie/surveys/how_many_online). It is estimated that over 1.9 billion individuals are Internet users, which is almost 29 percent of the world's population (Internet World Stats, 2011). In the United States, 76 percent of kids use the Internet three to four times per week for one hour (Nielson, 2010).

One of the most wired countries in the world is South Korea. By the end of 2012, every South Korean home will be connected at one gigabit per second (M. McDonald, 2011). This speed is more than two hundred times as fast as the average household setup in the United States. Why such high speed? South Koreans use the large bandwidth largely for Internet access and entertainment—multiplayer gaming, streaming Internet TV, and fast video downloads. Higher speeds mean companies can use high-definition videoconferencing with multiple overseas clients. Thus, Internet and innovative technology can advance existing businesses and can enhance intercultural negotiations and transactions.

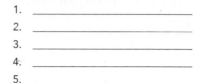

HIT-OR-MISS 11.1   TOP FIVE INTERNET LANGUAGES USED ON THE WEB

See if you "Hit" or "Miss" by identifying the top five languages used on the Internet:

1. _____

2. _____

3. _____

4. _____

5. _____

Answers: 1: German (78.6% Internet penetration); 2: Japanese (78.2%); 3: Korean (55.2%); 4: Russian (42.8%); 5: English (42%).

Internet penetration: the ratio between the sum of Internet users speaking a language and the total population estimate that speaks that language.

Source: Retrieved April 1, 2011, from http://www.internetworldstats.com/stats7.htm

Wired Communication

Personal use of the Internet has changed the way we communicate intra- and interpersonally across the globe. Online blogging has mass appeal and encourages individual creativity. According to Nielson (2010), Japanese Internet users are the most avid bloggers, posting more than 1 million blogs per month—this is more than any other country in the region. Japan is equally fascinated with Twitter. Adoption of Twitter accounts has jumped from less than 200,000 in 2009 to more than 10 million in 2010. In India, more than half of Twitter users (57%) have signed up in the past year and they "tweet" at least once per day (Nielson, 2010).

More importantly, we now have shared experiences across time and space, allowing us to communicate in real time about events that unfold thousands of miles away. By communicate, we mean by the various media outlets. The Beijing Summer Olympics became a worldwide event with more than 2 billion people—almost one-third of the world's population—watching the opening ceremony (Nielson Wire, 2008). The wedding of Prince William and the Duchess Kate was watched by 23 million Americans alone, and Michael Jackson's death caused big traffic spikes in Web video use. The death of Osama bin

Laden broke Twitter records: Twitter said it recorded the highest rate of Tweets in its history on May 1, 2011, when an average of 3,440 tweets per second were sent between 10:45 p.m. EST and 12:30 a.m. EST (Twitter, 2011). In the past, major events became headlines in local and national newspapers about a day after the event occurred. But now, when news goes viral, we have access in an instant, together sharing history and events across the world.

If we stop for a moment and reflect on what impact technology has on intercultural communication and our identity, we are confident that you can identify at least two positive or two negative factors. Past studies have assumed, incorrectly, that the ethnicity of an individual (via biological ties) automatically guarantees group membership. However, as we learned in Chapter 4, ethnicity is not a static phenomenon; it is a subjective experience that involves the active management of ingroup and outgroups. As we add the complex layer of the Internet, we as global citizens are at the crossroads of redefining, exploring, and reinventing our contemporary identities. In this next section, we define local versus global culture. Next, we expand on how media (via technology and the Internet) and pop culture have contributed to the changed trajectories of global and local identities. Let's now examine the clash between local and global identities.

THE TRANSFORMATION OF LOCAL AND GLOBAL IDENTITIES

What does it mean to be local or global? Twenty-two-year-old Thuy Nguyen was a contestant for Miss Vietnam, Florida, 2008. Throughout the pageant, she expressed pride in wanting to show others that she was a strong Vietnamese woman. It was not always this easy. Born in Vietnam, she was raised in the United States and went back to Vietnam when she was twelve. Her grandmother was ashamed of her granddaughter, Thuy, because she hardly spoke Vietnamese and felt she was too American (Persaud, 2008). Or what about the case of Governor Bobby Jindal of Louisiana? Jindal has downplayed his ethnic background throughout his political life. He changed his Indian name during childhood and, against his father's wishes, he converted from Hinduism to Christianity (Kashyap,

2009). Recall our earlier discussion in which identity differentiation and identity inclusion appear to be the repeated themes that run through the old and new generations of the twenty-first century. What Thuy and Bobby reflect is a constant shift between wanting to be an "individual" and wanting to remain a part of the group as well. However, there is a sense that they are separated from the group for not being ethnic enough. Both long for a sense of group belonging and connection *and*, at the same time, feel compelled to assert their unique personality stamps. This internal and external pull can also be a reflection of local versus global identity across cultural and international borders.

The **local identity** is made up of the ethnic values, practices, and traditions of the local identity communal group. In a sense, "the strengthening of local ties offers a way of grounding identity and loyalty in a very fast-paced and much criticized global world" (Selznick, 2008, p. 2). Ethnic assertion and the traditional ways of viewing entertainment, media, and culture resist conforming to global standards. Thus, some local cultures in the age of the Internet resist technological advances, reliance on global programming and products, and any attempt to "fuse" culture with contemporary trends. On the other hand, the **global identity** is made up of individuals who adopt and embrace international practices and values over local practices. In an attempt to replace the preference of local culture, global culture keeps up with the latest trends, technological advances, international programming, and consumer materialism.

The impact of "choosing global" over local implies the loss of a local culture. Or does it? For example, when we think about weddings, traditional customs and practice take precedence over global branding or consumerism. In Hong Kong, starting in 2012, couples can have a McWedding reception for approximately US$1,280. The package includes food and drinks for fifty people, a "cake" made of stacked apple pies, gifts for the guests, invitation cards, and a wedding photo of the couple (Lau, 2011). Sundaes, not alcohol, are used as toasts during the McWedding. The director of Hong Kong McDonalds announced McWeddings on October 10, 2010, because "10–10-10" is a numerical lucky combination for local Chinese (Lau, 2011). This McWedding global identity is the fusion of using trendy branding, name recognition, and some local cultural practices fused for commercialism purposes.

Although this is only one example, researchers argue that changes in local culture are the consequence of cultural imperialism and exposure to western media (Schiller, 1993; Sinclair, Jacka, & Cunningham, 1996). Mass media serves as one of the most efficient sources of such a culture (Featherstone, 1996). The morphing of a third identity, the combination or fusion of global and local, is influenced by television, music, and pop culture. Let's now examine these three factors contributing to global and local identity change.

The Lens of Television: Identity Imitation

Just how does a person's identity develop? If you think back to prior chapters, the influence of our parents, socialization, and peers is especially relevant. Growing up, did you ever watch *Sesame Street? Dora the Explorer? Teletubbies?* As you watched the show, did you ever ask yourself, "Gee, I wonder if kids in India are watching the same show?" Probably not. But outside the United States, children are happily forced to watch these U.S.-branded shows because they are easily accessible in the international market.

What are children watching nowadays? The international children's television landscape is a shared experience, filled with children having the same interests, watching the same programming, playing the same games, and sharing in the same media preferences available in their living rooms. The most dominant global networks are Nickelodeon (Viacom), the Cartoon Network (AOL/Time Warner), and the Disney Channel (Disney). All have managed to successfully internationalize their brand with a packaged variety of media products to markets across the globe. The success of both programming and products has led to the widespread availability and appeal for more goods and shows. With global and mass-market appeal, children are persuaded every day to incorporate the values from the television characters that come to life on the screen, such as *Dora the Explorer, Spiderman,* or *Spongebob Square Pants.* The aura of global cultural values tied to consumerism and pop culture may persuade local children to incorporate these values. Although children in Germany may integrate some elements more than a child in India or even Spain, the commonality is that each child is viewing the same message. This message carries more weight and influence by the same global system, in a way that is very appealing to children and teenagers around the globe.

What we can observe directly is that through the explosion of technology, the intersection of global and local identities is on the edge, standing at the crossroads. Children, youth, and adults are seeking ways to dance to their own beat but are still bound by tradition and local culture. As we discussed earlier, how an individual views him- or herself is significantly influenced by the significant persons within his or her social world (Espiritu, 1992). Thus, the process of identity negotiation is a complex and intersecting web of interacting with our social environment that teaches us what we should value or devalue. Children learn from their environment and one part of that environment includes the mass media.

Comstock (1993) argues that the "components of identity reflect and are a result from social interactions with family, friends, peers, authorities, and others as well as from mass media images and values. Indeed, since the mass media influence how people treat us, as clusters of demographic and cultural characteristics, social interactions are in part informed by the shared understandings or stereotypes about people that the media provide" (p. 311). Individuals, especially children, are intrigued by international media (whether they recognize it as foreign or not) and are influenced by the underlying cultural messages that are preferred in Western culture. The global child is more open to receiving nontraditional information and may select the foreign product because it is different from the local culture. The global child may be eager to embrace a new custom and challenge the tradition of the local space. The global versus local child becomes the struggle to be part of the global whole but a part of the group as well. When we add the impact of television, the result is the constant friction between local and global identity issues.

Television as the identity supplier provides the escape from traditional-based cultural values and forges a sense of communal belonging when children do not relate to their cultural–ethnic group. Although children are experiencing a sense of alienation from the norm, television provides a communal identity with other global children who share the same existence. While searching for the sense of belonging to a group, children end up finding each other in cyberspace. Sharing this intersecting space and time has only surfaced through the powerful means of the Internet. Although it is difficult to calculate the total amount of time children around the world spend watching television and other media, it is safe to assume that it is a significant part of their lives. Let's take a break for Hit-or-Miss 11.2! Can you guess the average amount of time children watch TV across the globe—and which country is the highest in TV viewing?

Did you guess correctly? Surprisingly, these numbers do not include Internet, games, and other social network media. The increase in minutes is in part the result of more programming targeted at children, including video on demand, where kids can watch the same show repeatedly (Gold, 2009). As the reliance on media for entertainment increases, the consumption of international media is influencing the way children are being socialized (Moran & Chung, 2008). Check out Figure 11.1 to see the graphics of what children in China are doing online.

If the impact of television affects children, how about the rest of us? How do we watch and how much do we watch? Despite the proliferation of mobile devices and online video, television continues to

---

HIT-OR-MISS 11.2   CHILDREN'S TV VIEWING AROUND THE WORLD

See if you "Hit" or "Miss." Match the average numbers of hours of television watched by children with the following countries:

letter:

_____ 1. 5 hours 18 minutes   a) Australia

_____ 2. 3 hours 30 minutes   b) Germany

_____ 3. 3 hours   c) Italy

_____ 4. 2 hours 44 minutes   d) Spain

_____ 5. 2 hours 38 minutes   e) United Kingdom

_____ 6. 1 hour 33 minutes   f) United States

Answers: 1e; 2f; 3a; 4c; 5d; 6b

Source: EuroData (2010); Nielson (2009); *The Times* (2009); *The Telegraph* (2009).

---

capture the most viewers. How people are watching television has evolved and it is these advances that have made television more relevant than ever. They aren't necessarily "watching TV" on TV—they are increasingly likely to watch TV programs on the Internet or on their cell phones (Stross, 2009). In a 2010 study Nielson addressed current findings about how we are supplied with alternative methods of watching:

• Online video: Approximately 70 percent of global online consumers watch online video; more than half in the workplace.

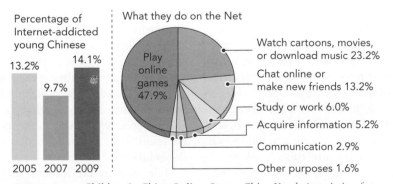

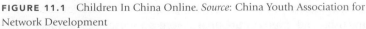

FIGURE 11.1   Children In China Online. *Source*: China Youth Association for Network Development

- Mobile video: is already used by 11 percent of global online consumers; highest in Asia-Pacific and among consumers in their late twenties.

- Tablet PCs: Globally, 11 percent of online consumers already own or plan to purchase a tablet PC (e.g. iPad) in 2011.

- HDTV (high-definition TV): improving the TV viewing experience for as many as 30 percent of global online consumers. Adoption is highest among older consumers and in North America, where HD content has proliferated.

- 3DTV (three-dimensional TV): has a small but important audience: 12 percent of global online consumers own or have definite intent to purchase a 3DTV in 2011.

- "Over the Top" TV: televisions with Internet connections are gaining interest. About one in five (22%) global online consumers owns or has definite interest in buying a television with Internet connection in the next year (Nielson, 2010).

Global Television Impact

With all these figures and data, television shapes the way we see our world. It is a compelling aspect of marketing culture, lifestyle, trends, and news. It also influences how we form our stereotypes of people in different cultures and ethnic groups. Three types of television shows are consistently in demand in the global market: action, drama, and reality television. Action shows are enticing because of their combination of action, violence, and sex. Viewers do not need to really listen to the show's words when they have vivid images and a lot of visual action stimulations. Drama shows have also done very well in the international market, and they are also usually dubbed into the local language. For example, in Argentina, the cast from two youth-oriented English language telenovelas ("Almost Angels" and "Rebel's Way") gave sold-out performances in Israel, with over forty thousand tickets sold. Equally startling is the dramatic rise and influence of the Korean drama, or "K-drama." But more importantly, Korean dramas have surpassed telenovelas in terms of global popularity.

When the K-drama *Winter Sonata* ended its massive run, travel agencies in Hawaii, Philippines, Malaysia, Singapore, and Japan bought tickets to the *"Winter Sonata"* tour, taking fans to the locations shot in the series. This brings up a question: Exactly how global are we? In the United States, entertainment is the second-largest export (Webb, 2009). U.S. television is everywhere. Different countries have different tastes and many are captivated by U.S. exported television shows, in particular shows like *Lost, Law and Order,* and *Two and a Half Men.* As more countries produce their own television shows, the international variety increases with availability and funding.

U.S. networks are purchasing international and homegrown productions, a reverse flow of globalization. International TV gives us a comparison of culture-specific and culture-universal display rules (e.g., nonverbal cues). Individuals in the United States have the opportunity to take a snapshot of the similarities and differences in communication. The result? We are hooked on reality TV—something for which we can thank Japan (*Iron Chef*), the UK (*American Idol*), and the Netherlands (*Big Brother*)! The international community can thank the United States for successful shows such as *America's Next Top Model, The Biggest Loser,* and, most of all, *Jersey Shore.*

According to the *Guinness Book of World Records,* can you name the most successful reality show ever? The correct answer is *Dancing with the Stars.* This show is licensed in thirty-five nations and shown in seventy-five more (Clarke, 2010). This international phenomenal hit series has the kind of ingredients needed for easy global translation: the cast, audience voting, and light-hearted interviews. When paired with a smooth dancer, a target pop culture figure creates buzz among viewers, who can judge their skills among friends and with online communities. The stars bring in a mix of controversy, beauty, brains, and two left feet, in some cases. *Dancing with the Stars* can credit its success to the unscripted events that unfold during real time, such as stars falling, shoes flying off, or wardrobe malfunctions.

Reality TV comes in many forms, but the most common focus of these shows is the development of interpersonal relationships. The desire to watch real-life people on camera has extended to various contexts and situations. For example, *Jersey Shore* is MTV's highest rated television series of all time, culminating in the January 20, 2011, most watched telecast of all time. So popular is this reality show that filming was delayed in Italy amid a contract dispute and very serious resistance from Italian nightclubs and hotels who refused to have cameras on their property.

Be Hip, Be Hot, and Pop Culture Impact

Pop culture has both positive and negative implications in the contemporary social world. Broadly speaking, pop culture creates a cultural interdependence on the global economy, e-commerce, mass media, and social network platforms. Individuals who support pop culture see the world as constantly changing, interdependent, and hip.

From a different analytical standpoint, opponents view pop culture as negative because of the connotation with commercialism, shallow effort, and mass production. Pop culture can damage cultural boundaries and Westernizes many intact, indigenous cultural groups. For example, pop culture has exported images of U.S. wealth, consumerism, and other mass media images throughout the world and created many "consuming" colonies with a strong U.S.-dominant flavor. Opponents argue pop culture dilutes culture, language, cultural etiquette, values, and traditions. See, for example, the top five all-time worldwide box office grossing movies (Jeopardy Box 11.1) and check out the global influence of Hollywood. Let's further explore how pop culture has changed local culture through music.

JEOPARDY BOX 11.1   TOP FIVE WORLDWIDE BOX OFFICE FILMS

1. Avatar (2009)
2. Titanic (1997)
3. Lord of the Rings: The Return of the King (2003)
4. Pirates of the Caribbean: Dead Man's Chest (2006)
5. Toy Story 3 (2010)

Source: http://www.boxofficemojo.com/alltime/world/ (retrieved July 17, 2011).

Outsourced Beats: You Are What You Can Dance To

Through music, we can find a common identity expression and connection with others—especially because music expresses exactly what we may be feeling. Music inspires trends, fashion, and alternative ways of communicating and makes a statement. Music may also bring controversy, conflict, and resistance. In the past, radio was the most common medium used to listen to popular tunes and catch live shows. Currently, radio is on the brink of extinction. One major reason is technology. We can burn music off of MP3 players, download it from iTunes, or use our music blogs to watch the newest and latest music videos. As a result, music creates our rhythmic identity and sparks a communal sense of space and time. Local cultures may aspire to "be like" a singer, a group, or a band. Nothing has influenced global pop culture as much as hip-hop music; in essence, they are one and the same. Hip-hop music, when combined with music videos, has cross-pollinated popular media and changed the dynamics of identity formation across the globe. Remember Adriana from our opening section of this chapter? Hip-hop has influenced more youth across the globe than any other trend in history.

Hip-hop music (or rap, as it was once called and is still referred to by some) sprang from the inner-city ghettos of the United States in the mid-1970s. Rap music has been associated with graffiti (or tagging), dance trends (breakdancing), scratching (a deejay simultaneously mixing two or more records), and artifacts (bling). Hip-hop music came from African American youth who were discouraged by racial oppression and the inequality of life. Rapping was an art, a way of expressing the problems they faced living on the outer edges of society. As the music increased in popularity and progressed from the inner city to the suburbs, rap music and hip-hop became big business when white teenagers started to listen and buy the music (Zwingle & McNally, 1999). At that point, hip-hop exploded. In the past three years, hip-hop has continued to generate the highest music sales in the United States and it is easy to see the worldwide influence of this genre of music that is cast across diverse cultural borders.

Outside the United States, the rise of the hip-hop identity can be linked to MTV. South Korea has exploded into the music industry, changing the identity and look of South Koreans. The South Korean music is called K-Pop or *gayo*. K-pop singers are known for their unique and hip style of music but are heavily influenced by U.S. styles. Taking rap and hip-hop trends (e.g., breakdancing) and adding unique dance twists and styles have resulted in a global fusion identity. The music combines elements of U.S. music (reggae and rap), fashion (surf wear, blonde hair, and baggy clothes), and Korean styles to make a new form of music. Dyed hair, baggy jeans, and designer labels are all features of K-pop singers (see Blog Pic 11.1).

In 2011, a South Korean newspaper examined K-pop by looking at uploaded videos on YouTube for the year 2010. The results showed that the videos by the Korean performers got 793.57 million hits from people in almost every country worldwide. Over 500 million views were from the Asian continent, 120 million from the American continent, and 55 million from Europe (Chung, 2011).

MTV Europe also has extensive showcases for hip-hop. In 1999, MTV Europe launched three twenty-four-hour digital programming services in the UK and is still going strong. MTV Base in England, the first music channel dedicated exclusively to R&B and dance music, reflects pop culture global hip-hop music trends. The success of rap and hip-hop covers MTV Latin America, MTV Australia, and MTV Asia. As music inspires dance, thirty-one affiliated countries are involved in Hip-Hop International, a dance contest for all countries to participate in. And who was the winner last year for World Hip-Hop adult dance team? *Request*—from New Zealand.

As cultural boundaries blur, music is no longer ethnic-specific or genre-specific. This is pop culture at its finest. K-pop bands flock to U.S. producers for outsourced beats (e.g., Kanye West, Timberland), while Hollywood revives the ukulele, making it the latest outsourced instrument trend (Sisario, 2011). Music has crafted a communal space or global sound stage for enthusiasts to relate to one another, move together as in *Pop Drop & Lock*, vent, and to be heard at the soulful level. What is fashionable and soulful in Asian, Latin American, and European regions is also fashionable in the United States or Belarus. Even President Obama has his foot in the pop culture door. During his 2008 Presidential inauguration ball, will.i.am of the Black Eyed Peas wrote, produced, and sang "Yes We Can" for President Obama. We can thank YouTube for allowing music and entertainment to be shared anytime, anyplace—as long as an individual downloaded it for us.

You Are What You Wear: Pop Culture as Fashion

Fashion is another component of global popular culture. Fashion, like pop culture, implies change: in the production, marketing, and purchase of clothes, change is fast and furious. The hip styles in both music and clothing are coordinated by designers, performers, and e.netizens. Recent elements of pop culture trends in fashion may be traced back to ethnic groups, sports teams, and leisure-interest groups. You've got the "look" or you're "it" when an individual's appearance is associated with a preference for music (heavy metal or hip-hop) or sports (skateboarding and golfing). Yet fashion is not cheap. An e.netizen's sense of alienation from the actual cultural world often pushes her or him to search for the latest fashion. In past years, you might have noticed young girls in Japan known as

Blog Pic 11.1 Trendy K-pop

Blog Pic 11.2   The *ganguro* trend in Japan

ganguro or *yamanba*. *Ganguro* ("black faces") visit tanning salons regularly to maintain a dark-brown tan or apply a dark-brown foundation. They dye their hair brown or gold and wear blue contact lenses. The result is a combination of the California beach girl and disco era looks. The centerpiece of their look is the six-inch, or higher, platform shoes or sandals. Despite the hazards of wearing platforms, these shoes have been in fashion for some time now.

Although the trend is fading, it is part of an ongoing identity evolution of Japan's female teenagers and part of the constructed e.netizen identity: keeping up with the trendy pop culture. To understand this fashion statement in Japan, we must probe a little deeper. The image of Japanese *ganguro* girls exists because they perceive themselves as not fitting into the "norms" of any groups. These outgroup members (or *ganguro* girls) seek out clubs that advocate difference, and in these clubs, they find a sense of community acceptance. The Japanese traditional values of conformity and collectivism appear to be too confining to them. They intentionally "darken" their skin colors to imitate African American women in the United States—as part of a disenfranchised or marginal group. Of course, the African American women might find this fashion odd or even "distasteful." In carving out their borrowed identities, the *ganguro* girls are making a clear statement of rebellion against the traditional idea of white/ pale skin as the standard of beauty and are advocating

their own imitational brand of identity uniqueness. Styles like Lolita and Goth are quite popular now (see Blog Pic 11.3).

Fashion and *music* are large markets for many e.netizens. Being hip and up to date is a reflection of differentiating themselves from their traditional parents and a traditional society. Being fashionable also means global social belonging and upgraded social status. This e.netizen consumerism culture may also reflect the transitional stages and changes between the local culture and the global culture.

As global impact fuses with local culture, we observe one outcome, the morphing of global and local culture. Morphing can be seen as visual formula: $A + B + C = X$. If A, B, and C are three mutually exclusive groups, X is the creative combination of the three, creating a new identity—the x-factor—based on distinct cultural groups and a result of the Internet. Morphing implies individuals who embrace their local values, the function of individual privacy and expression, but who also long for global belonging and connection that transcends traditional ethnic–cultural boundaries. The Internet, somehow, provides the ideal link to bridge these diametrically opposite values and desires.

Think back for a moment to the discussion of value orientations in Chapter 3. Our values allow us to attach meanings and explanations concerning people and events that are happening around us. Both cultural and personal values give us a sense of direction in terms of what is good or bad, right or wrong, fair or unfair. Cultural and personal values also change over time. They are not static entities. The role of the Internet connection adds another layer of complexity to our understanding of changing values in the twenty-first century. The following sections explain the authors' perspective of the global–local morphing process and the crystallization of the *e-netizen identity*.

WHO AND WHAT ARE E.NETIZENS?

e.netizen stands for a new generation of individuals, from any age group, wired to the Internet via intersecting space. e.netizens have both a local self and a global self. Some may call this a "hybrid" identity because it is a blend of many aspects of the local and global

Blog Pic 11.3 Fashion forward: (a) Goth, (b) punk, and (c) the Lolita look.

environment that is shared by all. Some may call this the "third culture" because we are rooted in the local context but connected to the global village. Although it is a hybrid global phenomenon, the e.netizen identity is also an outcome of power and popular culture.

Defining the Background of e.netizens

The aspect of power comes from the fact that wireless and daily access to the Internet is limited. So is the purchase of every upgraded mobile phone, tech gadget, and innovative computer game. Not everyone can afford the upgrade. Almost 75 percent of North Americans are online, whereas fewer than 10 percent of Africans are online (http://www.internetworldstats.com/stats.htm.). Behind the medium of identity reconstructions and image shaping are teams of corporations, start-up companies, marketers, and public relations specialists who intend to spread the latest trendy "in" product. One of the primary purposes of image reshaping is for profit making and profit recycling. In essence, every attempt to update technology allows e.netizen individuals to *distinguish* themselves as being the "first-wave users" while, simultaneously, also belonging to a fast-track, disposable culture.

The e.netizen identity is inexorably linked to pop culture. Pop culture is not only *mass* produced; it is simply culture that is widely favored and well enjoyed by many people (Storey, 2006). In addition, popular culture fosters a climate in which "globally ethnic" is actually appealing to diverse groups on a global level. One example of someone who is globally ethnic is Tiger Woods, who calls himself "Caublasian," a mixture of Caucasian, African American, and Asian. The new ambivalent-looking, *global-ethnic* celebrity has mass appeal in any ethnic market. She or he can connect with the masses on various levels and can also appeal to those who do not define themselves clearly within a particular ethnic group. This type of celebrity icon has at once no clear ethnic–cultural identity and so reflects a distinctive global-ethnic identity because of her or his fusion look and hybrid tastes. Think for a moment about your own identity: How do you think technology has shaped your identity? How do you think pop culture has influenced your sense of self? What would happen if you woke up tomorrow morning and your computer and cell phone disappeared?

Could you survive for two days without all these electronic gadgets? Are you one of many who rely so much on your tech devices that should your smartphone break, you will be completely out of touch?

Characteristics of an e.netizen Identity

We can view an **e.netizen identity** as a composite identity that is shaped by technology, popular culture, and mass consumption. An e.netizen can have both internal and external facets. Internally, one can hold hybrid components of ethnic–cultural values (e.g., collectivism and individualism) and contemporary aspects of being-in-doing value orientations. In addition, the e.netizen can swing flexibly between the HCC and LCC systems. An individual with an e.netizen identity has a sense of communal belonging on a global level. She is linked in with diverse yet like-minded individuals who actively carve out a social network community fervently via blogs, Twitter, and Facebook. In essence, they are flexible communicators and highly adaptable.

Let's examine some of these *e-characteristics* and how they relate to communication:

exclusive: The e.netizen is an exclusive group of individuals who are on the edge of becoming and are transitioners who feel entirely comfortable in the in-between groups. They may be members of specific ethnic or racial groups, but they are also loyal to the Internet community. For e.netizens, the Internet serves as the main connection to the world.

evolved: The e.netizen includes individuals who may have ties with their ethnic groups. However, they often tend to display more solidarity with their technoglobal networks or, as Pankraz (2011) claims, tribal behavior. e.netizens form their identities by choosing their own group allegiance and sense of particular belonging. Their social group identities are multifaceted and network-based. They also feel comfortable "borrowing" identities, making them chameleon-like, in terms of surface appearances and use of ethnic artifacts.

explorers: As a consumer-based identity, the e.netizen is in search of the *next* big thing, whether it is fashion, music, trends, or Web sites. Trendy and cutting-edge, the Web serves as a way of creating a space and a community to which they can find new places and belonging. e.netizens are willing to spend large amounts of money to keep up to date.

emoticons: The e.netizens prefer to communicate with emoticons for efficiency of time and space. Emoticons (see Chapter 7) are conveyed through texting and Tweeting. A simple emoticon is worth three sentences—who has time to go in depth?

entertained: To quote Nirvana, "here we are now, entertain us!" The entertainment industry in the United States is an estimated $754 billion dollar industry in 2011 (Mitchell, 2007). Most e.netizens have an insatiable appetite for entertainment. With video on demand, phone apps, movies, DVDs, and games, why leave the house? Europeans are deserting cable television in favor of services that provide streaming programming directly through Web browsers and, according to D. Takahashi (2010), the UK, Germany, and France spend over $3 billion on games per year.

engaged: Among e.netizens, decision-making is a group effort enhanced by social media platforms. Purchases are reviewed and rated. Opinions are shared, tagged, approved—but mostly rated. For example, how many stars would you give this section? Why?

energized: The e.netizens get bored easily: they need variety, they need constant sensory stimulation, they need instant gratification, via instant breaking news, visuals, sounds, or touches.

These are only a few of many characteristics of an e.netizen identity, a self that reflects a new generation of technosavvy individuals. Can you come up with your own e.netizen-ness? What other e-words can you think of? Use your imagination and stretch your e.boundary.

If ethnic group membership can be elastic, fluid, and flexible, what does an e.netizen identity look like? We propose that the e.netizen identity reflects an inverted pyramid: the widest part at the top represents *"gliding e.netizen identity"* who are individuals who have weaker attachment with the wired community and reflect the larger international group membership. These individuals have stronger ties with the local culture and see the Internet and technology as

a hobby and a way to gather information and to be provided with surface entertainment. Although surfing the Net is fun, gliding e.netizens have little, if any strong affiliation with groups sites on the Internet. There is surface-level influence on their communication behavior, purchasing power, and decision-making outcomes.

The midsection layer refers to the *"interfaced e.netizen identity"* in which individuals have moderately strong ties to the Internet. These individuals have interfaced ties with the global Internet community on one hand and also continue their local community ties with other individuals in real time. They are connected to the latest news, trends, and pop culture via the wired and the wireless community and also have a selective "buy in" factor with certain sites (e.g., interest hobby sites, blogs, or online dating sites) via the Internet. The interfaced e.entizens are influenced by global and local trends. They use social media platforms to communicate and follow some online communities.

Finally, the *"fixated e.netizen identity"* lies at the deep layer of our triangle. These individuals have strong attachment and solidarity to their e-netizen identity. These fixated e.netizens are continuously hooked and wired up, expressing their daily lives via a multitude of social media platforms. They live their daily reality via the virtual reality. Savvy and curious, the fixated e.netizen is a tribal community member and an ultimate online consumer—of news, brands, and products (see Figure 11.2). These global, fixated e.netizens are vigilant advocates of the Internet and spend much of their time looking at the screen in front of them, or texting, or Tweeting even if they are in a face-to-face group. Which one best describes you?

THE DIALECTICAL PULLS OF AN E.NETIZEN

The e.netizen identity is a cornerstone of contemporary identity development. This section highlights some of the important issues that concern the interplay between technology and global identity development. Perhaps one of the most striking challenges of e.net interaction is the aspect of dialectics. **Dialectical tensions** are conflicts that come from two opposing forces that exist at the same time (Baxter &

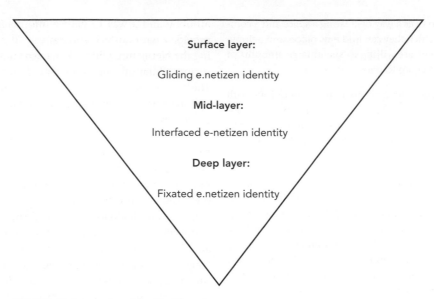

Surface layer:

Gliding e.netizen identity

Mid-layer:

Interfaced e-netizen identity

Deep layer:

Fixated e.netizen identity

FIGURE 11.2   e.netizen Identity: Three Layers

Montgomery, 1996). For example, tensions can exist when you want to be spontaneous but your friends want to preplan every step, cramping your style or making you feel bored by the everyday monotony. Any tension has the potential to create challenges for an individual and for his relationships. However, such dialectical tensions can also spark interpersonal collaboration and creativity—if the dialectics are managed flexibly and adaptively. The following pages discuss the dialectical pulls of time and space on the e.netizen identity (see Table 11.1).

Before launching into this discussion, please check your reactions on my.blog 11.1.

Spatial Zone Dialectics

For an e.netizen, the Internet provides privacy and anonymity in the safe environment of one's free space. The e.netizen culture transforms the way we look at space in such a way that individuals can experience both the *solitude pole* and the *tribal pole* in instant space and time zones. If you have checked words on both the left-hand and right-hand columns of my.blog 11.1, you're not going crazy; you're just one of the many individuals who interpret the use of the Internet from both dialectical poles. Within the solitude pole, the smart phone and iPad are typically accessed

TABLE 11.1   GLOBAL IDENTITY: DIALECTICAL CHALLENGES

Space:	Solitary space ⟷ Tribal space
Time:	Monotrack tempos ⟷ Multitrack tempos

my.blog 11.1

Please check the words or phrases that best describe your overall attitude toward the use of the Internet and compare your results with a classmate's:

Alone time	_____	Communal time	_____
Quietness	_____	Bustling noises	_____
Focused	_____	Excitement	_____
Work	_____	Playful	_____
Effort	_____	Action	_____
Fun	_____	Reaching out	_____

in private, personal space. We need not be confined to a public space, such as a computer lab, to access the Internet. We can be "virtual" on an airplane or subway, in a sports stadium, at the movies, sitting in the park, and even in a bathroom stall. Oftentimes, our communication exchanges happen within seconds. And the same holds true with news going viral—it is brief, speedy, and transcends space and time. If you swing too much toward the solitude pole, one result is a shut-in, or hikikomori in Japan. These are individuals, typically younger Japanese males, who stay in the privacy of their room typically on the Internet and find little solace in the outside world or the larger society (Zielenziger, 2006).

Simultaneously, the Internet is a social media platform providing shared tribal space. Chat rooms, blogs, Twitter, Facebook, and fan-based pages offer an individual a sense of communal connection and belonging to a particular group. Sharing this *public* space allows individuals to engage, explore, and interact with each other across cultural boundaries without actual face-to-face contact. e.netizens view the Internet as a top resource to reconnect with long-lost friends and high school sweethearts, create new relationships, enhance global team creativity, and empower people through human rights and international support groups. College students can collaborate across cultures via online discussion boards or e-mails. Faculty and researchers who have never met each other face to face can engage in online collaboration and research projects across national borders. At the same time, however, with the click of a button, all these sounds, images, sights, and actions can instantaneously vanish. The individual can reclaim her quiet space or privacy in seconds. This peculiar sense of reality versus fiction exists as a blurry line in the virtual reality world. Too much in the tribal pole and one may find themselves addicted. Hartvig (2010) found that South Korea has 2 million citizens addicted to the Internet, a result of being one of the world's most wired countries. Boot camps to rehab citizens and break their Internet addictions are very popular.

Temporal Dialectics

The Internet has also drastically reoriented our sense of time. It contracts and expands space and time via its multichannel, multiclicking, and instantaneous screen-to-screen delivery format. It offers e.netizens simultaneous opportunities to move quickly back and forth between monochronic amd polychronic time schedules. Externally, e.netizens may experience tensions by constantly shifting between **monotrack focus** (i.e., working on one project at a time) and **multitrack focus** (i.e., tending to multiple e.net tasks or activities)

on the Internet. With regard to communication, individuals with monotrack focus can also often bump into misunderstandings with individuals who enjoy multitrack focus because of their multitasking habits on the Internet.

More specifically, *monotrack e.netizens* concentrate on one task at a time. While they are working on a task project on the computer, they may find it difficult to e-mail, text, and talk to someone right next to them at the same time. They enjoy the focused energy of mulling over the unfolding online news or watching a YouTube video intensely and reflecting on its implications. However, *multitrack e.netizens* can be quite adept at multitracking—working on multiple projects, such as surfing, texting, and blogging. The e.net multitrack individuals also adhere to a being-in-doing value philosophy. While on the Net, they can chat with friends across the globe, access daily newspapers in several languages, and download new song releases. The **being-in-doing e.net philosophy** means that e.net multitrack individuals can fuse the "being mode" value dimension with the "doing mode" value dimension—they can be fully enjoying the here-and-now moment, spending *being* time with their multiple friends on Facebook and Twitter, and also *doing* other task activities. There is no doubt that the e.netizen is a changed generation in terms of traditional cultural values and norms held by their parents' or grandparents' generation.

Although the e-netizen monotracker can focus only on one thing at a time and tends to compartmentalize task projects and relational *fun* chat on the net, the multitrackers can move in and out smoothly between task activities and relational activities in a split second. Which temporal pull do you move to? If you are at a baseball game, do you watch the game with a gadget in your hand? If you are monotrack, you probably do not and will take issue with your friend(s) who do. It is obvious that both monotrack individuals and multitask individuals have to make greater efforts to apply all the skills that we have discussed in this book to manage their e.net cultural habits adaptively and flexibly. Monotrack individuals must be aware that they may misread cues and offend multitrack e.netizens. Likewise, multitrack individuals must realize the dangers of doing too many tasks at once and not doing one with poise and mindful attention. For example, when studying, talking, and driving, Haddington and Rauiomaa (2011) found drivers are distracted when the phone rings: drivers avert their eyes from the road, take one hand off the wheel, and look for the phone.

As global cultures become more interconnected through technology and pop culture, the e.netizen identity reflects the dynamic interplay between solitary space and shared tribal space, with monotrack tempo and multitrack rhythm. To further understand the effects of the e.netizen, two specific areas will be discussed: communication patterns and self presentation.

THE TIPPING POINT: COMMUNICATION PATTERN CHANGES

Thanks to technology, we now find ourselves sitting more than ever. Our new communication patterns are based on the time spent sitting. We sit and watch shows. We sit and type. We sit and play games. All with an on/off button. How does all of these sitting and typing with computer keys affect us? Today, one in three of the world's adults is overweight and one in ten is obese. By 2015, the World Health Organization estimates the number of chubby adults will balloon to 2.3 billion—equal to the combined populations of China, Europe, and the United States (Cunningham, 2010). Another outcome is the compression of time: we experience time in bursts of duration and in staccato rhythms. We experience the farness and closeness of space via a simple push of a button: we can travel to Tibet or New Zealand right in our own bedroom with a virtual tour. This sense of compressed time and space influences the pragmatics of our communication: how we talk to others no longer depends on what particular channel we use or in what situational context. This free-flowing context can have both pros and cons in our face-to-face interactions with an actual person from that far-flung culture. We form virtual images of places and people that are seemingly familiar but yet probably still have an edge of unfamiliarity and unpredictability to them. What is clear is that technology has changed the face of our communication, whether it is face to face, language styles, or interaction patterns. We believe that

innovative gadgets have been one of the primary sources of change. In this section, we will discuss how technology has influenced our communication across a variety of contexts: language use, relationship development, and the workplace.

Gadget Communication Patterns: Fast and Furious

Gadgets have transformed the way we communicate with each other. A tipping point has been passed in the competition between print and screen that has been underway since the beginnings of broadcast TV and now continues with video and other media. e.netizens increasingly avoid newspapers (and books) simply because there is a clear preference for a fully formed video experience that comes ready to play on a screen, requiring nothing but our passive attention (Stross, 2009). In the past, individuals waited for the morning newspaper to read both international and local news, cutting out stories and calling friends and family on land-line phones. This extinct way of communication gives us the basic question to ask: How did we change?

Technology gave us an answering machine, pager, and fax to contact people across time and space. But the diffusion of the *mobile phone* is our game-changer, which came primarily from Japan. This gadget, the mobile/smart/iPhone (*msi phone* for short), is our champion distracter from face-to-face conversation. In the past, face-to-face conversations could last for hours. Now, our verbal conversations are short and specific. How much time do you spend talking or texting? According to Chung and Kim (2010), normal users spent an average of 209 minutes per day with their phone. The reason is thought to be an increase in functions like Internet access and mobile TV, games, and other applications. In fact, more individuals in the United States use only cell phones and do not subscribe to land-line service (Fram & Merchant, 2011). This ability for everyone to be connected quickly is now economically even cheaper. Youth aged twelve to twenty-four in the United States are more connected, more tech savvy, and more likely to use personal devices such as smartphones, laptops, and other gadgets for video viewing. Driven by lifestyle choices, this trend is likely to increase as the younger becomes the older generation (Nielson, 2010).

As a result, gadgets have changed the way we communicate. Common e.netizens and students often text others in class or friends located in the same room. Subways and buses across the world are filled with individuals hooked up to a gadget. No one looks at each other. Stops are missed because one can be highly distracted by the drama unfolding on their iPad. If you are waiting for a friend who is late, what is the first thing you do? No doubt, get your phone or a small gadget to distract you. Technology also influences how we talk to others in public. Texting occurs as a frequent source of communication simply because we may not want others to hear our conversation and the challenge to engage in civil social rules. Ling (2008) argues that mobile phones tip the balance of our interactions; instead of talking with strangers while waiting for a bus or in line, we engage in more intimate conversation with our friends and family members via our smartphones.

For the amount of time it takes to have face-to-face communication, the fast and efficient style appears to be the preferred method among e.netizens. With the ongoing growth in popularity of connected devices such as touchscreen tablets, eReaders, and media players, mobile apps are likely to continue to dominate our lives. Games are the most popular app category on all connected devices, just as they are on smartphones and feature phones, whereas the iPod Touch currently leads all connected devices in apps downloads. Why talk when we can play?

At the same time, gadgets allow us to communicate with others across time in space. Skyping is a way of life for some. Just imagine if the early immigrants who fled their countries because of war, famine, or romance had the Internet: would they suffer less loneliness and depression? Modern technology brings change—fast and furious, and, inevitably, as we approach the twenty-second century, we must develop a nimble mindset and a sense of flexible "being" to get ready for the onslaught of the next set of technological gadgets.

Sharing Intimate Partners with a Gadget

Given the fact that we spend a majority of our time online or with a gadget, it is not surprising that our relationships may be affected. Mesch (2006), for example, found that if an individual spent time online for social purposes (e.g., playing games, chatting, group discussions), there were more family conflicts. Indeed, as we spend more time with a handheld device, we can see the impact on our friendships, romantic partners, and marital partners. In a study conducted with newly married couples, Kerkhof, Finkenauer, and Muusses (2011) found that if one partner was a compulsive Internet user, the other partner reported low intimacy, low passion, and feeling excluded.

The lack of communication with relational partners is affecting the sex lives of e.netizens as well. In Japan, over one-third of men aged sixteen to nineteen had no interest in sex, double the figure from 2008, and over 40 percent of those married have been sexless for at least the past month (Martin, 2011). And in France, French women are becoming increasingly assertive in their sexual habits, whereas one in five younger French men "has no interest in sex," according to one of the most comprehensive surveys of the nation's love lives (Samuel, 2008). Kunio Kitamura, director of the Clinic of the Japan Family Planning Association, examined the findings, stating that the younger generation of Japanese males finds it difficult to have face-to-face communication because of the proliferation of cell phones and the impact of the struggling economy (Martin, 2011). In this global technological age, individuals' attention is much more diffused and diluted.

Language Styles: Text, Tweet, Talk

As we discussed in Chapter 6, everyday language serves as a prism through which individuals interpret "meaningful" versus "meaningless" events. One meaningful event has been the transformation of cultural display rules via the Internet. As we progress with our advanced technology, we often use truncated language and emoticons to replace long sentences, words, and expressions of our feelings with a quick keyboard symbol. This truncated style is now part of our everyday lexicon. In 1981, when the music star Prince released his fourth album, *Controversy*, his lyrics contained a single letter to replace a word, *u* for *you*. His innovative and future-oriented thinking became his trademark on lyrical writing, with another song "I would die 4 u." No one ever thought the day would come when his shortened writing would become our way of life.

Abbreviations, as with emoticons, allow us to communicate with efficiency and shared meaning, possibly as a result of text and SMS messaging. Some language rules for this form of communication are as follows:

- single letters can replace words, such as *d* or *da* for *the*
- single digits can replace words, such as *ate* becomes *8*
- single letter or digit can replace a syllable, such as *foreign* becomes *4n*.

Many are unhappy with this style, especially traditionalists. British journalist Humphrys growls, "It is the relentless onward march of the texters, the SMS (Short Message Service) vandals who are…destroying it: pillaging our punctuation; savaging our sentences; raping our vocabulary. And they must be stopped.…The danger—for young people especially—is that they will come to dominate. Our written language may end up as a series of ridiculous emoticons and ever-changing abbreviations" (Humphrys, 2007).

Another language trend in the Internet age is our shortened words and word combinations. The younger generation, updated with innovation, has given us words like *ridic* (ridiculous), *delish* (delicious), and *vacay* (vacation). Word combinations include *staycation* (stay at home vacation) and *fantastical* (fantasy and magical). Can you name famous couples whose names have been shortened into combined names? Let's play Hit-or-Miss 11.3 (for a bonus, who was first?)

HIT-OR-MISS 11.3 ONE-NAME COUPLES

See if you "Hit" or "Miss" by naming a Hollywood couple who share a name together. Can you guess which one was first?

1. _____ TomKat
2. _____ Bennifer
3. _____ Brangelina
4. _____ Billary
5. _____ Bennifer 1.0

Answers: Tom Cruise and Katie Holmes; Ben Affleck and Jennifer Lopez; Brad Pitt and Angelina Jolie; Bill and Hillary Clinton; Ben Affleck and Jennifer Garner.

The first: Ben Affleck and Jennifer Lopez.

How did you do? As with any trend, language is elastic and flexible. We should be open to the communication styles that are shaped and molded by the latest technological advances.

Communicating to Be Social Change Agents

The Internet has become a global town square of the twenty-first century. Open to all, social networking allows for active engagement and involvement. Australia leads the world in social media engagement, with the highest global average for time spent per month engaging with social media, averaging over seven hours per month. In comparison to other countries, 62 percent of Australian Internet users visited a message board or forum in 2009 (Nielson, 2010). According to Japan's Foreign Ministry, 116 countries and 28 international organizations offered humanitarian aid to Japan after the devastating earthquake, tsunami, and nuclear disaster. This quick global response is a reflection of the power of social networking: inspiring people to become proactive change agents. In 2008, the Obama campaign for the presidency demonstrated the power of social media to mobilize support and raise money.

Popular author Malcolm Gladwell (2010) argued recently that social networks will not lead to serious activism. By implying that Internet exchanges are not high risk, we believe Gladwell underestimated the power of e.netizens and tribal communities. Social networking has expanded our intercultural relationships and allows us to better connect with the rest of humanity. Social networking may bring deep changes in the way we relate to each other and the way we work together. MSNBC anchor Lawrence O'Donnell traveled to Malawi in the summer of 2010 to raise awareness: students had no desks or chairs. Their education was based on sitting on dirty floors. Mr. O'Donnell launched a partnership with UNICEF to create Kids in Need of Desks, expecting to raise a couple thousand dollars. Instead, within one week, he raised 1 million dollars! This story reflects what social change is about via social networks. "It has created new avenues for sharing, discovering and learning about the world around us. It brings users small moments of delight. And, as we've seen in the Middle East, it's played a role in organizing the unrest that's shaken even long-serving dictators" (O'Brien, 2011, p. 14).

The peaceful civic activism in Egypt occurred on the Internet in coordination with rallies in the streets. Global citizens united on the Internet to connect to one another, sample a universe of news and information, or make their voices heard. And through this kind of communication discourse, online or face to face, new dimensions of debates emerged: how best to govern, administer justice, pursue prosperity, and create the conditions for long-term progress, both within and across borders (Stevens, 2011). This transformative connection that the Internet provides has only added a dimension of ideas, innovation, and economic growth.

Present but Virtual

One of the fastest growing trends in the business economy has been virtual teams and meetings. Individuals across the globe communicate and collaborate across different time zones and geographic locations. As more companies and businesses are integrated with other countries (e.g., Hyundai in the United States and Korea), virtual teams make sense, reducing costs and increasing productivity. At the same time, there still exist many intercultural misunderstandings, mistrust issues, and language barriers. According to Horwitz, Bravington, and Silvis (2006), the most important factors for successful cross-cultural teams are improved communication, role clarification, and relationship building. Teams with advanced technology have more successful interactions with virtual members than teams that lack the advanced technology experience.

During one of our worst economic disasters in U.S. history, virtual meetings and teams are the wave of the future. Cisco currently conducts its conferences via online streaming. Businesses in the United States are adopting virtual video conferences and Web casts to save on travel funds. And in other cases, virtual games are part of the training for employees. One especially interesting example is the Virtual Cultural Awareness Trainer (VCAT), a four-hour cultural awareness gaming simulation created by a private corporation for use by U.S. military personnel. This Web game prepares soldiers for the appropriate cultural

awareness prior to deployment to Iraq, Afghanistan, and other countries.

As more companies ride the wave of virtual technology, one of the key communication outcomes is the tolerance for ambiguity. Recall from our language discussion in Chapter 6 that our verbal styles frames *how a message should be interpreted or understood*. Online communication in a virtual "digital" context makes it difficult to read the intentions, interaction goals, relationship types, and the situation. Ambiguity of style refers to delayed messages, misinterpreted actions, and camouflaged intentions. As flexible communicators, be open to ambiguity and uncertainty and even technological glitches as you engage in a virtual meeting.

PERSONAL IDENTITIES IN FLUX: THE GLOBAL FACE

As the winds of globalization sweep across cultural borders, one of the most important issues we can address is the issue of our personal identity. Who we are is a reflection of our interactions with others. Oftentimes, we may not be happy with our identity, choosing to question or compare ourselves with others. This is normal. Developing a secure sense of who we are takes time and inner patience, moments of struggling and experiencing. In an age where time is not a commodity, our self view can be transformed in an instant.

Aboujaoude (2011) believes that the Internet does more harm than good; it can appeal to our worst instincts. We can conceal our identity, speed though transactions, pick and choose news items while avoiding others. More importantly, he argues that the Internet makes us more like-minded. Making us like-minded is an outcome of the Internet. If we think about our time spent with technology and the Internet, we must consider the images that we receive on a daily basis—images of thin models, well-proportioned men and women, and products announcing enhancements or replacements for better living. How can we not be persuaded? As devout e.netizens continually stream these messages, we are fairly certain some answer to the call of change: the change of their image (see Blog Pic 11.4).

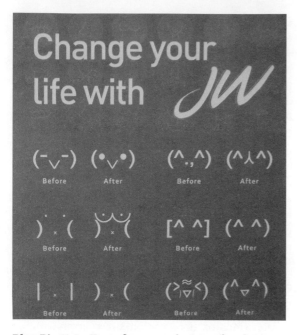

Blog Pic 11.4 Try to figure out the icons for plastic surgery in this ad. *Answers—across: eye surgery, nose, breast enhancement, cheekbone, liposuction, and Botox for the forehead.*

e.netizens are not only connected, but also chameleon-like. e.netizens have the ability to morph and fuse their identities based on recent trends and the "hot" factor. One outcome of this behavior is beauty, or the measurement of what is beautiful. Images that define beautiful are consistently discussed and ranked on Web sites, blog journals, and online communities. The constant rank of "hot" or "ugly" comes, inevitably, with our own social comparison. As more local cultures are choosing global image values, the ambiguous global identity is defined as the lack of ties to any particular local culture, but one in which slick Western values (e.g., materialism, violence, and consumerism) are privileged, among both men and women. Not wanting to be "unique," this global ambiguity is an indefinable image created for a common look. By taking the time to change one's looks based on Western magazines and Western products, this implies leaving behind local cultural standards of beauty. This pursuit of Western standards of beauty and disregarding of one's unique and culturally based physical traits may be one of the harms resulting from the Internet that Aboujaoude (2011) warns us about.

INTERCULTURAL REALITY CHECK: DO-ABLES

This chapter explored technology-driven, shifting value patterns and the development of an e.netizen global identity. The morphing of local and global cultures has been shaped in large part by technology, the Internet, and mass media. Watching television via multiple platforms encourages individuals to be a part of the pop culture movement, in particular, imported and exported television shows, hip-hop music, and fashion. We believe that the e.netizen culture started a new communication revolution that drastically transforms our sense of space and time issues on a global level. The dialectical challenges that e.netizens face in their contemporary communication process are issues of solitude versus tribal community and monotrack versus multitrack orientations. New generations of individuals have changed their communication patterns with others, molded by the gadgets used in everyday life. Living in compressed time and space, we have modified our everyday language use, we live in an almost-virtual world, and our relationships have the complex layer of a third-party crasher. Finally, our self-identity is vulnerable to the global images we see on a daily basis. We must take mindful pauses as we develop e.netizen communication flexibility by reflecting on some of the following checkpoints:

- Our identity is changing and becoming more fractured because of the Internet influence. Try to develop a deeper understanding with those who share our physical space and virtual space. We are now, in some select aspects, more similar than we have been because of virtual reality influences. There is a sense of shared common-ground community with others who live across the globe. Seek them out!
- Flexibility allows one not to become so Internet-centric or face-to-face contact-centric. Gliding e.netizens who may not be "technosavvy" must understand how the Internet can help them

communicate on a different playing field. Internet-centric individuals must learn from contact-centric individuals that their behaviors may appear rude by being too fixated into the newest techno gadgets.

- Try to understand that an open-minded attitude can help both fixated e.netizens and gliding e.netizens gain better insights into the other group. Remember—we learn most from people who are different from us. Creativity also blossoms because of diverse mindsets and diverse work habits.

- Be aware of the impact of the export of U.S. pop culture. Technology has blurred distinctive cultural lines. Be open to those who think they share aspects of U.S. culture (at least the tip of the iceberg of U.S. culture) and who form impressions and stereotypes about U.S. culture based on this exported, surface-level culture.

- Ask questions in a culture-sensitive manner! Do not be afraid to seek additional information when you are not sure about the e.net identity of another. Learn to be patient with globally fixated e.netizens and ask them to be patient with you.

- Because of the influence of different gadgets, we are going to communicate more and more with individuals who have diverse learning styles (e.g., visual, auditory, tactile/kinesthetic); we must be mindful of our own learning styles and also be respectful of culturally dissimilar individuals' learning styles and learning tempos.

Like it or not, technology is here to stay—learn to flow with it, play with it, adapt, and innovate—make it work for you, and not the other way around.

CHAPTER 12

HOW CAN WE BECOME ETHICAL INTERCULTURAL COMMUNICATORS?

CHAPTER OUTLINE

On Tuesday, January 12, 2010, at 4:53 p.m., a 7.0 magnitude earthquake struck Haiti ten miles west of Porte-au-Prince with its 2 million inhabitants. In the aftermath of the worst earthquake in Haitian history, Haitian authorities promptly arrested ten U.S. Americans who were attempting to bring thirty-three Haitian children to an orphanage in the neighboring Dominican Republic. It emerged that several of the children were not, in fact, orphans but that the parents of those children had apparently given them to the Americans willingly. The Haitian parents told reporters that they expected the children to be educated away from their families but not actually to be put up for adoption by the Baptist group from the United States.

The Idaho-based American members of the New Life Children's Refuge said that they were only trying to provide a better life for the children and denied that the group had done anything wrong. Meanwhile, Prime Minister Max Bellerive denounced the group's "illegal trafficking of children" and called it an "abduction case" because the group could not produce any Haitian government-issued paperwork consenting to these adoptions.

According to an age-old Haitian tradition, children from poor families in rural areas are often sent to live in cities with acquaintances or relatives. The Haitian Creole term for these children is "restavek," which is derived from the French words "rester avec," or "stay with." But critics of the restavek system say that it is closer to child slavery than any kind of foster care because many of the children are forced to engage in backbreaking work in return for their upkeep. A Haitian woman living in a tent after the devastating earthquake said that she could not support or feed her children and was prepared to give them to foreigners who could find good homes for them. What she would not consider, however, was giving up her children to live as restaveks.

Jean-Robert Cadet, a former restavek who set up a foundation to help such children, told Reuters: "A restavek is a child placed in domestic slavery." Mr. Cadet said that even today, "a twisted cowhide whip known as a rigwaz is still used to beat restaveks. It's the same whip that the French used during colonial times to beat slaves. You can buy them in the markets today."

—Adapted from Mackey, 2010

What do you think of this ethical dilemma situation? Do you think the Haitian parents were being cruel to their children by sending them away with the American group? What do you think of the actions of the American group? Were they taking advantage of a crisis situation or were they embarking on a courageous "orphan" rescue mission?

In any ethical dilemma situation, we have to make hard choices in considering the intent, the means or the action, the consequence, the end goal, the concrete situation, and the embedded sociohistorical cultural contexts of the real-life case. In an ambivalent intercultural decision-making case, in particular, we often have to make difficult choices between upholding our own cultural beliefs and values and considering the values of the other culture. Much of the complexity of an intercultural ethical decision-making process derives from the tension between whether ethics is a culture-bound concept or whether ethics should be understood apart from culture.

As cultural beings, we are socialized by the values and norms of our culture to think and behave in certain ways and to evaluate right from wrong actions. Our family, peer groups, educational institutions, mass media, socioeconomic and political systems, religious institutions, and historical traditions are some of the forces that shape and mold our cultural and personal values and also our everyday decisions. This cultural shared meaning system of "right or wrong" orientation often frames the outlook, interpretation, and evaluation of an ethical dilemma situation.

This chapter is organized in three sections. First, general contemporary ethical issues in global standard procedures versus local customary practices will be explored. Second, three intercultural ethical positions, namely, ethical absolutism, ethical relativism, and ethical universalism, will be discussed, and the central role of meta-ethics contextualism position will be explained. The chapter concludes by identifying a set of ten questions that we should all ask ourselves about ethical dilemma situations. Final passport "do-ables" will be presented concerning the continuous development of a set of principled personal ethics and the continuous practice of intercultural communication flexibility.

INTERCULTURAL COMMUNICATION ETHICS: CONTEMPORARY ISSUES

What is ethics? *Ethics* is a set of principles of conduct that governs the behavior of individuals and groups. *Ethics* has been defined as a community's perspective on "what is good and bad in human conduct and it leads to norms (prescriptive and concrete rules) that regulate actions. Ethics regulates what ought to be and helps set standards for human behavior" (Paige & Martin, 1996, p. 36; see also, Cheney, May, & Munshi, 2011). Thus, ethics is a set of standards that upholds the community's expectations concerning "right" and "wrong" conduct. The concept of ethics becomes more problematic and bewildering when the issue involves the interplay of global (or predominant Western) standards and local justice, corporate responsibility and local customary practices, and value clash and communication preference issues.

Global Standard Procedure and Local Justice Issues

First, let's check out a summary story excerpted from Adler and Gundersen (2008, p. 215). The story offers a dramatized critical incident to illustrate the clash of global standard procedures and local justice administration:

The Petty Theft Story
A major North American company operating in Asia discovered one of the local employees was stealing company property of minimal value...Following the company's standard worldwide procedure, the North American managing director reported the case to the

local police. Similar to many other North American companies, this company believed that it was best to let officials from the local culture deal with the theft and similar violations in whatever way they found most appropriate, rather than imposing the system of justice from their home culture. The local police arrived at the company, arrested the employee, took him to the police station, and interrogated him according to local procedures. The employee confessed. The police then took the employee outside and shot him dead.

Needless to say, the North American managing director was devastated and for the rest of his life felt remorseful and guilty about reporting the petty theft case to the local police, which resulted in the murder of a precious life.

As students of intercultural communication ethics, how can we make wise choices that reconcile the differences between global standard procedures and local justice issues? How can we leverage the laws, rules, and norms of the home-based environment with that of the local cultural setting? According to Adler and Gundersen (2008), in approaching the above "theft" case, we can start thinking of a cultural variability framework and applying it systematically to the following five-phase ethical decision-making model: *problem recognition, information search, construction of alternatives, decision-making choice,* and *implementation.*

In the *problem recognition phase,* we should learn to frame the petty theft case from both the North American cultural/legal standpoint and the local cultural/legal (e.g., "serious crime") lens. The cultural variability choice can range from problem solving/ change of attitude to situational rejection/acceptance. In the *information search phase,* the emphasis is on gathering multiple facts from different sectors of the Western and local cultures to gathering information concerning diverse ideas, possibilities, and potential consequences of "stealing." If the North American managing director had searched more closely for additional data, he might have uncovered the harsh punishment of death for anyone who violated the local law—whether the meaning of the crime is framed as petty or serious.

In the *construction of alternatives phase,* the emphasis is on how the North American company can craft culturally inclusive creative alternatives (e.g., deducting money from the employee's salary for a first-time offense and issuing a stern warning about corporate penalties for stealing) that reconcile its corporate integrity policy (e.g., "individuals can learn and change for the better") with that of the local culture's sense of underlying values (e.g., "once a thief, always a thief" notion). In the *decision-making choice phase,* perhaps forming a tripartite intercultural decision-making committee (i.e., members who comprise the North American region, the Asian region, and another third cultural region) to review the petty theft case might help to bring to light that the death consequence is awaiting the local employee if he were to be reported to the local police. The committee members may also want to rotate back to the construction of alternatives phase to bounce off some more creative solutions (e.g., devise a first-time warning system, firing the employee but not reporting the theft, demanding personal accountability of full self-disclosure, and/ or deducting money from the employee's year-end bonus). They may also want to slow down their timing in making a final decision about whether to report the theft to understand thoroughly the local legal and cultural punishment ramifications. The corporate culture may also want to be more intentional in assessing who should assume the primary responsibility for making the process decision and final outcome decision. For example, should the decision be made by an individual or a team-based approach? Should the decision-making procedure follow a top-down, sideways, or bottom-up process? Are diverse voices from different sectors of the workplace being heard and responded to in formulating a wise and productive outcome decision?

In the last *implementation phase,* the emphasis is on whether the new global corporate policy (e.g., implementing a first-time warning system for petty theft) should be implemented top-down (i.e., from the global headquarters) or involve the full participation and feedback cycles from subsidiaries from different cultural regions. Depending on the circumstances of each ethical dilemma case, a layered understanding of the relevant macro- and microfactors is needed to fine-tune our thinking, interpretations, process decisions, and outcome decisions of these complex dilemmas.

Corporate Responsibility and Local Customary Practice

Another set of contemporary ethical issues concerns the economically privileged position of a corporate culture operating in developing countries. Issues such as child labor, women's rights, human rights violations, working conditions, and corporate responsibility versus local discriminatory policies are also urgent ethical issues waiting to be addressed. For example, during the apartheid period in South Africa, many political groups claimed that international businesses had a "moral duty to boycott the apartheid regime—that is, either not to enter or pull out—while others, and in particular, the staying companies claimed that they were obligated to use their influence to better the life situation for the country's discriminated-against majority" (Brinkmann, 2006, p. 432). Perhaps with global corporate pressure and positive influence via constructive educational programs, social justice and other-awareness issues can be raised. More importantly, it is really through dedicated commitment and collective action of members inside the local culture who fervently want to promote breakthrough change that discriminatory practice in a national culture can be directly confronted.

On a more specific level, for example, on issues of local cultural hiring practices, Donaldson (1989) has developed what he describes as an ethical algorithm formula. He identified two conflict types: the country's moral reasoning related to the economic development of the country and the country's moral reasoning *not* related to economic development. In the first case, for example, a Latin American country has a lower minimum wage than in the United States because of its lower level of economic development. In the latter case, for example, hiring is done on the basis of clan or family network loyalty rather than based on individual merit. Donaldson's answer to the first case emphasizes that the practice is permissible *if and only if* the members of the home country would, under similar conditions of economic development, regard the practice as permissible. His answer to the "hiring family member" latter case entails two questions: (1) Is it possible to conduct businesses successfully in the local culture without undertaking this practice? (2) Is

the practice a clear violation of a fundamental international human right? The practice is permissible, *if and only if* the answer to both questions is "no."

Thus, assume that in Country X, a global company wants to open a manufacturing plant and in this country it is strict government policy that women be paid 50 percent of a man's salary for the same job. Thus, applying Donaldson's (1989) situational ethics formula, we can ask ourselves the twofold set of questions regarding this issue. The answer to the first question is "no:" it may not be possible to conduct business in the local culture and to pay women equally to men. However, the answer to the second question is "yes:" equal pay for equal work is a globally recognized right. Thus, the practice fails the overall situational ethics formula test (Brake, Walker, & Walker, 1995). In addition, Brake et al. (1995) recommend contemplation of the following questions in making a sound ethical intercultural decision:

(1) Are you ethically confident and comfortable in defending your action in both the private and the public sectors? Would you want your significant others, spouse, children, and parents to know about your problematic behavior? Would you want your colleagues and bosses to know about your shaky practice? Would you be comfortable if your questionable action were on the front page of a major newspaper or if it became the headline news of CNN?

(2) Would you want the same action to be happening to you or directed at a close member of your family? and

(3) What if everyone acted that way? What would be some of the cumulative harms? What would be some of the cumulative benefits? Would the resulting consequences be beneficial to the larger community or society on both the tangible and the principled ethics levels? Would the benefits sustain themselves without your corporate presence? Would you be comfortable teaching your children to act the same way? If you were designing an ideal global organization, would you want your employees to act that way? Are there better, more creative alternatives that rest on firmer ethical principles?

Cultural Value Clash and Communication Preference

The third contemporary issue concerns the cultural value clash of universalism and particularism (Parsons, 1951; Triandis, 1995). For example, Trompenaars and Hampden-Turner (1998) offered an intriguing critical incident to thirty thousand managers in thirty nations to respond to the following dilemma: you're riding in a car driven by a close friend, and your friend hits a pedestrian. The maximum allowed speed was twenty miles per hour, and your friend was driving at thirty-five miles per hour. Other than you, there are no witnesses. Your friend's lawyer says that if you testify under oath that your friend was driving at twenty miles per hour, your friend may avoid serious consequences. First, does your friend (a) have a definite right, (b) some right, or (c) no right to expect you to testify to the lower mph figure? Second, what would you do in view of the obligations of a sworn witness and the obligation to your friend: (d) testify that he was driving twenty miles per hour or (e) not testify that he was driving twenty miles per hour as requested?

According to the authors, if the manager's answer was a combo of (c) plus (e) or a combo of (b) plus (e), he or she was considered to possess "universalistic" value orientation, that is, a set of consistent rules should apply to all individuals, regardless of relationship types or circumstances. The general principle of what is legal or illegal, right or wrong, takes precedence over the particular details of who is involved in the particular situation. If the manager's response was a combo of (a) plus (d) or a combo of (b) plus (d), he or she was considered to possess "particularistic" value orientation, that is, the nature of the particular close friendship guided the manager's decision in protecting his or her close friend from legal harm and penalty. More than 90 percent of the managers in Switzerland, the United States, Canada, Ireland, Sweden, Australia, the UK, and the Netherlands claimed that society's rules were designed for everyone and, therefore, their friend had no right to expect them to testify falsely.

On the other hand, fewer than 55 percent of managers from Venezuela, Nepal, South Korea, Russia, China, and India made the same claim. Whereas the answers of the Swiss and U.S. managers reflected an "impartial" or "universalistic" value standpoint, the answers of the Venezuelan and Nepalese managers reflected a "particularistic" value pattern. Overall, the North American and Northern European respondents in this study tended to be more universalistic based and individualistic based in their decision making. Comparatively, the Latin American and Asian managers tended toward subscribing to particularistic-based and collectivistic-based value orientations in approaching the car accident scenario (Trompenaars & Woolliams, 2009).

The moral reasoning for the individualistic universalists stemming from the **"universalism"** viewpoint was, "as the seriousness of the accident increases, the obligation of helping their friend decreases . . . the law was broken and the serious condition of the pedestrian underlines the importance of upholding the law" (Trompenaars & Hampden-Turner, 1998, p. 34). Comparatively, the moral reasoning of the collectivistic particularists drawing from the **"particularism"** viewfinder was, "my friend needs my help more than ever now that he is in serious trouble with the law." As you can see, a rather straightforward critical incident such as this can generate multiple interpretations, dilemmas, and choices. Thus, a dilemma implies two equally compelling and competing premises, and an intercultural communicator must, at any given moment in time, select one of the two equally appealing or unappealing choices (Gannon, 2008; van Nimwegen, Soeters, & van Luijk, 2004; Williams, 2002). In reality, most intercultural ethical dilemmas have many layers of complexity, gradations, and nuances and are subject to different cultural interpretations from multiple spectrum dimensions.

MULTIPLE ETHICAL POSITIONS: ASSESSING PROS AND CONS

For the past fifteen years, interculturalists have struggled with the pros and cons of various ethical positions used to assess ethical violation situations in diverse cultural regions. These three ethical positions are *ethical absolutism, ethical relativism,* and *ethical universalism* (Ting-Toomey, 2011). This section will define each position and consider the merits and limitations of each viewpoint.

Ethical Absolutism Position

Before you read this section, take a couple of minutes to fill out the ethical orientation assessment (my.blog 12.1). Once you have determined whether you lean toward ethical absolutism or ethical relativism, read on.

Ethical absolutism emphasizes the principles of right and wrong in accordance with a set of

---

my.blog 12.1 DISCOVERING YOUR OWN ETHICAL POSITION: ETHICAL RELATIVISM OR ETHICAL ABSOLUTISM?

Instructions: The following items describe how people think about themselves and communicate in various conflict situations. Let your first inclination be your guide and circle the number in the scale that best reflects your overall value. The following scale is used for each item:

4 = SA = Strongly agree
3 = MA = Moderately agree
2 = MD = Moderately disagree
1 = SD = Strongly disagree

In making cultural judgments . . .	SA	MA	MD	SD
1. To treat each person consistently across cultures means fairness.	4	3	2	1
2. We should take cultural circumstances into account in making any judgments.	4	3	2	1
3. There should be one clear standard that all people in all cultures go by.	4	3	2	1
4. There are always exceptions to the rule— we should pay more attention to cultural insiders' viewpoints.	4	3	2	1
5. What is right is always right in all cultures.	4	3	2	1
6. What is wrong in one cultural situation may be deemed as right in another culture.	4	3	2	1
7. We should never be too flexible in applying clear, ethical principles.	4	3	2	1
8. We should understand the cultural contexts and customs before making any judgments.	4	3	2	1
9. Even if cultural circumstances change, rules are rules.	4	3	2	1
10. Without understanding the cultural traditions and values, we cannot judge fairly.	4	3	2	1

Scoring: Add up the scores on all the even-numbered items and you will find your ethical relativism score. Ethical relativism score: _____. Add up the scores on all the odd-numbered items and you will find your ethical absolutism score. Ethical absolutism score: _____.

Interpretation: Scores on each ethical position can range from 5 to 20; the higher the score, the more ethically relative and/or ethically absolute you are. If all the scores are similar on both ethical position dimensions, you hold a biethical value system.

Reflection probes: Compare your scores with a classmate's. Take a moment to think of the following questions: Where did you learn your ethics? What do you think are the pros and cons of holding an ethical relativist position? What do you think are the pros and cons of holding an ethical absolutist position? As a reminder, the ethical absolutist position can be an "imposed ethical universal" position put forward by many industrialized Western cultures to the rest of the world. Can you think of any current events that support or refute this last statement?

universally fixed standards regardless of cultural differences. Under the ethical absolutism position, the importance of cultural context is minimized. Thus, the idea of *universality* means that one set of consistent standards would guide human behavior on a global, universal level (Casmir, 1997; Pack-Brown & Williams, 2003).

Ethical absolutists believe that the same fixed standards should be applied to all cultures in evaluating *good* and *bad* behavior. Unfortunately, the dominant or mainstream culture typically defines and dominates the criteria by which ethical behavior is evaluated. Cultural or ethnic differences between membership groups are often minimized (Pedersen, 1997). For example, a dominant culture may view Western medicine as the best "civilized" way of treating a patient and thus impose this view on all groups. If a Hmong woman, for example, gives birth to a new baby and requests the nurse or doctor to give her the placenta, a Western doctor may find this request to be odd, strange, or bizarre and will likely refuse such an "uncivilized" request. However, within the Hmong culture, the act of burying the placenta has extremely important cultural significance and is related directly to the migration of one's soul and also to matters of life after death (Fadiman, 1997; see also, Ishii, 2009).

The positive aspect of ethical absolutism is that one set of fixed standards is being applied to evaluate a range of practices, thus preserving cross-situational consistency. The negative aspect is that ethical absolutism is a "culturally imposed" perspective that reflects the criteria set forth by members in the dominant cultures or groups (e.g., first-world nations vs. third-world nations). The ethical-absolutism approach often results in marginalizing or muting the voices of nondominant individuals and groups in both domestic and international arenas. It pushes a colonial ethnocentric worldview. Briefly, *colonial ethnocentrism* is defined as the rights and privileges of groups who are in a dominant power position in a society (whether it is at a political, economic, or social class or societal level), and these groups can impose their ethical standards on other nondominant groups or powerless individuals (Munshi, 2005; Ting-Toomey, 1999).

Ethical Relativism Position

A second approach, *ethical relativism*, emphasizes the importance of understanding the cultural context in which the problematic conduct is being judged. Under the ethical relativism position, the critical role of cultural context is maximized. It is important to elicit the interpretations and to understand problematic cases from the cultural insiders' viewpoint. The notion of relativism values understanding and evaluating behavior in accordance with the underlying traditions, beliefs, and values of the particular culture; these factors determine the evaluation of that behavior as appropriate or inappropriate.

Ethical relativists try to understand each cultural group on its own terms. They advocate the importance of respecting the values of another culture and using those value systems as standards for ethical judgments. They emphasize that *ethical* and *unethical* practices should be understood from a cultural insider lens (Barnlund, 1982). The positive implication of this approach is that it takes the role of culture seriously in its ethical decision-making process. It takes into account the importance of ethnorelativism rather than ethnocentrism (Bennett & Bennett, 2004).

However, the danger is that this view encourages too much cultural flexibility and ignores ethical principles that are developed beyond each cultural context. Thus, evaluative standards of ethical behavior are closely related to the conventional customs in each cultural context. These standards can then vary from place to place, group to group, and culture to culture. Furthermore, ethical relativism can continue to perpetuate intolerable cultural practices (e.g., female genital mutilation in Somalia and Sudan). Dominant groups in a society are often the ones that preserve cruel or intolerable cultural practices for their own gratification. They also perpetuate those practices that reinforce the status quo, which maintains its one-upmanship and keeps nondominant groups in subservient, powerless roles.

Ethical Universalism Position

A third approach, a *derived **ethical-universalism*** position, emphasizes the importance of deriving universal ethical guidelines by placing ethical judgments within the proper cultural context. Evaluations about "good" or "bad" behaviors require knowledge about the underlying similarities across cultures and about the unique features of a culture (Pedersen, 1997). A derived ethical universalism approach highlights an integrative culture-universal and culture-specific interpretive framework. Unfortunately, this is easier said than done.

Although a derived universalistic stance is an ideal goal to strive toward, it demands collaborative dialog, attitudinal openness, and hard work from members of all gender, ethnic, and cultural groups. It demands that all voices be heard and affirmed. It also demands equal power distributions among all groups that represent a diverse range of cultures. Furthermore, under authentic trusting conditions, representatives of diverse groups should also be able to speak up with no fear of sanctions. Most of the current "ethical universalism" approaches, unfortunately, are "imposed ethics" that rely heavily on Eurocentric moral philosophies to the exclusion of many coculture or minority group ethical philosophies or voices (see, for example, Cortese, 1990; Milhouse, Asante, & Nwosu, 2001). Beyond the Western codes of ethics such as virtue ethics, natural laws ethics, and utilitarian ethics and the occasional inclusion of feminist ethics, ethical codes from other cultural regions such as Confucian ethics, Taoist ethics, Buddhist ethics, Hindu ethics, Jewish ethics, Islamic ethics, Hispanic/Latino ethics, and pan-African ethics are seldom seen in mainstream readings on ethics (Houser, Wilczenski, & Ham, 2006). Ethical universalism is an ideal goal to strive for—especially when multinational and multicultural efforts have been made to include representative members from all disenfranchised groups to share their visions, dreams, and hopes.

Meta-Ethics Contextualism Position

A more reasonable, analytical perspective for guiding our ethical struggles in contemporary society may be that of the meta-ethics contextualism position (Ting-Toomey, 1999, 2011). This approach emphasizes the importance of understanding the problematic practice from a layered, contextual stance.

The term **meta-ethics** basically refers to the cultivation of an ethical way of thinking in our everyday lives that transcends any particular ideological position. A meta-ethics contextual approach means that the application of ethics can be understood only through a systematic analysis of the multiple layers of the ethical dilemma. Engaging in in-depth case-by-case analysis, individuals who hold a meta-ethics stance actively seek out panoramic 360-degree viewpoints on the ethical dilemma case. They also emphasize differentiated person-by-person considerations, situation-by-situation probes, intention-and-consequence comparative foci, and inclusion of macro (e.g., cultural worldviews), exo (e.g., formal institutions such as the court rulings), meso (e.g., media, community, or workplace standpoints), and micro (e.g., intercultural–interpersonal message exchanges) analytical lenses.

Subscribers to this meta-ethics contextual perspective tend to treat each ethical dilemma as a unique case with unique conditions and each context as a unique ethical context that deserves the full attention, effort, and time commitment of in-depth case analysis. Meta-ethics proponents emphasize the importance of systematic data collection from a wide range of sources plus the important consideration of taking the total situation—and the total cultural system—into account (Munshi, Broadfoot, & Smith, 2001). They also encourage the importance of cultivating creative options and seeking globally inclusive solutions to address these ethically wrangling situations. They try hard to move beyond polarized either–or thinking and advocate the importance of using human imagination and a creative mindset to come to some constructive resolution.

The strength of this approach is that it emphasizes in-depth fact-finding and layer-by-layer interpretations. It also takes into serious consideration the importance of culture, context, persons, intentions, means, consequences, and global humanism. The problem is that the meta-ethics contextual perspective is a time-consuming approach that involves a great amount of human power, hard work, fact-finding, and collaborative back-and-forth negotiation from diverse cultural groups. The plus side is that, in the long run, the time invested to understand a problematic practice from multiple contextual angles may ultimately help to save time and prevent further human suffering.

With clarity of understanding of the context that frames the behavior in question (on multiple sociohistorical, sociocultural, sociopolitical, socioeconomic, and situational levels), intercultural learners can make mindful choices concerning their own degree of commitment in approaching ethical situations. The position of meta-ethics contextualism is really a broader philosophical outlook on how an ethical dilemma should be conceptualized and approached. To prepare ourselves to develop an everyday meta-ethics mindset, we may use the recommendations from ethical experts (e.g., Moorthy, DeGeorge, Donaldson, Ellos, Solomon, & Textor, 1998) who outline the following preliminary procedures in analyzing problematic international business cases:

1. Collect factual data (i.e., before rushing to premature conclusions, check out the details and facts of the case from multiple, interpretive angles).
2. Consider the total situation and the cultural context (i.e., suspend ethnocentric judgment and be willing to see things from the other cultural frame of reference).
3. Identify the intentions and motives of others from three viewpoints: the intention independent of the action, the action independent of the intention, and both the intention and the action taken as a whole.
4. Analyze the weighted positive and negative consequences that follow from the intention and action taken together.

Good intentions are necessary for good action; however, you usually cannot know the true intentions of others. You can only observe their actions and infer backward. However, you do know and should systematically train yourself to know transparently what your own intentions or motives are for why you behave the way you behave in a particular situation. Thus, you can assume full responsibility for your own decision-making choices and, hence, strive to act ethically in both intentions and actions.

BECOMING ETHICAL INTERCULTURAL COMMUNICATORS: QUESTIONS TO CONSIDER

A *meta-ethical decision* is a discovery process, digging deeper into our own value system to find inconsistencies, resonating points, and creative problem-solving commitments. It also prompts us to gather multiple-level information to understand the reasons that give rise to problematic practices. After understanding the reasons behind an objectionable practice, we can then decide to accept or condemn such problematic "customs." Although some questionable behaviors across cultures can be deemed to be mildly offensive (and we may be using our ethnocentric lenses to evaluate such behaviors), other practices are completely intolerable on a humanistic scale.

You may also think of the following two questions in making a final meta-ethical decision: (1) Can you think of creative solutions other than the ones investigated? and (2) Is there any way to prevent similar ethical dilemmas from arising in the future in this culture? Grassroots movements and the commitment to change at the local culture level are two ways to eliminate traditional problematic practices.

In each problematic ethical case, we must mindfully place the ethical dilemma against our own personal standards and cultural judgments. We may not personally condone business bribery, but at the minimum we must understand the societal conditions that contribute to such a practice. We can then reason that "bribery, within this cultural context, is a common practice because of the following reasons..." or "unfair child labor practice originated in this cultural context because..." Once we thoroughly understand the sociohistorical, cultural, economic, situational, and realistic reasons for a particular practice, we can then employ imaginative solutions that can benefit the local people. The following meta-ethical guideline questions will further help you to clarify ambivalences you have about making informed and well-balanced meta-ethical choices and decisions.

In everyday life and on a personal level, we make choices that often have multiple consequences for our own lives and the lives of others. In the intercultural decision-making arena, we must mindfully ask ourselves the following questions when we encounter culture-based tug-and-pull ethical situations (Ting-Toomey, 1999):

1. Who or which group perpetuates this practice within this culture and with what reasons?

2. Who or which group resists this practice and with what reasons? Who is benefiting? Who is suffering—voluntarily or involuntarily?

3. Does the practice cause unjustifiable suffering to an individual or a selected group of individuals at the pleasure of another group?

4. What is my role and what is my "voice" in this ethical dilemma?

5. Should I condemn/reject this practice publicly and withdraw from the cultural scene?

6. Should I go along and find a solution that reconciles cultural differences?

7. Can I visualize alternative solutions or creative outcomes that can serve to honor the cultural traditions and at the same time get rid of the intolerable cultural practice?

8. At what level can I implement this particular creative solution? Who are my allies? Who are my enemies?

9. Should I act as a change agent in the local cultural scene via grassroots movement efforts?

10. What systematic changes in the culture are needed for the creative solution to sustain itself and filter through the system?

Let us take a look at Blog Post 12.1 and also Blog Post 12.2 in applying some of the above questions to a recent ethical courtroom case.

Use the ten suggested questions in your reflection on this story:

Other reflection questions may include the following:

• What is your connotative meaning for the term "honor?"

• Can ethics be separated from culture?

• Is honor killing merely a cultural problem?

• How do the notions of "face-saving" and "face-honoring" fit into this story about honor killing?

• How does the media taint the opinions of honor-killing related cases?

Many problematic cultural practices perpetuate themselves because of long-standing cultural habits or ignorance of alternative ways of doing things. Education or a desire for change from within the people in a local culture is usually how a questionable practice is ended. From a meta-ethics contextual framework, making a sound ethical judgment demands both breadth and depth of culture-sensitive knowledge, context-specific knowledge, and genuine humanistic concern. A meta-ethics contextual philosophy can lead us to develop an inclusive mindset and pave the way for a derived set of genuine, universal ethics. Struggling with ambiguous feelings and

---

BLOG POST 12.1   FALEH ALMALEKI/NOOR IRAQI AMERICAN CASE; PHOENIX, ARIZONA

The United Nations Population Fund estimates that 5,000 women are killed each year for dishonoring their families, and these numbers reflect reported cases only. Reports for the United Nations Human Rights bodies show that honor killings have occurred in Bangladesh, the United Kingdom, Brazil, Ecuador, Egypt, India, Israel, Italy, Jordan, Pakistan, Morocco, Sweden, Turkey, and Uganda. But there are also reports that the practice takes place in the U.S. and Canada, however, few of these cases are termed as honor killings and due to less media exposure we do not hear about it.

In October 2009, Faleh Almaleki ran over and killed his 20-year-old daughter, Noor (an Iraqi-American), in a Phoenix parking lot. He also injured his daughter's fiance's mother, whom she

had moved in with the previous year. After this incident, Faleh Almaleki fled the scene. Prosecutors said he attacked his daughter because he believed that she had become too westernized and that she had brought dishonor to the family. He had wanted her to stay a traditional Iraqi woman. However, she instead refused an arranged marriage, and went to college and had a boyfriend on her own.

After the parking lot incident, Almaleki fled to the United Kingdom via Mexico, but was extradited back to Phoenix to stand trial. The defense called the death an accident. They said he only wanted to spit on the boyfriend's mother whom Almaleki thought helped his daughter stay away from her own family. On April 15th 2011, Almaleki was sentenced to 34 ½ years in prison.

Source: http://www.cnn.com/2011/CRIME/04/15/arizona.honor.killing/index.html?hpt=T1

decisions while searching for the kernel of truth in an ethically foggy case is part of a maturing inquiry process.

BECOMING FLEXIBLE: FINAL PASSPORT DO-ABLES

To be flexible intercultural communicators, we must communicate with adaptability and creativity and develop a set of principled ethics to guide our everyday behaviors.

In delivering a keynote speech to an Honors Convocation Event, Stella shared her three personal principles that have guided her intercultural journey—from being an international undergraduate student in

America to becoming a U.S. immigrant in this adopted homeland (see Blog Post 12.3).

As you continue on your own intercultural and educational journey, we encourage you to identify and refine your own values and ethics (Ting-Toomey, 1997). To develop a set of personal principled ethics, we must constantly question our own intentions, actions, and decisions and the surrounding contexts that frame our personal choices. We also must learn to communicate appropriately, effectively, and respectfully in a variety of intercultural situations. To engage in flexible intercultural communication, we must take some risks and try out some new behaviors.

Concurrently, we should also make a strong commitment to consider the perspectives and experiences of our

---

BLOG POST 12.2 APPLICATION OF A META-ETHICS CONTEXTUALISM FRAMEWORK ON THE FALEH ALMALEKI/ NOOR IRAQI AMERICAN CASE; PHOENIX, ARIZONA

A meta-ethics perspective encourages us to move beyond polarized thinking so that we can make mindful choices concerning one's personal involvement in approaching this intercultural situation (Ting-Toomey, 2011). Ting-Toomey (2011) suggests asking these questions outlined below; see also the potential answers:

Who or which group perpetuates the practice of honor killing and why?

Honor killings are rampant all around the world. Reports from the United Nations Population Fund show that honor killings have occurred in many nonwestern nations, but there are also reports that the practice takes place in the United States and Canada. The practice of honor killings is perpetuated because of aged, patriarchal thinking against women.

Who or which group resists the practice of honor killing and why? Who is suffering?

Those who firmly believe in the basic human right of life reject this practice. Some may also argue that this practice is opposed by those that rely on Eurocentric morals and those that are trying to impose their views as universal; however, punishment for taking someone's life should be part of universal guidelines.

The judicial system and jurors in Phoenix clearly resist the practice of honor killing. But the interesting dilemma is whether or not the prosecutors seek the death penalty for Almaleki. He received 34 and ½ years of imprisonment for second degree murder. The main victims who are subjugated to this ill practice are women. However, we can also assume that all parties suffer, due to the emotional toil it takes on families as it tears them apart. It is important to consider what the males in the family have to deal with: consider that they may be pressured by external sources and eventually may have to bear some form of guilt. For example, his family or the Iraqi community

in Arizona may have pressured Almaleki because his daughter was becoming too westernized. Think about how and who gets to set these standards for women. Also, think about Almaleki's need to preserve his culture and traditions as an immigrant, something many Americans struggle with. Almaleki also stated that his daughter had "dishonored him" by living with her boyfriend. This external force and the idea of shame may have pushed him overboard, causing his family's demise.

Does honor killing cause unjustifiable suffering to an individual or a selected group of individuals at the pleasure of another group?

Yes, murder causes "unjustifiable suffering" to all parties involved and honor killing may cause unjustifiable terror to those women subject to scrutiny by those adhering to this practice. Almaleki may feel satisfied, because he fulfilled his duty to this group as his daughter had brought shame upon the family name.

What is my role and my "voice" in this ethical dilemma? Should I condemn this practice publicly?

Think about your role while reading this news story. Reflect on your demographics as college students in America, male or female, and your cultural-value system.

Should I find a solution that reconciles cultural differences? Alternative solutions to honor cultural traditions and stop intolerable practices?

Yes, education is the key. More important is getting the insiders' support. Because research efforts can be disconnected from the mainstream media, more efforts to promote collaborative dialog and appreciative inquiry are necessary. Collaborative dialog and negotiation from diverse cultural groups are required in order to gather culture-sensitive knowledge. There are several support groups online such as http://www.stophonourkillings.com.

Interpretations and answers prepared by N. Baig,
CSUF *graduate student*

intercultural partners on a global level. For example, take a look at the Blog Post 12.4 regarding the recent catastrophic earthquake in Japan.

We must also be willing to experiment with different styles of thinking, sensing, experiencing, valuing, behaving, and learning. In the process of changing our own approach to dealing with everyday intercultural communication, we can develop a more inclusive way of relating to individuals right next to us—in our classroom, workplace, and neighborhood.

We also need to practice more "**parallel thinking**." Parallel thinking means substituting any global or local event with people in your connected ingroup or intimate network and then cross-checking whether you would still arrive at a similar attribution process or a similar emotional reaction. Thus, for example, if you reread the opening story in this chapter concerning the Haitian mothers giving up their children for adoption to the American missionaries, if you substitute the "Haitian mothers" with your "own beloved sisters or best friends" in the scenario, would you still judge such action hastily or evaluatively? Likewise, if the American members of the New Life Children's Refuge were your "own brothers and sisters," would

you give them the benefit of the doubt and go on a fact-finding mission before arriving at a premature conclusion? Take another example, in the story in Blog Post 12.1, when we reported that Faleh Almaleki ran over and killed his twenty-year-old daughter, Noor (an Iraqi-American), in a Phoenix parking lot because she was deemed too westernized by her father. If you can substitute Noor as your "own sister" or your "closest best friend," would you feel more outrage at such "honor killing"? Would that prompt you to take social justice action or at least find out more about the issue of honor killing happening right in our own backyard? Practicing both parallel thinking technique and "perspective thinking" skill (i.e., stepping into the mindset and heartset of the other cultural person in viewing the same event) can help you to become a more flexible and compassionate individual in this global world. As His Holiness the Dalai Lama XIV observes succinctly, "If you think you are too small to make a difference, try sleeping with a mosquito."

His Holiness the fourteenth Dalai Lama also summarized his viewpoint on "Democracy and Peace" on his official website (http://www.dalailama.com):

Today, the values of democracy, open society, respect for human rights, and equality are becoming recognized all over the world as universal values. To my mind there is an intimate connection between democratic values and the fundamental values of human goodness. Where there is democracy there is a greater possibility for the citizens of the country to express their basic human qualities, and where these basic human qualities prevail, there is also a greater scope for strengthening democracy. Most importantly, democracy is also the most effective basis for ensuring world peace.

However, responsibility for working for peace lies not only with our leaders, but also with each of us individually. Peace starts within each one of us. When we have inner peace, we can be at peace with those around us. When our community is in a state of peace, it can share that peace with neighbouring communities and so on. When we feel love and kindness toward others, it not only makes others feel loved and cared for, but it helps us also to develop inner happiness and peace. We can work consciously to de-

Blog Pic 12.1　Be flexible and walk with peaceful thoughts.

BLOG POST 12.3 HONORS CONVOCATION KEYNOTE SPEECH, CALIFORNIA STATE UNIVERSITY, FULLERTON

It is my honor today to be standing here to celebrate with you this very joyous occasion and mark your stellar accomplishments and magical journey of arrival in this beautiful concert hall.

I have no doubt that many of you have overcome many obstacles, challenges, and hurdles to get to where you are today with joy and excitement. I salute YOU—all Summa Cum Laude graduates, University Honors Program graduates, and all special award recipients.

I also want to cheer on ALL your special family members, parents, intimate partners, and reliable friends—for I'm sure during your days of uncertainty, their encouraging words and soothing tones uplifted your spirit and motivated you to move forward.

There are three reflections I would like to share with you today. The First Thing is: Be ready to plunge into unfamiliar territory. Be prepared for surprises, unpredictability, and the thrill of discovery as you hike up the unfamiliar mountain in the next stage of your life. When I came to America as an international Chinese student more than thirty years ago, I landed in the middle of Iowa cornfields. I was totally lost, disoriented, and confused. However, I did persevere. To make a long story short, the constant culture shocks did test my own strengths and limits. However, you do learn more about yourself and your own priorities as you encounter the unknown and the unfamiliar. Take some risks and experiment with the unfamiliar. Learn to be playful, and balance your sense of self-discipline with imagination.

The Second Thing is: Be ready to take detours and enjoy the detoured scenery along the way. Your detoured trip may turn into a full-scale second stage journey. Honestly, I did not intentionally pursue the goal of being an intercultural communication professor. I had always thought I would become a television-film director when I was younger. My bachelor and master degrees were in the mass media area. However, my application to a Ph.D. media degree program was rejected. I took a detour and ended up finding my true passion in the teaching of and research in intercultural communication. Thus, a crossroads could be something stressful initially; however, the crossroads may lead you to a more vibrant landscape and terrain. Embrace your detours and challenges—everything will turn out OK.

Finally, the Third Thing is: Hold on to the precious people who help you to get to that amazing summit. As you trek to the top of the Japan's Mt. Fuji, or the China's Great Wall, or the Grand Canyon and take in the magnificent panoramic view, I hope you have someone special to share the breathtaking vista. At the end of the day, it's down to your beloved family members, your significant others, and your very loyal friends who are sitting here with you today who matter the most—they have gone through the bumpy and bouncy ride with you all the way. They have carried your backpacks and water for you. Create meaningful memories with them and honor yourself and your loved ones with dignity, joy, and appreciation.

CONGRATULATIONS and THREE CHEERS to all your hard work, tenacious spirit, and distinguished academic achievements!

Honors Convocation Keynote Speech presented by the 2008 Outstanding Professor, California State University, Fullerton, Dr. Stella Ting-Toomey, May 22, 2009.

BLOG POST 12.4

In March of 2011, one of the most powerful earthquakes ever, with a 9.0 magnitude, hit Japan. This earthquake triggered a destructive tsunami that killed over 15,000 people, with 11,000 still missing.

Professor Tanimoto from the University of Tokyo wrote a reflection about how the people of Japan are remaining civil and calm, because they have faith in their people and the government. He writes about the three-hour power blackouts and irregular metro schedules in Tokyo. But most surprising is how, he says, "most people seem to agree and are willing to share their burden. They trust that it's for the best. Along with electricity blackouts, the government is warning that water quality may suffer temporarily. Spurred on by my wife, I run to a convenience store nearby and find nearly empty rows of shelves and just ten bottles of water left. I am amazed that the owner is still selling the bottles at the regular price—$1 each—because I know I would pay twice as much. I briefly think about grabbing all ten bottles, but decide to buy just five, because I know others will need them. I also trust clean water will be available for me if I run out. Maybe my neighbor will provide it, and not the government, but I will have enough. I just trust I will."

The Japanese cultural value of harmony for the better of the group during this catastrophic crisis helps many of them get through this disaster in an orderly manner. In times of natural disasters it seems easy to become egocentric and ethnocentric against one's own people and make them the outgroup in a fight over scarce resources for basic survival. However, the people of Japan are making some other-centeredness and we-centeredness choices and taking the responsibility to help each other in times of desperate needs and emotional support.

Adapted from http://CNN.com. Retrieved March 25, 2011, from http://www.cnn.com/2011/OPINION/03/14/tanimoto.trust. japan.quake/index.html velop feelings of love and kindness. For some of us, the most effective way to do so is through religious practice. For others it may be non-religious practices. What is important is that we each make a sincere effort to take seriously our responsibility for each other and the world in which we live.

With compassion in the context of global human connection, we can all take mindful peaceful steps and spread peaceful thoughts to others. Do you recall the staircase model of intercultural communication competence in Chapter 2? Stumbling back and forth on the developmental staircase model and picking yourself up (and, hopefully, with your newfound knowledge and intercultural communication flexibility skills) and trying to walk again takes courage, humbleness, convictions, and open-mindedness.

We all are not perfect communicators, but we can constantly remind ourselves that we are works in progress. Thus, do not be discouraged—even the best intercultural communication specialists slip into intercultural accidents or puddles! The key is to be mindful of each step you take along the path and to try to refocus your energy and commitment to continue on your ethically guided intercultural journey.

A dynamic, flexible intercultural communicator tries to integrate knowledge, an open-minded attitude, and culture-sensitive skills and communicates ethically with culturally dissimilar others. The following quotation sums up the spirit of *dynamic flexibility:*

> The globally literate mind is a flexible mind. It remains agile and nimble as we learn to travel across boundaries and borders. Comfortable with chaos and change, it is able to contain conflicting and often opposing forces while creating cohesion and harmony from disparate parts. It's a mind that tolerates ambiguity and difference as it builds bridges across language, politics, and religions. And it's a mind that thinks and acts at the same time, all with a sense of tolerance and balance. By combining linear, logical reasoning with circular, systematic thinking, the global mind prepares us for the twenty-first century world. (Rosen, Digh, Singer, & Phillips, 2000, p. 174).

The dynamic, flexible communicator can swing comfortably from a low-context mode to a high-context mode and vice versa, code-switch from individualistic thinking to collectivistic thinking, hold both value sets simultaneously, and see the merits and filters in both value patterns. In essence, the dynamic, flexible communicator is mindful of the complex layers of self-identity and other-identity issues and is attuned to the situational context and the symbolic exchange process that flows between the two intercultural communicators.

We also must develop a sense of nimbleness to adapt to changing intercultural situations on a day-to-day basis. We should therefore take time to develop both analytical and emotional empathy to experience things from the other person's cultural frame of reference. For example, to be an ethical global leader, you can assume active responsibility at your campus or workplace to foster an inclusive climate and to cultivate a respectful vision for members from diverse walks of life. You can thus serve as a positive change catalyst to inspire others to learn about intercultural and domestic diversity issues in your very own backyard.

Finally, ethical intercultural communicators practice the following passport guidelines:

Blog Pic 12.2   Remember our stairs?

- Flexible intercultural communication is adaptive.
- Flexible intercultural communication is creative.

Blog Pic 12.3   Take the path to intercultural discovery.

- Flexible intercultural communication is experimental.
- Flexible intercultural communication is making detours and having the courage to try again.
- Flexible intercultural communication is knowing thyself on a continuous basis.
- Flexible intercultural communication is other-centered.
- Flexible intercultural communication is about identity respect issues.
- Flexible intercultural communication is the intentional development of mindfulness.
- Flexible intercultural communication is making hard, ethical choices.
- Flexible intercultural communication is a developmental, lifelong learning journey.

Blog Pic 12.4   Wrapping up the book and enjoying our pho (noodles).

IN CONCLUSION . . .

This book highlights some of the knowledge and skills that all of us can practice in approaching everyday intercultural situations. To engage in dynamic flexibility, we must be simultaneously adaptive and creative in synchronizing our words, movements, and breath with the words, movements, and breath of the culturally dissimilar other. Dynamic flexibility also calls forth our adventurous spirit and risk-taking abilities in reaching out to communicate respectfully with culturally dissimilar others.

An intercultural life is a creative life that demands both playfulness and mindfulness in transforming one's intercultural journey into a discovery process. Your journey may be filled with trials and tribulations and meandering paths. However, with the knowledge and skills presented in this book and with committed practice, you will surely uncover many hidden trails and unexpected delights. May you have the courage to experiment and to explore new terrain in your everyday intercultural walk, strolling and experiencing the diverse richness of the human spirit.

REFERENCES

Aboujaoude, E. (2011). *Virtually you: The dangerous power of the e-personality*. New York: W. W. Norton & Company.

Adelman, M. (1988). Cross-cultural adjustment. *International Journal of Intercultural Relations, 12,* 183–204.

Adler, N. (1997). *International dimensions of organizational behavior* (3rd ed.). Cincinnati, OH: South-Western College Publishing.

Adler, N., & Gundersen, A. (2008). *International dimensions of organizational behavior* (5th ed.). West Eagan, MN: Thomson.

Afewerki, F. *"looking at the world from my key hole."* 1995–2003. http://EdChange.org and Paul C. Gorski.

Agar, M. (1994). *Language shock: Understanding the culture of conversation*. New York: Morrow.

Alba, R. (1990). *Ethnic identity: Transformation of White America*. New Haven, CT: Yale University Press.

Allport, G. (1954). *The nature of prejudice*. Cambridge, MA: Addison–Wesley.

Almost all Millennials accept interracial dating and marriage. (2010, February 1). Pew Research Center for the People & the Press. Retrieved from http://pewresearch.org/pubs/1480/millennials-accept-iinterracial-dating-marriage-friends-different-race-generations

Altman, I., & Taylor, D. (1973). *Social penetration*. New York: Holt, Rinehart & Winston.

American Academy of Matrimonial Lawyers. (2010, February 10). *Big surge in social networking evidence says survey of nation's top divorce lawyers*. Retrieved from http://www.aaml.org/about-the-academy/press/press-releases/e-discovery/big-surge-social-networking-evidence-says-survey

Anand, R., & Lahiri, I. (2009). Intercultural competence in health care—Developing skills for interculturally competent care. In D. K. Deardorff (Ed.), *The Sage handbook of intercultural competence* (pp. 387–402). Thousand Oaks, CA: Sage.

Andersen, P. (2007). *Nonverbal communication: Forms and functions* (2nd ed.). Long Grove, IL: Waveland.

Andersen, P., Hecht, M., Hoobler, G., & Smallwood, M. (2003). Nonverbal communication across cultures. In W. Gudykunst (Ed.), *Cross-cultural and intercultural communication* (pp. 73–90). Thousand Oaks, CA: Sage.

Anderson, L. (1994). A new look at an old construct: Cross-cultural adaptation. *International Journal of Intercultural Relations, 18,* 293–328.

Applebome, P. (1996, December 20). School district elevates status of Black English. *The New York Times.* Retrieved from http://www.nytimes.com/1996/12/20/us/school-district-elevates-status-of-black-english.html

Archer, C. (1991). *Living with strangers in the U.S.A.: Communicating beyond culture.* Englewood Cliffs, NJ: Prentice Hall.

Asante, M., & Asante, K. (Eds.). (1990). *African culture: The rhythms of unity.* Trenton, NJ: African World Press.

Ash, R. (2006). *Top 10 of everything 2006.* Great Britain: Hamlyn.

Ash, R. (2011). *Top 10 of everything 2011.* Great Britain: Hamlyn.

Audit Bureau of Circulations. (2010). *Top 25 newsstand and circulation magazines 2010.* Retrieved from http://www.thewrap.com/media/column-post/newsstand-magazine-sales-slide-19986

Barge, J. K. (2006). Dialogue, conflict and community. In J. Oetzel & S. Ting-Toomey (Eds.), *The Sage handbook of conflict communication: Integrating theory, research and practice* (pp. 517–544). Thousand Oaks, CA: Sage.

Barna, L. M. (2009). The stress dynamic and its intersection with intercultural communication competence. In M. A. Moodian (Ed.), *Contemporary leadership and intercultural competence: Exploring the cross-cultural dynamics within organizations* (pp. 139–143). Thousand Oaks, CA: Sage.

Barnlund, D. (1962). Toward a meaning-centered philosophy of communication. *Journal of Communication, 2,* 197–211.

Barnlund, D. (1975). *Public and private self in Japan and the United States.* Tokyo: Simul Press.

Barnlund, D. (1982). The cross-cultural arena: An ethical void. In L. A. Samovar & R. E. Porter (Eds.) *Intercultural communication: A reader* (4th ed., pp. 394–399). Belmont, CA: Wadsworth.

Barnlund, D. (1989). *Communicative styles of Japanese and Americans: Images and realities.* Belmont, CA: Wadsworth.

Basso, K. (1970). To give up on words: Silence in Western Apache culture. *Southern Journal of Anthropology, 26,* 213–230.

Baxter, L. A., & Montgomery, B. M. (1996). *Relating: Dialogues and dialectics.* New York: Guilford.

Bello, M. (2010, April 15). Controversy shrouds Muslim women's head coverings. *USA Today.* Retrieved from http://www.usatoday.com/news/nation/2010–04-14-headscarves-muslim_N.htm

Benedictus, L. (2005, 21 January). *Every race, colour, nation and religion on earth.* Retrieved from http://www.guardian.co.uk/uk/2005/jan/21/britishidentity1

Bennett, J. M. (2003). Turning frogs into interculturalists: A student-centered developmental approach to teaching intercultural competence. In N. Boyacigiller, R. A. Goodman, & M. E. Phillips (Eds.), *Crossing cultures: Insights from master teachers* (pp.157–169). New York: Routledge.

Bennett, J. M. (2009). Cultivating intercultural competence: A process perspective. In D. K. Deardorff (Ed.), *The Sage handbook of intercultural competence* (pp. 121–140). Thousand Oaks, CA: Sage.

Bennett, J., & Bennett, M. (2004). Developing intercultural sensitivity: An integrative approach to global and domestic diversity. In D. Landis, J. Bennett, & M. Bennett (Eds.), *Handbook of intercultural training* (3rd ed., pp. 147–165). Thousand Oaks, CA: Sage.

Bennett, M. (1993). Towards ethnorelativism: A developmental model of intercultural sensitivity. In R. M. Paige, *Education for the Intercultural Experience* (pp. 21–71). Yarmouth, ME: Intercultural Press.

Bennett, M. F. (2009). Religious and spiritual diversity in the workplace. In M. A. Moodian (Ed.), *Contemporary leadership and intercultural competence: Exploring the cross-cultural dynamics within organizations* (pp. 45–59). Thousand Oaks, CA: Sage.

Bennett-Goleman, T. (2001). *Emotional alchemy: How the mind can heal the heart.* New York: Three Rivers.

Ben-Porath, E. N., & Shaker, L. K. (2010). News images and attribution in the wake of Hurricane Katrina. *Journal of Communication, 60,* 466–514.

Berg, M. V., & Paige, R. M. (2009). Applying theory and research: The evolution of intercultural competence in U.S. study abroad. In D. K. Deardorff (Ed.), *The Sage handbook of intercultural competence* (pp. 419–437). Thousand Oaks, CA: Sage.

Bernstein, B. (1971). *Class, codes, and control* (Vol. 1). London: Routledge and Kegan Paul.

Berry, J. (1994). Acculturation and psychological adaptation. In A. Bouvy, F. van de Vijver, P. Boski, & P. Schmitz (Eds.), *Journeys into cross-cultural psychology* (pp. 129–141). Lisse, The Netherlands: Swets & Zeitlinger.

Berry, J. (2004). Fundamental psychological processes in intercultural relations. In D. Landis, J. Bennett, & M. Bennett (Eds.), *Handbook of intercultural training* (3rd ed., pp. 166–184). Thousand Oaks, CA: Sage.

Berry, J. W. (2008). Globalisation and acculturation. *International Journal of Intercultural Relations, 32,* 328–336.

Berry, J., Kim, U., & Boski, P. (1987). Psychological acculturation of immigrants. In Y. Y. Kim & W. Gudykunst (Eds.), *Cross-cultural adaptation: Current approaches* (pp. 62–89). Newbury Park, CA: Sage.

Berscheid, E., & Reis, H. (1998). Attraction and close relationships. In D. Gilbert, S. Fiske, & G. Lindzey (Eds.), *The handbook of social psychology* (4th ed., pp. 193–281). Boston: McGraw–Hill.

Bhawuk, D. P. S., & Sakuda, K. H. (2009). Intercultural sensitivity for global managers. In M. A. Moodian (Ed.), *Contemporary leadership and intercultural competence: Exploring the cross-cultural dynamics within organizations* (pp. 255–267). Thousand Oaks, CA: Sage.

Bhawuk, D. P. S., Landis, D., & Munusamy, V. P. (2009). Understanding the basics of culture. In M. A. Moodian (Ed.), *Contemporary leadership and intercultural competence: Exploring the cross-cultural dynamics within organizations* (pp. 7–15). Thousand Oaks, CA: Sage.

Bianchi, A., & Sama, G. (2003, May 7). Brands enter lexicon in Latin America. *Wall Street Journal,* p. B6.

Biennial global survey. (2009). *International Society of Aesthetic Plastic Surgery.* Retrieved from http://www.isaps.org/stats.php

Bird, E. (1999). Images of the American Indian in popular media. *Journal of Communication, 49*(3), 61–83.

Bishop, J. (2009). Understanding and facilitating the development of social networks in online dating communities: A case study and model. In C. Romm-Livermore & K. Setzekorn (Eds.), *Social networking communities and e-dating services: Concepts and implications* (pp. 266–277). Hershey, PA: IGI Global.

Bochner, S. (1986). Coping with unfamiliar culture: Adjustment or culture learning? *Australian Journal of Psychology, 38,* 347–358.

Bogle, K. (2008). *Hooking up: Sex, dating, and relationships on campus.* New York: NYU Press.

Bolden, G. B. (2008). Reopening Russian conversations: The discourse particle-to and the negotiation of interpersonal accountability in closings. *Human Communication Research, 34,* 99–136.

Bond, M. H., et al. (2004). Culture-level dimensions of social axioms and their correlates across 41 cultures. *Journal of Cross-Cultural Psychology, 35,* 548–570.

Boucher, H. C., & Maslach, C. (2009). Culture and individuation: The role of norms and self-construals. *Journal of Social Psychology, 149,* 677–693.

Brabant M., Watson, B., & Gallois, C. (2010). Psychological perspectives: Social psychology, language, and intercultural communication. In D. Matsumoto (Ed.), *APA handbook of intercultural communication* (pp. 23–40). Washington, DC: American Psychological Association.

Brake, T., Walker, D. M., & Walker, T. (1995). *Doing business internationally: The guide to cross-cultural success.* New York: Irwin.

Bratter, J., & King, R. (2008). "But will it last?": Marital instability among interracial and same-race couples. *Family Relations, 57,* 160–171.

Brett, J. (2001). *Negotiating globally: How to negotiate deals, resolve disputes, and make decisions across cultural boundaries.* San Francisco: Jossey–Bass.

Brewer, M. (1991). The social self: On being same and different at the same time. *Personality and Social Psychology Bulletin, 17,* 475–482.

Brewer, M. (1997) The social psychology of intergroup relations: Can research inform practice? *Journal of Social Issues, 53,* 197–211.

Brewer, M. (2010). Social identity complexity and acceptance of diversity. In R. Crisp (Ed.), *The psychology of social and cultural diversity* (pp. 11–31). West Sussex, UK: Wiley–Blackwell.

Brewer, M., & Miller, N. (1996). *Intergroup relations.* Pacific Grove, CA: Brooks/Cole.

Brewer, M. B., & Pierce, K. P. (2005). Social identity complexity and outgroup tolerance. *Personality and Social Psychology Bulletin, 31,* 428–437.

Brinkmann, J. (2006). Business ethics and intercultural communication: Exploring the overlap between the two academic fields. In L. Samovar, R. Porter, & E. McDaniel (Eds.), *Intercultural communication: A reader* (11th ed., pp. 430–430). Belmont, CA: Thomson/Wadsworth.

Brislin, R. (2003, January 19). Culture clash: Understanding other cultures means moving beyond ethnocentrism and prejudice. *Star Bulletin.* Retrieved from http://www.starbulletin.com/columnist/column.php?%20id=2282&col_id= 19

Brislin, R., & Yoshida, T. (1994). *Intercultural communication training: An introduction.* Thousand Oaks, CA: Sage.

Brooks, D. (2003, November 8). Love, Internet syle. *The New York Times.* Retrieved from http://www.nytimes.com/2003/11/08/opinion/love-internet-style.html?scp=1&sq=love%20internet%20style&st=cse

Broome, B. J., & Jakobsson Hatay, A-S.(2006). Building peace in divided societies: The role of intergroup dialogue. In J. G. Oetzel & S. Ting-Toomey (Eds.), *Handbook of conflict communication* (pp. 627–662). Thousand Oaks, CA: Sage.

Brown, L. (2009). Worlds apart: The barrier between East and West. *Journal of International and Intercultural Communication, 2,* 240–259.

Brown, L., & Brown, J. (2009). Out of chaos, into a new identity: The transformative power of the international sojourn. *Journal of the Society for Existential Analysis, 20,* 341–361.

Brown, L., & Holloway, I. (2008). The initial stage of the international sojourn: Excitement or culture shock? *British Journal of Guidance & Counseling, 36,* 33–49.

Burgoon, J. (1995). Cross-cultural and intercultural applications of expectancy violation theory. In R. Wiseman (Ed.), *Intercultural communication theory* (pp. 194–214). Thousand Oaks, CA: Sage.

Burgoon, J. K., Guerrero, L. K., & Floyd, K. (2010). *Nonverbal communication.* Boston: Allyn & Bacon.

Burgoon, J., Buller, D., & Woodall, W. G. (1996). *Nonverbal communication: The unspoken dialogue* (2nd ed.). New York: McGraw–Hill.

Burritt, D. (2011, February 14). *Attention passengers: You are being watched.* Retrieved from http://www.news1130.com/news/local/article/183741—attention-passengers-you-are-being-watched

Buss, D. M., Abbott, M., Angleitner, A., Asherian, A., Biaggio, A., Blanco-Villasenor, A., et al. (1990). International preferences in selecting mates: A study of 37 cultures. *Journal of Cross-Cultural Psychology, 21*, 5–47.

Byram, M. (2009). Intercultural competence in foreign languages: Intercultural speaker and the pedagogy of foreign language education. In D. K. Deardorff (Ed.), *The Sage handbook of intercultural competence* (pp. 321–332). Thousand Oaks, CA: Sage.

Byrne, D. (1971). *The attraction paradigm.* New York: Academic Press.

Cai, D., & Fink, E. (2002). Conflict style differences between individualists and collectivists. *Communication Monographs, 69*, 67–87.

Canary, D. J., Cupach, W. R., & Serpe, R. T. (2001). A competence-based approach to examining interpersonal conflict. *Communication Research 28*, 79–104.

Canary, D. J., & Lakey, S. G. (2006). Managing conflict in a competent manner: A mindful look at events that matter. In J. G. Oetzel & S. Ting-Toomey (Eds.), *The SAGE handbook of conflict communication* (pp. 185–210). Thousand Oaks, CA: Sage.

Carbaugh, D. (1996). *Situating selves: The communication of social identities in American scenes.* Albany: State University of New York Press.

Carl, D., Gupta, V., & Javidan, M. (2004). Power distance. In R. J. House, P. J. Hanges, M. Javidan, P. W. Dorfman, & V. Gupta (Eds), *Leadership, culture, and organizations: The GLOBE study of 62 societies* (pp. 513–563). Thousand Oaks, CA: Sage.

Carroll, R. (1987). *Cultural misunderstandings: The French-American experience.* Chicago: University of Chicago Press.

Casmir, F. (1997) *Ethics in intercultural and international communication* Mahwah, NJ: Lawrence Erlbaum.

Chang, W. C., Chua, W. L., & Toh, Y. (1997). The concept of psychological control in the Asian context. In K. Leung, U. Kim, S. Yamaguchi, & Y. Kashima (Eds.), *Progress in Asian social psychology* (Vol. 1, pp. 96–117). New York: John Wiley.

Chang, Y. (2009). A qualitative study of temporary reentry from significant others' perspective. *International Journal of Intercultural Relations, 33*, 259–263.

Charon, J. (2004). *Ten questions: A sociological perspective* (5th ed.). Belmont, CA: Wadsworth.

Chazan, G., & Thomson, A. (2011, February 24). Irish Remedy for Hard Times: Leaving. *Wall Street Journal.* Retrieved from http://online.wsj.com/article/SB100014240527487038039045761524 22920009948.html

Chen, G.-M. (2001). Toward transcultural understanding: A harmony theory of Chinese Americans. In V. Milhouse, M. Asante, & P. Nwosu (Eds.), *Transcultural realities: Interdisciplinary perspectives on cross-cultural relations* (pp. 55–70). Thousand Oaks, CA: Sage.

Chen, L. (1997). Verbal adaptive strategies in U.S. American dyads with U.S. Americans or East Asian partners. *Communication Monographs, 64*, 302–323.

Chen, W. (2010). Internet-usage patterns of immigrants in the process of intercultural adaptation. *Cyberpsychology, Behavior, and Social Media, 13*, 387–399.

Chen, Y. W. (2006). Intercultural friendships from the perspective of East Asian international students. *Chinese Media Research, 2*(3), 43–58.

Chen, Y. W., & Nakazawa, M. (2010). Influences of culture on self-disclosure as relationally situated in intercultural and interracial friendships from a social penetration perspective. *Journal of Intercultural Communication Research, 38*(2), 77–98.

Cheney, G., May, S., & Munshi, D. (Eds.).(2011). *The handbook of communication ethics*. New York: Routledge.

Chinese Cultural Connection. (1987). Chinese values and the search for culture-free dimensions of culture. *Journal of Cross-Cultural Psychology, 18*, 143–164.

Choi, S., Kim, Y., Sung, Y., & Sohn, D. (2011). Bridging or bonding? A cross-cultural study of social relationships in social networking sites. *Information, Communication & Society, 14*, 107–129.

Chu, H. (2003, February 8). A South Korean star came out of the closet and fell into disrepute. *Los Angeles Times*, p. A3.

Chua, A. (2011). *Battle hymn of the tiger mother*. New York: Penguin.

Chung, K. H. (2011, January 21). *Top Korean pop stars are riding Hallyu's second wave*. Retrieved from http://joongangdaily.joins.com/article/view.asp?aid=2931261

Chung, L. C. (1998). *Ethnic identity and intergroup communication among Korean Americans and Vietnamese Americans in Oklahoma*. Unpublished doctoral dissertation, University of Oklahoma.

Chung, L. C., & Ting-Toomey, S. (1999). Ethnic identity and relational expectations among Asian Americans. *Communication Research Reports, 16*, 157–166.

Chung, S. K., & Kim, C. G. (2010). Influences of depression, stress, and self-efficacy on the addiction of cell phone use among university students. *Journal of Korean Academy of Adult Nursing, 22*, 41–50.

Church, A. (1982). Sojourner adjustment. *Psychological Bulletin, 91*, 540–572.

Clarke, C. H., & Lipp, G. D. (1998). *Danger and opportunity: Resolving conflict in US-based Japanese subsidiaries*. Yarmouth, ME: Intercultural Press.

Clarke, S. (2010, November 2). Fancy format pirouettes around the globe. *Variety Plus*. pp. A1, A3.

Cohen, R. (1987). Problems of intercultural communication in Egyptian–American diplomatic relations. *International Journal of Intercultural Relations, 11*, 29–47.

Cohen, R. (1991). *Negotiating across cultures: Communication obstacles in international diplomacy*. Washington, DC: U.S. Institute of Peace.

Coleman, L. J., & Bahnan, N. (2009). Segmentation practices of e-dating. In C. Romm-Livermore, & K. Setzekorn (Eds.), *Social networking communities and e-dating services: Concepts and implications* (pp. 233–265). Hershey, PA: IGI Global.

Coleman, S., & Raider, E. (2006). International/intercultural conflict resolution training. In J. G. Oetzel & S. Ting-Toomey (Eds.), *The SAGE handbook of conflict communication* (pp. 663–690). Thousand Oaks, CA: Sage.

Coleman, W. J., II (2007, November 28). *Accommodating emerging giants*. Retrieved from http://faculty.fuqua.duke.edu/~coleman/web/ColemanAEG.pdf

Collier, M. J. (1991). Conflict competence within African, Mexican, and Anglo American friendships. In S. Ting-Toomey & F. Korzenny (Eds.), *Cross-cultural interpersonal communication* (Vol. 15, pp. 132–154). Newbury Park, CA: Sage.

Collier, M. J. (Ed.). (2001). *Constituting cultural difference through discourse*. Thousand Oaks, CA: Sage.

Collier, M. J. (2005). Theorizing cultural identifications: Critical updates and continuing evolution. In W. B. Gudykunst (Ed.), *Theorizing about intercultural communication* (pp. 235–256). Thousand Oaks, CA: Sage.

Comstock, G. (1993). The role of television in American life. In G. L. Berry & J. K. Asamen (Eds.), *Children and television: Images in a changing sociocultural world* (pp. 117–131). Newbury Park, CA: Sage.

Cook, N. (2010, May 13). Where the jobs are: Amid the ongoing recession, freelancers are finding more and more work abroad. *Newsweek*. [Electronic version]. Retrieved from http://www.newsweek.com/blogs/jobbed/2010/05/13/where-the-jobs-are.html

Cortes, C. E. (2000). *The children are watching: How the media teach about diversity*. New York: Teachers College Press.

Cortes, C. E. (2002). *The making—and remaking—of a multiculturalist*. New York: Teachers College Press.

Cortes, C. E., & Wilkinson, L. C. (2009). Developing and implementing a multicultural vision. In M. A. Moodian (Ed.), *Contemporary leadership and intercultural competence: Exploring the cross-cultural dynamics within organizations* (pp. 17–31). Thousand Oaks, CA: Sage.

Cortese, A. (1990). *Ethnic ethics: The restructuring of moral theory*. Albany, NY: State University of New York Press-Albany.

Covarrubias, P. (2007). (Un)biased in Western theory: Generative silence in American Indian communication. *Communication Monographs, 74*, 265–271.

Crisp, R. (2010a). *The psychology of social and cultural diversity (Social issues and interventions)*. Malden, MA: Blackwell.

Crisp, R. J. (2010b). Prejudice and perceiving multiple identities. In J. F. Dovidio, M. Hewstone, P. Glick, & V. M. Esses (Eds.), *The Sage handbook of prejudice, stereotyping, and discrimination* (pp. 508–525). Thousand Oaks, CA: Sage.

Crocker, J., & Garcia, J. A. (2010). Internalized devaluation and situational threat. In J. F. Dovidio, M. Hewstone, P. Glick, & V. M. Esses (Eds.), *The Sage handbook of prejudice, stereotyping, and discrimination* (pp. 395–409). Thousand Oaks, CA: Sage.

Crohn, J. (1995). *Mixed matches: How to create successful interracial, interethnic, and interfaith marriages*. New York: Ballantine/Fawcett.

Cross, W., Jr. (1971). The Negro-to-Black conversion experience: Toward a psychology of black liberation. *Black World, 20*, 13–27.

Cross, W., Jr. (1978). The Thomas and Cross models on psychological Nigrescence: A literature review. *Journal of Black Psychology, 4*, 13–31.

Cross, W., Jr. (1991). *Shades of Black: Diversity in African-American identity*. Philadelphia: Temple University Press.

Cross, W., Jr. (1995). The psychology of Nigrescence: Revising the Cross model. In J. Ponterotto, J. Casas, L. Suzuki, & C. Alexander (Eds.), *Handbook of multicultural counseling* (pp. 93–122). Thousand Oaks, CA: Sage.

Cross, W., Jr., Smith, L., & Payne, E. (2002). Black identity: A repertoire of daily enactments. In P. Pedersen, J. Draguns, W. Lonner, & J. Trimble (Eds.), *Counseling across cultures* (5th ed., pp. 93–107). Thousand Oaks, CA: Sage.

Crystal, D. (2010). *The Cambridge encyclopedia of language* (3rd ed.). New York: Cambridge University Press.

Csikszentmihalyi, M. (1996). *Creativity: Flow and the psychology of discovery and invention*. New York: HarperCollins.

Cuddy, A. J. C., Fiske, S. T., & Glick, P. (2008). Warmth and competence as universal dimensions of social perception: The stereotype content model and the BIAS map. In *Advances in Experimental Social Psychology, 40*, 61–149.

Cuddy, A. J. C., Fiske, S. T., Kwan, V, S. Y., Glick, P., Demoulin, S., Leyens, J- P., et al. (2009). Stereotype content model across cultures: Towards universal similarities and some differences. *British Journal of Social Psychology, 48*, 1–33.

Cunningham, L. (2010, November 22). *Behold: the world's 10 fattest countries*. Retrieved from http://www.globalpost.com/dispatch/commerce/091125/obesity-epidemic-fattest-countries.

Cupach, W., Canary, D., & Spitzberg, B. (Eds.) (2010). *Competence in interpersonal conflict* (2nd ed.). Long Grove, IL: Waveland

Cushner, K., & Brislin, R. (Eds.). (1996). *Intercultural interactions: A practical guide* (2nd ed.). Thousand Oaks, CA: Sage.

Da Silva, A. (2007, March 7). Aloha has immigrants striving for citizenship: A study says Hawaii's newcomers are more likely to take steps to become American. *Honolulu Star Bulletin.* Retrieved from http://archives.starbulletin.com/2007/02/19/news/story02.htm

Daneshpour, M. (2009). Bridges cross, paths travelled: Muslim intercultural couples. In T. A. Karis & K. D. Killian (Eds.), *Intercultural couples: Exploring diversity in intimate relationships* (pp. 207–228). New York: Taylor & Francis.

Davis, B. (2010, November 10). As global economy shifts, companies rethink, retool. *Wall Street Journal.* Retrieved from http://online.wsj.com/article/SB100014240527487040499045755542 90932153112.html

Davis, W. (1999, August). Vanishing cultures. *National Geographic, 196* (2), 62–90.

Deardorff, D. K. (2009). Synthesizing conceptualizations of intercultural competence: A summary and emerging themes. In D. K. Deardorff (Ed.), *The Sage handbook of intercultural competence* (pp. 264–269). Thousand Oaks, CA: Sage.

D'Emilio, F. (2011 March 6). Italy tests immigrants on proficiency in Italian. *San Diego Union Tribune,* p. A10.

Devine, P., Hamilton, D., & Ostrom, T. (1994). *Social cognition: Impact on social psychology.* New York: Academic Press.

Digh, P (2008). *Life is a verb: 37 days to wake up, be mindful, and live intentionally.* Guilford, CT: The Globe Pequot Press.

Digh, P. (2011). *Creative is a verb: If you're alive, you're creative.* Guilford, CT: The Globe Pequot Press.

Dion, K. K., & Dion, K. L. (1996). Cultural perspectives on romantic love. *Personal Relationships, 3,* 5–17.

Dominici, K., & Littlejohn, S. (2006). *Facework: Bridging theory and practice.* Thousand Oaks, CA: Sage.

Donaldson, T. (1989*) The ethics of international business.* New York: Oxford University Press.

Dougherty, D. S., Mobley, S. K., & Smith, S. E. (2010). Language convergence and meaning divergence: A theory of intercultural communication. *Journal of International and Intercultural Communication, 3*(2), 164–186.

Dovidio, J. F., Gaertner, S. L., & Kawakami, K. (2010). Racism. In J. F. Dovidio, M. Hewstone, P. Glick, & V. M. Esses (Eds.), *The Sage handbook of prejudice, stereotyping, and discrimination* (pp. 312–327). Thousand Oaks, CA: Sage.

Dovido, J. F., Hewstone, M., Glick, P., & Esses, V. M. (Eds.). (2009). *Handbook of prejudice, stereotyping, and discrimination.* London: Sage.

Dovidio, J. F., Hewstone, M., Glick, P., & Esses, V. M. (2010a). Prejudice, stereotyping and discrimination: Theoretical and empirical overview. In J. F. Dovidio, M. Hewstone, P. Glick, & V. M. Esses (Eds.), *The Sage handbook of prejudice, stereotyping, and discrimination* (pp. 3–28). Thousand Oaks, CA: Sage.

Dovidio, J. F., Hewstone, M., Glick, P., & Esses, V. M. (Eds.). (2010b). *The Sage handbook of prejudice, stereotyping, and discrimination.* Thousand Oaks, CA: Sage.

Edwards, J. (1994). *Multilingualism.* London: Routledge.

Ekman, P. (2003). *Emotions revealed: Recognizing faces and feelings to improve communication and emotional life.* New York: Times Books.

Ekman, P., & Friesen, W. (1975). *Unmasking the face.* Englewood Cliffs, NJ: Prentice Hall.

Espiritu,. L. (1992*). Asian American panethnicity: Bridging institutions and identities*. Philadelphia: Temple University Press.

Facebook (2011). *Statistics.* Retrieved from http://www.facebook.com/press/info.php?statistics

Fackler, M. (2011, March 24). Severed from the world, villagers survive on tight bonds and to-do lists. *The New York Times*, p. A11.

Fadiman, A. (1997). *The Spirit catches you and you fall down.* New York: Farrar, Straus, & Giroux.

Farb, P. (1973). *Word play: What happens when people talk?* New York: Bantam Books.

Fassaert, T., Hesselink, A. E., & Verhoeff, A. P. (2009). Acculturation and use of health care services by Turkish and Moroccan migrants: A cross-section population-based study. *BMC Public Health, 9*, 1–9.

Feagin, J. R., & Feagin, C. B. (2011). *Racial and ethnic relations* (9th ed.). Upper Saddle River, NJ: Pearson.

Featherstone, M. (1996). Localism, globalism, and cultural identity. In R. Wilson & W. Dissanyake (Eds.), *Global/local: Cultural production and the transnational imaginary* (pp. 46–77). Durham, NC: Duke University Press.

Firmin, F. W., & Firebaugh, S. (2008). Historical analysis of college campus interracial dating. *College Student Journal, 42*, 782–788.

Fiske, A. P. (1991). *Structures of social life: The four elementary forms of human relations.* New York: Free Press.

Fiske, S. T., & Russell, A. M. (2010). Cognitive processes. In J. F. Dovidio, M. Hewstone, P. Glick, & V. M. Esses (Eds.), *The Sage handbook of prejudice, stereotyping, and discrimination* (pp. 115–130). Thousand Oaks, CA: Sage.

Fiske, S. T., Cuddy, A. J. C., Glick, P., & Xu, J. (2002). A model of (often mixed) stereotype content: Competence and warmth respectively follow from perceived states and competition. *Journal of Personality and Social Psychology, 82*, 878–902.

Fleck, S. (2009). *International comparisons of hours worked: An assessment of statistics.* Retrieved from http://www.bls.gov/opub/mlr/2009/05/art1full.pdf

Foeman, A. K., & Nance, T. (1999). From miscegenation to multiculturalism: Perceptions and stages of interracial relationship development. *Journal of Black Studies, 29*, 540–557.

Fram, A., & Merchant, N. (2011, April 21). Growing numbers use only cell phones. *San Francisco Chronicle*, p. A8.

Frankenberg, R. (1993). *White women, race matters: The social construction of whiteness.* Minneapolis, MN: University of Minnesota Press.

Freilich, M. (1989). Introduction: Is culture still relevant? In M. Frielich (Ed.), *The relevance of culture.* New York: Morgan & Garvey.

Furnham, A. (1988). The adjustment of sojourners. In Y. Y. Kim & W. Gudykunst (Eds.), *Cross-cultural adaptation* (pp. 42–61). Newbury Park, CA: Sage.

Furnham, A., & Bochner, S. (1982). Social difficulty in a foreign culture. In S. Bochner (Ed.), *Cultures in contact: Studies in cross-cultural interaction* (pp. 161–198). Elmsford, NY: Pergamon.

Galvin, K. M. (2006). Diversity's impact on defining the family: Discourse-dependence and identity. In L. H. Turner & R. West (Eds.), *The family communication sourcebook* (pp. 3–20). Thousand Oaks, CA: Sage.

Gannon, M. J. (2008). *Paradoxes of culture and globalization.* Los Angeles, CA: Sage.

Gannon, M., & Pillai, R. (2010). *Understanding global cultures: Metaphorical journeys through 28 nations, clusters of nations, and continents* (4th ed.). Thousand Oaks, CA: Sage.

Gao, G. (1991). Stability in romantic relationships in China and the United States. In S. Ting-Toomey & F. Korzenny (Eds.), *Cross-cultural interpersonal communication* (pp. 99–116). Newbury Park, CA: Sage.

Gao, G., & Ting-Toomey, S. (1998). *Communicating effectively with the Chinese.* Thousand Oaks, CA: Sage.

Garcia, W. R. (1996). Respeto: A Mexican base for interpersonal relationships. In W. Gudykunst, S. Ting-Toomey, & T. Nishida (Eds.), *Communication in personal relationships across cultures* (pp. 137–155). Thousand Oaks, CA: Sage.

Gardenswartz, L., & Rowe, A. (1998). *Managing diversity in health care.* San Francisco: Jossey–Bass.

Gardenswartz, L., & Rowe, A. (2009). The effective management of cultural diversity. In M. A. Moodian (Ed.), *Contemporary leadership and intercultural competence: Exploring the cross-cultural dynamics within organizations* (pp. 35–43). Thousand Oaks, CA: Sage.

Gareis, E. (2000). Intercultural friendship: Five case studies of German students in the USA. *Journal of Intercultural Studies, 21,* 67–91.

Gauthier-Villars, D. (2009, July 24). Mon Dieu! Sunday work hours upset French devotion to rest. *The Wall Street Journal,* p. A11.

Gibbs, J., Ellison, N., & Lai, C. (2011). First comes love, then comes Google: An investigation of uncertainty reduction strategies and self-disclosure in online dating. *Communication Research, 38,* 70–100.

Gitanjali. (1994). Second generation; once removed. In C. Camper (Ed.), *Miscegenation blues: Voices of mixed race women* [Interview excerpt: p. 133.]. Toronto, Canada: Sister Voices.

Gladwell, M. (2010, October 4). Small Change: Why the revolution will not be tweeted. *The New York Times.* Retrieved from http://www.nytimes.com/2011/02/22/technology/22iht-broadband22.html?_r=4

Glenn, C. L., & Cunningham, L. J. (2009). The power of black magic: The magical Negro and White salvation in film. *Journal of Black Studies, 40,* 135–152.

Glenn, F. (1981). *Man and mankind: Conflict and communication between cultures.* Norwood, NJ: Ablex.

Global mobility effectiveness survey. (2009). Ernst & Young. Retrieved from http://www.ey.com/Publication/vwLUAssets/Global_Mobility_Effectiveness_Survey_2010/$File/Global_mobility.pdf

Global trends relocation survey. (2010). Retrieved from http://www.articles.totallyexpat.com/global-relocation-trends-survey-2010/

Gold, M. (2009, October 27). Kids watch more than a day of TV each week. *Los Angeles Times.* Retrieved from http://articles.latimes.com/2009/oct/27/entertainment/et-kids-tv27

Goleman, D., Boyatzis, R., & McKee, A. (2002). *Primal leadership: Realizing the power of emotional intelligence.* Boston: Harvard Business School Press.

Gonzalez, A., Houston, M., & Chen, V. (Eds.). (20042011). *Our voices: Essays in culture, ethnicity, and communication* (4thFifth ed.). Los AngelesNew York: RoxburyOxford University Press.

Gottman, J., & Silver, N. (1999). *The seven principles for making marriage work.* New York: Crown.

Granovetter, M. (1973). The strength of weak ties. *American Journal of Sociology, 78,* 1360–1380.

Gudykunst, W. (2003). Intercultural communication theories. In W. Gudykunst (Ed.), *Cross-cultural and intercultural communication* (pp. 167–190). Thousand Oaks, CA: Sage.

Gudykunst, W. (2004). *Bridging differences: Effective intergroup communication* (4th ed.). Thousand Oaks, CA: Sage.

Gudykunst, W.B. (2001). Anxiety, uncertainty, and perceived effectiveness of communication across relationships and cultures. *International Journal of Intercultural Relations, 25(1),* 55–71.

Gudykunst, W. B. (2005a). An anxiety/uncertainty management (AUM) theory of effective communication: Making the mesh of the net finer. In W. B. Gudykunst (Ed.), *Theorizing about intercultural communication* (pp. 281–322). Thousand Oaks, CA: Sage.

Gudykunst, W. B. (2005b). An anxiety/uncertainty management (AUM) theory of strangers' intercultural adjustment. In W. B. Gudykunst (Ed.), *Theorizing about intercultural communication* (pp. 419–458). Thousand Oaks, CA: Sage.

Gudykunst, W., & Ting-Toomey, S., with Chua, E. (1988). *Culture and interpersonal communication.* Newbury Park, CA: Sage.

Gudykunst, W., Matsumoto, Y., Ting-Toomey, S., Nishida, T., Kim, K. S., & Heyman, S. (1996). The influence of cultural individualism–collectivism, self construals, and individual values on communication styles across cultures. *Human Communication Research, 22,* 510–543.

Guerrero, L., Andersen, P. A., & Afifi, W. (2010). *Close encounters: Communication in relationships* (3rd ed.). Thousand Oaks, CA: Sage.

Gullahorn, J. T., & Gullahorn, J. E. (1963). An extension of the U-curve hypothesis. *Journal of Social Issues, 19,* 33–47.

Guo-Ming, C., & Ran, A. (2009). A Chinese model of intercultural leadership competence. In D. K. Deardorff (Ed.), *The Sage handbook of intercultural competence* (pp. 196–208). Thousand Oaks, CA: Sage.

Gupta, S. R. (2009). Beyond borders: Leading in today's multicultural world. In M. A. Moodian (Ed.), *Contemporary leadership and intercultural competence: Exploring the cross-cultural dynamics within organizations* (pp. 145–158). Thousand Oaks, CA: Sage.

Haddington, P., & Rauniomaa, M. (2011). Technologies, multitasking and driving. *Human Communication Research, 37,* 223–254.

Hall, E. T. (1959). *The silent language.* New York: Doubleday.

Hall, E. T. (1966). *The hidden dimension* (2nd ed.). Garden City, NY: Anchor/Doubleday.

Hall, E. T. (1976). *Beyond culture.* New York: Doubleday.

Hall, E. T. (1983). *The dance of life.* New York: Doubleday.

Hall, E. T., & Hall, M. (1987). *Hidden differences: Doing business with the Japanese.* Garden City, NY: Anchor/Doubleday.

Halualani, R. T. (2008). "Where exactly is the Pacific?": Global migrations, diasporic movements, and intercultural communication. *Journal of International and Intercultural Communication, 1,* 3–22.

Halualani, R. T. (2010). Intercultural and interaction at a multicultural university: Students' definitions and sensemakings of intercultural interaction. *Journal of International and Intercultural Communication, 3,* 304–324.

Hammer, M. R. (2009). Solving problems and resolving conflict using the intercultural conflict style model and inventory. In M. A. Moodian (Ed.), *Contemporary leadership and intercultural competence: Exploring the cross-cultural dynamics within organizations* (pp. 219–231). Thousand Oaks, CA: Sage.

Harb, C., & Smith, P. (2008). Self-construals across cultures: Beyond independence–interdependence. *Journal of Cross-Cultural Psychology, 39,* 178–197.

Harris, I. M., & Shuster, A. L. (Eds.). (2007). *Global directory of peace studies and conflict resolution programs.* Retrieved from http://www.peacejusticestudies.org

Hartvig, N. (2010, March 25). *Virtually addicted: Weaning Koreans off their wired world.* Retrieved from http://www.cnn.com/2010/TECH/03/25/online.gaming.addic tion/index.html?iref=allsearch.

Haslam, S. A., & Dovidio, J. F. (2010). Prejudice. In J. M. Levine & M. A. Hogg, (Eds.), *Encyclopedia of group processes and intergroup relations* (Vol. 2, pp. 655–660). Thousand Oaks, CA: Sage.

Haslett, B. (1989). Communication and language acquisition within a cultural context. In S. Ting-Toomey & F. Korzenny (Eds.), *Language, communication, and culture.* (pp. 19–34). Newbury Park, CA: Sage.

Hawley, C. (2010, April 8). Crews fight flooding crisis in Mexico City. *USA Today.* Retrieved from http://www.usatoday.com/news/world/2010-04-08-sinking-city_N.htm

Hecht, M., Collier, M. J., & Ribeau, S. (1993). *African American communication: Ethnic identity and cultural interpretation.* Newbury Park, CA: Sage.

Hecht, M., & Ribeau, S. (1984). Sociocultural roots of ethnic identity. *Journal of Black Studies, 21,* 501–513.

Hecht, M., Ribeau, S., & Sedano, M. (1990). A Mexican American perspective on interethnic communication. *International Journal of Intercultural Relations, 14,* 31–55.

Helms, J. (Ed.). (1993). *Black and white racial identity: Theory, research, and practice.* Westport, CT: Praeger.

Hickson, M., III, Stacks, D., & Moore, N.-J. (2004). *Nonverbal communication: Studies and application* (4th ed.). Los Angeles: Roxbury.

Hof, R. D., McWilliams, G., & Saveri, G. (1998, June 22). The "click here" economy. *Business Week,* pp. 122–128.

Hofstede, G. (1991). *Cultures and organizations: Software of the mind.* London: McGraw–Hill.

Hofstede, G. (1998). *Masculinity and femininity: The taboo dimension of national culture.* Thousand Oaks, CA: Sage.

Hofstede, G. (2001). *Culture's consequences: Comparing values, behaviors, institutions, and organizations across nations* (2nd ed.). Thousand Oaks, CA: Sage.

Hofstede, G. J. (2009). The moral circle in intercultural competence. In D. K. Deardorff (Ed.), *The Sage handbook of intercultural competence* (pp. 85–99). Thousand Oaks, CA: Sage.

Hofstede, G., & Hofstede, G. J. (2005). *Cultures and organizations: Software of the mind* (Revised and expanded 2nd ed.). New York: McGraw–Hill.

Hofstede, G., & McCrae, R. R. (2004). Personality and culture revisited: Linking traits and dimensions of culture. *Cross-Cultural Research, 38,* 52–88.

Holmes, P. (2005). Ethnic Chinese students' communication with cultural others in a New Zealand university. *Communication Education, 54,* 289–311.

Horwitz, F., Bravington, D., & Silvis, U. (2006). The promise of virtual teams: Identifying key factors in effectiveness and failure. *Journal of European Industrial Training, 30,* 472–494.

House, R. J., Hanges, P. J., Javidan, M., Dorfman, P. W., & Gupta, V. (2004). *Leadership, culture, and organizations: The GLOBE Study of 62 Societies.* Thousand Oaks, CA: Sage.

Houser, R., Wilczenski, F. L., & Ham, M. (2006). *Culturally relevant ethical decision-making in counseling.* Thousand Oaks, CA: Sage.

Howell, W. (1982). *The empathic communicator.* Belmont, CA: Wadsworth.

Hulu continues ascent in U.S. online video market, breaking into top 3 properties by videos viewed for first time in March (2009, April 28). Retrieved from http://www.comscore.com/Press_Events/Press_Releases/2009

Humphrys, J. (2007, September 24). *I h8 txt msgs: How texting is wrecking our language.* Retrieved from http://www.dailymail.co.uk/news/article-483511/I-h8-txt-msgs-How-texting-wrecking-language.html#ixzz1LEn8ef9H

Hurh, W. M., & Kim, K. C. (1984). *Korean immigrants in America: A structural analysis of ethnic confinement and adhesive adaptation.* Cranbury, NJ: Associated University Presses.

Hvistendahl, M. (2008, March 25). China's Three Gorges Dam: An environmental catastrophe? *Scientific American*. Retrieved from http://www.scientificamerican.com/article.cfm?id=chinas-three-gorges-dam-disaster

Hyatt, L., Evans, L. A., & Haque, M. M. (2009). Leading across cultures: Designing a learning agenda for global praxis. In M. A. Moodian (Ed.), *Contemporary leadership and intercultural competence: Exploring the cross-cultural dynamics within organizations* (pp. 111–123). Thousand Oaks, CA: Sage.

Hymes, D. (1972). Models of the interaction of language and social life. In J. Gumperz & D. Hymes (Eds.), *Directions in sociolinguistics: The ethnography of communication* (pp. 3–47). New York: Holt, Rinehart & Winston.

Imahori, T. T., & Cupach, W. (2005). Identity management theory: Facwork in intercultural relationships. In W. B. Gudykunst (Ed.), *Theorizing about intercultural communication* (pp. 195–210). Thousand Oaks, CA: Sage.

Institute for International Education. (2011, March) *Open doors fast facts 2010*. Retrieved from http://www.iie.org/en/Research-and-Publications/Open-Doors/Data/US-Study-Abroad/Leading-Destinations/2007–09

Internet World Stats: Usage and Population Statistics. (2011, April). Retrieved from http://www.internetworldstats.com/

Iolana, P. (2006, March/April). *Tutu Pele: The living goddess of Haw'i'i's volcanoes*. Retrieved from http://oceanseminarycollege.academia.edu/PatriciaIolana/Papers/108678/TuTu_Pele_The_Living_Goddess_of_Hawaiis_Volcanoes

Ishii, S. (2009). Conceptualising Asian communication ethics: A Buddhist perspective. *Journal of Multicultural Discourses, 4*, 49–60.

Iyengar, S. (2010). *The art of choosing*. New York: Twelve-Hachette Group.

Iyer, P. (1989). *Video night in Kathmandu and other reports from the not-so-Far-East.* New York: Vintage Departures.

Jack, R. E., Blais, C., Scheepers, C., Schyns, P. G., & Caldara, R. (2009). Cultural confusions show that facial expressions are not universal. *Current Biology, 19*, 1543–1548.

Jackson, R. (1999). *The negotiation of cultural identity.* Westport, CT: Praeger.

Jackson, R. L. (2002). Cultural contracts theory: Toward an understanding of identity negotiation. *Communication Quarterly, 50 (No. 3 & 4)*, 359–367.

Jiang, C. C. (2011, April 25). Why more Chinese singles are looking for love online. *Time*. Retrieved from http://www.time.com/time/world/article/0,8599,2055996,00.html?xid=rss-fullworld-yahoo?xid=huffpo-direct

Jiang, L. C., Bazarova, N. N., & Hancock, J. T. (2011). The disclosure-intimacy link in computer-mediated communication: An attributional extension of the hyperpersonal model. *Human Communication Research, 37*, 58–77.

Johnson, D. W. (1986). *Reaching out: Interpersonal effectiveness and self- actualization* (3rd ed.). Englewood Cliffs, NJ: Prentice Hall.

Johnson, M. (1991). Commitment to personal relationships. In W. Jones & D. Perlman (Eds.), *Advances in personal relationship* (pp. 117–143). London: Kingsley.

Jones, J. (1997). *Prejudice and racism* (2nd ed.). New York: McGraw–Hill.

Joseph, A. L., & Afifi, T. D. (2010). Military wives' stressful disclosure to their deployed husbands: The role of protective buffering. *Journal of Applied Communication Research, 38*, 386–411.

Kakissis, J. (2011, January 4). Greece turns against migrants as economy collapses. *National Public Radio*. Retrieved from http://www.npr.org/2011/01/04/132643887/Greece-Turns-Against-Migrants-As-Economy-Collapses

Kale, S. H., & Spence, M. T. (2009). A trination analysis of social exchange relationships in e-dating. In C. Romm-Livermore & K. Setzekorn (Eds.), *Social networking communities and e-dating services: Concepts and implications* (pp. 314–328). Hershey, PA: IGI Global.

Kanayama, T. (2003). Ethnographic research on the experience of Japanese elderly people online. *New Media & Society, 5,* 267–288.

Karis, T. A. (2009). "We're just a couple of people": An exploration of why some black–white couples reject the terms of cross-cultural and interracial. In T. A. Karis & K. D. Killian (Eds.), *Intercultural couples: Exploring diversity in intimate relationships* (pp. 89–108). New York: Taylor & Francis.

Karis, T. A., & Killian, K. (Eds.). (2009). Intercultural couples: Exploring diversity in intimate relationships. New York: Routledge.

Kashima, Y., & Triandis, T. (1986). The self-serving bias in attributions as a coping strategy: A cross-cultural study. *Journal of Cross-Cultural Psychology, 17,* 83–97.

Kashyap, K. (2009, March 4). *The Bobby Jindal Racism Issue.* Retrieved from http://www.thedailybeast.com/articles/2009/03/04/the-bobby-jindal-racism-puzzle.html

Kayan, S., Fussell, S. R., & Setlock, L. D. (2006). Cultural differences in the use of instant messaging in Asia and North America. *Proceedings of CSCW 2006,* 525–528. New York: ACM.

Keaten, J. A., & Soukup, C. (2009). Dialogue and religious otherness: Toward a model of pluralistic interfaith dialogue. *Journal of International and Intercultural Communication, 2,* 168–187.

Kennedy, M., & Sakaguchi, T. (2009). Trust in social networking: Definitions from a global, cultural viewpoint. In C. Romm-Livermore & K. Setzekorn (Eds.), *Social networking communities and e-dating services: Concepts and implications* (pp. 225–238). Hershey, PA: IGI Global.

Kerkhof, P., Finkenauer, C. & Muusses, L. (2011). Relational consequences of compulsive internet use. *Human Communication Research, 37,* 147–173.

Kim, E. (1996). Personal story in Appendix. In E. Kim & E. Ying-Yu (Eds.), *East to America: Korean American life stories.* New York: New Press.

Kim, J., Lim, T., Dindia, K., & Burrell, N. (2010). Reframing the cultural differences between the East and the West. *Communication Studies, 61,* 543–566.

Kim, Y. Y. (1988). *Communication and cross-cultural adaptation: An integrative theory.* Clevedon, UK: Multilingual Matters.

Kim, Y. Y. (2001). *Becoming intercultural: An integrative theory of communication and cross-cultural adaptation.* Thousand Oaks, CA: Sage.

Kim, Y. Y. (2003). Adapting to an unfamiliar culture: An interdisciplinary overview. In W. Gudykunst (Ed.), *Cross-cultural and intercultural communication.* (pp. 243–258). Thousand Oaks, CA: Sage.

Kim, Y. Y. (2004). Long-term cross-cultural adaptation: Training implications of an integrative theory. In D. Landis, J. Bennett, & M. Bennett (Eds.), *Handbook of intercultural training* (3rd ed., pp. 337–362). Thousand Oaks, CA: Sage.

Kim, Y. Y. (2005). Adapting to a new culture: An integrative communication theory. In W. Gudykunst (Ed.), *Theorizing about intercultural communication* (pp. 375–400). Thousand Oaks, CA: Sage.

Kim, Y. Y. (2009). The identity factor in intercultural competence. In D. K. Deardorff (Ed.), *The Sage handbook of intercultural competence* (pp. 53–65). Thousand Oaks, CA: Sage.

Kimmel, M. M. (1992). *Men's lives* (2nd ed.). New York: Macmillan.

Kinsman, M. (2006, April 23). Baby boomer exodus. *San Diego Union-Tribune,* p. H-1.

Kitano, H., Fujino, D., & Sato, J. (1998). Interracial marriages. In L. Lee & N. Zane (Eds.), *Handbook of Asian American psychology* (pp.233–260). Thousand Oaks, CA: Sage.

Kito, M. (2005). Self-disclosure in romantic relationships and friendships among American and Japanese college students. *The Journal of Social Psychology, 145,* 127–140.

Kline, S. L., Horton, B., & Zhang, S. (2008). Communicating love: Comparisons between American and East Asian university students. *International Journal of Intercultural Communication, 32,* 200–214.

Kluckhohn, E., & Strodtbeck, E. (1961). *Variations in value orientations.* New York: Row, Peterson.

Knapp, M., & Hall, J. (2009). *Nonverbal communication in human interaction* (7th ed.). Belmont, CA: Wadsworth.

Kochman, T. (1981). *Black and white styles in conflict.* Chicago: University of Chicago Press

Kochman, T. (1990). Force fields in black and white communication. In D. Carbaugh (Ed.), *Cultural communication and intercultural contact* (pp. 219–224). Hillsdale, NJ: Erlbaum.

Kohls, L. R. (1996). *Survival kit for overseas living* (3rd ed.). Yarmouth, ME: Intercultural Press.

Kraus, E. (1991). *The contradictory immigrant problem: A socio-psychological analysis.* New York: Lang.

Krishnan, A., & Berry, J. (1992). Acculturative stress and acculturative attitudes among Indian immigrants to the United States. *Psychology and Developing Societies, 4,* 187–212.

Kroeber, A., & Kluckhohn, C. (1952). Culture: A critical review of concepts and definitions. *Papers of the Peabody Museum* (Vol. 47). Cambridge, MA: Peabody Museum.

Kudo, K., & Simkin, K. A. (2003). Intercultural friendship formation: The case of Japanese students at an Australian university. *Journal of Intercultural Studies, 24,* 91–114.

Kuhl, P. K., & Meltzoff, A. N. (1996). Infant vocalizations in response to speech: Vocal imitation and developmental change. *Journal of the Acoustical Society of America, 100,* 2425–2438.

Kwon, K., Barnett, G. A., & Chen, H. (2009). Assessing cultural differences in translations: A semantic network analysis of the universal declaration of human rights. *Journal of International and Intercultural Communication, 2,* 107–138.

Lacey, M. (2007, November 17). Child matadors draw Olés in Mexico's bullrings. *The New York Times.* Retrieved from http://www.nytimes.com/2007/11/19/world/americas/19bullfight.html?_r=2&hp=&oref=slogin&pagewanted=all

Lacey, M. (2008, December 6). A lifestyle distinct: The Muxe of Mexico. *The New York Times.* Retrieved from http://www.nytimes.com/2008/12/07/weekinreview/07lacey.html

LaFromboise, T., Coleman, H., & Gerton, J. (1993). Psychological impact of biculturalism: Evidence and theory. *Psychological Bulletin, 114,* 395–412.

Lah, K. (2010, February 18). *Olympic snowboarder's 'street' style offends Japanese.* Retrieved from http://www.cnn.com/video/#/video/sports/2010/02/18/lah.japan.snowboarder.cnn?iref=allsearch

Langer, E. (1989). *Mindfulness.* Reading, MA: Addison–Wesley.

Langer, E. (1997). *The power of mindful learning.* Reading, MA: Addison–Wesley.

Larimer, T. (2000, September 27). Failure is not just an individual matter. *Time Asia.* Retrieved from http://www.time.com/time/world/article/0,8599,2054482,00.html

Lau, J. H-C. L. (2011, February 28). Raising a milkshake to the bride and groom. *The New York Times,* p. A21.

LeBaron, M. (2003). *Bridging cultural conflicts: A new approach for a changing world.* San Francisco: Jossey–Bass.

Lee, C., & Gudykunst, W. (2001). Attraction in initial interethnic encounters. *International Journal of Intercultural Relations, 25,* 373–387.

Lee, H. E., & Park, H. S. (2011). Why Koreans are more likely to favor "apology," while Americans are more likely to favor "thank you." *Human Communication Research, 37,* 125–146.

Lee, J. A. (1977). A typology of styles of loving. *Personality and Social Psychology Bulletin, 3,* 173–182.

Lee, P. (2006). Bridging cultures: Understanding the construction of relational identity in intercultural friendship. *Journal of Intercultural Communication Research, 35,* 3–22.

Lee, P. (2008). Stages and transitions of relational identity formation in intercultural friendship: Implications for identity management theory. *Journal of International and Intercultural Communication, 1*, 51–69.

Lee, S., & Fernandez, M. (1998). Trends in Asian American racial/ethnic intermarriage: A comparison of 1980 and 1990 census data. *Sociological Perspectives, 41*, 323–343.

Leeds-Hurwitz, W. (2009). Ambiguity as a solution to the "problem" of intercultural weddings. In T. A. Karis & K. D. Killian (Eds.), *Intercultural couples: Exploring diversity in intimate relationships* (pp. 21–29). New York: Taylor & Francis.

Lennon, J. (1971). "Imagine" [John Lennon]. On *Imagine* [CD]. New York: Capital Records.

Leung, K. (1988). Some determinants of conflict avoidance. *Journal of Cross-Cultural Psychology, 19*, 125–136.

Leung, K., & Bond, M. H. (2004). Social axioms: A model of social beliefs in multi-cultural perspective. In M. P. Zanna (Ed.), *Advances in experimental social psychology* (Vol. 36, pp.119–197). San Diego, CA: Elsevier Academic Press.

Leung, K., Maddux, W. W., Galinsky, A. D., & Chiu, C. (2008). Multicultural experience enhances creativity: The when and how. *American Psychologist, 63*(3), 169–181.

Levin, S., Taylor, P. L., & Caudle, E. (2007). Interethnic and interracial dating in college: A longitudinal study. *Journal of Social and Personal Relationships, 24*, 323–341.

Levine, T., Aune, K., & Park, H. S. (2006). Love styles and communication in relationships: Partner preferences, initiation, and intensification. *Communication Quarterly, 54*, 465–486.

Lewin, K. (1936). *Principles of typological psychology.* New York: McGraw–Hill.

Leyens, J.-P., & Demoulin, S. (2010). Ethnocentrism and group realities. In J. F. Dovidio, M. Hewstone, P. Glick, & V. M. Esses (Eds.) *Sage handbook of prejudice, stereotyping, and discrimination* (pp. 194–208). Thousand Oaks, CA: Sage.

Leyens, J.-P., Yzerbyt, V., & Schadron, G. (1994). *Stereotypes and social cognition.* London: Sage.

Lim, T., Allen, M., Burrell, N., & Kim, S. (2008). Differences in cognitive relativity between Americans' and Koreans' assessments of self. *Journal of Intercultural Communication Research, 37*, 105–118.

Lin, C. (2006). Culture shock and social support: An investigation of a Chinese student organization on a US campus. *Journal of Intercultural Communication Research, 35*, 117–137.

Ling, R. (2008). *New tech, new ties: How mobile phone communication is reshaping social cohesion.* Cambridge, MA: MIT Press.

Lippman, W. (1936). *Public opinion.* New York: Macmillan.

Llerena-Quinn, R., & Bacigalupe, G. (2009). Constructions of difference among Latino/Latina immigrant and non-Hispanic White couples. In T. A. Karis & K. D. Killian (Eds.), *Intercultural couples: Exploring diversity in intimate relationships* (pp. 167–185). New York: Taylor & Francis.

Lo, M.- C. (2002). *Doctors within borders: Profession, ethnicity, and modernity in colonial Taiwan.* Berkeley, CA: University of California.

Locke, D. (1992). *Increasing multicultural understanding: A comprehensive model.* Newbury Park, CA: Sage.

Lorber, J. (1994). *Paradoxes of gender.* New Haven: Yale University.

Lucey, H. (2010). Families, siblings and identities. In M. Wetherell & C. T. Mohanty (Eds.), *The Sage handbook of identities* (pp. 476–491). Thousand Oaks, CA: Sage.

Lukens, J. (1978). Ethnocentric speech. *Ethnic Groups, 2*, 35–53.

Lysgaard, S. (1955). Adjustment in a foreign society. *International Social Science Bulletin, 7*, 45–51.

Mackey, R. (2010, February 25). Haitian tradition is criticized as child slavery. *The New York Times.* Retrieved from http://thelede.blogs.nytimes.com/tag/restaveks/

Maddux, W. W., & Galinsky, A. D. (2009). Cultural borders and mental barriers: The relationship between living abroad and creativity. *Journal of Personality and Social Psychology, 96,* 1047–1061.

Maltz, D., & Borker, R. (1982). A cultural approach to male-female communication. In J. Gumperz (Ed.), *Language and social identity* (pp. 195–216). Cambridge, UK: Cambridge University Press.

Manian, R., & Naidu, S. (2009). India: A cross-cultural overview of intercultural competence. In D. K. Deardorff (Ed.), *The Sage handbook of intercultural competence* (pp. 233–248). Thousand Oaks, CA: Sage.

Mansson, D. H., & Myers, S. A. (2011). An initial examination of college students' expression of affection through Facebook. *Southern Communication Journal, 76,* 155–168.

Markus, H., & Kitayama, S. (1991). Culture and the self: Implications for cognition, emotion, and motivation. *Psychological Review, 2,* 224–253.

Markus, H., & Kitayama, S. (1994). A collective fear of the collective: Implications for selves and theories of selves. *Personality and Social Psychology Bulletin, 20,* 568–579.

Martin, A. (2011, January 14). *Young men, couples shunning sex.* Retrieved from http://search.japantimes.co.jp/print/nn20110114a3.html

Martin, J. N., Bradford, L. J., Drzewiecka, J. A., & Chitgopekar, A. S. (2003). Intercultural dating patterns among young white U.S. Americans: Have they changed in the past 20 years? *Howard Journal of Communications, 14,* 53–73.

Martin, J., & Harrell, T. (1996). Reentry training for intercultural sojourners. In D. Landis & R. Bhagat (Eds.), *Handbook of intercultural training* (2nd ed., pp. 307–326). Thousand Oaks, CA: Sage.

Martin, J., & Harrell, T. (2004). Intercultural reentry of students and professionals: Theory and practice. In D. Landis, J. Bennett, & M. Bennett (Eds.), *Handbook of intercultural training* (3rd ed., pp. 309–336). Thousand Oaks, CA: Sage.

Mastro, D. E., Behm-Morawitz, E., & Kopacz, M. A. (2008). Exposure to television portrayals of Latinos: The implications of aversive racism and social identity theory. *Human Communication Research, 34,* 1–27.

Matsumoto, D. (2009). Culture and emotional expression. In C. Y. Chiu, Y. Y. Hong, S. Shavit, & R. S. Wyer, *Problems and solutions in cross-cultural theory, research and application* (pp. 271–287). New York: Psychology Press.

Matsumoto, D., & Juang, L. (2003). *Culture and psychology* (3rd ed.). Belmont, CA: Wadsworth.

Matsumoto, D., & Kudoh, T. (1993). American-Japanese cultural differences in attributions based on smiles. *Journal of Nonverbal Behavior, 17,* 231–243.

Matsumoto, D., Olide, A., Schug, J., Willingham, B., & Callan, M. (2009). Cross-cultural judgments of spontaneous facial expressions of emotion. *Journal of Nonverbal Behavior, 33,* 213–238.

Matsumoto, D., Yoo S. H., & LeRoux J. A. (2010). Emotion and intercultural adjustment. In D. Matsumoto (Ed.), *APA handbook of intercultural communication* (pp. 23–39). Washington, DC: American Psychological Association.

Matthews, T. J., & Hamilton, B. E (2009, August). Delayed childbearing: More women are having their first child later in life. *NCHS Data Brief, 21.* Retrieved from http://www.cdc.gov/nchs/data/databriefs/db21.pdf

Matusitz, J. (2005). *The acculturative experience of French students in a southwestern university apartment complex in the United States.* Paper presented at the annual conference of the International Communication Association, New York.

McCann, R., Honeycutt, J., & Keaton, S. (2010). Toward greater specificity in cultural value analyses: The interplay of intrapersonal communication affect and cultural values in Japan, Thailand, and the United States. *Journal of Intercultural Communication Research, 39,* 157–172.

McClure, S. (2002, December 28). Year in Asia. *Billboard Magazine, 114*(52/1), pYE-24.

McDonald, M. (2011, February 21). Home Internet may get even faster in South Korea. *The New York Times*. Retrieved from http://www.nytimes.com/2011/02/22/technology/22iht-broadband22.html?_r=4

McDonald, T. (2010, October 6). Feds get help translating Ebonics, reigniting debate. *The News & Observer* (Raleigh, NC). Retrieved from http://www.newsobserver.com

McIntosh, P. (2002). White privilege: Unpacking the invisible backpack. In A. Kasselman, L. D. McNair, & N. Scheidewind (Eds.), *Women, images, and realities: A multicultural anthology* (pp. 424–426). New York: McGraw–Hill.

McLachlan, D. A., & Justice, J. (2009). A grounded theory of international student well-being. *The Journal of Theory Construction & Testing, 13*, 27–32.

McLeod, P. L., Lobel, S. A., & Cox, T. H. (1996). Ethnic diversity and creativity in small groups. *Small Group Research, 27*, 248–264.

McNamara, R. P., Tempenis, M., & Walton, B. (1999). *Crossing the line: Interracial couples in the South.* Westport, CT: Praeger.

Medina-Lopez-Portillo, A., & Sinnigen, J. H. (2009). Interculturality versus intercultural competencies in Latin America. In D. K. Deardorff (Ed.), *The Sage handbook of intercultural competence* (pp. 249–263). Thousand Oaks, CA: Sage.

Mesch, G. S. (2006). Family relations and the Internet: Exploring family boundaries approach. *Journal of Family Communication, 6*, 119–138.

Milhouse, V., Asante, M., & Nwosu, P. (Eds.). (2001). *Transcultural realities: Interdisciplinary perspectives on cross-cultural communication.* Thousand Oaks, CA: Sage.

Mitchell, W. (2007). *Global entertainment industry to be worth 2.2 trillion in 2011.* Retrieved from http://www.screendaily.com/global-entertainment-industry-to-be-worth-2-trillion-by-2011/4033233.article

Miyamoto, N. (1999). What is the color of love? In A. Ling (Ed.), *Yellow light: The flowering of Asian American arts.* Philadelphia: Temple University Press.

Molinsky, A. (2007). Cross-cultural code-switching: The psychological challenges of adapting behavior in foreign cultural interactions. *Academy of Management Review, 32*, 622–640.

Moodian, M. A. (Ed.). (2010). *Contemporary leadership and intercultural competence: Exploring the cross-cultural dynamics within organizations.* Thousand Oaks, CA: Sage.

Moorthy, R., DeGeorge, R., Donaldson, T., Ellos, W., Solomon, R., & Textor, R. (1998). *Uncompromising integrity: Motorola's global challenge.* Schaumberg, IL: Motorola University Press.

Moran, K., & Chung, L. (2008, April). Global or local identity? A theoretical analysis of the role of Viacom on identity formation among children in an international context. *Global Media Journal, 7*(4), 1–14.

Moran, R. T., Youngdahl, W. E., & Moran, S. V. (2009). Intercultural competence in business—Leading global projects: Bridging the cultural and functional divide. In D. K. Deardorff (Ed.), *The Sage handbook of intercultural competence* (pp. 287–303). Thousand Oaks, CA: Sage.

Morry, M. M. (2005). Relationship satisfaction as a predictor of similarity ratings: A test of the attraction–similarity hypothesis. *Journal of Social and Personal Relationships, 22*, 561–584.

Mortenson, S. T., Burleson, B. R., Feng, B., & Liu, M. (2009). Cultural similarities and differences in seeking social support as a means of coping: A comparison of European Americans and Chinese an evaluation of mediating effects of self-construal. *Journal of Intercultural Communication, 2*, 208–239.

Mui, A. C., Kang, S.-Y., Kang, D., & Domanski, M. P. (2007). English language proficiency and healthy-related quality of life among Chinese and Korean immigrant elders. *Health & Social Work, 32*, 119–127.

Munshi, D. (2005). Through the subject's eye: Situating the other in discourses of diversity. In G. Cheney & G. Barnett (Ed.), *International and multicultural organizational communication* (pp. 45–70). Liberty Township, OH: Hampton.

Munshi, D., Broadfoot, K., & Smith, L. (2011). Decolonizing communication ethics: A framework for communicating otherwise. In G. Cheney, S. May, & D. Munshi (Eds.), *The ICA handbook of communication ethics* (pp. 119–132). Mahway, NJ: Lawrence Erlbaum.

Mutsvairo, B. (2006, March 17). Pass or fail to become Dutch. *San Francisco Chronicle*, p. A2.

Nash, D. (1991). The cause of sojourner adaptation: A new test of the U-curve hypothesis. *Human Organization, 50*, 283–286.

Neumann, R., Steinhauser, N., & Roeder, U. (2009). How self-construal shapes emotion: Cultural differences in the feeling of pride. *Social Cognition, 27*, 327–337.

Nguyen, A.-M., & Benet-Martinez, V. (2010). Multicultural identity: What is it and why it matters? In R. Crisp (Ed.), *The psychology of social and cultural diversity* (pp. 87–114). West Sussex, UK: Wiley–Blackwell.

Nielson. (2010). *State of the art report 2010*. Retrieved from http://blog.nielsen.com/nielsen wire/wp-content/uploads/2010/09/Nielsen-State-of-TV-09232010.pdf and http://blog.nielsen.com/nielsenwire/global/social-media-dominates-asia-pacific-internet-usage/

NielsonWire. (2008). *Cracking the Hispanic market—One segment at a time*. Retrieved from http://blog.nielsen.com/nielsenwire/consumer/cracking-the-hispanic-market-one-segment-at-a-time/

Norris, P. (2009). The impact of the Internet on political activism: Evidence from Europe. In C. Romm-Livermore & K. Setzekorn (Eds.), *Social networking communities and e-dating services: Concepts and implications* (pp. 123–141). Hershey, PA: IGI Global.

Nwosu, P. O. (2009). Understanding Africans' conceptualizations of intercultural competence. In D. K. Deardorff (Ed.), *The Sage handbook of intercultural competence* (pp. 158–178). Thousand Oaks, CA: Sage.

Oberg, K. (1960). Culture shock and the problems of adjustment to new cultural environments. *Practical Anthropology, 7*, 170–179.

O'Brien, C. (2011, February 27). "Social Network" tells us wrong story of our times. *San Mateo County Times*, pp. 1, 14.

O'Brien, C., & Witmer, J. (2003). *Images of Indians: How Hollywood stereotyped the Native American* [Documentary]. United States: Starz! Encore Entertainment.

Oetzel, J. G. (1998). Culturally homogeneous and heterogeneous groups: Explaining communication processes through individualism–collectivism and self-construal. *International Journal of Intercultural Relations, 22*, 135–161.

Oetzel, J. G. (1999). The influence of situational features on perceived conflict styles and self-construals in small groups. *International Journal of Intercultural Relations, 23*, 679–695.

Oetzel, J. G. (2005). Intercultural work group communication theory. In W. B. Gudykunst (Ed.), *Theorizing about intercultural communication* (pp. 351–371). Thousand Oaks, CA: Sage.

Oetzel, J. G. (2009). *Layers of intercultural communication*. New York: Allyn & Bacon.

Oetzel, J. G., & Ting-Toomey, S. (2003). Face concerns in interpersonal conflict: A cross-cultural empirical test of the face-negotiation theory. *Communication Research, 30*, 599–624.

Oetzel, J. G., Arcos, Mabizela, P., Weinman, M., & Zhang, Q. (2006). Historical, political, and spiritual factors for conflict: Understand conflict perspectives and communication in the Muslim world, China, Colombia, and South Africa. In J. G. Oetzel and S. Ting-Toomey (Eds.), *The Sage handbook of conflict communication: Integrating theory, research, and practice* (pp. 549–574). Thousand Oaks, CA: Sage.

Oetzel, J., Garcia, A., & Ting-Toomey, S. (2008). An analysis of the relationships among face concerns and facework behaviors in perceived conflict situations: A four-culture investigation. *International Journal of Conflict Management, 19,* 382–403.

Oetzel, J., Ting-Toomey, S., Masumoto, T., Yokochi, Y., Pan, X, Takai, J., et al. (2001). Face behaviors in interpersonal conflicts: A cross-cultural comparison of Germany, Japan, China, and the United States. *Communication Monographs, 68,* 235–258.

Oetzel, J. G., Ting-Toomey, S., & Rinderle, S. (2006). Conflict communication in contexts: A social ecological perspective. In J. G. Oetzel & S. Ting-Toomey (Eds.), *The SAGE handbook of conflict communication* (pp. 727–739). Thousand Oaks, CA: Sage.

Okabe, R. (1983). Cultural assumptions of East and West: Japan and the United States. In W. Gudykunst (Ed.), *Intercultural communication theory: Current perspectives* (pp. 21–44). Beverly Hills, CA: Sage.

Olson, P. (2008, May 21). The world's hardest working countries. *Forbes.* Retrieved from http://www.forbes.com/2008/05/21/labor-market-workforce-lead-citizen-cx_po_0521countries.html

Orbe, M. (1998). *Constructing co-culture-theory: An explication of cultures, power, and communication.* Thousand Oaks, CA: Sage.

Orbe, M. P., & Everett, M. A. (2006). Interracial and interethnic conflict and communication in the United States. In J. G. Oetzel & S. Ting-Toomey (Eds.) *The Sage handbook of conflict communication: Integrating theory, research, and practice* (pp. 575–594). Thousand Oaks, CA: Sage.

Orbe, M. P., & Spellers, R. E. (2005). From the margins to the center: Utilizing co-cultural theory in diverse contexts. In W. B. Gudykunst (Ed.), *Theorizing about intercultural communication* (pp. 173–191). Thousand Oaks, CA: Sage.

Orbe, M., & Harris, T. M. (2008). *Interracial communication: Theory into practice* (2nd ed.) Thousand Oaks, CA: Sage.

Osgood, C. E., Suci, G. J., & Tanenbaum, P. H. (1957). *The measurement of meaning.* Urbana, IL: University of Illinois.

Oskouei, M. (Writer/Director). (2006). *Nose Iranian style* [Documentary]. Tehran, Iran: Sheherazad Media International.

Osland, J. (1995). *The adventure of working abroad: Hero tales from the global frontier.* San Francisco: Jossey–Bass.

Pack-Brown, S., & Williams, C. (2003). *Ethics in multicultural contexts.* Thousand Oaks, CA: Sage.

Paige, M., & Martin, J. (1996). Ethics in intercultural training. In D. Landis & R. Bhagat (Eds.), *Handbook of intercultural training* (2nd ed., pp.35–60). Thousand Oaks, CA: Sage.

Paige, R. M., & Goode, M. (2009). Intercultural competence in international education administration—cultural mentoring: International education professionals and the development of intercultural competence. In D. K. Deardorff (Ed.), *The Sage handbook of intercultural competence* (pp. 333–349). Thousand Oaks, CA: Sage.

Palthe, J. (2009). Global human resource management. In M. A. Moodian (Ed.), *Contemporary leadership and intercultural competence: Exploring the cross-cultural dynamics within organizations* (pp.75–92). Thousand Oaks, CA: Sage.

Pankraz, D. (2011). *Tribal blending—self expression via mashing personas.* Retrieved from http://danpankraz.wordpress.com/tag/tribal-ideas/

Parham, T., & Helms, J. (1985). The relationship of racial identity attitudes to self-actualization of black students and affective states. *Journal of Counseling Psychology, 32,* 431–440.

Park, H. S., & Guan, X. (2006). The effects of national culture and face concerns on intention to apologize: A comparison of the USA and China. *Journal of Intercultural Communication Research, 35,* 183–204.

Park, H. S., & Guan, X. (2007). Cultural differences in self versus others' self-construals: Data from China and the United States. *Communication Research Reports, 24,* 21–28.

Park, H. S., & Guan, X. (2009) Culture, positive and negative face threats, and apology intentions. *Journal of Language and Social Psychology, 28,* 244–262.

Park, H. S., Lee, H. E., & Song, J. A. (2005). "I am sorry to send you SPAM:" Cross-cultural differences in use of apologies in email advertising in Korea and *U. S. Human Communication Research, 31,* 365–398.

Parsons, T. (1951). *The social system.* London: Routledge & Kegan.

Passel, J. S., & Cohn, D. (2008). U. S. Population Projections 2005–2050. *Pew Research Center.* Retrieved from http://pewhispanic.org/files/reports/85.pdf

Pearmain, E. (Ed.). (1998). *Doorways to the soul.* Cleveland, OH: Pilgrim.

Pedersen, P. (1997). Do the right thing: A question of ethics. In K. Cushner & R. Brislin (Eds.), *Improving intercultural interactions: Modules for cross-cultural training programs* (Vol. 2, pp. 149–164). Thousand Oaks, CA: Sage.

Pedersen, P., Crethar, H., & Carlson, J. (2008). *Inclusive cultural empathy: Making relationships central in counseling and psychotherapy.* Washington, DC: American Psychological Association.

Pell, D. (2011, March 25). Jimmy Wong saves the Internet. *Huffington Post.* Retrieved from http://www.huffingtonpost.com.

Pennington, D. (1990). Time in African culture. In A. Asante & K. Asante (Eds.), *African culture: The rhythms of unity* (pp. 123–139). Trenton, NJ: Africa World Press.

Persaud, B. (2008, February 17). Ethnic pride unfolds at minority women beauty contests. *Orlando Sentinel.* Retrieved from http://articles.orlandosentinel.com/2008–02-17/news/pageant17_1_miss-navajo-contests-miss-vietnam

Pettigrew, T. (1978). The ultimate attribution error: Extending Allport's cognitive analysis of prejudice. *Personality and Social Psychology Bulletin, 5,* 461–476.

Pettigrew, T. F., & Tropp, L. R. (2008). How does intergroup contact reduce prejudice? Meta-analytic tests of three mediators. *European Journal of Social Psychology, 38,* 922–934.

Pflug, J. (2011). Contextuality and computer-mediated communication: A cross cultural comparison. *Computers in Human Behavior, 27,* 131–138.

Philipsen, G. (1997). A theory of speech codes. In G. Philipsen & T. Albrecht (Eds.), *Developing communication theories.* Albany: State University of New York Press.

Philipsen, G. (2010). Researching culture in contexts of social interaction: An ethnographic approach, a network of scholars. illustrative moves. In D. Carbaugh & P. Buzzanell (Ed.), *Distinctive qualities of communication research* (pp. 87–105). New York: Routledge.

Phoenix, A. (2010). Ethnicities. In M. Wetherell & C. T. Mohanty (Eds.), *The Sage handbook of identities* (pp. 297–320). Thousand Oaks, CA: Sage.

Pieraccini, C., & Alligood, D. L. (2005). *Color television: Fifty years of African American and Latino images on prime-time television.* Dubuque, IA: Kendall/Hunt.

Pitts, M. J. (2009). Identity and the role of expectations, stress, and talk in short-term student sojourner adjustment: An application of the integrative theory of communication and cross-cultural adaptation. *International Journal of Intercultural Relations, 33,* 450–462.

Profile: Training of air marshals. (2010, December 20). *NBC Nightly News.* [Television broadcast]

Puentha, D., Giles, H., & Young, L. (1987). Interethnic perceptions and relative deprivation: British data. In Y. Y. Kim & W. Gudykunst (Eds.), *Cross-cultural adaptation: Current approaches.* Newbury Park, CA: Sage.

Purnell, L., & Paulanka, B. (2008). *Transcultural health care: A culturally competent approach* (3rd ed.). Philadelphia: F. A. Davis.

Pusch, M. D. (2009). The interculturally competent global leader. In D. K. Deardorff (Ed.), *The Sage handbook of intercultural competence* (pp. 66–84). Thousand Oaks, CA: Sage.

Pusch, M., & Loewenthall, N. (1988). *Helping them home: A guide for leaders of professional integrity and reentry workshops.* Washington, DC: National Association for Foreign Student Affairs.

Putnam, L. L. (2010). Communication as changing the negotiation game. *Journal of Applied Communication Research, 38,* 325–335.

Pyle, R. (2011, March 11). LPD: Annual racial profiling report doesn't indicate problems. *Lubbock Avalanche-Journal.* Retrieved from http://lubbockonline.com/crime-and-courts/2011–03-04/lpd-annual-racial-profiling-report-doesnt-indicate-problems

Racial rant inspires an Internet balladeer, A. (2011, March 24). *All Things Considered.* Received from http://www.npr.org/2011/03/24/134827085/a-racial-quarrel-inspires-an-internet-balladeer?ps=cprs

Radio and Television Business Report (2011, April 5). *Week 28: Univision #4 in primetime network.* Retrieved from http://www.rbr.com/tv-cable/tv-cable_ratings/week-28-univision-no-4-network-in-primetime.html

Rahim, M. A. (1992). *Managing conflict in organizations* (2nd ed.). Westport, CT: Praeger.

Ream, N. J. (2009). Astrological perspective on themes of 2009. *Kalapana Seaview Estates Community Association.* Retrieved from http://www.kalapanaseaviewhawaii.org/Newsletters/seaview-09.pdf

Redfield, R., Linton, R., & Herskovits, M. (1936). Memorandum for the study of acculturation. *American Anthropologist, 38,* 149–152.

Reicher, S., Spears, R., & Haslam, A. (2010). The social identity approach in social psychology. In M. Wetherell & C. T. Mohanty (Eds.), *The Sage handbook of identities* (pp. 45–62). Thousand Oaks, CA: Sage.

Remland, M. (2003). *Nonverbal communication in everyday life* (2nd ed.). Boston: Allyn & Bacon.

Remland, M., Jones, T., & Brinkman, H. (1995). Interpersonal distance, body orientation, and touch: Effects of culture, gender, and age. *Journal of Social Psychology, 135,* 281–298.

Richeson, J. A., & Shelton, J. N. (2010). Prejudice in intergroup dyadic interactions. In J. F. Dovidio, M. Hewstone, P. Glick, & V. M. Esses (Eds.), *Handbook of prejudice, stereotyping and discrimination.* Thousand Oaks, CA: Sage.

Richmond, V., & McCroskey, J. (2000). *Nonverbal behavior in interpersonal relations* (4th ed.). Boston: Allyn & Bacon.

Richmond, Y. (1996). *From nyet to da: Understanding the Russians* (2nd ed.). Yarmouth, ME: Intercultural Press.

Rideout, V. J., Foehr, U. G., & Roberts, D. F. (2010, January). Generation M2: Media in the lives of 8- to-18-year-olds. *A Kaiser Family Foundation Study.* The Henry J. Kaiser Family Foundation. Retrieved from http://www.kff.org

Ridley, C. R., & Udipi, S. (2002). Putting cultural empathy into practice. In P. Pedersen, J. Draguns, W. Lonner, & J. Trimble (Eds.), *Counseling across cultures* (5th ed., pp. 317–333). Thousand Oaks, CA: Sage.

Rink, F. A., & Jehn, K, A. (2010). Divided we fall, or united we stand? How identity processes affect faultline perceptions and the functioning of diverse teams. In R. Crisp (Ed.), *The psychology of social and cultural diversity* (pp. 281–296). West Sussex, UK: Wiley–Blackwell.

Rodriguez, G. (2008, February 28). White like us. *Los Angeles Times.* Retrieved from http://www.latimes.com/news/printedition/asection/la-oe-rodriguez25feb25,0,5964168.column

Rohrlich, B., & Martin, J. (1991). Host country and reentry adjustment of student sojourners. *International Journal of Intercultural Relations, 15,* 163–182.

Rokeach, M. (1972). *Beliefs, attitudes and values: A theory of organization and change.* San Francisco: Jossey–Bass.

Rokeach, M. (1973). *The nature of human values.* New York: Free Press.

Romano, R. (2003). *Race mixing: Black–white marriage in postwar America.* Cambridge, MA: Harvard University Press.

Romm-Livermore, C., Somers, T., Setzekorn, K., & King, A. L.-G. (2009). How e-daters behave online: Theory and empirical observations. In C. Romm-Livermore & K. Setzekorn (Eds.), *Social networking communities and e-dating services: Concepts and implications* (pp. 292–313). Hershey, PA: IGI Global.

Rosen, R., Digh, P., Singer, M., & Phillips, C. (2000). *Global literacies.* New York: Simon & Schuster.

Rosenblatt, P. C. (2009). A systems theory analysis of intercultural couple relationships. In T. A. Karis & K. D. Killian (Eds.), *Intercultural couples: Exploring diversity in intimate relationships* (pp. 3–19). New York: Taylor & Francis.

Rosenblatt, P., Karis, T., & Powell, R. (1995). *Multiracial couples: Black and white voices.* Thousand Oaks, CA: Sage.

Rosenfeld, M. (2007). *The age of independence: Interracial unions, same-sex unions, and the changing American family.* Cambridge, MA: Harvard University.

Ross, J., & Ferris, K. (1981). Interpersonal attraction and organizational outcome: A field experiment. *Administrative Science Quarterly, 26,* 617–632.

Rothman, J. (1997). *Resolving identity-based conflict in nations, organizations, and communities.* San Francisco: Jossey–Bass.

Rotter, J. (1966). Generalized expectancies for internal versus external control of reinforcement. *Psychological Monographs, 80,* 609.

Rowe, W., Bennett, S., & Atkinson, D. (1994). White racial identity development models: A critique and alternative proposal. *The Counseling Psychologist, 22,* 129–146.

Ruiz, A. (1990). Ethnic identity: Crisis and resolution. *Journal of Multicultural Counseling, 18,* 29–40.

Rustici, C. (2011, April 11). France burqa ban takes effect; two women detained. *Huffpost World.* Retrieved from http://www.huffingtonpost.com/2011/04/11/france-burqa-ban-takes-ef_n_847366.html

Rustogi, M. (2009). Asian-Indians in intercultural marriages: Intersections of acculturation, gender, and exogamy. In T. A. Karis & K. D. Killian (Eds.), *Intercultural couples: Exploring diversity in intimate relationships* (pp. 189–204). New York: Taylor & Francis.

Ryan, E. (2004). *Interpersonal attraction: The force that draws people together.* Retrieved from http://www.simplysolo.com/relationships/interpersonal_attraction_elizabeth_ryan.html

Safdar, S., Friedlmeier, W., Matsumoto, D., Yoo, S. H., Kwantes, C. T., Kakai, H., et al. (2009). Variations of emotional display rules within and across cultures. A comparison between Canada, USA, and Japan. *Canadian Journal of Behavioural Science, 41,* 1–10.

Said, E. (1978). *Orientalism.* New York: Pantheon Press.

Saletan, W. (2011, February 11). The computer made me do it. *New York Times Book Review,* p. 7.

Samuel, H. (2008, March 7). *French women are the new sexual predators.* Retrieved from http://www.telegraph.co.uk/news/worldnews/1581043/French-women-are-the-sexual-predators-now.html

Santamaría, A., de la Mata, M. L., Hansen T. G. B., & Ruiz, L. (2010). Cultural self-construals of Mexican, Spanish, and Danish college students: Beyond independent and interdependent self. *Journal of Cross-Cultural Psychology, 41,* 471–477.

Santilli, V., & Miller, A. N. (2011). The effects of gender and power distance on nonverbal immediacy in symmetrical and asymmetrical power conditions: A cross-cultural study of classrooms and friendships. *Journal of International and Intercultural Communication, 4,* 3–22.

Sapir, E. (1921). *Language: An introduction to the study of speech.* New York: Harcourt, Brace & World.

Saulny, S. (2011a, March 20). Race remixed: Black and white and married in the Deep South: A shifting image. *The New York Times,* pp. A1, A4.

Saulny, S. (2011b, March 25). Census data presents rise in multiracial population of youths. *The New York Times,* p. A3.

Schaefer, R. (2009). *Racial and ethnic groups* (12th ed.). New York: Prentice Hall.

Schaetti, B. F., Ramsey, S. J., & Watanabe, G. C. (2009). From intercultural knowledge to intercultural competence: Developing an intercultural practice. In M. A. Moodian (Ed.), *Contemporary leadership and intercultural competence: Exploring the cross-cultural dynamics within organizations* (pp. 125–137). Thousand Oaks, CA: Sage.

Schiller, H. (1993). Transnational media: Creating consumers worldwide. *Journal of International Affairs, 47,* 1–12.

Schmid, K., & Hewstone, M. (2010). Combined effects of intergroup contact and multiple categorization: Consequences for intergroup attitudes in diverse social contexts. In R. Crisp (Ed.), *The psychology of social and cultural diversity* (pp. 299–321). West Sussex, UK: Wiley–Blackwell.

Schwartz, S. (1990). Individualism–collectivism: Critique and refinement. *Journal of Cross-Cultural Psychology, 21,* 139–157.

Schwartz, S. (1992). Universals in the content and structure of values. In M. Zanna (Ed.), *Advances in experimental social psychology* (Vol. 25, pp. 1–65). New York: Academic Press.

Schwartz, S., & Bardi, A. (2001). Value hierarchies across cultures. *Journal of Cross-Cultural Psychology, 32,* 268–290.

Seligson, H. (2011, February 20). Jilted in the U.S., a site finds love in India. *The New York Times,* pp. BU1, BU5.

Selznick, B. (2008). Global television: Co-producing culture. Philadelphia: Temple University Press.

Seth, N., & Patnayakuni, R. (2009). Online matrimonial sites and the transformation of arranged marriage in India. In C. Romm-Livermore & K. Setzekorn (Eds.), *Social networking communities and e-dating services: Concepts and implications* (pp. 329–352). Hershey, PA: IGI Global.

Shackelford, T. K., Schmitt, D. P., & Buss, D. M. (2005). Universal dimensions of human mate preferences. *Personality and Individual Differences, 39,* 447–458.

Shakur, T. (1991). Words of wisdom. On *Jive 2Pacolypse Now* [CD]. New York: Interscope/Jive Records.

Shelton, J., Richeson, J., & Bergsieker, H. (2009). Interracial friendship development and attributional biases. *Journal of Social & Personal Relationships, 26,* 179–193.

Sherif, M. (1966). *In common predicament: Social psychology of intergroup conflict and cooperation.* New York: Octagon Books.

Shih, M., Sanchez, D., & Ho, G. (2010). Costs and benefits of switching among multiple social identities. In R. Crisp (Ed.), *The psychology of social and cultural diversity* (pp. 62–83). West Sussex, UK: Wiley–Blackwell.

Sias, P. M., Drzewiecka, J. A., Meares, M., Bent, R., Ortega, M., & White, C. (2008). Intercultural friendship development. *Communication Reports, 21,* 1–13.

Sinclair, J., Jacka, E., & Cunningham, S. (1996). *New patterns in global television: Peripheral vision.* Oxford, UK: Oxford University Press.

Sisario, B. (2011, April 17). Ukulele crazy. *The New York Times*, pp. AR9, 14.

Smith, P., Bond, M., & Kagitcibasi, C. (2006). *Understanding social psychology across cultures: Living and working in a changing world (Sage Social Psychology Program)*. Thousand Oaks, CA: Sage.

Smith, P., Dugan, S., Peterson, M. F., & Leung, K. (1998). Individualism collectivism and the handling of disagreement: A 23 country study. *International Journal of Intercultural Relations, 22*, 351–367.

Smith, P., Dugan, S., & Trompenaars, F. (1996). National culture and the values of organizational employees: A dimensional analysis across 43 nations. *Journal of Cross-Cultural Psychology, 27*, 231–264.

Spitzberg, B. H., & Changnon, G. (2009). Conceptualizing intercultural competence. In D. K. Deardorff (Ed.), *The Sage handbook of intercultural competence* (pp. 2–52). Thousand Oaks, CA: Sage.

Spitzberg, B., & Cupach, W. (1984). *Interpersonal communication competence*. Beverly Hills, CA: Sage.

Stathi, S., & Crisp, R. (2010). Intergroup contact and the projection of positivity. *International Journal of Intercultural Relations, 34*, 580–591.

Steinfatt, T. (1989). Linguistic relativity: Toward a broader view. In S. Ting-Toomey & F. Korzenny (Eds.), *Language, communication, and culture: Current directions* (pp. 35–78). Newbury Park, CA: Sage.

Stephan, C., & Stephan, W. (1992). Reducing intercultural anxiety through intercultural contact. *International Journal of Intercultural Relations, 16*, 89–106.

Stephan, W., & Stephan, C. (1996). *Intergroup relations*. Boulder, CO: Westview.

Stephan, W., & Stephan, C. (2001). *Improving intergroup relations*. Thousand Oaks, CA: Sage.

Sternberg, R. J. (Ed.). (1999). *Handbook for creativity*. Cambridge, UK: Cambridge University.

Stevens, K. (2011, February 23). *Internet freedom created investment and innovation*. Retrieved from http://english.chosun.com/site/data/html_dir/2011/02/23/2011022301176.html

Stewart, E., & Bennett, M. (2005). *American cultural patterns: A cross-cultural perspective* (2nd ed.). Boston: Nicholas Brealy.

Storey, J. (2006). *Cultural theory and popular culture: An introduction* (4th ed.). Athens, GA: The University of Georgia Press.

Storti, C. (2001). *Old world/new world*. Yarmouth, ME: Intercultural Press.

Storti, C. (2009). Intercultural competence in human resources—Passing it on: Intercultural competence in the training arena. In D. K. Deardorff (Ed.), *The Sage handbook of intercultural competence* (pp. 272–286). Thousand Oaks, CA: Sage.

Stringer, D., & Cassidy, P. (2003). *52 Activities for exploring values differences*. Yarmouth, ME: Intercultural Press.

Stross, R. (2009, February 7). Why television shines in a world of screens. *New York Times*. Retrieved from http://www.nytimes.com/2009/02/08/business/media/08digi.html?_r=1&scp=6%26sq=nielsen%26st=cse

Sue, D., & Sue, D. (1999). *Counseling the culturally different: Theory and practice* (3rd ed.). New York: Wiley.

Sussman, N. (1986). Reentry research and training: Methods and implications. *International Journal of Intercultural Relations, 10*, 235–254.

Tadmor, C., Hong, Y.-Y., Chiu, C.-Y., & No, S. (2010). What I know in my mind and where my heart belongs: Multicultural identity negotiation and its cognitive consequences. In R. Crisp (Ed.), *The psychology of social and cultural diversity* (pp. 115–144). West Sussex, UK: Wiley–Blackwell.

Tagg, B. (2008). "Dress as a man." New Zealand's men's netball as contested terrain. *Ethnography, 9*, 457–375.

Tajfel, H. (Ed.). (1979). *Differentiation between social groups: Studies in the social psychology of intergroup relations.* New York: Academic Press.

Takahashi, D. (2011, February 10). *Seven reasons why video games will grow in 2011.* Retrieved from http://venturebeat.com/2011/02/10/seven-reasons-why-video-games-will-grow-in-2011/

Tannen, D. (1994). *Talking 9 to 5.* New York: William Morrow.

Tausch, N., & Hewstone, M. (2010). Intergroup contact. In J. F. Dovidio, M. Hewstone, P. Glick, & V. M. Esses (Eds.), *The Sage handbook of prejudice, stereotyping, and discrimination* (pp. 544–560). Thousand Oaks, CA: Sage.

Tharp, T., with Reiter, M. (2003). *The creative habit: Learn it and use it for life.* New York: Simon & Schuster.

Thatcher, M. (1978, January 30). *Interview: World in Action Granada Television.* Retrieved from http://www.margaretthatcher.org/document/103485

Ting-Toomey, S. (1985). Toward a theory of conflict and culture. In W. Gudykunst, L. Stewart, & S. Ting-Toomey (Eds.), *Communication, culture, and organizational processes* (pp. 71–86). Beverly Hills, CA: Sage.

Ting-Toomey, S. (1986). Conflict communication styles in black and white subjective cultures. In Y. Y. Kim (Ed.), *Interethnic communication: Current research* (pp. 75–86). Newbury Park, CA: Sage.

Ting-Toomey, S. (1988). Intercultural conflict styles: A face-negotiation theory. In Y. Y. Kim & W. Gudykunst (Eds.), *Theories in intercultural communication* (pp. 213–235). Newbury Park, CA: Sage.

Ting-Toomey, S. (1991). Intimacy expressions in three cultures: France, Japan, and the United States. *International Journal of Intercultural Relations, 15,* 29–46.

Ting-Toomey, S. (1997). An intercultural journey: The four seasons. In M. Bond (Ed.), *Working at the interface of cultures* (pp. 202–215). London: Routledge.

Ting-Toomey, S. (1999). *Communicating across cultures.* New York: Guilford.

Ting-Toomey, S. (2004). Translating conflict face-negotiation theory into practice. In D. Landis, J. Bennett, & M. Bennett (Eds.), *Handbook of intercultural training* (3rd ed., pp. 217–245). Thousand Oaks, CA: Sage.

Ting-Toomey, S. (2005a). Identity negotiation theory: Crossing cultural boundaries. In W. B. Gudykunst (Ed.), *Theorizing about intercultural communication* (pp. 211–234). Thousand Oaks, CA: Sage.

Ting Toomey, S. (2005b). The matrix of face: An updated face-negotiation theory. In W.Gudykunst (Ed.), *Theorizing about intercultural communication* (pp. 71–92). Thousand Oaks, CA: Sage.

Ting-Toomey, S. (2007a). Intercultural conflict training: Theory-practice approaches and research challenges. *Journal of Intercultural Communication Research, 36,* 255–271.

Ting-Toomey, S. (2007b). Researching intercultural conflict competence: Some promising lenses. *Journal of International Communication, 13*(2), 7–30.

Ting-Toomey, S. (2009). A mindful approach to managing conflicts in intercultural-intimate couples. In T. A. Karis & K. Killian (Eds.), *Intercultural couples: Exploring diversity in intimate relationships* (pp. 31–49). New York: Routledge/Taylor & Francis.

Ting-Toomey, S. (2010a). Mindfulness. In R. Jackson (Ed.), *Sage encyclopedia of identity, Volume 1* (pp. 455–458). Thousand Oaks, CA: Sage.

Ting-Toomey, S. (2010b). Applying dimensional values in understanding intercultural communication. *Communication Monographs, 77,* 169–180.

Ting-Toomey, S. (2010c). Intercultural conflict competence. In W. Cupach, D. Canary, & B. Spitzberg (Eds.), *Competence in Interpersonal Conflict* (2nd ed., pp. 139–162). Long Grove, IL: Waveland.

Ting-Toomey, S. (2011). Intercultural communication ethics: Multiple layered issues. In G. Cheney, S. May, & D. Munshi (Eds.), *The ICA handbook of communication ethics* (pp. 335–352). Mahway, NJ: Lawrence Erlbaum.

Ting-Toomey, S., & Chung, L. C. (2005). *Understanding intercultural communication* (1st ed.). Los Angeles, CA: Roxbury Publishing Company.

Ting-Toomey, S., & Cole, M. (1990). Intergroup diplomatic communication: A face-negotiation perspective. In F. Korzenny & S. Ting-Toomey (Eds.), *Communicating for peace. Diplomacy and negotiation across cultures*. Newbury Park, CA: Sage.

Ting-Toomey, S., Gao, G., Trubisky, P., Yang, Z., Kim, H. S., Lin, S.-L., et al. (1991). Culture, face maintenance, and styles of handling interpersonal conflict: A study in five cultures. *International Journal of Conflict Management, 2*, 275–296.

Ting-Toomey, S., & Kurogi, A. (1998). Facework competence in intercultural conflict: An updated face-negotiation theory. *International Journal of Intercultural Relations, 22*, 187–225.

Ting-Toomey, S., & Oetzel, J. (2001). *Managing intercultural conflict effectively*. Thousand Oaks, CA: Sage.

Ting-Toomey, S., Oetzel, J., & Yee-Jung, K. (2001). Self-construal types and conflict management styles. *Communication Reports, 14*, 87–104.

Ting-Toomey, S., & Takai, J. (2006). Explaining intercultural conflict: Promising approaches and directions. In J.G. Oetzel & S. Ting-Toomey (Eds.), *The Sage handbook of conflict communication* (pp. 691–723). Thousand Oaks, CA: Sage.

Ting-Toomey, S., Yee-Jung, K., Shapiro, R., Garcia, W., Wright, T., & Oetzel, J. G. (2000). Cultural/ethnic identity salience and conflict styles in four U.S. ethnic groups. *International Journal of Intercultural Relations, 24*, 47–81.

Tobin, L. (2011, February 21). *Half of living languages face extinction*. Retrieved from http://www. guardian.co.uk/education/2011/feb/21/endangered-languages-research-project

Toyosaki, S. (2011). Critical complete-member ethnography: Theorizing dialectics of consensus and conflict in intracultural communication. *Journal of International and Intercultural Communication, 4*, 62–80.

Triandis, H. (1972). *The analysis of subjective culture*. New York: Wiley.

Triandis, H. (1990). Theoretical concepts that are applicable to the analysis of ethnocentrism. In R. Brislin (Ed.), *Applied cross-cultural psychology*. Newbury Park, CA: Sage.

Triandis, H. (1994). *Culture and social behavior*. New York: McGraw–Hill.

Triandis, H. (1995). *Individualism and collectivism*. Boulder, CO: Westview Press.

Trimble, J. E., Pedersen, P. B., & Rodela, E. S. (2009). The real cost of intercultural competence: An epilogue. In D. K. Deardorff (Ed.), *The Sage handbook of intercultural competence* (pp. 492–503). Thousand Oaks, CA: Sage.

Trompenaars, F., & Hampden-Turner, C. (1998). *Riding the waves of culture: Understanding diversity in global business*. Boston: McGraw–Hill.

Trompenaars, F., & Woolliams, P. (2009b 2009). Getting the measure of intercultural leadership. In M. A. Moodian (Ed.), *Contemporary leadership and intercultural competence: Exploring the cross-cultural dynamics within organizations* (pp. 161–173). Thousand Oaks, CA: Sage.

Twitter (2011, May 2). *Graphic of last night's activity*. Retrieved from https://twitter.com/#!/twitterglobalpr/status/65140762265915392

UNICEF. (2005). *A situation analysis of children, women, and youth*. Retrieved from http://www.unicef.org/eapro/SA_2005_Vanuatu.pdf

U.S. Bureau of Labor Statistics. (2008). *International comparisons of hours worked: An assessment of statistics*. Retrieved from http://www.bls.gov/opub/mlr/2009/05/art1full.pdf

U.S. Census Bureau International Data Base. (2000a). *Countries of origin of U.S. immigrants.* Retrieved from http://www.census.gov/ipc/www/idb/

U.S. Census Bureau International Data Base. (2000b). *Countries with the highest estimated net number of immigrants per 1000 population.* Retrieved from http://www.census.gov/ipc/www/idb/

U. S. Department of Justice. Office of Public Affairs. (2011, February 23) *Texas man pleads guilty to federal hate crime in connection with mosque arson in Arlington, Texas.* Retrieved from http://dallas.fbi.gov/dojpressrel/pressrel11/dl022311.htm

Van Dyne, L. Ang, S., & Koh, C. (2009). Cultural intelligence: Measurement and scale development. In M. A. Moodian (Ed.), *Contemporary leadership and intercultural competence: Exploring the cross-cultural dynamics within organizations* (pp. 233–254). Thousand Oaks, CA: Sage.

van Meijl, T. (2010). Anthropological perspectives on identity: From sameness to difference. In M. Wetherell & C. T. Mohanty (Eds.), *The Sage handbook of identities* (pp. 45–62). Thousand Oaks, CA: Sage.

van Meurs, N., & Spencer-Oatey, H. (2010). Multidisciplinary perspectives on intercultural conflict: The "Bermuda Triangle" of conflict, culture, and communication. In D. Matsumoto (Ed.), *APA handbook of intercultural communication* (pp. 59–77). Washington, DC: American Psychological Association.

Van Nimwegen, T., Soeters, J., & van Luijk, H. (2004). Managerial values and ethics in an international bank. *International Journal of Cross-Cultural Management, 4,* 101–122.

Verkuyten, M. (2010). Multiculturalism and tolerance: An intergroup perspective. In R. Crisp (Ed.), *The psychology of social and cultural diversity* (pp. 147–170). West Sussex, UK: Wiley–Blackwell.

Visson, L. (2009). Russian-American marriages: Cultures and conflicts. In T. A. Karis & K. D. Killian (Eds.), *Intercultural couples: Exploring diversity in intimate relationships* (pp. 147–164). New York: Taylor & Francis.

Walther, J. B., Van Der Heide, B., Kim, S.-Y., Westerman, D., & Tong, S. T. (2008). The role of friends' appearances and behavior on evaluations of individuals on Facebook: Are we known by the company we keep? *Human Communication Research, 34,* 28–49.

Wang, G., & Chen, Y.-N. K. (2010). Collectivism, relations, and Chinese communication. *Chinese Journal of Communication, 3,* 1–9.

Wang, G., & Liu, Z.-B. (2010). What collective? Collectivism and relationalism from a Chinese perspective. *Chinese Journal of Communication, 3,* 42–63.

Ward, C. (1996). Acculturation. In D. Landis & R. Bhagat (Eds.). *Handbook of intercultural training* (2nd ed.) (pp.124–147). Thousand Oaks, CA: Sage.

Ward, C. (2004). Psychological theories of culture contact and their implications for intercultural training and interventions. In D. Landis, J. Bennett, & M. J. Bennett (Eds.), *Handbook of intercultural training* (3rd ed., pp. 185–216). Thousand Oaks, CA: Sage.

Ward, C. (2008). Thinking outside the Berry boxes: New perspectives on identity, acculturation and intercultural relations. *International Journal of Intercultural Relations, 32,* 105–114.

Ward, C., Bochner, S., & Furnham, A. (2001). *The psychology of culture shock* (2nd ed.). Philadelphia, PA: Routledge.

Ward, C., & Kennedy, A. (1993). Where's the culture in cross-cultural transition? Comparative studies of sojourner adjustment. *Journal of Cross-Cultural Psychology, 24,* 221–249.

Waters, M. (1990). *Ethnic options: Choosing identities in America.* Berkeley: University of California.

Watzlawick, P., Beavin, J., & Jackson, D. (1967). *The pragmatics of human communication.* New York: Norton.

Webb, L. (2009, January 22). America's second largest export. *The WEBBlog*. Retrieved from http://blogs.cbn.com/thewebblog/archive/2009/01/22/americas-second-largest-export.aspx

Wetherell, M., & Mohanty, C. T. (Eds.) (2010). *The SAGE handbook of identities*. London, UK: Sage.

Wharton, B. (2011, February 28). Stop and Frisk stats place New York atop civil rights violators. *The Examiner*. Retrieved from http://www.examiner.com/bronx-county-independent-in-new-york/stop-and-frisk-stats-place-new-york-atop-civil-rights-violators

Wheeler, L., & Kim, Y. (1997). What is beautiful is culturally good: The physical attractiveness stereotype has different content in collectivistic cultures. *Personality and Social Psychology Bulletin, 23*, 795–800.

Whitty, M. T. (2009). E-dating: The five phases on online dating. In C. Romm-Livermore & K. Setzekorn (Eds.), *Social networking communities and e-dating services: Concepts and implications* (pp. 278–291). Hershey, PA: IGI Global.

Whorf, B. (1952). *Collected papers on metalinguistics*. Washington, DC: U.S. Department of State, Foreign Service Institute.

Whorf, B. (1956). *Language, thought and reality*. New York: Wiley.

Wikipedia. (2011). *List of countries by number of mobile phones in use* [Data file]. Retrieved from http://en.wikipedia.org/wiki/List_of_countries_by_number_of_mobile_phones_in_use

Williams, P. (2002). *The paradox of power*. New York: Warner Books.

Wilmot, W., & Hocker, J. (2011). *Interpersonal conflict* (8th ed.). Boston: McGraw–Hill.

Wisckol, M. (2011, April 21). Obama chimp email official meets the press. *The Orange County Register*. Retrieved from http://www.ocregister.com

Wiseman, R. (2003). Intercultural communication competence. In W. Gudykunst (Ed.), *Cross-cultural and intercultural communication* (pp. 191–208). Thousand Oaks, CA: Sage.

Wiseman, R., & Koester, J. (Eds.). (1993). *Intercultural communication competence*. Newbury Park, CA: Sage.

Wood, J. (1997). Diversity in dialogue: Commonalities and differences between friends. In J. Makau and R. Arnett (Eds.), *Communication Ethics in an Age of Diversity* (pp. 5–26). Urbana: University of Illinois Press, 1997.

Wood, J. (2004). *Gendered lives: Communication, gender, and culture* (6th ed.). Belmont, CA: Wadsworth.

Wood, J. (2009). *Gendered lives: Communication, gender, and culture* (8th ed.). Belmont, CA: Wadsworth.

Wyatt, T. (1995). Language development in African American English child speech. *Linguistics and Education, 7*, 7–22.

Yancey, G. (2007). Experiencing racism: Differences in the experiences of whites married to blacks and non-black racial minorities. *Journal of Comparative Family Studies, 38*, 197–213.

Young, L. (1994). *Crosstalk and culture in Sino-American communication*. Cambridge, UK: Cambridge University Press.

Yuki, M., Maddux, W., & Masuda, T. (2007). Are the windows to the soul the same in the East and West? Cultural differences in using the eyes and mouth as cues to recognize emotions in Japan and the United States. *Journal of Experimental Psychology, 43*, 303–311.

Zaharana, R. S. (2009). An associative approach to intercultural communication competence in the Arab world. In D. K. Deardorff (Ed.), *The Sage handbook of intercultural competence* (pp. 179–195). Thousand Oaks, CA: Sage.

Zakaria, F. (2011, February 17). Why there's no turning back in the Middle East. *Time, 177*(7), 31.

Zelizer, B. (2001). Popular communication in the contemporary age. In W. Gudykunst (Ed.), *Communication yearbook, 24*, 299. Thousand Oaks, CA: Sage.

Zhang, R., Ting-Toomey, S., Dorjee, T., & Lee, P. (2012, in press). Culture and self-construal as predictors of relational responses to emotional infidelity: China and the United States. *Chinese Journal of Communication, 4*.

Zhang, Y., & Van Hook, J. (2009). Marital dissolution among interracial couples. *Journal of Marriage and the Family, 71*, 95–107.

Zielenziger, M. (2006). *Shutting out the sun: How Japan created its own lost generation*. New York: Doubleday.

Zuckerman, P. (2006). Atheism: Contemporary rates and patterns. In M. Martin (Ed.), *The Cambridge companion to atheism* (pp. 47–68). New York: Cambridge University.

Zwingle, E., & McNally, J. (1999, August). A world together. *National Geographic, 196* (2), 6–34.

GLOSSARY

ACCENT   means the inflection or tone of voice that is perceived to be the distinctive characteristic of an individual.

ACCEPTANCE OF CULTURAL DIFFERENCE   is the cultural worldview state in which one's own culture is experienced as one of many possible diverse cultural experiences and a beginning positive attitude in acknowledging cultural differences.

ACCULTURATION   refers to the incremental identity-related change process of immigrants and refugees in a new environment from a long-term perspective.

ADAPTATION OF CULTURAL DIFFERENCE   is the cultural worldview state in which the experience of another culture yields perceptual shifting—seeing things from the other cultural angle— and also engaging in behavioral adaptation appropriate to that cultural frame of reference.

ADAPTORS   are hand gesture habits or movements that fulfill some kind of psychological or physical need.

AMBIVALENCE STAGE   refers to time when sojourners experience grief, nostalgia, and pride, with a mixed sense of relief and sorrow that they are going home.

APPROPRIATENESS   refers to the degree to which the exchanged behaviors are regarded as proper and match the expectations generated by the insiders of the culture.

ARTIFACTS   are ornaments or adornments we use to communicate just by wearing the actual item.

ATTITUDE   refers to both cognitive and affective predisposition and learned tendency that influence our thinking pattern.

ATTRIBUTIONS   are the explanations, causes, or reasons we ascribe to why people behave the way they behave or why certain events happen.

AUTHORITARIAN PERSONALITY APPROACH   causes prejudice to occur as it emphasizes personality features of the individual, including a rigid observance of (or adherence to) conventional norms, complete acceptance of authority, and a high concern for those in power.

AVOIDING STYLE   involves dodging the topic, the other party, or the situation altogether; it also involves behavior ranging from glossing over the topic and denying that conflict exists to; leaving the conflict scene.

"BEING-IN-BECOMING" SOLUTION   means living with an emphasis on spiritual renewal and regeneration.

BEING-IN-DOING E.NET PHILOSOPHY means that e.net multitrack individuals can fuse the "being mode" value dimension with the "doing mode" value dimension—they can be fully enjoying the here-and-now moment, spending *being* time with their multiple friends on Facebook and Twitter, and also *doing* other task activities.

"BEING" SOLUTION means living with emotional vitality and being relationally connected with significant others.

BLENDED FAMILY refers to the merging of different family systems from previous marriages.

BREADTH refers to the number of topics we are comfortable and willing to disclose to reveal our dynamic self during the self-disclosure.

CHRONEMICS is known as the study of time. It concerns how people in different cultures structure, interpret, and understand the time dimension.

CO-CULTURE THEORY refers to "minority" group members such as African American, Asian American, Hispanic American, and Native American groups on equal memberships with the dominant white group.

COLLECTIVISM refers to the broad value tendencies of a culture in emphasizing the importance of the "we" identity over the "I" identity, group rights over individual rights, and ingroup needs over individual wants and desires.

COMMUNICATION ADAPTABILITY refers to our ability to change our interaction behaviors and goals to meet the specific needs of the situation. It implies behavioral flexibility in dealing with the intercultural miscommunication episode.

COMMUNICATION COMPETENCE refers to the application of culture-sensitive knowledge, open- minded attitude, and the activation of appropriate, effective, and adaptive communication skills.

COMPENSATION means conflict parties can offer exchanges or concessions for conflict issues they value differently.

COMPROMISING STYLE involves a give-and-take concession approach to reach a mid-point agreement concerning the conflict issue. Individuals tend to use fairness appeals, trade-off suggestions, or other quick, short-term solutions.

CONFLICT is an aggravating disagreement process between two interdependent parties over incompatible goals and the interference each perceives from the other in her or his effort to achieve those goals.

CONFLICT COMMUNICATION STYLE refers to patterned verbal and nonverbal responses to conflict in a variety of frustrating conflict situations.

CONFLICT RESOURCES are tangible (e.g., money) or intangible (e.g., desires or needs) rewards that people want in a dispute.

CONNOTATIVE MEANING stresses the subjective, interpretive meanings of a word constructed by individual members based on their cultural and personalized language experience.

CONSCIOUS COMPETENCE STAGE refers to the intentional mindfulness stage in which individuals actively pursue new intercultural knowledge to improve their communication competencies and practice new interaction skills.

CONSCIOUS INCOMPETENCE STAGE refers to the troubling realization stage in which individuals have some notions (i.e., attitudinal openness) that they behave incompetently; however, they lack the knowledge or skills to operate adaptively in the new culture.

CONTENT GOALS are the tangible issues that are external to the individuals involved.

CONTENT MEANING refers to the factual (or digital) information that is being conveyed to the receiver through an oral channel or other communication medium.

CONTROLLING OR MASTERING THEIR ENVIRONMENT operates under the belief that if something is wrong in a system or organization, they can fix it, change it, or master it.

CULTURAL COMMUNITY refers to a group of interacting individuals within a bounded unit who uphold a set of shared traditions and way of life.

CULTURAL COMPETENCE SKILLS refer to the cultural knowledge you have internalized and the operational skills you are able to apply in the interaction scene.

CULTURAL DISPLAY RULES are the sociocultural norms and situational expectations that we have in terms of when to express what nonverbal emotions and also when to use what nonverbal gestures under what particular situational contexts.

CULTURAL DISTANCE refers to the major differences concerning cultural values, language, and verbal and nonverbal styles between one's home culture and the host society.

CULTURAL EMPATHY is the learned ability of the participants to understand accurately the self-experiences of others from diverse cultures and, concurrently, the ability to convey their understanding responsively and effectively to reach the "cultural ears" of the unfamiliar others.

CULTURAL IDENTITY is defined as the emotional significance that we attach to our sense of belonging or affiliation with the larger culture and we have internalized the larger sociocultural value patterns of that membership community.

CULTURAL IDENTITY SALIENCE refers to the strength of affiliation one has with the larger culture.

CULTURAL NORMS are the collective expectations of what constitutes proper or improper behavior in a given interaction scene.

CULTURAL VALUES refer to a set of priorities that guide "good" or "bad" behaviors, "desirable" or "undesirable" practices, and "fair" or "unfair" actions.

CULTURALLY SHARED BELIEFS refer to a set of fundamental assumptions or worldviews that people hold dearly to their hearts without question.

CULTURALLY SHARED TRADITIONS can include myths, legends, ceremonies, and rituals that are passed on from one generation to the next via an oral or written medium.

CULTURE is a learned meaning system that consists of patterns of traditions, beliefs, values, norms, meanings, and symbols that are passed on from one generation to the next and are shared to varying degrees by interacting members of a community.

CULTURE BUMP is defined as a cultural violation on the behavioral level when our meanings do not overlap with one another in viewing the same behavior and thus create communication awkwardness or embarrassment.

CULTURE SHOCK basically refers to a stressful transitional period when individuals move from a familiar environment into an unfamiliar one—the stress and confusion can occur on the affective, behavioral, and cognitive levels.

DEDUCTIVE REASONING refers to the primacy of conceptual models or big principles to start and then moves on to distill pertinent facts and inferences.

DEFENSE AGAINST CULTURAL DIFFERENCE is the cultural polarized worldview state in which one's own cultural (or adopted culture) practices are experienced as the only "superior" ones and all other cultural practices are second-rate or "backward."

DENIAL OF CULTURAL DIFFERENCE is the cultural worldview state in which one's own cultural community is experienced as the only "authentic" one and the individuals in this state tend to avoid any cultural difference situations.

DENOTATIVE MEANING of a word emphasizes its objective, dictionary definition shared and recognized by the majority members of a linguistic community.

DEPTH   refers to the intimate layers that reveal our emotionally vulnerable self during the self disclosure process.

DIALECTICAL TENSIONS   are conflicts that come from two opposing forces that exist at the same time.

DIFFERENT CULTURAL COMMUNITIES   is defined as a broad concept that refers to groups of interacting individuals within bounded units who uphold a set of shared traditions and way of life.

DIFFERENTIATION   means taking an active stance to acknowledge the different cultural perspectives and lenses in a conflict situation.

DIRECT INSTITUTIONAL DISCRIMINATION   occurs when there is a community-prescribed endorsement of discrimination.

DIRECT STYLE   is used to reveal the speaker's intentions with clarity and are enunciated with a forthright tone of voice.

DISAFFILIATES   is one of the identity forms of bicultural children where they distance themselves or claim not to be influenced by their parents' cultural backgrounds, and they often create their own identity labels and rebel against any existing label that is imposed on them as part of a particular racial or cultural group.

DISPOSITIONAL APPROACH   emphasizes that individuals do have predominant, stable conflict style tendencies in handling a wide variety of conflict situations in different cultures.

DISTANCE OF AVOIDANCE   is a form of moderate ethnocentrism, that reflects attempted linguistic or dialect switching in the presence of outgroup members, as well as displayed nonverbal inattention to accentuate ingroup connection and avoidance of outgroup members.

DISTANCE OF DISPARAGEMENT   is a high ethnocentrism, and refers to the use of racist jokes or hate-filled speech used to downgrade outgroup members.

DISTANCE OF INDIFFERENCE   is a low degree of ethnocentrism that reflects the lack of sensitivity in our verbal and nonverbal interactions in dealing with dissimilar others.

"DOING" SOLUTION   means living through action-based activities and emphasizing the achievement of concrete outcomes.

DOMINATING OR COMPETITIVE/CONTROLLING STYLE   emphasizes conflict tactics that push for one's own position above and beyond the other person's interest by using aggressive, defensive, controlling, and intimidating tactics.

DRAMATIC SPIRAL REASONING   refers to the use of effusive metaphors, stories, parables, and a wide range of flowery adjectives to reinforce a point.

EFFECTIVENESS   refers to the degree to which communicators achieve mutually shared meaning and integrative goal-related outcomes.

EMBLEMS   are culture-specific gestures that substitute for actual words or phrases.

ENCULTURATION   refers to the sustained, primary socialization process of strangers in their original home (or natal) culture wherein they have internalized their primary cultural values.

E.NETIZEN   stands for a new generation of individuals, from any age group, wired to the Internet via intersecting space.

E.NETIZEN IDENTITY   is a composite identity that is shaped by technology, popular culture, and mass consumption.

ENVIRONMENTAL BOUNDARIES   are defined as the claimed sense of space or privacy that is needed and the emotional attachment we have for marking our ingroup versus outgroup territories.

ETHICAL ABSOLUTISM   emphasizes the principles of right and wrong in accordance with a set of "universally" (yet ethnocentrically based) fixed standards regardless of cultural differences.

ETHICAL RELATIVISM emphasizes the importance of understanding the cultural context in which the problematic conduct is being judged.

ETHICAL UNIVERSALISM emphasizes the importance of deriving universal ethical guidelines by placing ethical judgments within the proper cross-cultural context.

ETHICS is defined as a community's perspective on what is good and bad in human conduct and leads to norms (prescriptive and concrete rules) that regulate actions.

ETHNIC IDENTITY refers to interpretive ancestral heritage and perceived ingroup communal ties, as well as beliefs about the origins of one's forebears, and can be based on historical origin, race, religion, language, or perceived distinctive traits as a particular group.

ETHNOCENTRIC MINDSET means staying stuck with our own cultural worldviews and using our own cultural values as the baseline standards to evaluate the other person's cultural behavior.

ETHNOCENTRISM means seeing our own culture as the center of the universe and seeing other cultures as insignificant or even inferior.

ETHNORELATIVE MINDSET means to understand a communication behavior from the other person's cultural frame of reference.

ETHNORELATIVISM means to understand a communication practice from the other person's cultural frame of reference.

EXPANSION means an active search for alternative paths or creative solutions to enlarge the amount, type, or use of available resources for mutual gains.

EXPLOITATION THEORY is mainly about power as a scarce resource: to maintain higher status and power, one restrains those of lower status to improve one's own group position and security.

EXTENDED FAMILY consists of extended kinship groups, such as grandparents, aunt and uncles, cousins, and nieces and nephews.

EXTERNAL LOCUS OF CONTROL emphasizes external conditions , karma, fate, and external forces shaping a person's life happenings and events.

FACE is about socially approved self-image and other-image consideration issues—on the surface level, it can be about give-and-take respect and disrespect attitudinal issues; on the deeper level, it is about honor and shame belief and value systems.

FACEWORK is about the verbal and nonverbal interaction strategies that we use to maintain, defend, or upgrade our own social self-image and attack or defend (or even "save") the social images of others.

FAVORABLE SELF-BIAS AND OTHER-DEROGATION PRINCIPLE is the tendency to favor ourselves and our ingroup in explaining our success and to create belittling explanations for others' or outgroup members' successes.

FEMININITY pertains to societies in which social gender roles are fluid and can overlap—that is, whatever a woman can do, a man can do.

FENG SHUI literally means "wind" and "water" in Chinese. Used for thousands of years, feng shui is the ancient Chinese philosophy of aesthetics in combining different elements of the laws of Heaven and Earth to attain good energy or qi within a room, a house, or an architectural design and including its harmonious blend with the surrounding environment.

FIXATED E.NETIZEN IDENTITY are individuals who have deep attachment and solidarity to their e-netizen identity. They are continuously hooked and wired up, expressing their daily lives via a multitude of social media platforms.

FLEXIBLE INTERCULTURAL COMMUNICATION emphasizes the importance of integrating knowledge and an open-minded attitude and putting them into adaptive and creative practice in everyday communication.

FLEXIBLE/MINDFUL STEREOTYPING   refers to treating our own stereotypic images as the "first-best guesses" and being aware that we are engaging in stereotyping others based on overgeneralizations or overexaggerated images because of unfamiliarity or ignorance.

FUNDAMENTAL ATTRIBUTION ERROR   occurs when we tend to engage in cognitively biased explanations by overestimating negative personality traits in explaining a stranger's undesirable actions and underestimating external, situational factors.

FUTURE-ORIENTED TIME SENSE   means planning for desirable short- to medium-term developments and setting out clear objectives to realize them.

GESTURES   are culturally specific and significant forms of nonverbal communication and can include dramatic to understated nonverbal hand and body movements.

GLIDING E.NETIZEN IDENTITY   are individuals who have weaker attachment with the wired community and they reflect the larger international group membership. These individuals have stronger ties with the local culture and see the Internet and technology as a hobby.

GLOBAL IDENTITY   is made up of individuals who adopt and embrace international practices and values over local practices.

HAPTICS   is a nonverbal function that examines the perceptions and meanings of touch behavior.

HARMONY-WITH-NATURE OR "FLOWING" VALUE SOLUTION   this value orientation emphasizes spiritual transformation or enlightenment rather than material gain. Those with this value orientation also tend to believe in living harmoniously with nature.

HATE CRIME   is typically motivated by hostility to the victim as a member of a group (e.g., on the basis of ethnicity/race, disability, age, religion, gender, or sexual orientation).

HIGH-CONTACT CULTURES   individuals in these cultures often look each other in the eye directly, face each other more closely, and touch more frequently in their everyday conversations.

HIGH-CONTEXT COMMUNICATION   is based on how intention or meaning can best be conveyed through the embedded contexts and the nonverbal channels of the verbal message. It refers to communication patterns of indirect verbal style and tactful nonverbal tone and emphasizes diplomatic talk, self-humbling speech, and listener-sensitive values.

HIP-HOP MUSIC (or HIP-HOP CULTURE)   originates from the African American youths of the United States in the mid-1970s who were discouraged by racial oppression. Hip-hop culture is an expressive, artistic culture that has been associated with rap music, dance trends, scratching (i.e., a deejay simultaneously mixing two or more records), graffiti, and artifacts (e.g., bling/jewelry).

HONEYMOON STAGE   is the initial landing phase, in which everything appears fresh and exhilarating as individuals are excited about their new cultural environment.

HORIZONTAL SELF-CONSTRUAL   involves the personality traits of preferring to treat others on an equal level regardless of age, rank, or status and tends to favor informal interactions.

HOSTILITY STAGE   is the serious culture shock stage in which nothing works out smoothly as sojourners experience major emotional upheavals.

HUMOROUS STAGE   is where sojourners learn to laugh at their cultural faux pas and start to realize that there are pros and cons in each culture.

IDENTITY   refers to our reflective views of ourselves and of other perceptions of our self-images—on both the social identity and the personal identity levels.

IDENTITY-BASED GOALS   are about self-respect (face-saving) and other-consideration (face-honoring) issues in a conflict situation—they can be about sociocultural identity, personal identity, and/or communication identity issues.

IDENTITY MEANING   refers to the following questions: "Who am I and who are you in this inter-action episode?" "How do I define myself in this interaction scene?" and "How do I define you in this interaction scene?" Identity meaning involves issues such as the display of respect or dis-respect and identity approval or disapproval.

ILLUSTRATORS   are nonverbal hand gestures that we use along with the spoken message.

INDEPENDENT-SELF CONFLICT LENS   follows an outcome-oriented model, which empha-sizes tangible conflict issues above and beyond relationship issues, a clear win-lose conflict approach, a "doing" angle, in which something tangible in the conflict is broken and needs fixing.

INDEPENDENT SELF-CONSTRUAL   involves the view that an individual is a unique entity with an individuated repertoire of feelings, cognitions, and motivations.

INDIRECT INSTITUTIONAL DISCRIMINATION   is a broad practice that indirectly affects group members without intending to.

INDIRECT STYLE   is used to camouflage the speaker's actual intentions and is carried out with a softer tone.

INDIVIDUALISM   refers to the broad value tendencies of a culture in emphasizing the importance of individual identity over group identity, individual rights over group rights, and individual needs over group needs.

INDUCTIVE REASONING   refers to the importance of establishing facts and evidence and then arriving at a general principle or conclusion.

INFLEXIBLE INTERCULTURAL COMMUNICATION   stresses the continuation of using our own cultural values, judgments, and routines in a rigid manner.

INFLEXIBLE/MINDLESS STEREOTYPING   occurs when one holds on to preconceived images of individuals or group members by operating on automatic pilot or subconscious reactions because of unfamiliarity.

INGROUP   members are people with whom you feel connected to or owe a sense of loyalty and allegiance, such as family members, close friends, or familiar others within the community.

INGROUP COLLECTIVISM   refers to the sentiment of loyalty and solidarity between the employee and his or her organization or ingroup community.

INGROUP FAVORITISM PRINCIPLE   states that there is a positive attachment to and predisposi-tion for norms that are related to one's ingroup.

INGROUPS   are groups with whom we feel emotionally close and with whom we share an inter-dependent fate, such as family or extended family, or people from our own cultural or ethnic group.

INSTITUTIONAL COLLECTIVISM   refers to the institutional perspective in enforcing ingroup norms, cohesion, and conformity.

IN-SYNC ADJUSTMENT STAGE   takes place when sojourners feel "at home" and experience iden-tity security and inclusion. The boundaries between outsiders and insiders become fuzzier, and sojourners experience social acceptance and support.

INTANGIBLE RESOURCES   include deeply felt desires or emotional needs, such as emotional security, inclusion, connection, respect, control, and meaning issues.

INTEGRATING OR COLLABORATIVE STYLE   reflects a commitment to find a mutual-inter-est solution and involves a high concern for self-interest and also a high concern for the other person's interest in the conflict situation. Individuals tend to use nonevaluative descriptive messages, qualifying statements, and mutual-interest clarifying questions to seek common-ground solutions.

INTEGRATION OF CULTURAL DIFFERENCE   is the cultural worldview state in which the individual intentionally (on cognitive, behavioral, and affective levels) incorporates diverse cultural worldviews into one's identity and is able to transform polarized value sets into complementary value resources.

INTERACTION GOAL   refers to the objective of the meeting.

INTERACTIVE SITUATION   refers to the idea that every communication episode occurs in a relational context, a psychological context, and a physical context.

INTERCULTURAL ADJUSTMENT   refers to the short-term and medium-term adaptive process of sojourners in their overseas assignments.

INTERCULTURAL CODE-SWITCHING   refers to intentionally adapting and moving between culturally ingrained systems of verbal and nonverbal behaviors relevant to the situation at hand.

INTERCULTURAL COMMUNICATION   is defined as the symbolic exchange process whereby individuals from two (or more) different cultural communities attempt to negotiate shared meanings in an interactive situation within an embedded societal system.

INTERCULTURAL COMPETENCE   refers to the intentional integration of culture-sensitive knowledge, open-minded attitude, and adaptive communication skills in an intercultural encounter.

INTERCULTURAL CONFLICT   is defined as the implicit or explicit emotional struggle or frustration between persons of different cultures over perceived incompatible values, norms, face orientations, goals, scarce resources, processes, and/or outcomes in a communication situation.

INTERCULTURAL-INTIMATE CONFLICT   is defined as any antagonistic friction or disagreement between two romantic partners caused, in part, by cultural or ethnic group membership differences.

INTERDEPENDENT-SELF CONFLICT LENS   views conflict from a relational process lens, which emphasizes relationship and feeling issues, a win–win relational approach, in which feelings and "faces" can both be saved, a "being" angle, in which relational trust must be repaired and loyalty must be amended to preserve relational harmony, and a long-term compromising negotiation mode that has no clear winner or loser in the ongoing conflict.

INTERDEPENDENT SELF-CONSTRUAL   involves an emphasis on the importance of fitting in with relevant others and ingroup connectedness.

INTERFACED E.NETIZEN IDENTITY   are individuals who have moderately strong ties to the Internet. These individuals have interfaced ties with the global Internet community on one hand and also continue their local community ties with other individuals in real time.

INTERGROUP COMMUNICATION   happens whenever individuals belonging to a sociocultural group interact—collectively or individually—with members from another sociocultural group based primarily on ingroup/outgroup (or social identity) membership traits.

INTERNAL LOCUS OF CONTROL   emphasizes internal drive, free will, personal motivation and effort, and individual responsibility over the success or failure of an assignment.

INTRAPERSONAL SPACE   refers to the need for information privacy or psychological distance and preferred solitude between the self and others.

ISOLATE DISCRIMINATION   occurs when an ingroup member engages in harmful verbal and nonverbal action that is intentionally targeted toward an outgroup member.

KARMA   means the quality of your present or even future lives is determined by your current life's actions or actions from your numerous past lives—it broadly equates destiny or fate.

KINESICS   is the study of posture, body movement, gestures, and facial expressions.

KNOWLEDGE   here refers to the systematic, conscious learning of the essential themes and concepts in intercultural communication flexibility.

LANGUACULTURE is the necessary interdependent tie between language and culture.

LANGUAGE is an arbitrary, symbolic system that labels and categorizes objects, events, groups, people, ideas, feelings, experiences, and many other phenomena.

LARGE POWER DISTANCE CULTURES tend to accept unequal power distributions, hierarchical rights, asymmetrical role relations, and rewards and punishments based on age, rank, status, title, and seniority.

LOCAL IDENTITY is made up of the ethnic values, practices, and traditions of the local identity communal group.

LOW-CONTACT CULTURES individuals in these cultures often engage in fewer touching behaviors, often preferring indirect eye gazes and less use of hand gesture movements.

LOW-CONTEXT COMMUNICATION is based on how intention or meaning is expressed through explicit verbal messages. It refers to communication patterns of direct verbal style and matter-of-fact tone and emphasizes verbal transparency, assertiveness, and sender-oriented values.

MAJORITY GROUP IDENTIFIERS is one of the identity forms that bicultural children claim where children identify with the parent from the dominant culture or religion, and they may or may not publicly acknowledge the identity of their other parent (in this case, from a minority-group background).

MASCULINITY pertains to societies in which social gender roles are clearly complementary and distinct.

MEANING is the interpretation we attach to a symbol.

META-ETHICS refers to the cultivation of an ethical way of thinking and philosophical outlook in our everyday lives that transcends any particular ideological position.

META-ETHICS CONTEXTUAL APPROACH means that the application of ethics can be understood only through a systematic analysis of the multiple macro–micro contexts and layers of the ethical dilemma situation.

MINDFUL LISTENING is a face-validation and power-sharing skill in attuning to the speaker's verbal and nonverbal messages and responding appropriately and sensitively.

MINDFULNESS refers to the heightened awareness of our own thinking patterns, affective reactions, and preferred behavioral routines and also extend this particular awareness to understand the culturally unfamiliar others' frames of reference.

MINDFUL REFRAMING is the process of using neutrally toned to positively toned language to change or alter the meaning frame in which each person interprets the conflict event with the goal of trying to generate alternative or multiple interpretation viewpoints.

MINIMIZATION OF CULTURAL DIFFERENCE is the cultural worldview state in which elements of one's own culture are viewed as "universals" and such "surface universals" are superimposed on all other cultural behaviors or practices.

MINORITY GROUP IDENTIFIERS is one of the identity forms that bicultural children claim where they identify with the parent who is a minority, and they may either acknowledge that their other parent is from a different background or deny (or minimize) their dual heritage background.

MODERATE-CONTACT CULTURES is a blend of both high-contact and low-contact cultures.

MONOCHRONIC TIME CULTURE emphasizes the importance of keeping track of clock time and keeping punctual appointment time and separating work activities from relational activities clearly.

MONOTRACK FOCUS is when you work on one project at a time on the Internet.

MORPHOLOGICAL RULES (or **MORPHOLOGY**) refers to how combinations of different sounds make up a meaningful word or different meaningful units of a particular word.

MOTIVATIONAL ORIENTATION involves the person's willingness or desire to enter into a new culture.

MULTITRACK FOCUS is when you tend to multiple e.net tasks or activities on the Internet.

NEGOTIATE SHARED MEANINGS refers to the general goal of any intercultural communication encounter.

NONLINGUISTIC CUES can include nonverbal eye contact, smiles, touch, hand gestures, or even silence.

NONVERBAL COMMUNICATION is defined as the message exchange process involving the use of nonlinguistic and paralinguistic cues that are expressed through multiple communication channels in a particular sociocultural setting.

OBLIGING OR ACCOMMODATING STYLE is characterized by a high concern for the other person's conflict interest above and beyond one's own conflict position. They tend to either smooth over the conflict or give in to the wishes of their conflict partners.

OTHER-ORIENTED FACE-SAVING BEHAVIORS are the attempts to support others' face claims and work with them to prevent further face loss or help them to restore face constructively.

OUTGROUP members are those with whom one feels emotionally and psychologically detached, such as strangers, unfamiliar others, or members who belong to a competitive or opposing group.

PARALANGUAGE is the sounds and tones we use in conversation and the speech behavior that accompanies the message.

PARALINGUISTIC CUES refer to the tone of voice, pitch, or volume of the sounds that accompany a verbal message.

PARALINGUISTIC FEATURES are the nonword sounds and characteristics of speech.

PARALLEL THINKING means substituting any global or local event with people in your connected ingroup or intimate network and then cross-checking whether you would still arrive at a similar attribution process or a similar emotional reaction.

PARAPHRASING SKILLS involve summarizing the content meaning of the other's message in your own words, and nonverbally echoing your interpretation of the emotional meaning of the other's message.

PARTICULARISM means depending on the particular relationship types or circumstances, rules or norms should be tailored to the particular individuals undergoing a particular set of experiences.

PAST-ORIENTED TIME SENSE means honoring historic and ancestral ties plus respecting the wisdom of the elders.

PERCEPTION is the process of selecting cues from the environment, organizing them into a coherent pattern and labeling such a pattern, and interpreting that pattern in accordance with our cultural and personal expectations.

PERCEPTION CHECKING is used to ensure that we are interpreting the speaker's nonverbal and verbal behaviors accurately during an escalating conflict episode.

PERSONAL COMMITMENT means an individual's desire or intent to continue an interpersonal relationship on the basis of his or her subjective emotional feelings and experiences, regardless of family or ingroup reactions.

PERSONAL EXPECTATIONS refer to the anticipatory process and predictive outcome of the upcoming situation.

PERSONAL FAMILY SYSTEM   refers to a democratic family system that emphasizes personal, individualized meanings and negotiable roles between parents and children.

PERSONAL IDENTITIES   include any unique attributes such as "smart," "shy," "optimistic," and "outgoing" that we associate with our individuated self in comparison with those of others.

PERSONALITY ATTRIBUTES   refer to stable dispositional traits such as independent and interdependent self characteristics.

PHONEMES   are the smallest distinctive sound units of a word in a language system.

PHONOLOGICAL RULES (or **PHONOLOGY**)   refers to the different accepted procedures for combining phonemes in a word.

PHYSICAL CONTEXT   refers to the immediate physical features and layouts surrounding the face-to-face or mediated interaction.

POLYCHRONIC TIME CULTURE   emphasizes the importance of relational connection time and places more emphasis on completing the ongoing human transactions than keeping track of strict clock time schedules.

POP CULTURE   refers to an integration of ideas and perspectives gleaned from global economy, e-commerce, mass media, social network platforms, and informal consensus of the media culture and expresses trendy taste, consumerism, and the export of attention-grabbing celebrity images worldwide.

POSITIONAL FAMILY SYSTEM   refers to a large power distance family system that emphasizes communal meanings and hierarchical respect, ascribed roles, and different statuses between parents and children; family rule conformity.

PRAGMATIC RULES (or PRAGMATICS)   refer to the contextual or situational rules that govern the appropriate versus inappropriate language usage in a particular cultural community.

PREJUDICE   refers to a prejudgment or a preconceived assumption toward an individual or outgroup members in a pejorative or negative direction based on limited knowledge or slim evidence.

PRESENT-ORIENTED TIME SENSE   means valuing the here and now, especially the interpersonal relationships that are unfolding currently.

PRINCIPLE OF NEGATIVITY   occurs when we typically place more emphasis on negative information concerning our competitors or outgroup members.

PRIVATE SELF   refers to those facets of the person that are potentially communicable but are not usually shared with generalized others.

PROCESS   refers to the interdependent nature of the intercultural encounter.

PROXEMICS   is the study of spatial distance between persons, physical contact or noncontact preference, and sociocultural and psychological influence on the use of space and space violations.

PSYCHOLOGICAL ADJUSTMENT   refers to feelings of well-being and satisfaction during cross-cultural transitions.

PSYCHOLOGICAL CONTEXT   refers to our psychological moods (e.g., anxious versus secure), meaning-making interpretations (e.g., perceived meanings of the formal or informal interactive setting), and normative role expectations of a given situation.

PUBLIC SELF   refers to those facets of the person that are readily available and are easily shared with others.

RACIAL PROFILING   is the singling out of one particular ethnic group in a police investigation.

RACISM   relates to a personal/institutional belief in the cultural superiority of one race and the perceived inferiority of other races.

REENTRY CULTURE SHOCK STAGE   is experienced when sojourners return to their home culture and face an unexpected jolt, because this shock is unanticipated.

REFRAMING   is the mindful process of using language to change the way each person defines or thinks about experiences and views the conflict situation.

REGULATORS   are nonverbal behaviors we use in conversation to control, maintain, or "regulate" the pace and flow of the conversation.

RELATIONAL CONFLICT GOALS   refer to how individuals define the particular relationship or would prefer or expect to define it in a particular manner in the interactive situation.

RELATIONAL CONTEXT   examples are intercultural acquaintance relationships, friendships, dating relationships, and business relationships to illustrate diverse relationship contexts.

RELATIONAL MEANING   offers information concerning the state of the relationship between the two communicators.

RELATIONAL WORLDVIEW   emphasizes a language system that focuses on "big picture" thinking and that is based on a relationship-based experience and also emphasizes the importance of family and ingroup relationship webs.

RELATIONSHIP EXPECTATION   refers to anticipation of how things should work out in a relationship situation.

"ROMEO AND JULIET" EFFECT   occurs in an intercultural-intimate relationship: the more the respective families are against this intimate relationship, the more the couple wants to rebel against their parents and "do their own thing" and, therefore, they find each other even more attractive.

RESOCIALIZATION STAGE   is when sojourners have moved past the reentry culture shock stage and they are assimilating back into their home culture. There are three types of individuals in this stage: resocializers, alienators, and transformers.

SADFISH   is an acronym that refers to these seven facial emotions: Sadness, Anger, Disgust, Fear, Interest, Surprise, and Happiness is the study of posture, body movement, gestures, and facial expressions.

SAPIR–WHORF HYPOTHESIS   has two forms—the strong form states that language determines our thinking pattern, and the weak form states that language only influences or shapes our thinking pattern.

SCAPEGOATING THEORY   suggests prejudiced individuals believe that they are the victims of society. If something is not going well in their life, they will blame a minority group instead of accepting the basic responsibility for some other type of failure.

SELECTIVE ATTENTION PROCESS   is used when we pick out cues quickly and especially selecting social stimuli or cues that grab our attention.

SELECTIVE INTERPRETATION   is when we attach meanings to the data we receive, and this meaning construction process often reflects our expectations and biases.

SELECTIVE ORGANIZATION AND LABELING PROCESS   is used when we organize our perceptions by grouping similar objects, people, or things together and labeling them with a symbol or name.

SELF-DISCLOSURE   involves the intentional process of revealing exclusive information about ourselves to others that the other individuals do not know.

SELF-EFFACEMENT BIAS   refers to the attributional explanation of individuals to use self-humbling or self-modesty interpretation to explain the failed events caused by their lack of ability or oversight.

SELF-ENHANCEMENT STYLE   emphasizes the importance of drawing attention to or exaggerates one's credentials, outstanding accomplishments, and special abilities.

SELF-HUMBLING STYLE emphasizes the importance of downplaying oneself via modest talk, restraint, hesitation, and the use of self-deprecation messages concerning one's performance or effort.

SELF-ORIENTED FACE-SAVING BEHAVIORS are used when one attempts to regain or defend one's image after threats to face or face loss.

SEMANTIC RULES (or SEMANTICS) of a language concern the features of meaning we attach to words.

SETTING can include the consideration of cultural context or physical context.

SINGLE-PARENT FAMILY refers to a household headed by a single parent.

SITUATIONAL APPROACH stresses the importance of the conflict topic and the conflict situation in shaping what conflict styles will be used in what types of relationships and in what contexts, or both of these.

SKILLS are our operational abilities to integrate knowledge and a responsive attitude with adaptive intercultural practice.

SMALL GROUP DISCRIMINATION occurs when individuals from an ingroup engage in hostile and abusive actions against outgroup members.

SMALL POWER DISTANCE CULTURES tend to value equal power distributions, equal rights and relations, and equitable rewards and punishments on the basis of performance.

SOCIAL IDENTITIES include cultural or ethnic membership, gender, sexual orientation, social class, political or religious affiliation, age, disability, professional, and also family and relational role identities.

SOCIETAL EMBEDDED SYSTEM refers to the multilayered contexts such as history, politics, economics, social class, formal institutions, and policies, as well as the community or organizational contexts that shape the process and the outcome of the intercultural communication process.

SOCIOCULTURAL ADJUSTMENT refers to the ability to fit in and execute appropriate and effective interactions in a new cultural environment.

SPEECH COMMUNITY is a group of individuals who share a common set of norms and rules regarding appropriate communication practices.

STEREOTYPES are exaggerated pictures we create about a group of people on the basis of our inflexible beliefs and expectations about the characteristics or behaviors of the group.

STRONG (or HIGH) UNCERTAINTY AVOIDANCE refers to cultural characteristics that promote the importance of spelling out clear procedures and valuing conflict-avoidance behaviors.

STRUCTURAL APPROACH causes prejudice to occur as it stresses the climate in one's society whereby institutions promote a "pecking order" among group members.

STRUCTURAL COMMITMENT refers to individuals taking into consideration various external social and family reactions in deciding either to continue or to break up an interpersonal relationship.

SUBJUGATION-TO-NATURE OR "YIELDING" VALUE SOLUTION. Individuals who subscribe to this solution tend to be more fatalistic than individuals who subscribe to the controlling nature value solution. They believe that nature is a powerful force that is beyond the control of individuals.

SYMBOL refers to a sign, artifact, word(s), gesture, or nonverbal behavior that stands for or reflects something meaningful.

SYMBOLIC EXCHANGE refers to the use of verbal and nonverbal symbols between a minimum of two individuals to accomplish shared meanings.

SYNTACTIC RULES (or **syntactics**) of a language refer to how words are sequenced together in accordance with the grammatical practices of the linguistic community.

SYNTHESIZERS is one of the identity forms that bicultural children claim, children who acknowledge the influence of both aspects of their parents' cultural backgrounds and synchronize and synthesize the diverse aspects of their parents' values into a coherent identity.

SYSTEMS APPROACH integrates both dispositional and situational approaches.

TANGIBLE RESOURCES refer to concrete resources including money available to spend on a new car, a sound system, or a vacation.

TEMPORAL REGULATION is defined as the psychological and emotional attitudes and rhythms we have about time.

TRADITIONAL FAMILY refers to a family structure consisting of a husband–wife/father–mother pair that has a child or children, with a father working outside the home and a homemaker mother.

TRANSACTIONAL INTERCULTURAL COMMUNICATION refers to the simultaneous encoding and decoding of the exchanged message between two or more interdependent communicators.

UNCONSCIOUS COMPETENCE STAGE refers to the "mindlessly mindful" intercultural sensitivity stage in which individuals move in and out of spontaneous, yet adaptive, communication with members of the new culture.

UNCONSCIOUS INCOMPETENCE STAGE refers to the "blissfully ignorant" stage in which individuals have neither culture-sensitive knowledge nor responsive attitudes to communicate competently with the host members of the new culture.

UNDERSTATED SPIRAL REASONING includes the use of subtle messages, implied hints, reserved talk, relational reasons, and tactful nonverbal gestures to convey an intended meaning and context.

UNIVERSALISM means that a set of consistent rules should apply to all individuals, regardless of relationship types or circumstances.

VALUES are shared ideas about what counts as important or unimportant, right or wrong, what is fair or unfair, and what counts as ethical or unethical conduct.

VERTICAL SELF-CONSTRUAL involves the personality traits of preferring to treat others based on age, rank, or status levels and tends to favor formal interactions.

WEAK (or **LOW**) **UNCERTAINTY AVOIDANCE** refers to cultural characteristics that promote risk-taking and conflict-approaching modes.

WORLDVIEW refers to one's larger philosophical outlook or way of perceiving the world and how this outlook, in turn, affects one's thinking and reasoning patterns.

AUTHOR INDEX

SUBJECT INDEX

Page numbers ending with *t* indicate a table; with *f* a figure; with *b* a box.